Third
Edition

THE MIND AND HEART OF THE NEGOTIATOR

Leigh L. Thompson

Kellogg School of Management
Northwestern University

PEARSON

Prentice
Hall

Upper Saddle River, New Jersey 07458

Library of Congress Cataloging-in-Publication Data

Thompson, Leigh L.
  The mind and heart of the negotiator / Leigh L. Thompson.—3rd ed.
    p. cm.
  Includes bibliographical references and indexes.
  ISBN 0-13-140738-4 (alk. paper)
    1. Negotiation in business.   I. Title.

HD58.6.T478 2004
658.4'052–dc22   2004044617

Editorial Director: Jeff Shelstad
Media Project Manager: Jessica Sabloff
Executive Marketing Manager: Shannon Moore
Marketing Assistant: Patrick Danzuso
Managing Editor: John Roberts
Production Editor: Renata Butera
Associate Director, Manufacturing: Vincent Scelta
Production Manager: Arnold Vila
Manufacturing Buyer: Michelle Klein
Design Director: Maria Lange
Cover Designer: Bruce Kenselaar
Cover Illustration: Robert Weeks
Manager, Multimedia Production: Christy Mahon
Composition: Integra
Full-Service Project Management: Jennifer Welsch, BookMasters, Inc.
Printer/Binder: Phoenix Booktech

Credits and acknowledgments borrowed from other sources and reproduced, with permission, in this textbook appear on appropriate page within the text.

Pearson Education LTD.
Pearson Education Singapore, Pte. Ltd
Pearson Education, Canada, Ltd
Pearson Education–Japan

Pearson Education Australia PTY, Limited
Pearson Education North Asia Ltd
Pearson Educación de Mexico, S.A. de C.V.
Pearson Education Malaysia, Pte. Ltd

10 9 8 7 6 5 4 3 2 1
ISBN 0-13-140738-4

To the loves of my life:
Bob, Sam, Ray, and Anna

Brief Contents

Contents

CHAPTER 2   Preparation: What to Do Before Negotiation   13

Preface

This book is dedicated to negotiators who want to improve their ability to negotiate—whether that be multimillion-dollar business deals or personal interactions. Many books address the issues of negotiation, so why this one? If I were to cite a single reason why I wrote a book in this saturated field it is this: *The science of negotiation can help people dramatically improve their ability to negotiate economically better deals and also psychologically better deals.* Simply stated: You can improve your monetary returns and feel better about yourself and the people you deal with. This book contains an integration of theory, scientific research, and practical examples. Moreover, the practical examples—selected from hundreds of real-world negotiations involving people from several companies—illustrate effective as well as ineffective negotiation skills.

Here is what you can expect when you read this book:

- **Illustrative case studies and real-life negotiations**: I have included several examples and actual cases of negotiating in managerial and executive contexts. Each chapter opens with a case analysis (often from the business world, but government, community, and personal life as well). Furthermore, many of the points in the chapters are supplemented with illustrations and examples drawn from actual negotiations, both contemporary and historical. I do not use these examples to *prove* a theory; rather, I use them to *illustrate* how many of the concepts in the book are borne out in real-world situations.
- **Skills-based approach**: I provide practical take-away points for the manager and the executive. A good example is Chapter 4 on integrative negotiation. A series of hands-on principles that have been proven to increase the value of negotiated deals are provided. Moreover, several students and clients have written, indicating how they utilized the tools in their actual business negotiations. Those examples are included as well.
- **Self-insight**: We included several ways that negotiators can test their own intuition and approach. For example, Chapter 5, Developing a Negotiating Style, allows negotiators to assess their "instinctive" bargaining style and provides suggestions for how to further develop their bargaining repertoire. Moreover, Chapter 10 provides a deep look at cultural differences in negotiation so that the negotiator can better understand his or her own cultural style and that of others.
- **Sophisticated bargaining skills**: The second and third sections of the book deal with complex, yet commonly occurring negotiating situations, such as negotiating with agents, mediation and arbitration, negotiating via e-mail and conference call, negotiating with competitor companies, and of course, negotiating cross-culturally.

I took the task of revising *The Mind and Heart of the Negotiator* very seriously. Every chapter has a new opening section that illustrates a real-world negotiation and no fewer than 135 examples from the business world have been added since the last edition. Also, I cited the ground-breaking results of more than 200 new scientific articles on negotiation. I benefit greatly from the advice, comments, and critiques given to me by my students and colleagues, and I hope that their advice keeps coming so that I am able to improve upon the book even further.

The research and ideas in this book come from an invaluable set of scholars in the fields of social psychology, organizational behavior, sociology, negotiation, and cognitive psychology. My research, thinking, and writing has been inspired in important ways by the following people: Wendi Adair, Cameron Anderson, Linda Babcock, Max Bazerman, Kristin Behfar, Terry Boles, Jeanne Brett, Susan Brodt, Karen Cates, Hoon-Seok Choi, Gary Fine, Craig Fox, Adam Galinsky, Wendi Gardner, Dedre Gentner, Robert Gibbons, Kevin Gibson, James Gillespie, Rich Gonzalez, Deborah Gruenfeld, Reid Hastie, Andy Hoffman, Peter Kim, Shirli Kopelman, Rod Kramer, Laura Kray, Terri Kurtzburg, Geoffrey Leonardelli, John Levine, Allan Lind, George Loewenstein, Jeff Loewenstein, Deepak Malhotra, Beta Mannix, Kathleen McGinn, Vicki Medvec, Tanya Menon, Dave Messick, Terry Mitchell, Don Moore, Michael Morris, Keith Murnighan, Janice Nadler, Maggie Neale, Kathy Phillips, Robin Pinkley, Ashleigh Rosette, Nancy Rothbard, Elizabeth Seeley, Marwan Sinaceur, Harris Sondak, Tom Tyler, Leaf Van Boven, Kimberly Wade-Benzoni, Laurie Weingart, and Judith White. In *The Mind and Heart of the Negotiator*, I use the pronoun "we" because so much of my thinking has been influenced and shaped by this set of eminent scholars.

The revision of this book would not have been possible without the dedication, organization, and editorial skills of Sean McMillan, who created the layout, organized hundreds of drafts, mastered the figures, and researched many case studies for this book.

In this book, I talk about the "power of the situation" and how strongly the environment shapes our behavior. The Kellogg School of Management is one of the most supportive, dynamic environments I have ever had the pleasure to be a part of. In particular, Dean Dipak Jain and Associate Deans Robert Magee and Robert Korajczyk have strongly supported research as well as teaching, and intellectual leadership as well as pedagogical leadership. I am particularly indebted to my wonderful visionary colleague, Jeanne Brett, who created the Dispute Resolution Research Center (DRRC) at Kellogg in 1986, and to the Hewlett Foundation for their generous support of the DRRC. Grants from the National Science Foundation's Decision Risk and Management Science program have made it possible for me to conduct several of the research studies that I discuss in this book. I am also grateful for a grant received by the Citigroup Research Council, which made possible many of the studies about learning and negotiation reviewed in this book.

This book is very much a team effort of the people I have mentioned here, whose talents are diverse, broad, and extraordinarily impressive. I am deeply indebted to my colleagues and my students, and I feel grateful that they have touched my life and this book.

Overview

This book is divided into three major sections. The first section deals with the essentials of negotiation—the key principles and groundwork for effective negotiation. Chapter 2 leads the manager through effective preparation strategies for negotiation. Chapter 3 discusses distributive negotiation skills, or how to optimally allocate resources in ways that are favorable to one's self—a process called "slicing the pie." Chapter 4 is probably the most important chapter in the book; it focuses on "win-win" negotiation or, more formally, integrative negotiation. This creative part of negotiation involves expanding the pie of resources in ways that provide more gains to go around.

The second section of the book deals with advanced and expert negotiation skills. Chapter 5 focuses on assessing and developing your negotiation style. This chapter invites readers to honestly appraise their own negotiation style in terms of three dimensions: motivation, approach, and emotion. The negotiator can accurately assess his or her own style and its limitations and learn to assess the styles adopted by other negotiators. Chapter 6 focuses on establishing trust and building a relationship. This chapter examines business and personal relationships and how trust is developed, broken, and repaired. Chapter 7 discusses power, persuasion, and influence tactics. This chapter looks at the topic of persuasion and influence as it occurs across the bargaining table, and also deals with the important issue of ethics in negotiation. In Chapter 8, the focus falls on problem solving and creativity. This chapter provides strategies for learning how to think out-of-the-box and provides techniques for using creativity and imagination in negotiation.

The third section deals with special scenarios in negotiation. Chapter 9 examines the complexities of negotiating with multiple parties, such as the conflicting incentives as they occur across the bargaining table, coalitions, voting rules, and how to leverage one's own bargaining position when negotiating with multiple parties. Chapter 10 focuses on cross-cultural negotiation, which addresses the key cultural values and negotiation norms across a variety of nationalities, along with some advice for cross-cultural negotiations. Chapter 11 deals with dilemmas, or situations in which negotiators make choices in a mixed-motive context, where cooperation involves building trust with the other party, and competition involves an attempt to increase one's own share of resources. The chapter examines the nature of social dilemmas and how to negotiate successfully within various types of dilemmas. Chapter 12 focuses on information technology and its impact on negotiation and uses a place-time model of social interaction to examine the challenges and opportunities of negotiation as it occurs in the technological age.

Finally, four appendices provide a variety of additional material: Appendix 1 invites readers to examine the rationality of their negotiation beliefs and preferences, Appendix 2 provides a short course on lie detection and nonverbal communication as they occur in negotiation, Appendix 3 reviews the essentials of third-party intervention, and Appendix 4 provides tips and a worksheet for negotiating a job offer.

CHAPTER

1

NEGOTIATION: THE MIND AND THE HEART

"Before the strangling and death threat, the [negotiation between David M. Colburn of America Online and executives at Music Boulevard] began innocently enough. Colburn sat back while [his business associate, Myer] Berlow, reviewed the proposed deal. Colburn and Berlow had already gone through the numbers: Music Boulevard, an online music service, was going to pay $8 million over three years to run ads on AOL. [However, Berlow suddenly saw the deal in an entirely different light:] If Music Boulevard launched an initial public offering of stock—and its parent company, N2K Inc., had already filed a registration statement with the Securities and Exchange Commission to do just that—then an ad deal with AOL would be worth more than $8 million. [Berlow began to think that these Music Boulevard executives in front of him] stood to personally gain millions from an IPO—[in which AOL would not share.] Berlow then quietly tore out the pricing page from the proposed contract: The $8 million figure vanished [and he wrote in $16 million.] The Music Boulevard execs were perplexed because, after all, this meeting was the final review of a contract to which they had already verbally agreed." Colburn looked at his partner and tried to salvage the situation by repeating the $8 million number. However, Berlow insisted the price should be $16 million. At that point, Berlow announced he was going to the bathroom and asked his partner, Colburn, to join him. During the bathroom conversation, Berlow explained his reasoning and then cursed Coburn for not picking up on his cues, "Since you [f-word] up the sale, David, every dime under $16 million you should pay out of your own pocket." At this point, enraged, Colburn grabbed Berlow by the throat and rammed him against the wall screaming, "I'm going to kill you!" Berlow was instantly overcome by tears of laughter—about the thought of the Music Boulevard execs seeing his face beaten by his own partner. Colburn and Berlow reentered the room and got $18 million (*Washington Post,* June 15, 2003).

Negotiations don't usually involve physical violence, and most of us are not making $18 million deals. However, one thing that business scholars and business people are in complete agreement on is that everyone negotiates nearly every day. *Getting to Yes* (Fisher & Ury, 1981) begins by stating, "Like it or not, you are a negotiator. . . . Everyone negotiates something every day" (p. xvii). Similarly, Lax and Sebenius, in *The Manager as Negotiator* (1986) state that "Negotiating is a way of life for managers . . . when managers deal with their superiors, boards of directors, even legislators" (p. 1). G. Richard Shell, who wrote *Bargaining for Advantage* (1999), asserts, "All of us negotiate many times a day" (p. 6). Herb Cohen, author of *You Can Negotiate Anything* (1980), dramatically suggests that "your world is a giant negotiation table" (p. 15). Perhaps these statements indicate why a recent business article on negotiation warned, "However much you think negotiation is part of your life, you're underestimating" (*Inc.*, Aug. 1, 2003a, p. 76). In this book we believe that *negotiation is your key communication and influence tool* in and outside of the company. Anytime you cannot achieve your objectives (whether it be a desired merger or a dinner date) without the cooperation of others, you are negotiating. We provide dramatic (and disturbing) evidence in this chapter that most people do not live up to their negotiating potential. The good news is that you can do something about it.

The sole purpose of this book is to improve your ability to negotiate in the contexts that matter most to you. We present this information through a marriage of scientific studies of negotiation and real business cases. And, in case you are wondering, it is not all common sense. We are frank about the fact that science drives the best practices covered in this book. We focus on business negotiations; understanding business negotiations helps people to be more effective negotiators in their personal lives as well (Gentner, Loewenstein, & Thompson, 2003).

In this book, we focus on three major negotiation skills: (1) creating value (also known as win-win negotiation); (2) claiming value (also known as staying in business!); and (3) building trust (also known as long-term sustainability). By the end of this book, you will have developed a mental set that will allow you to know what to do and say in negotiations. Moreover, the fact that you have a mental set (also called a *mental model*, van Boven & Thompson, 2003) will mean that you can prepare effectively for negotiations, and enjoy the peace of mind that comes from having a game plan. Things may not always go according to plan, but your mental set will allow you to update effectively and most important, to learn from your experiences.

NEGOTIATION: DEFINITION AND SCOPE

In this book we use the following working definition of negotiation: *Negotiation is an interpersonal decision-making process necessary whenever we cannot achieve our objectives single-handedly*. Negotiations not only include the one-on-one business meeting, but also multiparty, multicompany, and multimillion-dollar deals. Whether simple or complex, negotiations boil down to people, communication, and influence. Even the most complex of business deals can be broken down to a system of one-on-one relationships.

People negotiate in their personal life (e.g., with their spouses, children, school teachers, neighbors) as well as in their business life. Thus, the scope of negotiation ranges from one-on-one to highly complex multiparty and multination interactions. In the business world, people negotiate at multiple levels and contexts — within departmental or business units, between departments, between companies, and even across industries. For this reason, managers must understand enough about negotiations to be effective negotiating within, between, and up and across all of these business environments.

NEGOTIATION AS A CORE MANAGEMENT COMPETENCY

Negotiation skills are increasingly important for executives, leaders, and managers in the business world. The five key reasons for the importance of negotiation skills include (1) the dynamic nature of business, (2) interdependence, (3) competition, (4) the information age, and (5) globalization.

Dynamic Nature of Business
Mobility and flexibility are the dictates of the new world of work. Most people do not stay in the same job that they take upon graduating from college or receiving their MBA degree; furthermore, most people will not have the same job as their predecessor. According to the U.S. Department of Labor (2002), the average person born in the later years of the baby boom held nearly 10 jobs between the ages of 18 and 36, with two-thirds of those jobs being held before age 28. The dynamic, changing nature of business means that people must negotiate and renegotiate their existence in organizations throughout the duration of their careers. The advent of decentralized business structures and the absence of hierarchical decision making provide opportunities for managers, but they also pose some daunting challenges. People must continually create possibilities, integrate their interests with others, and recognize the inevitability of competition both within and between companies. Managers must be in a near-constant mode of negotiating opportunities. According to Linda Greene, associate vice chancellor for academic affairs at the University of Wisconsin–Madison, "Many important events essential to professional success and professional satisfaction happen every day in the workplace and they are not always announced in advance" (*The Capital Times*, Jan. 1, 2000, p. 1E). In truth, negotiation comes into play when people participate in important meetings, get new assignments, head a team, participate in a reorganization process, and set priorities for their work unit. Negotiation should be second nature to the business manager, but often it is not.

Interdependence
The increasing interdependence of people within organizations, both laterally and hierarchically, implies that people need to know how to integrate their interests and work together across business units and functional areas. For example, when

Chrysler and Mercedes Benz merged in 1998, there was extreme reluctance among different groups in the company to utilize synergies. For the first few years, Mercedes executives closely guarded their parts and designs for fear of eroding the Mercedes mystique. And Chrysler engineers tried to preserve some independence, even though it meant reinventing the wheel (*The Wall Street Journal*, Mar. 12, 2003). This reluctance not only occurs within companies, as people from different departments and units integrate their knowledge to create a product or service, but it also occurs between people from different companies, as is the case with strategic alliances. The increasing degree of specialization and expertise in the business world implies that people are more and more dependent on others to supply the components for a complete service or product. It is unwise to assume that others have similar incentive structures, so managers need to know how to promote their own interests while simultaneously creating joint value for their organizations. This task requires negotiation. For example, consider the strategic decision of Best Buy, the electronics company that sells nearly 10 percent of all consumer PCs sold in the United States, to develop its own brand of PCs in 2002 (*Business 2.0*, Aug. 1, 2003a). Before the product PC launch, Best Buy was concerned that because PCs account for more than 9 percent of all sales, the existing major computer manufacturers—Compaq, HP, Sony, Toshiba, and others—would be in a position to dictate terms of supply. Moreover, if the recession led to shutdowns of any of these companies, the holes in Best Buy's product lines might drive customers to other suppliers or to their competitor, Dell. Yet, by entering the field, Best Buy would now compete with the most powerful companies in the low-margin, competitive PC business—companies that were currently Best Buy's suppliers.

Competition

Business is increasingly competitive. Nearly 40,000 businesses filed for bankruptcy in 2002, a 10.7 percent increase over the previous year (Associated Press, May 16, 2002). Five of the nation's eight largest bankruptcies in history occurred in 2002, according to BankruptcyData.com—and those data did not include Enron's December 2001 filing (Associated Press, Jan. 15, 2003). In today's economy, a few large companies are emerging as dominant players in the biggest markets. These industry leaders often enjoy vast economies of scale and earn tremendous profits. The losers are often left with little in the way of a market, let alone a marketable product (Frank & Cook, 1995). Consider Oracle's hostile 2003 bid for rival software maker, PeopleSoft, which effectively killed the previously announced merger between PeopleSoft and J.D. Edwards (*Business 2.0*, Aug. 1, 2003d). As Deutsche Bank software analyst Brian Skiba put it, "The software business has become more Darwinian. Over the next five years, the big [will] get bigger and the small [will] disappear" (p. 90). Larry Ellison of Oracle has bluntly stated that 1,000 more tech firms must die, and, one month before making his offer on PeopleSoft, Ellison methodically mapped out all possible merger permutations in his industry.

This reality means that companies must be experts in competitive environments. Managers not only need to function as advocates for their products and services, but they must also recognize the competition that is inevitable between companies and, in some cases, between units within a given company. Understanding how to navigate this competitive environment is essential for successful negotiation.

Information Age

The information age also provides special opportunities and challenges for the manager as negotiator. The information age has created a culture of 24/7 availability. With technology that makes it possible to communicate with people anywhere in the world, managers are expected to negotiate at a moment's notice. Computer technology, for example, extends a company's obligations and capacity to add value to its customers. Prior to 2001, 80 percent of transactions at Starbucks were conducted with bills and coins. Among other things, this form of exchange meant that Starbucks had no knowledge about its customers—the more than 3 million people who daily plunk down more than $3 for a cup of coffee (*Business 2.0*, Aug. 1, 2003b). The return business—or the fact that many java junkies return more than 16 times each month—should be the core of Starbucks' customer focus. However, when you don't know anything about your customers, it is more difficult to serve them. To capitalize on the powers of the information age and give its customers added boost, Starbucks launched the plastic prepaid card in 2001. Among other things, it allowed Starbucks to understand its customers, as well as offer perks, such as a free half-pound of coffee.

Globalization

Most managers must effectively cross cultural boundaries in order to do their jobs. Setting aside obvious language and currency issues, globalization presents challenges in terms of different norms of communication. Managers need to develop negotiation skills that can be successfully employed with people of different nationalities, backgrounds, and styles of communication. Consequently, negotiators who have developed a bargaining style that works only within a narrow subset of the business world will suffer unless they can broaden their negotiation skills to effectively work with different people across functional units, industries, and cultures (Bazerman & Neale, 1992). It is a challenge to develop a negotiation skill set general enough to be used across different contexts, groups, and continents, but specialized enough to provide meaningful behavioral strategies in any given situation. This book provides the manager with such skills.

MOST PEOPLE ARE INEFFECTIVE NEGOTIATORS

On the question of whether people are effective negotiators, managers and scholars often disagree. Many people regard themselves to be effective at negotiation. These same people believe most of their colleagues are distinctly ineffective at the negotiation table. However, our performance speaks louder than our self-proclaimed prowess. Most people often fall extremely short of their potential at the negotiation table, judging from their performance on realistic business negotiation simulations (for reviews, see Neale & Bazerman, 1991; Thompson & Hrebec, 1996; Loewenstein, Thompson, & Gentner, 2003). Numerous business executives describe their negotiations as win-win only to discover that they left hundreds of thousands of dollars on the table. Fewer than 4 percent of managers reach win-win outcomes when put to the test (Nadler, Thompson, & van Boven, 2003); and the incidence of outright lose-lose outcomes is 20 percent (Thompson & Hrebec, 1996). In addition to these data, our controlled scientific investigations (hereafter referred to as CSIs), which allow scholars to infer direct cause-and-effect relationships, indicate that most negotiators leave money on the table. Consider another example: Even on issues for which people were in perfect agreement, they fail to realize it 50 percent of the time (Thompson & Hrebec, 1996). Moreover, we make the point several times throughout this book that effective negotiation is not just about money—it is equally about relationships and trust.

NEGOTIATION SANDTRAPS

In our research, we have observed and documented four major shortcomings in negotiation:

1. **Leaving money on the table** (also known as "lose-lose" negotiation) occurs when negotiators fail to recognize and exploit win-win potential.
2. **Settling for too little** (also known as "the winner's curse") occurs when negotiators make too-large concessions, resulting in a too-small share of the bargaining pie.
3. **Walking away from the table** occurs when negotiators reject terms offered by the other party that are demonstrably better than any other option available to them. (Sometimes this shortcoming is traceable to hubris or overweening pride; other times, it results from gross miscalculation.)
4. **Settling for terms that are worse than the alternative** (also known as the "agreement bias") occurs when negotiators feel obligated to reach agreement even when the settlement terms are not as good as their other alternatives.

This book teaches you how to avoid these errors, create value in negotiation, get your share of the bargaining pie, reach agreement when it is profitable to do so, and quickly recognize when agreement is not a viable option in a negotiation.

WHY PEOPLE ARE INEFFECTIVE NEGOTIATORS

The dramatic instances of lose-lose outcomes, the winner's curse, walking away from the table, and the agreement bias raise the question of why people are not more effective at the bargaining table. Because negotiation is so important for personal and business success, it is rather surprising that most people do not negotiate very well. Stated starkly: It just does not make sense that people would be so poor at something that is so important for their personal and business life. The reason is not due to a lack of motivation or intelligence on the part of negotiators. The problem is rooted in three fundamental problems: faulty feedback, satisficing, and self-reinforcing incompetence.

Faulty Feedback

Most of us have plenty of opportunities to negotiate, but little opportunity to learn how to negotiate effectively. As we will see, arguably the most important component of learning is feedback. Three things about feedback are key: accuracy, immediacy, and specificity. The problem is not lack of experience but a shortage of timely and accurate feedback. Even those people who have daily experiences in negotiation receive little feedback on their negotiating effectiveness. The absence of feedback results in two human biases that further prevent negotiators from optimally benefiting from experience. The first problem is the **confirmation bias**, or the tendency for people to see what they want to see when appraising their own performance. The confirmation bias leads individuals to selectively seek information that confirms what they believe is true. Whereas the confirmation bias may seem perfectly harmless, it results in a myopic view of reality and can hinder learning. Consider, for example, mathematician John Allen Paulos' disastrous foray into the stock market (*The Guardian*, July 17, 2003). At first, he invested only an unexpected cash windfall, but slowly he began to use up more and more of his savings. Even though Paulos knew all about logic and rationality, he had fallen victim to inventing reasons to support his purchases and ignoring information that did not support it.

A second problem associated with the absence of relevant and diagnostic feedback is **egocentrism**, which is the tendency for people to view their experiences in a way that is flattering or fulfilling for themselves. For example, this potentially inaccurate view may increase a manager's self-esteem; however, in the long run, it does a disservice by preventing a manager from learning effectively. For example, egocentrism and the suspension of reality certainly influenced executives at Citigroup and J.P. Morgan Chase & Co. to manipulate cash flows at Enron (*BusinessWeek*, Aug. 11, 2003a). The belief that they could mislead Enron shareholders and minimize perceived risk of being accused of deception was likely fueled by unwarranted beliefs about their role. Egocentrism also played a role in the American Airlines negotiations in April 2003 in which bankruptcy was narrowly avoided. American said it had to have $1.8 billion in annual cuts from all employee groups as part of a $4 billion effort to restructure the company. The airline was losing $5 million a day. The three major groups involved—pilots union, professional flight attendants, and the ground workers of the transport workers union—all believed that they deserved more than what they believed others were entitled to (*Dallas Morning News*, Apr. 3, 2003).

Satisficing

The second reason why people often fall short in negotiation is due to the human tendency to satisfice (Simon, 1955). According to Nobel Laureate Herb Simon (1955), **satisficing** is the opposite of *optimizing*. In a negotiation situation, it is important to optimize one's strategies by setting high aspirations and attempting to achieve as much as possible; in contrast, when people satisfice, they settle for something less than they could otherwise have. For example, Anchor Bay settled for $10 million from Storm Ventures and Venrock Associates in venture financing. CEO of Anchor Bay, Laurence Thompson, comments that it was exactly the valuation they asked for, meaning that "Maybe we did not ask for enough" (*Private Equity Week*, June 9, 2003). Over the long run, satisficing (or the acceptance of mediocrity) can be detrimental to both individuals and companies, especially when a variety of effective negotiation strategies and skills that can be cheaply employed to dramatically increase profit. (We discuss these strategies in detail in the next three chapters.)

Self-Reinforcing Incompetence

To achieve and maintain effectiveness in the business world, people must have insight into their limitations. The same is true for negotiation. However, most people are "blissfully unaware of their own incompetence" (Dunning, Johnson, Ehrlinger, & Kruger, 2003, p. 83). Moreover, it creates a cycle in which the lack of skill deprives them not only of the ability to produce correct responses, but also of the expertise necessary to surmise that they are not producing them. As a case in point, Dunning and colleagues examined the question of whether students taking a test had insight into their performance. The students were grouped into four quartiles based on their performance. The lowest-performing quartile greatly overestimated their performance on the test. Even though they were actually in the 12th percentile, they estimated themselves in the 60th percentile. This example is not an isolated case, according to Dunning. People overestimate their percentile ranking relative to others by as much as 40 to 50 points (Kruger & Dunning, 1999). Moreover, the problem cannot be attributed to a lack of incentives. The overestimation pattern even appears after people are promised significant financial rewards for accurate assessments of their performance (Ehrlinger, Johnson, Banner, Dunning, & Kruger, 2003).

Related to the principle of self-reinforcing incompetence is the fact that people are reluctant to change their behavior and experiment with new courses of action because of the risks associated with experimentation. In short, the fear of losing keeps people from experimenting with change. Negotiators instead rationalize their behavior in a self-perpetuating fashion. The fear of making mistakes may result in a manager's inability to improve his or her negotiation skills. In this book, we remove the risk of experimentation by providing several exercises and clear demonstrations of how changing one's behavior can lead to better results in negotiation.

Argyris (2002) suggests that people can diagnose their incompetence and increase their effectiveness if they engage in double-loop learning. Unfortunately, most people practice single-loop learning. **Single-loop learning** occurs when errors are corrected without altering the underlying, governing values (e.g., the fundamental principles of negotiation). **Double-loop learning** occurs when errors are corrected by changing the governing values and then the actions. Sebenius's (2001) article on the "six habits of merely effective negotiators" makes the point about working with the right assumptions very clear: "Understanding your counterpart's interests and shaping the decision so the other side agrees for its own reasons is the key to jointly creating and claiming sustainable value from a negotiation" (p. 88). In this sense, we invite managers to be active learners in terms of understanding their own values when it comes to negotiation.

DEBUNKING NEGOTIATION MYTHS

When we delve into managers' theories and beliefs about negotiation, we are often startled to find that they operate with faulty beliefs. Before we start on our journey toward developing a more effective negotiation strategy, we need to dispel several faulty assumptions and myths about negotiation. These myths hamper people's ability to learn effective negotiation skills and, in some cases, reinforce poor negotiation skills. In the following section, we expose six of the most prevalent myths about negotiation behavior.

Myth 1: Negotiations Are Fixed-Sum

Probably the most common myth is that most negotiations are fixed-sum in nature, such that whatever is good for one person must *ipso facto* be bad for the other party. The truth is that most negotiations are not purely fixed-sum; in fact, most negotiations are variable-sum in nature, meaning that if parties work together, they can create more joint value than if they are purely combative. However, effective negotiators also realize that they cannot be purely trusting because any value that is created must ultimately be claimed by someone at the table. Our approach to negotiation is based on Walton and McKersie's (1965) conceptualization that negotiation is a mixed-motive enterprise, such that parties have incentives to cooperate as well as compete.

Myth 2: You Need to Be Either Tough or Soft

The fixed-sum myth gives rise to a myopic view of the strategic choices that negotiators have. Most negotiators believe they must choose between either behaving in a tough (and sometimes punitive fashion) or being "reasonable" to the point of soft and concessionary. We vehemently disagree. Along with Bazerman and Neale (1992), we believe that the truly effective negotiator is neither tough-as-nails nor soft-as-pudding, but rather, principled (Fisher & Ury, 1981). Effective negotiators follow an "enlightened" view of negotiation and correctly recognize that to achieve their own outcomes, they must work effectively with the other party (and hence, cooperate), but must also leverage their own power and strengths.

Myth 3: Good Negotiators Are Born

A pervasive belief is that effective negotiation skills are something that people are born with, not something that can be readily learned. This notion is false because most excellent negotiators are self-made. In fact, naturally gifted negotiators are rare. We tend to hear their stories, but we must remember that their stories are *selective*, meaning that it is always possible for someone to have a lucky day or a fortunate experience. This myth is often perpetuated by the tendency of people to judge negotiation skills by their car-dealership experiences. Purchasing a car is certainly an important and common type of negotiation, but it is not the best context by which to judge your negotiation skills. The most important negotiations are those that we engage in every day with our colleagues, supervisors, coworkers, and business associates. These relationships provide a much better index of one's effectiveness in negotiation. In short, effective negotiation requires practice and feedback. The problem is that most of us do not get an opportunity to develop effective negotiation skills in a disciplined fashion; rather, most of us learn by doing. Experience is helpful, but not sufficient.

Myth 4: Experience Is a Great Teacher

We have all met that person at the cocktail party or on the airplane who boasts about his or her great negotiation feats and how he or she learned on the job (Bazerman & Neale, 1992). It is only partly true that experience can improve negotiation skills; in fact, experience in the absence of feedback, is largely ineffective in improving negotiation skills (Loewenstein, Thompson, & Gentner, 2003; Nadler,

Thompson, & van Boven, 2003; Thompson & DeHarpport, 1994; Thompson, Loewenstein, & Gentner, 2000). Natural experience as an effective teacher has three strikes against it. First, in the absence of feedback, it is nearly impossible to improve performance. For example, can you imagine trying to learn mathematics without ever doing homework or taking tests? Without diagnostic feedback, it is very difficult to learn from experience.

The second problem is that our memories tend to be selective, meaning that people are more likely to remember their successes and forget their failures or shortcomings. This tendency is, of course, comforting to our ego, but it does not improve our ability to negotiate.

Finally, experience improves our confidence, but not necessarily our accuracy. People with more experience grow more and more confident, but the accuracy of their judgment and the effectiveness of their behavior do not increase in a commensurate fashion. Overconfidence can be dangerous because it may lead people to take unwise risks.

Myth 5: Good Negotiators Take Risks

A pervasive myth is that effective negotiation necessitates taking risks and gambles. In negotiation, this approach may mean saying things like, "This is my final offer" or "Take it or leave it" or using threats and bluffs. It is what we call a "tough" style of negotiation. Tough negotiators are rarely effective; however, we tend to be impressed by the tough negotiator. In this book, we teach negotiators how to evaluate risk, how to determine the appropriate time to make a final offer, and, more importantly, how to make excellent decisions in the face of the uncertainty of negotiation.

Myth 6: Good Negotiators Rely on Intuition

An interesting exercise is to ask managers and anyone else who negotiates to describe their approach to negotiating. Many seasoned negotiators believe that their negotiation style involves a lot of "gut feeling," intuition, and "in-the-moment" responses. We believe that intuition does not serve people well. Effective negotiation involves deliberate thought and preparation and is quite systematic. The goal of this book is to help managers effectively prepare for negotiation, become more self-aware of their own strengths and shortcomings, and develop strategies that are **proactive** (i.e., those that anticipate the reactions of their opponent) rather than **reactive** (i.e., those that are dependent upon the actions and reactions of their opponent). Thus, excellent negotiators do not rely on intuition; rather, they are deliberate planners. As a general rule, don't rely on your intuition unless you are an expert.

LEARNING OBJECTIVES

This book promises three things: First (and most important), reading this book will *improve your ability to negotiate successfully*. You and your company will be richer, and you will experience fewer sleepless nights, because you will have a solid framework and excellent toolbox for successful negotiation. However, in making this promise, we must also issue a warning: Successful negotiation skills do not come through passive learning. Rather, you will need to actively challenge yourself. We can think of no better way to engage in this challenge than to supplement this book with classroom experiences in negotiation in which managers can test their negotiation skills, receive timely feedback, and refine their negotiation strategies on a repeated basis. Moreover, within the classroom, data suggest that students who take the course for a grade will be more effective than students who take the course pass-fail (Craver, 1998).

Second, we provide you with a *general strategy for successful negotiation.* Take a look at the table of contents. Notice the distinct absence of chapter titles such as "Negotiating in the Pharmaceutical Industry" or "Real Estate Negotiations" or "High-Tech Negotiations." We don't believe that negotiations in the pharmaceutical world require a fundamentally different set of skills from negotiations in the insurance industry or the software industry. Rather, we believe that negotiation skills are transferable across situations. In making this statement, we do not mean to imply that all negotiation situations are identical. This assumption is patently false because negotiation situations differ dramatically across cultures and activities. However, certain key negotiation principles are essential in all these different contexts. The skills in this book are effective across a wide range of situations, ranging from complex, multiparty, multicultural deals to one-on-one personal exchanges.

Finally, this book offers *an enlightened model of negotiation.* Being a successful negotiator does not depend on your opponent's lack of familiarity with a book such as this one or a lack of training in negotiation. In fact, it would be ideal for you if your key clients and customers knew about these strategies. This approach follows what we call a *fraternal twin model,* which assumes that the other person you are negotiating with is every bit as motivated, intelligent, and prepared as you are. Thus, the negotiating strategies and techniques outlined in this book do not rely on "outsmarting" or tricking the other party; rather, they teach you to focus on simultaneously expanding the pie of resources and ensuring the resources are allocated in a manner that is favorable to you.

In summary, our model of learning is based on a three-phase cycle: experiential learning, feedback, and learning new strategies and skills.

THE MIND AND HEART

Across the sections of this book, we focus on the *mind* of the negotiator as it involves the development of deliberate, rational, and thoughtful strategies for negotiation. We also focus on the *heart* of the negotiator, because ultimately we care about relationships and trust. We don't need to trade off dollars and give up value to build relationships and trust. In fact, the opposite is true. We base all our teachings and best practices on scientific research in the areas of economics and psychology—again reflecting the idea that the bottom line *and* our relationships are both important (Bazerman, Curhan, Moore, & Valley, 2000). The corporate scandals that first began to rock the corporate world in 2001 have fueled a backlash against the business world and its inhabitants. Perhaps these incidents are what rekindled negative perceptions of businesspeople, and MBAs in particular. "[The] emphasis on analysis has produced a generation of MBAs who are critters with lopsided brains, icy hearts, and shrunken souls" (Leavitt, 1989, p. 39). Such an assessment provides all the more reason to put the focus on the heart and relationships in business.

2

PREPARATION: WHAT TO DO BEFORE NEGOTIATION

Like many managers, Tom Britton, a senior network analyst at American Suzuki Motor Corporation in Brea, California, felt he was underpaid. His annual performance review was coming up in a few months and he decided to prepare. So he surfed the Web to find up-to-date information about salaries—and this cost him some money. However, the way he figured it, if the research helped him get a raise, it would be worth it; if it did not, he would at least be better informed about his talents vis-à-vis the industry. Armed with a lot of information by the time his performance review rolled around, Tom provided documentation to his direct supervisor and asked for an opportunity to review everything with him. The documentation revealed that there was a marked difference between what the industry was paying locally and what Tom Britton was earning. The result? Britton got his raise. To be sure, Britton's supervisor had done his own research, but Tom's data—objective and clear—actually helped Tom's supervisor justify a salary increase to upper management (*Christian Science Monitor,* July 29, 2002).

As the opening example in this chapter illustrates, preparation is the key to successful negotiation. The work that you do prior to negotiation pays off substantially when you finally find yourself seated at the table. The 80–20 rule applies to negotiation: About 80 percent of your effort should go toward preparation; 20 percent should be the actual work involved in the negotiation. Most people clearly realize that preparation is important, yet they do not prepare in an effective fashion. Faulty preparation is not due to lack of motivation; rather, it has its roots in negotiators' faulty perceptions about negotiation.

We noted in Chapter 1 that most negotiators view negotiation as a **fixed-pie** enterprise. Most negotiators (about 80 percent of them) operate under this perception (Thompson & Hastie, 1990). Negotiators who have fixed-pie perceptions usually adopt one of three stances when preparing for negotiation:

1. They resign themselves to capitulating to the other side (also known as *soft bargaining*).

2. They prepare themselves for an attack (also known as *hard bargaining*).
3. They *compromise* in an attempt to reach a midpoint between their opposing desires (often regarded to be a win-win negotiation, but in fact, is not).

Depending on what the other party decides to do in the negotiation, fixed-pie perceptions can either lead to a battle of wills (e.g., if both parties are in attack mode), mutual compromise (i.e., if both parties are soft), or a combination of attack and capitulation. The common assumption among all three approaches is that concessions are necessary by one or both parties to reach an agreement. The fixed-pie perception is usually *always* wrong; thus, choosing between capitulation, attack, and compromise is not an effective approach to negotiation.

A more accurate model of negotiation is a *mixed-motive* decision-making enterprise. As a mixed-motive enterprise, negotiation involves both cooperation and competition. In this chapter, we review the essentials of effective preparation, whether it be with a next-door neighbor, a corporate executive officer, or someone from a different culture. We argue that excellent preparation encompasses three general abilities:

1. Self-assessment
2. Assessment of the other party
3. Assessment of the situation

Next, we systematically review each of these abilities and the skills they require. For each, we pose questions that a negotiator should ask himself or herself when preparing for negotiation.

SELF-ASSESSMENT

The most important questions a negotiator needs to ask of himself or herself at the outset of negotiation are "What do I want?" and "What are my alternatives?" By far, the first question is the more intuitive and easier of the two to answer. Even so, many people do not think carefully about what they want before entering negotiations. The second question defines a negotiator's power in the negotiation and influences the ultimate outcome of the negotiation. We take up these questions in more detail.

What Do I Want?

In any negotiation scenario, a negotiator needs to determine what constitutes an ideal situation. This specific description is known as a **target** or **aspiration** (sometimes called a **target point** or **aspiration point**). Identifying a target or aspiration may sound straightforward enough, but three major problems often arise at this point:

1. The first problem is the case of the *underaspiring negotiator*, who sets his or her target or aspirations too low. The underaspiring negotiator opens the negotiation by requesting something that is immediately granted, resulting in a regrettable state of affairs known as the **winner's curse** (Akerlof, 1970; Neale & Bazerman, 1991). The winner's curse occurs when a negotiator makes an offer that is immediately accepted by the other party. Consider what happened to Joseph Bachelder who was

representing a grocery executive in critical negotiations. Bachelder demanded that his client—the grocer—get a 4.9% stake in the business. The words barely left his mouth when the company's controlling shareholder jubilantly agreed. Says Bachelder, "I just died. I knew right away that I had underbid. We could have had more if I had just asked for it" (*The Wall Street Journal*, June 25, 2003). The immediate acceptance of one's offer by an opponent signals that a negotiator did not ask for enough. Another example is that of an army sergeant returning from a tour of duty in the Gulf War. Recently engaged, the sergeant wanted to bring back a beautiful gold necklace for his bride-to-be. When he entered the Saudi Arabian jewelry store, he knew enough not to offer full price for the gold necklace, so he offered exactly half of the marked price. At that moment, the shopkeeper offered to also include the matching earrings and bracelet! The sergeant's key mistake: His initial offer was too generous because he had not adequately prepared.

2. The second problem is the case of the *overaspiring* or *positional negotiator*. This type of negotiator is too "tough"; he or she sets the target point too high and refuses to make any concessions. Take the case of Will Vinton, who received no fewer than three termination offers from Phil Knight of Nike. One of the offers totaled to two years' salary as severance and $180K for his company stock. Vinton rejected all of the offers and ended up with only $50K (*The Oregonian*, May 25, 2003).

3. The third problem is what we call the *grass-is-greener negotiator*. These negotiators do not know what they really want—only that they want what the other party does not want to give them and do not want what the other party is willing to offer. This type of negotiation behavior is also known as **reactive devaluation** (Ross & Stillinger, 1991; Curhan, Neale, Ross, & Rosencranz-Engelmann, 2004). For example, in a survey of opinions regarding possible arms reductions by the United States and the Soviet Union, respondents were asked to evaluate the terms of a nuclear disarmament proposal, a proposal that was either allegedly taken by the United States, Soviet Union, or a neutral third party (Ross & Stillinger, 1991). In all cases, the proposal was identical; however, reactions to it depended upon who allegedly initiated it. The terms were seen as unfavorable to the United States when the Soviets were the initiators, even though the same terms appeared moderately favorable when attributed to a neutral third party and quite favorable when attributed to the United States (see also Oskamp, 1965).

What Is My Alternative to Reaching Agreement in This Situation?

A negotiator needs to determine his or her best alternative to a negotiated agreement. This step is so important that it has been made into an acronym: **BATNA** (**B**est **A**lternative **t**o a **N**egotiated **A**greement (Fisher & Ury, 1981). A BATNA determines the point at which a negotiator is prepared to walk away from the negotiation table. In practice, it means that negotiators should be willing to accept any set of terms that is superior to their BATNA and reject outcomes that are worse than their BATNA. Surprising as it may seem, negotiators often fail on both counts.

BATNAs and Reality

Despite its simple appeal, the BATNA concept is something that is consistently difficult to convey to most manager-negotiators. When we ask them to tell us about their BATNA, we usually hear a sermon about how much they deserve. A BATNA is not something that a negotiator wishes for; rather, it is determined by objective reality. In short, if the world does not recognize how great you are, then you do not have a desirable BATNA. A common problem we have seen in our training of MBA students and executives is that negotiators are reluctant to recognize their real BATNAs, and they fall prey to wishful thinking and unrealistic optimism.

Your BATNA Is Not a Passive Concept

Your BATNA—once properly identified—is not a passive concept. Rather, it is *dynamic*, meaning that at any point in time, it is either improving or deteriorating. Thus, we don't suggest that negotiators simply identify their BATNAs. Once their BATNAs are identified, negotiators should constantly be improving them. One strategy for improving BATNAs is to follow Bazerman and Neale's (1992) "falling in love" rule, which applies to most negotiation situations. According to this rule, negotiators should not fall in love with one house, one job, or one set of circumstances, but instead, try to identify two or three options of interest. Del Monte strategically kept their options open in 2002 when their own board had an offer to sell the company in an all-cash deal. At the same time, H. J. Heinz chairman William R. Johnson offered to give Del Monte a few businesses that would double its size. For two months, Del Monte kept negotiations open with two competing parties offering dramatically different outcomes. They did so to be able to leverage their bargaining position. Del Monte's board wisely directed its chairman, Richard G. Wolford, to keep his options open, which eventually resulted in a better deal for the company (*Pittsburgh Post-Gazette*, Aug. 29, 2002). By following this strategy, the negotiator has a readily available set of alternatives that represent viable options should the current alternative come at too high a price or be eliminated. The "falling in love" rule is difficult to follow because most people set their sights on one target job, house, or set of terms and exclude all others. Many negotiators are reluctant to recognize their BATNAs and get them confused with their aspiration point. Another problem associated with the failure to properly identify one's BATNA is that it can be influenced and manipulated by the other party during the course of negotiation.

Do Not Let the Other Party Manipulate Your BATNA

We just argued that you should be constantly attempting to improve your BATNA based upon objective information. However, it is important to realize that the source of objective information does not usually emanate from the other party. Simply stated: The other party always has an incentive to minimize the quality of your BATNA, and thus will be motivated to provide negative information vis-à-vis your BATNA. If you have not properly prepared, you might be particularly influenced by such persuasive appeals. However, we argue that your BATNA should *not* change as a result of the other party's persuasion techniques. Your BATNA should only change as a result of objective facts and evidence. Many savvy negotiators attempt to manipulate the other party's perception of their own BATNA. Negotiators are most likely to fall prey to this ploy when they have not adequately prepared for the negotiation and have conjured up a BATNA that is not based on objective information.

In a negotiation, the person who stands to gain most by changing our mind should be the *least* persuasive. Thus, it is important to develop a BATNA before commencing negotiations and to stick to it during the course of negotiations. It is helpful to write your BATNA in ink on a piece of paper and put it in your pocket before negotiating. If you feel tempted to settle for less than your BATNA, it may be a good time to pull out the paper, call a halt to the negotiation process, and engage in an objective reassessment.

Determine Your Reservation Point

Once the negotiator has identified her BATNA, she is in an excellent position to determine her reservation point. The **reservation point** is not determined by what the negotiator wishes and hopes for, but rather, by what her BATNA represents. Consider the example of an MBA student negotiating her employment terms. Let's imagine that the MBA student has a $90,000 job offer from company A, with some stock options, moving expenses, and a signing bonus. The student is interested in getting an offer from company B. Thus, company A is her BATNA. The question the student should ask herself is, What does company B need to offer me so that I feel it is identical to the offer made by company A? The answer to this question represents her reservation point, which includes all things relevant to the job offer: not only salary, stock options, moving expenses, and signing bonus, but also quality of life and feelings about the city to which she will move. A reservation point, then, is a *quantification* of a negotiator's BATNA.

Many negotiators fail to assess their reservation point when they prepare for negotiation. This failure is a serious strategic error because the negotiator's reservation point has the most direct influence on his or her final outcome. In particular, when three types of information—market price, reservation price, and aspiration—were made available to negotiators, only reservation prices drove final outcomes (Blount-White et al., 1994).

Failure to assess reservation points can lead to two unfortunate outcomes. In some instances, negotiators may agree to an outcome that is worse than their BATNA. In our example, the student could agree to a set of employment terms at company B that are actually worse for her than what company A is offering. A second problem is that negotiators may often reject an offer that is better than their BATNA. For example, the MBA student may reject a package from company B that is actually more attractive than the offer from company A. Although this example may seem completely ludicrous, the incidence of agreeing to something worse than one's BATNA and rejecting an offer better than one's BATNA is quite high. To avoid both of these errors, we suggest that the negotiator follow the steps outlined in Box 2-1.

BOX 2-1

DEVELOPING A RESERVATION POINT

Step 1: Brainstorm Your Alternatives. Imagine that you want to sell your house. You have already determined your target point—in this case, $275,000. That is the easy part. The real question is, What is the lowest offer you will accept for your home? This step involves thinking about what you will do in the event that you do not get an offer of $275,000 for your house. Perhaps you may reduce the list

continued

price by $10,000 (or more), perhaps you may stay in the house, or you may consider renting. You should consider as many alternatives as possible. The only restriction is that the alternatives must be feasible—that is, realistic. This requirement involves research on your part.

Step 2: Evaluate Each Alternative. In this step, you should order the various alternatives identified in step 1 in terms of their relative attractiveness, or value, to you. If an alternative has an uncertain outcome, such as reducing the list price, you should determine the probability that a buyer will make an offer at that price. For example, suppose that you reduce the list price to $265,000. You assess the probability of a buyer making an offer of $265,000 for your house to be 70 percent, based on recent home sale prices in the area. Your reservation price is based on research, not hope. The best, most valuable, alternative should be selected to represent your BATNA.

Step 3: Attempt to Improve Your BATNA. Your bargaining position can be strengthened substantially to the extent that you have an attractive, viable BATNA. Unfortunately, this step is the one that many negotiators fail to develop fully. To improve your BATNA in this case, you might contact a house rental company and develop your rental options, or you may make some improvements that have high return on investment (e.g., new paint). Of course, your most attractive BATNA is to have an offer in hand on your house.

Step 4: Determine Your Reservation Price. Once you have determined your most attractive BATNA, it is now time to identify your reservation price—the least amount of money you would accept for

your home at the present time. Once again, it is *not* effective to pull this number out of thin air. It *must* be based on fact.

For example, you assess the probability of getting an offer on your house of $265,000 (or higher) to be 60 percent. Suppose that you assess the probability that you will get an offer of $250,000 or higher to be 95 percent. You think there is a 5 percent chance that you will not get an offer of $250,000 and will rent your house. You can use this information to assess your expected probabilities of selling your house:

Reduce the price of your home to $265,000
$$P_{sale} = 60\%$$
Reduce the price of your home to $250,000
$$P_{sale} = 35\%$$
Rent the house
$$P_{rent} = 5\%$$

The probabilities represent the chances that you think your house will sell at a particular price or will have to be rented. Thus, you think that if the list price of your house is reduced to $265,000, it is 60 percent likely that you will receive an offer of that amount within six weeks. If you reduce the price of your home to $250,000, you are 95 percent certain that you will get an offer. (Note that we write this probability as 35 percent because it includes the 60 percent probability of receiving an offer of $265,000.) Finally, you think there is a 5 percent chance that you will not get an offer of $250,000 or more in the next six weeks and that you will have to rent your house—a value you assess to be worth only $100,000 to you at the present time.

Note that in our calculation, the probabilities always sum to exactly 100 percent, meaning that we have considered all possible events occurring. No alternative is left to chance. An overall value for each of these "risky" alternatives is assessed by multiplying the value of each option by its probability of occurrence:

Value of reducing price to $265,000

$= \$265,000 \times 0.6 = \$159,000$

Value of reducing price to $250,000

$= \$250,000 \times 0.35 = \$87,500$

Value of renting the house

$= 100,000 \times 0.05 = \$5,000$

As a final step, we add all of the values of the alternatives to arrive at an overall evaluation:

$= 0.6(\$265,000) + 0.35(\$250,000)$
$\quad + 0.05(\$100,000)$
$= \$159,000 + \$87,500$
$\quad + \$5,000 = \$251,500$

_____

* After six weeks, you may reduce the price of your home to $250,000.

This value is your reservation price. It means that you would never settle for anything less than $251,500 in the next six weeks.* It also means that if a buyer were to make you an offer right now of $251,000, you would seriously consider it because it is very close to your reservation price. Obviously, you want to get a lot more than $251,500, but you are prepared to go as low as this amount at the present time.

The offers that you receive in the next six weeks can change your reservation point. Suppose a buyer offers to pay $260,000 for the house next week. It would be your reservation point by which to evaluate all subsequent offers.

Be Aware of Focal Points

Negotiators who make the mistake of not developing a reservation point before they negotiate often focus on an arbitrary value that *masquerades* as a reservation price. Such arbitrary points are **focal points**. Focal points can be salient numbers, figures, or values that appear to be valid but have no basis in fact—your roommate's job offer, for example. A good example of the arbitrariness of focal points is provided by an investigation in which people were asked for the last four digits of their Social Security number (Lovallo & Kahneman, 2003). They were then asked whether the number of physicians in Manhattan was larger or smaller than the number formed by those last four digits. Finally, they were asked to estimate how many physicians are in Manhattan. Despite the fact that it was obvious to everyone that Social Security digits are random and therefore, could not possibly be related to the number of doctors in Manhattan, a strong correlation emerged between the digits and people's estimates. It would seem absurd to base judgments on random digits, but people did.

Beware of Sunk Costs

Sunk costs are just what they sound like—money you have invested that is, for all practical purposes, gone. Economic theory asserts that only future costs and benefits should affect decisions. However, the problem is that people have a hard time forgetting the past, and they often try to recoup sunk costs. This mindset can lead to trouble. One type of sunk cost is the purchase price that home sellers paid for their house. Simply stated, at some point in the past, a person purchased her house for a certain price. That price, by economic standards, is a sunk cost and should, for all practical purposes, be irrelevant to the negotiation the seller has with a buyer today. However, most people are affected by the past. To examine this phenomenon, Diekmann and colleagues (1996) conducted a simulation of sellers and buyers in real estate negotiations. In all cases, the Multiple Listing Service (MLS) sheet describing the house was identical, as was the current real estate market. However, negotiators were given different information about their previous purchase price. Buyers offered significantly higher amounts for a condominium with larger sunk costs, indicating that the seller's sunk costs influenced the buyer's behavior. Moreover, sellers' BATNAs were significantly lower when they had low, as opposed to high, sunk costs. Final settlements were significantly lower in the low (as opposed to high) sunk cost situations. When preparing for negotiations, negotiators need to be aware that sunk costs will not only influence their own behavior but the behavior of their opponents.

Do Not Confuse Your Target Point with Your Reservation Point

Negotiators often make the mistake of using their target point as their reservation point. Thus, the negotiator has a clear sense of what he or she would like to achieve but has not thought about the least acceptable terms he or she could live with. This poor negotiation strategy can result in one of two fatal flaws. The negotiator who lacks a well-formed reservation point runs the risk of agreeing to a settlement that is worse than what he or she could do by following another course of action. In other cases, the negotiator may walk away from potentially profitable deals. For example, many home sellers reject early offers on their house that are superior to their reservation point, only to be forced to accept an offer of less value at some later point in time. For example, consider the negotiations involving the naming of the New Orleans Superdome (*Times-Picayune*, June 1, 2003). The state of Louisiana received two offers after putting the Superdome naming rights on the market in September 2001. The state rejected the first offer and, since then, the market has run dry.

Identify the Issues in the Negotiation

Many negotiators make the mistake of identifying only a single issue to negotiate. Usually, this issue is money (e.g., sales price or salary, etc.). It is a grave mistake to focus on a single issue in a negotiation because, in reality, more issues are at stake in most negotiation situations. The problem is that they remain "hidden" unless negotiators do the work of unbundling them. By identifying other issues, negotiators can add value to negotiations. For example, in the purchase of a car, the payment terms, cash up-front, loan agreement, or warranty could all be negotiable issues. Negotiators should take time to brainstorm how a single-issue negotiation may be splintered into multiple issues (Lax & Sebenius, 1986). Unbundling negotiations into several issues is not intuitive because people have a tendency to simplify situations into single issues. However, negotiators should try to make single-issue negotiations more complex by adding issues.

Identify the Alternatives for Each Issue

Once the negotiator has identified the issues to be negotiated, it is a good idea to identify several alternative courses of action within each issue. For example, in a negotiation for a new car, payment terms might be broken down into percentage paid up front or percentage of interest on a loan; a loaner agreement might involve how many months or years the option to buy is available. By identifying issues and alternatives, negotiators create a matrix in which the identified issues in the negotiation are located along the columns and the alternatives are located along the rows.

Identify Equivalent Packages of Offers

Once a negotiator has identified the issues in a negotiation and identified alternatives within each issue, the next step of preparation is to determine a variety of different combinations of the issues that all achieve the target or aspiration point. For example, an MBA student in a job interview might identify starting salary, signing bonus, and vacation days as key issues and identify several alternatives within these issues. The student might then take the step of identifying highly attractive packages that she could present as opening offers in the negotiation; for example, a starting salary of $90,000, three weeks of vacation per year, and a signing bonus of $10,000 might be psychologically equivalent to a starting salary of $100,000, 10 days of vacation per year, and a signing bonus of $12,000. Negotiators attempt to identify as many multiple-issue packages of offers as possible to present to the other party. This approach creates more degrees of freedom in negotiation. *The most important aspect of identifying packages of offers is that the packages should all be of equivalent value or attractiveness to oneself.* This task requires that negotiators ask themselves some important questions about what they value and what is attractive to them. (The task can be accomplished in a variety of ways; as a first step, it is wise to consult Appendix 1, which helps prepare a negotiator to identify packages of equivalent value by testing the negotiator's rationality.)

We strongly discourage negotiators from stating a range (e.g., a salary range). This limited perspective is not in any way equivalent to identifying packages of offers. By stating a range, the negotiator gives up important bargaining ground and moves too close to his or her BATNA. We call it a *premature concession.* By stating a range ("I would be interested in a salary between $90,000 and $100,000") a negotiator has already made a concession (implicitly agreeing to a salary of $90,000). Ideally, a negotiator should exhaust possible packages of a given value before making a concession, which can be best achieved by determining more than one way to satisfy the negotiator's interests and aspirations. Another benefit of identifying packages of offers is that the negotiator does not give his or her opponent the impression that he or she is a *positional negotiator.* (A positional negotiator is a person who determines a set of terms desired in a negotiation, presents those terms, and refuses to budge on any dimension of any issue; see Fisher, Ury, & Patton, 1991.) By identifying multiple issues and multiple alternatives within each issue, a negotiator is more likely to achieve his or her target.

Assess Your Risk Propensity

Negotiations always involve risk. The key question is not necessarily how to minimize risk or how to brace oneself psychologically to take risks, as many practitioner-oriented books might lead one to believe. Rather, the key is to understand the nature of risk and how that risk affects decision making. As an exercise, suppose you are offered a choice between the following two options:

>   Option A: Receiving a cashier's check for $5,000
>   Option B: Playing a game that offers a 50 percent chance of winning a $10,000 cashier's check and a 50 percent chance of winning nothing

When presented with a choice between a sure thing and a gamble of equivalent value, most people choose option A, the sure thing. Note that the expected value of each choice is $5,000, which would mean that negotiators should be indifferent (or risk-neutral) between the two. However, the strong preference for option A over B reflects a fundamental principle of negotiator behavior: **risk aversion**.

Now, imagine yourself facing the following unenviable choice:

>   Option C: Paying $5,000 for an unexpected expense
>   Option D: Playing a game that offers a 50 percent chance of paying nothing and a 50 percent chance of paying $10,000

Most people find it difficult to choose between options C and D because these choices are undesirable. However, when forced to make a decision, the majority of negotiators choose option D, even though the expected value of C and D is exactly the same—$5,000. Option D represents the "risky" alternative. The dominant choice of D over C reflects a fundamental principle of human psychology:

Most people are risk-seeking when it comes to losses. In contrast, when it comes to gains, most people are risk-averse. A *reference point* defines what a person considers to be a gain or a loss. Thus, rather than weighing a course of action by its impact on total wealth, people generally "frame" and evaluate outcomes as either "gains" or "losses" relative to some arbitrary reference point (Kahneman & Tversky, 1979).

So, what are the implications for negotiation? According to Bottom (1998), negotiators should consider the differential impact of three sources of risk in any negotiation. Each type of risk may affect risk-seeking and risk-averse behavior differently. The three sources of risk in negotiation include: strategic risk, BATNA risk, and contractual risk.

Strategic Risk

Strategic risk refers to the riskiness of the tactics that negotiators use at the bargaining table. As mentioned earlier, negotiators often choose between extremely cooperative tactics (such as information-sharing and brainstorming) and, at the other extreme, competitive tactics (such as threats and demands). Consider the risk that AOL's David Colburn took when negotiating with Microsoft to get the AOL icon on Microsoft Windows start page—valuable real estate on the computer desktop because it gave AOL access to untold millions of Microsoft customers who might sign up for the online service (*Washington Post*, June 15, 2003). It would mean that AOL would not have to send free disks to get people to sign up for AOL because the software would already be installed on the computer. During the negotiation, Colburn threatened to use the browser of Microsoft's archenemy—Netscape—if Microsoft did not agree to put the AOL icon on the Windows start page. Microsoft agreed. Consider also the extremely calculated risk that Joseph Bachelder took when negotiating

Michael Valentino's CEO compensation at a major pharmaceutical company. Bachelder told Valentino that he knew on day one that Valentino would get everything he wanted. When Valentino asked why, Bachelder said that the hiring company had mistakenly put its own general counsel in charge of the talks, "When this is over, you're going to be that guy's boss. He knows that. He can't fight you too hard on anything" (*The Wall Street Journal*, June 25, 2003).

Kray, Paddock, and Galinsky (2003) reasoned that negotiators who had recently experienced a string of failures would adopt a "loss frame" and would feel less "in control" in a negotiation; conversely, negotiators who had experienced a recent string of successes might feel greater control. Consequently, loss-framed negotiators were reluctant to reveal information that could be used to exploit them; instead, they preferred to manage risk by delaying outcomes.

One way of assessing the amount of risk that people are willing to take is to examine how they behave in an ultimatum situation. In a typical ultimatum situation, one player must propose how to divide a fixed sum (e.g., $10) and the other player can only accept the offered share or reject it, leaving both people with nothing. Dividers who propose a very large share for themselves relative to the other party (a risky strategy) often have their proposal rejected by the other party, even if the proposal is better than the other party's BATNA (Pillutla & Murnighan, 1995).

BATNA Risk

Whereas the negotiator can and should be fairly sure that he or she can resort to his or her BATNA in the event that the present negotiation does not result in agreement, most negotiation situations involve an element of risk. In actual practice, many people's BATNAs are uncertain because potential alternatives arrive sequentially. For example, consider a student who has seven sequentially scheduled interviews over the next 10 weeks, but no actual offers. In this sense, the student's BATNA is a guess about the likely attractiveness of future alternatives. Bottom (1998) gives another example of a car dealer's uncertain BATNA: "A car dealer who decides not to make the one last concession needed to close a deal is rarely doing so because an alternative buyer in the next room is waiting to buy the same car at a higher price. The seller must make a conjecture about the likelihood that a more attractive offer will be made in the near future. Rejecting an offer entails a risk that the car will remain on the lot indefinitely, costing the dealer money, with no better offer forthcoming" (p. 94).

Under most circumstances, we might expect that negotiators who are in a "gain frame" to be more risk-averse (and therefore, more concessionary) than negotiators who hold a "loss frame" (who might hold out). This gain-loss basis can be a potential problem in negotiation because negotiators can be "framed." To see how, consider the following example: Negotiators who are instructed to "minimize their losses" make fewer concessions, reach fewer agreements, and perceive the settlements to be less fair compared to those who are told to "maximize their gains" (Bazerman, Magliozzi, & Neale, 1985; Neale & Northcraft, 1986; Neale, Huber, & Northcraft, 1987; for reviews, see Neale & Bazerman, 1991). In short, the negotiators who are told to "minimize their losses" adopt more risky bargaining strategies (just as the majority of people choose option D over C in the earlier example), preferring to hold out for a better, but more risky, settlement. In contrast, those who are told to "maximize their gains" are more inclined to accept the sure thing (just as most people choose option A over B in the earlier example). Negotiators who view the glass as "half full" are more inclined to reach agreement, whereas negotiators who view the glass as "half empty" are more inclined to use threats and resort to their BATNAs. If one negotiator has a negative frame and the other has a positive frame, the negotiator with the negative frame reaps a greater share of the resources (Bottom & Studt, 1993). Thus, a negotiator needs to be aware of the important psychological impact his or her reference point can have on his or her own behavior. Obviously, negotiators should carefully examine their reference points and be wary when their opponents attempt to manipulate those reference points.

A negotiator's BATNA acts as an important reference point from which other outcomes are evaluated. Outcomes and alternatives that fall short of one's BATNA are viewed as losses; outcomes that exceed a negotiator's reservation point or BATNA are viewed as gains. The more risk-averse the negotiator, the more likely it is that she or he will make greater concessions (Neale & Bazerman, 1985). Thus, given BATNAs of equal expected value, the more risk-averse negotiator will be in a weaker bargaining position (Crawford & Sobel, 1982). Making a concession is the best way to avoid taking a risk.

Contractual Risk

According to Bottom (1998), **contractual risk** refers to the risk associated with the willingness of the other party to honor its terms. For example, signing a peace treaty with one's adversaries may lead to genuine peace, or it may lead to a military disadvantage if the other side fails to honor the agreement. For example, during the 1960s, the U.S. government negotiated the sale of weapons to the Iraqi government. At the time, the agreement appeared to serve mutually beneficial purposes as a defense against Communist aggression. However, the same agreement became a threat to U.S. interests when Iraq nationalized its oil fields and announced a friendship treaty with the Soviet Union. Moreover, even with full commitment of the parties, the value of a contract is influenced by circumstances that are outside control of the parties—something known as exogenous hazards (Bottom, 1998).

Another example of contractual risk comes from the business world: The Mitsubishi Estate Company provided a dramatic example of the risk of erroneous estimates in negotiation (Bottom, 1996). In October 1989, Mitsubishi agreed to pay the Rockefeller family trust $846 million in exchange for a controlling interest in the Rockefeller Group, Inc., which owns Rockefeller Center. Unfortunately, Mitsubishi, along with many others, failed to foresee the collapse of the New York real estate market, which dramatically lowered the value of the acquisition. In May 1995, Mitsubishi Estate Company was forced to seek bankruptcy protection primarily in an attempt to stem the $600 million in losses they had incurred on the investment (*The Wall Street Journal*, May 12, 1995; June 9, 1995). Clearly, the Mitsubishi negotiators expected a much better payoff when they signed the original agreement to acquire control of the property.

How does such contractual risk affect negotiator behavior? Under contractual risk, negotiators with negative frames (risk-seeking) are more likely to reach integrative agreement than those with positive frames (risk-averse). Why? The only route capable of attaining high aspirations entails some creative risk. Thus, if integrative negotiation outcomes involve "sure things," positive frames are more effective; however, if the integrative outcomes require negotiators to "roll the dice," negative frames are more effective. In a series of studies involving contractual risk, Bottom (1998) reports that negotiators with a "loss frame" are more cooperative and more likely to settle than those with a "gain frame." Further, "loss frame" negotiators create more integrative agreements.

Endowment Effects

According to basic principles of rationality, the value or utility we associate with a certain object or outcome should not be influenced by irrelevant factors, such as who owns the object. Simply stated, the value of the object should be about the same, whether we are a buyer or a seller. (*Note*: Buyers and sellers might want to adopt different *bargaining positions* for the object, but their *private valuations* for the object should not differ as a consequence of who has possession of it.) However, negotiators' **reference points** may lead buyers and sellers to have different valuations for objects. Someone who possesses an object has a reference point that reflects his or her current endowment. When someone who owns an object considers selling it, he or she may view the situation as a loss. The difference between what sellers demand and what buyers are willing to pay is a manifestation of loss aversion, coupled with the rapid adaptation of the reference point. Therefore, we should expect that sellers will demand more for objects than buyers are willing to pay.

One example comes from a class of MBA students who were "endowed" with coffee mugs worth $6, as charged by the university bookstore (Kahneman, Knetsch, & Thaler, 1990). The students who were not given a coffee mug were told that they had the opportunity to buy a mug from a student who owned one, if the student who owned the mug valued it less. The buyers' willingness to pay for the mug and the sellers' willingness to sell the mug were inferred from a series of choices (e.g., "receive $9.75" versus "receive mug," "receive $9.50 versus a mug," etc.). Basic rationality would predict that about half of the buyers will value the mug more than the seller and therefore trade will occur; similarly, about half of the sellers will value the mug more than the buyer and trade will not occur. The reference point effect, however, predicts that because of the loss-aversion behavior engendered by the seller's loss frame, trade will occur less than expected. Indeed, although 11 trades were expected, on average, only four took place. Sellers demanded in excess of $8 to part with their mugs; prospective buyers were only willing to pay list price (Kahneman, Knetsch, & Thaler, 1990).

If sellers are risk-seeking by virtue of their endowment, how can it be that horses, cars, furniture, companies, and land are bought and sold every day? The endowment effect operates only when the seller regards himself or herself to be the owner of the object. If a seller expects to sell goods for a profit and views the goods as currency (for example, when MBA students are endowed with tokens rather than coffee mugs), the endowment effect does not occur.

Am I Going to Regret This?

People evaluate reality by comparing it to its salient alternatives (Kahneman & Miller, 1986). Sometimes we feel we made the "right" decision when we think about alternatives. Other times, we are filled with regret. What determines whether we feel we did the right thing (e.g., took the right job, married the right person) or whether we feel regret? An important component in determining whether a person experiences regret is counterfactual thinking (Gilovich & Medvec, 1994). **Counterfactual thinking**, or thinking about what might have been but did not occur, may be a reference point for the psychological evaluation of actual outcomes. In negotiation, immediate acceptance of a first offer by an opponent often means a better outcome for the proposing negotiator; however, the outcome is distinctly less satisfying (Galinsky, Seiden, Kim, & Medvec, 2002). One of the benefits of having a first offer accepted is that it can positively affect preparation. Negotiators whose first offer is accepted by the opponent are more likely to prepare longer for a subsequent negotiation; it also makes negotiators reluctant to make the first offer again (Galinsky, Seiden, Kim, & Medvec, 2002).

As an example, consider feelings of regret experienced by athletes in the Olympic games (Medvec, Madey, & Gilovich, 1995). Although silver medalists should feel happier than bronze medalists because their performance is objectively superior, counterfactual reasoning might produce greater feelings of regret and disappointment in silver medalists than in bronze. Specifically, the bronze medalist's reference point is that of not placing at all, so winning a medal represents a gain. In contrast, the silver medalist views himself or herself as just missing the gold. With the gold medal as the referent, the silver medalist feels a loss. Indeed, videotapes of medalists' reactions (with the audio portion turned off) reveal that bronze medalists are perceived to be happier than silver medalists (Medvec, Madey, & Gilovich, 1995). Further, silver medalists report experiencing greater feelings of regret than do bronze medalists.

Violations of the Sure Thing Principle

Imagine that you face a decision between going to graduate school X on the East Coast or graduate school Y on the West Coast. You must make your decision before you find out whether your start-up company has received funding from a venture capitalist. In the event you get the funding, the East Coast provides access to many more of your potential customers. In the event that funding does not come through, by going to the East Coast, you would be closer to your family, who could help you with finances. This sounds pretty straightforward so far: School X is your dominant choice no matter what the venture capitalist does. In other words, you have chosen school X regardless of whether you get funding. Making a decision between X and Y should not be hard—or should it?

When faced with uncertainty about some event occurring (such as whether your company will be funded), people are often reluctant to make decisions and will even pay money to delay decisions until the uncertain event is known. This is paradoxical because no matter what happens, people choose to do the same thing (Tversky & Shafir, 1992). Consider a situation in which a student has just taken a tough and exhausting qualifying examination (see Shafir, 1994). The student has the option of buying a very attractive five-day Hawaiian vacation package. The results of the exam will not be available for a week, but the student must decide whether to buy the vacation package now. Alternatively, she can pay a nonrefundable fee to retain the right to buy the vacation package at the same price the day after the exam results are posted. When presented with these three choices, most respondents (61 percent) choose to pay a nonrefundable fee to delay the decision. Two other versions of the scenario are then presented to different groups of participants. In one version, the student passed the exam, and in the other version, the student failed. In both of these situations, respondents overwhelmingly preferred to go on the vacation. Thus, even though we decide to go on the vacation no matter what the results of the exam, we are willing to pay money to delay making this decision.

This behavior violates one of the basic axioms of rational theory of decision making under uncertainty: the **sure thing principle** (Savage, 1954). According to the sure thing principle, if an alternative X is preferred to Y in the condition that some event, A, occurs, and if X is also preferred to Y in the condition that some event, A, does not occur, then X should be preferred to Y, even when it is not known whether A will occur.

Why would people pay a fee to a consultant or intermediary to delay the decision when they would make the same choice either way? Violations of the sure thing principle are rooted in the *reasons* people use to make their decisions. In the earlier example, people have different reasons for going to Hawaii for each possible event. If they pass the exam, the vacation is a celebration or reward; if they fail the exam, the vacation is an opportunity to recuperate. When the decision maker does not know whether he or she has passed the exam, he or she may lack a clear reason for going to Hawaii. In the presence of uncertainty, people may be reluctant to think through the implications of each outcome and, as a result, they violate the sure thing principle.

Do I Have an Appropriate Level of Confidence?

Consider a situation in which you are assessing the probability that a particular company will be successful. Some people might think the probability is quite good; others might think the probability is low; still others might make middle-of-the-road assessments. For the negotiator, what matters most is making an assessment that is accurate. How accurate are people in judgments of probability? How do they make assessments of likelihood, especially when full, objective information is unavailable?

Judgments of likelihood for certain types of events are often more optimistic than is warranted. The *overconfidence effect* refers to unwarranted levels of confidence in people's judgment of their abilities and the occurrence of positive events and underestimates of the likelihood of negative events. For example, in negotiations involving third-party dispute resolution, negotiators on each side believe the neutral third party will adjudicate in their favor (Farber & Bazerman, 1986, 1989; Farber, 1981). Obviously, a decision favoring both parties cannot happen. Similarly, in final-offer arbitration, wherein parties each submit their final bid to a third party who then makes a binding decision between the two proposals, negotiators consistently overestimate the probability that the neutral arbitrator will choose their own offer (Neale & Bazerman, 1983; Bazerman & Neale, 1982). Obviously, the probability is only 50 percent that a final offer will be accepted; nevertheless, both parties' estimates typically sum to a number greater than 100 percent. The message is to be aware of the overconfidence effect. When we find ourselves to be highly confident of a particular outcome occurring (whether it be our opponent caving in to us, a senior manager supporting our decision, etc.), it is important to examine why. On the other hand, evidence suggests that overconfidence about the value of the other party's BATNA might serve the negotiator well. Specifically, negotiators who are optimistically biased (i.e., they think that their counterpart will concede more than he or she really can) have a distinct bargaining advantage (Bottom & Paese, 1999).

SIZING UP THE OTHER PARTY

Once the negotiator has gone through the preparation procedure for evaluating what he or she wants in a negotiation situation, it is time to think about the other party (or parties).

Who Are the Other Parties?

It is always important to identify who are the players in a negotiation. A **party** is a person (or group of people with common interests) who acts in accord with his or her preferences. Parties are readily identified when they are physically present, but often, the most important parties are not present at the negotiation table. Such parties are known as the **hidden table** (Friedman, 1992). When more parties are involved in the negotiations, the situation becomes a team or multiparty negotiation, and the dynamics change considerably. A variety of issues crop up as more parties enter the bargaining room. For example, with more than two parties, coalitions may develop, and teams of negotiators may form. Team and multiparty negotiations are so important that we devote an entire chapter to them in this book (Chapter 9). Sometimes, it is obvious who the other parties are, and they have a legitimate place at the table. However, in other situations, the other parties may not be obvious at all, and their legitimacy at the table may be questionable. The negotiator should take the time to carefully ascertain who the parties are. Sometimes, the power of the most important and influential parties comes, in part, from being away from the table.

Are the Parties Monolithic?[1]

Monolithic refers to whether parties on the same side of the table are in agreement with one another concerning their interests in the negotiation. Although it would make sense for parties on the same side to be of one voice, often they are not. Frequently, the parties are composed of people who are on the same side but have differing values, beliefs, and preferences. For example, as twin vice chairmen of Toys "R" Us, Michael Goldstein and Robert Nakasone presented a united front when negotiating for big initiatives. They made many important decisions jointly. However, their styles were not the same. Over time, their interests and styles clashed greatly, leading Robert Nakasone to ask Michael Goldstein to stop attending the all-important top-management Monday noontime meetings. Sometime later, Michael Goldstein asked Robert Nakasone to resign (*The Wall Street Journal*, Dec. 2, 1999).

Issue Mix

As we noted earlier, a negotiator takes the time to fractionate a single-issue negotiation into multiple issues. However, the other party may have a different set of issues that they have identified. The two parties then are, in a sense, talking "apples and oranges" once they come to the negotiation table.

Others' Interests and Position

A negotiator should do as much research and homework as possible to determine the other parties' interests in the negotiation. For example, of the multiple issues

---

[1]This question is raised by Raiffa (1982) in his seminal book, *The Art and Science of Negotiation*.

identified, which issues are most important to the other party? What alternatives are most preferable to the other party?

Other Negotiators' BATNAs

Probably the most important piece of information a negotiator can have in a negotiation is the BATNA of the other party. Unfortunately, unless you are negotiating with an extremely naïve negotiator, it is unlikely that opponents will reveal their BATNAs. However, a negotiator can and should do research about the other party's BATNA before negotiating. Most negotiators severely underresearch their opponent's BATNA. For example, most people, when purchasing cars, have access to a wealth of information about dealers' costs; however, they do not access this information prior to negotiating with car salespersons. This lack of information, of course, limits their ability to effectively negotiate. Along the same lines, many people do not adequately utilize real estate agents when purchasing houses. Real estate agents can provide a wealth of valuable information about the nature of the market and the history of a house that is for sale—all of which can be valuable when trying to determine an opponent's BATNA. The other party's aspiration point will be quite clear; however, the negotiator who determines only the other party's aspiration point and not the BATNA is in a severely disadvantageous negotiation position because her opponent's aspiration may act as an anchor in the negotiation process.

SITUATION ASSESSMENT

In addition to sizing up oneself and sizing up the other party in a negotiation, the negotiator is well advised to assess the negotiation situation. In some types of business interactions, certain norms differ radically from those of other business situations. Assess the following *before* negotiating (see Raiffa, 1982).[2]

Is the Negotiation One Shot, Long Term, or Repetitive?[3]

In a one-shot negotiation, a transaction occurs, and no future ramifications accrue to the parties. Most negotiation situations are not one-shot situations in which the parties involved come together only at one point in time to conduct business. One of the few situations that has been identified as a truly one-shot negotiation is the interaction that occurs between customers and wait staff at interstate roadside diners—neither party will likely ever see one another again. (Incidentally, economists are baffled as to why diners leave tips—because tipping is usually a mechanism used in long-term relationships.)

Even if the parties to negotiation change over time, negotiators' reputations precede them to the table. Because most people negotiate in the context of social networks, most negotiations are long term in nature because reputation information is carried through those social networks. Repetitive negotiations are situations in which negotiators must renegotiate terms on some regular basis (e.g., unions and their management). In long-term and repetitive negotiations, parties must consider

---

[2]Many of the questions that follow are suggested by Raiffa (1982); we also expand his list.
[3]H. Raiffa (1982), *The Art and Science of Negotiation*, Cambridge, MA: Belknap.

how their relationship evolves and how trust is maintained over time. Probably the most important long-term relationship that involves negotiation is the job employment negotiation. Because people want to negotiate economically attractive deals but not sour long-term relationships, this negotiation is generally regarded as uncomfortable (see Sidebar 2-1). This topic is so important that we devote a special chapter to trust and relationships (Chapter 6) and a separate appendix on negotiating a job offer.

> ### Sidebar 2-1. Job Negotiation
> "Even in a sluggish economy, job seekers should try to negotiate the best possible pay package and departure deal for a new job" (CareerJournal.com, as cited in *Business Wire*, May 22, 2001). Employers have an incentive to treat people well because they want to preserve the morale of the workforce. Moreover, most employers are ready to negotiate: 82 percent of all HR professionals expect job candidates to counteroffer, and a whopping 92 percent say that salaries are indeed negotiable.

Do the Negotiations Involve Scarce Resources, Ideologies, or Both?

The two major types of conflict are consensus conflict and scarce resource competition (Aubert, 1963; Druckman & Zechmeister, 1973: Kelley & Thibaut, 1969; Thompson & Gonzalez, 1997). **Consensus conflict** occurs when one person's opinions, ideas, or beliefs are incompatible with those of another, and the two seek to reach an agreement of opinion. For example, jurors' beliefs may differ about whether a defendant is innocent or guilty; two managers may disagree about whether someone has project management skills; two people may argue over whether gun ownership should be controlled. Consensus conflict is about ideology and fundamental beliefs and, as you might imagine, is difficult to resolve because it involves values and emotions. **Scarce resource competition** exists when people vie for limited resources. For example, when business partners are in conflict concerning how to divide responsibilities and profits, each may feel he or she deserves more than the other feels is appropriate.

Many conflict situations involve not only scarce resources but ideologies. People who are in conflict about interests (e.g., money and resources) are more likely to make value-added trade-offs and reach win-win outcomes than people who are in conflict about values or beliefs (Harinck, DeDreu, & Van Vianen, 2000). For example, the Israeli-Palestinian conflict involves the allocation of land (a scarce resource) but stems from fundamentally different religious beliefs and ideologies.

Is the Negotiation One of Necessity or Opportunity?

In many cases, we must negotiate to meet our needs; in other situations, negotiations are more of a luxury or opportunity. As an example, consider a couple selling their house because they have been transferred to a different location. They must negotiate a contract on their house. Even if they have an attractive BATNA, they eventually must negotiate with someone to achieve their needs. In contrast, a person who is interested in enhancing her salary and benefits might want to improve her employment situation. No pressing need to negotiate exists; rather, negotiation is initiated for opportunistic reasons. Consider how the CEO of United, Jim Goodwin, avoided a negotiation of *necessity* (negotiation with his pilot unions) and instead focused on a negotiation of *opportunity* (a possible acquisition of US Airways). The problem for Goodwin was that his failure to focus on the negotiation of necessity led to serious problems (*Denver Post*, June 9, 2003).

Many people avoid negotiations of opportunity because they feel that they lack skills. Indeed, having confidence in one's self as a negotiator is important for success (Sullivan, O'Connor, & Burris, 2003). Some people are comfortable with negotiations, to the point that they are always involved in them. Consider, for example, deal maker extraordinaire Ed Lampert (*BusinessWeek*, Aug. 11, 2003b). In 2003, he was the second-largest stockholder in Sears. He sold $1.5 million in shares of stock after Sears disclosed its intention to sell the credit unit. In the following quarter, he bought back $1 million in shares.

Is the Negotiation an Exchange or Dispute Situation?

In the typical negotiation, parties come together to attempt to exchange resources. In the classic example, a buyer sees greater value in a seller's goods than the seller wants for them, and an exchange takes place (money is paid for goods or services). In other situations, negotiations take place because a claim has been made by one party and has been rejected by the other party. These aspects characterize a **dispute situation** (Ury, Brett, & Goldberg, 1988). For example, consider the dispute that involved Michael Capellas, the CEO of WorldCom (renamed MCI), whose rivals allegedly avoided hundreds of millions of dollars in fees over a decade by disguising long-distance calls as local calls or as calls originated by its long-distance competitor, AT&T (*BusinessWeek*, Aug. 11, 2003c). The difference between exchanges and disputes concerns the alternatives to mutual settlement. In an exchange situation, parties simply resort to their BATNAs; in a classic dispute situation, they often go to court.

Are Linkage Effects Present?[4]

Linkage effects refer to the fact that some negotiations affect other negotiations. Probably the most obvious example is in the case of law and setting precedent. Resolutions in one situation have implications for other situations. For example, when the Teamsters union negotiated with the corporate parent of Jewel supermarkets in 2003, company management feared that if the Teamsters won a strong contract, it would serve as a template for unions at its other stores around the country (*Chicago Tribune*, Aug. 13, 2003). Albertsons, for example, had more than 400 labor contracts. Often direct linkages will occur when a multinational firm has operations in several countries and a decision made in one country carries over to other countries. Sometimes, indirect linkage effects are also a factor, such as when a decision made at the negotiation table affects some interest group in a fashion that no one anticipates fully. For example, a key reason why mergers are often unsuccessful is that companies do not think about linkage effects with current employees. In most merger scenarios, employees of the purchased company are given little information about the turn of

---

[4]Raiffa (1982).

events until well after the deal is settled. Rumors fly about what's going on, and employees are left in limbo, bitter about changes, and worried about their jobs and colleagues. Human resource specialists should be involved in the negotiation process to make the linkages for the employees smoother. For example, when baking soda product manufacturer Church & Dwight sought to acquire pharmaceutical company Carter-Wallace, Steven P. Cugine, the vice president of human resources, was involved from the beginning to manage the linkages. Within days of the acquisition, he held group meetings to explain the situation and lay out the transition strategy (*Workforce*, Feb. 1, 2003).

Is Agreement Required?[5]

In many negotiation situations, reaching agreement is a matter of preference. For example, in a salary negotiation, a person might be willing to decline an offer from one company and either stay with the current company, start his or her own company, or delay negotiations indefinitely. However, in other situations, reaching agreement is not only the only course of action—it is required. For example, on August 17, 1981, when more than 85 percent of the 17,500 air traffic controllers went on strike for better working conditions and improved wages, President Ronald Reagan told the controllers to return to work or the government would assume that the striking controllers had quit. By the end of that week, more than 5,000 Professional Air Traffic Controllers Organization (PATCO) members received dismissal notices from the FAA. Reagan stated that Congress had passed a law in 1947 forbidding strikes by government employees, including a nonstrike oath that each air controller must sign upon hiring. Another example: The Taylor Law bars public employees from striking. This legislation affected the negotiations between New York governor George Pataki and the 14 bargaining units representing 190,000 state employees. Negotiations can be automatically extended under the Taylor Law if no new agreement is reached at the time of expiration (*The Times Union–Albany*, Mar. 2, 2003).

Is It Legal to Negotiate?

In the United States, it is illegal to negotiate the selling of human organs. In September 1999, the online auction house eBay had to retract a seller's posted auction for a human kidney (*New York Times*, Sept. 3, 1999). The bidding went up to $5.7 million before eBay called off the auction. However, in the Philippines, it is legal to sell kidneys, despite ongoing debate about the issue (see Sidebar 2-2).

> **Sidebar 2-2. Is It Legal to Negotiate?**
> Consider the desperation that must have lead Romeo Roga, 36, of the Philippines to do what he did. Romeo's one-year-old son was sick with measles, and Roga needed cash to pay medical bills. He earned $1.25 a day carrying sacks of rice at the harbor—not enough to support his family of five children. Roga's stepfather told him he could earn $2,125 by selling his kidney. Said Roga, "I was forced to do it.

---

[5]Raffia (1982).

It was a matter of survival" (*Newsweek*, Nov. 1, 1999, p. 50). The Roman Catholic Church denounces the business as unethical and exploitative. However, kidney patients are usually willing to pay any price just to live. Doctors are seeking a middle ground, with the objective of preventing people from commercializing organ donation. Roga's kidney did not get him much. His son died, and the money has since run out. He tires easily with only one kidney. Says Roga, "At least I've helped someone" (p. 50).

Sometimes, no specific laws govern what can or cannot be negotiated; rather, individuals rely on strong cultural norms that are highly situation-specific. For example, most people in the United States do not negotiate the price of fruit at major grocery stores, but they do it freely in farmer's markets, such as the Pike Place Market in Seattle, Washington. But farmer's markets are not the only place to haggle. For example, Bill Meyer, 41-year-old father of six, rarely pays full price for anything. In grocery stores, he tries to get bargains on food that is going to spoil if it is not sold. In thrift stores, he gathers up a pile of stuff and offers a single price for it. At pizza parlors, he asks for pizzas that have not been picked up and gets them for $3 each (*The Oregonian*, Apr. 30, 1996). Most home electronic stores will negotiate, as well as stores that sell large, durable goods. And, when it comes to college financial aid packages, families often have more options than they realize and may be able to negotiate larger aid awards for their children. Colleges will usually balk at the idea of "negotiations," but will take another look if they see compelling reasons to do so. Colleges don't want every parent asking for more money, but about 60 percent of the time, when parents inquire and are prepared, they get more money (*Dow Jones Newswires*, Apr. 22, 2003).

Is Ratification Required?[6]

Ratification refers to whether a party to the negotiation table must have any contract approved by some other body or group. For example, a corporate recruiter may need to have the salary and employment packages offered to recruits ratified by the company's human resources group or the CEO. In some circumstances, negotiators may tell the other side that ratification is required when it is not.

Are Time Constraints or Other Time-Related Costs Involved?[7]

Virtually all negotiations have some time-related costs. Although the negotiator who desperately needs an agreement, or for whom the passage of time is extremely costly, is likely to be at a disadvantage (Stuhlmacher, Gillespie, & Champagne, 1998), more time pressure is not necessarily bad. It is important to distinguish *final deadlines* from *time-related costs* (Moore, 2004). Two negotiators may face radically different time-related costs, but a deadline for one is a deadline for the other. The shortest final deadline is

---

[6]Raffia (1982).
[7]Raffia (1982).

the only one that counts, and if they don't have a deal by that point, the two negotiators must exercise their BATNAs.

Time Pressure and Deadlines

A final deadline is a fixed point in time that ends the negotiations. The rate of concessions made by negotiators increases as negotiators approach final deadlines (Lim & Murnighan, 1994). According to Moore (2004), negotiators believe that final deadlines (i.e., time pressure) are a strategic weakness, and so avoid revealing their deadlines for fear that their "weakness" will be exploited by opponents. However, in point of fact, because deadlines restrict the length of the negotiation for all parties, they place all parties under pressure. One person's final deadline is also the other's final deadline (Roth, Murnighan, & Schoumaker, 1988). For example, consider how Adam Chesnoff revealed his deadline when in negotiations with Haim Saban (*Reuters*, Aug. 11, 2003). When time ran out on the negotiations, Chesnoff came back with his own deadline: his wedding date. "If we can't get [the deal] done by Friday, you won't have a problem with Haim or me, you'll have to deal with my fiancée, which is a much more difficult conversation." However, when negotiators keep their deadlines secret, the result is that they rush to get a deal before the deadline, whereas their opponents, who expect longer negotiations, concede at a more leisurely pace (Moore, 2004). (For another example of strategic use of deadlines at AOL, see Sidebar 2-3.)

Sidebar 2-3. Strategic Deadline Pressure

AOL used their knowledge of time pressure and deadlines in a strategic fashion. AOL's strategy of creating an "insane deadline" would always begin with a delicate courtship that would end up with an ultimatum that would leave the client reeling and usually acquiescing. AOL would begin negotiations as a "slow waltz" between AOL and a prospective client, involving "lots of wooing and pretty words about how great the client's business was, how neat it would be if the two sides hooked up, how wonderful it would be if the client bought ads on AOL. Naturally, AOL wouldn't mention that it was having precisely the same slow dance with multiple partners. Weeks would go by—then AOL would suddenly demand immediate action. Abruptly, deal makers would draw up a contract, slam it on the table and order the prospective client to sign it within 24 hours or, worse, by the end of the day, or else AOL would take the offer to another party, which happened to be standing by." What's more, the contracts would always be of mammoth size—impossible to penetrate in the time constraints. Moreover, AOL executives made deal makers of other companies sit around for hours, in a so-called waiting game, just to signal to them that they were not important (*Washington Post*, June 15, 2003).

The reason why negotiators so often incorrectly predict the consequences of final deadlines in negotiation has to do with the more general psychological tendency to focus egocentrically on the self when making comparisons or predictions (Moore & Kim, 2003). Negotiators focus on the deadline's effect on themselves more than its effect on their negotiating partners. The same tendency leads people to predict that they will be above average on simple tasks and below average on difficult tasks (Kruger, 1999; Windschitl, Kruger, & Simms, 2003).

Time-Related Costs

Setting a final deadline on the negotiations can be helpful, especially if the passage of time is particularly costly to you (Moore, 2004). This strategy was used successfully to reach an agreement in the National Basketball Association strike of 1998 to 1999. The owners set a final deadline and threatened to walk out if they could not come to agreement with the players by January 5, 1999. The two sides came to agreement on January 4 on terms that dramatically favored the owners.

Time Horizon

Another time-related question concerns what Okhuysen and colleagues (2003) refer to as the **time horizon**—the amount of time between the negotiation and the consequences or realization of negotiated agreements. As a general principle, the longer the temporal distance between the act of negotiation and the consequences of negotiated agreements, the better the agreement (Okhuysen et al., 2003). The reason is that parties are less contentious since the realization is in the distance. Moreover, this time benefit is particularly pronounced in the cases where negotiations concern "burdens" as opposed to "benefits," because time gives people opportunity to discount the effects of burdens.

Are Contracts Official or Unofficial?

Many negotiation situations, such as the purchase of a house or a job offer, involve official contracts that legally obligate parties to follow through with stated promises. However, in several negotiation situations of equal or greater importance, negotiations are conducted through a handshake or other forms of informal agreements. Considerable cultural variation surrounds the terms of what social symbols constitute agreement (handshakes versus taking tea together) as well as which situations are treated officially or unofficially. Awkwardness can result when one party approaches the situation from a formal stance and the other treats it informally. Consider the negotiations between city commissioners in Florida and firefighters (*South Florida Sun-Sentinel*, June 3, 2003). Pension fund increases were part of a handshake and verbal agreement. However, when it came to the actual signing, the commissioners refused to ratify the concessions they had previously agreed to. Obviously, ill will can result when implicit contracts are broken. (We take up the topic of broken trust in Chapter 6.)

Where Do the Negotiations Take Place?

Common wisdom holds that it is to one's advantage to negotiate on one's own turf, as opposed to that of the other side. So important is this perception that great preparation and expense are undertaken to find neutral ground for important negotiations. For example, for the summit between former president Ronald Reagan and Soviet leader Mikhail Gorbachev, the site was carefully selected. The two met at the Chateau Fleur d'Eau in Geneva, Switzerland. Similarly, the multiparty Irish talks were stalled in 1991 when conflict broke out concerning where the next set of talks would be held. The Unionists, who agreed to talk directly to Irish government ministers about the future of Northern Ireland, were anxious to avoid any impression of going "cap in hand" to Dublin, and therefore wanted the talks held in London, the capital to which they were determined to remain connected. In contrast, the Social Democratic and Labor Party, which represented the majority of Catholic moderates in the province, preferred that the talks be held in Dublin, the capital to which they felt a strong allegiance (*Baltimore Sun*, May 7, 1991). Similarly, when John Mack, of Credit Suisse First Boston, negotiated with Frank Quattrone, the investment firm's powerful tech banker, Mack insisted that they not meet in New York, where the firm had its headquarters, and not in Palo Alto, where Quattrone was based, but in Kansas City, Missouri, because it was "halfway between" (*Fortune*, Sept. 1, 2003).

Are Negotiations Public or Private?[8]

In many areas, the negotiation dance takes place in the public eye. In other negotiation situations, negotiations occur privately. For example, Kelman's (1991) work with the Israeli-Palestinian negotiations occurred under strict privacy. As Kelman notes, privacy was instrumental for progress between parties:

> The discussions are completely private and confidential. There is no audience, no publicity, and no record, and one of the central ground rules specifies that statements made in the course of a workshop cannot be cited with attribution outside the workshop setting. These and other features of the workshop are designed to enable and encourage workshop participants to engage in a type of communication that is usually not available to parties involved in an intense conflict relationship. (p. 214)

In contrast, one of the unique aspects of sports negotiations is that they take place in a fishbowl atmosphere, with fans and the media observing every move at the bargaining table (Staudohar, 1999). Staudohar notes that this kind of attention can lead to a media circus, with owners and players projecting their opinions on issues and events:

> The dickering back and forth makes for entertaining theater, but is a hindrance to the rational settlement of differences. It is customary, therefore, for both owners and players to be advised by their leaders to hold their tongues. NBA owners were made subject to fines of $1 million by the league for popping off in the media.

---

[8]Raffia (1982).

Is Third-Party Intervention a Possibility?[9]

In many negotiation situations, third-party intervention is commonplace (and even expected). Most commonly, third-party intervention takes the form of mediation or arbitration. However, in other areas, third-party intervention is unheard of. The mere presence of third parties may serve to escalate the tensions in negotiation situations, if the initial parties egocentrically believe that third parties will favor their own position. In other situations, it is less common (and perhaps a sign of personal failure) to involve third parties. Third-party intervention is so important that we devote Appendix 3 to it in this book.

What Conventions Guide the Process of Negotiation (Such as Who Makes the First Offer)?

In many negotiations, people have complete freedom of process. However, in other negotiations, strong conventions and norms dictate how the process of negotiation unfolds. For example, when people buy or sell houses in the United States, the first offer is typically made by a prospective buyer, and all offers are formalized in writing. However, marked differences characterize the process across the country, with some home negotiations being conducted via spoken word and some via official contract.

Do Negotiations Involve More Than One Offer?

In some situations, it is typical to go back and forth several times before a mutually agreeable deal is struck. In other situations, this type of dealing is considered unacceptable. In the real estate world, for example, buyers and sellers expect to negotiate. These same people, however, would not dream of negotiating in Nordstrom.

As another example, many employers now expect that job candidates will attempt to negotiate what is initially offered to them, but for many, extending the haggling is not acceptable. Carl Kusmode, founder of the Tiburon Group, an Internet recruiter in Chicago, said he withdrew an offer to a database administrator who kept upping his price. "It became insulting," Kusmode said (*U.S. News & World Report*, Nov. 1, 1999). Thus, a negotiation should go one or two rounds, not 10. Negotiation norms, however, vary from industry to industry. As an example, consider what happened to Jay Kaplan, real estate entrepreneur (*The Arizona Republic*, Jan. 9, 1994). He had traveled through the southeastern United States for eight consecutive days and met with five different owners, trying to purchase apartment buildings and shopping centers. Each meeting was a marathon session, with offers and counteroffers, lasting until dawn before an agreement was made. By the eighth day, with one meeting left, Kaplan was tired and decided to use a single-offer strategy. After asking for some aspirin and putting on his most exhausted face, Kaplan said to the other party: "You're asking $4.3 million for your property. I want to buy it for $3.7 million. Let's save ourselves the trouble of a long negotiation. I'm going to make you only one offer. It will be my best shot, and it will be a fair one. If you're a reasonable man, I'm sure you'll accept it." (p. E6). The strategy backfired. Kaplan then offered the other party $4.025 million, and the other party rejected it. They haggled for four

---

[9]Raffia (1982).

hours until they agreed on $4.275. The opponent later told Kaplan that no way was he going to accept the first offer made—no matter what it was.

Do Negotiators Communicate Explicitly or Tacitly?

In a typical buyer-seller negotiation or employment negotiation, negotiators communicate explicitly with one another. However, in other situations, communication is not explicit but tacit, and people communicate through their actions. This issue is so important that we devote an entire chapter to it (Chapter 11, in a discussion of social dilemmas).

Is a Power Differential a Factor Between Parties?

Technically, negotiation occurs between people who are interdependent, meaning that the actions of one party affect those of the other party, and vice versa. If one person has complete authority over another and is not affected by the actions of others, then negotiation cannot occur. However, it is often the case that low-power people can affect the outcomes of high-powered others. For example, a CEO has more power than a middle-level manager in the company, but the manager can undoubtedly affect the welfare of the company and the CEO. The presence or absence of a power differential between negotiating parties can strongly affect the nature of negotiations. This topic is so important that we devote an entire chapter to power and influence in this book (Chapter 7).

Is Precedent Important?

In many negotiation situations, precedent is important, not only in anchoring negotiations on a particular point of reference, but also in defining the range of alternatives. Often the major argument that negotiators must confront when attempting to negotiate for themselves is the other side's statement that he or she must follow precedent. In a sense, the negotiator fears that making a decision in one case will set him or her up for future negotiations. Of course, most precedents allow for a great deal of interpretation on the part of the precedent-follower and the person attempting to challenge the precedent. Oftentimes, negotiators will invoke precedent as a way of cutting off negotiations.

CONCLUSION

Effective preparation places the negotiator at a strategic advantage at the bargaining table. We outlined three general areas of preparation: the self, the other party, and the context or situation. In terms of personal preparation, the negotiator who has identified a personal BATNA and set a reservation price and a target point is in a much better position to achieve the desired objectives. The negotiator who has prepared for negotiation knows when to walk away and how much is reasonable to concede. The negotiator who has adequately researched an opponent's BATNA and interests is less likely to be tricked or confused by that other party. We outlined several issues concerning the negotiation situation that the negotiator should consider prior to commencing negotiations. A summary preparation form is presented in Table 2-1. We suggest the negotiator use it when preparing for negotiations. The next two chapters focus on pie-slicing and pie-expanding strategies in negotiations.

TABLE 2-1 Preparation Worksheet for Negotiations		
Self-Assessment	*Assessment of the Other Party*	*Assessment of the Situation*
• What do I want? (Set a target point) • What is my alternative to reaching agreement? (Identify your BATNA) • What is my reservation point? (See Box 2-1) • What focal points could influence me? • What are my "sunk costs"? • Have I ensured that my target point is not influenced by my reservation point? • What are the issues in the negotiation? • What are the alternatives for the issues? • Have I identified equivalent multi-issue offers? • Have I assessed my risk propensity?	• Who are the other parties? • Are there parties who are likely to not be at the table? • Are the parties monolitic? • What issues are relevant to the other party? • What are the other party's interests? • What are the other party's alternatives for each issue? • What is the other party's position? • What is the other negotiator's BATNA?	• Is the negotiation one shot, long term, or repetitive? • Do the negotiations involve scarce resources, conflict of ideologies, or both? • Is the negotiation of necessity or opportunity? • Is the negotiation an exchange or dispute situation? • Are there linkage effects? • Is agreement required? • Is it legal to negotiate? • Is ratification required? • Are there time constraints or other time-related costs? • Are contracts official or unofficial? • Where do negotiations take place? • Are negotiations public or private? • Is third-party intervention a possibility? • Are there conventions in terms of the process of negotiation? • Do negotiations involve more than one offer by each party? • Do negotiators communicate explicitly or tacitly? • Is there a power differential among parties? • Is precedent important?

3

DISTRIBUTIVE NEGOTIATION: SLICING THE PIE

Several years ago, Lindsey McAlpine, now CEO of the McAlpine Group in Charlotte, North Carolina, was a young man, eager to work on his first real estate project. He met with a much older industry leader who was selling a piece of land in Charlotte. Sensing that the guy on the other side of the table did not take him seriously, Lindsey said, "Look, I have an experienced partner. I can't tell you who he is, but he won't agree to these terms." Of course, there was no partner; Lindsey now needed to find someone who looked the part. Says Lindsey, "My entire goal was to find a man who was older than 50 with gray hair—what I call, to this day, my gray-headed equity." Lindsey pulled in a friend whom he told to not talk but to simply sit in the meeting and "look mature." The strategy worked (*Inc.*, Aug. 1, 2003a, p. 76).

Unfortunately, too much pop psychology substitutes for solid negotiation strategy. In this example, the young negotiator ended up with a larger slice of the bargaining pie than he ever imagined; however, the strategy might not work well a second time. We don't believe that such a strategy is sustainable in the long term or, for that matter, advisable in the short term. In this chapter, we focus on how negotiators can best achieve their outcomes—both economic (e.g., money and resources) as well as social (i.e., preserving the relationship and building trust). The strategies are all based on controlled scientific investigations (CSIs), so we can infer direct cause-and-effect relationships. We also provide several examples of how they are used in actual business negotiations. In this chapter, we address the first of the two central goals of negotiation: slicing the pie. This chapter discusses who should make the first offer, how to respond to an offer made by the other party, the proper amount of concessions to make, and how to handle an aggressive negotiator.

The entire process of making an opening offer and then reaching a mutually agreeable settlement is known as the **negotiation dance** (Raiffa, 1982). Unfortunately, most of us never took dancing lessons or know what to do once we find ourselves on the dance floor. Should we lead? Should we follow? A few hard and fast rules of thumb apply, but the negotiator must make many choices that are not so clear-cut. We wrestle with these issues in this chapter.

Although this chapter deals with slicing the pie, it is important to realize that most negotiations involve a win-win aspect (*expanding* the pie), which we discuss in detail in the next chapter. However, even in win-win negotiations, the pie of resources created by negotiators eventually has to be sliced, and it is pie slicing that we discuss first because it tends to be more straightforward and intuitive. First, we discuss the bargaining zone. Then we discuss 10 ways to increase your slice of the pie. Finally, we take up the topic of fairness as it applies to slicing the pie.

THE BARGAINING ZONE AND THE NEGOTIATION DANCE

You analyzed the negotiation situation as best you can. You thought about your target point and your BATNA in a realistic fashion, developed a reservation point, and used all available information to assess your opponent's BATNA. Now it is time for face-to-face negotiation. Typically, negotiators' target points do not overlap: The seller wants more for the product or service than the buyer is willing to pay. However, it is often (but not always) the case that negotiators' reservation points *do* overlap, meaning that the most the buyer is willing to pay is more than the least the seller is willing to accept. Under such circumstances, a mutual settlement is profitable for both parties. *However, the challenge of negotiation is to reach a settlement that is most favorable to oneself and does not give up too much of the bargaining zone.* The **bargaining zone**, or **zone of possible agreements (ZOPA)** (Lax & Sebenius, 1986) is the region between each party's reservation point. The final settlement of a negotiation will fall somewhere above the seller's reservation point and below the buyer's reservation point (Raiffa, 1982).

Every negotiator should know certain important principles when it comes to slicing the pie. First, it is important to realize that the bargaining zone can be either positive or negative (see Figures 3-1A and 3-1B).

In a positive bargaining zone, negotiators' reservation points overlap, such that the most the buyer is willing to pay is greater than the least the seller will accept. This overlap means that mutual agreement is better than resorting to BATNAs. For example, consider the bargaining zone in Figure 3-1A. The seller's reservation point is $11; the buyer's reservation point is $14. The most the buyer is willing to pay is $3 greater than the very least the seller is willing to accept. The bargaining zone is between $11 and $14, or $3. If the negotiators reach agreement, the settlement will be somewhere between $11 and $14. If the parties fail to reach agreement in this situation, the outcome is an impasse and is **suboptimal,** because negotiators leave money on the table and are worse off by not reaching agreement than reaching agreement.

In some cases, the bargaining zone may be nonexistent or even negative. However, the negotiators may not realize it, and they may spend fruitless hours trying to reach an agreement. This situation can be costly for negotiators; during the time in which they are negotiating, their opportunities may be worsening (i.e., negotiators have time-related

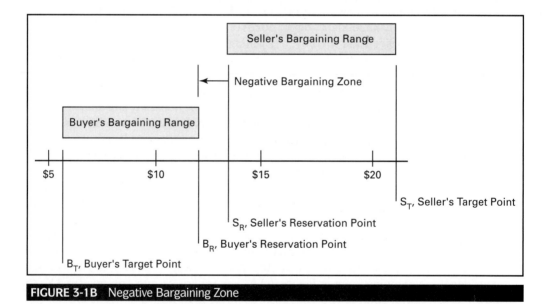

FIGURE 3-1A   Positive Bargaining Zone

FIGURE 3-1B   Negative Bargaining Zone

costs; see Chapter 2). For example, consider the bargaining zone in Figure 3-1B, in which the seller's reservation point is $14 and the buyer's reservation point is $12. The most the buyer is willing to pay is $2 less than the seller is willing to accept at a minimum. This **negative bargaining zone** offers is no positive overlap between the parties' reservation points. In this situation, negotiators should exercise their best alternatives to agreement. Because negotiations are costly to prolong, it is in both parties' interests to determine whether a positive bargaining zone is possible. If not, the parties should not waste time negotiating; instead, they should pursue other alternatives. Consider, for example the negotiations between the Green Bay Packers and football receiver, Antonio Freeman, in 2002 (*Wisconsin State Journal*, June 4, 2002). The Green Bay Packers offered Freeman $1 million in base salary. However, Freeman refused, indicating he had better alternatives elsewhere.

Bargaining Surplus
So far, we stressed the point that mutual settlement is possible when parties' reservation points overlap and impossible when parties' reservation points do not overlap. **Bargaining surplus** is the amount of overlap between parties' reservation points. It is a measure of the size of the bargaining zone (what we refer to in this chapter as "the pie"). The bargaining surplus is a measure of the value that a negotiated agreement offers to both parties over the alternative of not reaching settlement. Sometimes it is very large; other times it is very small. Skilled negotiators know how to reach agreements when the bargaining zone is small.

Negotiator's Surplus
We noted that negotiated outcomes will fall somewhere in the bargaining zone. But what determines *where* in this range the settlement will occur? Obviously, each negotiator would like the settlement to be as close to the other party's reservation point as possible, thereby maximizing his or her slice of the pie. In our example in Figure 3-1A, the seller would prefer to sell close to $14; the buyer would prefer to buy close to $11. *The best possible economic outcome for the negotiator is one that just meets the other party's reservation point, thereby inducing the other party to settle, but allows the focal negotiator to reap as much gain as possible.* This outcome provides the focal negotiator with the greatest possible share of the resources to be divided. In other words, one person gets all or most of the pie.

The positive difference between the settlement outcome and the negotiator's reservation point is the **negotiator's surplus** (see Figure 3-2). Notice that the total surplus of the two negotiators adds up to the size of the ZOPA or bargaining surplus. Negotiators want to maximize their surplus in negotiations; surplus represents

FIGURE 3-2 Bargaining Range and Surplus

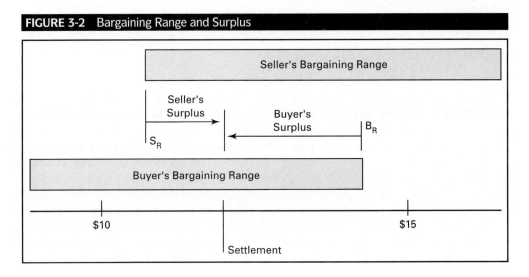

resources in excess of what is possible for negotiators to attain in the absence of negotiated agreement.

The fact that negotiated settlements fall somewhere in the ZOPA and that each negotiator tries to maximize his or her share of the bargaining surplus illustrates the **mixed-motive** nature of negotiation. Therefore, negotiators are motivated to cooperate with the other party to ensure that settlement is reached in the case of a positive bargaining zone, but they are motivated to compete with one another to claim as much of the bargaining surplus as they can.

PIE-SLICING STRATEGIES

The most frequently asked question about negotiation is, "How can I achieve the most of the bargaining surplus for myself?" Stated another way: "How can I get a deal that is much better than my BATNA?" For example, a new deal maker at Amazon.com had just negotiated a $5 million ad deal with a dot-com, but he was convinced he could get more because the dot-com was a publicly traded company (meaning that he could see their finances). So, he told his boss he wanted to get $10 million for the deal (*Washington Post*, June 15, 2003). Another example: If you are a potential home buyer and you discern that the seller's reservation point is $251,000, that is an ideal offer to make, assuming it well exceeds your reservation point. However, this feat is easier said than done. How do you get information about the other party's reservation price? Most negotiators will never reveal their reservation point, but it may emerge unintentionally. Raiffa (1982) cautions negotiators not to reveal their reservation points and cites a humorous story wherein one party opens with a direct request for information about his opponent's reservation price:

> "Tell me the bare minimum you would accept from us, and I'll see if I can throw in something extra." The opponent, not to be taken in, quips, "Why don't you tell us the very maximum that you are willing to pay, and we'll see if we can shave off a bit?" (p. 40)

This example illustrates the essence of negotiation: How do people make sure they reach agreement if the ZOPA is positive but still claim as much of the pie as possible?

Another problem emerges as well. Even if someone reveals her reservation point, the other party has no way to verify that the first party is telling the truth. In fact, the most commonly used phrase in any negotiation is "That's my bottom line." When the other party tells us his or her reservation point, we are faced with the dilemma of determining whether the information is valid. The negotiator is always at an information deficit because the other party's reservation point is usually not verifiable—it includes subjective factors—whereas a BATNA is based on objective factors and can therefore be verifiable.

Given that "private" information about reservation points is inherently unverifiable, negotiation seems rather pointless. After all, if you can never tell if the other person is telling the truth, then communication would be seen as fruitless (economists refer to such discussions as "cheap talk," [Croson, Boles, & Murnighan, 2003]). However, in our research, cheap talk does, in fact, matter (Bazerman, Gibbons,

Thompson, & Valley, 1998). Even so, we know that people negotiate all the time in the absence of such information. When people negotiate, they are constantly making judgments about the other person's reservation point and interests.

Some conditions allow negotiators to be more *confident* about the other party's reservation point. For example, a car buyer openly invites the dealer to call the competitor in the next suburb as a way of verifying that the buyer can indeed get the same car for less money. Similarly, if a person says something that is not in his or her interest, we may have more reason to believe it. For example, if a seller tells us she does not have another buyer and is under pressure to sell, we might believe her because this statement is not in her interest. This factor leads to an important cautionary note: It is not necessarily in your best interest to misrepresent your reservation point because you risk the possibility of disagreement. For example, imagine that you are trying to sell your used CD player because you have been given another, nicer model as a gift. You would be willing to accept $100 for the used model (your reservation point, based upon a pawnbroker's offer), but you would ideally like to get $200 (your target point). You place an ad, and a potential buyer calls offering to pay $110. If you tell the caller that you have an offer of $120 (when in fact, you do not), you risk the possibility that the potential buyer will not accept because he or she might have a better BATNA. Obviously, it is in your interest not to let potential buyers believe that your reservation price is $200 (see Farrell & Gibbons, 1989).

With regard to slicing the pie, negotiators should be willing to settle for outcomes that exceed their reservation point and reject offers that are worse than their reservation point. This rule of thumb seems infinitely rational; however, as noted earlier when discussing the "sandtraps" of negotiation (in Chapter 1), people frequently settle for outcomes worse than their BATNA (the agreement bias) and often reject offers that are better than their BATNA (hubris). As a case in point, most strikes are eventually settled on terms that could have been reached earlier, without parties incurring the costs that the strike imposes (Keenan & Wilson, 1993; Roth, 1993). The key question is why this seemingly irrational behavior occurs. The problem can usually be traced to either cognitive or emotional biases. We will elaborate on some of these biases later in this chapter.

If negotiators follow 10 basic strategies, they can substantially increase the probability that they will obtain a favorable slice of the pie. Although these strategies don't come with guarantees, they are the best advice we can offer for enhancing one's ability to garner more resources for one's self.

Strategy 1: Assess Your BATNA and Improve It

It is truly surprising how many negotiators do not think about their BATNA prior to entering negotiation. Even those who think about their BATNA often do not attempt to improve it. We realize that for most negotiators, BATNAs involve some uncertainty (see Chapter 2). However, uncertainty is not a good excuse for failure to assess one's BATNA. *Nothing can help a negotiator get a bigger slice of the pie than having a great BATNA.*

The risk a negotiator takes from not accurately assessing his or her BATNA prior to negotiation is that the negotiator will be unduly influenced by the opponent negotiator. We strongly prescribe that negotiators spend a considerable amount of time attempting to improve upon their BATNA before entering into a negotiation (remember the "falling in love" principle from Chapter 2).

Strategy 2: Determine Your Reservation Point, But Do Not Reveal It

Unless you are willing to settle for your reservation point, do not reveal your BATNA or your reservation price during the course of negotiation, even in the friendliest of situations. If you do, the other party will simply offer you your reservation price and you will not have any surplus for yourself. Further, your threats to "hold out" won't work because the other negotiator will know that rationally, you are better off accepting the offer.

In only two circumstances do we think it is appropriate to truthfully reveal your reservation price.

> **Situation #1:** You have exhausted your time to negotiate and are about to walk out without a deal and you sense that the bargaining zone may be very small or perhaps negative. Prior to stepping on the plane or leaving the meeting, you could reveal your reservation price. For example, in California in August 2003, the clock ticked toward the deadline for submitting petition signatures for a privacy bill that would require banks and other financial institutions to obtain customers' permission before they could share or sell information about them to other companies (*San Francisco Chronicle*, Aug. 20, 2003). As the deadline approached, Chris Larsen, chairman and CEO of E-LOAN, kicked in $1 million of his and his company's money to bankroll the petition initiative to guarantee it a place on the ballot—the most he could spend.
>
> **Situation #2:** You have a great BATNA and, consequently, an aggressive reservation price, and you would be happy if your opponent matched or barely exceeded your reservation point. In this sense, negotiators "signal" their BATNA. For example, consider how US Airways' Stephen Wolf would signal his BATNA in negotiations with United (who was interested in acquiring US Airways). Wolf's opening offer was $88 per share. United regarded this price to be unreasonable because the stock was trading below $30 a share. However, Wolf signaled that United's archrival—American—might be interested. And consequently, United agreed to pay $60 per share—a price that some United advisers considered to be $10 to $15 too high (*Denver Post*, June 9, 2003).

Consider how another company, AOL, would signal its BATNA: One tactic involved an AOL deal maker pitching a deal to a prospective dot-com client. The AOL rep's PowerPoint presentation would include the logo of the client's rival—as if AOL had accidentally mixed up some of the slides from another presentation. The AOL rep would then feign embarrassment and apologize. However, the slip-up was completely intentional and meant to signal to the dot-com that AOL had a BATNA (*Washington Post*, June 15, 2003).

Many negotiators reveal their true reservation price if they trust and like the other party or desire a long-term relationship. However, we think this is ill-advised. Negotiators have available many other ways to demonstrate trust and relationship-building, short of revealing a BATNA. Further, revealing information about a BATNA or reservation point is not a pie-expanding strategy; it is a pie-slicing strategy, and as a pie-slicing strategy, it has the effect of reducing a negotiator's power in a negotiation.

Many negotiators, after studying the rationality of BATNAs and reservation prices, conclude that strategic misrepresentation of their reservation price might be advantageous. We do not believe that negotiators should lie about their BATNA or reservation price during negotiation. Lying is problematic for ethical reasons (which we will discuss in Chapter 7) but also can strategically backfire. If you lie about your reservation price you effectively reduce the size of the bargaining zone, because the bargaining zone is defined as the overlap of each party's reservation price. It means that a positive but small bargaining zone may be transformed into a negative bargaining zone, and you may reach an impasse because your lie falsely indicated a negative bargaining zone. It will be difficult to save face in such a situation because you risk appearing foolish if you retract your offer.

Strategy 3: Research the Other Party's BATNA and Estimate Their Reservation Point

Even though determining the other party's BATNA may be easier said than done, negotiators often fail to do sufficient research, which reduces their power more than anything. Negotiators can use a variety of ways to garner information that may reveal something about the opponent's alternatives.

Be careful when the other party discloses, however. When a negotiation opponent discloses his or her BATNA at the outset of the negotiation, negotiators actually make less demanding offers, disclose more truthful information, and settle for less profit than when the opponent does not disclose a BATNA (Paese & Gilin, 2000). This tendency points to the powerful effect reciprocity has on our own behavior.

Strategy 4: Set High Aspirations (Be Realistic, But Optimistic)

Your aspiration, or target point, defines the upper limit on what you can ever expect to get in a negotiation. Because you will never get more than your first offer, your first offer represents the most important **anchor point** in the negotiation. As a case in point, consider how United Airlines captain Rick Dubinsky, known for his toughness, began by dropping an anchor in his negotiations with CEO of United, Jim Goodwin, in January 2000. Using a pad of paper on Goodwin's own desk, Dubinsky drew two lines, one about an inch above the other. The bottom line, Dubinsky explained, was the current pilots' pay. The top was where Dubinsky expected it to go. Then, Dubinsky drew a delta sign indicating the difference between the two and wrote the number 21. "You are going to settle at 21%. That's the number, Jim. You are going to go there easy or you are going to go there hard, but you are going to go there" (*Denver Post*, June 9, 2003).

According to Raiffa (1982), the final outcome of any negotiation can be reliably predicted as a statistical average between the first two offers that fall within the bargaining zone. Note that this fact argues against negotiators making unrealistic proposals, because they do not fall within true bargaining zone. In our own research, we use the first offer made by each party as a measure of his or her aspirations (see Kray, Thompson, & Galinsky, 2001). Moreover, aspirations or target points determine the "final demands" made by negotiators, more so than do BATNAs (Thompson, 1995a). Stated simply, negotiators who set high aspirations end up with more of the pie than those who set lower aspirations. And, negotiators whose aspirations exceed those of their opponents get more of the bargaining zone (Chen, Mannix, & Okumura, 2003). For example, negotiators who have unattractive reservation points and high aspirations actually demand more from their opponents than do negotiators with attractive BATNAs and low aspirations. Thus, it pays to set your aspirations high during a negotiation.

However, this generalization does not mean asking for the outrageous. To be sure, sometimes the "outrageous offer" will pay off. For example, Joe Costello, CEO of Think3, a product-design software company in Santa Clara, California, recounted a time when he negotiated with 27 Toshiba engineers and executives. At best, Costello hoped to land a $5 million deal. When Costello opened, he wrote $27 million on the whiteboard. He admits that he made the number up. Costello was lucky that Toshiba had an unattractive BATNA and needed the software (*Business 2.0*, Sept. 1, 2002). If you ask for something outrageous, you run risk of souring the relationship. Strategically, it is far more effective to make your first offer slightly worse than the other party's reservation point and then bargain them up to their reservation point. Stated differently: Most people are not going to *immediately* accept your first offer, but they *ultimately* might accept an offer that is their reservation point.

Setting specific, challenging, and difficult goals results in greater profit than does setting easy or nonspecific goals (Huber & Neale, 1986, 1987; Neale, Northcraft, & Earley, 1990; Thompson, 1995a). In many cases, nonspecific or easy goals lead to compromise agreements, which (as we will argue in the next chapter) are suboptimal. High aspirations exert a self-regulating effect on negotiation behavior. Negotiators who are assigned easy goals tend to set harder new goals; however, in spite of adjustments, their new goals are significantly easier than the goals chosen by the difficult-goal negotiators. Thus, it is to a negotiator's advantage to set a high, somewhat difficult aspiration point early in the negotiation.

When a negotiator focuses on his or her target point during negotiation, this increases the value of the eventual outcome he or she receives (Galinsky, Mussweiler, & Medvec, 2002; Thompson, 1995a). Similarly, negotiators who focus on "ideals" rather than "oughts" do better in terms of slicing the pie (Galinsky & Mussweiler, 2001). However, the negotiator who focuses on ideals does not *feel* as satisfied as the negotiator who focuses on his reservation point or BATNA. Thus, focusing on targets leads people to do very well in negotiations, but feel worse; in contrast, focusing on reservation points leads people to *do* worse, but *feel* better. These findings demonstrate that gut feeling or intuition can be misleading. How, then, can successful but unhappy negotiators feel better? If negotiators think about their BATNA after the negotiation, they feel psychologically better (Galinsky, Mussweiler, & Medvec, 2002).

We strongly advise negotiators to avoid the **winner's curse** in which your first offer is immediately accepted by the other side because it is too generous. This outcome signals that you did not set your aspirations high enough. Furthermore, we caution negotiators to avoid a strategy known as **boulwarism.** Boulwarism is named after Lemuel Boulware, former CEO of General Electric, who believed in making one's first offer one's final offer. As you might expect, this strategy is not very effective, and it often engenders hostility from the other side.

Another piece of advice: Do not become psychologically "anchored" by your reservation point. Stated simply: Do not let your reservation point drive your aspiration point; the two should be separate. Many negotiators who have learned to assess their BATNA and set an appropriate reservation point fail to think about their aspiration or target point. Consequently, the reservation point acts as a psychological anchor for their aspiration point and, in most cases, people make insufficient adjustments—they do not set their target high enough. We discourage negotiators from using any kind of multiplier of their reservation point to determine their target because no logical reason supports doing so.

Strategy 5: Make the First Offer (If You Are Prepared)

Folklore dictates that negotiators should let the opponent make the first offer. "The experts say it's better to let your adversary make the opening offer" (*Inc.*, Aug. 1, 2003a, p. 79). However, that statement is the pop view of what the experts really say. Letting the other party make the first offer is good advice if you are unprepared or if the other party knows more about you than you know about them (i.e., recall the winner's curse). However, scientific investigation of real bargaining situations does not support this intuition. Whichever party—buyer or seller—makes the first offer, that person obtains a better final outcome (Galinsky & Mussweiler, 2001). Why? First offers act as an anchor point (Galinsky & Mussweiler, 2001). First offers correlate at least 0.85 with final outcomes, which suggests how important they are (Galinsky & Mussweiler, 2001). Negotiators need to think about a number of factors when making an opening offer. First and foremost, an opening offer should not give away any part of the bargaining zone, which puts a negotiator at a pie-slicing disadvantage. Second, many people worry that they will "insult" the other party if they open too high (if they are selling) or too low (if they are buying). However, the fear of insulting the other party and souring the negotiations is more apparent than real, especially if your demands are supported with logic. Managers tell us that when they are faced with an extreme opening offer from the other party, they are not insulted; instead, they prepare to make concessions.

Distinct advantages are associated with making the first offer in a negotiation. The first offer that falls within the bargaining zone can serve as a powerful anchor point in negotiation. Recall, in the previous chapter, the example of people's Social Security numbers affecting their estimates of the number of physicians in Manhattan. That was a case of insufficient adjustment from an arbitrary anchor. Making the first offer protects negotiators from falling prey to a similar anchoring effect when they hear the opponent's offer. Ideally, a negotiator's first offer acts as an anchor for the opponent's counteroffer. For example, Northwest Airlines asked its pilots very early in their 2003 negotiations to take a 17.5 percent pay cut and forgo raises, including a 5.5 percent hike scheduled in the future (*The Commercial Appeal*, July 16, 2003).

Your first offer should not be a range. For that matter, we don't advise stating ranges at any point. For example, employers often ask prospective employees to state a range in salary negotiations. Do not fall victim to this bargaining ploy. By stating a range, you are giving up precious bargaining ground. Your opponent will consider the lower end of the range as your target and negotiate down from there. A far better strategy is to respond to your opponent's request for a range by giving him or her several offers that would all be equally satisfying to you. This point is an important one, and we will return in the next chapter.

One more thing about making the first offer: If you have made an offer to an opponent, then you should expect to receive some sort of counteroffer or response. Once you put an offer on the table, be patient. It is time for your opponent to respond. In certain situations, patience and silence can be important negotiation tools. Do not interpret silence on the other person's part to be a rejection of your offer. Many negotiators make what we call "premature concessions"—they make more than one concession in a row before the other party responds or counteroffers. Always wait for a response before making a further concession. For example, Lewis Kravitz, an Atlanta executive coach and former outplacement counselor, advises patience and knowing when not to speak in the heat of negotiations. In one instance, he was coaching a young man who had just been sacked by his team. The young man felt desperate and told Kravitz he was willing to take a $2,000 pay cut and accept $28,000 for his next job. Kravitz told the man to be quiet at the bargaining table and let the prospective employer make the first offer. At the man's next job interview, the employer offered him $32,000, stunning the overjoyed job seeker into momentary silence. The employer interpreted the silence as dissatisfaction and upped the offer to $34,000 on the spot (*The Wall Street Journal*, Jan. 27, 1998).

Strategy 6: Immediately Reanchor if the Other Party Opens First

If your opponent makes an offer, then the ball is in your court. It is wise to make a counteroffer in a timely fashion. This move does two things. First, it diminishes the prominence of the opponent's initial offer as an anchor point in the negotiation. Second, it signals a willingness to negotiate. It is an essential part of preparation that you plan your opening offer before hearing the other party's opening—otherwise you risk being anchored by the other party's offer. Moreover, Galinsky and Mussweiler (2001) coached some negotiators who received an offer from the other party to focus on information that was inconsistent with that offer; others were not given such coaching. The result? *Thinking* about the opponent's BATNA or reservation price or even one's own target point completely negates the powerful impact that the other party's first offer might have on you. Above all, do not adjust your BATNA based upon your opponent's offer, and do not adjust your target. It is extremely important not to be "anchored" by the opponent's offer. An effective counteroffer moves the focus away from the other party's offer as a reference point.

Strategy 7: Plan Your Concessions

Concessions are the reductions that a negotiator makes during the course of a negotiation. First offers are "openers." It is rare (but not impossible) for a first offer to be accepted. Note: If a first offer is immediately accepted by the other party, negotiators are likely to engage in counterfactual thoughts about how they could have done better (e.g., "what could have been different?) and are therefore less satisfied than negotiators whose first offers are not immediately accepted (Galinsky, Seiden, Kim, & Medvec, 2002). Most negotiators expect to make concessions during negotiation. (One exception is the bargaining style known as *boulwarism*, which we discussed previously.) What is the best way to make such concessions so as to maximize your share of the bargaining zone? Negotiators need to consider three things when formulating counteroffers and concessions: (1) the **pattern of concessions,** (2) the **magnitude of concessions,** and (3) the **timing of concessions.**

Pattern of Concessions

Unilateral concessions are concessions made by one party; in contrast, *bilateral concessions* are concessions made by both sides. Negotiators who make fewer and smaller concessions are more effective in terms of maximizing their slice of the pie, compared to those who make larger and more frequent concessions (Siegel & Fouraker, 1960; Yukl, 1974). It is an almost universal norm that concessions take place in a *quid pro quo* fashion, meaning that negotiators expect a back-and-forth exchange of concessions between parties. People expect others to respond to concessions by making concessions in kind. However, negotiators *should not* offer more than a single concession at a time to an opponent. Wait for a concession on the opponent's part before making further concessions. An exception would be a situation in which you feel that the opponent's offer is truly near his or her reservation point.

Magnitude of Concessions

Even though negotiators may make concessions in a back-and-forth method, this exchange does not say anything about the degree of concessions made by each party. Thus, a second consideration when making concessions is to determine how much to concede. The usual measure of a concession is the amount reduced or added (depending upon whether one is a seller or buyer) from one's previous concession. It is unwise to make consistently greater concessions than one's opponent.

The **graduated reduction in tension (GRIT) model** (Osgood, 1962) is a method in which parties avoid escalating conflict so as to reach mutual settlement within the bargaining zone. The GRIT model, based on the reciprocity principle, calls for one party to make a concession and invites the other party to reciprocate by making a concession. The concession offered by the first party is significant, but not so much that the offering party is tremendously disadvantaged if the opponent fails to reciprocate.

Hilty and Carnevale (1993) examined the degree of concessions made by negotiators over different points in the negotiation process (e.g., early on versus later). They compared black hat/white hat (BH/WH) negotiators with white hat/black hat (WH/BH) negotiators. BH/WH negotiators began with a tough stance, made few early concessions, and later made larger concessions. WH/BH negotiators did the opposite: They began with generous concessions and then became tough and unyielding. The BH/WH concession strategy proved to be more effective than the WH/BH strategy in eliciting concessions from an opponent. Why? The BH-turns-WH sets up a favorable contrast for the receiver. The person who has been dealing with the BH feels relieved to now be dealing with the WH.

Timing of Concessions

By timing of concessions, we mean whether concessions are immediate, gradual, or delayed (Kwon & Weingart, 2004). In an analysis of buyer-seller negotiations, sellers who made immediate concessions received the most negative reaction from the buyer—who showed least satisfaction and evaluated the object of sale most negatively. In contrast, when the seller made gradual concessions, the buyer's reaction was most positive—high satisfaction.

Strategy 8: Use an Objective-Appearing Rationale to Support Your Offers

The way in which an offer is presented dramatically affects the course of negotiations. Ideally, present a rationale that appears to be objective and invites the opponent to buy into your rationale. If your proposals are labeled as "fair," "even splits," or "compromises," they carry more impact. The importance of having a rationale cannot be overestimated. Oftentimes, people simply want to hear that you have a rationale and don't even bother to assess the details of it. For example, Langer, Blank, and

Chanowitz (1978) examined how often people were successful in terms of negotiating to cut in line at a photocopy machine. Those that did not provide a rationale were the least successful (60%); those who presented a logical rationale were the most successful (94%). Interestingly, those who presented a meaningless rationale (e.g., "I have to cut in line because I need to make copies") were remarkably successful (93%). The next section of this chapter takes up the topic of fairness in detail.

Strategy 9: Appeal to Norms of Fairness

Fairness is a "hot button" in negotiation because most negotiators view themselves as fair, or wanting to be fair. The ideal pie-slicing strategy is to determine which norms of fairness would be appropriate for the situation and then use these norms to argue for your own target point. As a negotiator, you should be aware that fairness is subjective and therefore egocentric, meaning that a variety of norms of fairness exist, and negotiators usually focus on norms of fairness that serve their own interests (Loewenstein, Thompson, & Bazerman, 1989). Thus, negotiators should realize that fairness is an arbitrary concept that can be used as a bargaining strategy with an opponent; however, the negotiator should simultaneously be prepared to counterargue when an opponent presents a fairness argument that does not serve his or her own interests.

Strategy 10: Do Not Fall for the "Even Split" Ploy

A common focal point in negotiation is the "even split" between whatever two offers are currently on the negotiation table. In many negotiation situations, such as in car and house buying, negotiators' offers do not overlap. Inevitably, one person has the bright idea of "splitting the difference." The concept of the even split has an appealing, almost altruistic flavor to it. To many of us, it seems unreasonable to refuse to compromise or meet the other person halfway. So what is the problem with even splits? The problem is that they are *based on arbitrarily arrived-at values.* Consider a car-buying situation. Suppose you initially offered $33,000 for the car, then $34,000, and then, finally, $34,500. Suppose the salesperson initially requested $35,200, then reduced it to $35,000, and then to $34,600. The salesperson then suggests that you split the difference at $34,550, arguing that an even split of the difference would be "fair." However, the pattern of offers up until that point was not "even" in any sense. You made concessions of $1,500; the salesperson made concessions of $600. Further, even concessions that were of equal magnitude do not guarantee that the middle value is a "fair" value. It behooves a negotiator to begin with a high starting value and make small concessions. Often, the person who suggests the even split is in an advantageous position. Before accepting or proposing an even split, make sure the anchors are favorable to you.

THE MOST COMMONLY ASKED QUESTIONS

Should I Reveal My Reservation Point?

Revealing your reservation point is generally not a good strategy unless your reservation point is especially good and you suspect that the bargaining zone is narrow. If you reveal your reservation price, be prepared for the other party to offer you your reservation price, but not more.

As we saw earlier, the most valuable piece of information you can have about your opponent is his or her reservation point. This knowledge allows you to make your opponent an offer that barely exceeds his or her reservation point and claim the entire bargaining surplus for yourself. However, you should assume your opponent is as smart as you are and therefore not likely to reveal his or her reservation point. By the same token, if you reveal your reservation point, little would stop your opponent from claiming the bargaining surplus in the negotiation.

Some negotiators reveal their reservation point to demonstrate that they are bargaining in good faith and trust the other party. These negotiators rely on their opponent's goodwill and trust their opponent not to take undue advantage of this information. Other, more effective ways can be used build trust rather revealing your reservation price. For example, you could show a genuine, expressed interest in the needs and interests of the other party. The purpose of negotiation is to maximize your surplus, so why create a conflict of interest with the other party by "trusting" them with your reservation point?

Should I Lie About My Reservation Point?

If negotiators do well for themselves by not revealing their reservation point, perhaps they might do even better by lying, misrepresenting, or exaggerating their reservation point. Lying is not a good idea for three important reasons.

First, lying is unethical. Lewicki and Stark (1996) identified five types of behavior that are considered to be unethical in negotiations, including traditional competitive bargaining (e.g., exaggerating an initial offer or demand), attacking an opponent's network (e.g., attempting to get your opponent fired or threatening to make him or her look foolish), misrepresentation and lying (e.g., denying the validity of information your opponent has that weakens your negotiating position even though the information is valid), misuse of information (e.g., inappropriate information gathering), and false promises (e.g., offering to make future concessions that you know you won't follow through on; guaranteeing your constituency will uphold the settlement, even though you know they won't).

Our examination of egocentrism and lying in tight social networks revealed that even though 40 percent of people believed that others in the network lied over a 10-week period, these same people admitted lying only about 22 percent of the time. Perhaps these egocentric perceptions drive the lawsuits that often occur in negotiations. For example, Textron was accused by its union of lying during labor negotiations (*Textron v. United Automobile*, 1998). Digital Equipment Corporation was accused of lying during pretrial negotiations (*Digital v. Desktop Direct Co.*, 1994), and Woolworth was accused of misrepresenting the amount of asbestos in a building during the negotiation of a lease (*Century 21, Inc. v. F. W. Woolworth*, 1992; all examples reported in Schweitzer & Croson, 1999). The conclusion? A double standard: We are much more likely to see others as deceptive than we are to admit deceiving others. The message: Don't take chances!

Second, lying does not make sense strategically. Lying about your reservation point reduces the size of the bargaining zone. It means that negotiations in which the negotiator would prefer to reach an agreement will sometimes end in impasse. Negotiators who lie about their reservation point often find it difficult to save face. The most common lie in negotiation is "This is my final offer." It is embarrassing to

Multiple Methods of Fair Division

Fairness comes in many forms and types. Most often, negotiators use one of three fairness principles when it comes to slicing the pie: equality, equity, and need (Deutsch, 1985):

1. **Equality rule,** or blind justice, prescribes equal shares for all. Outcomes are distributed without regard to inputs, and everyone benefits (or suffers) equally. The education system and the legal system in the United States are examples of equality justice: Everyone receives equal entitlement. In a university, all students have equal entitlement to health services and career placement services.

2. **Equity rule,** or proportionality of contributions principle, prescribes that distribution should be proportional to a person's contribution. The free market system in the United States is an example of the equity principle. In many universities, students bid for classes; those who bid more points have greater entitlement to a seat in the course. Equity is such an important fairness rule that we later discuss it in detail.

3. **Needs-based rule,** or welfare-based allocation, states that benefits should be proportional to need. The social welfare system in the United States is based on need. In many universities, financial aid is based on need.

Situation-Specific Rules of Fairness

Different fairness rules apply in different situations (Schwinger, 1980). For example, most of us believe that our court/penal justice system should be equality based: Everyone should have the right to an equal and fair trial regardless of income or need (equality principle). In contrast, most of us believe that academic grades should be assigned on the basis of an equity-based rule: Students who contribute more should be rewarded with higher marks (equity principle). Similarly, most people agree that disabled persons are entitled to parking spaces and easy access to buildings (need principle). However, sometimes fierce debates arise (e.g., affirmative action, with some arguing that it is important for people who have been historically disadvantaged to have equal access and others arguing for pure equity-based, or merit-only, rules).

The *goals* involved in a negotiation situation often dictate which fairness rule is employed (Mikula, 1980). For example, if our goal is to minimize waste, then a needs-based or social welfare policy may be most appropriate (Berkowitz, 1972). If our goal is to maintain or enhance harmony and group solidarity, equality-based rules are most effective (Leventhal, 1976). If our goal is to enhance productivity and performance, equity-based allocation is most effective (Deutsch, 1953).

Similarly, a negotiator's *relationship to the other party* strongly influences the choice of fairness rules. When negotiators share similar attitudes and beliefs, when they are physically close to one another, or when it is likely that they will engage in future interaction, they prefer equality rule. When the allocation is public (others know what choices are made), equality is used; when allocation is private, equity is preferred. Friends tend to use equality, whereas nonfriends or acquaintances use equity (Austin, 1980). Further, people in relationships with others do not consistently employ one rule of fairness but, rather, use different fairness rules for specific incidences that occur within relationships. For example, when people in relationships are asked to describe a recent incident from their own relationship illustrating a particular justice principle (equity, equality, or need), need-based fairness is related to incidents involving nurturing and personal development, whereas equity and equality-based fairness are related to situations involving the allocation of responsibilities (Steil & Makowski, 1989). In general, equality-based pie-slicing strategies are associated with more positive feelings about the decision, the situation, and one's partner.

Fairness rules also depend on whether people are dealing with rewards versus costs (recall our discussion about the "framing effect" in Chapter 2). Equality is often used to allocate benefits, but equity is more commonly used to allocate burdens (Sondak, Neale, & Pinkley, 1995). For example, in one investigation, people were involved in a two-party negotiation concerning a joint project (Ohtsubo & Kameda, 1998). In the benefit-sharing condition, negotiators were told that their joint project produced a total earning of 3,000 GL (a hypothetical monetary unit) and that their task was to reach an agreement about how to divide this amount with their partner. Participants were told that they had personally incurred a cost of 1,350 GL for this project and that their final profile would be determined by subtracting 1,350 from the negotiated agreement amount. In the cost-sharing condition, the situation was exactly the same, except participants were told that they had personally invested 1,650 GL. Thus, the bargaining situation was identical in both situations, with the exception of the personal investment. Obviously, an equal split of 3,000 would mean 1,500 apiece that would result in a gain in the benefit condition and a loss in the cost condition. As it turned out, negotiators were more demanding and tougher when bargaining how to share costs than benefits. Furthermore, fewer equal-split decisions were reached in the cost condition.

The selection of fairness rules is also influenced by extenuating circumstances. Consider, for example, a physically handicapped person who attains an advanced degree. A person who overcomes external constraints is more highly valued than a person who does not face constraints but contributes the same amount. When a situation is complex, involving multiple inputs in different dimensions, people are more likely to use the equality rule. Thus, groups often split dinner bills equally rather than compute each person's share. This approach can lead to a problem, however. Group members aware of the pervasive use of equality may actually spend more individually. No group member wants to pay for more than he or she gets; if people cannot control the consumption of others, they consume more. Of course, when everyone thinks this way, the costs escalate, leading to irrational group behavior—a topic we discuss in the chapter on social dilemmas (Chapter 11).

The multiple orientations are a potential source of conflict and inconsistency (Deutsch, 1985). For example, people who are allocating resources choose different rules of fairness than do people who are on the receiving end. Allocators often distribute resources equally, even if they have different preferences. In contrast, recipients who have been inequitably, but advantageously, treated, justify their shares—even when they would not have awarded themselves the resources they received (Diekmann, Samuels, Ross, & Bazerman, 1997).

Social Comparison
Social comparison is an inevitable fact of life in organizations and relationships. Even if we do not desire to compare ourselves with others, we inevitably hear about someone's higher salary, larger office, special opportunities, or grander budget. Social situations are constant reminders of how others—strangers, acquaintances, and friends—compare

with us in terms of fortune, fame, and happiness. How do we react to social comparisons? Are we happy for other people—do we bask in their glory when they achieve successes—or are we threatened and angry?

When does performance of another individual enhance our personal self-evaluation, and when does it threaten our self-worth? When we compare ourselves to one another, we consider the relevance of the comparison to our self-concept. People have beliefs and values that reflect their central dimensions of the self. Some dimensions are highly self-relevant; others are irrelevant. It all depends on how a person defines himself or herself. The performance of other people can affect our self-evaluation, especially when we are psychologically close to them. When we observe someone who is close to us performing extremely well in an area that we highly identify with, our self-evaluation is threatened. Such "upward" comparisons can lead to envy, frustration, anger, and even sabotage. Upon hearing that a member of one's cohort made some extremely timely investments in companies that have paid off multifold and is now a millionaire three times over, people probably feel threatened if they pride themselves on their financial wizardry. The fact that our colleague excels in an area that we pride ourselves on rubs salt in the wounds of the psyche. When another person outperforms us on a behavior that is irrelevant to our self-definition, the better their performance and the closer our relationship, the more we gain in self-evaluation. We take pride in their success.

When it comes to pay and compensation, people are more concerned about how much they are paid relative to other people, whom they consider to be their peers, than the absolute level of their pay. (The irrepressible need to compare oneself to others has led to the development of Web sites, such as SalaryScan [*Business Wire*, June 10, 2002], in which radiologists can access a salary comparison database.) This type of behavior reveals that people often care more about how their slice of the pie compares to other people than the size of the slice in an absolute sense (Adams, 1965; Blau, 1964; Deutsch, 1985; Homans, 1961; Walster, Berscheid, & Walster, 1973; see Box 3-1 for an example of social comparison).

With whom do people compare themselves? Three social comparison targets may be distinguished: upward comparison, downward comparison, and comparison with similar others.

1. **Upward comparison** occurs when people compare themselves to someone who is better off, more accomplished, or higher in status. The young entrepreneur starting his own software company may compare himself to Bill Gates. Oftentimes, people compare themselves upward for inspiration and motivation.
2. **Downward comparison** occurs when people compare themselves to someone who is less fortunate, able, accomplished, or lower in status. For example, when a young manager's marketing campaign proves to be a complete flop, she may compare herself to a colleague whose decisions led to the loss of hundreds of thousands of dollars. Downward comparison often makes people feel better about their own state.
3. **Comparison with similar others** occurs when people choose someone of similar background, skill, and ability with whom to compare. For example, an individual looks at other first-year MBA students when assessing their skills in finance. Comparison with similar others is useful when people desire to have accurate appraisals of their abilities.

BOX 3-1

SELF-INTEREST VERSUS SOCIAL COMPARISON

Imagine that you are being recruited for a position in firm A. Your colleague, Jay, of similar background and skill, is also being recruited by firm A. Firm A has made you and Jay the following salary offers:

Your salary: $75,000

Jay's salary: $95,000

Your other option is to take a position at firm B, which has made you an offer. Firm B has also made your colleague, Ines, an offer:

Your salary: $72,000

Ines's salary: $72,000

Which job offer do you take, firm A's or firm B's? If you follow the principles of rational judgment outlined in Appendix 1, you will take firm A's offer—it pays more money. However, if you are like most people, you prefer firm B's offer because you do not like feeling you are being treated unfairly (Bazerman, Loewenstein, & White, 1992).

What drives the choice of the comparison other? A number of goals and motives may drive social comparison, including the following:

1. **Self-improvement:** People compare themselves with others who can serve as models of success (Taylor & Lobel, 1989). For example, a beginning chess player may compare skill level with a grand master. Upward comparison provides inspiration, insight, and challenge, but it can also lead to feelings of discouragement and incompetence.
2. **Self-enhancement:** The desire to maintain or enhance a positive view of oneself may lead people to bias information in self-serving ways. Rather than seek truth, people seek comparisons that show them in a favorable light. People make downward comparisons with others who are less fortunate, less successful, and so forth (Wills, 1981).
3. **Accurate self-evaluation:** The desire for truthful knowledge about oneself (even if the outcome is not favorable).

The Equity Principle

When it comes to relationships and slicing the pie, people make judgments about what is fair based on what they are investing in the relationship and what they are getting out of it. Inputs are investments in a relationship that usually entail costs. For example, the person who manages the finances and pays the bills in a relationship incurs time and energy costs. An output is something that a person receives from a relationship. The person who does not pay the bills enjoys the benefits of a financial service. Outputs, or outcomes, may be positive or negative. In many cases, A's input is B's outcome, and B's input is A's outcome. For example, a company pays (input) an employee (outcome) who gives time and expertise (input) to further the company's goals (outcome).

Equity exists in a relationship if each person's outcomes are proportional to his or her inputs. Equity, therefore, refers to equivalence of the outcome/input ratio of parties; inequity exists when the ratio of outcomes to inputs is unequal. Equity exists when the profits (rewards minus costs) of two actors are equal (Homans, 1961). However, complications arise if two people have different views of what constitutes a legitimate investment, cost, or reward, and how they rank each one. For example, consider salaries paid to basketball players in the NBA. With star players taking the greatest slice of the salary pie (capped at a fixed amount), little is left over to pay the last three or four players on a 12-person team roster. The minimum salary of $272,500 might seem extraordinarily high to the average person, but in the context of the team—with an average salary of $2.6 million and a star salary of $30 million per year to the Chicago Bulls' Michael Jordan in 1997—it reflects a sizeable disparity (Staudohar, 1999).

Equity exists when a person perceives equality between the ratio of his or her own outcomes (O) to inputs (I) and the ratio of the other person's outcomes to inputs, where a and b represent two people (Adams, 1965):

$$\frac{O_a}{I_a} = \frac{O_b}{I_b}$$

However, this equity formula is less applicable to situations in which inputs and outcomes might be either positive or negative. The basic equity formula may be reconstructed as follows:

$$\frac{O_a - I_a}{|I_a|^{ka}} = \frac{O_b - I_b}{|I_b|^{kb}}$$

This formula proposes that equity prevails when the disparity between person *a*'s outcomes and inputs and person *b*'s outcomes and inputs are equivalently proportional to the absolute value of each of their inputs. The numerator is "profit," and the denominator adjusts for positive or negative signs of input. Each k takes on the value of either +1 or −1, depending on the valence of participants' inputs and gains (outcomes−inputs).

Restoring Equity

Suppose that you were hired by your company last year with an annual salary of $85,000. You felt happy about your salary until you learned that your colleague at the same company, whom you regard to be of equivalent skill and background, is paid $5,000 more per year. How do you deal with this inequity? When people find themselves participating in an inequitable relationship, they become distressed; the greater the perceived inequity, the more distressed people feel. This distress drives people to attempt to restore equity to the relationship.

People who believe they are underpaid feel dissatisfied and seek to restore equity (Walster, Berscheid, & Walster, 1973). For example, underpaid workers lower their level of effort and productivity to restore equity (Greenberg, 1988), and in some cases, they leave organizations characterized by inequity to join an organization where wages are more fairly distributed, even if they are less highly paid in absolute terms (Schmitt & Marwell, 1972).

Consider what happened when two vice presidents of a major *Fortune* 100 company were promoted to senior vice president at about the same time in the late 1990s

(*Washington Post*, June 15, 2003). Both of them moved into new offices, but one of them suspected an inequity. He pulled out blueprints and measured the square footage of each office. His suspicions were confirmed when it turned out the other guy's office was bigger than his by a few feet. A former employee said, "He blew a gasket." Walls were moved, and his office was reconfigured to make it as large as his counterpart's.

People use the following six means in order to eliminate the tension arising from inequity (Adams, 1965):

1. Alter the inputs. (The senior VP could work less hard, take on fewer projects or take more days off, etc.)
2. Alter the outcomes. (The senior VP could make his office bigger—which he did.)
3. Cognitively distort inputs or outcomes. (The senior VP could minimize the importance of his contributions and maximize the perceived value of his office—for example, by deciding that his office was quieter than that of his counterpart.)
4. Leave the situation. (The senior VP could quit his job.)
5. Cognitively distort either the inputs or the outcomes of an exchange partner. (The senior VP may view the other VP as contributing more, or perhaps regard the big office to be less attractive than it actually is.)
6. Change the object of comparison. (The senior VP may stop comparing himself to the other SVP and start comparing himself to someone else in the company.)

The use of the first two strategies depends on whether the person has been over- or underrewarded. Overrewarded individuals can increase their inputs or decrease their outcomes to restore equal ratios, whereas underrewarded people must decrease their inputs or increase their outcomes. For example, people work harder if they think they are overpaid. Conversely, people may cheat or steal if they are underpaid (Greenberg, 1990).

Given the various methods of restoring equity, what determines which method will be used? People engage in a cost-benefit analysis and choose the method that maximizes positive outcomes. Usually, this method minimizes the necessity of increasing any of one's own inputs that are difficult or costly to change and also minimizes the necessity of real changes or cognitive changes in inputs/outcomes that are central to self-concept. Simply put, it is often easier to rationalize a situation than to do something about it. Further, this type of change minimizes the necessity of leaving the situation or changing the object of social comparison once it has stabilized. Thus, we are not likely to ask for a salary cut if we think we are overpaid, but we are more inclined to regard the work we do as more demanding. (See Sidebar 3-1 for an examination of factors that can lead to reactions to inequity.)

Sidebar 3-1. Distributed Versus Concentrated Unfairness
Within an organizational setting, many acts of unfair or unjust behavior may occur. For example, a person of color may be passed over for a promotion. A woman with managerial skills may be relegated to administrative and secretarial tasks. How do employees react to injustice in the organization? Consider two hypothetical companies: A and B. In each company, the overall incidence of unfair

continued

behavior is identical. In company A, the unfair incidences (i.e., percentage of total acts) are targeted toward a single individual—a black female. In company B, the unfair incidences are spread among three individuals—a black female, a Hispanic male, and an older, handicapped white male. The fact that the incidences are concentrated on a single individual or spread out over many organizational members should be irrelevant, if the overall incidence of unfairness in each organization is the same. In practice, however, these situations are viewed quite differently.

In a simulated organization, each of three employees was victimized in one out of three interactions with a manager. In another company, one of the three employees was victimized in all three out of three interactions with a manager; the two other employees were treated fairly. Thus, in both companies, the incidence of unfairness was identical. However, groups' overall judgment of the unfairness of the manager was greater when the injustice was spread across members than when it was concentrated on one individual. Most disconcertingly, targets of discrimination were marginalized by other group members. Blaming-the-victim effects may be more rampant when individuals are the sole targets of discrimination— ironically, when they need the most support (Lind, Kray, & Thompson, 1996).

The equity drive is so strong that people who are denied the opportunity to restore equity will derogate others, thereby restoring *psychological equity*. If distortion must occur, people focus on the other person's inputs or outcomes before distorting their own, especially if such distortion threatens their self-esteem. Leaving the situation and changing the object of comparison involve the highest costs, because they disrupt the status quo and violate justice beliefs.

Procedural Justice

In addition to their slice of the pie, people are concerned with the way resources are distributed (Thibaut & Walker, 1975, 1978; Leventhal, 1976, 1980). People evaluate not only the fairness of outcomes, but also the fairness of the procedures by which those outcomes are determined. People's evaluations of the fairness of procedures determine their satisfaction and willingness to comply with outcomes. For example, managers who educate employees (i.e., explain to them why change is occurring, such as in the case of a merger) find that it increases employee commitment to the change (Kotter & Schlesinger, 1979). The process of explaining decisions in a change context helps employees adapt to the change, whereas the lack of an explanation is often regarded by employees as unfair, generating resentment toward management and toward the decision (Daly & Geyer, 1994). Indeed, Daly (1995), in an investigation of 183 employees of seven private-sector organizations that had each just completed a relocation, found perceived fairness was higher when justification was provided in the case of unfavorable change.

Fairness in Relationships

Consider the following situation: You and a college friend developed a potentially revolutionary (and profitable) idea for a new kind of water ski (see Loewenstein, Thompson, & Bazerman, 1989). You spent about half a year in your dorm basement developing a prototype of the new invention. Your friend had the original idea; you developed the design and materials and assembled the prototype. The two of you talk to a patent lawyer about getting a patent, and the lawyer tells you a patent is pending on a similar product, but the company will offer you $3,000 for one of the innovative features of your design. You and your friend gladly accept. What division of the $3,000 between you and your friend would you find to be most satisfying?

People's preferences for several possible distributions of the money for themselves and the other person were assessed (Loewenstein, Thompson, & Bazerman, 1989). People's utility functions were <u>social</u> rather than <u>individual</u>, meaning that individual satisfaction was strongly influenced by the payoffs received by the other as well as the payoffs received by the self (see Figure 3-3). Social utility functions were tent-shaped. The most satisfying outcome was equal shares for the self and other ($1,500 apiece). Discrepancies between payoffs to the self versus the other led to lower satisfaction. However, social utility functions were lopsided in that advantageous inequity (self receives more than other) was preferable to disadvantageous inequity (other receives more than self). Further, the relationship people had with the other party mattered: In positive or neutral relationships, people preferred equality; in negative relationships, people preferred advantageous inequity. (See Sidebar 3-2 for an examination of different types of profiles.)

Sidebar 3-2. Profiles of Pie Slicers

Have you ever wondered whether most people are truly interested in other people or are only concerned about their own profit? To examine this question, MBA students were given several hypothetical scenarios, such as the situation involving the ski invention, and asked what division of resources (and in some cases, costs) they preferred. Further, people made responses for different kinds of relationships: friendly ones, antagonistic ones, and neutral ones (Loewenstein, Thompson, & Bazerman, 1989). Three types of people were identified:

- **Loyalists** prefer to split resources equally, except in antagonistic relationships (27%).
- **Saints** prefer to split resources equally no matter whether relationships are positive, neutral, or negative (24%).
- **Ruthless competitors** prefer to have more resources than the other party, regardless of relationship (36%).

People will pass up outcomes that entail one person receiving more than others and settle for a settlement of lower joint value but equal-appearing shares (McClelland & Rohrbaugh, 1978). This arrangement is especially true when resources are "lumpy" (i.e., hard to divide into pieces), such as an oriental rug (Messick, 1993).

Egocentrism

What is fair to one person may not be fair in the eyes of another. For example, consider a group of three people who go out for dinner. One person orders a bottle of expensive wine, an appetizer, and a pricey main course. Another abstains from drinking and orders

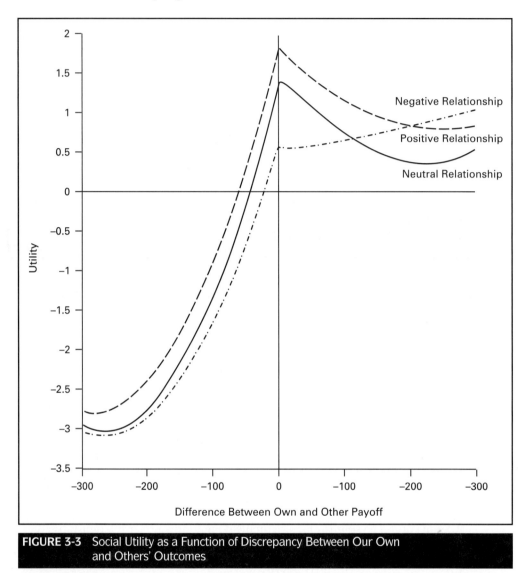

FIGURE 3-3   Social Utility as a Function of Discrepancy Between Our Own
and Others' Outcomes

Source: "Social Utility and Decision Making in Personal Contexts", G.F. Lowenstein, I. Thompson, M.H. Bazerman (1989), *Journal of Personality* and *Social Psychology*, 57(3), 426-441. Copyright © 1989 by the American Psychological Association. Reprinted with permission.

an inexpensive side dish. The third orders a moderately priced meal. Then the bill arrives. The wine drinker immediately suggests that the group split the bill into thirds, explaining that this approach is the simplest. The teetotaler winces and suggests that the group ask the waiter to bring three separate bills. The third group member argues that, because he is a graduate student, the two others should cover the bill, and he invites the two over to his house the next week for pizza. This example illustrates that any situation can have as many interpretations of fairness as it has parties involved. Two people may both truly want a fair settlement, but they may have distinctly different and equally justifiable ideas about what is fair. Consider, for example, "fairness opinions" that underpin mergers and acquisitions. Some are written by independent firms unconnected to the

BOX 3-2

EGOCENTRIC INTERPRETATIONS OF FAIRNESS

You worked for 7 hours and were paid $25. Another person worked for 10 hours. It is piecemeal work. How much do you think the other person should get paid? If you are like most people, you believe the other person should get paid more for doing more work—about $30.29 on average. It is hardly a self-serving response. Now, let's turn this question on its head: The other person worked for 7 hours and was paid $25. You worked for 10 hours. What is a fair wage for you to be paid? The average response is $35.24 (Messick & Sentis, 1979). The difference between $35.24 and $30.29 is about $5, which illustrates the phenomenon of egocentric bias: People pay themselves substantially more than they are willing to pay others for doing the same task.

deal, but the majority aren't (*BusinessWeek*, Nov. 24, 2003a). Banks can rack up millions of dollars in fees by acting simultaneously as agents and appraisers, presumably fueled by self-serving interests.

Why are people self-serving? People want or prefer more than what they regard as fair (basic hedonism). In short, our preferences are more primary, or immediate, than our social concerns. People are more in touch with their own preferences than with the concerns of others. We have immediate access to our preferences; fairness is a secondary judgment. For this reason, fairness judgments are likely to be tainted by preferences. Because preferences are primary and immediate, they often color a person's evaluation of fairness in a self-serving fashion. In a sense, our preferences act as a self-serving prime on our judgments of fairness.

Allocating more money to ourselves (see Box 3-2) is only one way that people show egocentric bias. Egocentric judgments of fairness also emerge in other ways. For example, people select fairness rules in a self-serving fashion: When people make minimal contributions, they often prefer equality rather than equity; however, when people's contributions are substantial, they opt for equity rather than equality (van Avermaet, 1974). Even if people agree to use the same fairness rule, they think it is fair for them to get more than others in a similar situation because they think they would have contributed more (Messick & Rutte, 1992).

Another way people can engage in egocentric evaluation is to selectively weight different aspects of the exchange situation in a way that favors themselves. Consider a situation in which participants are told how many hours they worked on a task of assembling questionnaires as well as how many questionnaires they completed. The key dimensions are hours worked and productivity. Participants are then asked to indicate what they believe is fair payment for their work. Those who worked long hours but did not complete many questionnaires emphasize the importance of hours; in contrast, those who worked short hours but completed many questionnaires emphasize quantity completed. Thus, people emphasize the dimension that favors themselves (van Avermaet, 1974).

Appeals to equality can also be self-serving (Messick, 1993). At a superficial level, equality is trivially simple. Employing equality as a division rule in practice, however, is complex because of the several dimensions on which equality may be established (see

Harris & Joyce, 1980). Furthermore, equality is not consistently applied. For example, when the outcome is evenly divisible by the number in the group, people will use equality more than when even division is not possible (Allison & Messick, 1990).

The major problem with egocentric judgment is that it makes negotiations more difficult to resolve. (See Sidebar 3-3 for an example.)

Sidebar 3-3. Fairness and Strikes

The likelihood and length of strikes may be directly predicted by the difference in perceived fair wages between management and union (Thompson & Loewenstein, 1992). In other words, if management and union have widely differing perceptions of what constitutes a fair settlement, a strike is more likely. Even more disconcertingly, providing each party (management and labor) with additional unbiased information concerning the dispute has the effect of exaggerating each party's perceptions of fair settlement outcomes and excluding parties in their positions. It is a good example of how more information is not always better in negotiations.

The preceding examples suggest that people immediately seize upon any opportunity to favor themselves. However, in many situations, people would ultimately be better off by not having egocentric views. Consider arbitration situations: People's predictions of judges' behavior are biased in a manner that favors their own side. Efforts to de-bias litigants meet with virtually no success. Informing parties of the potential bias or providing them with information about the opponent's point of view does little to assuage biased perceptions of fairness, suggesting that egocentric biases are deeply ingrained (Babcock, Loewenstein, Issacharoff, & Camerer, 1995).

People really do care about fairness but usually do not realize that they are behaving in a self-interested fashion. Egocentric judgments of responsibility and fairness are attributable to ways in which people process information. Several cognitive mechanisms allow the development of egocentric judgments:

- **Selective encoding and memory.** Our own thoughts attract attention away from thinking about the contributions of others. We rehearse our own actions and fit them into our own cognitive schemas, which facilitates retention and subsequent retrieval. If encoding mechanisms lead to self-serving judgments of fairness, then a person who learns of the facts before knowing which side of a dispute he or she is on should not be egocentric. However, the egocentric effect still emerges even when the direction of self-interest occurs subsequent to the processing of information, suggesting that encoding is not the sole mechanism producing egocentric judgment.
- **Differential retrieval.** When making judgments of responsibility, people ask themselves, "How much did I contribute?" and they attempt to retrieve specific instances (Ross & Sicoly, 1979). Because it is cognitively easier to retrieve instances involving oneself, a positive correlation exists between recall and responsibility attributions (Kahneman & Tversky, 1982).
- **Informational disparity.** People are often not privy to the contributions made by others, which suggests that information, not goals, mediates the self-serving

effect. Even when information is constant but goals are manipulated, however, the self-serving effects emerge (see Thompson & Loewenstein, 1992), suggesting that information itself is not solely responsible for the egocentric effect (see Camerer & Loewenstein, 1993).

Most situations are ambiguous enough that people can construe them in a fashion that favors their own interests. One unfortunate consequence is that people develop different perceptions of fairness even when they are presented with the same evidence. Consider a strike situation in which people are provided with background information on a hypothetical teachers' union and board of education. The background material is constructed so that some facts favor the teachers and other facts favor the board of education. On balance, the facts are equal. In one condition, both disputants are presented with extensive, identical background information concerning the dispute. In another condition, disputants are presented with abbreviated, much less extensive background information. Those who have extensive information are more likely to go on strikes that last longer and are more costly to both parties, compared to disputants who do not have extensive information, even though information is identical for both sides (Thompson & Loewenstein, 1992). Information, even when shared among parties, creates ambiguity and provides fertile ground for unchecked self-interest to operate.

WISE PIE SLICING

The distribution of resources (pie slicing) is an unavoidable and inevitable aspect of negotiation. What qualities should we live by when slicing the pie? Messick (1993) suggests the following qualities: consistency, simplicity, effectiveness, and justifiability. To this list of qualities, we add consensus, generality, and satisfaction (Levine & Thompson, 1996).

Consistency
One of the hallmarks of a good pie-slicing heuristic is consistency or invariance across settings, time, and respect to the enforcer of the procedure. For example, most of us would be outraged if those managers up for performance review did better if the meeting was scheduled in the morning versus the afternoon. This example represents a clear bias of the interviewer. Fairness procedures are often inconsistent because of heuristic decision making. Heuristic judgment processes are necessary when normative decision procedures are absent or when their application would be inefficient. Unfortunately, people are typically unaware of the powerful contextual factors that affect their judgments of fairness.

Simplicity
Pie-slicing procedures should be clearly understood by the individuals who employ them and those who are affected by them. Group members should be able to easily articulate the procedure used to allocate resources. This allows the procedure to be implemented with full understanding and the outcomes of the procedure to be evaluated against a clear criterion.

Effectiveness

Pie-slicing policies should produce a choice, meaning that the allocation procedure should yield a clear decision. If the procedure does not produce such a decision, then conflict may erupt among group members who try to identify and implement a decision post hoc.

Justifiability

Pie-slicing procedures should be justifiable to other parties. A fairness rule may be consistent, simple, and effective, but if it cannot be justified, it is not likely to be successful. For example, suppose that a manager of an airline company decides that raises will be based upon hair color: Blondes get big raises, brunettes do not. This policy is consistent, simple, and effective, but hardly justifiable.

Consensus

Group members should agree upon the method of allocation. Effective pie-slicing procedures are often internalized by group members, and norms act as strong guidelines for behavior and decision making in groups. Because social justice procedures often outlive current group members, new members are frequently indoctrinated with procedures that the group found useful in the past (Bettenhausen & Murnighan, 1985; Levine & Moreland, 1994).

Generalizability

The pie-slicing procedure should be applicable to a wide variety of situations. Procedures and norms develop when intragroup conflict is expected, enduring, or recurrent, and effective policy therefore specifies outcome distribution across situations.

Satisfaction

The pie-slicing procedure should be satisfying to negotiators in order to increase the likelihood they will follow through with their agreements.

CONCLUSION

When it comes to slicing the pie, the most valuable information is a negotiator's best alternative to reaching agreement (BATNA). Nothing can substitute for the power of a strong BATNA. Negotiators can enhance their ability to garner a favorable slice of the pie by engaging in the following strategies: determine their BATNA prior to negotiations; attempt to improve upon their BATNA; research the other party's BATNA; set high aspirations; make the first offer; immediately re-anchor if the other party opens with an "outrageous" offer; resist the urge to state a range; make bilateral, not unilateral, concessions; use objective-appearing rationales to support offers; and appeal to norms of fairness. We strongly advise that negotiators not reveal their reservation price (unless it is very attractive) and never about their BATNA. A negotiator who is well-versed in the psychology of fairness is at a pie-slicing advantage in negotiation.

4

WIN-WIN NEGOTIATION: EXPANDING THE PIE

Sequim's mayor and Wal-Mart's attorney fired verbal shots at the county as the appeals hearing for approving Wal-Mart's construction plans concluded. Shortly thereafter, appeals were filed by the Clallam County Department of Community Development, the Jamestown S'Kallam Indian tribe, and the community group, Sequim First, to block the city planning director from allowing a Wal-Mart complex to be built in the small town of Sequim (fewer than 5,000 people). The groups opposed to the new 575,000 square-foot shopping center complex argued that the Wal-Mart would create a traffic nightmare, causing "unsafe driving conditions" on the roads, and that the storm-water runoff (from all the concrete and pavement) would put toxins in the city's rivers and streams; they argued the impact could cause anywhere between a 280 and 500 percent increase in traffic. And they wanted Wal-Mart to pay—in advance—something to the tune of $100 million to fix the roads. However, Wal-Mart and the mayor of Sequim viewed these protests as a thinly veiled ploy to squeeze a "deep pocket to pay for [the city's] neglect [of its roads]." According to Wal-Mart and the mayor, the county's road maintenance around Sequim had been downright negligent and the county had not kept up the roads. A Wal-Mart analysis of the same roads predicted only a 7 percent traffic increase. For a while it appeared to be a standoff and the two sides seemed to be working off completely different data. Then, a breakthrough solution was proposed by Mayor Walt Schubert: An independent body would conduct an analysis of possible traffic impacts on the country roads, and Wal-Mart would give the city up to $100,000 if substantial traffic impacts were proven through the independent study. Through this plan, the Wal-Mart could be built and the city could have money to fix the roads (*Sequim Gazette,* July 9, 2003; *Sequim Gazette,* July 30, 2003a, p. 1).

Most negotiations are not win-or-lose enterprises. Unfortunately, however, most people approach them as though they are. Win-win negotiation strategies are anything but intuitive, and many people who regard themselves to be win-win negotiators are often the people who leave money on the table without even realizing it. We need to be hypervigilant concerning the creation and maximization of the pie of resources. This chapter provides managers with strategies for realizing all of the potential from negotiation situations.

WHAT IS WIN-WIN NEGOTIATION ANYWAY?

Many negotiators, upon reaching agreement, will proudly describe their negotiations as win-win. However, closer inspection usually reveals that money was squandered, resources wasted, and potential joint gain untapped. Clearly, negotiators' minds and hearts were in the right places, but they did not achieve what they really wanted—an integrative agreement that fully leveraged parties' interests and all available options. Win-win negotiation is a nice idea that is too often poorly understood and poorly acted upon. Most people erroneously equate win-win negotiations to mean splitting the pie evenly. Obviously, dividing the pie is always necessary in negotiation, and people can feel emotional about it. However, win-win means something entirely different. Win-win is *not:*

- **Compromise:** Compromise is middle ground between negotiators' positions. Usually, it means any space within the bargaining zone (Chapter 3). Win-win negotiation does not pertain to how the pie is divided (Chapter 3), but rather, to how the pie is *enlarged* by negotiators. In several instances negotiators may make compromises, yet leave money on the table.
- **Even split:** Even splits, like compromises, refer to how the bargaining zone is divided among the negotiators. For example, two sisters who quarrel over an orange and ultimately decide to cut it in half have reached an even split. However, if they fail to realize that one sister wants all of the juice and the other wants all of the rind, it is painfully clear that the even split is not win-win (Follet, 1994). An even split of resources in no way ensures that an integrative agreement has been reached.
- **Feeling good:** Happiness, or feeling good, is no guarantee that money and resources have not been wasted; in fact, many "happy" negotiators do not expand the pie (Thompson, Valley, & Kramer, 1995).
- **Building a relationship:** Building a relationship and establishing trust is an important aspect of negotiation. However, it is not sufficient to proclaim a negotiation as win-win. Even people with a genuine interest in the other party may not be thinking creatively and crafting win-win deals. In fact, people who would seem to have the most interest in building a relationship with the other party (for example, husbands and wives, dating couples, and long-term partners) often fail to reach integrative agreements (Fry, Firestone, & Williams, 1983; Thompson & DeHarpport, 1998; Kurtzberg & Medvec, 1999).

Win-win negotiation *really* means that all creative opportunities are exploited and no resources are left on the table. We call these outcomes **integrative negotiations.** In hundreds of examples, money is left on the table in real-world negotiations; the problem is that people do not realize it. It is, of course, an example of the faulty feedback problem discussed in Chapter 1. This chapter provides strategies for reaching true win-win deals.

TELLTALE SIGNS OF WIN-WIN POTENTIAL

Integrative potential exists in just about every negotiation situation. However, people often fail to see it or do not believe that win-win is possible. Most negotiations do not appear to have win-win potential. Consequently, most people do not immediately see opportunities for reaching integrative agreements. It takes hard work to create integrative opportunities. The following questions are designed to determine the *possibility* for win-win negotiation. They are excellent questions for negotiators to ask when assessing the potential of a negotiation situation.

Does the Negotiation Contain More Than One Issue?

Most negotiation situations present themselves as single-issue negotiations. By definition, single-issue negotiations are not win-win because whatever one party gains, the other party loses. However, even in the simplest of negotiations, it is possible to identify more than one issue. The probability that negotiators will have identical preferences across all issues is small, and, as we will see, *it is differences in preferences, beliefs, and capacities that may be profitably traded off to create joint gain* (Lax & Sebenius, 1986). For example, in the peace treaty talks between Syria and Israel, technical experts formed committees to identify several issues, including the extent of an Israeli withdrawal from the Golan Heights, water rights, security measures, and the timetable for implementing an agreement. Israel put the emphasis on security guarantees, and Syria placed greater weight on the withdrawal from the Golan Heights, thus allowing a more integrative agreement to emerge (*USA Today,* Jan. 5, 2000).

Can Other Issues Be Brought In?

Another strategy is to bring other issues not previously considered into the negotiation. For example, in a four-day negotiation between San Marino, California, and the local firefighters association, the key issue was salary. Firefighters wanted an increase. The negotiators began searching for several options to reach this goal by connecting benefits to wages, allowing cost savings to be distributed to firefighters, and taking on additional duties (thereby increasing incomes). In addition, management spent a great deal of time providing the firefighters with information on cost-benefit analyses, operating costs, and other relevant budgetary information so that all parties could evaluate which options were the most practical and beneficial. This information sharing contributed not only to this negotiation but provided helpful information for future organizational discussions (Quinn, Bell, & Wells, 1997). Similarly, when Mark Lazarus, of Turner Broadcasting was negotiating with NBA Commissioner David Stern in 2001, he brought in several issues, including the number of regular season games, rights to Western Conference finals, rights to the NBA All-Star game, and a stake in the new cable network, and the integration of AOL into the deal (*Adweek,* June 9, 2003). In short, the more moving parts, the better is the potential deal.

Can Side Deals Be Made?

In many situations, people are strictly cautioned not to make side deals or side payments. In contrast, the ability to bring other people into negotiations to make side deals may increase the size of the bargaining pie. For example, consider the side deal that AT&T cooked up with Comcast Corporation in 1999. For a while, AT&T was in a vigorous battle with Comcast Corporation for the acquisition of MediaOne Group, Inc. A win-win side deal was created when AT&T provided Comcast with a number of its cable systems and about 2 million additional cable subscribers; in return, Comcast paid AT&T $9 billion, or about $4,500 per subscriber, for the additional customers. Most important for AT&T, Comcast withdrew its $48 billion bid for MediaOne. Thus, by offering a valuable side deal, AT&T was able to satisfy its competitor (Dow Jones Business News, December 27, 1999).

Do Parties Have Different Preferences Across Negotiation Issues?

If parties have different strengths of preference across the negotiation issues, by definition, it is a win-win negotiation (Froman & Cohen, 1970). Again, consider the orange-splitting example. Essentially, the situation involves two issues: the juice and the rind. Moreover, with regard to preferences, one sister cares more about the juice; the other cares more about the rind. If only a single issue (the orange) was involved or if both sisters wanted the juice much more than the rind, then an integrative agreement would not be possible. The key is to determine each party's preferences and devise a means of satisfying each party's most important interests while inducing them to make concessions on lower-priority issues. Another example: The war over Colorado River water pitted cities against farmers, fomented tensions among seven states, and dominated the attention of Native American Indian tribes, environmentalists, federal officials, and Mexico (*Baltimore Sun,* Aug. 17, 2003). However, by understanding the different capabilities of some of the players, an integrative agreement can be formulated. Under a proposed deal, the city of San Diego would pay the Imperial Valley $2.5 billion over 45 years to receive about 7 percent of the valley's water supply. The water would compensate for the cutback California faces because of higher usage in Arizona, which stores river water underground, leaving less for its western neighbor. This arrangement means that San Diego would get a reliable source of new water while the Imperial Irrigation Distributor would be able to sell water to San Diego at a rate 16 times what its own farmers pay. In this situation, San Diego placed a higher priority on water supply; the Imperial Valley placed a higher priority on income from selling the water.

A PYRAMID MODEL

True win-win or integrative negotiations leave no resources underutilized. We distinguish three "levels" of integrative, or win-win, agreements. The pyramid model presented in Figure 4-1 depicts the three levels of integrative agreements. Beginning at the base, each successive level subsumes the properties of the levels below it. Ideally, negotiators should always strive to reach level 3 integrative agreements. Higher levels are progressively more difficult for negotiators to achieve, but they are more beneficial to negotiators.

Level 1 integrative agreements exceed parties' no-agreement possibilities, or reservation points. Reaching an agreement that exceeds parties' no-agreement possibilities creates value relative to their best alternative. Negotiators create value by reaching settlements that are better than their reservation points, or disagreement alternatives.

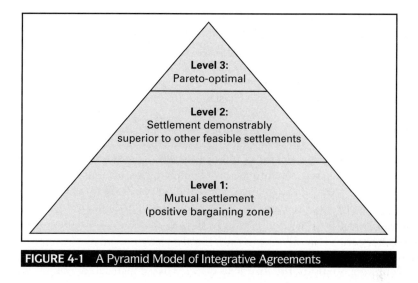

FIGURE 4-1 A Pyramid Model of Integrative Agreements

Level 2 integrative agreements are better for both parties than are other feasible negotiated agreements. In other words, negotiators create value with respect to one negotiated outcome by finding another outcome that all prefer.

The existence of such agreements, by definition, implies that the bargaining situation is not purely fixed-sum: Some agreements yield higher joint gain than do others. By definition, in purely fixed-sum situations, all outcomes sum to the same joint amount, and, therefore, no alternative agreement exists that improves one party's outcome while simultaneously improving or not reducing the outcome of the other party. If negotiators fail to reach agreement in a fixed-sum negotiation when the bargaining zone is positive, they have failed to reach a level 1 agreement. Unlike the pure fixed-sum case, integrativeness is much more difficult to assess in the more common mixed-motive case.

Level 3 integrative agreements are impossible to improve upon from the perspective of *both* parties. Technically speaking, level 3 integrative agreements are settlements that lie along the **Pareto-optimal frontier** of agreement, meaning that no other feasible agreement exists that would improve one party's outcome while simultaneously not hurting the other party's outcome. Therefore, *any* agreement reached by negotiators in a purely fixed-sum situation is level 3, leaving no way to improve any negotiator's outcome without making the other party worse off. In reality, it is difficult to determine whether an agreement is level 3, but we will present some helpful techniques.

Reaching level 3 integrative agreements may sound easy enough, but observation of hundreds of executives' performance in business negotiation simulations reveals that fewer than 25 percent reach level 3 agreements, and of those, approximately 50 percent do so by chance.[1]

---

[1]This data is based on executives' performance on negotiation simulations that involve integrative (win-win) potential.

MOST COMMON PIE-EXPANDING ERRORS

If reaching win-win negotiation agreements is the objective of most negotiators, what prevents them from doing so? Negotiators encounter two key problems, which we describe next.

False Conflict

False conflict, also known as **illusory conflict,** occurs when people believe that their interests are incompatible with the other party's interests when, in fact, they are not. For example, in the Cuban Missile Crisis, unbeknownst to the United States, Russia preferred to constrain the Cubans from provocative behavior and to minimize the contributions of the Chinese—an interest held by the United States (Walton & McKersie, 1965). Similarly, in a labor strike at Dow Chemical Company, both union and management preferred the same wage increase; however, neither party realized this fact at the time of the strike (Balke, Hammond, & Meyer, 1973).

In 1990, Thompson and Hastie uncovered a particularly insidious and widespread effect in negotiations: **the lose-lose effect.** They constructed a negotiation situation in which the parties involved had compatible interests on a subset of the negotiation issues, meaning both parties wanted the same outcome. At first, it seemed absurd to imagine any other outcome occurring other than the parties settling for what was obviously the best solution for themselves and the other person. However, a substantial number of negotiators not only failed to realize that the other person had interests that were completely compatible with their own, but they reached settlements that were less optimal for both parties than some other readily available outcome. A situation in which people fail to capitalize on compatible interests is a lose-lose agreement (Thompson & Hrebec, 1996). In an analysis of 32 different negotiation studies across more than 5,000 people, we found that negotiators failed to realize compatible issues about 50 percent of the time and fell prey to the lose-lose effect about 20 percent of the time (Thompson & Hrebec, 1996).

What should negotiators do to avoid lose-lose agreements? First, negotiators should be aware of the fixed-pie perception and not automatically assume that their interests are opposed by the other party. Second, negotiators should avoid making **premature concessions** to the other party (i.e., giving up ground on issues before even being asked). Finally, negotiators should develop an accurate understanding of the other party's interests—a skill we will explore soon.

Fixed-Pie Perception

The **fixed-pie perception** is the belief that the other party's interests are directly and completely opposed to one's own interests (Fisher & Ury, 1981; Bazerman & Neale, 1983; Thompson & Hastie, 1990). Most untrained people have a fixed-pie understanding of negotiation. Most untrained negotiators view negotiation as a pie-slicing task: They assume that their interests are incompatible, that impasse is likely, and that issues are settled one by one rather than as packages (O'Connor & Adams, 1996). For example, in one investigation, negotiators' perceptions of the other party's interests were assessed immediately before, during, and then following a negotiation (Thompson & Hastie, 1990). Most negotiators (68%) perceived the other's interests to be completely opposed to their own. In fact, negotiators shared interests that could be profitably traded off and completely compatible. In short, negotiators with fixed-pie perceptions literally throw money away.

Unfortunately, banishing the fixed-pie perception is difficult. It is not enough to warn negotiators of its existence (Thompson, 1991). Further, it is not enough for negotiators to have experience (Thompson, 1990a, 1990b). It is not even enough for negotiators to receive feedback about their opponents' interests to eliminate the fixed-pie perception (Thompson & DeHarpport, 1994). We will talk more about how to successfully challenge the fixed-pie perception when we examine biases and creativity (Chapter 8).

Lack of time and effort do not explain lose-lose outcomes and the fixed-pie perception. The biggest detriment to the attainment of integrative agreements is the faulty assumptions we make about our opponent and the negotiation situation. One of the first realizations negotiators should make is that negotiation is not a purely competitive situation. Rather, most negotiation situations are mixed-motive in nature, meaning that parties' interests are imperfectly correlated with one another. Thus, the gains of one party do not represent equal sacrifices by the other. For example, consider a negotiation between two collaborators on a joint project: One is risk-averse and values cash up front more than riskier long-term payoffs; the other is more interested in long-term value than in current gains. The two may settle on a contract in which a large lump sum is paid to the risk-averse negotiator, and the other party reaps most of the (riskier) profits in the long term.

In fact, few conflicts are win-or-lose enterprises (Deutsch, 1973). In most mixed-motive negotiations, parties realize at some level that they have two incentives vis-à-vis the other party: cooperation (so that they can reach an agreement and avoid resorting to their BATNAs) and competition (so that they can claim the largest slice of the pie). However, what this analysis misses is the incentive to create value, which is the key to win-win negotiation.

STRATEGIES THAT DO NOT REALLY WORK

We want to save negotiators time and heartache in their quest to expand the pie by outlining several strategies that, on a superficial level, might seem to be effective in expanding the pie and reaching win-win agreements, but in fact, do not really work.

Commitment to Reaching a Win-Win Deal

Many negotiators approach the negotiation table committed to reaching a win-win deal. However, commitment to reaching a win-win deal does not guarantee that negotiators will reach a win-win agreement, primarily because they are working with an incorrect idea about what win-win is. In fact, it may lull them into a false sense of security.

Compromise

Negotiators often mistake win-win negotiations for equal-concession negotiations. Equal concessions or "splitting the difference" does not really ensure that a win-win negotiation has been reached. Compromise pertains to slicing the pie, not expanding the pie.

Focusing on a Long-Term Relationship

Oftentimes, negotiators believe that focusing on the long-term nature of their relationship with the other party will ensure a win-win deal. Obviously, the long-term relationship is key in negotiation—and we spend an entire chapter discussing how to foster the relationship—but, establishing a long-term relationship does not translate directly into win-win. Rather, it means that negotiators should have an easier time working to reach win-win. It is a nice intention, but it does not guarantee that all the resources will be discovered and optimally exploited in the negotiation.

Adopting a Cooperative Orientation

It is nice when negotiators approach the negotiation table with benevolent attitudes and a cooperative orientation. However, negotiators' intentions to cooperate often keep them from focusing on the right information at the right time. For example, negotiators often attempt to cooperate by revealing their BATNA to the other party; revealing one's BATNA is a pie-slicing issue, not a pie-expanding issue. Negotiators often think cooperation means compromise, and compromises often mean lose-lose negotiation. For example, in 1996, MasterCard International wanted to figure out why the credit card company was losing money on some of its promotional deals. Subsequent analysis revealed that MasterCard was attempting to form good relationships with others (i.e., being cooperative), but they were giving away money and promotions and not asking for sufficient compensation in return (*Training,* Oct. 1, 1999). This type of situation prompted Pruitt and Carnevale (1993) to develop a *dual-concern* model of effective negotiation: high concern for the other party coupled with high concern for one's own interests.

Taking Extra Time to Negotiate

Negotiators often think that, with a little extra time, they can achieve all the joint gains possible in a negotiation. Extra time does not guarantee that negotiators will reach an integrative agreement (most negotiators wait until the last few moments of a negotiation to reach an agreement), and the quality of the negotiation does not improve with additional time. Furthermore, people tend to work to fill their time (McGrath, Kelly, & Machatka, 1984). The same is true for negotiation. For example, we recently gave some people one hour, others two hours, and still others a week (via e-mail) to complete a two-party negotiation exercise. If time really makes a difference in terms of the quality of negotiated agreements, then the one-hour group should be expected to have inferior outcomes in terms of expanding the pie. However, this expectation was not realized: No discernable differences appeared between the three groups, which suggests that more time to negotiate does not improve the quality of negotiated agreements.

STRATEGIES THAT WORK

So much for the strategies that do not work. What does work when it comes to expanding the pie? We identify nine strategies that can help negotiators expand the pie and create win-win negotiations (see also Bazerman & Neale, 1982). We ordered them in terms of the most obvious and intuitive strategies—the ones that your grandmother probably could have told you about—to strategies that are more sophisticated. The first few strategies are especially good to use when negotiating with someone who seems cooperative and trustworthy; the strategies that come later on this list are useful when dealing with "problem people" or extremely tough negotiators. And, most important, all of them are based on controlled scientific investigations (CSIs).

Build Trust and Share Information

Negotiators who build a trusting relationship and share information greatly increase the probability that a win-win outcome will be reached (Bazerman & Neale, 1992). It is important to realize that the information that negotiators need to share is not information about their BATNAs, but rather, information about their *preferences* and *priorities* across the negotiation issues. For example, the International Brotherhood of Electric Workers Local 300 and Central Vermont Public Service approach negotiations by sharing each other's needs at the start of their labor contract negotiations (*Business Wire,* Dec. 27, 2001). At the outset, George Clain, the Local 300 president, had doubts about sharing such information: "[B]oth sides had doubts about the process when it was first used three years ago, but it proved a valuable tool in maintaining a mutually beneficial working relationship" (para. 6).

Negotiators can exchange six key types of information during negotiation. The skilled negotiator knows how to recognize each. Even more important, the skilled negotiator knows what information is safe (and even necessary) to reveal in order to reach win-win outcomes. Table 4-1 outlines the six types of information that negotiators can exchange. Table 4-2 (on page 79) supplements Table 4-1 by providing a worksheet to complete prior to negotiation.

Ask Diagnostic Questions

A negotiator could ask the other party in a negotiation any number of questions (see Table 4-1). However, of the six types of information listed in Table 4-1, only two are truly directly helpful types of questions to ask in terms of expanding the pie—questions about underlying interests and questions about priorities (Bazerman & Neale, 1992). A negotiator who asks the other party about his or her preferences is much more likely to reach an integrative agreement than a negotiator who does not ask the other party about his or her priorities (Thompson, 1991). The disappointing news, however, is that left to their own devices, negotiators fail to ask diagnostic questions. For example, only about 7 percent of negotiators seek information about the other party's preferences during negotiation, when it would be dramatically helpful to know such information (Thompson, 1991).

Why are these questions diagnostic with respect to increasing the likelihood of win-win agreements? Two reasons: First, such questions help negotiators discover where the value is. For example, consider how Frank McKenna of New Brunswick attracted new investment to the province: "We had to know what was a 'win' for the other party because if you don't know what that is, you can't meet it. [When we] negotiated to get call centres to come into our province, we had to know about their interests as far as location, turnover, and quality of the work force and how they *prioritized* each of these interests" (*The Globe and Mail,* June 17, 2002). Second, diagnostic questions do not tempt the other party to lie or to misrepresent himself or herself. It is easy

TABLE 4-1 Types of Information in Negotiation and How Each Affects Distributive and Integrative Agreements

Type of Information	Definition (example)	Claiming Value	Creating Value
BATNA (and reservation price)	The alternatives a negotiator has outside of the current negotiation (e.g., "If I don't buy your car, I can buy my uncle's car for $2,000")	Revealing this information severely hurts ability to maximize negotiator surplus (i.e., the difference between your reservation price and the final outcome)	Revealing or obtaining this information does not affect ability to reach level 2 or 3 integrative agreements; might help negotiators reach level 1 integrative agreements
Position (stated demand)	Most often, a negotiator's opening offer; the behavioral manifestation of his/her target point (e.g., "I will give you $1,500 for your car")	Opening with an aggressive target point significantly increases the negotiator's surplus (share of the bargaining zone)	Does not affect integrative agreements
Underlying interests	The underlying needs and reasons a negotiator has for a particular issue or target (e.g., "I need a car because I need transportation to my job site, which is 15 miles away in a rural zone")	Revealing this information generally increases likelihood of obtaining a favorable slice of pie because negotiators who provide a rationale for their demands are more adept at realizing their targets	Very important for reaching win-win deals; by (truthfully) revealing underlying interests, negotiators can discover winwin agreements (e.g., one sister tells the other that she wants the orange because she needs to make juice and has no need for rinds)
Priorities	A judgment about the relative importance of the issues to a negotiator (e.g., "I am more concerned about the down payment than I am about the financing for the car")	Increases a negotiator's surplus (slice of the pie) indirectly, because if more value is created via sharing priorities, then the probability that a negotiator will get a larger slice of the pie increases	Vitally important for maximizing the pie (e.g., the sister who said she cared more about the rinds *relative to* the juice created potential for integrative agreement)
Key facts	Pertains to information that bears on the quality and the value of the to-be-negotiated issues (e.g., "The car has a rebuilt engine and has been involved in a major collision"; "The oranges are genetically modified")	This information can affect the slice of the pie the negotiator obtains in that facts either increase or decrease the value of the to-be-negotiated issues	Affects the quality of win-win agreements in that failure to reveal key information may lead a negotiator to over- or undervalue a particular resource (e.g., someone who sells "fresh organic orange juice" does not want to have genetically modified oranges as an ingredient)
Substantiation	Argument either made to support one's own position or to attack the other party's position (e.g., "You will get lots of dates if you buy my car because women like it")	Most dominant type of distributive tactic (24% to 27% of all statements, Carnevale & Lawler, 1986); can increase a negotiator's slice of the pie because providing a rationale (even an absurd one) can often be effective in obtaining a demand	Considered to be a distributive tactic; does not increase win-win negotiation and may, in fact, reduce likelihood of win-win (Pruitt, 1981; Hyder, Prietula, & Weingart, 2000)

TABLE 4-2 Information Preparation Sheet

Issue	Self		Other	
	position * underlying interest		other party's position on this issue other party's underlying interest	
	*			
	*			
	*			
	*			
Reservation price				
Target				
BATNA				

Instructions:

1. Negotiators should first complete the left-most column by identifying the issues to be negotiated.
2. Then, negotiators should indicate their "position" in the top part of the triangle and their underlying interest in the lower part of the triangle in the middle column.
3. Next, negotiators should rank-order the issues from most to least important (using, say, 1 through 5 in the small boxes).
4. Next, negotiators should make their best assessment of the other party's position, interests, and priorities across the issues.
5. Negotiators should indicate their reservation price (and attempt to assess the RP of the other party).
6. Negotiators should indicate their target point (which will serve as their first offer).
7. Negotiators should indicate their BATNA (and attempt to assess the other party's BATNA).

Note: *Rating/ranking of importance (e.g. 0-100, 1-5, etc.)
Source: J. Brett. (2003). "Negotiation Strategies for Managers," Executive Program, Kellogg School of Management.

to see how asking a person about his or her BATNA or reservation price might well lead that person to exaggerate or lie, but it is not immediately clear why or how a negotiator would lie about his or her underlying needs. Thus, diagnostic questions are effective in part because they do not put negotiators on the defensive. Ideally, it is important to understand how the negotiation impacts the company's business goals. For example, negotiating teams at one of Mexico's largest banks collaborated with financial analysts to determine the best way to work with clients who were not repaying their loans following the country's 1994 currency crisis. The analysts helped team members understand the bank's priorities and use them to devise options for reaching agreements with debtors (Ertel, 1999).

Provide Information

It is a fallacy to believe that negotiators should never provide information to their opponent (Bazerman & Neale, 1992). Negotiations would not go anywhere if negotiators did not communicate their interests to the other party. Remember, you should negotiate as you would with your fraternal twin: If you do not provide information, neither will the other party. A negotiator should never ask the other party a question that he or she is not willing to answer truthfully. The important question, then, is not *whether* to reveal information, but *what* information to reveal.

In negotiation, people are often reluctant to share information. Despite what many popular approaches to negotiation argue, it is not effective to refuse to share information. Thus, in addition to seeking information about the other party, negotiators are wise to provide information about their own interests to the other party (see Table 4-1). Most important, by signaling your willingness to share information about your interests (not your BATNA), you capitalize on the important psychological principle of reciprocity. That is, if you share information, the other party will often share as well. Negotiators who provide information to the other party about their priorities are more likely to reach integrative agreements than negotiators who do not provide this information (Thompson, 1991). Further, the disclosing negotiator is not placed at a strategic disadvantage. The disclosing negotiator does not earn significantly more or less resources than his or her opponent.

A distinct time course emerges in terms of the unraveling of information during negotiation. Adair and her colleague (Adair & Brett, 2003) divided the negotiation into four quarters. They found that during the first quarter, people are more likely to use influence strategies as they battle for power and influence. During the second quarter, priority information peaks as negotiators began to discuss the issues and share information about their priorities. In the third quarter, negotiators often engage in a dance of making offers and counteroffers and either support or reject them on the basis of rational argument. In the fourth quarter, negotiators begin to work toward agreement by building on each other's offers.

Even though many negotiators believe that they provide information during a negotiation, their opponent does not necessarily understand the information. This faulty assumption may be traceable to the **illusion of transparency** (Gilovich, Savitsky, & Medvec, 1998). The illusion of transparency means that negotiators believe they are revealing more than they actually are (i.e., they believe that others have access to information about them when in fact they do not). For example, in one investigation, negotiators judged whether an observer to the negotiation could accurately discern their negotiation goals from their behavior (Vorauer & Claude, 1998). Negotiators consistently overestimated the transparency of their objectives. Thus, people feel more like an "open book" with respect to their goals and interests in negotiation than they actually are. Negotiators are also not as clear in their messages as they should be. Indeed, when the information exchanged is amenable to multiple interpretations, it can lead to settlement delays and divergence of expectations (Loewenstein & Moore, 2004). Conversely, when a single interpretation is obvious, information sharing leads to convergence of expectations and speeds settlement.

Unbundle the Issues

One reason negotiations fail is because negotiators haggle over a single issue, such as price. By definition, if negotiations contain only one issue (e.g., price), they are purely distributive (i.e., fixed-pie). Skilled negotiators are adept at expanding the set of nego-tiable issues. Adding issues, unbundling issues, and creating new issues can transform a single-issue, fixed-pie negotiation into an integrative, multi-issue negotiation with win-win potential (Lax & Sebenius, 1986). Integrative agreements require at least two issues and, in the case of negotiation issues (not *parties*), the more the merrier. Roger Fisher tells of a time when he was helping the president of a company sell a building he owned (*CFO Magazine*, Sept. 1, 2001): "He was retiring and wanted $2 million, which he con-sidered a fair price. He had a buyer, but the buyer wouldn't pay that price. I asked the seller, 'What's the worst thing about selling this building?' And he said, 'All of my papers for 25 years are mixed up in my corner office. When I sell the building, I can't throw everything away. I've got to go through that stuff. That's the nightmare I have'" (para. 9). Then Fisher asked the buyer why he wanted the building. The buyer explained he hoped to use it for hoteling. This knowledge gave Fisher the idea of suggesting that the seller offer the buyer a lease with an option to buy with one contingency: that the president's name be on the corner office for three years. The buyer agreed. In this example, Fisher notes that the key underlying needs are not about money, but more about convenience.

Make Package Deals, Not Single-Issue Offers

Most negotiators make the mistake of negotiating each issue one by one. This approach is a mistake for several reasons: First and foremost, negotiating each issue separately does not allow negotiators to make trade-offs between issues. To capitalize on different strengths of preference, negotiators need to compare and contrast issues and trade them off. Second, it may mean that impasse is more likely, especially if the bargaining zone is narrow and trade-offs are necessary to reach a mutually profitable outcome. Finally, single-issue offers lure negotiators into compromise agreements, which, as we have seen, are usually not the best approach for win-win negotiations.

Make Multiple Offers Simultaneously

In some cases, negotiators are disappointed and frustrated to find that their attempts to provide and seek information are not effective. It happens most commonly in the face of high distrust and less than amicable relations. Now what? Is all hope lost? Can the negotiator do anything to change the situation? Fortunately, the answer is yes. The strategy of **multiple simultaneous offers** can be effective even with the most uncooperative of negotiators (Bazerman & Neale, 1992; Kelley & Schenitzki, 1972; Kelley, 1966). The strategy involves presenting the other party with at least two (and preferably more) proposals of *equal value* to oneself. For example, in the Wal-Mart negotiation discussed at the beginning of this chapter, Sequim county engineer, Don McInnes responded to the planning director's protests by outlining three different options: (1) widening three roads to a standard 40-foot width; (2) bringing the road-ways up to a higher standard (but not to full standards) through a major overhaul; or (3) creating a cul-de-sac at two of the roads (*Sequim Gazette*, July 30, 2003b).

The multiple-offer strategy is threefold:

1. **Devise multiple-issue offers**, as opposed to single-issue offers (to get away from sequential bargaining, which can lock people into lose-lose outcomes).
2. **Devise offers that are all of equal value to yourself** (leaving yourself many ways to get what you want before making a concession).

3. Make the offers all at the same time. This last point is the hardest for most people to do because they negotiate like playing tennis: They make one offer and then wait for the other party to "return" a single offer; then they make a concession, and so on and so forth. In the multiple-offer strategy, a negotiator presents a "dessert tray" of offers to the other party and invites a reaction. *Note:* The other party should be cautioned that "cherry-picking" (e.g., selecting the terms from each option that most suit him or her) is not permissible. Rather, the offers are truly "package deals" (Schatzki, 1981).

Negotiators who make multiple equivalent offers enjoy more profitable negotiated outcomes and are evaluated more favorably by the other party (Medvec, Leonardelli, Claussen-Schultz, & Galinsky, 2004). Specifically, they are seen as being more flexible by the other side. And, they are more satisfied at the end of the negotiation. Multiple offers increase the discovery of integrative solutions (Hyder, Prietula, & Weingart, 2000). When issues are packaged together in a single proposal, rather than considered as separate entities, it is easier to arrange trades or concession. Moreover, when issues are dealt with individually, negotiators tend to compromise on each issue in a sequential fashion (Thompson, Mannix, & Bazerman, 1988; Weingart, Bennett, & Brett, 1993). More importantly, it is **substantiation** (arguments for one's own position or against the other's position) that interferes the most with win-win arguments. According to Hyder and colleagues (2000), "Substantiation, by its very nature, is a seductive strategy that seems not only to be a default behavior, but a persistent one that feeds upon itself and the cognitive resources of the negotiators" (p. 194). Substantiation begets more substantiation (Weingart, Hyder, & Prietula, 1996).

According to Medvec and Galinsky (2004), the negotiator who makes multiple, equivalent offers has an edge in five critical aspects: They can (1) be more aggressive in terms of anchoring the negotiation favorably, (2) gain better information about the other party, (3) be more persistent, (4) signal their priorities more effectively, and (5) overcome concession aversion on the part of the other side.

Be Aggressive in Anchoring

Consider how our colleague used this strategy to effectively anchor the negotiation: Ken Alex, an attorney at a major international law firm was negotiating a business news database.[2] For the law firm, the database was critical and they had to renew it. Not doing so would mean a lot more research librarian time, and recent staff cutbacks had reduced the number of librarians. The amount the firm paid for the renewal in the previous year was $52,000. Ken had budgeted $58,000 for this year's renewal. Ken's strategy was to use the simultaneous multiple-offer strategy. Because he knew that one of the key issues for the database service was the contracted value of the database, he reasoned that a two-year contract with a major firm would be quite valuable for the database company. Moreover, signing up for two years was a low-risk strategy for Ken, because he was confident that the firm would want the database again next year. Moreover, it also would represent budget certainty for the firm in highly volatile times. Ken made two proposals that he called A and B. Proposal A was a one-year renewal at $45,000; proposal B was a two-year renewal for $43,000 for year 1 and

---

[2]Personal communication, December 4, 2002. (*Note:* Names have been altered.)

$47,000 for year 2. Ultimately, the database company opted for proposal B, the two-year renewal.

Gain Better Information About the Other Party

The multiple-offer strategy is based on the strategy of **inductive reasoning,** meaning that a negotiator can unilaterally deduce what the other party's true interests are and where the joint gains are. (We talk more about inductive, as well as deductive, reasoning, in Chapter 8 in a discussion of advanced negotiations and creativity.) By listening to the opponent's response, the negotiator learns about the other party's preferences. Thus, the negotiator acts as a "detective" by drawing conclusions based on the opponents' responses to the multiple offers.

Be More Persistent and More Persuasive Regarding the Value of an Offer

Consider how the multiple-offer strategy helped a negotiation team at a major pharmaceutical firm maintain his ground in a particular tense negotiation.[3] "The situation was a divestiture and we had an issue surface from our side (regarding much more inventory than was originally estimated), a significant surprise that appeared as if we had provided incorrect information at the due diligence stage. The issue was of a very significant magnitude relative to the size of the deal (meaning that they would have to pay a higher amount in some very significant way.)" The pharmaceutical firm proposed five options, all of equivalent value, that involved various trade-offs between deferred payment terms, cash on close, not taking some of the inventory, among other options. The team made the five proposals and then held their collective breath, "We had already had multi-day tirades on issues of who owned the pencil sharpeners, so we were braced for the worst attacks." The other team calmly said, "We understand," and the very next day selected one of the options. Says the pharmaceutical team members, "If we had taken the single-option approach, their obvious position would have been to say, 'That is your problem, you misled us . . . provide us with the excess inventory for free.'" However, this potential deal-killer was avoided and the deal closed much more successfully than ever anticipated.

Overcome Concession Aversion

When people perceive themselves as having more choices (as opposed to only one), they may be more likely to comply. For example, when Ross Johnson, a member of the California Senate was faced with a legislative bill that he hated, he did not kill it outright. Rather, he strategically offered up three amendments that he knew would not be accepted, but which would make the non-Orange county legislators aware of some things that Johnson felt were important (*Orange County Register*, Jan. 6, 2002).

Structure Contingency Contracts by Capitalizing on Differences

Negotiators not only have differences in interest and preference, but they view the world differently (Lax & Sebenius, 1986). A book author may believe that the sales will be high; the publisher believes they will be more modest. Different interpretations of the facts may threaten already tenuous relations. Attempts to persuade the

---

[3]Personal communication, September 14, 2003.

other person may be met with skepticism, hostility, and an escalating spiral of conflict. The surprising fact is that differences in beliefs—or expectations about uncertain events—pave the way toward integrative agreements. For example, in the Wal-Mart negotiation presented at the beginning of this chapter, the parties had wildly differing beliefs about the impact that the shopping complex would have on the local traffic, with the city estimating a 500 percent increase in traffic and Wal-Mart estimating only 7 percent. Given these differing predictions, it is somewhat ironic to think that they might be leveraged to create a workable solution. In fact, it is differences, rather than commonalities, that can be more advantageous in negotiations (Lax & Sebenius, 1986). The enlightened negotiator realizes that differences in beliefs, expectations, and tastes can create greater value than when both negotiators have identical preferences. The problem is that most people are uncomfortable when they encounter differences and, instead of leveraging this opportunity, they either downplay their differences or ignore them.

Negotiators can exploit differences to capitalize on integrative agreements in a variety of ways (Lax & Sebenius, 1986). Consider the following differences and the opportunities they create:

- Differences in the valuation of the negotiation issues
- Differences in expectations of uncertain events
- Differences in risk attitudes
- Differences in time preferences
- Differences in capabilities

Differences in Valuation

Negotiators have different strengths of preference for each issue. For example, in a negotiation for scarce office space, one person is more interested in a large office than a nice view; the other negotiator is more interested in a view than having extra space. They reach an agreement in which one person gets a large, windowless office and the other gets a small office with a great view. By trading off these issues, both were better off than by simply compromising on each issue. The strategy of trading off so as to capitalize on different strengths of preference is known as **logrolling** (Froman & Cohen, 1970).

Differences in Expectations

Because negotiation often involves uncertainty, negotiators differ in their forecasts, or beliefs, about what will happen in the future. Consider the case of a woman and her brother who inherited a tool store from their father.[4] The sister expected the profitability of the store to decline steadily; the brother expected the store to succeed. The sister wanted to sell the store; the brother wanted to keep it. A contingent contract was constructed: The brother agreed to buy his sister's share of the store over a period of time at a price based on her bleak assessment of its worth. The sister is guaranteed a certain return; the brother's return is based on how well the store does.

Consider another example. A city planner contracted with a building corporation to build and manage a condominium/retail center. The city's assessment of future sales was bleak, and so the city wanted to tax the units heavily. The corporation did not like

---

[4]Personal communication, April 1993.

the prospect of high taxes and believed that sales would be high in the coming year. A contingent contract was developed. The city promised the corporation a tax cap over 10 years as a function of yearly sales: Higher sales meant a lower tax cap; lower sales meant a higher tax cap. Each party was confident that its best-case scenario would prevail.

Differences in Risk Attitudes

In other situations, negotiators agree on the probability of future events but feel differently about taking risks (Lax & Sebenius, 1986). For example, two colleagues may undertake a collaborative project, such as writing a novel, for which they both agree that the probability of success is only moderate. The colleague with an established career can afford to be risk-seeking; the struggling young novelist may be risk-averse. The two may capitalize on their different risk-taking profiles with a contingent contract: The more risk-averse colleague receives the entire advance on the book; the risk-seeking colleague receives the majority of the risky profits after the publication of the novel. Negotiators who have a gain-frame (i.e., see the glass as half full) are more likely to logroll or trade-off issues in a win-win fashion; conversely, those with a loss-frame (i.e., see the glass as half empty) are more likely to accept a contingent contract (Kray, Paddock, & Galinksy, 2003).

Differences in Time Preferences

People may value the same event quite differently depending on when it occurs (Lax & Sebenius, 1986). If one party is more impatient than the other, mechanisms for optimally sharing the consequences over time may be devised. Two partners in a joint venture might allocate the initial profits to the partner who has high costs for time, whereas the partner who can wait will achieve greater profits over a longer, delayed period.

Differences in Capabilities

People differ not only in their tastes, probability assessments, and risk preferences; they differ in their capabilities, endowments, and skills. Consider two managers who have different resources, capital, and support staff. One manager has strong quantitative, statistical skills and access to state-of-the-art computers; the other has strong marketing and design skills. Together, they may combine their differing skills and expertise in a mutually beneficial way, such as in the design of a new product concept. The development of successful research collaborations is fostered by differences in skills and preferences (Northcraft & Neale, 1993).

Cautionary Note

Capitalizing on differences often entails **contingency contracts,** wherein negotiators make bets based upon different states of the world occurring. For contingency contracts to be effective, they should satisfy the following four criteria. First, they should not create *a conflict of interest.* For example, if a book author, optimistic about sales, negotiates a contingency contract with her publisher such that royalty rates will be contingent upon sales, the contract should not create an incentive for the publisher to attempt to thwart sales. Second, contingency contracts should be *enforceable* and therefore may often require a written contract. Third, contingency contracts should be *clear, measurable, and readily evaluated,* leaving no room for ambiguity. Conditions and measurement techniques should be spelled out in advance (Bazerman & Gillespie, 1999). Further, a date or time line should be mutually agreed upon. Finally, contingency contracts require *continued interaction* among parties. We go into more detail about contingency contracts in Chapter 8 (creativity in negotiation).

Presettlement Settlements (PreSS)

Presettlement settlements (PreSS), engineered by Gillespie and Bazerman (1998), have three characteristics: They are *formal,* in that they encompass specific, binding obligations; *initial,* because they are intended to be replaced by a formal agreement; and *partial,* in that the parties do not address or resolve all outstanding issues. According to Gillespie and Bazerman (1998), PreSSs involve more than a simple handshake or "gentleman's agreement." Rather, a PreSS occurs in advance of the parties undertaking full-scale negotiations and is designed to be replaced by a long-term agreement. A PreSS resolves only a subset of the issues on which the parties disagree (i.e., partial). In some cases, instead of resolving any of the outstanding issues, a PreSS may simply establish a concrete framework for final negotiations.

Gillespie and Bazerman (1998) note that a famous example of PreSS is the 1993 Oslo accords between Israel and Palestine. The Oslo accords sought to establish an incremental process of negotiation and reciprocation that would lead to what both parties termed "final-status" talks. The parties agreed to wait to resolve the most difficult issues (e.g., borders, settlements, Jerusalem) until the final-status talks. As an initial step, the Israelis and Palestinians sought to resolve less difficult issues, thereby establishing a political dialogue and working toward formalized relations. For example, the Israelis agreed to release female prisoners, transfer disputed money, and withdraw from Hebron. The Palestinians agreed to revise their national charter, transfer suspected terrorists, and limit the size of the Palestinian police force. Gillespie and Bazerman also noted that the PreSS framework has subsequently floundered due to heated rhetoric and escalating violence. (For another type of PreSS, see Box 4-1.)

BOX 4-1

NO-FIST (NORMAL OPERATIONS WITH A FINANCIAL STRIKE)

Lax and Sebenius (1997) proposed a type of presettlement settlement (PreSS) in a letter to the editor of *The Wall Street Journal.* Lax and Sebenius noted that a planned strike by American Airlines pilots would result in the airline suffering revenue losses of more than $200 million per day. To avoid such a catastrophe, they recommended the following: "Once the [strike] deadline is imminent and negotiations are irretrievably stuck, the parties would agree to continue normal operations but to put some or all of their revenues and salaries into an escrow account controlled by a trusted outside party" (Lax & Sebenius, 1997, p. A22). No matter how the escrow fund is eventually divided, both parties will be better off relative to a typical strike. NO-FIST produces a Pareto-superior outcome for all concerned parties, including pilots, shareholders, customers, and nonpilot airline employees.

Search for Postsettlement Settlements

A final strategy for expanding the pie is one in which negotiators reach an initial settlement that both agree to but spend additional time attempting to improve upon (each from their own perspective). In the **postsettlement settlement strategy,** negotiators agree to explore other options with the goal of finding another that both prefer more than the current one, or that one party prefers more and the other is indifferent to (Raiffa, 1982). The current settlement becomes both parties' new BATNA. For any future agreement to replace the current one, both parties must be in agreement; otherwise, they revert to the initial agreement. It may seem counterintuitive, and perhaps downright counterproductive, to resume negotiations once an acceptable agreement has been reached, but the strategy of postsettlement settlements is remarkably effective in improving the quality of negotiated agreements (Bazerman, Russ, & Yakura, 1987) and in moving an agreement from a level 1 agreement to a level 2 or 3 agreement.

The postsettlement settlement strategy allows both parties to reveal their preferences without fear of exploitation, because they can safely revert to their previous agreement. If better terms are found, parties can be more confident they have reached a level 2 or 3 settlement. If no better agreement is found, the parties may be more confident that the current agreement is level 3.

A STRATEGIC FRAMEWORK FOR REACHING INTEGRATIVE AGREEMENTS

The discovery and creation of integrative agreements is much like problem solving. Problem solving requires creativity. Integrative agreements are devilishly obvious after the fact, but not before. Because negotiation is an ill-structured task, with few constraints and a myriad of possible "moves," a royal road for reaching integrative agreement does not exist. Look at the decision-making model of integrative negotiation in Figure 4-2. The model is prescriptive; that is, it focuses on what negotiators should do to reach agreement, not what they *actually* do. The model has five major components: resource assessment, assessment of differences, construction of offers and trade-offs, acceptance/rejection of a decision, and renegotiation.

Resource Assessment

Resource assessment involves the identification of the bargaining issues and alternatives. For example, consider an employment negotiation. The bargaining issues may be salary, vacation, and benefits. The feasible salary range may be $60,000 to $100,000, vacation time may be one to five weeks, and benefits may include stock options or a company car. In this stage, parties identify the issues that are of concern to them in the negotiation. A superset emerges from the combination of both parties' issues.

The union of both parties' issue sets forms the **issue mix** of the negotiation. In addition to specifying the issue mix, parties also define and clarify the alternatives for each issue. The ultimate set of options for each issue is a superset of both parties' alternatives.

Later stages of resource assessment move beyond the mere identification of issues and alternatives to two higher-order processes: the **unbundling** of issues and

FIGURE 4-2   Decision-Making Model of Integrative Negotiation

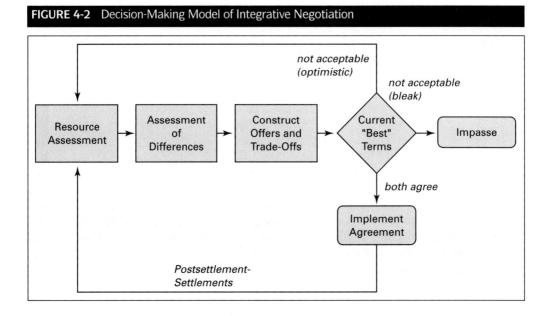

alternatives, and the addition of new issues and alternatives. Unbundling (Lax & Sebenius, 1986) of issues is important in negotiations that center around a single issue. Because mutually beneficial trade-offs require a minimum of two issues, it is important to fractionate conflict into more than one issue. In other instances, it may be necessary to add new issues and alternatives. The process of adding issues and alternatives is facilitated by discussing parties' interests.

Assessment of Differences

Once the issue mix and set of alternatives are identified, negotiators should focus on assessing their differences in valuation, probability assessment, risk preferences, time constraints, and capabilities (Lax & Sebenius, 1986). Two concerns should guide the assessment of interdependencies. First, each party should focus on its most important issues. Second, parties should focus on issues that are of high value to one party and of low cost for the other party to provide.

Offers and Trade-Offs

In this phase, parties should consider several potential trade-offs among valuations, forecasts, risks, time preferences, and capabilities, and eliminate those dominated by other alternatives. It makes no sense to pursue a trade-off unless what you are offering is more valuable to the other party than what it costs you to provide.

Acceptance/Rejection Decision

At some point, negotiators may land on an outcome both find minimally acceptable: It exceeds both parties' reservation points and constitutes a level 1 integrative agreement. Parties may end negotiations with this agreement, but the identification of a minimally acceptable agreement does not necessarily mean that settlement is efficient.

Negotiators should continue to explore the possibilities, depending on their costs for time and their subjective assessments of the likelihood of reaching a superior solution. Negotiators' aspirations and goals may influence the search process in negotiation; negotiators who set specific, challenging goals are more likely to continue to search for integrative agreements than do those who do not set goals or who set easy goals (Huber & Neale, 1986).

Prolonging Negotiation and Renegotiation

Two feedback loops emanate from the decision stage: the decision to prolong negotiations and the decision to renegotiate. Negotiators should prolong negotiations when the best agreement on the bargaining table fails to meet both parties' reservation points. Negotiators should reassess the resources by unpacking the initial set of issues and breaking them down to smaller issues that may be traded off. In addition to unpacking issues, negotiators may add issues and alternatives to the bargaining mix. If parties have identified all the issues and alternatives, identified differences to trade off, and a mutually agreeable solution has not been found, then they should call a halt to the negotiation and pursue their BATNAs.

DO NOT FORGET ABOUT CLAIMING

Sometimes, when negotiators learn about integrative agreements and expanding the pie, they forget about the distributive (pie-slicing) element of negotiation. It is not an effective negotiation strategy to focus exclusively on expanding the pie; the negotiator must simultaneously focus on claiming resources. After all, if a negotiator focused only on expanding the pie, he or she would be no better off because the other party would reap all the added value.

Negotiators acquire reputations for claiming (Weber, Loewenstein, & Thompson, 2003; Tinsley, O'Connor, & Sullivan, 2002). Negotiators who get a distributive reputation are responded to with a greater use of distributive tactics (e.g., substantiation, stating positions) and fewer integrative tactics (e.g., sharing preferences and priorities). Consequently, negotiators with a distributive reputation are actually less effective in maximizing the pie, because they engender the use of distributive strategies in their counterparts (to the detriment of pie-expanding strategies).

We have witnessed three stages in the evolution of the integrative negotiator. The first stage is what we call the "old-fashioned" negotiator. This type of negotiator comes from the old school of bargaining and believes that to successfully negotiate, one must adopt a tough, hard stance. The second stage in the evolution of the negotiator is what we call the "flower child" negotiator, or one who gets "turned on" to win-win negotiations and is so busy expanding the pie that he or she forgets to claim resources. Thus, the "flower child" is at a disadvantage in terms of slicing the pie. The third stage is what we call the "enlightened" negotiator, who realizes that negotiation has a pie-expanding aspect but at the same time does not forget to claim resources. Thus, this negotiator protects his or her interests while expanding the pie. If you follow all the strategies outlined in this chapter, you will be an enlightened negotiator.

CONCLUSION

Virtually all negotiators want to reach integrative (or win-win) agreements; however, most negotiators fail to do so—meaning that money and resources are left on the table. In reality, people are usually not aware that their negotiation outcomes are inefficient. The key reasons for lose-lose outcomes are illusory conflict and the fixed-pie perception. The successful creation of win-win negotiation deals involves trust and sharing information about priorities and preferences (not BATNAs!); asking diagnostic questions; providing your opponent information about your priorities and preferences (not your BATNA!); unbundling issues; making package deals (not single-issue offers); making multiple offers simultaneously; structuring contingency contracts that capitalize on differences in negotiators' beliefs, expectations, and attitudes; and using pre- and postsettlement settlement strategies. In their attempts to expand the pie, negotiators should not forget about claiming resources.

CHAPTER 5

DEVELOPING A NEGOTIATING STYLE

Rick Dubinsky was the guy who organized the 1985 pilots' strike at United, which earned him the nicknames "Mad Dog" and "Bomb Thrower." He "helped oust CEO Dick Ferris; and led attempted buyouts of United during the late 1980s and early 1990s." Dubinsky was just the man that the United pilots wanted going into 2000: He was smart, fearless, and passionate about organized labor. "Rick intimated a lot of people. They either fought back, ignored him, or rolled over." United's management team saw Dubinsky as a dangerous, manipulative bully who could do real damage, especially with a seat on the board. They were concerned that mild-mannered, people-oriented CEO Jim Goodwin would be putty in his hands. When Goodwin announced his interest in acquiring US Airways, Dubinsky put on his boxing gloves because he feared that the acquisition would cost many United pilots their seniority, because their pilot counterparts at US Airways had more experience and seniority, which determine the type of aircraft and routes pilots fly, their pay scale, scheduling, and vacation. So, Dubinsky's tactic was simple and lethal: "I don't see anything wrong with labor's philosophy of walking in and grabbing management firmly by the throat and saying we want our money." Dubinsky's assessment of United's BATNA was summed up by his statement, ". . . you can't kill the golden goose, and I don't believe we were anywhere near doing that. This goose had all kinds of eggs in 2000" (*Denver Post,* June 9, 2003, p. A1).

TOUGH VERSUS SOFT NEGOTIATORS

Negotiators often choose between one of two completely different negotiation styles or approaches: being tough or being soft (Bazerman & Neale, 1992). Rick Dubinsky is a tough negotiator. The tough negotiator is unflinching, makes high demands, concedes little, holds out until the very end, and often rejects offers that are within the bargaining zone. In contrast, the soft negotiator typically offers too many and too-generous concessions, reveals his or her reservation point, and is so concerned that the other party feels good about the negotiation that he or she gives away too much of the bargaining pie to the other party. About 78 percent of MBA students describe their style as "cooperative"; 22 percent describe themselves as "aggressive" (Lewicki & Robinson, 1998).

About 73 percent of attorneys are considered by their colleagues to be cooperative, and 27 percent to be competitive (Williams, 1983). Neither approach is particularly effective in simultaneously expanding and slicing the pie, and both approaches are likely to lead to outcomes that negotiators regret. The tough negotiator is likely to walk away from potentially profitable interactions and may gain a reputation for being stubborn. This reputation may intimidate others, but it will not change the size of the bargaining zone. On the other hand, the soft negotiator agrees too readily and never reaps much of the bargaining surplus.

The good news is that being tough or soft is not the negotiator's only choice. This chapter is designed to help you create a comfortable and effective negotiating style that allows you to (1) expand the pie, (2) maximize your slice, and (3) feel good about the negotiation.

MOTIVATION-APPROACH-EMOTION

The rest of this chapter focuses on three key dimensions of bargaining style: your goals (or your motivational drives), your approach, and your use of emotion. Our view is that basic motivations, such as self-interest or competition, influence behavior in negotiations. Similarly, the approach that a negotiator takes—interests-based, legalistic (or rights-based), or power-based (i.e., via threats)—affects the course of negotiations. Finally, the use of emotions (or lack thereof) is also a type of bargaining style.

We will review each dimension and profile negotiators that characterize each style. Your job is to do an honest self-assessment of what your current negotiation style is. If you are like most people—you will see your style as a little bit of everything, depending upon the situation. However, most people tend to adopt more of one style than others. Simply put, most people have a dominant, or instinctive, style. (See Sidebar 5-1 for a description of Charlene Barschefsky's style). Furthermore, the people with whom you negotiate tend to see you as being more like one style rather than a blend of all of them.

> ### Sidebar 5-1. Charlene Barshefsky's Negotiation Style
> When Charlene Barshefsky was U.S. trade representative, she would don her signature silk scarves before going to the negotiation table to hammer out deals. Once, she went without sleep for 51 hours to pound out a trade agreement with Japan; speaking in perfect turns of phrase, she was able to grind down the other side. Her colleagues were so impressed that they nicknamed her "Stonewall." She was also called "Dragon Lady": In a negotiation with China, she threatened to pack her bags and leave for the airport, cueing her negotiation partner, Gene Sperling, a White House aide, to stalk theatrically away from the table after her. Some described Barshefsky as a "sharp instrument," a "woman warrior who is genuinely responsive to people" (*Straits Times*, Nov. 21, 1999, p. 42). Armed with the precise speech of a litigator, Barshefsky was enormously skilled in wresting concessions from trading partners. In one negotiation, she did not even need to utter a single word to disconcert her

counterpart—when a Japanese finance master said that the U.S. delegation had to "take or leave" the offer that was on the table, Barshefsky just laughed out loud. Through years of expertise, Barshefsky developed her own effective bargaining style (*Straits Times*, Nov. 21, 1999).

Your first response in a negotiation situation is often a good indicator of your instinctive style. Take an honest look at yourself negotiating (tape-record or videotape yourself if you have to). Then ask people who are not afraid to give you frank feedback how they view you, in terms of style. You will probably be surprised at their responses!

Next, we review the various styles and discuss the pros and cons of each. Once you know your style, you are not locked into it forever. You have choices, and this chapter suggests ways to change your behavior.

MOTIVATIONS

People have different orientations toward the process of negotiation. Some people are individualists, seeking only their own gain; others are cooperative, seeking to maximize joint interests; and others are competitive, seeking to maximize differences. For a complete chart of motivational orientations, see Figure 5-1, which depicts eight distinct motivational orientations, ranging from altruism (high concern for others' interests) to aggression (desire to harm the other party) to masochism (desire to harm one's self) and individualism (desire to further one's own interests). Cooperation represents a midpoint between altruism and cooperation; martyrdom represents a midpoint between altruism and masochism; sadomasochism represents a midpoint between masochism and aggression; and competition represents a midpoint between aggression and individualism.

Assessing Your Motivational Style

Although Figure 5-1 depicts several motivational orientations (MOs), the following three are most common: individualism, competition, and cooperation, so we'll focus most on them. (See Table 5-1, specifically.)

1. The **individualistic** negotiator prefers to maximize his or her own gain and has little or no concern for how much the other person is getting.
2. The **competitive** negotiator prefers to maximize the difference between his or her own profits and those of the other party (i.e., "beat" the other side).
3. The **cooperative** negotiator seeks equality and to minimize the difference between negotiators' outcomes.

For a quick assessment of your own motivational orientation, complete the nine questions in Box 5-1.

Your ability to understand how your goal is shaped by various external factors is a key step toward self-insight. Richard Shell (1999) has identified helpful strategies and tips designed for cooperative types and competitive types. According to Shell, if you are a cooperative negotiator, you need to become more assertive, confident, and

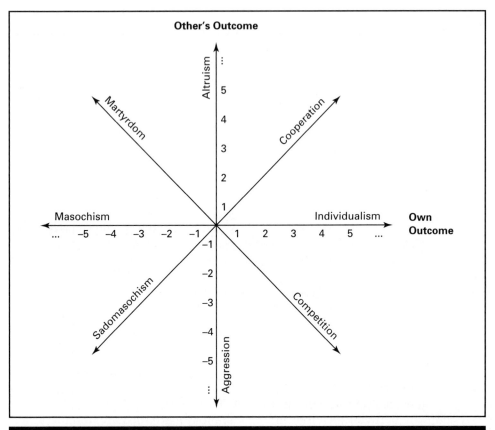

FIGURE 5-1   Subset of Social Values

Source: Reprinted from *Cooperation and Helping Behavior*, C. G. McClintock and E. van Avermaet, "Social Values and Rules of Fairness: A Theoretical Perspective," pp. 43–71, Copyright © 1982, with permission from Elsevier.

TABLE 5-1   Motivational Styles

	Motivational Style		
	Individualistic	*Competitive*	*Cooperative*
Objective	Self-interested	Victory	Joint welfare
View of others	Self-interest	Competitive	Heterogeneous: Some cooperators, some competitive; some individualistic
Situational factors that trigger this MO	Incentives to maximize own gain	Group competition; when organizations make interpersonal comparisons salient	Social identity; superordinate goals

BOX 5-1

MOTIVATIONAL STYLE ASSESSMENT

Each question presents three possible distributions of money (A, B, and C) to you and an opponent. Your task is to choose which of these distributions you most pre-fer. Indicate your true preference, not what you think you should choose. Be honest with yourself and circle only one alternative per question (Kuhlman & Marshello, 1975).

	Payoff to You *Payoff to Other*	A	B	C
1	You	$4,800	$5,400	$4,800
	Other party	$ 800	$2,800	$4,800
2	You	$5,600	$5,000	$5,000
	Other party	$3,000	$5,000	$1,000
3	You	$5,200	$5,200	$5,800
	Other party	$5,200	$1,200	$3,200
4	You	$5,000	$5,600	$4,900
	Other party	$1,000	$3,000	$4,900
5	You	$5,600	$5,000	$4,900
	Other party	$3,000	$5,000	$ 900
6	You	$5,000	$5,000	$5,700
	Other party	$5,000	$1,000	$3,000
7	You	$5,100	$5,600	$5,100
	Other party	$5,100	$3,000	$1,100
8	You	$5,500	$5,000	$5,000
	Other party	$3,000	$1,000	$5,000
9	You	$4,800	$4,900	$5,400
	Other party	$4,800	$1,000	$3,000

Compute your **cooperative** score by giving yourself one point for:
#1-C, #2-B, #3-A, #4-C, #5-B, #6-A, #7-A, #8-C, #9-A.

Compute your **competitive** score by giving yourself one point for:
#1-A, #2-C, #3-B, #4-A, #5-C, #6-B, #7-C, #8-B, #9-B.

Compute your **individualist** score by giving yourself one point for:
#1-B, #2-A, #3-C, #4-B, #5-A, #6-C, #7-B, #8-A, #9-C.

prudent in negotiations to be more effective at pie-expanding and pie-slicing. He outlines seven tools for the overly cooperative negotiator:

1. **Avoid concentrating too much on your bottom line**. Instead, spend extra time preparing your goals and developing high aspirations.
2. **Develop your BATNA**. Know your options to negotiating.
3. **Get an agent and delegate the negotiation task**. It is not an admission of failure to appoint an agent, if you think that person can act more assertively for you than you can yourself.
4. **Bargain on behalf of someone or something else, not yourself**. Sometimes people feel selfish when they negotiate; to get away from this limiting perception, think

about other people, such as your family, your staff, even your "retired self," and negotiate on their behalf.

5. **Create an audience**. People negotiate more assertively when they have an audience. So, tell someone about your negotiation, make promises, and then report results.

6. **Say, "You will have to do better than that because ... ," not "yes."** Cooperative people are programmed to say yes to almost anything. Rehearse not saying yes to everything that is proposed. Indeed, a historical analysis of four crises (e.g., Bay of Pigs and the Cuban Missile Crisis) reveals that leaders with cooperative-affiliative motivation are more likely to offer concessions (Langner & Winter, 2001).

7. **Insist on commitments, not just agreements**. An agreement puts too much trust in the other party; instead, insist upon commitments and specific promises from the other party, with consequences if they are not followed.

Shell also outlines seven tools for competitive people. He cautions that competitive negotiators need to become more aware of others and legitimate their needs.

1. **Think about pie expansion, not just pie slicing**. Remember that you can increase your slice of the pie by creating a bigger pie.

2. **Ask more questions than you think you should**. It pays to really understand the other party's objectives and needs.

3. **Rely on standards**. Other people respond well to arguments based upon standards of fairness and objectivity.

4. **Hire a relationship manager**. It is not a sign of failure to consult with someone concerning how to manage the "people side" of negotiations.

5. **Be scrupulously reliable**. Keep your word. Remember the egocentric bias: You see yourself as more honorable than others do, so you have to go overboard. (Remember the data on the "lying" study presented in Chapter 3.)

6. **Do not haggle when you can negotiate**. Do not view the negotiation as a contest of wills on every little issue. Spend time thinking about all the issues and the big picture. Remember that trade-offs mean that you may lose on some issues in return for big gains on other issues.

7. **Always acknowledge the other party and protect that person's self-esteem**. Do not gloat or brag. Remember that Dale Carnegie said the word other people most like to hear is their own name. So shower them with honest respect.

Strategic Issues Concerning Motivational Style

Once you know your own (and the other party's) motivational style, how can you best use this information? Several strategic issues are relevant when it comes to motivational style.

The Myth of the Hard Bargainer

According to Andrea Kupfer Schneider (2002), the myth of the "effective hard bargainer" should be destroyed. In her analysis of more than 700 practicing attorneys, adversarial behavior is regarded by peers to be distinctly ineffective. In fact, more than 50 percent of the negotiators viewed as adversarial were regarded as ineffective. Simply put: As negotiators become more irritating, stubborn, and unethical, their effectiveness ratings drop.

Moreover, similar findings have been obtained by directly observing negotiators (as opposed to self- and other-reports). When both negotiators have a cooperative orientation, they can be more effective in terms of maximizing the pie (Olekalns & Smith, 1998, 1999, 2003; Pruitt & Lewis, 1975; Weingart, Bennett, & Brett, 1993; Weingart, Brett, & Olekalns, 2003). For example, in a study of multiparty negotiations, cooperative groups outperformed individualists in terms of pie expanding (Weingart, Bennett, & Brett, 1993). Highly cooperative negotiators use more integrative strategies (such as information exchange), make more proposals for mutual coordination, and use fewer distributive tactics (Olekalns & Smith, 1999). Moreover, the more cooperatively motivated people present in a negotiation, the more integrative (pie-expanding) information is exchanged (Weingart, Brett, & Olekalns, 2003). And, when individualistically motivated negotiators are at the table, a greater increase occurs in distributive strategies (e.g., positional statements and substantiation). According to Olekalns and Smith (2003), cooperators and individualists take different roads to reach win-win outcomes. Individualists use the multiple-offer strategy and indirect information exchange; in contrast, cooperators share information about interests and priorities directly.

Do Not Lose Sight of Your Own Interests

By arguing that competitive, hard bargaining is not effective, we do not mean that negotiators should turn into "cream puffs" (Glick & Croson, 2001). In any negotiation situation, it is important not to lose sight of your own interests. Individualists do not need to worry about this possibility, but cooperators and competitors do. Often, two cooperators end up with a lose-lose agreement because they fail to make their interests known to the other party (Thompson & DeHarpport, 1998). Similarly, competitors are often so intent on "beating" the other side that they do not pay attention to their own interests. In a sense, they win the battle but lose the war. Thus, it is important that you maintain a high level of concern for your own interests as well as those of the other party (Pruitt & Carnevale, 1993; De Dreu, Weingart, & Kwon, 2000). (Some gender differences have been documented as well when it comes to motivational orientation; see Sidebar 5-2.)

Sidebar 5-2. Why Do Women Settle for Less?
"Lisa Barron became interested in studying women and money while she was in graduate school, after noticing that men in her master of business administration classes spent a lot of time talking about money—and the women didn't" (*Orange County Register*, July 5, 2003). Barron watched men and women negotiate in mock job interviews (Barron, 2003). To enhance realism, she had real MBA students negotiate with real hiring managers for marketing positions. She told them to ask for more than the $60,000 starting salary. Men believed that they had to advocate for themselves; in contrast, women believed that if they did a good job, the organization would eventually reward them. Whereas 85 percent of the men felt comfortable measuring their worth in dollars; 83 percent of the women were uncomfortable doing so and unsure of their monetary value. At least 70 percent of men believed they were entitled to more than others, but 71 percent of the women believed that they were entitled to the same as others (cooperative motivation).

Social Comparison Can Cause Breakdowns in Negotiation

In the negotiations between United and its pilots in 1999, the union doubled its pay raise demand from 14.5 to 28 percent immediately upon learning that pilots at Delta had gotten a 20 percent jump above industry-leading rates (*Denver Post*, June 9, 2003). As noted in Chapter 3, people are concerned with the payoffs received by others. In one investigation, people were given several choices concerning the division of a pie between themselves and another person (e.g., $300 you/$300 other versus $500 you/$800 other, etc.; Loewenstein, Thompson, & Bazerman, 1989). They were asked to indicate how satisfactory each division of the pie was. If people were purely individualistic, satisfaction would only be driven by the amount of money for oneself. In fact, people were highly concerned with how much the "other person" received, so much so that people often preferred to earn less money, if it meant that this would equate outcomes between themselves and another person. For example, many people preferred $300 self/$300 other over $500 self/$800 other. When faced with a choice between $300 self/$300 other versus $800 self/$500 other, people still tended to prefer equality, but not nearly as strongly as when the self was disadvantaged.

The relationship we have with the other party can affect our own motivational orientation. Consider the following choice (from Loewenstein, Thompson, & Bazerman, 1989):

Choice A: $4,000 for yourself
Choice B: 50 percent chance at $3,000; 50 percent chance at $5,000

Which do you choose? We asked 111 MBA students, and most of them (73 percent) chose the sure thing: choice A. This example confirms the risk-aversion principle we discussed in Chapter 2. We then asked a separate, but comparable, group of MBA students to choose between:

Choice C: $4,000 for yourself
            $6,000 for another person
Choice D: Self: 50 percent chance at $3,000, 50 percent chance at $5,000
            Other: 50 percent chance at $7,000, 50 percent chance at $5,000

A close look at all four choices (A, B, C, and D) reveals that the C choice is identical to the A choice (except for the payoff to the other person), and the D choice is identical to the B choice (except for the payoff to the other person). Thus, if people were perfectly rational and consistent, they would choose C over D (given that most choose A over B). However, this outcome is not what actually happens. People's choices are driven, in large part, by their *relationship* with the other party. Negotiators who have a positive relationship with the other person prefer the sure thing (C; 56%) over the gamble (D); in contrast, those who had a negative relationship with the other person preferred to gamble on D (67%) over C. Apparently, the type of relationship we have with another person affects our motivational orientation.

Perhaps it is this concern for equality that led to the removal of American Airlines CEO Donald Carty in 2003. When Donald Carty became CEO of American Airlines in 1998, he was well-liked and was thought to have personal charm. However, in the aftermath of the September 11, 2001, terrorist attacks, Carty was forced from his position because of "poisoned" relations with American's powerful unions and in the end, his own board of directors. The reason? The union members, who had recently taken serious wage cuts, discovered that Carty and other executives had privately been given bonus plans and lavish pension benefits. It seemed like an inequity of the grandest sort and they would have no part of it (*Tulsa World*, Apr. 25, 2003).

Distinct differences are evident between the pie-expanding and pie-slicing strategies used by cooperators versus those used by competitors. Cooperators not only increase the size of the pie, they also prefer an equitable division of the pie in comparison to individualists and competitors. Furthermore, cooperation is strongly related to reciprocity: Relative to individualists and competitors, cooperators are more likely to engage in the same level of cooperation as their opponent (Van Lange, 1999).

Use the Principle of Reinforcement to Shape Behavior

Negotiators can use basic principles of reinforcement (and punishment) to shape the behavior of their opponents. Use of reinforcement and punishment can be subtle, and the other party may not even be aware that you are using it. As an example, in one study, a lecturer stood in front of a class. Half of the class was instructed to look interested, nod their heads, and smile approvingly (positive reinforcement); the other half of the class was told to look bored and disinterested (punishment). After a short time, the instructor moved to the side of the class that was reinforcing his behavior. One of the best ways to encourage an opponent to engage in a behavior is to positively reinforce it when you see that person using it. (*Note*: Reinforcement for a child is candy; reinforcement for an adult is a smile or flattery.) It is important to reinforce the behavior immediately after it occurs, rather than delaying it. Similarly, one of the fastest ways to extinguish behavior you *do not* want your opponent to use is to simply not respond.

Recognize the Power of Reciprocity

Integrative (pie-expanding) and distributive (pie-slicing) behaviors tend to be reciprocated (Brett, Shapiro, & Lytle, 1998; Donohue, 1981; Putnam, 1983). Similarly, the tendency is for people to reciprocate the MO of the other party. If you want to discourage a competitive MO in your opponent, then you need to resist the urge to reciprocate it.

Anticipate Motivation Clashes at the Bargaining Table

It is unlikely that your partner will have the same negotiation motivation as you, at least initially. Consider what happens when a person with a cooperative orientation negotiates with a competitive person. The cooperator begins the negotiation in a cooperative fashion, but when she realizes that she is facing a competitor, she changes her own style. People with a cooperative orientation behave competitively when paired with a competitive opponent, whereas competitive players do not change (Kelley & Stahelski, 1970). In another study, when different types of players were faced with a prosocial (cooperative) opponent, prosocial and individualistic players were more likely to cooperate than were competitive players, but they would compete when the other party competed; competitive players competed regardless of the behavior of the other party (McClintock & Liebrand, 1988).

Anticipate Convergence

A negotiator's goal orientation (individualistic, cooperative, or competitive) provides an initial strategic approach to negotiations. During negotiation, people's strategies often change in response to how they view the other party and the situation. In particular, when a cooperator meets a competitor, the cooperator is the one to change. Thus, a strong tendency toward convergence of styles is likely to occur at the bargaining table (Weingart & Brett, 1998).

Convergence of outcomes, as well as bargaining styles, occurs in later stages of negotiation (Gulliver, 1979). As deadlines approach, people exchange specific proposals and make concessions (Lim & Murnighan, 1994; Stuhlmacher, Gillespie, & Champagne, 1998).

APPROACH[1]

According to Ury, Brett, and Goldberg (1988), negotiators use one of three types of approaches when in the process of conflict or dispute resolution:

1. ***Interests:*** Negotiators who focus on interests attempt to learn about the other's underlying needs, desires, and concerns (see also Fisher & Ury, 1981; interests-based negotiation). Negotiators with an interests-based approach often attempt to reconcile differing interests among parties in a way that addresses parties' most pressing needs and concerns.
2. ***Rights:*** Negotiators who focus on rights apply standards of fairness to negotiation. Standards may include terms specified by contracts, legal rights, precedent, or expectations based upon norms.
3. ***Power:*** Negotiators who focus on power use status, rank, threats, and intimidation to get their way. Interestingly, entire books are focused on use of power, such as *Guerilla Negotiating: Unconventional Weapons and Tactics to Get What You Want* (Levinson, Smith, & Wilson, 1999) and Fox and Nelson's (1999) *Sue the Bastards!*

As an example of the difference between interests, rights, and power-based approaches, consider this statement made by an employer: "I am afraid that I cannot meet your desired salary requirements, but I do hope that you will realize that working in our company is a wonderful opportunity and join us." Before reading further, take a moment to consider how you would respond if an employer made this statement to you. Three different negotiators might respond to the opponent's statement in ways unique to their own approach:

1. ***Interests-based response:*** "I am very interested in joining your company if my interests can be met. I would like to share some of my key goals and objectives. I want to learn more about the company's interests, from your standpoint. I should mention right now that salary is a key concern on several levels for me, not the least of which is the fact that I am a single-wage earner in my family and I have a number of educational loans. You did not mention other aspects of the offer, such as stock options, vacations, and flex time. Can we discuss these issues at this point?"

---

[1]Ideas in this section are based on Ury, Brett, and Goldberg's (1988) interests, rights, and power model in dispute situations. We apply their model to a negotiation context.

2. ***Rights-based response:*** "I am very interested in joining your company if we can come up with a fair employment package. I would like to point out that my salary requirements are in line with those of other people joining similar companies. I would think it would be a competitive advantage for your company to offer employment packages that are competitive with those being offered by other companies. I believe that my record and previous experience mean that a higher salary would be fair in this case."

3. ***Power-based response:*** "I am very interested in joining your company, but I must tell you that other companies are offering me more attractive deals at this point. I would like to invite you to reconsider the offer so that I do not have to resort to turning your offer down, given that I think that we make a good match for one another. I hope that you will be able to make a competitive offer."

For a more complete description of interests-, rights-, or power-based approaches, see Table 5-2.

During the process of negotiating or resolving disputes, the focus may shift from interests to rights to power and back again. For example, in one investigation (Lytle, Brett, & Shapiro, 1999), negotiators' statements were tape-recorded during a negotiation. Each statement that negotiators made was coded in terms of whether it reflected an interests-, rights-, or power-based approach. Parties moved frequently

TABLE 5-2 Approaches to Negotiation

	Approach		
	Interests	*Rights*	*Power*
Goal	Self-interest Dispute resolution Understanding others' concerns	Fairness Justice	Winning Respect
Temporal focus	Present (what needs and interests do we have right now?)	Past (what has been dictated by the past?)	Future ("What steps can I take in future to overpower others?")
Distributive strategies (pie slicing)	Compromise	Often produces a "winner" and a "loser"; thus, unequal distribution	Often produces a "winner" and a "loser"; thus, unequal distribution
Integrative strategies (pie expansion)	Most likely to expand the pie via addressing parties' underlying needs	Difficult to expand the pie unless focus is on interests	Difficult to expand the pie unless focus is on interests
Implications for future negotiations and relationship	Greater understanding Satisfaction Stability of agreement	Possible court action	Resentment Possible retaliation Revenge

among interests, rights, and power in the same negotiation (23/25 dyads), with more emphasis on rights and power in the first and third quarters than in the second and fourth.

Assessing Your Approach

Continuing with our analysis of the United pilots' negotiation we can analyze the series of moves in the negotiation in terms of interests, rights, and power:

- Union POWER MOVE: When United's pilots expected a new contract on April 12, 2000, many were angry when it did not happen. They began refusing to work overtime and started calling in extra sick days. This reaction caused immediate disruptions to United's flight schedule, which required voluntary overtime by pilots to function normally. Management also noticed that pilots were taxiing more slowly, correcting flight plans at the last minute, and insisting on repairs of minor items.
- Management RIGHTS MOVE: Management warned that if such tactics were organized by the union, they would be illegal. The company began compiling evidence it could take to court, including union communiqués encouraging pilots to "work to rule" (in other words, to do everything to the letter of the contract).
- Union POWER MOVE: Pilots stopped conducting training flights for new hires, leaving a pool of 120 pilots who could not fly. In July, 20 California-based first officers called in sick in one day, forcing the company to cancel virtually its entire schedule of Asia-bound fights. In Colorado Springs, pilots abandoned a plane full of passengers on the ramp because their duty-time was up and United couldn't find replacements to get them from Denver. A clandestine pilot newsletter circulated in August urging pilots to "slow down" and give United "a Labor Day that they'll never forget."
- Management RIGHTS AND POWER MOVE: In November, with the busy Thanksgiving weekend approaching, United took its mechanics to court, seeking $66 million in damages [rights]. The company also fired and disciplined some of them [power].

Next, we present each approach in greater detail. Which one characterizes you?

Interests

Interests are a person's needs, desires, concerns, fears—in general, the things a person cares about or wants. Interests underlie people's positions in negotiation (the things they *say* they want). Reconciling interests in negotiation is not easy. It involves probing for deep-seated concerns, devising creative solutions, and looking for trade-offs. We discussed some negotiation strategies in Chapters 3 and 4, such as fashioning trade-offs or logrolls among issues, searching for compatible issues, devising bridging solutions, and structuring contingency contracts. It is difficult to immediately address interests in a negotiation because people adopt positional tendencies, and emotions can often conceal interests. Negotiators who use an interests-based approach frequently ask other parties about their needs and concerns and, in turn, disclose their own needs and concerns.

Rights

In a clearly rights-based move, Steve Clayborn, of Grovetown, Georgia, shocked a nurse and caused a scene at Doctors Hospital when he refused to sign a standard consent form unless he could "pencil in some changes" (*Augusta Chronicle*, July 12, 2003). Consider the moves of Nike CEO Phil Knight and Will Vinton of Vinton Studios that resembled a complicated game of corporate chess (*The Oregonian*, May 25, 2003). Each time Knight tried to make a move, Vinton blocked it, using his rights under the company's complicated stock ownership structure. Knight would not put more money into the company unless it issued new stock. However, Vinton found a legal loophole that would allow him to buy enough stock to regain control of Vinton Studies. Eventually, Knight fired Vinton and paid him no severance.

These examples illustrate that a common negotiation style is to rely on some independent standard with perceived legitimacy or fairness to determine who is right in a situation. Some rights are formalized by law or contract. Others are socially accepted standards of behavior, such as reciprocity, precedent, equality, and seniority in an organization (e.g., "I want a higher salary because it would be consistent with the incentive structure in this organization"). Rights are rarely clear-cut. They often differ from situation to situation and sometimes, contradictory standards apply. For example, a productive employee may want a salary increase based upon extreme productivity, yet the organization may focus on seniority. Reaching an agreement on rights, where the outcome will determine who gets what, can often be exceedingly difficult—frequently leading negotiators to involve a third party to determine who is right. The prototypical rights procedure involves **adjudication**, in which disputants present evidence and arguments to a neutral third party who has the power to hand down a binding decision. Negotiators who use a rights-based approach frequently say things like, "I deserve this," or "This is fair." For example, consider the following rights-based argument that occurred between John Mack of Credit Suisse First Boston and Frank Quattrone, the investment firm's powerful tech banker. The following conversation occurred between them as they were sitting in a private dining room in the Fairmont Hotel (*Fortune*, Sept. 1, 2003):

> MACK: "I am going to tear up your contract."
> QUATTRONE: "You can't do that. It's a contract."
> MACK: "I can do it. I believe I have legal grounds, and I'm prepared to go to court." (p. 98)

See the cartoon in Figure 5-2 for a humorous example of a rights-based move.

Power

Power is the ability to coerce someone to do something he or she would not otherwise do. Exercising power typically means imposing costs on the other side or threatening to do so. Exercising power may manifest itself in acts of aggression, such as sabotage, physical attack, or withholding benefits derived from a relationship. A prime example of a power move occurred when Time Warner yanked ABC stations off its systems in 11 cities at the beginning of the May sweeps period in 2000, a critical time for setting ratings and ad rates. Television viewers instead saw the words, "DISNEY HAS TAKEN ABC AWAY FROM YOU" in block letters scrolling across the screen (*Adweek*, May 1, 2000; see Sidebar 5-3 for the complete story).

"*Your wife's also asking that you rot in hell for eternity, but I think that's negotiable.*"

FIGURE 5-2 Humorous Example of a Rights-Based Move in a Divorce

Source: © The New Yorker Collection 1999 Michael Masline from cartoonbank.com. All Rights Reserved.

Sidebar 5-3. Power Moves

At 12:01 on the morning of May 1, 2000, the TV screen went blue on Time Warner Cable's WABC-TV feed, and a scrolling message in block letters began: "DISNEY HAS TAKEN ABC AWAY FROM YOU." After four months of fruitless negotiations over the rights to retransmit ABC signals over cable, Time Warner yanked ABC stations off its systems in 11 cities, including Houston, Philadelphia, Raleigh, and New York, during a period critical for setting ratings and ad rates. The "alert" aired on WABC-TV Channel 7 in New York, whose cable subscribers in 3.5 million homes went without their local ABC station. Time Warner said it wanted to extend talks until the end of the year, but ABC only offered an extension through May 24—the end of the sweeps. Time Warner laid blame squarely on Disney, ABC's corporate parent. "Disney is trying to inappropriately use its ownership of ABC television stations to extract excessive and unreasonable terms for its cable TV channels—terms that would add hundreds of millions of dollars in cost for Time Warner and its cable customers," said Fred D. Ressler, senior vice president of programming for Time Warner Cable (*Adweek*, May 1, 2000). Disney wanted higher fees for the cable rights to ABC and broader distribution by Time Warner for Disney's own cable programming, especially ESPN. The Cable Act of 1992 entitles over-the-air networks to compensation from cable systems that carry network signals. The agreement between Disney's ABC and Time Warner Cable expired on December 31, 1999. ABC blamed the impasse on Time Warner: "This is a punitive act, but Time Warner is only punishing their own customers through their cable system," said Tom Kane, president and general manager of WABC (*Adweek*, May 1, 2000).

Within a relationship of mutual dependence (e.g., labor and management; employee and employer), the question of who is more powerful rests on who is more dependent. In turn, one's degree of dependency on the other party rests on how satisfactory the alternatives are for satisfying one's interests. The better the alternative, the less dependent one is. Power moves include behaviors that range from insults and ridicule to strikes, beatings, and warfare. For example, the former chairman of Allied Capital, David Gladstone, was aggressive in his business dealings, to the point of using physical violence (*Forbes*, Sept. 2, 2002b). Allied's board forced Gladstone to retire in February 1997 after he smacked a female executive in the back of her head two times, so hard that her head snapped forward.

The variety of power tactics have in common the intent to coerce the other side to settle on terms more satisfactory to the wielder of power. For example, Kim Jong Il, president of North Korea, was described by some as "cunning and cruel, with street-fighter instincts" (*Patriot-News Harrisburg,* Jan. 12, 2003, para. 5). Moreover, he was not above using brinksmanship—threatening to drive himself and others over the edge. However, Wendy Sherman, the former senior State Department official who negotiated with Kim in the Clinton administration, said, "He is not crazy. . . . He is intelligent and he is totally conscious about what he is doing" (para. 7). His strategy is to push just far enough—just before the U.S. government gets really angry, he stops the provocations and comes to the negotiation table.

The two types of power-based approaches are *threats* in which one or both parties makes a threat and *contests* in which parties take action to determine who will prevail (Ury, Brett, & Goldberg, 1988). Determining who is more powerful without a decisive and potentially destructive power contest may be difficult because power is ultimately a matter of perception. Despite objective indicators of power (e.g., financial resources), parties' perceptions of their own and each other's power do not often coincide. Moreover, each side's perception of the other's power may fail to take into account the possibility that the other will invest greater resources in the contest than expected, out of fear that a change in the perceived distribution of power will affect the outcomes of future disputes. Many power contests involve threatening avoidance (e.g., divorce), actually engaging in it temporarily to impose costs on the other side (e.g., a strike or breaking off diplomatic relations), or ending the relationship altogether.

Strategic Issues Concerning Approaches

The Principle of Reciprocity

Negotiators should anticipate that the style they use in negotiation will often be reciprocated by the other party. In one investigation, the reciprocal rates were interests (42%), followed by power (27%) and rights (22%) (Lytle, Brett, & Shapiro, 1999). Thus, before negotiation, you should evaluate the pros and cons of interests, rights, and power. In general, interests are less risky than rights and power, as we will see later.

Interests Are Effective for Pie Expansion

Focusing on interests can usually resolve the problem underlying the dispute more effectively than focusing on rights or power. A focus on interests can help uncover "hidden" problems and help identify which issues are of the greatest concern to each party. Our advice is to put the focus on interests early in the negotiations. This suggestion raises an obvious question: If interests are effective, why doesn't everyone use them? Ury, Brett, and Goldberg (1988) identify several reasons, including lack of skill, the tendency to reciprocate rights and power, and strong cultural or organizational norms.

How to Refocus Your Opponent on Interests (and Move Them from Rights and Power)

Suppose that you enter a negotiation with an interests-based approach, but your opponent is focusing steadily on rights or power. This situation is making you angry, and you find yourself starting to reciprocate power and rights out of sheer self-defense. Yet you also realize that this behavior is creating a lose-lose situation. How do you break out of the spiral of reciprocity? Next, we identify two sets of strategies that you can use: personal strategies (that you, as a person, can use in a face-to-face situation) and structural strategies (steps that an organization can take to create norms that engender an interests-based culture; Ury, Brett, & Goldberg, 1988).

Personal Strategies   *Do Not Reciprocate!* Reciprocation is a form of reward and encouragement of behavior. If you want to extinguish a behavior, resist the urge to reciprocate (Fisher, Ury, & Patton, 1991; Ury, Brett, & Goldberg, 1988). By not reciprocating, you can refocus your opponent. When the other negotiator reciprocated, the focal negotiator stayed with rights and power arguments 39 percent of the time; however, when the other did not reciprocate, the focal negotiator stayed with rights and power arguments only 22 percent of the time (and hence, was refocused 78 percent of the time; Lytle, Brett, & Shapiro, 1999). Consider how John Chen, CEO of Sybase, dealt with a full-out power blast launched by one of the company's largest shareholders. "You have 5 minutes," the investor said angrily, "to tell me why I ought to hold this piece of garbage" (*Business 2.0*, Aug. 1, 2003c, p. 64). Chen resisted the temptation to fight back, and instead turned the focus back to interests by focusing on the customers who had entrusted critical data to Sybase software and could not afford to rip it out. Chen suggested that the focus should be on regaining customers' confidence (shared interest) and successfully refocused the discussion.

Provide Opportunities to Meet   Often, rights- and power-based approaches emerge when parties are out of touch and uncertain about the intentions of the other side. Getting parties together for informal discussions can move them toward interests.

When people are face-to-face, they often can't help but feel some compassion for the other party. Moreover, differences don't have an opportunity to fester. For example, Justice Warren Winkler, an Ontario Superior Court Justice, is a believer in resolving disputes face-to-face. In one negotiation, Winkler intervened between the pilots union of Air Canada and its low-cost regional carrier, Jazz Airlines, whose animosities go back a decade. After three days of talks and no progress, Winkler rounded up the key pilot leaders with just five hours before a deadline. With no warning, he had them all go into his own office suite boardroom. It was the first time through the whole process that they had met face-to-face (*Toronto Star*, June 2, 2003).

Don't Get Personal—Use Self-Discipline   Make sure that you stay focused on the conflict and the issues. Many negotiators begin to attack the other party's character. In their classic book, *Getting to Yes*, Fisher and Ury (1981) advocate separating the people from the problem. Moreover, the same phenomenon characterizes successful marriages. Gottman and Levenson (2000) tracked couples over a 14-year period. Based upon an initial observation of the couples' fighting style early in their marriage, they were able to predict which couples got divorced and which stayed together with 93 percent accuracy. The biggest determinant of divorce was not the amount of arguing, nor the amount of anger, but the use of personal attacks.

Use Behavioral Reinforcement   Make sure that you are not rewarding the other party's rights- or power-based behavior. In other words, if you have been planning on making a concession, do not offer it up to the other party immediately after he or she has misbehaved or acted out. If you do, you reward the very behavior that you want to extinguish. One of the most effective ways to extinguish a behavior is simply not to react. If you do react, you may be unconsciously rewarding the behavior (e.g., if the other party benefits from the attention associated with a conflict spiral). Recall that rewards include things like eye contact, head nods, smiling, and other types of nonverbal approval.

Making unilateral concessions is not effective for refocusing negotiations. In one study, concession making was less effective in refocusing negotiations from rights and power (60% refocused) as were other noncontentious communications (77% refocused; Lytle, Brett, & Shapiro, 1999). Why? A unilateral concession may be seen as a reward for contentious behavior; therefore, it may encourage the repetition of such behavior.

Send a Mixed Message   In other words, reciprocate, but add an interests-based proposal. Reciprocation is instinctive, especially under stress (Lerner, 1985). Thus, you may find that your opponent is making you angry, and you need to "flex your muscles." One effective strategy is to reciprocate rights or power, but *combine* it with interests-based questions or proposals (Ury, Brett, & Goldberg, 1988). As an example, consider this statement from a computer company embroiled in a bitter dispute with a printing company (Lytle, Brett, & Shapiro, 1999):

> You know, your reputation could be seriously compromised by suing us, as we could just as easily go to all the other printing companies and let them know how you have cheated us . . . but this is not going to solve the problem. Right now, we don't have any money to pay you and, even if you sue us, you will not be able to collect. Why don't we try to find a way to discuss this problem that might give both of us a chance to get what we really want out of this situation? (p. 44)

Sending the opponent this kind of "mixed message" (rights and interests) gives them a chance to choose what to reciprocate—interests, rights, or power.

Try a Process Intervention   Process interventions are tactics that are interests-based with the goal of moving the opponent back to interests-based negotiation. Effective processes can include any of the pie-expanding strategies we discussed in Chapter 4 (e.g., multiple offers, revealing information about priorities, etc.) as well as several other dispute resolution strategies (indicated next). In a direct test as to the effectiveness of process interventions, Ury, Brett, and Goldberg (1988) examined the percent of time that a negotiator successfully extinguished a rights or power move by the opponent. Least effective was reciprocation (66%); the most effective method was the process intervention (82% success rate), mixed-message approach (74% success rate), and simply resisting the urge to reciprocate (self-discipline; 76% success rate).

Let's Talk and Then Fight   Another strategy is to agree to talk for 20 minutes or so, and to then argue. By agreeing up front on a process, both parties commit implicitly to listening to one another at least temporarily.

Strategic Cooling-Off Periods   It is easy to muster a rights-based response or power display in the heat of conflict. After all, an interests-based approach requires deeper levels of cognitive processing and the ability to get past the more obvious rights and power issues that are likely to surface. Thus, it often serves parties' interests to build in some cooling-off periods that allow them to better assess their own needs and interests, independent of rights and power issues.

Paraphrasing   Many times, negotiators will have difficulty in their attempts to turn a rights- or power-based argument into an interests-based discussion. It is important for negotiators not to abandon their interests-based approach, but rather, to persist in their attempt to understand the other party's underlying needs. Stephen Covey (1999) suggests that parties to conflict should be forced to empathize with each other. He has a strict ground rule: "You can't make your point until you restate the other person's point to his or her satisfaction" (Covey, 1999, p. 5). People are often so emotionally invested that they cannot listen. According to Covey, they pretend to listen. So he asks the other party, "Do you feel understood?" The other party always says, "No, he mimicked me, but he doesn't understand me." The negotiator gets to state a point only after satisfying the other party (for an example of this interaction, see Sidebar 5-4).

Sidebar 5-4. Resolving Differences
The following is a quote from Steven Covey, chairman of the Franklin Covey Company and author of *Seven Habits of Highly Effective People* and *Families and Principle-Centered Leadership*:

> Once the president of a company came to me and said, "Will you be a third-party facilitator in a lawsuit we face? None of us trusts the other party."
> And I said, "You don't need me. You can do it yourself. Just put everything up front, and then ask if they would be willing to search

for a better solution." So he called the president of the other company and made the invitation. The other president said, "No, let the legal process handle it." He probably thought, "He's just playing softball now. Let's stick with hardball."

My friend then said, "Listen, I'll send you our material, and then let's meet. I won't bring my attorney. Bring your attorney if you like. You don't even have to say a word. We'll just have lunch. You have nothing to lose and possibly something to gain."

So they came together, and he basically said, "I'm going to see if I can make your case for you, since you're not going to speak." He tried to show genuine empathy, and he described the other party's position in depth, surprising the other president with his empathy. He then said, "Do I have an accurate understanding?"

At that point, the president spoke up and said, "That's about half accurate, but I need to correct some inaccuracies."

His attorney said, "Don't say another word." He then told his attorney to essentially shut up because he could feel the power of this communication.

My friend captured every major point of the other case, using a flip chart, and then made his points. They then started discussing possible alternatives that would meet their needs. Shortly after lunch, they had their disagreement resolved.

You can experience the magic of synergy that comes from sincere empathy if you seek a creative, win-win third alternative to two opposing positions (Covey, 1999, pp. 5–6).

Label the Process   If you recognize that your opponent is using a rights- or power-based approach after you have tried to focus on interests, it might be useful to point out and label the strategy you see the opponent using. Recognizing or labeling a tactic as ineffective can neutralize or refocus negotiations (Fisher, Ury, & Patton, 1991). Consider, for example, how one manager used the labeling strategy to defuse an opponent's rights-based argument:

We can argue all afternoon as to whether the language in the contract pertains to application software. I think it does not; you think it does. We are never going to agree about that. Let's see if we can move on. What about . . . . (p. 45)

Similarly, Justice Warren Winkler uses the power of language, "I don't have time for you guys to go on a 'wants' hunt. Draw up a new list of concessions based on need, not greed" (*Toronto Star*, June 2, 2003).

Structural Strategies   The following structural strategies are ones suggested by Ury, Brett, and Goldberg (1988) in their book, *Getting Disputes Resolved* (p. 42). The authors suggest several methods whereby dispute resolution systems can be designed and used within organizations, some of which are described here in detail. Each of these strategies is designed to reduce the costs of handling disputes and to produce satisfying, durable resolutions.

Put the Focus on Interests   The parties involved should attempt to negotiate, rather than escalate to adjudication, which can be achieved by establishing a known negotiation procedure. For example, Ury, Brett, and Goldberg (1988, pp. 42–43) note that when International Harvester introduced a new procedure for oral (rather than written) handling of grievances at the lowest possible level, the number of written grievances plummeted to almost zero. Some organizations stay focused on interests via use of a *multistep negotiation procedure*, in which a dispute that is not resolved at one level of the organizational hierarchy moves to progressively higher levels. Another strategy is the *wise counselor*, in which senior executives are selected to consider disputes. By creating *multiple points of entry*, negotiators can have several points of access for resolving disputes. In some instances, *mandatory negotiations* can provide a way for reluctant negotiators to come to the table. By providing *skills and training* in negotiation, people will be better prepared to negotiate in an interests-based fashion. Finally, by providing opportunities for *mediation*, in which a third party intervenes, negotiators can often focus on interests. Again, Justice Warren Winkler decided to put the issue of who flies what planes in the Air Canada negotiations before an impartial third party for resolution (*Toronto Star*, June 2, 2003).

Build in "Loop-Backs" to Negotiation   According to Ury, Brett, and Goldberg (1988), interests-based procedures will not always resolve disputes, yet a rights or power contest can be costly and risky. Excellent structural solutions provide procedures that encourage negotiators to turn back from contests to negotiation. These methods are what Ury, Brett, and Goldberg call "loop-back" procedures:

- ***Looping back from rights.***   Some loop-back procedures provide information about a negotiator's rights as well as the likely outcome of a rights contest. Consider *information procedures* in which databases are created that can be accessed by negotiators who want to research the validity and outcome of their claims. *Advisory arbitration* is a method whereby managers are provided with information that would likely result if arbitration were to be carried out or the dispute were to go to court. *Minitrials* are procedures whereby "lawyers" (high-level executives in the organization who have not been previously involved) represent each side and present evidence and arguments that are heard by a neutral judge or advisor. Minitrials put negotiation in the hands of people who are not emotionally involved in the dispute and who have the perspective to view it in the context of the organization's broad interests.
- ***Looping back from a power conflict.***   A variety of strategies can be used to move parties away from power contests back to interests. *Crisis procedures*, or guidelines for emergency communication written in advance, can establish communication mechanisms between disputants. For example, in disputes between the United States and the Soviet Union, a hotline served a crisis procedure purpose; in addition, U.S. and Soviet officials established nuclear risk reduction centers, staffed 24 hours in Washington and Moscow, for emergency communications (Ury, Brett, and Goldberg 1988, p. 55). Finally,

intervention by third parties can halt power contests (a topic we take up in Appendix 3). For example, consider the musicians' strike against producers of Broadway shows in 2003. New York City mayor Michael Bloomberg called both sides into a round-the-clock negotiating session to move away from entrenched positions. Although Bloomberg has no official authority, the stature of his office made it impossible for either side to turn him down. Indeed, both sides were looking for a way to resolve the dispute and save face (*The Record*, Mar. 12, 2003).

Provide Low-Cost Rights and Power Backups   Should interests-based negotiation fail, it is useful to have low-cost rights and power backup systems. *Conventional arbitration* is less costly than court or private adjudication. Ury, Brett, and Goldberg (1988) note that 95 percent of all collective bargaining contracts provide for arbitration of disputes. *Med-arb* is a hybrid model in which the mediator serves as an arbitrator, if mediation fails. With the threat of arbitration in the air, parties are often encouraged to reach a negotiated solution. In final-offer arbitration, the arbitrator does not have authority to compromise between parties' positions, but rather, must accept one of the final offers made. Thus, each party has an incentive to make a final offer appear the most reasonable in the eyes of the neutral third party. *Arb-med* is also a hybrid model traced from South Africa in which an arbitrator makes a decision and places it in a sealed envelope. The threat of the arbitrator's decision sits on a table and is destined to be opened unless the parties reach mutual agreement. Arb-med is more effective than conventional arbitration (Conlon, Moon, & Ng, 2002).

Build in Consultation Beforehand and Feedback Afterwards   *Notification and consultation* between parties prior to taking action can prevent disputes that arise through sheer misunderstanding. They can also reduce the anger and hostility that often result when decisions are made unilaterally and abruptly. *Postdispute analysis and feedback* is a method whereby parties learn from their disputes to prevent similar problems in the future. Similarly, by establishing a *forum*, consultation and postdispute analysis can be institutionalized so as to create an opportunity for discussion.

Provide Skills and Resources   Oftentimes, people find themselves embroiled in conflict and negotiation when they never expected it. The extent to which they do not have the resources or skills to resolve disputes can often lead to rights- and power-based actions (i.e., suing or firings). However, when these same people have been given skills in interests-based negotiations, they can often create opportunity from conflict in a way that is beneficial for everyone concerned.

High Costs Associated with Power and Rights

Focusing on who is right or who is more powerful usually leaves at least one person perceiving himself or herself as a loser. Even if you are the winner in these situations, the problem is that often, losers do not give up, but appeal instead to higher courts or plot revenge. Rights are less costly than power, generally—power costs more in resources consumed and opportunities lost. For example, strikes cost more than arbitration, and violence costs more than litigation. Costs are incurred not only in efforts invested, but from the destruction of each side's resources. Power contests often create new injuries and a desire for revenge. Interests are less costly than rights. In summary, focusing on interests, compared to rights and power, produces higher satisfaction with outcomes, better working relationships, and less recurrence; it may also mean lower transaction costs.

Know *When* to Use Rights and Power

Despite their general effectiveness, focusing on interests is not enough: Resolving all disputes by reconciling interests is neither possible nor desirable (Ury, Brett, & Goldberg, 1988). The problem is that rights and power procedures are often used when they are not necessary; a procedure that should be the last resort too often becomes the first move. Rights and power may be appropriate to use when (Ury, Brett, & Goldberg, 1988):

- *The other party refuses to come to the table.* In this case, no negotiation is taking place, and rights and power are necessary to face engagement.
- *Negotiations have broken down and parties are at an impasse.* A credible threat, especially if combined with an interests-based proposal, may restart negotiations. For example, when American Airlines was negotiating with its pilot unions in 2003, they had their lawyers standing in clear view in the lobby ready to file bankruptcy papers at exactly 5 P.M. (*Dallas Morning News*, Apr. 3, 2003). Often, parties cannot reach agreement on the basis of interests because their perceptions of who is right or more powerful are so different that they cannot establish a range in which to negotiate. In this case, a rights procedure may be needed to clarify the rights boundary within which a negotiated resolution can be sought.
- *The other party needs to know you have power.* Sometimes, people need to wield power simply to demonstrate that they have it (Ury, Brett, & Goldberg, 1988). However, the consequences of imposing will can be costly. Your threats must be backed up with actions to be credible. Furthermore, the weaker party may fail to fully comply with a resolution based on power, thus requiring the more powerful party to engage in expensive policing.
- *Interests are so opposed that agreement is not possible.* Sometimes, parties' interests are so disparate that agreement is not possible. For example, when fundamental values are at odds (e.g., abortion beliefs), resolution can only occur through a rights contest (a trial) or power contest (a demonstration or legislative battle).
- *Social change is necessary.* To create social impact, a rights battle may be necessary. For example, consider the case of *Brown v. Board of Education*, which laid important groundwork for the elimination of racial segregation.
- *Negotiators are moving toward agreements and parties are "positioning" themselves.* In other words, parties are committed to reaching a deal, and now they are dancing in the bargaining zone.

Know *How* to Use Rights and Power

We made the point that negotiators need to know when to use rights and power. However, simply recognizing when to use these strategies does not guarantee success. Following are some key things the negotiator needs to take into consideration when using rights and power and, in particular, when making a threat (Brett, 2001).

Threaten the Other Party's Interests   To effectively make a threat, a negotiator needs to attack the other party's underlying interests. Rights and power should challenge the opponents' long-term and highly valued interests. Otherwise, the other party will feel little incentive to comply with your threat. Consider how American Airlines attempted to jump-start negotiations with their union members in 2003 by threatening their most basic interests (*Dallas Morning News*, Apr. 3, 2003). Company negotiators gave a written "outline" to each union group called a "term sheet" that clearly laid out the financial impact that bankruptcy would entail: $500 million in pay and benefits cuts beyond the $1.62 billion that the airline asked for. The result was that the union leaders were now anchored on this number: For example, the pilot's board quickly huddled at union offices and came up with 10 concessions that would raise the needed amount.

Clarity   Negotiators need to be clear about what actions are needed by the other party. For example, nine days after al Qaeda's terrorist attacks on the United States in 2001, President Bush issued a clear threat: He demanded that the Taliban turn over Osama bin Laden and the leaders of his terrorist network, and that it shut down the terrorist training camps in Afghanistan; otherwise, the U.S. would "direct every resource at our command—every means of diplomacy, every tool of intelligence, every instrument of law enforcement, every financial influence and every necessary weapon of war—to the destruction and to the defeat of the global terror network" (*Associated Press*, Sept. 20, 2001).

Credibility   Power-based approaches typically focus on the future (e.g., "If you do not do such-and-such, I will withdraw your funding"). To be effective, the other party must believe that you have the ability to carry out the threat. If you are not seen as credible, people will call your bluff. Ideally, it is desirable to convince the other party that you have power without actually having to exert it.

Do Not Burn Bridges   We made the point that rights and power are risky. It is important that you leave a pathway back to interests-based discussion. Ury, Brett, and Goldberg (1988) call it the "loop-back to interests." Threats are expensive to carry out; thus, it is critical that you are able to turn off a threat. This ability allows the other party to save face and reopen negotiations. If you do not provide yourself with a loop back to interests, you force yourself to carry out the threat. Furthermore, after you use your threat, you lose your power and ability to influence. Lytle, Brett, and Shapiro (1999, p. 48) suggest that if you are going to use rights or power, you should use the following sequence: (1) state a specific, detailed demand and deadline; (2) state a specific, detailed, credible threat (which harms other side's interests); and (3) state a specific, detailed, positive consequence that will follow if the demand is met.

EMOTIONS[2]

If approach (interests, rights, and power) is the *packaging* of negotiators' goals, then emotions are the *delivery* of the package. For example, we can imagine a power-based argument or threat delivered in any of these three ways: calm, cool, and collected;

---

[2]Ideas in this section have been strongly influenced by collaboration with Shirli Kopelman, Vicki Medvec, Deepak Malhotra, Ashleigh Rosette, and Vanessa Seiden.

TABLE 5-3 Emotional Styles

	Rational	*Positive*	*Negative*
Focus	Conceal or repress emotion	Create positive emotion in other party Create rapport	Use irrational-appearing emotions to intimidate or control other party
Distributive strategies (pie slicing)	Citing norms of fair distribution	Compromise for the sake of the relationship	Threats Often tough bargaining
Integrative strategies (pie expansion)	Systematic analysis of interests	Positive emotion stimulates creative thinking	Negative emotion may inhibit integrative bargaining
Implications for future negotiations and relationship	Not likely to say or do anything regrettable, but also may come across as "distant"	Greater feelings of commitment to relationship partner	Pressure to carry out threats or lose credibility

positive and constructive; or negative and heated. Thompson, Medvec, Seiden, and Kopelman (2000) outlined three distinct emotional styles:

1. **Unemotional and rational** (i.e., the "poker face" approach)
2. **Positive** (i.e., the friendly and nice approach)
3. **Negative** (i.e., the "squeaky wheel" or "rant 'n' rave" approach)

Table 5-3 depicts these three emotional styles (rational, positive, and negative) and describes their implications for distributive bargaining, integrative bargaining, and the relationship among negotiators. Kopelman, Rosette, and Thompson (2004) tested the effectiveness of each of these styles in a dispute situation. The positive and rational emotional strategies were distinctly more effective than the negative emotional strategy in obtaining desirable outcomes in an ultimatum setting. Negotiators who strategically employ the positive approach are more likely to develop a constructive future relationship than negotiators who employ rational or negative approaches.

Assessing Your Emotional Style

One way to assess your emotional style is to take the test in Box 5-2. It is also a good idea to ask two or three colleagues who are not afraid to give you honest feedback to complete the test according to how they view your emotional style in negotiations.

The Rational Negotiator: Keeping a Poker Face

A common piece of advice in negotiation is to "keep a poker face." This advice stems from a belief that showing emotion is a sign of weakness and that emotion makes a negotiator vulnerable to giving away too much of bargaining pie. The absence of emotions is consistent with principles of rationality. In his book *The Art and Science of Negotiation*, Raiffa (1982, p. 120) lists "self-control, especially of emotions and their visibility" as the thirteenth most-important characteristic of effective negotiators (out of 34 key characteristics). Similarly, Nierenberg (1968) claims that:

BOX 5-2

EMOTIONAL STYLE QUESTIONNAIRE

Read each statement, and indicate whether you think it is true or false for you in a negotiation situation. Force yourself to answer each one as generally true or false (i.e., do not respond with "I don't know").

1. In a negotiation situation, it is best to "keep a cool head."

2. I believe that in negotiations you can "catch more flies with honey."

3. It is important to me that I maintain control in a negotiation situation.

4. Establishing a positive sense of rapport with the other party is key to effective negotiation.

5. I am good at displaying emotions in negotiation to get what I want.

6. Emotions are the downfall of effective negotiation.

7. I definitely believe that the "squeaky wheel gets the grease" in many negotiation situations.

8. If you are nice in negotiations, you can get more than if you are cold or neutral.

9. In negotiation, you have to "fight fire with fire."

10. I honestly think better when I am in a good mood.

11. I would never want to let the other party know how I really felt in a negotiation.

12. I believe that in negotiations, you can "catch more flies with a fly-swatter."

13. I have used emotion to manipulate others in negotiations.

14. I believe that good moods are definitely contagious.

15. It is very important to make a very positive first impression when negotiating.

16. The downfall of many negotiators is that they lose personal control in a negotiation.

17. It is best to keep a "poker face" in negotiation situations.

18. It is very important to get the other person to respect you when negotiating.

19. I definitely want to leave the negotiation with the other party feeling good.

20. If the other party gets emotional, you can use it to your advantage in a negotiation.

21. I believe that it is important to "get on the same wavelength" as the other party.

22. It is important to demonstrate "resolve" in a negotiation.

23. If I sensed that I was not under control, I would call a temporary halt to the negotiation.

24. I would not hesitate to make a threat in a negotiation situation if I felt the other party would believe it.

Scoring Yourself

Computing your "R" score: Look at items #1, #3, #6, #11, #16, #17, #20, #23. Give yourself 1 point for every "true" answer and subtract 1 point for every "false" answer. Then combine your scores for your R score (rational).

Computing your "P" score: Look at items #2, #4, #8, #10, #14, #15, #19, #21. Give yourself 1 point for every "true" answer and subtract 1 point for every "false" answer. Then combine your scores for your P score (positive).

Computing your "N" score: Look at items #5, #7, #9, #12, #13, #18, #22, #24. Give yourself 1 point for every "true" answer and subtract 1 point for every "false" answer. Then combine your scores for your N score (negative).

"People in an emotional state do not want to think, and they are particularly susceptible to the power of suggestion from a clever opponent . . . [an] excitable person is putty in the hands of a calm, even-tempered negotiator." (p. 46)

Moreover, Fisher, Ury, and Patton, in *Getting to Yes* (1991), caution that emotions may quickly bring a negotiation to an impasse or end. Emotions can impair the effective decision making necessary for negotiation. According to Janis and Mann (1977), decision makers experiencing high levels of emotional stress often undergo incomplete search, appraisal, and contingency-planning thought processes. As a result, they make defective decisions.

It is important, however, to draw a distinction between *expressing* and *feeling* emotion. Even though a negotiator may *feel* emotion, he or she dares not express it, lest it lead to less-than-desirable outcomes. According to economists, the negotiator who expresses relief, satisfaction, and approval risks settling for a worse outcome than does the poker-faced negotiator. Raiffa (1982) strictly cautions negotiators from displaying emotion: "Don't gloat about how well you have done" (p. 130).

The Positive Negotiator: You Can Catch More Flies with Honey

A different emotional style is the "positive emotion" approach. Instead of repressing emotion and using a poker face, this negotiator believes that, when it comes to negotiation, "you can catch more flies with honey." Three critical steps are involved in the positive-emotion process: (1) feeling positive emotion, (2) expressing it, and (3) engendering it in the opponent.

Former president Ronald Reagan was a skilled negotiator who capitalized on positive emotion at the bargaining table. For example, during the Geneva Summit negotiations with Gorbachev, Reagan endeared himself to the Soviet leader by making jokes. On one occasion, Reagan told a joke about an American who says that his country is the best because he can walk into the White House and tell the president he is doing a lousy job; a Russian responds that his country is better because he can go into the Kremlin and tell Gorbachev the same thing—that Reagan is doing a lousy job running the United States. Gorbachev laughed, and the parties successfully moved forward in negotiations (*Washington Post*, Nov. 23, 1985).

The obvious question is whether positive emotion is effective. Indeed, empirical investigations reveal that positive emotion enhances the quality of negotiated settlements, as compared to poker-faced negotiations (Kumar, 1997; Kramer, Pommerenke, & Newton, 1993). Two key reasons explain the effectiveness behind positive emotion: one deals with how people process information when they are in a good mood, and the other is based on the effect a good mood creates in others.

Positive Emotions and Information Processing   People process information differently when in a positive mood, as opposed to a negative or neutral mood (Isen, 1987). A good mood promotes creative thinking (Isen, Daubman, & Nowicki, 1987), which, in turn, leads to innovative problem solving (Carnevale & Isen, 1986). For example, Carnevale and Isen (1986) conducted an experiment in which some negotiators watched a funny movie and were given a gift. These negotiators reached more integrative negotiations and generated more creative ideas than negotiators who did not watch the movie and were not given a gift (see also Allred, Mallozzi,

Matsui, & Raia, 1997; Barry & Oliver, 1996; Forgas, 1996). In general, positive-mood negotiators use more cooperative strategies, engage in more information exchange, generate more alternatives, and use fewer contentious tactics than negative or neutral-mood negotiators (Carnevale & Isen, 1986).

Positive Emotions and Their Effect on the Opponent   Emotion in negotiation is a self-fulfilling prophecy; that is, negotiators' own emotions can determine the emotions of the other party and the nature of the conflict resolution. For example, in one investigation, people in a job-contract negotiation achieved lower joint gains when they experienced high levels of anger and low levels of compassion toward each other than when they experienced positive emotion (Allred, Mallozzi, Matsui, & Raia, 1997). Furthermore, angry negotiators were less willing to work with each other and more likely to overretaliate (Allred, Mallozzi, Matsui, & Raia, 1997). Malaysia's ambassador to France, Datuk Tunku Nazihah Mohamed Rus, knows the effect that positive emotions have on the opponent. Tunku Nazihah was hosting a lunch for a group of French businessmen with a fearsome reputation for being tough negotiators. Unfazed, she asked the men, "How do you like my cooking?" (*New Sunday Times*, June 1, 2003, para. 2). She is a tough negotiator—but combines it with stories that make others laugh helplessly. Tunku Nazihah is passionate about the "people aspect" of negotiating and devotes as much time to laying groundwork as she does to high-level negotiations (*New Sunday Times*, June 1, 2003). However, faking positive emotion can take its toll in terms of increasing stress and lessening your influence at the bargaining table. People who fake positive emotion are more likely to feel stress and actually get lower service delivery ratings (e.g., ratings by customers; Grandey, 2003).

The Negative Negotiator: Rant 'N' Rave

Quite a different negotiation approach is to demonstrate blatant, negative emotions, such as anger, rage, indignation, and impatience. The negative negotiator uses wild displays of negative emotion to coerce the other party to meet stated demands. A key difference distinguishes the truly angry person from the strategically angry negotiator. Negotiators who are really angry and feel little compassion for the other party are less effective in terms of expanding the pie than are happy negotiators (Allred, Mallozzi, Matsui, & Raia, 1997). Moreover, they are not as effective in terms of slicing the pie (for a review, see Allred, 2000). In contrast, negotiators who are "strategically angry" are more likely to gain concessions from their opponent because the other party will assume that the angry person is close to their reservation point (van Kleef, De Dreu, & Manstead, 2004). Angry negotiators induce fear in their opponent, and their opponents are most likely to succumb when they are motivated (van Kleef, De Dreu, & Manstead, 2004).

   The irrational negotiator is, in reality, *highly rational*. Sometimes, the more out of control and crazy a negotiator appears to be, the more effective he or she can be in a negotiation. By appearing unstable and volatile, the irrational negotiator convinces the opponent that he or she would sooner walk away from the table without having reached an agreement than settle for anything less than desired. As a case in point, consider how the head of AOL's advertising division, Myer Berlow, started playing with a large knife during a negotiation with Amazon.com's Jeff Bezos (*Washington Post*, June 15, 2003). The blade was about 8 inches long. It wasn't a hunting knife; it was a pocket knife. Bezos's eyes became the size of saucers. Why did Berlow pull out the knife? AOL was trying to pitch Amazon the benefits of advertising goods on AOL. However, Neil Davis (AOL) wanted to buy Amazon and had included a slide in the presentation that Berlow had explicitly warned him not to use—the one about how Amazon should be integrated within the AOL service. Berlow glared at Davis and said, "If you don't take that slide out, I'm going to stab you." He was not only pointing the knife at Davis, he started approaching him with the weapon and Bezos thought he would get stabbed. Thus, irrational negotiators are effective to the extent that they can convince the other party that they will follow through with what seems to be an extreme course of action, perhaps because they have nothing to lose (i.e., they convince the other party that they would be willing to take great risks that would perhaps hurt both parties if they do not get what they want).

Grave examples of such tactics can be found throughout history. For example, before the German annexation of Austria, Hitler met to negotiate with the Austrian Chancellor von Schuschnigg. At some point in this dark historical meeting, Hitler's emotional style became irrational:

> [He] became more strident, more shrill. Hitler ranted like a maniac, waved his hands with excitement. At times he must have seemed completely out of control. . . . Hitler may then have made his most extreme coercive threats seem credible. . . . [He threatened to take von Schuschnigg into custody, an act unheard of in the context of diplomacy.] He insisted that von Schuschnigg sign an agreement to accept every one of his demands, or he would immediately order a march into Austria. (Raven, 1990, p. 515)

The irrational negotiator is manipulative and downright Machiavellian at times. A negotiator who is faced with an irate opponent may capitulate to the other party to end the interaction quickly (Frank, 1988). This move, of course, only reinforces the irrational-appearing behavior, making it more likely to be used in the future. The irrational negotiating style does not just mean displaying anger. Displays of helplessness, pouting, and hurt feelings can be used to manipulate others in negotiations as well. Similarly, acting somewhat insane can achieve similar effects, such as when AOL's Berlow would announce to his opponents during the middle of negotiations that his favorite movie was *The Godfather*, his philosopher-hero was Machiavelli, and quote that "it is safer to be feared than loved" (*Washington Post*, June 15, 2003).

What are the specific psychological principles that make the irrational negotiator effective? Consider the following (Thompson, Medvec, Seiden, & Kopelman, 2000):

- **The Door-in-the-Face Technique** When a person makes an outlandish initial request, they are more likely to secure agreement to a subsequent, smaller request. This "door-in-the-face technique" is based on principles of perceptual contrast: If we lift a heavy object, set it down, and then lift a light object, we perceive the light object to be much lighter than it actually is (Cialdini, 1975; Cann, Sherman, & Elkes, 1975). Skilled negotiators have been profiting from perceptual contrast for years (Cialdini, 1993). Consider the savvy car salesperson who shows the potential buyer the most expensive models before showing him the model in which he is actually interested. Compared to the $40,000 price tag of the expensive model, the $20,000 price tag of the intended sale seems much more reasonable. Similarly, the irrational negotiator who calms down a bit following a wild display of emotion may get what he or she wants.

- *Negative Reinforcement* Negative reinforcement, or escape behavior, explains the increased likelihood of behavior that eliminates or removes an aversive stimulus (Skinner, 1938). For example, if a radio is playing obnoxious music, you will turn it off, thus eliminating the unpleasant sounds. In a similar vein, because most people find it unpleasant to be around someone who is openly hostile, negative, and a "loose cannon," they may be willing to capitulate to the other party just to remove themselves from this aversive situation. Unfortunately, this behavior acts as positive reinforcement for the opponent. If someone acts irrational and you acquiesce, you increase the likelihood of that person engaging in negative behavior in the future. Thus, irrational negotiators may capitalize on, and be reinforced for, their negative emotional behavior. One type of negative reinforcement is the pressure that people feel to stop another person from having a tantrum or crying. For example, Effa Manley, a female baseball player, was not above shedding tears to get what she wanted at the negotiation table. Pittsburgh sports writer Wendell Smith recalls, "If she did not get what she wanted, Mrs. Manley would wrinkle up her pretty face and turn on the sprinkling system" (*New York Daily News*, June 20, 2003). Hall of Famer Larry Doby remembered a time when he ignored a contract that Manley had sent him. She wrote Larry a letter: "I have not had the courtesy of a reply from you. Having met your mother, I know you were not raised this badly" (*New York Daily News*, June 20, 2003).
- *Self-Regulation* Most people like to prolong positive moods and exposure to positive stimuli and minimize negative moods. In fact, people "self-regulate" by actively working to maintain a desired positive mood (Baumeister, Leith, Muraven, & Bratslavsky, 1998). One way to self-regulate is to avoid negative stimuli. Most people find it unpleasant to interact with an irrational negotiator and, in order not to ruin their day, capitulate to the other side.
- *Squeaky Wheel Principle* The **squeaky wheel principle** (Singelis, 1998) states that a negotiator should demonstrate an unwillingness to move away from a stated position by escalating the level of hostility and using threats. Schelling (1960) describes the situation of two people (we will call them A and B) in a rowboat. A threatens B that if he does not row, A will tip the boat over. Simply stating the threat will not be as powerful as when A rocks the boat fervently while yelling to B that if B wants him to stop, he must row the boat. Thus,

Initiating steady pain, even if the threatener shares the pain, may make sense as a threat, especially if the threatener can initiate it irreversibly so that only the other's compliance can relieve the pain they both share. (Schelling, 1960, p. 196)

Strategic Advice for Dealing with Emotions at the Table

Keeping a Cool Head Is Easier Said Than Done

Often, our emotions are not under our control. The very act of trying to keep a poker face may backfire, especially if people try too hard to do so. For example, when people tell themselves not to conjure up certain thoughts, they find it virtually impossible to refrain from thinking those exact thoughts. Indeed, people who spend more time trying to repair their negative moods are the most likely to suffer from persistent emotional problems such as depression and anxiety (Wegner & Wenzlaff, 1996). Thus, it may be difficult not to express emotions if you are feeling them.

Controlling Emotion May Interfere with the Process of Entrainment

Entrainment is the process whereby one person's internal feelings are felt and acted upon by another person, such as when one person in a positive mood "affects" the mood of the other person with whom he or she is interacting (Kelly, 1988). When people negotiate, they each synchronize their behavior in accordance with the behavioral and emotional states of the other person. In a sense, people develop an interpersonal rhythm that reflects a shared emotional and behavioral state. Entrainment is a natural biological process that is conducive to social relationships and rapport building (Kelly, 1988). A negotiator who is deliberately focused on repressing emotion may interfere with this process, and an awkward, strained relationship may develop. For example, a poker-faced negotiator could create a more stilted interaction if the other party starts to react to and reflect his or her emotional state.

Emotions Are Contagious

If one negotiator conveys positive emotion, the other negotiator is likely to "catch" this positive emotional state and convey positive emotion as well (Hatfield, Caccioppo, & Rapson, 1992). However, the same is true for negative emotion.

Positive Emotions Promote Integrative Bargaining

Examinations of positive affect on creative ability suggest that when people are experiencing a positive mood, they are more creative, generate integrative information, and are more flexible in conveying their thoughts (Baron, 1990; Isen, Daubman, & Nowicki, 1987; Isen, Niedenthal, & Cantor, 1992). Why does positive emotion work? It is largely due to a combination of the self-fulfilling prophecy, information processing, and the fact that positive affect is associated with more creative and varied cognitions. For example, people who experience positive emotion, see relationships among ideas and link together nontypical category exemplars (Forgas & Moylan, 1996; Isen, Niedenthal, & Cantor, 1992). This response builds rapport, which, in turn, helps to avoid impasse (Drolet & Morris, 1995, 2000; Moore, Kurtzberg, Thompson, & Morris, 1999; Thompson, Nadler, & Kim, 1999) and facilitates the negotiation process.

Negative Emotion Must Be Convincing to Be Effective

Schelling (1960) offers the example of two negotiators playing a game of "chicken" in their cars—a highly risky game. One person assumes an advantage if she rips the steering wheel out of her car and throws it out the window, as long as her opponent sees her doing this. The other party is then forced into moving out of the way; in other words, he is forced to concede if both are to survive the game. But not just any behavior will suffice to evoke such concessions from the other party (Frank, 1988): "For a signal between adversaries to be credible, it must be costly (or, more generally, difficult) to fake" (p. 99). Frightened that the negotiation may end in an impasse, the other party may be pressured to concede to what would normally be considered outrageous demands. This type of negotiation strategy is best characterized by the expression "The squeaky wheel gets the grease," and can be highly effective.

The Timing of Emotion Matters

People tend to remember an experience in terms of how they felt at the end of it (Fredrickson & Kahneman, 1993; Kahneman, Fredrickson, Schreiber, & Redelmeier, 1993; Redelmeier & Kahneman, 1996). Indeed, the endpoint of an interaction bears critical negotiation power. For example, when opponents end the negotiation on a humorous note (i.e., "I will throw in my pet frog"), acceptance rates are higher than when they do not end on a positive note (O'Quin & Aronoff, 1981). Although we want to leave the other party feeling good, we should not show our opponent that we feel good. Conveying elation or gloating at the end of a negotiation makes our opponent feel less successful and less satisfied with the negotiation (Thompson, Valley, & Kramer, 1995).

CONCLUSION

We systematically considered three different stylistic issues in negotiation: motivational orientation (individualistic, cooperative, or competitive); approach (interests-, rights-, or power-based); and emotional style (rational/cool-headed; positive; or negative/irrational). We discussed the pros and cons of each stylistic issue. The key messages of this chapter are as follows:

- *Get in touch with your own style in an honest and straightforward way.* If you still think you are out of touch, then ask someone else to appraise you honestly, using the diagnostic tools presented in this chapter.
- *Know your limits and your strengths.* We have seen that it is not better to adopt one particular style because each has its own weaknesses and strengths. Knowing your own stylistic limits and strengths is important.
- *Understand your opponent better.* Most naïve negotiators just assume that their opponent has the same orientation that they do. However, with 27 different style combinations, this assumption is not likely. We hope that the styles we described in this chapter act as a type of "wake-up call" on diversity. With these styles in mind, you can better size up your opponent and perhaps change an opponent's style through the various techniques discussed.
- *Expand your repertoire.* We often find that people do not feel comfortable with their bargaining style or do not find it effective. This chapter gives negotiators options for expanding their repertoire, especially at critical points during negotiation.

Although we talked about negotiator style, almost equally important is the *confidence* that a negotiator has in his or her abilities. According to Sullivan, O'Connor, and Burris (2003), negotiators' self-efficacy (the belief that they can do something) affects their performance. Sullivan and colleagues distinguish two types of self-efficacy that map onto pie-slicing and pie-expanding skills: distributive self-efficacy and integrative self-efficacy (see Table 5-4). As might be expected, negotiators high in distributive self-efficacy do well in terms of claiming value; negotiators high in integrative self-efficacy do well in creating value. Moreover, the type of self-efficacy influences the tactics a negotiator uses.

TABLE 5-4 Distributive and Integrative Self-Efficacy

For each of the following tactics, rate your confidence in your ability to use each tactic.

1. Establish a high level of rapport with the other negotiator.
2. Convince the other negotiator to agree with you.
3. Prevent the other negotiator from exploiting your weaknesses.
4. Build a high level of trust between you and the other negotiator.
5. Make few concessions.
6. Find trade-offs that benefit both parties.
7. Find and exploit the other negotiator's weaknesses.
8. Gain the upper hand against the other negotiator.
9. Use persuasive arguments to support your position.
10. Exchange concessions.
11. Disguise your true interests.
12. Look for an agreement that maximizes both negotiators' interests.
13. Make each concession look difficult.
14. Persuade the other negotiator to make the most of the concessions.
15. Reach an agreement on each issue before going on to the next one.

Note: Distributive efficacy items: #2, #3, #5, #7, #8, #9, #11, #13, #14, #15
     Integrative efficacy items: #1, #4, #6, #10, #12

Source: B. Sullivan, K. M. O'Connor, and E. Burris (2003), "Negotiator Confidence: The Impact of Self-Efficacy on Tactics and Outcomes," Paper presented at the Academy of Management Annual Meeting, Seattle, WA.

CHAPTER

6

ESTABLISHING TRUST AND BUILDING A RELATIONSHIP

John Mack, of Credit Suisse First Boston, believes in relationships and trust as the foundation of negotiations and business relationships. Says Mack, "You can't build a culture unless you get to know people in a relaxed atmosphere." Mack makes it a point to get to know the person behind the business. In one situation, he was negotiating a multimillion-dollar pay contract with Bennett Goodman, who heads CSFB's merchant-banking and leveraged-finance business. Mack noticed a Duke basketball book on Goodman's table and learned that the junk bond buyer was a big Duke fan who takes his kids to the Duke versus North Carolina game every spring. Mack, a Duke grad, pitched Goodman on decency and fair pay and left him to decide whether he would relinquish his contract. Goodman opted to be a team player and told Mack that his group did not want to be pigs and would give back $50 million. An hour later, Goodman received a call from Coach K, as Duke's fabled Mike Krzyewski is known. Coach K told Goodman, "I'm best friends with John Mack . . . what you did today warmed his heart. That's what good leadership is all about." The coach went on to tell Goodman that he was the "Shane Battier of CSFB"—referring to Duke's selfless star player. Goodman was floored! In awe, he hung onto Coach K's every word for an hour. And coach K said, "I told him he'd need to give back more if he wanted longer phone calls." In fact, Goodman did. In 2002, he and his group gave back another $50 million (*Fortune*, Sept. 1, 2003).

THE PEOPLE SIDE OF WIN-WIN

In Chapter 4, we said that win-win is important, and we made the point that people often fail to fully exploit all of the potential value in the negotiation. We gave several examples of how people often resort to compromise, when it would be much better to make value-added trade-offs. We said several times that people leave money on the table. However, successful negotiation is not just about money or economic value. And, despite the fact that rational behavior is often equated with the maximization of monetary wealth, the truth is that economic models focus on the maximization of utility—and utility can be defined as money, but it can also be defined as other things, such as trust, security, happiness, and peace of mind. The true definition of win-win is agreements that allow negotiators to fully maximize whatever they care about, whether it's money, relationships, trust, peace of mind, or something else. Curhan, Elfenbein, & Xu (2004) surveyed a broad spectrum of lay people, negotiation researchers, and negotiation practitioners about what they value in a negotiation. Results suggested that negotiators tend to care about four basic domains—feelings about instrumental outcomes, feelings about themselves, feelings about the process, and feelings about their relationships. Curhan, Elfenbein, & Xu's **Subjective Value Inventory (SVI)** helps negotiators learn to conceptualize their performance in a negotiation along multiple dimensions—dimensions that may constitute precursors to long-term negotiation value. (See Table 6-1 for the Subjective Value Inventory.)

Negotiators are at complete liberty to care about anything that has value to them, however subjective or objective. Moreover, economic outcomes are imperfectly correlated with psychological outcomes. Stated another way, making more money may not always make us feel more successful (Thompson, 1995a; Thompson, Valley, & Kramer, 1995), or more satisfied (Thompson Valley, & Kramer, 1995; Galinsky, Mussweiler, & Medvec, 2002). For example, even though it is wise to unbundle single-issue negotiations into multi-issue negotiations, negotiators who negotiate a lot of issues actually

---

TABLE 6-1   Curhan, Elfenbein, and Xu's (2004) Subjective Value Inventory

Think about your most recent negotiation. Rate your response to each question below on a 1–7 scale with 1 being not true or not characteristic, and 7 being very true or very characteristic.

1. I am satisfied with my own outcome (i.e., the extent to which the terms of my agreement benefit me).
2. I feel like I forfeited or "lost" in this negotiation.
3. I am satisfied with the balance between my own outcome and my counterpart's outcome.
4. I feel like I "lost face" (i.e., damaged my sense of pride) in this negotiation.
5. I behaved according to my own principles and values.
6. This negotiation made me feel more competent as a negotiator.
7. The negotiation process was fair.
8. The other party listened to my concerns.
9. I achieved a sense of closure in the negotiation.
10. I trusted the other party.
11. The other party and I built a good foundation for our future relationship.
12. The terms and commitments in this agreement will be adhered to over time by both parties.

Note about scoring:
- Instrumental outcome (average items 1–3; reverse score #2)
- Feelings about oneself (average items 4–6; reverse score #4)
- Feelings about the process (average items 7–9)
- Feelings about the relationship (average items 10–12)

Source: Curhan, J. R., H. A. Elfenbein, and A. Xu. (2004), "What Do People Value When They Negotiate?: Establishing Validity for the Subjective Value Inventory of Negotiation Performance." Working paper, Massachusetts Institute of Technology, Cambridge, MA. To obtain a full version of the SVI, or to learn more about research related to this topic, see www.subjectivevalue.com.

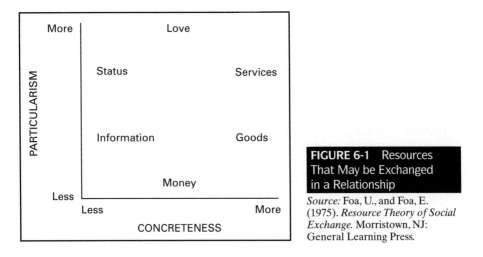

FIGURE 6-1   Resources That May be Exchanged in a Relationship

Source: Foa, U., and Foa, E. (1975). *Resource Theory of Social Exchange.* Morristown, NJ: General Learning Press.

feel psychologically worse about their outcomes (Naquin, 2003). Why? They are more likely to ponder "what might have been" and experience doubts.

Businesspeople often tell us that you cannot negotiate things like trust, respect, caring, or relationships. However, we think that through our actions we negotiate these things every day. We just don't realize that we are doing so. Consider Figure 6-1, which identifies six different types of resources that people can exchange: love, money, services, goods, status, and information (Foa & Foa, 1975). Each of these resources varies in terms of particularism (how much utility we derive depends on who is providing it—a kiss from one's own child is valued much more than a kiss from a complete stranger) and concreteness (how tangible it is). Love and social status are less concrete than services or goods, and love is more particular than money.

TRUST AS THE BEDROCK OF NEGOTIATION

Trust is essential in any human relationship. The same principle applies to negotiation. Trust is an expression of confidence in another person or group of people that you will not be put at risk, harmed, or injured by their actions (Axelrod, 1984). On a practical level, trust means that we could be exploited by someone. Moreover, most relationships hold some incentive for people to behave in an untrustworthy fashion (Kramer, 1999; Kramer, Brewer, & Hanna, 1996).

Three Types of Trust in Relationships

People form three major types of trust relationships with others: deterrence-based trust, knowledge-based trust, and identification-based trust (Shapiro, Sheppard, & Cheraskin, 1992; Lewicki & Bunker, 1996).

Deterrence-Based Trust

Deterrence-based trust is based on consistency of behavior, meaning that people will follow through on what they promise they are going to do. Behavioral consistency, or follow-through, is sustained by threats or promises of consequences that will result if consistency and promises are not maintained. The consequences most often used are punishments, sanctions, incentives, rewards, legal implications, and others. Deterrence-based trust often involves contracts and various forms of bureaucracy and surveillance. Deterrence-based trust mechanisms are more common than you might think. An estimated 35 percent of the online workforce in the United States is monitored by their employers (CNN, Sept. 6, 2001). Other forms of deterrence are also used. For example, in the Hawthorne plant in the 1940s, the established norm was that workers would not deviate from acceptable levels of production. Deviation from this norm would result in some people being labeled as overperformers (also known as "rate-busters") and some being labeled as underperformers (also known as "shirkers"). Whenever a worker was caught over- or underperforming, other plant workers would give them a sharp blow to the upper arm (called "binging"). (For another example, see Sidebar 6-1.)

Sidebar 6-1. Deterrence-Based Trust

Another striking example of deterrence-based trust is the negotiated agreement between explorer Christopher Columbus and King Ferdinand and Queen Isabella. Ferdinand and Isabella offered Columbus ships, men, and money to carry the faith and the Spanish flag to the West. However, Columbus refused to agree until his demands were met in writing. He insisted that he be knighted, made admiral of the Ocean Sea, and viceroy and governor general of all the lands that he would discover. He further demanded 10 percent of whatever would be acquired overseas. A handshake would not suffice. He insisted that the deal be set in writing, and so drafted a lengthy, detailed agreement between himself and the crown. This move was astonishingly bold, considering that the king and queen held the power of life and death over him. The haggling went back and forth, and on April 17, 1492, the Pact of Santa Fe was agreed to by the rulers (*Investors' Business Daily*, Dec. 11, 1998).

Two key problems arise with deterrence-based trust. First, they are expensive systems to develop and maintain—they require development, oversight, maintenance, and monitoring—and second, a backfiring effects is likely. The backfiring is based upon psychological principles of **reactance**; in popular culture, this concept is also known as *reverse psychology*. For example, empirical evidence demonstrates that the presence of signs reading "Do Not Write on These Walls Under Any Circumstances" actually increases the incidence of people's violations of the vandalism norm (as compared to signs that say "Please Do Not Write on These Walls" or the complete absence of signs; Pennebaker & Sanders, 1976). Similarly, people take longer to vacate a parking space when they know someone else is waiting for it (Ruback & Juieng, 1997). People often have a negative reaction whenever they perceive that someone is controlling their behavior or limiting their freedom. When people think their behavior is under the control of extrinsic motivators, such as sanctions and rewards, intrinsic motivation is reduced (Enzle & Anderson, 1993). Thus, surveillance may undermine people's motivation to engage in the behaviors that such monitoring is intended to ensure.

For example, the fear of monitoring adversely impacted trust among flight attendants at Delta Airlines (Hochschild, 1983). Flight attendants came to fear and distrust their passengers because of a policy allowing passengers to write letters of complaint about in-flight service. The climate of distrust was further intensified when flight attendants became suspicious that undercover supervisors were posing as passengers. The system backfired. We will further discuss deterrence-based trust later.

Knowledge-Based Trust

Knowledge-based trust is grounded in behavioral predictability, and it occurs when a person has enough information about others to understand them and accurately predict their behavior. Whenever informational uncertainty or asymmetry characterizes a relationship, it provides opportunity for deceit, and one or both parties risk exploitation. Paradoxically, if no risk is present in an exchange situation, exploitation cannot occur, but high levels of trust will not develop (Thibaut & Kelley, 1959). Thus, trust is a consequence or response to uncertainty (Kollock, 1994; Granovetter, 1973).

An intriguing example of the development of knowledge-based trust among negotiators concerns the sale of rubber and rice in Thailand (Siamwalla, 1978; Popkin, 1981). For various reasons, rubber is a product in which quality cannot be determined at the time of sale but only months later. Thus, when rubber is sold, the seller knows the quality of the rubber, but the buyer does not. It presents a classic case of one-sided informational asymmetry. In contrast, in the rice market, the quality of rice can be readily determined at the time of sale (no informational uncertainty). It would seem that the rubber market, because of its informational asymmetries, would be characterized by exploitation on the part of sellers who would only sell cheap rubber at high prices, creating a market of lemons (Akerlof, 1970). However, buyers and sellers in the rubber market have abandoned anonymous exchange for long-term exchange relationships between particular buyers and sellers. Within this exchange framework, growers establish reputations for trustworthiness, and rubber of high quality is sold.

Knowledge-based trust increases dependence and commitment among parties (Dwyer, Schurr, & Oh, 1987; Kollock, 1994). For example, suppliers who regularly negotiate with certain customers develop highly specialized products for their customers. Such product differentiation can create barriers to switching suppliers. In addition to economic dependence, people become emotionally committed to some relationships. For example, in markets characterized by information asymmetries, once negotiators develop a relationship with someone they find to be trustworthy, they remain committed to the relationship, even when it would be profitable to trade with others (Kollock, 1994). When switching does occur, the party who is "left" feels indignant and violated. For example, the decision of major car manufacturers to switch to lower-cost suppliers left their higher-cost longtime suppliers feeling betrayed. Similarly, people who expect to interact with others in the future are less likely to exploit them, even when given an opportunity (Marlowe, Gergen, & Doob, 1966). When negotiators anticipate extended relationships, they are more likely to cooperate with customers, colleagues, and suppliers, but not with competitors (Sondak & Moore, 1994). These relationships and the perception of low mobility among individuals promote development of integrative agreements across interactions, rather than only within given transactions (Mannix, Tinsley, & Bazerman, 1995).

Identification-Based Trust

Identification-based trust is grounded in complete empathy with another person's desires and intentions. In identification-based trust systems, trust exists between people because each person understands, agrees with, empathizes with, and takes on the other's values because of the emotional connection between them; thus, they act for each other (Lewicki & Bunker, 1996). Identification-based trust means that other people have adopted your own preferences.

In Table 6-2, we list the three types of relationships (personal, business, and embedded) and the three types of trust (deterrence-based, knowledge-based, and identification-based). We indicate the type and nature of interaction that may occur when different types of trust and different types of relationships intersect. Whereas it may seem that personal relationships would or should be completely grounded in knowledge-based or identification-based trust, it does not always occur. For example, a deterrence-based trust system is put in place when couples get prenuptial agreements, when husbands or wives pay private investigators to monitor the actions of their spouses, and when parents install video cameras to monitor childcare providers. In business relationships, the extreme form of *theory X management* has deterrence-based trust at the heart of its assumptions about human behavior. According to theory X management, workers are inherently lazy and need to be monitored within a punishment system so that they will perform their tasks. Theory Y and other enlightened forms of management assert that workers perform for the joy of working, and monitoring systems only decrease intrinsic interest.

Building Trust: Rational and Deliberate Mechanisms

With a little bit of thinking, people can take some proactive steps to build trust in their relationships with others. The following techniques can be used in personal as well as

TABLE 6-2   Trust/Relationship Grid

	Relationship		
Trust	*Personal Relationship*	*Business Relationship*	*Embedded Relationship*
Deterrence-based	Lack of trust Prenuptial agreements Surveillance	Theory X management Use of threats, punishments, sanctions Surveillance	Use of threats, punishments, sanctions
Knowledge-based	Sympathy for the other	Customer-driven focus Assessment of clients' needs	Understand and appreciate partners
Identification-based	True empathy for other Investment in other's welfare	Theory Y management Selection of employees who fit corporate culture and its values Restructuring to serve customer	Empathy Development of social identity

professional situations. For an examination of how businesspeople attempt to secure trust, see Figure 6-2.

Transform Personal Conflict into Task Conflict

Two basic types of conflict can occur in relationships. **Personal conflict**, also known as **emotional conflict**, is personal, defensive, and resentful (Guetzkow & Gyr, 1954; Jehn, 2000). Personal conflict is often rooted in anger, personality clashes, ego, and tension. **Task conflict**, also known as **cognitive conflict**, is largely depersonalized. It consists of argumentation about the merits of ideas, plans, and projects, independent of the identity of the people involved. Task conflict is often effective in stimulating the creativity necessary for integrative agreement because it forces people to rethink problems and arrive at outcomes that everyone can live with. As a general principle, personal conflict threatens relationships, whereas task conflict enhances relationships, provided that

---

FIGURE 6-2   How Managers Secure Commitment in the Absence of Binding Contracts

We recently conducted a survey to examine how businesspeople attempt to secure trust in relationships. We asked 52 MBA students to "imagine that you are involved in a negotiation situation where you need to get commitment (i.e., follow-through) from one or more of the people involved. The nature of the negotiation does not involve 'binding contracts.' How do you try to instill a sense of commitment in the absence of any binding contracts?" The responses varied dramatically.

Review of Categories (Left to Right on X-Axis):

- *Persuasion and consciousness-raising* (e.g., "I would reinforce the idea that this is the beginning of a long-term, multiple-contact relationship, and that it is in my counterparty's best interest to think about the repercussions of reneging on future negotiations")

- *Coercion and threat tactics* (e.g., humiliation, punishment, etc.)

- *Nonverbal strategies* (e.g., handshakes, establishing rapport, ". . . look people in the eye, have them look at you, and say to you that they will do what you want them to do . . .", etc.)

- *Verbal agreements*

- *Behavior modification* (e.g., tit for tat; social modeling)

- *Rewards and benefits*

- *Public commitments* (e.g., ". . . by making the outcome public, the erring party would suffer public embarrassment and suffer loss of reputation . . .")

- *Alignment of incentives*

- *Collecting information about other's BATNA*

- *Written (nonbinding) agreements*

- *Creation of mutual enemy*

- *Creating escrow* or collateral arrangements

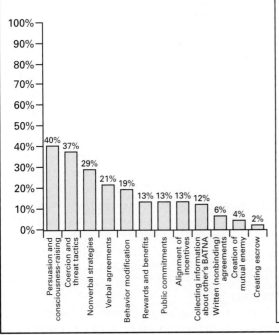

BOX 6-1

CREATING A FORUM FOR CONFLICT

Bovis Construction Corporation, who has worked on the renovation of Los Angeles City Hall and the construction of a football stadium in Nashville, deals with conflict in an open fashion (*Los Angeles Times*, May 1998). Prior to each project, Bovis construction teams hold a planning session in which team members openly address potential conflicts. These planning sessions are conducted by company facilitators who encourage the project owner, architects, contractors, and other players to map out processes they plan to follow to get the job done. During the session, participants draft and sign a "win-win agreement," which includes a matrix that lays out what team members expect from one another. The first box in a matrix may detail the owner's responsibilities on the project, whereas the next box may look at the owner's expectations of the construction manager. Teams then use this matrix to review their progress on the project. Bovis managers agree that the process has not only decreased the adversity that is so prevalent on construction sites, but the firm has also saved millions of dollars and has completed projects on time.

people are comfortable with it (see Jehn, 1997). As an example of how companies create a forum for conflict, see Box 6-1.

Agree on a Common Goal or Shared Vision

The importance of a common goal is summed up in a quote by Steve Jobs, who is associated with three high-profile Silicon Valley companies—Apple, NeXT, and Pixar: "It's okay to spend a lot of time arguing about which route to take to San Francisco when everyone wants to end up there, but a lot of time gets wasted in such arguments if one person wants to go to San Francisco and another secretly wants to go to San Diego" (Eisenhardt, Kahwajy, & Bourgeois, 1997, p. 80). Shared goals do not imply homogeneous thinking, but they do require everyone to share a vision. Steve Jobs is not alone in his thinking. Colin Sewell-Rutter, a director of The Results Partnership, a consultancy that specializes in improving board-level communications, concludes that "The single most important source of problems within the boardroom is the lack of a shared vision, and shared corporate goals. . . . All the major difficulties ultimately stem from that" (Lynn, 1997, p. 31).

The 1993 departure of Ernest Mario as chief executive of the pharmaceutical firm Glaxo (as it was then known) illustrates how conflicts can also mask the fact that people never fundamentally agree on what the company is about. Mario was thought to have been preparing a takeover of American rival Warner-Lambert, even though the then-chairman, Sir Paul Girolami, believed that the company should stick with its strategy of investing for organic growth. The result was a bitter conflict that culminated in Mario's departure with a $3 million payoff (it was only after Girolami retired that Glaxo made its first takeover in decades, when it bid for Wellcome).

Capitalize on Network Connections

Negotiators who do not know each other may attempt to build a more trusting relationship by trying to find a common node in their social networks. In other words, they engage in enough discussion to attempt to single out someone whom they both know. It has been said that there are only six degrees of separation between people (Burt, 1999). Finding a common link in social networks signals not only similarity of interests, but it also creates accountability via common network relations.

Find a Shared Problem or a Shared Enemy

It is remarkable how the presence of a common enemy can unite people and build trust (Sherif, Harvey, White, Hood, Sherif, 1961). This phenomenon happens for several reasons. First, it is often necessary for people to join forces to compete against a common enemy (e.g., a shared goal of sorts was created during the Reagan-Gorbachev Summit talks). One evening, Reagan and Soviet leader Mikhail Gorbachev were drinking coffee after dinner on Lake Geneva. Secretary of State George P. Shultz turned to Georgi Kornienko, the Soviet first deputy foreign minister, and accused him of trying to stall summit negotiations on bilateral issues. "You, Mr. Minister, are responsible for this," Shultz declared. Then, turning to Gorbachev, the secretary of state added forcefully: "This man is not doing what you want him to do. He is not getting done what you want done." Reagan took advantage of the situation to create a common bond and looked at Gorbachev: "To hell with what they're doing. You and I will say, 'We will work together to make it come about.'" Reagan and Gorbachev then shook hands. That moment marked a critical turning point in the meeting (*Washington Post*, Nov. 23, 1985). A common goal, or common enemy, removes the perception that parties' interests are completely opposed and builds a new value that represents a higher-order principle that all parties find motivating.

Focus on the Future

It is difficult for negotiators to agree on what happened in the past, but if they can forgive and forget and focus on their future together, this intention can go a long way toward building trust. For example, Sean M. Haley, warehousing operations manager for Sage Products Inc., an 800-employee medical device manufacturer, considers negotiation of critical importance in managing the company's relationship with its distribution and transportation provider. Because his company gives all its freight to this third party, trust is essential. Once Haley identifies the appropriate contact for issues that arise, he negotiates a resolution of shipment problems. Haley has found that not assigning blame for occasional problems and focusing instead on what both parties must do in the future to ensure better customer service produces integrative outcomes (*Warehousing Management*, Sept. 1, 1998).

Building Trust: Psychological Strategies

A variety of psychological tools can be used to enhance and build trust between people. These psychological mechanisms distinguish themselves from the rational, cognitive mechanisms discussed earlier in that people tend not to talk about these factors explicitly; rather, savvy negotiators know how to capitalize on them intuitively.

Similarity

People who are similar to each other like one another (Griffin & Sparks, 1990). The **similarity-attraction effect** may occur on the basis of little, and sometimes downright trivial, information. Simply put, we like people whom we perceive to be similar to us. Negotiators are more likely to make concessions when negotiating with people they know and like. Savvy negotiators increase their effectiveness by making themselves similar to the other party. Many sales training programs urge trainees to "mirror and match" the customer's body posture, mood, and verbal style, because similarities along each of these dimensions actually lead to positive results (LaFrance, 1985; Locke & Horowitz, 1990; Woodside & Davenport, 1974). Similarity in dress also has dramatic effects. For example, marchers in a political demonstration not only are more likely to sign the petition of a similarly dressed requester, but do so without bothering to read it first (Suedfeld, Bochner, & Matas, 1971).

Mere Exposure

The more we are exposed to something—a person, object, or idea—the more we come to like it. The mere exposure effect (Zajonc, 1968) is extremely powerful and occurs below the level of our awareness. Advertisers know about the mere exposure effect. The more we are exposed to TVs, the more we come to like the product—up to a point.

Savvy negotiators increase their effectiveness by making themselves familiar to the other party. Instead of having a single-shot negotiation, they suggest a preliminary meeting over drinks and follow with a few phone calls and unexpected gifts. By the time of the final negotiation, the target negotiator feels as though he or she is interacting with an old friend. U.S. Senator George Mitchell developed a "quality time" strategy for helping to bridge relationships in the Northern Ireland peace process. In September 1999, he moved the talks between Ulster Unionist leader David Trimble and Sinn Fein president Gerry Adams to the London residence of U.S. Ambassador Phil Lader. Over meals, cocktails, and informal get-togethers, Mitchell brought the men closer together (*Newsweek International*, Nov. 8, 1999). (See Sidebar 6-2 for an example of how mere exposure increases liking in classrooms.)

Sidebar 6-2. Mere Exposure Increases Liking

The effects of mere exposure on liking are demonstrated clearly in the classroom. In one investigation, student A attended 15 sessions of a course. For each session, she arrived before the class began, walked down the aisle, and sat at the front, where other students could see her. Student B did the same thing, but attended only 10 lectures. Student C came to class only five times. Student D never showed up. At the end of the term, the students in the class were shown slides of students A, B, C, and D, and were asked to indicate how "familiar" they found each one; how attractive they found each one, and how similar they believed each one was to them. The number of classes attended had a dramatic impact on attraction and similarity, but not familiarity (Moreland & Beach, 1992).

Good Mood

People in a good mood are more agreeable (Carnevale & Isen, 1986; Forgas & Moylan, 1996). Funny cartoons, unexpected little gifts, small strokes of fortune, and thinking positive thoughts all engender a good mood (see Isen & Baron, 1991, for a review). Even "incidental emotions" that grow out of events that are not even part of the negotiation (such as a fight with a spouse, etc.) can influence our emotions at the bargaining table (Dunn & Schweitzer, 2003). As an example of how mood and the immediate situation affect the course of negotiation, consider how superagent and attorney Leigh Steinberg negotiated quarterback Drew Bledsoe's multiyear contract with New England Patriots owner Bob Kraft. The two of them were sitting in a loud, crowded hotel lobby during the National Football League (NFL) Owners' Conference. As they led up to their bargaining positions, other people were interrupting them, thus making it difficult to talk or build a connection. In the midst of the interruptions and chaos, Kraft proposed $29 million over seven years. Steinberg countered with $51 million. Insulted, angry, and shaking his head, Kraft got up and walked out. Steinberg had made a mistake, but instead of inflaming the situation, he gave it more time. Six months later, Steinberg asked Kraft to dinner at a quiet Italian restaurant. He let Kraft vent anger and frustration over Bledsoe's proposed salary. It came out that Kraft had interpreted the high counteroffer as a signal that Bledsoe wanted nothing to do with the team and instead wanted to be a free agent. Calmly, Steinberg assured Kraft that Bledsoe wanted to stay. He explained that in the hubbub of the lobby six months earlier, Steinberg had not been able to create the solid rapport that they had that evening and had not been able to establish an atmosphere of trust. That night, they settled on $42 million. Says Steinberg, "The key to successful negotiations is to develop relationships, not conquests" (*Investors' Business Daily*, Sept. 22, 1998).

A surefire way to engender a good mood is through laugher or humor. Consider how Greg Matusky "warmed up" the other side of the table, who just happened to be U.S. Technologies. Matusky was involved in a high-stakes negotiation that involved buying back a company he'd sold to U.S. Technologies some time earlier. When he walked into the D.C. downtown office, he opened the meeting by whipping out a fake million-dollar bill with a dramatic flourish, saying, "The real offer is for $900,000. I'll take my $100,000 in change on the way out." Laughter filled the room and Matusky had succeeded in breaking the ice (*Inc.*, Aug. 1, 2003b).

Physical Presence

People form both personal and business relationships to others who are literally physically close to them. For example, when students are seated alphabetically in a classroom, friendships are significantly more likely to form between those whose last names begin with the same or nearby letter (Segal, 1974). This is what is called the **propinquity effect**. This point may not seem important until you consider the fact that you may meet some of your closest colleagues, and perhaps even a future business partner, merely because of an instructor's seating chart! Similarly, those people given a corner seat or an office at the end of a corridor make fewer friends in the organization (Maisonneuve, Palmade, & Fourment, 1952). If an instructor changes seat assignments once or twice during the semester, each student becomes acquainted with additional colleagues (Byrne, 1961). To further see the power of the propinquity effect, consider the entering class of the Maryland State Police Training Academy (Segal, 1974). Trainees were assigned to their classroom seats and to their dormitory rooms by the alphabetical order of their last names. Sometime later, trainees were asked to name their three best friends in the group; their choices followed the rules of alphabetization almost exactly. Larsons were friends with Lees, not with Abromowitzes or Xiernickes, even though they were separated by only a few yards (Byrne, 1961; Kipnis, 1957).

As another example, consider friendship formation among couples in apartment buildings. In this particular case, residents had been assigned to their apartments at random as vacancies opened up, and nearly all of them were strangers when they moved in. When asked to name their three closest friends in the entire housing project, 65 percent named friends in the same building. Among those living in the same building, the propinquity effect was in play: 41 percent of next-door neighbors indicated they were close friends, compared to only 22 percent who lived two doors apart, and only 10 percent who lived on the opposite ends of the hall.

The propinquity effect has an impact on **functional distance**. Certain aspects of architectural design make it more likely that some people will come into contact with each other more often than with others, even though physically, the distances between them might be the same. For example, more friendships were made with people on the same floor than on another floor, presumably because climbing stairs requires more effort than walking down the hall.

Reciprocity

According to the **reciprocity principle**, we feel obligated to return in kind what others have offered or given to us. We referred to this powerful principle earlier as the law of the universe. Although sounding like an overstatement, this principle is one that all human societies subscribe to—it is a rule permeating exchanges of all kinds (Gouldner, 1960). Feelings of indebtedness are so powerful that if unresolved, they carry on into the future and are passed on to the next generation to repay. People feel upset and distressed if they have received a favor from another person and are prevented from returning it.

Madeleine Albright (U.S. Secretary of State, 1997–2001) knows the powers of reciprocity. One of Albright's first public meetings with members of Congress was an appearance to testify before the House Appropriations Subcommittee, chaired by Republican Harold Rogers. Albright needed to be on good terms with Rogers because his subcommittee's jurisdiction included the State Department's operating budget. For the occasion, Albright carried with her a big box, gift-wrapped in red, white and blue ribbon. Inside was a book of photographs. Albright had learned that Rogers had lost all his papers and photographs in a fire at his home, a disaster that had erased many souvenirs of his career and compounded the grief caused by the recent death of his wife. Albright instructed embassies in countries he had visited to provide copies of photos taken on those occasions, and compiled them in an album she bestowed on him right there in the committee hearing room (*National Journal*, June 3, 2000).

Not surprisingly, people are aware of the powerful grip that reciprocity has on them. Often people will turn down favors and rewards from others because they do not want to be obligated.

So far we have said that reciprocity is powerful, but we find nothing inherently illogical or dangerous with reciprocity with regard to negotiation. Usually, reciprocity pertains more to the pattern of concessions than to the degree of concessions. Therefore, if someone does us a favor or makes a concession, we feel obligated to return the favor or concession. However, unless we are careful, we could be victimized by an opponent who preys on our feelings of indebtedness.

For example, suppose the opponent provides us with a favor, gift, or service that we never invited and perhaps even attempted to avoid. Our attempts to return it have been denied, and we are left with the unwanted gift. Even under these circumstances, the reciprocity rule may operate. Thus, we should beware of the unsolicited gift from our real estate agent, the courtesy token from our business associate, and the free lunch from the consulting firm. When faced with these situations, we should acknowledge the favor and then, if we still feel indebted, return the favor on a similar level.

Don't Gloat

Negotiators should resist the urge to gloat or show signs of smugness following negotiation (see also Raiffa, 1982). In one investigation, some negotiators gloated following their negotiation ("I really feel good about the negotiation;" "I got everything I wanted"). Other negotiators made self-effacing remarks, such as "I really didn't do that well." Later, negotiators who overheard the other party gloat or make self-effacing remarks were given an opportunity to provide valuable stock options to these same parties. Those parties who gloated received significantly fewer stock options than those who made the self-effacing remarks (Thompson, Valley, & Kramer, 1995).

Schmoozing

Small talk often seems to serve no obvious function. The exchange of pleasantries about the weather or our favorite basketball team seems to be purposeless, except for conforming to social etiquette. However, on a *preconscious* level, schmoozing has a dramatic impact on our liking and trust of others. For example, even a short exchange can lead people to develop considerably more trust in others than in the absence of interaction (Nadler, Kurtzberg, Morris, & Thompson, 1999). According to Susan Pravda, comanaging partner of the Boston law office of Epstein, Becker, and Green, schmoozing is an important part of negotiations. She advises, "Don't walk in and start going through your list. If they have a baby picture on the desk, it doesn't hurt to say, 'oh, is that a new grandchild?' People like to talk about themselves. It can segue into what you're trying to achieve" (*The Wall Street Journal*, Jan. 27, 1998). Peter J. Pestillo, executive vice president of corporate relations for Ford Motor and one of the auto industry's leading labor negotiators, is known for his golf dates with union negotiators. Says Pestillo, "If you know someone, you know something that might be more important to him than to you" (*The Wall Street Journal*, Jan. 27, 1998, p. B1).

Flattery

People like others who appreciate and admire them. People are more likely to trust others who like them, and respond more favorably when they are flattered. It would seem that the positive pie-slicing effects of flattery would be reversed if the flatterer is suspected of having ulterior motives; however, even if people suspect that the flatterer has another reason for flattering them, this behavior can still increase liking and trust under some conditions (Jones, Stires, Shaver, & Harris, 1968). The most strategic type of flattery, in terms of advancing one's own interest, is to flatter another person on a dimension that is important to him, but that he feels somewhat insecure about (Jones, Stires, Shaver, & Harris, 1968). John Wakeham, previous chief whip for Margaret Thatcher, says about Westminster politics: "I was absolutely fascinated by how Westminster actually works . . . the smoke-filled rooms, the nods and the winks. As a businessman, I found it more comprehensible than most politicians do. One thing I learnt as chief whip was the infinite capacity of human beings to absorb flattery" (*The Guardian*, Jan. 15, 2000, p. 6).

Self-Disclosure

Self-disclosure means sharing information about oneself with another person. It is a way of building a relationship with another person by making oneself vulnerable, in that the self-disclosing negotiator is providing information that could potentially be exploited. Self-disclosure also explicitly invites the other person to reciprocate the disclosure, thereby increasing trust.

What Leads to Mistrust?

One of the biggest threats to trust in a relationship is what is known as a **breach**, or **defection**. A breach occurs when one or both people violate the trust that has been built between them. For example, on March 19, 2003, U.S. President George W. Bush issued orders to begin "striking selected targets of military importance to undermine Saddam Hussein's ability to wage war." According to the United States, Saddam Hussein had engaged in a breach of trust by placing "Iraqi troops and equipment in civilian areas, attempting to use innocent men and women as shields for his own military," and demonstrating disregard for "conventions of war [and] rules of morality" (CNN, Mar. 19, 2003).

Miscommunication

In some cases, a real breach of trust does not occur between persons, but somehow, a miscommunication occurs that causes one or more parties to interpret it as such. Miscommunication is more likely when parties are not in regular contact, especially when they have little face-to-face contact.

Poor Pie Expansion

To the extent that negotiators are not skilled in using pie-expanding strategies (as we discussed in Chapter 4 on integrative negotiation), trust between parties can be threatened. Therefore, it is imperative that negotiators be skilled in expanding the pie so as to increase and sustain trust between themselves and the other party.

Dispositional Attributions

Negotiators often make dispositional, as opposed to situational, attributions for the questionable behavior of the other party, which can threaten trust levels (Morris, Larrick, & Su, 1999). A **dispositional attribution** is one that calls into question another person's character and intentions by citing them as the cause of a behavior or incident (e.g., arrogance, greed, etc.). In contrast, a situational attribution cites one or more situational factors as the cause of a behavior or incident (e.g., a traffic jam, the faulty mail-delivery system, etc.). Making these dispositional attributions for their opponents' behaviors can threaten the trust between negotiators and the other party, because it is much more difficult for people to respond to a dispositional attribution than a situational one. For example, Kramer and Wei (1999) examined how people interpret ambiguous and slightly negative social interactions (i.e., when a person you know does not acknowledge you when you walk past him). It turns out that the power or status differential is significant in interpreting these situations. The high-power person who does not acknowledge a colleague usually reported having a busy day, or more often, not even being aware of the other person. In contrast, the low-power person was often extremely paranoid and upset, believing that the high-power person was attempting to ostracize or punish them. Thus, the low-power person makes a dispositional attribution for what is really a situational case.

Focusing on the "Bad Apple"

In a team or group, one person may have a reputation for being less trustworthy, tougher, or less easy to work with than other members of the group. This person is what we call the "bad apple," and bad apples can stand out. The problem is that people's impression of the bad apple can spoil their impression of the entire bunch. For example, Naquin (1999) found that in negotiations between labor and management groups in a simulated interaction, negotiators were significantly less likely to trust the group as a whole than any individual in the group. It seems that the "bad apple" in the group called the entire group's trustworthiness into question.

Social Comparison

Social comparison—or the need and desire of people to compare themselves to others in terms of competence, attractiveness, success, benefits, and many other qualities—inevitably leads to feelings of distrust. It is always possible to find some dimension on which we feel less equitably treated than others. Therefore, it is important for negotiators to realize that social comparison generally tends to be a losing proposition in terms of creating positive bonds between people.

Repairing Broken Trust

When trust has been broken, it is often in both parties' interests to attempt to repair the trust because broken relationships are often costly in terms of the emotions involved and the opportunities lost. However, it is possible to rebuild trust that has been broken (see Bottom, Gibson, Daniels, & Murnighan, 2000). Next, we outline a process for repairing broken trust (see Box 6-2 for a quick summary).

Step 1: Suggest a Personal Meeting

When trust has been violated, one person (party) either directly (or indirectly) accuses the other (target) of doing something that was unfair. The target's first reaction is often one of surprise combined with denial, and he or she may feel a need to exonerate himself or herself. The target should suggest a face-to-face meeting with the party as quickly as possible. Indeed, verbal explanations are more effective than written explanations (Shapiro, Buttner, & Barry, 1994).

Step 2: Put the Focus on the Relationship

Instead of launching into discussions of who is right or who is wrong, put the focus on what both people care about: the relationship. Often, both people will readily agree that the relationship is worth saving. At the root of the bitter breakup of Pennsylvania health plans Highmark and Capital Blue-Cross was the fact that each party accused the other of causing the split. Both sides claimed that the other tossed the first salvo. CEO of Capital, Jim Mead, said that CEO of Highmark, John Brouse, called him incompetent. Mead responded by reminding consumers that Highmark desires to "gorge itself on acquisitions." The tragic aspect was that the two CEOs were friends and neighbors (*Best's Review*, Oct. 1, 2002).

Step 3: Apologize

Sincerity is important. Targets should apologize for their behavior and accept responsibility for their actions. The expression of remorse following a wrongful act can mitigate punishment. The target should apologize in a way that takes ownership for his or her actions or behavior, yet does not necessarily accept the party's version

BOX 6-2

STEPS TOWARD REPAIRING BROKEN TRUST

Step 1: Suggest a personal meeting.

Step 2: Put the focus on the relationship.

Step 3: Apologize.

Step 4: Let them vent.

Step 5: Do not get defensive.

Step 6: Ask for clarifying information.

Step 7:   Test your understanding.

Step 8:   Formulate a plan.

Step 9:   Think about ways to prevent a future problem.

Step 10: Do a relationship checkup.

of the violator's intentions. For example, a target might tell a party, "I am very sorry that I did not consult you before preparing the report." By saying this, the target does not agree with the party's accusation that the violator attempted to take more credit for the report; rather, the target only identifies the action as being hurtful for the victim. Indeed, when companies acknowledge that they have committed acts that threaten their legitimacy (e.g., newspaper claims of illegal conduct), they are more successful in blunting criticism when they point to external, mitigating circumstances (e.g., company norms, budgetary problems, etc.; Elsbach, 1994; Bies, Shapiro, & Cummings, 1988).

Step 4: Let Them Vent

It is important for people to express their anger, rage, disappointment, and feelings of betrayal over the event. Merely talking about negative events can actually be part of the cure (Pennebaker, Hughes, & O'Heeron, 1987). Research on procedural justice (Lind & Tyler, 1988) indicates that having a chance to express their disappointment, often helps people take a significant step in the healing process.

Step 5: Do Not Get Defensive

Instinctively, targets will attempt to defend their own honor. However, it is important not to behave defensively, no matter how misinformed or wrong you believe the other party to be. It is appropriate to tell the other person that you view the situation differently and to point out that the situation can be viewed in many ways. Only after the party has had an opportunity to vent and explain his or her perspective should the violator attempt to tell the party, in clear and simple terms, what his or her intentions were. For example, a target might say, "My intention was to submit the report and not bother too many people with unnecessary requests to edit it."

Step 6: Ask for Clarifying Information

Targets should invite the party to provide clarifying information in a nondefensive fashion. For example, a target might say, "Am I wrong in thinking that you did not ask to be listed on the report?" or "Did you receive the draft copy that I sent the previous week?"

Step 7: Test Your Understanding

If a person feels that they are understood, the chances for rebuilding trust are greatly increased. It is helpful if one party can truly empathize with the other's perspective (e.g., "I can understand why you felt out-of-the-loop. I have felt that way before, too."). The ability to understand emotion in others is one aspect of emotional intelligence (Mayer, Salovey, & Caruso, 2000). Indeed, a negotiator's ability to understand emotion is directly related to how satisfied the other party feels, independent of the monetary value of the outcome (Mueller & Curhan, 2004).

Step 8: Formulate a Plan

A major stumbling block in the trust rebuilding process is that parties have different ideas about what is fair. The egocentric bias once again rears its ugly head with most harmdoers perceiving themselves as more beneficent than the harmed. However, the mere fact of asking the harmed what he or she needs can go a long way toward rebuilding trust. In an empirical investigation of breaches of trust, harmdoers who asked "What can I do?" were more successful in rebuilding cooperation than those who did not ask or asked "What will it take?" (Bottom, Gibson, Daniels, & Murnighan, 2000). According to Bottom and colleagues (2000), penance is critical to trust in mixed-motive relationships. Aggravating a counterparty after a breach by making offers of penance that do not seem sincere may further antagonize. In contrast, volunteering to do penance, even in small amounts, is particularly effective.

In a major investigation of the how people repair trust, a key finding was that the speed and amount of "trust recovery" is significantly moderated by the *promises* that a person makes (Schweitzer, Hershey, & Bradlow, 2003). No one should underestimate the power of the spoken word, especially when it contains an apology. For example, verbal explanation can dramatically dampen people's negative reactions to aversive behavior (Bottom, Gibson, Daniels, & Murnighan, 2002). However, when it comes down to truly rebuilding cooperation, the power of the deed exceeds the power of the spoken word. "Substantive amends have significantly more positive effects than explanations alone [on rebuilding cooperation]" (p. 497).

Step 9: Think About Ways to Prevent a Future Problem

Do not just try to remedy the past; rather, think about a way to make sure that this problem, and any others like it, does not occur in the future. This effort may take some time, but it is well worth it.

Step 10: Do a Relationship Checkup

It is often wise to pull out your planners and decide upon a lunch or coffee meeting in a month or so to discuss how each party is feeling about the situation and occurrences since the breach of trust occurred. It is also helpful to schedule this date during the first meeting, because after this time, it may seem awkward to bring it up. This step ensures that parties will have a reason to meet and an opportunity to talk things through at a later date.

REPUTATION

One thing a negotiator definitely needs to protect is his or her reputation. According to Glick and Croson (2001), you don't have to be a famous real estate tycoon for others to have an impression of you. Glick and Croson (2001) argue that managers' reputations are built fairly quickly in negotiation communities. And the reputations that people gain affect how others deal with them. As a case in point, they describe the reputation held by Donald Trump:

> Real estate developer Donald Trump has a well-publicized reputation as a hard-line negotiator. In an article describing Trump's negotiations with the Taj Mahal Casino Resorts' bondholders, Trump's advisors tell how after a deal is agreed upon, he always comes back requesting something more. Well-informed counterparts, familiar with his reputation, are prepared for this tactic and anticipate it in deciding how many concessions to make during the pre-agreement stage. Similarly, Trump has a reputation for storming out of negotiations in the middle of talks. An anonymous participant in the bondholders negotiation above said, "You know Donald's going to get up and leave, you just don't know when" (Glick & Croson, 2001, p. 177).

Glick and Croson cite the Silicon Valley as an example of a negotiation community, where an active technology trade press helps generate a rich flow of information regarding reputations. Because venture capitalists co-invest with various firms, they share information. Moreover, because time is money, you might not even get on a calendar unless your reputation is good.

Our impressions of others are formed quickly and immediately, sometimes within the first few minutes of meeting someone, because the judgments we make about people are often automatic (Bargh, Lombardi, & Higgins, 1988). Not surprisingly, we form impressions of people on the basis of limited information. Reputations are often more extreme and polarized than the person they represent; they can be summed up by four words: *judgmental, consistent, immediate,* and *inferential.* The reputations assigned to others tend to be highly evaluative, meaning that they are either "good" or "bad" (Osgood, Suci, & Tannenbaum, 1957). Furthermore, the reputations we assign to others are highly internally consistent. Once we decide that someone is trustworthy, other qualities about this person are perceived as consistent with this favorable impression. This tendency gives rise to the **halo effect**, which is the propensity to believe that people we trust and like are also intelligent and capable.

Of course, the halo effect can work in the opposite direction. The **forked-tail effect** means that once we form a negative impression of someone, we tend to view everything else about them in a negative fashion. For this reason, it is difficult to recover from making a bad impression.

Glick and Croson (2001) note that reputations are based on a combination of firsthand and secondhand information. Firsthand information is based on our direct experience with someone. Secondhand information is we hear about someone else's experience with someone.

Glick and Croson (2001) undertook an investigation of the reputations earned by 105 students enrolled in a class. They rated one another, on the basis of firsthand experience, from the least cooperative to the most cooperative:

- **Liar-manipulator** (will do anything for advantage)
- **Tough but honest** (very tough negotiator, but does not lie, and makes few concessions)

- **Nice and reasonable** (will make concessions)
- **Cream puff** (will make concessions and be conciliatory regardless of what the other does)

The major finding from their multiweek investigation was that people act much tougher when dealing with someone who has reputation of being a liar (61% reported using classic distributive, pie-slicing tactics with these people). Against tough negotiators, this behavior dropped to 49 percent and integrative tactics (pie-expanding tactics) were used 35 percent of the time. Against nice negotiators, only 30 percent used distributive tactics and 64 percent used integrative tactics. And, against cream puffs, 40 percent used distributive tactics and only 27 percent used integrative tactics. The key conclusion is that people use tough or manipulative tactics in a defensive fashion with liars and tough negotiators, and use them in an opportunistic fashion with cream puffs.

Repairing a tarnished reputation is a lot like attempting to build trust. People will look at your behavior more than your words, so it is important to act in a trustworthy fashion—not just talk in a trustworthy fashion.

RELATIONSHIPS IN NEGOTIATION

The past dealings we have had with another person shape how we act with them in the present. Indeed, the quality of the deals that negotiators reach is powerfully affected by their previous bargaining experiences. For example, negotiators who reach impasse find themselves getting caught in "distributive spirals" in which they interpret their performance as unsuccessful, experience negative emotions, and develop negative perceptions of their negotiation counterparts and the entire negotiation process (O'Connor & Arnold, 2001). Moreover, negotiators who reach an impasse in a prior negotiation are more likely to impasse in their next negotiation or to reach low-value (lose-lose) deals compared to negotiators who were successful in reaching agreement (i.e., reaching a level 1 agreement; O'Connor, Arnold, & Burris, 2003). Moreover, this effect holds true even when the negotiator is dealing with a different person. Thus, if a negotiator has "baggage" from the past, it affects his or her ability to go forward. Even more dramatically, incidental emotions from the past (e.g., anger stemming from an argument with a spouse) can influence trust in an unrelated setting (e.g., the likelihood of trusting a coworker; Dunn & Schweitzer, 2003). In short, anger about anything—even in our past with another person—makes us less likely to trust anyone else in the future.

People often feel better about pie-slicing and are in a better position to expand the lie when they have a good relationship and trust one another. For example, Pruitt and Carnevale (1993) find that a high concern for oneself and the other party is most likely to lead to integrative (win-win) outcomes (for an overview, see Rubin, Pruitt, & Kim, 1994). Levels of cooperation decrease as social distance increases between people (Buchan, Croson, & Dawes, 2002). And, in our own research, we find when reaching agreement is important, negotiators who have a relationship are more likely to reach a win-win agreement than negotiators who do not have a relationship (Kray, Lind, & Thompson, 2004).

Most people negotiate in their personal lives. For example, people negotiate with spouses, friends, and neighbors (see Valley, Neale, & Mannix, 1995). People also negotiate on a repeated basis with others in their personal life who do not necessarily fall into the categories of "friends" or "family" (e.g., homeowners negotiating with contractors;

parents negotiating with other parents concerning carpool arrangements; parents negotiating with nannies concerning child care; etc.). In addition to negotiating in our personal lives, we also negotiate in our business lives, with colleagues, supervisors, and staff members. In some cases, our personal life is intermingled with our business life in relationships that we cannot easily classify as strictly personal or strictly business, but rather a little or a lot of both. We refer to this type of relationship as an "embedded" relationship (Uzzi, 1997). We will expose the relevant implicit norms and rules that lurk under each of these three types of relationships and their implications for trust in negotiations. The behavior of people in relationships is guided by shared sets of rules (see Argyle & Henderson, 1984; Clark & Mills, 1979). Individuals in relationships seek to abide by the rules of relationships and not violate the expectations of others.

Negotiating with Friends

Most people negotiate quite often, even in the most intimate of personal relationships. For example, consider how James and Lloyd Maritz decided to negotiate their differences about how to manage their company business. In 1950, they decided to cut the company in half and, following Solomon's rule, one brother did the dividing and the other brother got to choose first (*The Wall Street Journal*, Aug. 12, 2002). What do we know about doing "business" with friends and family?

McGinn and Keros (2002) examined negotiations among strangers and friends and found that one of three patterns emerges early on:

- Opening up: complete and mutual honesty
- Working together: cooperative problem solving
- Haggling: competitive attempt to get the best possible deal for oneself

These negotiators use one of three dynamic processes—trust-testing, process clarification, and emotional punctuation—when they have difficulty moving through the interaction. When strangers interact, they often immediately begin in haggling mode. In contrast, friends almost immediately begin to open up.

Why People Are Uncomfortable Negotiating with Friends

A motto followed by many people is "friends should not do business." People are extremely reluctant to negotiate with friends, if it means that money, goods, or services change hands. People who do negotiate with friends report feeling uncomfortable (Kurtzberg & Medvec, 1999). According to Kurtzberg and Medvec, "Friendship dictates that we should be concerned with fairness and the other person's welfare, while negotiations dictate that we should get a good deal for ourselves" (p. 356). These two dictates are in conflict with one another. The reason for the discomfort is traceable to the fact that most friendships are built on *communal norms*, which basically mandate that we should take care of people we love, respond to their needs, and not "keep track" of who has put in what (Clark & Mills, 1979). Thus, the communal norm prescribes that we should be sensitive to the needs of people we love or like and attempt to meet those needs, rather than trying to maximize our own interests. The opposite of communal norms are *exchange norms*, which basically say that people should keep track of who has put what into a relationship, and that they should be compensated based on value and quality of their inputs. Thus, people need to have a mental accounting system of sorts that enters who has done what.

The truth is that we negotiate with our friends all the time. For example, we make childcare arrangements with neighbors, plan parties and vacations together, and even purchase jointly shared equipment together (e.g., snowblowers). Friends don't call these things "negotiations"; rather, they say they are "working things out," "making plans," "figuring things out," and so on. Above all, in these interactions, people are careful not to exchange money, and sometimes go to great and strange lengths in order not to.

Friends Are Less Competitive with Each Other

Not surprisingly, friends are less competitive with each other than they are with strangers (for a review, see Valley, Neale, & Mannix, 1995). Friends exchange more information, make more concessions, and make fewer demands. Consequently, negotiators who are in a relationship are often unable to profitably exploit opportunities to create value. Curhan, Neale, Ross, and Rosencranz-Engelmann (2004) refer to the oft-observed pattern where people in close relationships reach monetarily inefficient outcomes but increase their relational satisfaction as the "O. Henry Effect." In O. Henry's story, "The Gift of the Magi," the main characters—husband and wife—are madly in love with each other, but engage in an inefficient exchange in a desperate attempt to provide each other with a Christmas gift. Curhan, Neale, Ross, and Rosencranz-Engelmann (2004) tested this idea with actual negotiators and found that when relationship partners sacrifice instrumental value, they actually increase their relational satisfaction.

Friends May Not Reach Level 3 Integrative Agreements

Friends and lovers are too willing to compromise (Fry, Firestone, & Williams, 1983; Thompson & DeHarpport, 1998). Friends are reluctant to engage in the firm flexibility maxim that is often required to reach level 3 integrative agreements. In short, friends believe that reaching an impasse may permanently damage their relationship, so they settle quickly. Yet, as we have seen in our discussion of integrative agreements in Chapter 4, it is important to focus on differences of interest and maintain high aspirations to reach level 3 integrative outcomes. When people compromise quickly because they want to avoid conflict and minimize threat of impasse, they are likely to leave value on the table. In short, they satisfice, rather than optimize. They often justify this satisficing behavior as necessary so as to avoid conflict, but we think that they are selling themselves short. Just think once again about the example of the sisters and the orange in Chapter 4. The sisters most likely immediately compromised because they did not want to risk a permanent rift in their relationship. Yet their outcome is not really win-win. It would be far better if the sisters had a conversation about their individual needs. Friends who really want to reach win-win need to explore the other's needs.

Friendship and the Myth of Mind Reading

People in intimate and friendship relationships are often hurt and annoyed that their needs are not met. What's more, they often expect others to be able to understand their needs. For this reason, they are reluctant to express these needs. Thus, begins an escalating cycle of hurt feelings compounded by anger.

Friendship and the Mismanagement of Agreement

Organizational psychologist Jerry Harvey's (1974) story of the road to Abilene (see Box 6-3) epitomizes the notion that among family and friends, conflict is to be avoided at all costs, even if it means a lose-lose outcome for all involved. The need for friends to

BOX 6-3

THE ABILENE PARADOX

The July afternoon in Coleman, Texas (population 5,607), was particularly hot—104 degrees as measured by the Walgreen's Rexall Ex-Lax temperature gauge. In addition, the wind was blowing fine-grained West Texas topsoil through the house. But the afternoon was still tolerable—even potentially enjoyable. There was a fan going on the back porch; there was cold lemonade; and finally, there was entertainment. Dominoes. Perfect for the conditions. The game required little more physical exertion than an occasional mumbled comment, "Shuffle 'em," and an unhurried movement of the arm to place the spots in the appropriate perspective on the table. All in all, it had the markings of an agreeable Sunday afternoon in Coleman—that is, it was until my father-in-law suddenly said, "Let's get in the car and go to Abilene and have dinner at the cafeteria."

I thought, "What, go to Abilene? Fifty-three miles? In this dust storm and heat? And in an un-air-conditioned 1958 Buick?"

But my wife chimed in with "Sounds like a great idea. I'd like to go. How about you, Jerry?" Since my own preferences were obviously out of step with the rest I replied, "Sounds good to me," and added, "I just hope your mother wants to go."

"Of course I want to go," said my mother-in-law. "I haven't been to Abilene in a long time."

So into the car and off to Abilene we went. My predictions were fulfilled. The heat was brutal. We were coated with a fine layer of dust that was cemented with perspiration by the time we arrived. The food at the cafeteria provided first-rate testimonial material for antacid commercials.

Some four hours and 106 miles later we returned to Coleman, hot and exhausted. We sat in front of the fan for a long time in silence. Then, both to be sociable and to break the silence, I said, "It was a great trip, wasn't it?"

No one spoke. Finally my mother-in-law said, with some irritation, "Well, to tell the truth, I really didn't enjoy it much and would rather have stayed here. I just went along because the three of you were so enthusiastic about going. I wouldn't have gone if you all hadn't pressured me into it."

I couldn't believe it. "What do you mean 'you all'?" I said. "Don't put me in the 'you all' group. I was delighted to be doing what we were doing. I didn't want to go. I only went to satisfy the rest of you. You're the culprits."

My wife looked shocked. "Don't call me a culprit. You and Daddy and Mama were the ones who wanted to go. I just went along to be sociable and to keep you happy. I would have had to be crazy to want to go out in heat like that."

Her father entered the conversation abruptly. "Hell!" he said.

He proceeded to expand on what was already absolutely clear. "Listen, I never wanted to go to Abilene. I just thought you might be bored. You visit so seldom I wanted to be sure you enjoyed it. I would have preferred to play another game of dominoes and eat the leftovers in the icebox."

After the outburst of recrimination we all sat back in silence. Here we were, four reasonably sensible people who, of our own volition, had just taken a 106-mile trip across a godforsaken desert in a furnace-like temperature through a cloud-like dust storm to eat unpalatable food at a hole-in-the-wall cafeteria in Abilene, when none of us had really wanted to go. In fact, to be more accurate, we'd done just the opposite of what we wanted to do. The whole situation simply didn't make sense (Harvey, 1974).

maintain the illusion of agreement means that important differences in preferences, interests, and beliefs are often downplayed or buried. Paradoxically, it is precisely these kinds of differences that *should* surface in any negotiation, to enable negotiators in personal relationships to fashion value-added trade-offs and develop contingency contracts. Somehow, friends and families need a way of making their differences known, so as to capitalize on them in a win-win fashion.

If We Have to Negotiate, We Should Divide It Down the Middle

When it comes to dividing the pie, friends use an **equality rule** (thereby allocating equal shares to everyone involved), whereas strangers and business associates used an **equity rule**—otherwise known as a **merit-based rule**—in which those who have contributed more are expected to receive more (Austin, 1980). Unfortunately, equality norms may promote compromise agreements, thereby inhibiting the discovery of integrative trade-offs. However, norms of equality are not blindly applied by people in close relationships. For example, friends who differ in their ability and effort in a joint task will favor the less able, but more diligent, partner in the allocation of resources (Lamm & Kayser, 1978). Similarly, people in communal relationships will meet the other's needs, with no expectation of remuneration (Clark & Mills, 1979). Equity, in which outcomes are allocated proportional to inputs, is a hallmark feature of the business world. For example, most of us do not expect to earn the same exact salary as our colleagues; we earn salaries based upon various contributions and inputs to the specific business situation. However, equity does not seem to have a legitimate role in personal relationships.

Negotiating with Businesspeople

In contrast to friendship negotiation, businesspeople are much more likely to use an exchange norm. Exchange norms are rooted in concept of market pricing. **Market pricing** is a method by which everything is reduced to a single value or utility metric that allows for the comparison of many qualitatively and quantitatively diverse factors (Fiske, 1992). Market pricing allows people to negotiate by making references to ratios of this metric, such as percentage share in a business venture. Money is the prototypical medium of market pricing relationships. Capitalism is the ultimate expression of market pricing. Market pricing can be viewed from another angle as a social influence device. In a true market pricing relationship, people will do virtually anything if offered enough money because "everyone has his price." However, just because this approach is the predominant business mode, it does not mean that people will follow it.

We Choose Our Friends, but Not Our Coworkers

Basically, we (usually) like our friends, but we do not necessarily like the people we do business with. Yet this generalization does not excuse us from having to negotiate and deal with them. In fact, we must often deal with people whom we do not like and whom we may regard to be offensive. For example, a woman might find herself having to negotiate with a male who is a blatant sexist. It is often difficult for people to separate their feelings about someone as a person from the business at hand. (See Sidebar 6-3 for an example of an uncomfortable business relationship.)

Sidebar 6-3. Uncomfortable Business Relationships

Uncomfortable business relationships occur when a negotiation involves engaging in interactions that, in a personal context, would take on a different meaning, and thus, might be regarded as inappropriate. For example, consider two managers, a man and a woman, each married, who have late flights arriving in their destination city and very busy schedules, and nevertheless need to negotiate. They agree to meet at a bar, because it is the only location open that late at night. However, when they arrive at the bar, the waitstaff treats them as a couple. The situation is embarrassing for the business associates because their relationship is viewed in a different way by those outside the business context than by those on the "inside." This perception has implications for the negotiation; for example, if the waitstaff presents the check to the man, it can potentially create an uncomfortable power dynamic between them. (We will discuss this further in Chapter 7.) Quite often, business opportunities are conducted in the context of social relationships (Uzzi, 1997). For this reason, it is difficult to form close relationships across gender lines if they are built through social activities such as playing golf, going to the theater, or meeting for dinner, because these practices often have a different meaning between men and women than they do between persons of the same gender (Etzkowitz, Kemelgor, & Uzzi, 1999).

Business Relationships Often Have Status and Rank Issues Associated with Them

Most friendships are not hierarchical—meaning that in friendships, people do not have different status and rank. In contrast, businesses are generally organized around rank and status—either explicitly (e.g., an organizational chart) or implicitly (e.g., salaries, number of supervisees, office space, etc.). Differences in power, as we shall see in Chapter 7, set the stage for "hot" negotiations. Thus, negotiating in the business world is often considerably more challenging because negotiations about a given issue are embedded in a larger status negotiation among the actors in the organization. Status issues, of course, can vary across cultures as well as organizations. As we will see in Chapter 10, in some cultures, it is perfectly acceptable for members of different status and rank to meet each other at the bargaining table. However, in other cultures, people find this uncomfortable and insulting.

The Need for Swift Trust

The dynamic, changing nature of business interactions means that we need to build trust with people more rapidly, on basis of less information (often, with no past history) and, in many cases, with no expected meaningful future interaction. For example, a new temporary partnership involving the need for immediate trust was formed recently between auctioneer Sotheby's Holdings, Inc., and Rossi & Rossi, a London art dealer for an exhibition and sale of Tibetan art (*The Wall Street Journal*, Mar. 19, 1999). The partnership was well-timed, as long-neglected art and objects from Tibet and the Himalayas are of interest to both collectors and buyers. This exhibition marked the first time a major auction house partnered with an independent dealer to sell artwork publicly and far away from the auction block. Normally, the auction house does not own inventory; the new partnership, though, makes Sotheby's a dealer with its own inventory to protect and push. Sotheby's offered Rossi & Rossi the use of its gallery space and promoted the show with its sizeable marketing power in return for a share of the profits from the sale.

The partnership between Sotheby's and Rossi & Rossi is an example of **swift trust**. Swift trust is the mechanism that allows people to build trust quickly (Meyerson, Weick, & Kramer, 1996). Many new business relationships require that strangers come together and produce a product, service, or carry out some task, and then immediately disband, perhaps never to see one another again. In contrast, our personal relationships are longer term; we have a past history with family and friends, and we expect to have future interactions with them. Business situations of the twenty-first century increasingly require swift trust, which is necessary among people who have a finite life span in a temporary system. The question is, how do we build trust with no past and no likely future? We deal with this issue later.

No Such Thing as a One-Shot Business Situation

Taken alone, this notion contradicts the idea of swift trust. On the surface, it would seem that swift trust epitomizes the one-shot business situation, wherein people who do not know each other must somehow trust each other enough to do business and then terminate the relationship, never to see each other again. However, in the business world, through its web of networked relationships, it is impossible to not experience the consequences of our interactions with others. If these consequences percolate through our business networks, then the situation is technically not a one-shot interaction. Social networks mean that even though the particular people in a business interaction may never interact nor see one another again, their companies will interact again, or others in their social network will become apprised of the interaction, which will, in turn, affect the nature of future business interactions. Therefore, it is important to realize that the one-shot business situation may be a virtual impossibility.

When in Business with Friends and Family

In 1999, Eric Hunter who had given up his CEO post to his brother Neal, in his family-owned company Cree Inc., began to think that his younger brother was mismanaging the company. The tension boiled over one night when the brothers were having a snowball fight and Neal slammed Eric to the ground, cutting his leg. The fight escalated into a high-tech family feud, complete with lawsuits, allegations of fraud and harassment, and even death threats (*BusinessWeek*, Aug. 11, 2003d). When friends and family do business, the relationship is more complex and known as an **embedded relationship**. The classic embedded relationship is the family business—like Eric and Neal Hunter—wherein people who are related are doing business together.

The embedded relationship would seem to have several advantages, the most important of which is facilitating the nature of business exchange by initiating self-organizing governance arrangements that operate through expectations of trust and reciprocity, rather than expensive deterrence mechanisms (Uzzi, 1999a). For example, in one empirical investigation, firms that embedded their bank exchanges in social attachments were more likely to have access to capital and received more favorable interest rates on loans (Uzzi, 1999b).

Another example of an embedded relationship is that between Magic Johnson (former Los Angeles Lakers' star basketball player) and Jerry Buss (the Lakers' owner).

They always socialized away from basketball and spent nearly every dinner together during home games. Formally, they were employer and employee: The employer would pay, and the employee would play. According to Magic Johnson, the two of them developed a relationship outside of the formal business because "he saw me as one of his kids" (*Los Angeles Times*, Apr. 23, 1996). Says Johnson, "That's why I've never negotiated with him. . . . We never had a negotiation. He said, 'I want to give you this.' I said, 'OK.' He said, 'I want you to coach this team.' I said, 'OK.' It's been like that. It's no contract, you just say, 'OK.' That's how we have it" (p. 1). Buss calls Johnson his hero; Johnson calls Buss his surrogate father.

However, pitfalls to an embedded relationship can also happen. We describe some of them next.

The Emotional Potential Is Higher

The emotional potential of embedded relationships is higher because more dimensions occur with the self-involved. When business and friendship combine, the emotional potential can often be overwhelming, and interpersonal conflict can result. For example, if someone has a poor exchange with a neighbor that leaves the friendship in question, it is quite disturbing, but the person can at least travel to work knowing that the situation is "contained." Similarly, a person may have a terrible day at work and still be able to go home that evening to take solace in friends and family. Somehow, the separation of work and friendship creates a "buffer zone" for the parties involved. However, when things go awry in an embedded relationship during the course of negotiation, all systems can potentially fail. Consider the Maritz Company, who suffered through three generations of feuding (*The Wall Street Journal*, Aug. 12, 2002). Before Bill Maritz passed away, he wrote at the end of his memoir, "I still find it virtually impossible to understand and accept the lack of respect and feeling my two sons, Peter and Flip, have shown me." The mother, Phyllis Maritz said, "It would be my greatest hope to see the company sold and out of the family forever. Then perhaps the family could heal."

Internal Value Conflict

Personal relationships are driven by people's need for acceptance, love, and identity, whereas business relationships are generally guided by a need for achievement and utilitarian goals. In embedded relationships, people often experience more internal value conflict because competence and liking are at battle with one another. For example, we may find someone to be a delightful friend, a wonderful and empathic listener, and a good person to spend time with; however, this person may be incompetent at the business task at hand. Conversely, the person who is more competent may be annoying to us. The question is, which of these factors do we respond to in the situation, competence or liking?

Myopia

We have seen that embedded relationships can often reduce the costs associated with surveillance. However, embedded relationships may create myopia if people are reluctant to move beyond their own networks. At the extreme, imagine a cliquish network in which people engage only in business matters with their friends. This interaction may eventually result in a myopic view of reality, if people within the network are biased in their perceptions and not connected to others who may have more or better information. Valley and T. Thompson (1998) refer to these types of relationships as "sticky ties"—describing the resistance to change that emanates from ingrained habits of past social interaction. Further, mandating changes in social ties creates passive resistance or inertia, in that most people are reluctant to turn to new, untried partners for information, resources, and the variety of interactions that are required in organizations.

Bottom Line on Relationships

Virtually all of the relationships a person has fit into one of the three types we described: friendship, pure business, or business friends. How can a negotiator assess the quality of the relationship he or she has with a given person? As a start, you can consider where your relationship stands on each of the dimensions listed in Table 6-3 on page 150. If the majority of the dimensions of your relationship are listed on the right-hand side, you can deduce that an effective relationship has developed.

CONCLUSION

In this chapter, we argued that social outcomes, such as goodwill, trust, and respect, are just as important as economic outcomes. Establishing trust and building relationships are essential for effective negotiation. We discussed three types of "trust" relationships, including deterrence-based trust (based on sanctions and monitoring), knowledge-based trust (based on predictability and information), and finally identification-based trust (based on true empathy). We discussed trust-building and trust-repairing strategies, including transforming personal conflict into task conflict, agreeing on a common goal, recognizing a shared problem, and focusing on the future. We reviewed psychological strategies that often engender trust, such as similarity, mere exposure, good mood, physical presence, reciprocity, small talk, flattery, and self-disclosure. We reviewed three common types of relationships in negotiation: business-only, friendship-only, and multiplex relationships that involve both.

Nielsen Pocket Piece and tell me where the numbers come from" (*Advertising Age*, Oct. 1, 2001). Similarly, David Colburn, of AOL, would actually rehearse before negotiating: He was devoted, sending e-mails to people at midnight to review particular details concerning the negotiation (*Washington Post*, June 15, 2003).

Status

Two types of status are relevant in most negotiation situations: primary status characteristics and secondary status characteristics. **Primary status characteristics** refer to marks and indicators of legitimate authority; for example, a person's rank within an organizational chart, the number of supervisees in that person's unit, and a person's various titles and degrees all denote primary status. The impact of status on the conduct of bargaining can be quite enormous. (Recall the opening example of Chapter 3 in which the negotiator used the "gray-haired equity.") High-status individuals talk more, even when they do not necessarily know more. A high-status person will also generally control when he or she speaks in a conversation; furthermore, a low-status person will defer to the high-status person in terms of turn-taking in the conversation. These factors can affect pie-slicing in a negotiation.

When primary status cues (such as rank and stature in an organization) are absent, or when people of equal status negotiate, people often pay attention to **secondary status characteristics**, which are cues and characteristics that have no legitimate bearing on the allocation of resources or on the norms of interaction, but nevertheless exert a powerful influence on behavior. Secondary status characteristics are also known as **pseudostatus characteristics** that include sex, age, ethnicity, status in other groups, and cultural background. The three most common secondary status characteristics are gender, age, and race. Quite simply put, men have more influence than women; older people have more influence than younger people; and white people have more influence than black people when it comes to interpersonal interaction (Mazur, 1985). Typically, pseudostatus characteristics are highly visible. Pseudostatus characteristics, of course, have little to do with ability, but people act as if they do.

Status cues are noted quickly, often within minutes after negotiators are seated at the bargaining table. Pseudostatus characteristics should not, in any normative or rational sense, exert an effect on the negotiation; however, they often do. Furthermore, even when a negotiator does not regard these pseudostatus cues to be significant (or even rejects them outright), if someone else at the bargaining table considers them significant, he or she can create a **self-fulfilling prophesy**. For an example of how the self-fulfilling prophesy works in another domain, consider the following: African-Americans who were asked to indicate their race prior to taking a scholastic aptitude test (SAT) performed significantly worse than African-Americans who were not asked to indicate their race beforehand (Steele & Aronson, 1995). Presumably, African-American students, as well as the larger population, are well aware that one (false) stereotype of African-Americans is that they are not as intellectually competent as their white peers. When an African-American person is made aware of the faulty stereotype, and the fact that the activity in which the person is engaging is relevant to that stereotype, presumably, he or she is vulnerable to fulfilling that stereotype. This phenomenon is called **stereotype threat** (Steele, 1997). At a cognitive level, stereotypical attributes such as lack of intelligence, laziness, and athleticism are connected to a person's behavioral repertoire, which is why the mere mention of a false stereotype can lead to stereotypically consistent behaviors. Most important, people who seem most resistant to negative stereotyping (e.g., high-achieving, gifted African-Americans) often fall prey to stereotype threats. This tendency suggests that the self-fulfilling prophesy occurs because erroneous stereotypes are activated that hinder performance.

In a related study, Spencer, Steele, and Quinn (1999) examined the self-fulfilling prophesy effect among women in the domain of mathematics. A pervasive stereotype is that women are worse than men at solving difficult math problems (Benbow & Stanley, 1980). According to Spencer and colleagues (1999), women only perform worse than men in situations in which they perceive themselves to be at risk of confirming the gender stereotype. Indeed, when women were told that no gender differences had been observed for a test they were about to take, no differences between men's and women's test scores were observed. However, when women were told that gender differences had been shown to exist, men outperformed women on the same tests.

Thus, in both of these examples, we find that traditionally disadvantaged persons (in this case, African-Americans and women) are vulnerable to fulfilling the negative stereotypes held about them, even when they do not regard these stereotypes to be true of themselves. A similar dynamic can happen in negotiations. For example, when a male who has traditional sex role values negotiates with a woman, his belief system may imperil the fair division of the bargaining pie (see Sidebar 7-1).

Sidebar 7-1. Determinants and Consequences of Salary Negotiations by Male and Female MBA Graduates

When the salary-negotiating behaviors and starting salary outcomes of 205 MBA graduate students were investigated, no differences were observed between men and women in terms of the proclivity to negotiate—meaning that women were just as likely as men to attempt to renegotiate the initial offers made to them by their employers. However, women did obtain lower monetary returns from negotiations (4.3% starting salary increment for men versus 2.7% for women). Over the course of a career, the accumulation of such differences may be substantial. One estimate is that the present value of women's cumulative pay shortfall would be more than $29,000, in terms of a 30-year career (Gerhart & Rynes, 1991).

We wanted to directly analyze how the different genders fare at the bargaining table, so my colleagues Laura Kray, Adam Galinsky, and I created a series of highly realistic negotiation simulations between MBA females and males in a research investigation that came to be known as the "Battle of the Sexes" (Kray, Thompson, & Galinsky, 2001). What we found surprised us. First, we found that across the board, men were more successful than women in terms of pie-slicing—they inevitably got a bigger slice (Kray, Thompson, & Galinsky, 2001; Kray, Galinsky & Thompson, 2002). Second, when negotiators believed that the simulations were actually predictive of their true negotiation ability, men did even better. Apparently, the women—in this case, highly successful managers from major companies—were getting tripped up because of the pervasive cultural stereotype that "women are docile." Even though these successful females were anything but docile, the mere knowledge that this stereotype about women exists was enough to form a mental roadblock in the negotiations. We speculated that if the cultural stereotype about women was positioned more prominently that women would be able to mentally attack it. We created a simulation in which we deliberately mentioned the classic female stereotype, and the tide turned. These highly competent female MBA students not only actively dismissed the stereotype, they claimed more of the pie than did their male MBA students. The message? Stereotypes that lurk below the surface have a way of creeping into the subconscious recesses of our minds and negatively interfering with our performance. By exposing those negative stereotypes—getting them out in the open and then mentally attacking them—women can do much better.

These results gave us the idea of completely turning the stereotype of women on its head: We created a negotiation simulation in which we clearly told the men and women MBAs that success in negotiation requires *people skills*—listening, verbal prowess, nonverbal acumen, and so on—all the elements of the classic female stereotype. Sure enough, women performed better under these conditions (Kray, Galinsky, & Thompson, 2002). The key conclusion is that if any task (such as negotiation) can be positively linked to your own gender stereotype, you can perform better. Perhaps this reasoning explains in part why Oprah is so powerful. (See also Sidebar 7-2 for an example of how a powerful female leader has leveraged her role.)

Sidebar 7-2. The Verbal and Nonverbal Skills of Power
Madeleine Korbel Albright is the first female Secretary of State in U.S. history and the highest-ranking woman ever to serve in the executive branch of government. The tough-talking, wisecracking, former Georgetown University professor sought the job and accepted it eagerly, making no pretense of reluctance and offering no sham modesty about her stellar credentials (*National Journal*, June 3, 2000). In her reign as Secretary of State, "Last Word" Albright has an impressive list of powerful accomplishments: She forged an alliance that finally faced down Serb aggression in the Balkans and held it together during the war, and she did it without a total rupture with Moscow. At the same time, she kept the Israeli-Palestinian peace negotiations from falling apart completely while Benjamin Netanyahu was prime minister so that Netanyahu's successor, Ehud Barak, could build on a foundation that was still intact. She nursed the relationship with China and opened the door to better relations with Iran. Her secret to power: "Interrupt!" At least it is the advice she gives to young women: "Don't wait for men to solicit your input" (*National Journal*, June 3, 2000). And she walks the talk: In her course at Georgetown, she instituted a no-hand-raising rule because she believes that if students are told to raise their hands before speaking, women will do so, but men will not. Her successes with the variety of people she has dealt with reveal her remarkable persuasive skills and her bargaining power.

Social Networks

Whereas information power in a negotiation refers to the power associated with *what* you know, network power refers to the power associated with *who* you know. **Social capital** is the power that results from managers' access to other people within and outside their organization. Social capital is a value that comes from who, when, and how to coordinate through various contacts within and beyond the organization. Mark Isakowitz made an entire company based on the power of networks. His job is to act as a negotiator-mediator for businesspeople who want to influence Capitol Hill. The hospital association sought his negotiation skills to kill the Medicare bill. The legislation was supported by high-ranking Republicans, so Isakowitz used networks of a higher order—the party's leadership—to prevent the bill's passage. One day, he staked out at the busy crossroads on the second floor of the Capitol between the Rotunda and the door to the House. Standing there, he was guaranteed to spot Majority leader Tom DeLay (R-Texas) and Whip Roy Blunt (R-Missouri). When they appeared, he issued his threat: The hospital industry had produced TV ads that would label any lawmaker supporting the bill an enemy of health care. The group was willing to spend $4 million to air commercials and Isakowitz was willing to give them a demo tape right on the spot. The Republicans declined the tape, but accepted his threat. Within weeks, the Ways and Means committee killed the Medicare decrease. Hospital stocks stablilized and the commercials never aired. Such is the power of networks and social capital (*Fortune*, Aug. 11, 2003b, p. 121).

You don't have to be a Capitol Hill lobbyist to leverage social networks. Managers with more social capital get higher returns on their human capital because they are positioned to identify and develop more rewarding opportunities (Burt, 1992). Negotiators with high network power are those who act as **boundary spanners**, bridging functional gaps in organizations and units. In other words, they are the critical link between people who otherwise would not be in contact. As boundary spanners, they fill a unique spot within the organizational network by bringing together people, knowledge, and information that would not otherwise be brought together. A negotiator's position as a unique link in a network of relationships means that he or she can broker more opportunities than other members of the network who do not represent unique links within the organization and beyond. Furthermore, negotiators who are boundary spanners are in a position to make or break opportunities for other people. Negotiators who act as boundary spanners broker the flow of information between people and control information. Negotiators who bridge gaps are the people who know about, have a hand in, and exercise more control over rewarding opportunities. They have broader access to information because of their diverse contacts. This access means that they are more often aware of new opportunities and have easier access to these opportunities than do their peers—even their peers of equivalent or greater human capital. For this reason, they are also more likely to be discussed as suitable candidates for inclusion in new opportunities and are more likely to be able to display their capabilities because they have more control over the substance of their work, defined by relationships with subordinates, superiors, and colleagues.

Physical Appearance

It is a somewhat disturbing fact that physically attractive people are more effective in getting what they want than are less physically attractive people, independent of their actual skills. For example, the work produced by allegedly attractive people is more highly valued than that produced by less-attractive people. As a case in point, in one investigation, men evaluated an essay with a photo of the supposed author attached—either an attractive or an unattractive woman (as judged by an independent group of people; for a review, see Feingold, 1992). Even though the essays were identical in all instances, men's judgments of the essay were strongly affected by how attractive the woman in the picture was: The more attractive the person in the photo, the better the grade given (Landy & Sigall, 1974). People think that attractive people are more talented, kind, honest, and intelligent (Eagly, Ashmore, Makhijani, & Longo, 1991). As a consequence, attractive people are more persuasive in terms of changing attitudes (Chaiken, 1979) and getting what they want (Benson, Karabenick, & Lerner, 1976). Physical attractiveness has a favorable impact on sales effectiveness (Kivisilta, Honkaniemi, & Sundvi, 1994; Reingen & Kernan, 1993) and on income levels across a wide range of occupations (Hamermesh & Biddle, 1994). By the way, attractiveness is usually achieved through dress and grooming in most of these investigations.

As might be expected, the benefits of attractiveness carry through to the negotiation table. Consistent with the idea of a "beauty premium," attractive people are offered more money, but also more is demanded of them (Solnick & Schweitzer, 1999).

The evaluation of an employment applicant can be affected by physical attractiveness as well (Dion, 1972). Attractive people are evaluated more positively and are treated better than unattractive people. Attractive communicators and salespeople are more effective in changing other people's attitudes than unattractive ones (Kiesler & Kiesler, 1969). For this reason, sales campaigns often feature an attractive person attempting to sell a product or service. Attractive people are often presumed to have other positive qualities as well; for example, they are regarded to be more poised, interesting, sociable, independent, dominant, exciting, sexy, well-adjusted, socially skilled, and successful than unattractive persons (Dion & Dion, 1987; Moore, Graziano, & Millar, 1987). This attribution of positive qualities to attractive people is part of the "halo effect" described in Chapter 6. The underlying message: Be aware of how your judgment (and others') is affected by physical appearance.

The Effects of Power on Those with Less Power

What are the psychological effects of those who have more power on those who have less power? In terms of perception and accuracy, those with less power are highly accurate in perceiving the behaviors and attitudes of those with higher power (Fiske & Dépret, 1996). This capability makes a lot of sense, especially because those of lesser power are dependent upon those of higher power for important organizational rewards. If someone is in a position to control a variety of organizational benefits that could dramatically affect your well-being, you would probably closely scrutinize his or her behavior. However, this greater accuracy may come at a price. Those who are low in power may exhibit signs of paranoia, believing that they are being constantly scrutinized and evaluated by those who are higher in power (Kramer & Hanna, 1988).

The Effects of Power on Those Who Hold Power

People who are high in power are often oblivious to people who have less power (Gruenfeld, Keltner, & Anderson, 1998). Presumably, people who are high in power have little or no reason to pay attention to those who are less powerful. After all, the powerful are in control of the situation, and the actions of those who are not as powerful have little effect on the high-power person's well-being. Consequently, those who have more power tend to be less accurate about the situation. In terms of negotiation, people who are higher in power (whether it is a legitimate form of power or not) may be less vigilant and thorough in collecting information from those of lesser power. Those with more power also engage in less "self-monitoring," meaning that they don't change their behavior to fit the situation (Snyder, 1974; Gruenfeld, Keltner, & Anderson, 1998). For example, in one investigation, highly powerful people were secretly videotaped as they interacted with less powerful people. The interchange took place at a social gathering where refreshments were being served. High-power people ate more and messier foods, which resulted in a disheveled appearance (Gruenfeld, Keltner, & Anderson, 1998). The more powerful people were less concerned with how they appeared to other people because they considered others' perceptions to be largely inconsequential. In contrast, those of lesser power engaged in a much higher level of monitoring their own behavior (i.e., ate less and were less messy in appearance).

PERSUASION TACTICS

You do not necessarily have to have power to be persuasive. Some negotiators are masters of attitude and behavior change. We identify techniques that negotiators can use to induce attitude and behavior change in their opponents. However, we need to caution negotiators that power can be used against them as well.

Two desires are especially important in negotiation: the need to be liked and approved of, and the need to be rational and accurate. Savvy negotiators prey upon people's need to be approved of and respected by others and their need to believe that they are rational and logical. Next, we identify two primary routes to persuasion that tap into these two needs.

Two Routes to Persuasion

The two routes to persuasion (Chaiken, Wood, & Eagly, 1996) roughly correspond to our distinction between the mind and the heart of the negotiator. The first route is called the *central route* to persuasion. The central route is direct, mindful, and information-based. Here, activities such as evaluating the strength or rationality of an opponent's argument and deciding whether its content agrees or disagrees with a negotiator's beliefs tend to occur. When an opponent's messages are processed via this central route, persuasion will occur, to the extent that the arguments presented by a negotiator are convincing and the facts marshaled on their behalf are strong ones. *The central route is ideal when dealing with analytical people who tend to focus on information, facts, and data.*

The other route is the *peripheral route* to persuasion. In contrast to the central route, little cognitive or mindful work is performed when attempting to persuade someone via the peripheral route. Rather, persuasion, when it occurs, involves a seemingly automatic response to various cues. Typically, the cues relating to a person's prestige, credibility, or likability are the ones that will be successful when navigating the peripheral route. Persuasion is more likely to occur through the peripheral route when the negotiator is distracted or highly emotionally involved in the situation.

The central and peripheral routes create two different "languages" by which to negotiate and persuade: The central route is rational, direct, cognitive, and information-based; the peripheral route is emotional and motivational. In the next sections, we deal with tactics that can be used via the central route and via the peripheral route. Again, we caution negotiators that all of these tactics can and probably will be used against them at some time in their negotiation career. Therefore, when describing each of these tactics, we indicate a defense strategy that a negotiator can use if he or she suspects that a particular tactic is being used against him or her. However, it is worthwhile to note that the best defensive system is awareness of these tactics and excellent preparation prior to entering into a negotiation.

Central Route Persuasion Tactics
Central route persuasion tactics involve rational and deliberate strategies that can be used to organize the content and flow of information during a negotiation.

The Power of Agenda
In a negotiation, players explicitly or implicitly follow an agenda. Most commonly, negotiators discuss the issues in a one-by-one, "laundry list" fashion. Negotiations often concern who controls the agenda. Tom Smerling, Washington director of the Israel Policy Forum, a group that supports an active U.S. role in Middle East peace talks, notes that virtually every international negotiation starts with a quarrel over the agenda (*USA Today*, Jan. 5, 2000).

As we indicated in Chapter 4 on integrative negotiation, we strongly dissuade negotiators from considering issues one at a time. Rather, it is through the *packaging of issues* that integrative opportunities can be discovered. Nevertheless, the savvy negotiator may use the power of agenda not only to expand the pie, but to slice the pie in a manner favorable to himself or herself. The negotiator who lays out the issues in a way that reflects his or her own highest priorities may be more likely to achieve gains on his or her high-priority issues.

Defense   It is a good idea to discuss what may seem to be an implicit or unspoken agenda (e.g., "I get the sense that you have an agenda of how you would like to cover the issues. I would like to hear your ideas and then tell you mine. Maybe we can come up with an agenda that makes sense for both of us, after hearing each other out.").

The Power of Alternatives
Negotiators who are able to generate alternatives within each of the issues may have a bargaining advantage because they formulate alternatives that benefit themselves. Obviously, an infinite number of alternatives may be possible for any given bargaining situation; the savvy negotiator will specify alternatives that are most favorable to himself or herself.

Defense   You do not need to be too much on the defensive if your opponent is laying out the alternatives. This factor is helpful for you in trying to assess your opponent's needs and interests. Make sure that you have thought about your own alternatives and get those on the table.

The Power of Options
In our chapter on integrative bargaining (Chapter 4), we strongly advocated that negotiators generate several options, all of equal value to themselves. The negotiator who takes control of generating options is at a power advantage in the negotiation.

Defense   If you find your opponent suggesting several options, it is actually good news because it suggests that your opponent is not a positional negotiator. However, make sure that you do not offer unilateral concessions. The best way to avoid making unilateral concessions is to generate several options to present to the other party.

Attitudinal Structuring

If a negotiator suspects that an opponent has an uncertain or unspecified BATNA, he or she can influence the opponent's perception of his or her BATNA. Thus, a negotiator may manipulate his or her opponent into revealing his or her BATNA.

Defense   The best strategy to use when an opponent attempts to manipulate your perception of your own BATNA is to have researched your BATNA and developed your reservation price well before entering into the negotiation. We frequently witness instances in which a negotiator is manipulated into revealing the BATNA when an opponent makes the assumption that the negotiator's BATNA is weak. As an example, consider the following interchange between negotiators:

NEGOTIATOR A: You know, it is really a buyer's market out there. I would strongly suggest that you think about my offer [on your house] before you turn it down. There may not be any more buyers for a while.

NEGOTIATOR B: Actually, I have received a lot of interest on my house.

NEGOTIATOR A: In this market? That does not sound very likely to me. In fact, my sister is selling her house, and she has not had an offer yet.

NEGOTIATOR B: Actually, just last week, a buyer from out of state saw my house and said he would most likely make an offer of $230,000 this week. You can ask my agent about it, if you do not believe me.

NEGOTIATOR A: That is so interesting. Just last night my husband and I decided that we would most likely offer $231,000 for your house . . . imagine that!

From this interchange, we see that negotiator A was successful in getting negotiator B to reveal her BATNA by putting her on the defensive.

The Power of Contrast

Negotiators may often invent and present irrelevant alternatives for their opponent to consider. Often, the negotiator who proposes these irrelevant alternatives knows the other party will find them unacceptable, but psychologically, these alternatives can create a **contrast effect**. As an example of how the contrast effect works, consider the behavior of some real estate agents (see Cialdini, 1993). Agents who want a prospective buyer to make an offer on a house may show the buyer several houses. They will arrange a house-shopping day such that they first show the prospective buyer some "doghouses" that may have been on the market for several months, are extremely unattractive, or are overpriced. The buyer may become somewhat depressed at the sight of these houses or at the high price tags they carry. At this point, the agent will show the buyer the houses that he or she really expects the buyer to consider. This tactic creates a psychological contrast effect because the potential buyer will look upon these houses much more favorably than the more dilapidated, overpriced alternatives and will be more motivated to make an offer. In negotiation, contrast is often used when an opponent makes an extreme initial offer and then follows with an offer that appears more reasonable. Acceptance rates of the second offer are higher when it follows the initial extreme offer.

Defense   The best defense against the contrast effect is a well-formed target point set prior to negotiation. For example, the prospective home buyer should research the market enough to realize what value is available. In many negotiation situations, it is wise to counter a low offer made by the opponent with your target point. At all costs, negotiators need to avoid making premature concessions—concessions that they make before they have tried to get what they want.

Commitment and Consistency

The **consistency principle** is the fundamental need to be consistent in our beliefs, feelings, and behaviors, not only to others, but also to ourselves. To contradict ourselves, whether in thought or in deed, is a sign of irrationality. Thus, savvy negotiators will often attempt to get a verbal commitment from their opponent.

What are the implications of the consistency principle for the negotiator? If a negotiator agrees to something (i.e., particular set of terms, etc.), he or she is motivated to behave in a fashion consistent with his or her verbal commitment. A common bargaining ploy of salespeople is to ask customers about their intentions to buy (for example, "Are you ready to buy a car today at the right price?"). Most people would agree to this statement because it does not obligate them to buy a particular car. However, powerful psychological commitment processes begin to operate once we acknowledge ourselves to be a "buyer."

Defense   Be careful what you agree to. If a car seller asks whether you are ready to buy a car, do not immediately say "Yes!" but rather, "That depends on how things go in terms of finding what I want and the terms I want."

Framing Effects: Capitalizing on the Half-Full or Half-Empty Glass

As we saw in Chapter 2, people are risk-averse for gains and risk-seeking when it comes to losses. Recall that the **reference point** defines what a person considers to be the status quo from which gains and losses are evaluated. Savvy negotiators know that if they want to induce their opponent to maintain the status quo—that is, induce risk aversion or conservatism—they should present options as gains relative to a reference point. Similarly, if they want to induce change, they frame choices as losses.

Defense   Determine your reference point prior to entering into a negotiation to avoid being "framed."

Fairness Heuristics: Capitalizing on Egocentric Bias

Fairness is a hot button in negotiation. To the extent that negotiators can characterize their offer as "fair," they increase the likelihood that it will be accepted by the other party. However, multiple indexes and measures of fairness exist.

Defense   Be aware of the many rules of fairness (e.g., equity, equality, and need). When an opponent puts forth a fairness ploy, the negotiator should be ready to present a counterargument that is favorable to and consistent with one's own perceptions of fairness (see Chapter 3).

Time Pressure

Common intuition has it that the negotiator who is under the most time pressure is at a disadvantage in a negotiation. Whereas it is true that the negotiator who needs to come to an agreement more quickly (because his or her BATNA may deteriorate with time) is at a disadvantage, time limits may be an advantage for the negotiator (Moore, 2004).

Defense   Remember, the party who has the deadline in effect sets the deadline for the other party. Set a limit on how long you will negotiate. A final deadline limits the potential time-related costs. If you face a final deadline, whether or not you set it yourself, make sure that those with whom you are negotiating know about the time constraint it puts on them. If they want any deal at all, they will have to work to come up with an agreement before the deadline (Moore, 2004).

Peripheral Route Persuasion Tactics

The strategies we describe next work through a fundamentally different mechanism—people's inherent need to be liked, approved of, and respected by others. The negotiator who uses the following strategies manipulates an opponent's sense of his or her own identity and, through these strategies, attempts to change the opponent's behavior. Marshaling defense strategies is more difficult in the case of peripheral route persuasion tactics, because they often catch us off guard. A good defense is an awareness of common strategies.

Delayed Liking

Should you show your liking for the other party immediately or wait awhile? In terms of gaining compliance from the other party, it is far more effective to *grow* to like the other party (Aronson & Linder, 1965). The most effective type of liking—in terms of getting what you want from someone—is to not like the other person immediately. Rather, people who *grow* to like someone are more effective in getting what they want than if they show their liking for the other person immediately. For example, consider an investigation of evaluative feedback in which people were given one of four types of evaluations by a peer: completely positive, initially negative and then positive, relentlessly negative, and initially positive and then negative. The recipient of the evaluation feedback was then asked to indicate how much he or she liked the other party. Liking was highest for the other party who was initially negative and later became positive (Aronson & Linder, 1965).

To Err Is Human

Negotiators are naturally suspicious of smooth-talking and attractive negotiators. Therefore, it is important to show your opponent that you are human and have your own foibles and faults. Showing the other person that you have flaws may endear you to them. For example, in one investigation, people listened to someone who was highly competent (i.e., got 92% of difficult exam questions correct). During a subsequent interview, it was revealed that this person was also very competent in other areas—an honor student, editor of the yearbook, and excellent at sports. In another situation, people heard the same person, but this time, he spilled coffee on himself during the interview. Even though the person had identical qualifications in both instances, when he made the human error (spilling coffee), he was liked much more than when he was "perfect." In fact, liking increased by 50 percent (Aronson, Willerman, & Floyd, 1966).

Priming the Pump

People's judgments and behaviors are affected by **unconscious priming**, which refers to the impact that subtle cues and information in the environment have on our behavior (at a level below our conscious awareness).

Consider the following hypothetical scenario: You and a business associate are formulating strategy for the next round of negotiations with an important client. The two of you are discussing your strategy at a local bar, where a big-screen TV is broadcasting a particularly vicious boxing match. You and your associate are not really watching the fight but hear the referee's calls and description of the action in the background. You notice that your associate talks about "packing a punch" and "hitting below the belt" and you wonder whether the social context is affecting your associate's judgment about negotiation. You suggest that the two of you walk down the street to the Honey Bear Cafe; the local music that night is a folk group called Brotherly Love. As the two of you are sipping coffee, your associate once again starts talking about the upcoming negotiations. You listen as he talks about "harmony" and "building a community" and wonder again whether features of your location are influencing your friend's judgment. This scenario illustrates how people are often manipulated by cues in the environment that act as primes. Sometimes these cues are random or naturally occurring products of the environment (such as in the bar); sometimes they may be "planted" (by a savvy negotiator). Obviously, it is important to understand how priming certain aspects of the situation may affect our own behavior.

Reinforcement

Although people may not be aware of it, simple, nonverbal gestures such as nodding, smiling, and eye contact are forms of social reinforcement. When negotiators offer these reinforcements to their opponent when the opponent is saying things that the negotiator finds acceptable, but withholds reinforcement at other points during the negotiation, they may be successful in manipulating the behavior of the opponent. Consider, again, the interpersonal prowess of Madeleine Albright. Conservative Southern politicians like Republican Sonny Callahan generally have little in common with liberal Democrats like Albright, that is, until she turns on the charm via reinforcement. During a Chamber of Commerce dinner in Mobile, Alabama, Callahan presented Albright with a personally autographed copy of the book *Forrest Gump* by Winston Groom. Albright instinctively knew that she should reinforce the bond, and she told the crowd, "Well, taking a line out of this book, dealing with Sonny is a little bit like having a box of chocolates. You never know what you're going to get, but with Sonny you always know you've got a very sweet center" (*National Journal*, June 3, 2000).

Social Proof

In the movie *When Harry Met Sally*, Sally (Meg Ryan) is having lunch with Harry (Billy Crystal) and demonstrating how women can fake sexual pleasure. An older woman at a nearby table sees Sally moaning in ecstasy and tells the waitress, "I'll have what she's having." The woman used the principle of social proof to guide her own behavior.

According to the **social proof principle**, we look to the behavior of others to determine what is desirable, appropriate, and correct. This behavior is sensible in many respects; if we want to get along with others, it only makes sense to know what they expect. However, this fundamental psychological process can work against us in negotiations if we look toward others—especially our opponent—to determine an appropriate offer or settlement. For example, new-car dealers target the neighbors of recent customers. Bartenders often "seed" their tip jars, and church ushers "prime" collection baskets with coins. Social proof is why advertisers use the slogans "largest-selling" and "fastest-growing." One tactic, called the *list technique*, involves making a request after a target person has been shown a list of similar others who have already complied. For example, college students and homeowners donated money or blood to a charitable cause in much greater numbers when shown a list of others who had already done so (Reingen, 1982). People do not realize the extent to which our behavior is influenced by those around us. Further, the more ambiguous the situation, the more likely we are to rely on situational cues and the behavior of others to tell us what to do.

Reactance Technique

Reactance technique (also known as *reverse psychology* or the *boomerang effect*) refers to people's innate need to assert their individual freedom when others attempt to take it away (Brehm, 1983). Negotiators can use an interesting form of reverse psychology to extract what they want and need from their opponent. (*Warning*: This technique can be extremely risky to use; we argue that negotiators practice with it before negotiating so as not to make fatal errors.)

One strategy for getting a "reaction" from your opponent is to paraphrase their position in a way that makes it sound more extreme than it actually is. For example, consider the following interchange that occurs after two hours of a negotiation in which each negotiator has stopped making concessions:

NEGOTIATOR A (*with deep sincerity and respect*): So, what you seem to be saying is that you have put your best offer on the table. That is your final best offer; there are no other possibilities of any kind. Your offer is a line drawn in the sand.

NEGOTIATOR B (*looking slightly perplexed*): Well, no, it is not entirely like that. I have tried to be clear about my company's position and feel committed to achieving our goals. And the final offer I made reflects my company's goals.

NEGOTIATOR A (*with resignation*): I respect a person who makes a commitment, who draws a line in the sand and who will not move an inch from that position. Who has the resolve to stick to his guns, and the tenacity and firmness of an army and . . .

NEGOTIATOR B (*interrupting negotiator A*): Look, I am not drawing a line in the sand, or anything like that. I am a reasonable person, and I am willing to consider reasonable offers.

NEGOTIATOR A (*looking incredulous*): You mean you have the power and the freedom to create more options? I was under the impression that you were tied to your position . . .

NEGOTIATOR B (*somewhat defensively*): Well, of course, I can do anything I want here—within reason. I can come up with other alternatives.

NEGOTIATOR A (*with interest*): I am most interested in hearing about your ideas.

Foot-in-the-Door Technique

In the **foot-in-the-door technique**, a person is asked to agree to a small favor or statement (such as agreeing with a question like "Are you ready to buy a car today at the right price?" or signing a petition). Later, the same person is confronted with a larger request (e.g., buying a car or voting with a particular coalition in a departmental meeting). The probability that the person will agree to the larger request increases when the person previously agreed to the smaller request (Beaman, Cole, Preston, Glentz, Steblay, 1983). This strategy plays upon people's need to demonstrate consistent behavior.

Door-in-the-Face Technique

Another strategy for gaining compliance is called the **door-in-the-face technique** (or the **rejection-then-retreat tactic**) in which a negotiator starts off the negotiation by asking for a very large concession or favor from the other party—one that the opponent is almost certain to refuse (Cialdini, 1975). When the refusal occurs, the negotiator makes a much smaller request, which is, of course, the option they wanted all along. We described this principle in Chapter 3, which admonishes negotiators to state high aspirations. The high aspiration creates a contrast effect, in that the opponent views any request that is less extreme than the original to be more reasonable.

That's-Not-All Technique

Many negotiators engage in the **that's-not-all technique** (also known as **sweetening the deal**) by offering to add more to a negotiated package or deal. For example, car dealers often add options to the car in question as a "deal closer." Evidence suggests that the that's-not-all technique actually works: In a study involving a bake sale, when patrons asked about cupcake prices and were told that two cupcakes cost $0.75, 40 percent bought the cupcakes. However, when they were told that one cupcake cost $0.75 and another cupcake would be "thrown in" for free, 73 percent bought the cupcakes (Burger, 1986).

ETHICAL NEGOTIATION

The distributive aspect of negotiation may create incentives for people to violate ethical standards of behavior. Some hard and fast rules dictate what is ethical in negotiation, but more often, negotiators must deal with many shades of gray. Ethics are a manifestation of cultural, contextual, and interpersonal norms that render certain strategies and behaviors unacceptable. According to Robinson, Lewicki, and Donahue (2000) negotiators evaluate tactics on a continuum of "ethically appropriate" to "ethically inappropriate" when deciding whether to use tactics. We address the question of what behaviors are regarded as unethical or questionable in negotiations, what factors give rise to them, and how to develop personal ethical standards.

Lying

More than anything else, lying is regarded to be unethical (as well as illegal in some cases). A given statement may be defined as *fraudulent* when the speaker makes a knowing misrepresentation of a material fact on which the victim reasonably relies and which causes damage. Unpacking this definition, we find several key aspects to lying: (1) The speaker is aware that he or she is misrepresenting information (2) regarding a material fact. The other party (3) relies on this fact, and (4) by doing so is damaged in some way—economically or emotionally. Consider the case in which a New York City landlord told a prospective tenant that if he did not rent the condo, the landlord would rent it immediately to someone else. In this situation, the landlord misrepresented interest in the apartment; the tenant relied on this fact to make a lease decision and was economically damaged.

Using this standard of lying, let's examine some of the key concepts we have discussed thus far, namely: positions, interests, priorities, BATNAs, reservation prices, and key facts.

1. ***Positions:*** In a negotiation, positions are largely subjective demands made by one party to another, and therefore, negotiators are under no obligation to truthfully state their position. For example, a prospective employee negotiating a job contract may tell the employer that she feels entitled to a salary of $100,000 per year, when in fact, she is willing to accept $85,000. Note that this negotiator is not lying about her BATNA, nor is she implying that she has another job offer; she is just stating that she feels entitled to $100,000.

2. ***Interests:*** In negotiation, it is generally assumed that people are self-interested with no "general duty of good faith." Specifically, according to the U.S. Court of Appeals, 7th Circuit:

> In a business transaction, both sides presumably try to get the best deal. That is the essence of bargaining and the free market. . . . No legal rule bounds the run of business interest. So, one cannot characterize self-interest as bad faith. No particular demand in negotiations could be termed dishonest, even if it seemed outrageous to the other party. The proper recourse is to walk away from the bargaining table, not sue for "bad faith" negotiations. (*Feldman v. Allegheny International, Inc.,* 1998)

3. ***Priorities and preferences:*** With regard to priorities, just like interests, a negotiator is entitled to his or her preferences, however idiosyncratic they might be; further, a negotiator misrepresenting his or her interests is not a material fact.

> "Estimates of price of a value placed on the subject of a transaction and a party's intentions as to an acceptable settlement of a claim" are not material facts for purposes of the rule prohibiting lawyers from making false statements to a third person. (Model Rules of Professional Conduct of the American Bar Association, 2004)

You can appreciate the complexities of sharing (or failing to share) information with the following example: Consider two people who have been hired to act as a project team in a company. The two associates (*A* and *B*) are given a large office to share, and they begin to arrange their workplace. The office contains two desks, and the only window can be enjoyed from one of the desks. A conversation between *A* and *B* reveals that *A* wants the desk with the window view and is ready to make sacrifices on other joint resources to get it—like giving up the close parking space and the storage areas. Unbeknownst to *A*, *B* has a terrible fear of heights; the window overlooks a steep precipice outside, and frankly, *B* prefers the other desk that is near an attractive saltwater aquarium. *B* considers not mentioning her true preference, hoping that she can *appear* to make a sacrifice, and so extract more resources. This strategy is known as **passive misrepresentation** because a negotiator does not mention true preferences and allows the other party to arrive at an erroneous conclusion. Now, imagine that *A* surprises *B* by asking her point-blank which desk *B* prefers—the one by the windows or the aquarium. Does *B* lie about her preferences? If so, she commits an act of **active misrepresentation** if she deliberately misleads her opponent. The strategic manipulation ploy is used about 28 percent of the time (O'Connor & Carnevale, 1997).

4. ***BATNAs:*** As stated in Chapter 2, a negotiator's BATNA is an objective state of affairs and therefore *is* material and subject to litigation. The message: Don't make up offers that don't exist! Negotiators who make up offers that don't exist (or even allude to them) are bluffing. According to Lewicki (1983), a bluff can be a false promise or false threat. A false promise (e.g., "if you do *x*, I will reward you") and a false threat (e.g., "if you do not do *x*, I will punish you") are false in the sense that the person stating the threat does not intend to or cannot follow through.

5. ***Reservation prices:*** As stated in Chapter 2, a negotiator's reservation price is the quantification of a negotiator's BATNA. Thus, a negotiator's stated reservation price (the least or most at which he or she will sell or buy) is not a material fact per se, and thus, while it may be reprehensible to lie about one's reservation price, it is not unethical, legally speaking.

6. ***Key facts:*** The falsification of erroneous, incorrect information is unethical (and subject to punishment). For example, a home seller who does not disclose known foundation problems in a house is guilty of falsification. Consider the charges being brought by Chrysler shareholder Kirk Kerkorian against DaimlerChrysler regarding their "merger" (*BusinessWeek*, Nov. 24, 2003b). According to Kerkorian, Daimler's CEO, Jürgen E. Schrempp promoted the $36 billion deal as a "merger of equals" rather than a "takeover." Although the wording may seem to be a trivial difference, it had an important consequence for Chrysler shareholders, who owned nearly 14 percent of the company at the time: They were not paid a takeover premium. In fact, their shares have lost 56 percent of their value.

Other Questionable Negotiation Strategies

In addition to lying about positions, interests, preferences, priorities, BATNAs, reservation prices, or material facts, some people have cited at least five other behaviors as unethical:

- **Traditional competitive bargaining:** In an analysis of MBA students' perceptions of unethical behavior, traditional competitive bargaining behavior, such as hiding one's real bottom line, making very high or low opening offers, and gaining information by asking among one's contacts, was considered to be unethical (Lewicki & Robinson, 1998). Indeed, self-rated "aggressive" negotiators are more accepting of such tactics than are self-rated "cooperative" negotiators (Lewicki & Robinson, 1998).
- **Manipulation of an opponent's network:** This tactic involves an attempt to weaken an opponent's position by influencing his or her associate or constituency. For example, consider how state labor unions attempted to use access to social networks to defeat an antitax initiative in the state of Washington (*Seattle Times*, Apr. 4, 2002). Labor union groups sent e-mails, pretending to be from campaign supporters who were requesting petitions, signs, and stickers. The idea was to get the protax group to waste a lot of money and time sending people pamphlets, stickers, and other items that would ultimately be thrown away. The political director of the Washington State Labor Council, Diane McDaniel said, "It will cost [the other side] valuable campaign resources to mail hundreds and possibly thousands of packets."
- **Reneging on negotiated agreements:** In many important negotiations, deals are closed without formal contracts. For example, even in the purchase of houses and

cars, an understanding is often reached before official papers have been signed. Even after formal contracts are signed, a period of recision exists, wherein either party can legally exit from the agreement. However, considerable disagreement and ethical debate concerns the issue of whether parties have a right to renege on an agreement once an informal closing (such as a handshake) has occurred.

- **Retracting an offer:** According an unwritten rule, once a negotiator puts an offer on the table, he or she should not retract it. This action would be bargaining in bad faith. Even so, negotiators may need to retract offers because a mistake has been made: For example, a department store publishes winning lottery numbers, but a typo was made, and a large number of people believe themselves, mistakenly, to be winners (see Sidebar 7-3). However, what the offering negotiator may see as a mistake is often viewed by the recipient negotiator as bargaining in bad faith.

- **Nickel-and-diming:** The strategy of continually asking for "just one more thing" after a deal has presumably been closed is annoying to most people. Most people are reluctant to make concessions when they fear that the other party will continue to prolong negotiations. Negotiators are more likely to make concessions if they feel that they will be successful in closing the deal. Thus, it is often an effective strategy to inform the other party of the terms you need to make the agreement final. Even better, prepare the official paperwork and indicate that you will "sign today" if your terms are met. The prospect of closing a deal is often enough of an enticement for negotiators to agree to the terms proposed by the other party.

Sidebar 7-3. Retracting an Offer

On November 5, 1999, the *New York Daily News* printed the wrong numbers in a Scratch 'N' Match lottery game. The *News*, citing game rules, said it would not honor "false winners," but it did announce that they would award the day's regular sum of $192,500 in prizes by holding a drawing the next month between all who sent in winning game cards. Not surprisingly, calls of anger and frustration flooded the hotline and telephone system, and people swarmed the lobby of the *News* building in New York. An elderly security guard in the building was punched and suffered a black eye, and irate game players threatened lawsuits (*New York Times*, Nov. 6, 1999).

Sins of Omission and Commission

It is widely believed that sins of commission (active lying) are more unethical than sins of omission (failing to provide information, see Box 7-1). After all, a negotiator could claim that the opponent did not "ask the right questions" or that she did not think the information was relevant. For an example of the complexity of sins of omission, consider the scenario in Box 7-2. It is possible to withhold information and not be regarded as unethical, but willful shielding from material information does not exculpate the negotiator. In other words, a businessperson should not refuse to see company reports in order to maintain a stance that the company is in financial health.

BOX 7-1

LESSONS IN THE ART OF SPIN

Offer Candor, Not Truth. "Fleischer never promises the whole truth. He only promises to say what he knows. That way, the White House can withhold the truth by limiting what Fleischer knows. On January 10, he announced that two Cabinet secretaries had recently discussed Enron's financial situation with Enron executives. When reporters asked why he was just now admitting this fact after they had inquired 'for weeks about contacts between the company and the President and the administration,'

Fleischer explained that he had just found out and that 'every question you've asked me before. . . was about the President. I speak for the President.' A reporter then asked whether Cheney had talked to Enron executives. 'Nothing that was brought to my attention or that I'm aware of,' said Fleischer. So if it turns out that Cheney had such conversations, reporters can't accuse Fleischer of lying. He's blameless. The fact that he's also useless is their problem, not his." (*Slate*, Jan. 23, 2003)

Note: For more on Arie Fleisher, see http://slate.msn.com/?id=2061084.

BOX 7-2

SINS OF OMISSION

A couple interested in purchasing a house had almost all aspects of a deal worked out. The realtor was aware that the couple would have strongly preferred to make an offer on House B, which had sold in the previous month to someone else and, therefore, had not been on the market when the couple was house shopping. The realtor showed the couple House A, and the couple made an offer on it, which was accepted. Prior to the closing on House A, House B came on the market again, due to a set of completely unforeseeable circumstances. The realtor was aware that House B was now on the market, but did not inform the couple prior to their closing on House A. It was only following the closing (and

after a 7.5 percent commission was paid to the realtor) that the realtor informed the couple that House B was now on the market and asked the couple whether they wanted to put their newly purchased House A on the market and purchase House B.

Did the agent engage in unethical behavior? In the eyes of the real estate agent, because House B was not officially listed, and because the couple did not inquire about whether House B was on the market, he did not engage in unethical behavior. In the eyes of the couple, it was unethical for the realtor not to inform them that their preferred house had become available when it did.

Costs of Lying

Senator Sam Ervin remarked that, "the problem with lying is you have to remember too damn much" (Senate Watergate Hearings, 1974). Several costs, or disadvantages, are associated with lying, the first of which is that the liar can be caught and face criminal charges. Even if the liar is not caught, one's reputation and trustworthiness can be damaged. This event, when it happens repeatedly, can then lead to an entire poisonous culture in which everyone in the organization lies and general suspiciousness increases. Lying also may not be strategic: Because a negotiator who lies about his or her reservation price effectively decreases the size of the bargaining zone, the probability of impasse increases.

Under What Conditions Do People Engage in Deception?

It is not clear how often or what factors trigger the use of deception in negotiation. To help shed light on this issue, we conducted a survey of MBA students enrolled in a negotiations class. We asked students to describe the conditions under which they personally would engage in deception (defined as lying) in negotiations. Somewhat surprisingly, most people were able to identify situations in which they would lie. Only two people out of 47 said that they would never deceive. More than 25 percent said that they would use "white lies" or exaggerations in nearly any negotiation. The most common reason for lying is when we think the other party is lying (see Figure 7-1 on page 172).

Psychological Bias and Unethical Behavior

Ethics are often a problem in negotiations, not so much because people are inherently evil and make trade-offs between profit and ethics or fail to consider other people's interests and welfare, but rather because of psychological tendencies that foster poor decision making (Messick & Bazerman, 1996). People may often *believe* they are behaving ethically, but due to self-serving tendencies, problems result and negotiators cry foul. Some of the human biases that give rise to ethical problems in negotiation are the illusion of superiority, illusion of control, and overconfidence (see Messick & Bazerman, 1996).

- **Illusion of superiority:** People tend to view themselves and their actions much more favorably than others view them (Taylor & Brown, 1988). People tend to focus on their positive characteristics and downplay their shortcomings. In relative terms, people believe that they are more honest, ethical, capable, intelligent, courteous, insightful, and fair than others. It is likely that Frank Quattrone, the previous head of CSFB's technology investment banking business, fell prey to the illusion of superiority in his fascination with risk and thirst for power.
- **Illusion of control:** People tend to think that they have more control over events than they really do. For example, in games of chance, people often feel that they can control outcomes (Langer, 1975). Obviously, this thinking can lead to a type of gambler's fallacy in decision making. However, it can also give rise to ethical problems, such as when people make claims of quality control that cannot be met.
- **Overconfidence:** Most people are overconfident about their knowledge. For example, when people are asked factual questions and then asked to judge the probability that their answers are true, the probability judgments far exceed the actual accuracy measures of the proportion of correct answers. On average, people claim to be 75 percent certain, when they are actually correct only

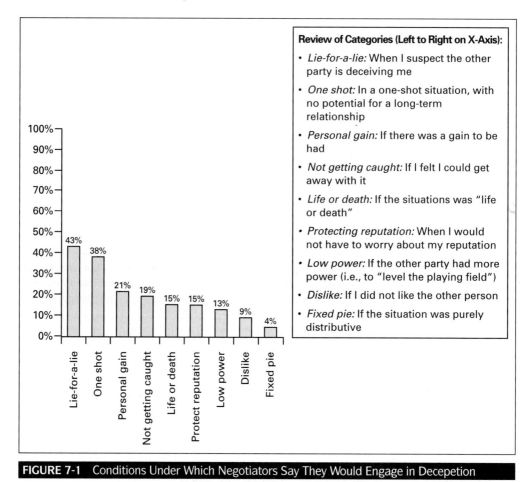

Review of Categories (Left to Right on X-Axis):

- *Lie-for-a-lie:* When I suspect the other party is deceiving me
- *One shot:* In a one-shot situation, with no potential for a long-term relationship
- *Personal gain:* If there was a gain to be had
- *Not getting caught:* If I felt I could get away with it
- *Life or death:* If the situations was "life or death"
- *Protecting reputation:* When I would not have to worry about my reputation
- *Low power:* If the other party had more power (i.e., to "level the playing field")
- *Dislike:* If I did not like the other person
- *Fixed pie:* If the situation was purely distributive

FIGURE 7-1   Conditions Under Which Negotiators Say They Would Engage in Decepetion

60 percent of the time (Fischhoff, Slovic, & Lichtenstein, 1977). And, people who have unmet goals (presumably because of overconfidence) are more likely to engage in unethical behavior (Schweitzer, Ordóñez, & Douma, 2004).

Given that our judgments of ethical behavior will be biased, how can negotiators best answer the question of whether a given behavior is ethical? Consider the following:

1. **The front-page test:** The front-page test, or light-of-day test, poses the following ethical challenge to negotiators: Would you be completely comfortable if your actions and statements were printed in full on the front page of the local newspaper or were reported on the TV news? If not, then your behavior or strategies in question may be regarded as unethical. Another version: "How would I feel if I had to stand before a board of inquiry and describe what I have done?"

2. **Reverse Golden Rule:** The Golden Rule states, "Do unto others as you would have them do unto you." In this strategy, the negotiator asks himself or herself, "If the tables were turned, how would I feel if my opponent did this to me?" If the answer is "I wouldn't like it very much," then it means that the behavior in question may be regarded as unethical.

3. ***Role modeling:*** "Would I advise others to do this?" or "Would I be proud to see my child act this way?" or "What if everyone bargained this way? Would the resulting society be desirable?"

4. ***Third-party advice:*** It is wise to consult a third party—someone who takes an impartial view of the negotiation—to see how that person regards your planned behavior. When consulting the third party, do not reveal your own vote. Describe the event or situation in third-person.

5. ***Strengthen your bargaining position:*** Negotiators who have prepared adequately will be less tempted to lie. For example, a negotiator who initiates efforts to improve her BATNA does not need to lie about her BATNA. A negotiator who has thought about the factors that affect his reservation price can simply inform the other party, "It's none of your business." And, a negotiator who has considered the facts can express an "opinion" based on the facts.

CONCLUSION

A negotiator's BATNA is the most important source of power in a negotiation. Having said that, effective use of power is not simply the threat of exercising one's BATNA. The enlightened negotiator knows that a larger slice of the pie can be gotten by creating a larger pie. We outlined two types of influence strategies that appeal to the mind and heart, respectively. The mindful strategies are based upon strategic use of information and include controlling the agenda, generating alternatives within issues, generating options across issues, attitudinal structuring and persuasion, consistency, and strategic framing. The psychological strategies we discussed included delaying liking, a certain degree of self-effacing behavior, strategic priming, reinforcement, social proof, reactance, foot-in-the-door, door-in-the-face, and that's-not-all.

All negotiators need to be concerned about ethical behavior in negotiation and know that, as with everything else, we don't always see our actions the way others see them. We discussed the moral and strategic disadvantages of lying with respect to the six things that negotiators most often lie about (positions, interests, priorities, BATNAs, reservation prices, and key facts). We discussed how the illusion of superiority, the illusion of control, and overconfidence might contribute to a negotiator's decision to engage in deception. We suggest that negotiators engage in five "tests" when struggling to decide whether a given behavior is ethical: the front-page test, reverse Golden Rule, role modeling, third-party advice, and strengthening their bargaining position.

8

CREATIVITY AND PROBLEM SOLVING IN NEGOTIATIONS

In 1991, two West Coast energy producers found a new way to help Columbia River salmon and improve Southern California's dirty air without spending a dime. Southern California Edison Co. and the Bonneville Power Administration entered into an agreement in 1991 that helped to protect young salmon in the Pacific Northwest. Under the agreement, Bonneville Power increased its release of water in the Columbia River during the summer, and Edison accepted the hydroelectric power that was generated. The flows helped young salmon swim through reservoirs more quickly, as large numbers of these fish get lost or eaten in slack water. In the fall and winter, Edison returned the power it borrowed from Bonneville. This arrangement meant that the company wouldn't need to run oil and coal-fired plants during the summer. This exchange of about 200 megawatts of power, enough for about 100,000 households, improved the downstream migration of young salmon in the river. It enhanced Southern California air quality by reducing the need to operate fossil fuel power plants during the smoggy summer months. Edison said that the arrangement cut the amount of pollution entering the Los Angeles basin by about 46 tons, the equivalent of taking about 5,000 cars off the highways. In this creative agreement, no money changed hands (*The Oregonian,* Mar. 7, 1991).

CREATIVITY IN NEGOTIATION

The creative aspect of negotiation is too often ignored by negotiators, who fixate on the competitive aspect of negotiation. This tendency is largely driven by the pervasive **fixed-pie perception,** or the belief that negotiation is a win-or-lose enterprise. Even negotiators who believe in win-win potential frequently misconstrue "expanding the pie" to mean compromising, rather than a true joint gain process. Successful negotiation requires a great deal of creativity and problem solving, and the process of slicing the pie can be a lot easier when the pie has been enlarged via creative and insightful problem-solving strategies, such as in the case of Bonneville Power and Edison. This chapter is the "advanced course" in integrative bargaining—using problem solving and creativity to reach win-win outcomes.

This chapter provides the means by which negotiators can transform their negotiations into win-win enterprises. For starters, we invite negotiators to put their problem-solving skills and creativity to the test. Then we take up the topic of creativity in negotiation and what creative negotiation agreements look like. Next, we consider the biggest threats or killers of creative problem solving in negotiations. We conclude by offering an "exercise regimen" for keeping your creative mind sharp for a variety of managerial activities including, but not limited to, negotiation.

Test Your Own Creativity

Box 8-1 contains 13 problems. Take 30 minutes right now to try to solve these problems. When in doubt, make your best guess, but make an honest attempt at solving each problem. As you go along, make a mental note of your thoughts about each problem as you try to solve it. Read the rest of the chapter before you look up the answers in Box 8-7 (at the end of this chapter). As you read the chapter, see whether any insights come to you and make note of them.

WHAT IS YOUR MENTAL MODEL OF NEGOTIATION?

Interviews with managers, the research literature, and the most popular published books on negotiation reveal five distinct mental models of negotiation, including "haggling," "cost-benefit analysis," "game playing," "partnership," and "problem solving" (Thompson & Loewenstein, 2003). Negotiators' mental models shape their behavior. In other words, if I approach negotiation as a "dog-eat-dog" enterprise, I am going to be much tougher than if I approach negotiation as a "partnership." As you read about these five mental models, think about which one best characterizes how you approach negotiation.

Haggling

Probably the most common mental model of negotiation is what we call the *haggling model*. The image this approach might conjure up is of two dogs fighting over one bone. For example, Joe Bachelder, who negotiates contracts for top corporate executives, is a haggler. "From a small conference room he calls 'the cave,' Mr. Bachelder will haggle on the phone for hours to win multimillion-dollar executive-pay packages, which sometimes evoke astonishment or anger when made public. On a given day, he may battle for something as major as a chief executive's $19 million pension plan or as minute as a client's right to take home office photos if fired. 'Joe is relentless,' says John Wood, an executive recruiter at Spencer Stuart. 'He will go back repeatedly on issues until he gets as much as he can'" (*The Wall Street Journal*, June 25, 2003, para. 3). Resolution in this model comes down to a struggle between two parties, in which each is trying to obtain the biggest share of the pie. The haggling model is based upon a fixed-pie perception of negotiation.

BOX 8-1

CREATIVITY TEST

CARD DECISION[1]

Look at the following numbers/letters. Each number/letter represents a card. On each of the four cards, a letter appears on one side and a number on the other. Your task is to judge the validity of the following rule: "*If a card has a vowel on one side, then it has an even number on the other side.*" Your task is to turn over only those cards that have to be turned over for the correctness of the rule to be judged. What cards will you turn over? [*Circle those cards that you will turn over to test the rule.*]

    E   K   4   7

PERSON IN A ROOM DECISION[2]

A person has been chosen at random from a set of 100 people, consisting of 30 engineers and 70 lawyers. What is the probability that the individual chosen at random from the group, Jack, is an engineer?

"Jack is a 45-year-old man. He is married and has four children. He is generally conservative, careful, and ambitious. He shows no interest in political and social issues and spends most of his free time on his many hobbies, which include home carpentry, sailing, and mathematical puzzles."

Jack is [*circle one*]:
an engineer   a lawyer

BETTING DECISION[3]

Which gamble would you rather play? [*Circle either A or B.*]

A: 1/3 chance to win $80,000

B: 5/6 chance to win $30,000

Now, imagine that you have to choose one of the following gambles. Which one will you play? [*Circle either C or D.*]

C: 50% chance to win $10,000 and 50% chance to lose $10,000

D: $0

WATER JUGS[4]

You have been given a set of jugs of various capacities and unlimited water supply. Your task is to measure out a specified quantity of water. You should assume that you have a tap and a sink so that you can fill jugs and empty them. The jugs start out empty. You are allowed only to fill the jugs, empty them, and pour water from one jug to another. As an example, consider problems #1 and #2:

Example Problem#	Capacity of Jug A	Capacity of Jug B	Capacity of Jug C	Quantity Desired
1	5 cups	40 cups	18 cups	28 cups
2	21 cups	127 cups	3 cups	100 cups

---

[1]Wason, P. C., & Johnson-Laird, P. N. (1972). *Psychology of Reasoning: Structure and Content.* Cambridge, MA: Harvard University Press.

[2]Kahneman, D., & Tversky, A. (1973). On the psychology of prediction. *Psychological Review, 80,* 237–251.

[3]Tversky, A., & Kahneman, D. (1981). The framing of decisions and the psychology of choice. *Science, 211,* 453–458.

[4]Luchins, A. S. (1942). Mechanization in problem solving. *Psychological Monographs, 5*(46), whole no. 248.

To solve problem #1, you would fill jug A and pour it into B, fill A again and pour it into B, and fill C and pour it into B. The solution to this problem is denoted by **2A + C.**

To solve problem #2, you would first fill jug B with 127 cups, fill A from B so

that 106 cups are left in B; fill C from B so that 103 cups are left in B; empty C and fill C again from B so that the goal of 100 cups in jug B is achieved. The solution to this problem can be denoted by **B-A-2C.**

Real Problems

Problem #	Capacity of Jug A	Capacity of Jug B	Capacity of Jug C	Desired Quantity	Solution
1	14	163	25	99	
2	18	43	10	5	
3	9	42	6	21	
4	20	59	4	31	
5	23	49	3	20	
6	15	39	3	18	
7	28	76	3	25	
8	18	48	4	22	
9	14	36	8	6	

STICK PROBLEMS[5]

You have six sticks, all of equal length. You need to arrange them to form four triangles that are equilateral and with each side one stick long. (You cannot break any sticks.) Indicate how you would do this.

LETTER SEQUENCE[6]

What is the next letter in the following sequence?

OTTFFSS___

GOLD CHAIN

Isaac is staying at a motel when he runs short of cash. Checking his finances, he discovers that in 23 days he will have plenty of money, but until then, he will be broke. The motel owner refuses to let Isaac stay without paying his bill each day, but because

Isaac owns a heavy gold chain with 23 links, the owner allows Isaac to pay for each of the 23 days with one gold link. Then, when Isaac receives his money, the motel owner will return the chain. Isaac is very anxious to keep the chain as intact as possible, so he does not want to cut off any more of the links than absolutely necessary. The motel owner, however, insists on payment each day, and he will not accept advance payment. How many links must Isaac cut while still paying the owner one link for each successive day?

_____links

SUSAN AND MARTHA

Susan and Martha are discussing their children when Susan asks Martha for the ages of her three sons. Martha says, "The sum of their ages is 13 and the product of

---

[5]Scheer, M. (1963). *Scientific American, 208,* 118–218.
[6]Letter sequence: Source unknown.

continued

their ages is the same as your age." Susan replies, "I still do not know their ages." What must Susan's age be?

   a. 24 b. 27 c. 63 d. 36 e. 48

NECKLACE[7]

A woman has four pieces of chain. Each piece is made of three links. She wants to join the pieces into a single closed ring of chain. To open a link costs 2 cents; to close a link costs 3 cents. All links are now closed. She has only 15 cents. How does she do it?

NINE DOT PROBLEM[8]

Consider the following nine dots. Draw four or fewer straight lines *without lifting your pencil from the paper* so that each of the nine dots has a line through it.

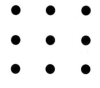

PIGPEN[9]

Nine pigs are kept in a square pen, as shown in the figure. Build two more square enclosures that would put each pig in a pen by itself.

WATERLILIES[10]

Water lilies on a certain lake double in an area every 24 hours. On the first day of summer, there is one water lily on the lake. On the sixtieth day, the lake is completely covered with water lilies. On what day is the lake half-covered?

BARTENDER PROBLEM[11]

A man walks into a bar and asks for a glass of water. The bartender points a shotgun at the man. The man says "Thank you," and walks out. What is going on in this situation?

---

[7]Wickelgren, W. A. (1974). *How to Solve Problems.* San Francisco, CA: W. H. Freeman.

[8]Weisberg, R. W., & Alba, J. W. (1981). An examination of the alleged role of "fixation" in the solution of several insight problems. *Journal of Experimental Psychology: General,* 110, 169–192.

[9]Fixx, J. F. (1972). *More Games for the Super-Intelligent.* New York: Warner Books.

[10]Sternberg, R. J., & Davidson, J. E. (1983). Insight in the gifted. *Educational Psychologist,* 18, 51–57.

[11]Dayton, T., Durso, F. T., & Shepard, J. D. (1990). A measure of the knowledge reorganization underlying insight. In R. W. Schraneveldt (Ed.), *Pathfinder Associative Networks: Studies in Knowledge Organization.* Norwood, NJ: Ablex.

Cost-Benefit Analysis

Some negotiators think of negotiation as a rational, decision-making model, in which they map out a cost-benefit analysis, and attempt to maximize their returns. For example, Robert Rubin, former U.S. Treasury secretary calculates the odds of almost every decision he faces, using both real and mental yellow pads (*Fortune*, Dec. 22, 2003). As a case in point, he once suggested to the board of the American Ballet Theatre, on which he sat, that it enact a cost reduction by cutting 10% of the swans in "Swan Lake."

Game Playing

The *game-playing model* of negotiation is a game of wits and nerve. It might very well be called a "poker game" mental model. The chess game model of negotiation elevates negotiation from "fighting in the streets" to battle of wits between two or more highly intelligent people. In game-playing, each person has his or her own interests in mind and, in many cases, a competitive motive, such that they attempt to beat the other party at the "game" of negotiation. This game is carried out, however, in an extremely civil and refined fashion. For example, Jerry Ford, CEO of First Nationwide Corporation is soft-spoken and genial, with an easy, self-confident demeanor. He is not the kind of negotiator to pound the table, raise his voice, or try to win by intimidation; he is respectful and a good listener. "With his adversary charmed and disarmed, he moves in for the kill" (*US Banker*, Feb. 1, 1997, p. 28). It's a formula that Ford has used repeatedly in 22 years of buying and selling banks and thrifts.

Partnership

A quite different mental model of negotiation is what we call the *partnership model*, which is often embraced by salespeople and companies that believe in treating their clients as partners. Negotiators who ascribe to the relationship model believe it is important to build rapport between people to nurture a long-term relationship, and in many cases, to make sacrifices in the name of creating long-term goodwill.

Problem Solving

The *problem-solving model* is a mental model of negotiation in which people consider negotiation to be the task of defining and solving a problem. In problem-solving negotiations, two people sit on the same side of the table and attempt to solve a puzzle together. This model focuses on the collaborative or cooperative aspects of the task, and involves a great deal of creativity, reframing of the problem, and out-of-the-box thinking.

We investigated negotiators' mental models and how they affect performance (van Boven & Thompson, 2003). First, negotiators who reach win-win outcomes have mental models that are more accurate about the other party's underlying interests compared to negotiators who fail to reach win-win outcomes. Second, comparison of the negotiators who reach win-win outcomes reveal that they have mental models that are more similar to one another than do negotiators who fail to reach win-win outcomes. In short, negotiators who craft win-win outcomes are literally thinking along the same lines. Finally, experience-based training was effective in helping negotiators to develop mental models that looked more like expert, win-win models; didactic lecturing was uniquely ineffective—a topic that we take up in detail in this chapter.

CREATIVE NEGOTIATION AGREEMENTS

Creativity in negotiation often follows the pattern of the "Monday morning quarterback," meaning that in hindsight, it is easy to see creative opportunity in negotiations; however, it often eludes us in the moment. Next, we outline the hallmark characteristics of truly creative negotiations (see also Pruitt & Carnevale, 1993).

Fractionating Problems into Solvable Parts

Most negotiation situations present themselves to us as single-issue negotiations (that is, until some creative negotiator finds a way to break the problem into smaller parts and, in the process of doing so, prioritizes the issues and trades them off) (Lax & Sebenius, 1986). The hallmark of a highly creative negotiated agreement is when negotiators can see integrative possibilities in a situation that appears to have only a single issue. Fractionating problems into solvable parts and creating multiple-issue negotiations from what appear to be single-issue negotiations is probably the most important aspect of creative negotiation (Lax & Sebenius, 1986). For example, consider how the negotiations between members of the United Food and Commercial Workers Local 175 and Wilfrid Laurier University avoided strike, even when they had a $300,000 deficit to deal with. They fractionated the bargaining issue from a single issue—wage increases—to several issues that included job security, controls over uniforms, parking fees, access to athletic facilities, and overtime costs (*Kitchener-Waterloo Record*, July 29, 2003). People are good at solving problems when the problems are presented directly to them; however, people are not very good at *defining* problems. Negotiation is mostly about defining a problem rather than solving it (i.e., searching for differences in such a way that trade-offs can be creative). Psychologists call this task **problem representation,** as opposed to problem solving, which is not to say that problem solving is not an important skill. Rather, how a negotiator frames a problem can either set limits or create important opportunities in the problem-solving process.

Finding Differences: Issue Alignment and Realignment

Before negotiators can find differences that can be traded off, they need to align the issues in such a way that permits the issues to be negotiated independently and, ideally, traded off (Lax & Sebenius, 1986). Linking issues creates a lot of constraints that limit negotiators' abilities to trade off issues. Ideally, negotiators should create issues that are **orthogonal** to one another, such that they can be traded off without having too many implications for other issues. Skilled negotiators know how to realign issues so as to find pockets of opportunity. Consider, for example, the negotiation between architect Daniel Libeskind and developer Larry Silverstein concerning the rebuilding of the World Trade Center site (*New York Times*, July 16, 2003a). By identifying additional issues and realigning issues, a negotiated agreement was reached, ending months of heated battles between Silverstein and Libeskind. The impasse centered on how much influence the architect (Libeskind) would have on the design of the first office building to go up at the site—the 1,776-foot tower that defines the rebuilt Trade Center's presence on the Lower Manhattan skyline. The developer (Silverstein) wanted to involve other architects for the largest tower and make changes to the master plan. An agreement was reached between the two by carving out another issue—namely, the development of commercial design guidelines governing future commercial development on the site. Libeskind won this issue. But Silverstein got to hire another firm to serve as design architect and project manager for the Freedom tower, the first commercial building to be constructed on site.

Expanding the Pie

Expanding the pie is an important method by which to create integrative agreements. When negotiators effectively expand the pie, they can avoid suboptimal compromise. Rather, the key is to find enough for all parties involved. At first glance, it may not seem that expanding the pie is a viable option in many negotiation situations. However, negotiators who labor under the fixed-pie perception may limit their options unnecessarily. Consider for example, how a negotiation between a fire station and elementary school was transformed from an impasse to a creative arrangement by expanding the pie (*Richmond-Times Dispatch*, Feb. 18, 1998). Initially, the school wanted to acquire land to expand, but the fire station blocked their move. So the pie was expanded such that each party paid an unrelated third party for a separate parcel of land. In the final deal, the city gave a three-acre parcel of land to a private owner, who then gave 7.5 of his own acres (located nearer to the school and fire station) back to the city. At this point, the fire station and the school successfully expanded the pie of available land to accomplish both of their goals. Thus, by expanding the pie to include another plot of land that could be "swapped," both parties ultimately achieved what they wanted—the school was able to expand and the firehouse could make its entrances and exits more convenient and safe.

Bridging
Oftentimes, it is not possible for negotiators to find a compromise solution, and expanding the pie does not work. Furthermore, perhaps neither party can get what they want in a trade-off that meets their interests. A **bridging** solution creates a new alternative that meets parties' underlying interests. Bridging alerts us to yet another reason to understand the other party's interests and to avoid positional bargaining. If negotiators understand the basic needs of their opponent, they are more likely to fashion bridging agreements. The opening example of the energy producers and the Pacific Northwest salmon is a bridging solution.

Cost Cutting
Sometimes, people are reluctant to negotiate because reaching a resolution seems costly to them. Most people are risk-seeking when it comes to loss, meaning that they are extremely reluctant to make concessions, and may behave irrationally when they believe they will have to make concessions. Cost cutting is a way of making the other party feel whole by reducing their costs. An example of value-added cost cutting occurred in the negotiations between the Nature Conservancy and the Great Northern Paper Company (National Public Radio, Aug. 28, 2002). On the surface, we might expect the interests of these two to be a classic fixed pie—the Nature Conservancy, dedicated to preserving everything from trees to water, should hardly want to work with a company that makes its money by cutting down trees for consumer and industrial use. Kent Wommack of the Nature Conservancy said, "In my 20 years with the Nature Conservancy, I have heard far too often from skeptics that environmentalists and the paper industry can never see eye to eye" (National Public Radio, Aug. 28, 2002). But in an unprecedented partnership, the Nature Conservancy assumed $50 million worth of Great Northern's debts. In return, Great Northern Paper agreed to protect a quarter-million acres from development.

Nonspecific Compensation
In a nonspecific-compensation negotiated agreement, one negotiator receives what he or she wants, and the other is compensated (or paid) by some method that was initially outside the bounds of the negotiation. For example, Phil Jones, managing director of

Real Time, the London-based interactive design studio, recalls an instance where he used nonspecific compensation in his negotiations. The problem was that his client, a Formula 1 motor-racing team, wanted to launch Internet Web sites but did not have the budget to pay him. However, in Phil Jones's eyes, the client was high profile and had creative, challenging projects that Real Time wanted to get involved with. Formula 1 came up with a nonspecific compensation offer to make the deal go through: tickets to some of the major Formula 1 meetings. It worked. Says Phil Jones: "The tickets are like gold dust . . . and can be used as a pat on the back for staff or as an opportunity to pamper existing clients or woo new ones" (*Management Today*, Nov. 1, 1998).

Structuring Contingencies

In 2003, a breakthrough gas deal was signed by Royal Dutch/Shell and Total Group in Saudi Arabia. Unlike previous arrangements, wherein gas companies made enormous financial commitments in return for limited access to Saudi hydrocarbons, Shell and Total agreed to spend $200 million over five years of exploration. If they found nothing, they could walk away. If they found oil, they could sell whatever gas they found and report the reserve on their books (*BusinessWeek,* Aug. 4, 2003a). The Shell-Total negotiation with the Oil Minister of Saudi Arabia is an example of a contingency contract.

Often, a major obstacle to reaching negotiated agreements concerns negotiators' beliefs about some future event or outcome (Lax & Sebenius, 1986). Impasses often result from conflicting beliefs that are difficult to surmount, especially when each side is confident about the accuracy of his or her prediction and consequently suspicious of the other side's forecasts. Often, compromise is not a viable solution, and each party may be reluctant to change his or her point of view. Fortunately, contingent contracts can provide a way out of the mire. With a **contingency** (or contingent) **contract,** differences of opinion among negotiators concerning future events do not have to be bridged; they become the core of the agreement (Bazerman & Gillespie, 1999). According to Bazerman and Gillespie, companies can bet on the future rather than argue about it. In some areas of business, contingency contracts are commonplace. For example, CEOs regularly agree to tie their salary to a company's stock price, and, in the textbook publishing business, royalty rates to authors are often tied to sales.

However, in many business negotiations, contingency contracts are either ignored or rejected out of hand for several basic reasons (Bazerman & Gillespie, 1999): First, people are unaware of how to construct contingency contracts. It often never occurs to people to bet on their differences when they are embroiled in conflict. Second, contingency contracts are often seen as a form of gambling, a high-risk enterprise. Third, no systematic way of thinking about the formulation of such contracts is usually available, meaning that they *appear* to be a good idea, but how to formalize and act upon them remains an enigma. Fourth, many negotiators have a "getting to yes" bias, meaning that they focus on reaching common ground with the other party and are reluctant to accept differences of interest, even when this might create viable options for joint gain (Gibson, Thompson, & Bazerman, 1994). In fact, most negotiators believe that differences of belief are a source of problems in a negotiation. The paradoxical view suggested by the contingency contract strategy states that differences are often constructive. With a contingency contract, negotiators can focus on their real mutual interests, not on their speculative disagreements (Bazerman & Gillespie, 1999). When companies fail to find their way out of differences in beliefs, they often go to court, creating expensive delays, litigation costs, loss of control by both parties, and deteriorating BATNAs. (For an example of how negotiators failed to use contingency contracts and suffered costs, see Sidebar 8-1.)

Sidebar 8-1. Failure to Use Contingency Contracts

"Consider how a contingent contract might have changed the course of one of the century's most famous and most fruitless antitrust cases. In 1969, the U.S. Department of Justice [DOJ] filed a suit against IBM, alleging monopolistic behavior. More than a decade later, the case was still bogged down in litigation. Some 65 million pages of documents had been produced, and each side had spent millions of dollars in legal expenses. The DOJ finally dropped the case in 1982, when it had become clear that IBM's once-dominant share of the computer market was eroding rapidly.

"During the case's thirteen futile years, IBM and the government had essentially been arguing over differences in their expectations about future events. IBM assumed that its market share would decrease in coming years as competition for the lucrative computer market increased. The government assumed that IBM, as a monopolist, would hold its large market share for the foreseeable future. Neither felt the other's view was valid, and so neither had a basis for compromise.

"An efficient and rational way to settle this dispute would have been for IBM and the government to have negotiated a contingent contract—to have placed a wager on the future. They might have agreed, for example, that if by 1975 IBM still held at least 70 percent of the market—its share in 1969—it would pay a set fine and divest itself of certain businesses. If, however, its market share had dropped to 50 percent or lower, the government would not pursue antitrust actions. If its share fell somewhere between 50 percent and 70 percent, another type of contingency would take effect.

"Constructing such a contingent contract would not have been easy. There were, after all, an infinite number of feasible permutations, and many details would have to have been hammered out. But it would have been far more rational—and far cheaper—to have the two sides' lawyers devote a few weeks to arguing over how to structure a contingent contract than it was for them to spend years filing motions, taking depositions, and reviewing documents."

Source: Bazerman and Gillespie, 1999, pp. 4–5.

Another wonderful feature of contingency contracts is that they provide a nearly perfect lie-detection device. In business negotiations, the fear of being deceived can be a major impediment to reaching agreements. Contingency contracts are a powerful method for uncovering deceit and neutralizing its consequences; they are particularly useful because they allow negotiators to test the opponent's veracity in a nonconfrontational manner, thereby allowing parties to save face. Contingency contracts also allow parties who are concerned about being cheated to safeguard themselves. This fear of being cheated is precisely what Christopher Columbus was worried about when he negotiated an agreement to the new world with Queen Isabella and King

BOX 8-2

THE SIX BENEFITS OF CONTINGENCY CONTRACTS

1. Contingency contracts allow negotiators to *build on their differences*, rather than arguing about them. Do not argue over the future. Bet on it.

2. Contingency contracts allow negotiators to *manage decision-making biases.* Although overconfidence and egocentrism can be barriers to effective agreements, contingency contracts use these biases to create a bet.

3. Contingency contracts allow negotiators to *solve problems of trust,* when one side has information that the other side lacks. The less-informed party can create a contingency to protect itself against the unknown information possessed by the other side.

4. Contingency contracts allow negotiators to *diagnose the honesty of the other side.*

When one party makes a claim that the other party does not believe, a bet can be created to protect a negotiator against the lie.

5. Contingency contracts allow negotiators to *reduce risk through risk sharing.* The sharing of upside gains and losses not only can reduce risk, but it can also create goodwill by increasing the partnership between the parties.

6. Contingency contracts allow negotiators to *increase the incentive of the parties to perform* at or above contractually specified levels. Contingency contracts should be specifically considered when the motivation of one of the parties is in question.

Source: Bazerman and Gillespie, 1999.

Ferdinand. Worried that he would risk life and opportunity and not gain anything, Christopher Columbus insisted that he be offered an opportunity to contribute one-eighth of the costs of future expeditions and be guaranteed one-eighth of all profits. Unfortunately, the crowns reneged on the deal upon his return, and Columbus had to go to court (*Investors' Business Daily*, Dec. 11, 1998).

By the same token, contingency contracts can build trust and good faith between negotiators, because incentives can be provided for each company to deliver exceptional performance. For example, when Phil Jones, Real Time's managing director, negotiated a deal with the Football Association (FA) for an e-commerce Web site dedicated to the U.K. bid for the 2006 World Cup, Real Time was responsible for the bid's logo and original Web site. "The FA have a limited budget to spend across a range of media, so I'm talking to them about perhaps receiving a percentage of what's sold from the new site. . . . That's really putting your money where your mouth is" (*Management Today*, Nov. 1, 1998, p. 128). Therefore, contingency contracts provide a safety net, limiting each company's losses should an agreement unexpectedly go awry. (For a summary of the benefits of contingency contracts, see Box 8-2.)

Although we believe that contingency contracts can be valuable in many kinds of business negotiations, they are not always the right strategy to use. Bazerman and Gillespie (1999) suggest three key criteria for assessing the viability and usefulness of contingency contracts in negotiation:

1. Contingency contracts require *some degree of continued interaction between the parties*. Because the final terms of the contract will not be determined until sometime after the initial agreement is signed, some amount of future interaction between parties is necessary, thereby allowing them to assess the terms of their agreement. Therefore, if the future seems highly uncertain, or if one of the parties is suspected of preparing to leave the situation permanently, contingency contracts may not be wise.

2. Parties need to think about the *enforceability* of the contingency contract. Under a contingency contract, one or more of the parties will probably not be correct about the outcome because the contract often functions as a bet. This outcome creates a problem for the "loser" of the bet, who may be reluctant to reimburse the other party when things do not go his or her way. For this reason, the money in question might well be placed in escrow, thereby removing each party's temptation to defect.

3. Contingency contracts require a high degree of *clarity* and *measurability*. If an event is ambiguous, nonmeasurable, or of a subjective nature, overconfidence, egocentric bias, and a variety of other self-serving biases can make the objective appraisal of a contingency contract a matter of some opinion. Thus, we strongly suggest that parties agree upfront on clear, specific measures concerning how the contract will be evaluated. For this reason, it is often wise to consult a third party.

THREATS TO EFFECTIVE PROBLEM SOLVING AND CREATIVITY

A variety of human biases and shortcomings can threaten a person's ability to think creatively. People think along particular, well-worn lines and are often impervious to new ideas and insights. Next, we illuminate the most common threats to effective problem solving and creativity and make suggestions on how to avoid them. A key first step to preventing these biases is *awareness* of their existence.

The Inert Knowledge Problem

People's ability to solve problems in new contexts depends on the accessibility of their relevant knowledge. Simply stated, if a manager is confronted with new business challenges, he or she often consults his or her knowledge base for previous problems that have cropped up in an attempt to see which previous problem-solving strategies might be useful in solving the new problem. The **inert knowledge problem** is the inability to access relevant knowledge when we most need it (Whitehead, 1929). Simply, the information necessary to solve a particular new problem is part of a manager's cognitive repertoire but is not accessible at the right time. This unavailability is not due to senility or amnesia, but rather, to the peculiar way that our long-term memories are constructed.

A striking dissociation occurs between what is most *accessible* in our memories and what is most *useful* in human problem solving and reasoning. People often fail to recall what is ultimately most valuable for solving new problems (Forbus, Gentner, & Law, 1995; Gentner, Rattermann, & Forbus, 1993). For example, consider an example from B. H. Ross (1987). People studied examples containing principles of probability theory and then attempted to solve problems requiring the use of those principles.

BOX 8-3

THE TUMOR PROBLEM

Suppose you are a doctor faced with a patient who has a malignant tumor in his stomach. It is impossible to operate on the patient, but unless the tumor is destroyed, the patient will die. A kind of ray can be used to destroy the tumor. If the rays reach the tumor all at once at a sufficiently high intensity, the tumor will be destroyed. Unfortunately, at this intensity, the healthy tissue that the rays pass through on the way to the tumor will also be destroyed. At lower intensities, the rays are harmless to healthy tissue, but they will not affect the tumor either. What type of procedure might be used to destroy the tumor with the rays and, at the same time, avoid destroying the healthy tissue? (Gick & Holyoak, 1980; adapted from Duncker, 1945)

If the study and test stories were from the same context, people were more likely to be reminded of them than if the stories were from different contexts.

In another example, participants were given a story to read about a hawk giving feathers to a hunter (Gentner, Rattermann, & Forbus, 1993). Participants were then given one of four stories resulting from the crossing of surface and structural similarity (i.e., a story with similar characters and plot, different characters but same plot, similar characters but different plot, or different characters and different plot). People were over four times more likely to recall this story when later shown a story with similar characters than when shown a story with different characters. The conclusion is that people often fail to recall what is ultimately most valuable for solving new problems (Forbus, Gentner, & Law, 1995; Gentner, Rattermann, & Forbus, 1993). Upon being informed of the correct approach to a negotiation, management students often express regret: "I knew that, I just did not think to use it."

Unfortunately, negotiators in the real world typically do not experience regret because they are not told when they have just made learning and application errors. Thus, the ability of managers to *transfer* knowledge from one context to another is highly limited. Transfer is the ability to apply a strategy or idea learned in one situation to solve a problem in a different, but relevant, situation. It is important to distinguish **surface-level transfer** from **deep transfer**. Surface-level transfer occurs when a person attempts to transfer a solution from one context to a superficially similar context. However, in most situations, it is desirable for people to apply solutions and strategies that have deep, meaningful similarities, rather than superficial ones. Unfortunately, this task proves quite difficult for most managers to do. In general, if two problems have similar surface (or superficial) features, managers are more likely to transfer knowledge from one problem situation to the other. Ideally, however, managers want to be able to transfer solutions to problems that have similar deep (or structural) features but that may have significantly different superficial features.

As a case in point, consider the "tumor problem" presented in Box 8-3. When presented with this problem, few people successfully solve it; if it is preceded by the fortress problem in Box 8-4, the solution rate rises dramatically (Gick & Holyoak,

BOX 8-4

THE FORTRESS STORY

A small country fell under the iron rule of a dictator. The dictator ruled the country from a strong fortress. The fortress was situated in the middle of the country, surrounded by farms and villages. Many roads radiated outward from the fortress like spokes on a wheel. A great general arose, who raised a large army at the border and vowed to capture the fortress and free the country of the dictator. The general knew that if his entire army could attack the fortress at once, it could be captured. His troops were poised at the head of one of the roads leading to the fortress, ready to attack. However, a spy brought the general a disturbing report. The ruthless dictator had planted mines on each of the roads. The mines were set so that small bodies of men could pass over them safely because the dictator needed to be able to move troops and workers to and from the fortress. However, any large force would detonate the mines. Not only would this blow up the road and render it impassable, but the dictator would destroy many villages in retaliation. A full-scale direct attack on the fortress therefore appeared impossible.

The general, however, was undaunted. He divided his army into small groups and dispatched each group to the head of a different road. When all was ready, he gave the signal, and each group charged down a different road. All of the small groups passed safely over the mines, and the army then attacked the fortress in full strength. In this way, the general was able to capture the fortress and overthrow the dictator (Gick & Holyoak, 1980; adapted from Duncker, 1945).

1980). Even though a similar solution can be applied in both problems, because the surface information in each problem is quite different (one deals with a medical situation; the other, a political situation), people are often unable to access their knowledge about one of these problems to help them solve the other.

The same problem occurs in negotiation. Studies of MBA students, executives, and consultants acquiring negotiation skills reveal a dramatic inert knowledge problem (Loewenstein, Thompson, & Gentner, 1999, 2003; Thompson, Loewenstein, & Gentner, 2000; Gentner, Loewenstein, & Thompson, 2003; for a review, see Loewenstein & Thompson, 2000). Transfer rates are quite low when a key principle needs to be applied to different negotiation situations that involve different surface features. For example, when people are challenged with a negotiation situation involving a theater company that contains the potential for a contingency contract, they are often unable to employ the principle of contingency contracts even when they have received extensive training on this principle in a previous negotiation case involving a different context, such as a family-owned farm. The reason why is that we tend to use our previous knowledge only when it seems similar to a new problem. People do not appear to be able to recognize problems that may benefit from similar problem-solving principles and strategies.

The obvious question is: What can decrease the inert knowledge problem and increase people's ability to transfer knowledge they possess when faced with a situation that could potentially benefit from that knowledge? One answer appears to be quite simple and powerful. It involves making an explicit comparison between two or more relevant cases (Thompson, Loewenstein & Gentner, 2000). To the extent that people mentally compare cases or situations, they are able to create a problem-solving schema that is uncluttered by irrelevant surface information. Thus, problem-solving schemas created through this process of mental comparison are more portable and more likely to be called upon when negotiators are challenged with a novel problem. In the absence of comparison, it is not clear to negotiators which information about a situation is relevant or irrelevant. Furthermore, as helpful as making comparisons can be, recognizing *when* to make them is not always obvious. For example, in our training of MBA students and executives, we frequently present negotiators with several training cases, usually on the same page. Very rarely did negotiators actively compare the cases printed on the same page, even though they contained a similar underlying principle. Thus, the key appears to be making comparisons among experiences, a strategy we elaborate upon later.

Availability Heuristic

Which is more common: Words that start with the letter *K*—for example, *king*—or words with *K* as the third letter—for example, *awkward* (Kahneman & Tversky, 1982)? In the English language, there are more than twice as many words with *K* as the third letter than there are words with *K* as the first letter. Despite this fact, the majority of people guess incorrectly, in that they assume that there are more words with *K* as the first letter, due to the **availability heuristic.** According to the availability heuristic, the more prevalent a group or category is judged to be, the easier it is for people to bring instances of this group or category to mind. This heuristic affects the quality of negotiators' judgments in that they may be biased by the ease with which information can be brought to mind. For example, in one investigation, people were presented with a list of 39 names of well-known people (Tversky & Kahneman, 1973). Nineteen of these people were female; 20 were male. The women on the list happened to be more famous than the men. Afterwards, people were asked to judge how many women's names appeared on the list. People dramatically overestimated the number of female names, presumably because they were easier to recall—another illustration of the availability heuristic.

The availability heuristic is associated with the **false consensus effect** (Sherman, Presson, & Chassin, 1984). The false consensus effect refers to the fact that most people think that others agree with them more than is actually warranted. For example, people who smoke estimate that 51 percent of others are smokers, but nonsmokers estimate that only 38 percent of people are smokers (Sherman, Presson, & Chassin, 1984). Furthermore, people overestimate the proportion of people who agree with them about their attitudes concerning drugs, abortion, seatbelt use, politics, and even Ritz™ crackers (Nisbett, Krantz, Jepson, & Kunda, 1995). When a negotiator falls victim to the availability heuristic, the likelihood of employing creative strategies (which are often less available) is severely undermined.

Representativeness

Imagine that you have just met your new boss. She is thin, wears glasses, is soft-spoken, and dresses conservatively. Later, you realize that you and your supervisor never discussed your hobbies and outside interests. Is your supervisor into reading books or sporting events? In answering such questions, people make judgments on the basis of a relatively simple rule: The more similar a person is to a group stereotype, the more likely he or she is to also belong to that group. Most people assume the supervisor is a book reader. Basically, the more a person *looks* like the stereotype of a group member, the more we are inclined to stereotype them as belonging to that group. The **represent-ativeness** heuristic is based on stereotypes of people, which may often have a basis in reality, but are frequently outdated and wrong. For example, when most people hear the name "Betty Pat McCoy," they assume she is from Texas and has big hair. However, she is a savvy advertising executive in charge of her agency's $700 million of media buying (*Advertising Age*, Oct. 1, 2001). Furthermore, reliance on stereotypical informa-tion can lead people to overlook other types of information that could potentially be useful in negotiations. The most important type of information is related to base rates. **Base rates** are the frequency with which some event or pattern occurs in a general population. For example, consider a negotiator interested in purchasing a new car. One source of information concerning the new car is a popular consumer report. This report is based upon thousands and thousands of consumer data and research and therefore is highly reliable. However, in addition to consulting this source, people interested in pur-chasing a new car often consult their neighbors and friends. Sometimes, a neighbor or friend may have had a personal experience with a car that is quite different from what is reported in the consumer report magazine. Oftentimes, however, people who consult their neighbors and friends will discount perfectly valid information (i.e., the base rate information) and choose to rely upon a single, vivid data point. This error is known as the **base rate fallacy.**

Faulty judgments of probability are associated with what is known as the **gambler's fallacy,** the tendency to treat chance events as though they have a built-in, evening-out mechanism. However, each event is independently determined. As an example, con-sider the following problem: Suppose you flip a coin and it comes up heads five times in a row. What do you think the next outcome will be? Most people feel that the prob-ability is high that the coin will come up tails. Actually, of course, the probability of a heads or tails outcome is always the same—50 percent—for each flip, regardless of the previous result. However, most people think that some sequences (such as heads, tails, heads, tails) are far more likely to occur than others (such as a string of heads or a string of tails; Tversky & Kahneman, 1974).

Anchoring and Adjustment

Job candidates are often asked by recruiters what their salary range is. The job candi-date, wanting to maximize his or her salary but at the same time not remove himself or herself from consideration because of unrealistic demands, faces a quandary. Similarly, the prospective home buyer struggles with what to make as an opening offer. What fac-tors determine how we make such assessments of value?

According to Tversky and Kahneman (1974), people use a reference point as an anchor and then adjust that value up or down as deemed appropriate. For example, a prospective job recruit may have a roommate who just landed a job with a salary of $80,000. The candidate decides to use $80,000 as a starting point. Two fundamental con-cerns arise with the anchoring-and-adjustment process. The first is that the anchors we use to make such judgments are often arbitrary (Tversky & Kahneman, 1974). Oftentimes, anchors are selected on the basis of their temporal proximity, not their relevance to the judgment in question. The second is that we tend to make insufficient adjustments away from the anchor; we are weighed down by the anchor. (Remember how people's estimates of the number of doctors in Manhattan were affected by their social security number!) The message for the negotiator is clear: Carefully select anchors, and be wary if your opponent attempts to anchor you.

Unwarranted Causation

Consider the following facts:

- Women living in the San Francisco area have a higher rate of breast cancer.
- Women of lower socioeconomic status are less likely to breast-feed their babies.
- People who marry at a later point in life are less likely to divorce.

Before reading further, attempt to explain each fact. When people are asked to do so, they frequently conclude the following:

- Living in San Francisco causes breast cancer.
- People of lower socioeconomic status are not given postnatal care.
- People become wiser as they grow older.

All of these explanations are reasonable, but they are all unwarranted based upon the information given. The tendency to infer a **causal relationship** between two events is unwarranted because we do not know the direction of causality (for example, it is possible that women with cancer are attracted to the Bay Area). Further, a third variable could be the cause of the event (people who marry later may be richer or more educated). Maybe older, more professional women are attracted to the Bay Area, and this group is statistically more susceptible to cancer. Maybe women of lower socioeconomic status are younger and less comfortable breast-feeding, more likely to be targeted by formula companies, or less likely to get maternity leave. The point is that each situation comes with a myriad of possible explanations.

Belief Perseverance

The perseverance effect is the tendency of people to continue to believe that something is true even when it is revealed to be false or has been disproved (Ross & Lepper, 1980). For example, imagine that you have taken an aptitude test and have been told you scored poorly. Later, you learn the exam was misscored. Are you able to erase this experience? Not if you are like most college students, who continue to persevere in their beliefs (Ross & Lepper, 1980). Why is this tendency so prevalent? Once a causal explanation is constructed, it is difficult to change it. If you or your negotiation opponent has an erroneous belief about the other, even when it is proven wrong, the belief may still prevail. The important implication is to carefully examine the beliefs you hold about your opponent and be cognizant of faulty beliefs they may have about you.

Illusory Correlation

Illusory correlation is the tendency to see invalid correlations between events. For example, people often perceive relationships between distinct pieces of information as a mere consequence of their being presented at the same time (Hamilton & Gifford, 1976). For example, in one investigation, people read diagnoses of mental patients

(Chapman & Chapman, 1967, 1969). Specifically, people were shown pictures allegedly drawn by these patients and then were given the patients' diagnoses to read. In actuality, there was no correlation at all between the types of pictures the patients allegedly drew and the nature of their diagnoses (paranoia, schizophrenia). Nevertheless, the people reviewing the evidence believed that they saw correlations—for example, between a diagnosis of paranoia and a drawing of a very large eye. Even when people are presented with contradictory or ambiguous evidence, they are extremely reluctant to revise their judgments. As another example, suppose you learn during the course of a negotiation with a business representative from country X that 60 percent of country X's male population is uneducated. Suppose that the same day you learn that 60 percent of crimes committed in that country are violent. Although no logical relation connects the two statistics, most people assume a correlation; that is, they assume that uneducated men from country X are responsible for violent crimes. In fact, no relationship exists between the two—it is illusory. Such correlations between separate facts are illusory because they lack an objective basis for the relationships. Rather, our implicit theories are constructed so that we interpret relations between temporally proximate events.

Just World

Most of us believe that the world is a fair place: People get out of life what they deserve and deserve what happens to them (Lerner, 1980). This mindset leads to positive evaluations of others who have good things happen to them; for example, most people believe that "good" people are likely to win lotteries. Unwarranted negative impressions are produced when others suffer misfortune; for instance, we assume that bad people or ignorant people are victims of crimes (Saunders & Size, 1986). **Blaming-the-victim attributions** are **defensive attributions** because they enable observers to deal with the perceived inequities in others' lives and maintain the belief that the world is just (Thornton, 1992). In short, if we believe that bad things could easily happen to us (e.g., dying in an airplane crash or losing a limb), the world is scary and less predictable.

Hindsight Bias

The **hindsight bias** refers to a pervasive human tendency for people to be remarkably adept at inferring a process once the outcome is known but be unable to predict outcomes when only the processes and precipitating events are known (Fischhoff, 1975). The hindsight bias, or the "I knew it all along" effect, makes integrative solutions to negotiation situations appear to be obvious when we see them in retrospect, although before they were discovered, the situation appeared to be fixed-sum.

We are frequently called upon to explain the causes of events, such as the demise of an organization or the success of a particular company. We often perceive events that have already occurred as inevitable. Stated another way, once we know the outcome of an event, we perceive the outcome to be an inevitable consequence of the factors leading to the outcome. This **creeping determinism** (Fischhoff, 1975) accounts for the "Monday morning quarterback" or the "I knew it all along" phenomenon. Therefore, once someone knows the outcome, the events leading up to it seem obvious. The hindsight bias also accounts for why negotiators often think integrative agreements are obvious after the fact but fail to see them when encountering a novel negotiation.

Functional Fixedness

Functional fixedness occurs when a problem solver bases a strategy on familiar methods (Adamson & Taylor, 1954). The problem with functional fixedness is that previously learned problem-solving strategies hinder the development of effective strategies in new situations. The person fixates on one strategy and cannot readily switch to another method of solving a problem. In other words, experience in one domain produces in-the-box thinking in another domain. Reliance on compromise as a negotiation strategy may produce functional fixedness.

The notion here is that past experience can limit problem solving. Consider the tumor problem presented in Box 8-3. The solution rate, when people are given the problem by itself, is 37 percent; however, when people are shown a diagram of an arrow going through a black dot and then given the problem, the solution rate drops to 9 percent (Duncker, 1945). The diagram of the arrow going through the black dot depicted the function of the X-ray as a single line going through the human body; thus, it blocked people's ability to think of several rays focused on the tumor. Functional fixedness occurs when people have a mental block against using an object in a new way in order to solve a problem. In another example, people are challenged with the problem of how to mount a candle vertically on a nearby screen to function as a lamp. The only materials they are given are a box of matches, a box of candles, and a box of tacks. The creative solution is to mount the candle on top of the matchbox by melting the wax onto the box and sticking the candle to it, then tacking the box to the screen. This elegant solution is much harder to discover when the boxes are presented to people filled with tacks (i.e., the way the boxes are normally used), rather than emptied of their contents (Anderson, 1995).

Set Effect

Closely related to the problem of functional fixedness is the **set effect,** in which prior experience can also have negative effects in new problem-solving situations. Also known as **negative transfer,** prior experience can limit a manager's ability to develop strategies that are of sufficient breadth and generality. Consider the water jug problem presented in Box 8-1. People who had the experience of working on all the water problems typically used a longer, costlier method to solve the problems. People without the experience of solving the problems almost always discovered the short, direct solution. Mechanized thought and set effects are the arthritis of managerial thinking and the wet blanket on the fires of creativity in negotiation.

Selective Attention

In negotiations, we are bombarded with information—the opponents' physical appearance, his or her opening remarks, hearsay knowledge, nonverbal behavior, and so on. However, we perceive about 1 percent of all information in our stimulus field (Kaplan & Kaplan, 1982). We perceive only a tiny fraction of what happens in the negotiation room. How do we know if we are paying attention to the right cues?

The basic function of our sensory information buffers is to parse and code stimulus information into recognizable symbols. Because external stimuli cannot get directly inside our heads, we cognitively represent stimuli as internal symbols and their interrelations as symbol structures. The sensory buffers—visual, auditory, and tactile—maintain the stimulus as an image or icon while its features are extracted. This activity occurs rapidly and below our threshold of awareness. The features extracted from a given stimulus object comprise a coded description of the object. For example, our interaction with a colleague concerning a joint venture is an event that is real, but our minds are not video cameras that record everything; rather, we use a process known as **selective attention.**

Overconfidence

Consider a situation in which you are assessing the probability that a particular company will be successful. Some people might think the probability is quite good; others might think the probability is low; others might make middle-of-the-road assessments. For the decision maker, what matters most is making an assessment that is accurate. How accurate are people in judgments of probability? How do they make assessments of likelihood, especially when full, objective information is unavailable?

Judgments of likelihood for certain types of events are often more optimistic than is warranted. The **overconfidence effect** refers to unwarranted levels of confidence in people's judgment of their abilities and the occurrence of positive events and underestimates of the likelihood of negative events. For example, in negotiations involving third-party dispute resolution, negotiators on each side believe the neutral third party will adjudicate in their favor (Farber, 1981; Farber & Bazerman 1986, 1989). Obviously, this outcome cannot happen; the third party cannot adjudicate in favor of both parties. Similarly, in final-offer arbitration, wherein parties each submit their final bid to a third party who then makes a binding decision between the two proposals, negotiators consistently overestimate the probability that the neutral arbitrator will choose their own offer (Neale & Bazerman, 1983; Bazerman & Neale, 1982). Obviously, the probability is only 50 percent that a final offer will be accepted; nevertheless, typically, both parties' estimates sum to a number greater than 100 percent. The message is to beware of the overconfidence effect. When we find ourselves to be highly confident of a particular outcome occurring (whether it be our opponent caving in to us, a senior manager supporting our decision, etc.), it is important to examine why.

The Limits of Short-Term Memory

Short-term memory is the part of our mind that holds the information currently in the focus of our attention and conscious processing. Unfortunately, short-term memory has severely limited capacity; only about five to nine symbols or coded items may be currently active. The "seven plus-or-minus two" rule extends to just about everything we try to remember (Miller, 1956). Consider, for example, an interaction you might have with the president of a company concerning the details of a consulting engagement. The president tells you many facts about her company; you will recall, on average, five to nine pieces of information. Without deliberate rehearsal, the information in your short-term memory will disappear and be replaced with new information perceived by your sensory registers. Obviously, we perceive much more information than we ultimately store and remember.

CREATIVE NEGOTIATION STRATEGIES

The following strategies are designed to sharpen your creative mind. Thus, they are not specific to negotiation; rather, they are an exercise program for enhancing creativity. Because negotiation, like exercise, is an activity we need to engage in regularly, these strategies can be extraordinarily beneficial for increasing creativity in negotiation.

Multiple Roads Lead to Rome (and an Expert Understanding)

In our research, we have carefully examined the ability of managers to apply what they learn in the classroom to their real life negotiations. The rates of "positive transfer" (applying knowledge learned in one situation to another) is markedly limited (Thompson, Loewenstein, & Gentner, 2000; Loewenstein, Thompson, & Gentner, 2003). Moreover, even the ability to benefit from our own direct experience is limited. For example, 100 percent of the respondents reading a negotiation case that contained win-win potential suggested (suboptimal) compromises (Gentner, Loewenstein, & Thompson, 2003). We have found dramatic evidence that when attempting to learn something new (e.g., a key strategy, a principle, etc.), it is important to have two (or more) cases or examples, rather than just one. The reason is clear: What is essential about any example or any case taught in a business school is not the details of the case, but rather the key underlying idea. The ability of a manager to separate the wheat from the chaff, or the core idea from the idiosyncrasies of the example, is limited if faced with only one case. In fact, our research indicates that one case is no more effective than no cases at all (Loewenstein, Thompson, & Gentner 2003). However, it is not enough to simply be presented with two cases; the manager needs to actively mentally compare the two cases. Moreover, even if the instructor does not provide more than one case, if the manager (or trainee) can think of examples from his or her own experience, it can help a lot.

Feedback

No one can get better without feedback. For example, even star golfers regularly seek feedback on their swings. And when it comes to learning, the more intense and pointed the feedback is, the better. For example, power golf guru Jim McLean charges $500 per hour to give business leaders like Henry Kravis, Charles Schwab, Ken Chenault, and David Rockefeller direct feedback on just how bad their swing looks (*Fortune*, Aug. 11, 2003c). His teaching style is simple and powerful: analyze, be direct, and focus on what needs work. Says McLean, "These [business] people are used to getting results on the job. They want the same from their golf games" (p. 126). If we consider the fact that a near-perfect correlation exists between our ability to negotiate and our ability to successfully run a company, doesn't it make sense to seek feedback on our negotiation ability?

Of course, we've put our money where our mouth is and have conducted the controlled, scientific investigations with regard to the importance of feedback for improving results, which showed a direct, causal effect of receiving feedback on the ability to improve (Thompson & DeHarpport, 1994; Nadler, Thompson, & van Boven, 2003).

The type and method of feedback matter. For example, in one investigation of business managers' negotiations, negotiators were given one of four types of feedback (allegedly from their opponent) following a negotiation, ranging from positive to negative, which focused on their abilities or their ethics (Kim, Diekmann, & Tenbrunsel, 2003).

- **Positive-ability feedback** (" . . . what a skilled negotiator you seemed to be.")
- **Negative-ability feedback** (" . . . what an unskilled negotiator you seemed to be.")
- **Positive-ethicality feedback** (" . . . what an ethical negotiator you seemed to be.")
- **Negative-ethicality feedback** (" . . . what an unethical negotiator you seemed to be.")

The key question was how the feedback would affect the performance of the negotiators in a subsequent negotiation situation. Negotiators who received the negative-ability feedback were the least competitive and achieved the worst individual performance. Negotiators who received the negative-ethicality feedback were the most honest. Negotiators who received the positive-ethicality feedback were the most cooperative (Kim, Diekmann, & Tenbrunsel, 2003).

In addition to the type of feedback that negotiators give to one another, we examined the type of feedback that a coach might give to a negotiator (Nadler, Thompson, & van Boven, 2003). We first measured managers' baseline performance in an initial negotiation. Then, we separated them into one of five different "feedback groups": no feedback (our scientific "control" condition); traditional lecture-style feedback (also known as "didactic feedback"); information-based feedback (wherein negotiators learned about other party's underlying interests); observational feedback (wherein negotiators got to watch experts-in-action via videotape for about 15 minutes); and finally, analogical learning (wherein negotiators were given relevant cases that all closed in on a single key negotiation skill). The results? Nearly everything is better than no feedback at all. And nearly anything is better than traditional, classroom-style, didactic learning. (See Figure 8-1; see also van Boven & Thompson, 2003, for another illustration of how experience-based training is better than instruction-based training.)

Creativity Templates

Jacob Goldenberg and his colleagues (Goldenberg, Nir, & Maoz, in press) have developed a method for stimulating creativity in product innovation that extends to negotiations. The Creative Negotiation Template approach enables a negotiator to identify and

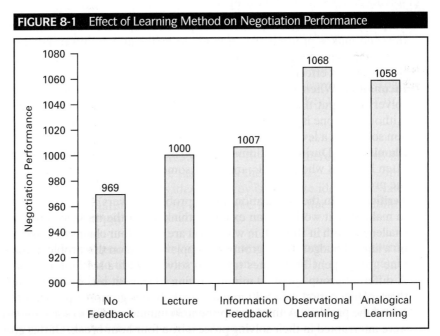

FIGURE 8-1   Effect of Learning Method on Negotiation Performance

Source: Reprinted by permission, J. Nadler, L. Thompson, L. van Boven. "Learning Negotiation Skills: Four Models of Knowledge Creation and Transfer," *Management Science,* 49(4), pp. 529–540. Copyright © 2003, The Institute for Operations Research and the Management Sciences, 901 Elkridge Landing Road, Suite 400, Linthicum, MD 21090 USA.

As a way of thinking about these three indexes of creativity, do the following exercise: See how many possible uses you can think of for a cardboard box. (Give yourself about 10 minutes for this exercise.) Suppose that one person who completed this exercise, Geoff, generated two ideas: using the box as a cage for a hamster and as a kennel for a dog. Geoff would receive two points for fluency of ideas because he offered two different ideas, but only one point for flexibility because the ideas are of the same category (i.e., a home for animals). Creative people generate more novel and unusual ways to use a cardboard box. Another person, Avi, generated these unusual ideas for a cardboard box: using it as a god, using it as a telephone (e.g., two boxes and some string), and trading it as currency. Avi would get a score of three points for fluency and three points for flexibility, because three separate categories of ideas for use, involving religion, communication, and economics were used. In addition, Avi's ideas are extremely original.

It is easy to see how flexibility in thought—that is, thinking about different categories of use—can influence originality. Thus, one simple key for enhancing creativity is to *diversify the use of categories*. By listing possible categories of use for a cardboard box (containers, shelter, building material, therapy, religion, politics, weaponry, communication, etc.), a person's score on these three dimensions could increase dramatically. Thus, a key strategy is to think in terms of *categories* of ideas—not just *number* of ideas. This approach can often help negotiators out of a narrow perspective on a conflict and open up new opportunities for creative solutions.

Brainstorming

Alex Osborn, an advertising executive in the 1950s, wanted to increase the creativity of organizations. He believed that one of the main blocks to creativity was the premature evaluation of ideas. He was convinced that two heads were better than one when it came to generating ideas, but only if people could be trained to defer judgment of their own and others' ideas during the idea generation process. Therefore, Osborn developed the most widespread strategy used by organizations to encourage creative thought: brainstorming.

Brainstorming is a technique used by a large number of companies and organizations to unleash the creative group mind and avoid the negative impact of group dynamics on creativity. The goal of brainstorming is to maximize the quantity and quality of ideas. Osborn aptly noted that quantity is a good predictor of quality: A group is more likely to discover a really good idea if it has a lot of ideas from which to choose, but brainstorming involves more than mere quantity. Osborn believed that the ideas generated by one person in a team could stimulate ideas in other people in a synergistic fashion.

Osborn believed that the collective product could be greater than the sum of the individual parts if certain conditions were met. Hence, he developed rules for brainstorming. Contrary to popular corporate lore that brainstorming sessions are wild and crazy free-for-alls where anything goes, brainstorming has defined rules (Osborn, 1957, 1963). They are still widely used today, and several companies post the brainstorming guidelines and roles prominently in their meeting rooms (see Table 8-1). However, people do not often use them for negotiations.

Convergent Versus Divergent Thinking

Two key skills are involved in creative thinking: divergent thinking and convergent thinking (Guilford, 1959, 1967). **Convergent thinking** is thinking that proceeds toward a single answer, such as the expected value of a 70 percent chance of earning $1,000 is

TABLE 8-1	Rules for Brainstorming

Expressiveness: Group members should express any idea that comes to mind, no matter how strange, weird, or fanciful. Group members are encouraged not to be constrained nor timid. They should freewheel whenever possible.

Nonevaluation: Do not criticize ideas. Group members should not evaluate any of the ideas in any way during the generation phase; all ideas should be considered valuable.

Quantity: Group members should generate as many ideas as possible. Groups should strive for quantity; the more ideas, the better. Quantity of ideas increases the probability of finding excellent solutions.

Building: Because all of the ideas belong to the group, members should try to modify and extend the ideas suggested by other members whenever possible.

Source: Adapted from Osborn, A. F. (1957). *Applied Imagination* (rev. ed.). New York: Scribner.

obtained by multiplying $1,000 by 0.7 to reach $700. **Divergent thinking** moves outward from the problem in many possible directions and involves thinking without boundaries. It is related to the notion of flexibility of categories and originality of thought. Divergent thinking *is* out-of-the-box thinking.

Many of the factors that make up creative problem solving seem most closely related to divergent thinking. However, ideas eventually need to be evaluated and acted upon, which is where convergent thinking comes in. In convergent thinking, a negotiator judges and evaluates the various ideas presented as to their feasibility, practicality, and overall merit.

People working independently excel at divergent thinking because no cognitive or social pressures constrain their thought. In short, they are not subject to conformity pressures. In contrast, people are much less proficient at divergent thinking. The key reasons have to do with conformity pressures. To avoid social censure, people assess the norms of the situation and conform to them. In contrast, groups excel compared to individuals when in comes to convergent thinking. Groups are better at judging the quality of ideas. This ability suggests that an effective design for promoting creativity in negotiation involves separating the generation of ideas—leaving this task to individual team members—and then evaluating and discussing the ideas as a team. (However, divergent thinking is not always looked upon favorably; see Sidebar 8-3.)

Sidebar 8-3. Divergent Thinking

Divergent thinking (or creative thinking) is often not rewarded in schools and organizations. For example, Getzels and Jackson (1962) observed that teachers prefer students who have high IQs but are not high in creativity. High-IQ students and managers tend to gauge success by conventional standards (i.e., to behave as teachers expect them to and seek careers that conform to what others expect of them). In contrast, highly creative people use unconventional standards for determining success, and their career choices do not usually conform to expectations. Most educational training, including that of MBAs, favors logical or convergent thinking and does not nurture creative or divergent thinking.

Deductive Reasoning

To be effective at negotiation, negotiators need to be good at deductive, as well as inductive, reasoning. First we take up the topic of **deductive reasoning,** or the process of drawing logical conclusions. For example, most people have some kind of training in solving logical syllogisms like the ones in Box 8-5. The difficulty in solving these syllogisms does not imply that managers are stupid; rather, it indicates that formal logic and individual (or psychological) processes are not necessarily the same. However, many people violate rules of logic on a regular basis. Some of the most common violations of the rules of logic are the following:

- **Agreement with a conclusion:** The desirability of the conclusion often drives people's appraisal of reality. This behavior, of course, is a form of wishful thinking, as well as an egocentric bias. The tendency is strong for people to judge the conclusions they agree with as valid, and the conclusions they disagree with as invalid.
- **Cognitive consistency:** People have a tendency to interpret information in a fashion that is consistent with information that they already know. The tendency for people to judge conclusions to be true, based upon whether the information agrees with what they already know to be true, illustrates the need for consistency in one's belief structure.
- **Confirmation bias:** People have a strong tendency to seek information that confirms what they already know. A good example of this bias is the card task presented in Box 8-1.

Inductive Reasoning

Inductive reasoning is a form of hypothesis testing, or trial and error. In general, people are not especially good at testing hypotheses, and they tend to use confirmatory methods. A good example is the card task in Box 8-1. Another example is the availability heuristic we discussed earlier, such that judgments of frequency tend to be biased by the ease with which information can be called to mind.

For example, people make inaccurate judgments when estimating probabilities. Consider the problem in Box 8-6 (Tversky & Kahneman, 1974). When people are asked to answer this question, 22 percent select the first answer (i.e., the larger hospital), 22 percent select the second answer (i.e., the smaller hospital), and 56 percent select the third answer (i.e., both hospitals). They seem to make no compensation for large versus small sample sizes. They believe that an extreme event—for example, 60 percent of births being male—is just as likely in a large hospital as in a small one. In fact, it is actually far more likely for an extreme event to occur within a small sample because fewer cases are included in the average. People often fail to take sample size into account when they make an inference.

In summary, managers do not form generalizations (reason inductively) in ways that statistics and logic suggest. When people make inferences about events based on their experience in the real world, they do not behave like statisticians. Rather, they seem to be heavily influenced by salient features that stand out in their memory, and they are swayed by extreme events even when the sample size is small.

BOX 8-5

SAMPLE SYLLOGISMS

Pick the conclusions that you can be sure of (Stratton, 1983):

1. All S are M. All M are P. Therefore,
   a. All S are P.
   b. All S are not P.
   c. Some S are P.
   d. Some S are not P.
   e. None of these conclusions is valid.

2. As technology advances and natural petroleum resources are depleted, the securing of petroleum from unconventional sources becomes more imperative. One such source is the Athabasca tar sands of northern Alberta, Canada. Because some tar sands are sources of refinable hydro-carbons, these deposits are worthy of commercial investigation. Some kerogen deposits are also sources of refinable hydrocarbons. Therefore:
   a. All kerogen deposits are tar sands.
   b. No kerogen deposits are tar sands.
   c. Some kerogen deposits are tar sands.
   d. Some kerogen deposits are not tar sands.
   e. None of the above.

3. The delicate Glorias of Argentina, which open only in cool weather, are all Sassoids. Some of the equally delicate Fragilas, found only in damp areas, are not Glorias. What can you infer from these statements?
   a. All Fragilas are Sassoids.
   b. No Fragilas are Sassoids.
   c. Some Fragilas are Sassoids.
   d. Some Fragilas are not Sassoids.
   e. None of the above.

If you think like most people, problem #1 is probably the easiest to solve (the answer is a). However, problems #2 and #3 generate much higher error rates (75 percent error rate for problem #2, with most errors due to picking answer c instead of e; 90 percent error rate for problem #3, mainly due to picking d instead of e).

BOX 8-6

THE HOSPITAL PROBLEM

A certain town is served by two hospitals (Tversky & Kahneman, 1974). In the larger hospital, about 45 babies are born each day, and in the smaller hospital, about 15 babies are born each day. As you know, about 50 percent of all babies are boys. However, the exact percentage varies from day to day. Sometimes it may be higher than 50 percent, sometimes lower. For a period of one year, each hospital recorded the days in which more than 60 percent of the babies born were boys. Which hospital do you think recorded more such days?

1. The larger hospital

2. The smaller hospital

3. About the same (within 5 percent of each other)

Flow

According to Csikszentmihalyi (1997), **autotelic experience,** or **flow,** is a particular kind of experience so engrossing and enjoyable that it becomes worth doing, even though it may have no consequences beyond its own context. Creative activities in life, such as music, sports, games, and so on, are typical sources for this kind of experience. Of course, people never do anything purely for its own sake—their motives are always a combination of intrinsic and extrinsic considerations. For example, filmmakers may make films for the joy of creating something artistic, but also because the film may make money or win an Academy Award™. Similarly, managers and executives create new products and ideas not only because they enjoy doing so, but because the products will make the company more profitable. However, if people are only motivated by extrinsic rewards, they are missing a key ingredient in terms of experience. In addition to the external rewards, they can also enjoy an activity, such as negotiation, for its own sake.

This kind of intense flow experience is not limited to creative endeavors. It is also found in the most mundane activities in the personal and business world, such as going to work every day, interacting with people, and so on. An important condition for the flow experience is that a person feels that his or her abilities match the opportunities for action. If the challenges are too great for a person's skill, intense anxiety, or **choking,** can occur. However, if the person's skills outweigh the challenges of the experience, he or she may feel bored. The message is that process is more important than the outcome of the interaction. In a negotiation, this effect of flow means that the process of working through differences, satisfying underlying needs, and creating value is more important than the content of the particular negotiation. To the extent that negotiation is viewed as unpleasant, uncomfortable, or a struggle, flow (and the creative process that can ensue from flow) is less likely to occur.

CONCLUSION

Effective negotiation requires creative thinking. The ability to think creatively is affected by a negotiator's mental model of negotiation. We identified five common mental models: haggling, cost-benefit analysis, game-playing, partnership, and problem-solving. We noted that creative negotiations include fractionating problems into several, simpler parts; finding differences to exploit; expanding the pie; bridging; cost cutting; nonspecific compensation; and structuring contingency contracts. We reviewed several of the biggest threats to creativity in negotiation, including the inert knowledge problem, availability bias, representativeness, anchoring and adjustment, unwarranted causation, illusory correlation, hindsight bias, functional fixedness, selective attention, and overconfidence. We described several strategies for re-thinking almost any negotiation problem, including feedback, incubation, brainstorming, divergent (as opposed to convergent) thinking, deductive as well as inductive reasoning, and psychological flow.

BOX 8-7

ANSWERS TO CREATIVITY TEST

CARD DECISION

Correct answer: E and 7

Averaging over a large number of experiments (Oaksford and Chater 1994), it has been found that 89 percent of people select E, which is a logically correct choice because an odd number on the other side would disconfirm the rule. However, 62 percent also choose to turn over the 4, which is not logically informative because neither a vowel nor a consonant on the other side would have falsified the rule. Only 25 percent elect to turn over the 7, which is a logically informative choice because a vowel behind the 7 would have falsified the rule. Only 16 percent elect to turn over K, which would not be an informative choice.

PERSON IN A ROOM DECISION

Correct answer: Jack is a lawyer.

This problem illustrates a classic base-rate problem. We are given information that the probability of any one person selected is equivalent to the stated base rates; the normatively appropriate solution is 30 percent, thus making it more likely that Jack is a lawyer. Yet, most people choose to ignore base rate information and assume that Jack is an engineer. An answer that goes against explicitly stated probability theory runs the risk of being one based on stereotypes. Groups may be more likely to defend the stereotype decision.

BETTING DECISION

Correct answer: A (for the first bet)

The normatively appropriate logic here is to use expected value theory, in which the expected value of a risky choice is determined by the value of the payoff multiplied by its probability. Using this technique, the expected value of bet A is $8 \times 0.3333 = \$2.66$. The expected value of bet B is ($3 \times 0.8333 = \$2.5$). Thus, bet A maximizes expected value. However, many people overweight high probabilities and end up choosing bet B. Groups tend to be riskier than individuals, so groups often choose riskier decisions, whether they are normatively appropriate or not. For the second bet, either answer is normatively correct because their expected values are the same.

WATER JUGS

Problem solvers can become biased by their experiences to prefer certain problem-solving operators in solving a problem. Such biasing of the problem solution is known as a set effect. Also known as the Einstellung effect, or mechanization of thought, this can paradoxically lead to worsened performance. The Einstellung effect involves remembering a particular sequence of operations, and it is memory for this sequence that is blinding managers to other possibilities. In this series of problems, all problems except 8 can be solved by using the B-2C-A method. For problems 1 through 5, this solution is the simplest, but for problems 7 and 9, the simpler solution of A + C also applies. Problem 8 cannot be solved by the B-2C-A method but can be solved by the simpler solution of A-C. Problems 6 and 10 are also solved more simply as A-C than B-2C-A.

Of the participants who received the whole setup of 10 problems, 83 percent

continued

used the B-2C-A method on problems 6 and 7, 64 percent failed to solve problem 8, and 79 percent used the B-2C-A method for problems 9 and 10. The performance of people who worked on all 10 problems was compared with the performance of people who saw only the last five problems. These people did not see the biasing B-2C-A problems. Fewer than 1 percent of these people used B-2C-A solutions, and only 5 percent failed to solve problem 8. Thus, the first five problems can create a powerful bias for a particular solution. This bias hurt solution of problems 6 through 10.

STICK PROBLEM

Correct answer: Form a tetrahedron (kind of like a pyramid)

Most people take the six sticks and form a square with an X in it. However, this solution is not acceptable because the triangles are not equilateral—each has a 90 degree angle. Another incorrect answer that is common is to form three of the sticks in a triangle and overlay them on another triangle upside down; this produces four triangles, but the sides of the triangle are not one stick in length. In order to solve the problem, the solver must think in three dimensions, making a pyramid with a triangle base. This is a general class of problem situations that often involve "insight"—a rearrangement of the parts in a certain way to solve a problem.

LETTER SEQUENCE

Correct answer: E

The answer to this Eureka problem is E. The letters are the first seven letters of the first eight digits: one, two, three, four, five, six, seven, and eight.

GOLD CHAIN

Correct answer: 2

The chain puzzle is a Eureka problem. Many groups answer 11 because that would involve cutting only every other link. The correct answer, however, is two. If the fourth and eleventh links are cut, all the values from 1 to 23 can be obtained by getting "change" back from the motel owner. Separate links (the fourth and the eleventh) are given on days 1 and 2, but on day 3, the three-link unit is given to the owner, who returns the separate links. These links are then used to pay on days 4 and 5, but on day 6, the six-link unit is used, and the owner returns the others as change. The process can be continued for 23 days.

SUSAN AND MARTHA

Correct answer: 36

This is a disjunctive decision task. It is a Eureka problem, and the answer must be calculated. Only 14 combinations yield a total of 13 (e.g., 1, 1, 11; 1, 2, 10; 1, 3, 9, etc.), and only two of these have the identical product (1, 6, 6 and 2, 2, 9). If we assume that Susan knows her own age, she would still be confused only if she were 36.

NECKLACE

Initially, people tend to break a link on each chain, attach it to another chain, and then close it. The more elegant (and cheaper) solution is to break a single three-link piece and use its links to attach others. It costs 6 cents to open three links. The total connection cost is 9 cents, yielding a 15-cent necklace.

NINE DOT PROBLEM

Correct answer: See Panels 3 and 4

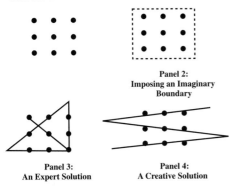

Panel 2:
Imposing an Imaginary
Boundary

Panel 3:
An Expert Solution

Panel 4:
A Creative Solution

Most people implicitly assume that the lines must be drawn within an imaginary boundary, as shown in the second panel of the diagram. One possible solution that is preferred by "experts" is given in the third panel of the diagram. The problem solver must go outside the self-imposed square boundary. Another creative solution uses lines that do not go through the center of the dots, as shown in the fourth panel of the diagram. This solution involves overcoming another self-imposed limit on the problem— namely, realizing that it is not necessary to draw the lines through the center of each dot. Thus, one major kind of conceptual block is the tendency to impose too many constraints on the problem (that is, to represent the problem in a way that limits the potential kinds of solutions). Overcoming the conceptual blocks is similar to overcoming functional fixedness or Einstellung; instead, look for alternative ways of representing the problem.

PIGPEN

Correct answer: See diagram

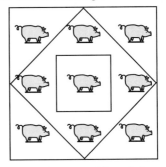

This is an "insight" problem. Most people assume that each pigpen must be square. The solution involves diamond-shaped pens.

WATERLILIES

Correct answer: Day 59

This is a pure "insight" problem. People initially approach the problem as one involving a linearly increasing quantity and simply divide the total time in half. However, because the lilies increase exponentially in area, this approach is incorrect, and another representation is called for. Such a change in representation can occur when the participant tries to imagine what happens as the pond fills up and he or she works backward from the last day, rather than carrying out a formal analysis of the problem.

BARTENDER PROBLEM

The man who walked into the bar had the hiccups. The bartender realized this and attempted to scare the daylights out of the man by pointing a gun at him. Some people are able to solve this problem immediately; others are not. This is a Eureka problem.

C H A P T E R

9

MULTIPLE PARTIES, COALITIONS, AND TEAMS

In May 2003, CEOs at every company on the *Fortune* 1000 and *Fortune Global 500* opened a letter to discover that they would be sued if anyone anywhere in their company had used Linux—the free, open-source operating system sweeping corporate IT departments. A little known company called SCO Group, headquartered in Lindon, Utah, had sent the letter. Two months earlier, SCO had filed a $1 billion lawsuit against IBM, claiming that Big Blue had taken chunks of SCO-owned Unix code and sprinkled it into Linux. According to Darl McBride, the CEO of SCO, some companies were misusing Unix code by inserting it into other programs they were using, a privilege they needed to pay SCO for in the form of an additional license. The leverage that SCO had in fighting IBM was by involving IBM's customers. The more SCO could scare Big Blue's customers, the more power SCO had. To make things more complicated, Ralph Yarro, the head of Canopy Group, owns 43 percent of SCO. Canopy, owned by Noorda, is made up of 35 start-up companies. When McBride got rebuffed by IBM, he flew to the Florida office of Boies, Schiller, and Flexner for a meeting with the anti-Microsoft litigator David Boies, who agreed to take up the case on a combination contingency-and-hourly-fee basis. In the meantime, Microsoft called BayStar Capital managing partner, Lawrence Goldfarb, to ask if he would consider investing in SCO (*Fortune,* July 21, 2003; *BusinessWeek,* Mar. 22, 2004).

The SCO negotiation illustrates the complexity of a multiparty negotiation. At the primary table are SCO and IBM. When IBM becomes a reluctant negotiator, SCO puts leverage on IBM's hidden or secondary table—its customers. SCO's second table includes the Canopy Group, which is an extension of Noorda, and BayStar Capital, which is connected to SCO. Additionally, agents and law firms are involved, which add more dynamics to the bargaining table.

Thus far, we have been in a two-party world of negotiation. In the opening example of this chapter, however, is a complex assortment of players. Some are negotiators; some are agents; others are constituents. Often, negotiation situations are not purely one-on-one situations. Often other people are at the table and behind the scenes. To negotiate effectively in groups, negotiators need all of the skills we have described thus far, and then some. We discuss the skills specific to multiparty negotiation in this chapter.

ANALYZING MULTIPARTY NEGOTIATIONS

How might we analyze the negotiation between SCO and IBM? The negotiation involves a myriad of players, relationships, and issues (see Figure 9-1). In the example in Figure 9-1, two principals are involved in the multiparty negotiation: SCO and IBM. Noorda, the Canopy Group, and BayStar Capital are potential principals. A coalition may include SCO and Microsoft, SCO and IBM customers, or IBM and the law firm of Boies, Schiller, and Flexner. Further, other companies are in similar positions as IBM (in terms of receiving the letter) and may act as coalition partners. Negotiations within and between organizations are embedded in an intricate web of interdependent relationships and interests. Just as a complete understanding of human anatomy requires analyses at the levels of cell chemistry, tissues, organs, and organ systems, a complete understanding of negotiation within and between organizations requires analysis at several levels (Thompson & Fox, 2000).

In this chapter, we review six levels of analysis beyond one-on-one negotiation: (1) multiparty negotiations; (2) coalitions; (3) principal-agent relationships;

FIGURE 9-1 SCO-IBM Negotiations Structure

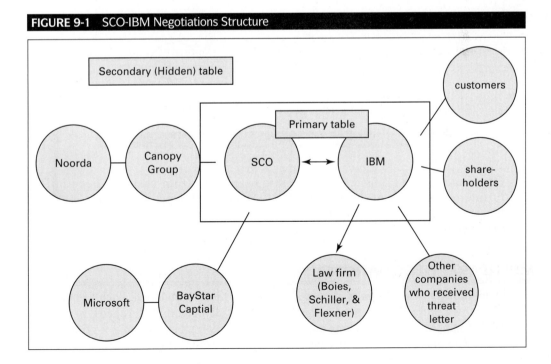

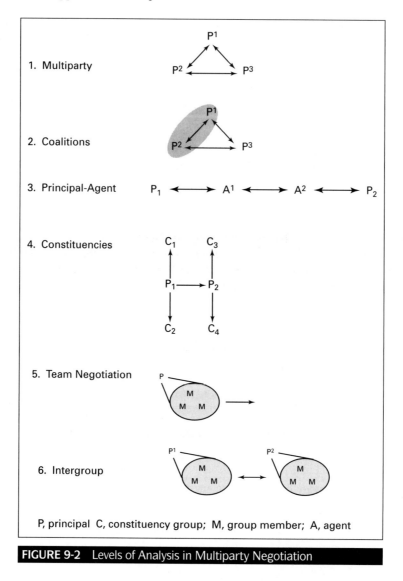

1. Multiparty

2. Coalitions

3. Principal-Agent

4. Constituencies

5. Team Negotiation

6. Intergroup

P, principal C, constituency group; M, group member; A, agent

FIGURE 9-2   Levels of Analysis in Multiparty Negotiation

(4) constituencies; (5) team negotiation; and (6) team-on-team negotiations, or intergroup negotiations (see Figure 9-2). For each level, we identify key challenges and then suggest practical advice and strategies for maximizing negotiation effectiveness.

MULTIPARTY NEGOTIATIONS

A **multiparty negotiation** is a group of three or more individuals, each representing their own interests, who attempt to resolve perceived differences of interest (Bazerman, Mannix, & Thompson, 1988; Kramer, 1991). For example, a group of students who must collectively prepare and present a group project for a course grade is involved in a multiparty negotiation, as is a group of specialists in an architectural firm who must design a house for a client. The parties to a negotiation may be individuals, teams, or groups. For example, Governor-elect Jim Doyle of Wisconsin prefers to negotiate the terms of the state-tribal gaming compacts with the state's Native American tribes as a group, rather than by individual tribe. These group negotiations depart from the process used by former Governor Tommy Thompson, who negotiated with each of Wisconsin's 11 tribes individually (Associated Press, Dec. 3, 2002). The involvement of more than two principals at the negotiation table complicates the situation enormously. Social interactions become more complex, information-processing demands increase exponentially, and coalitions can form. Yet, groups make more accurate judgments and more readily aggregate information than do individuals (Bottom, Ladha, & Miller, 2002).

Key Challenges of Multiparty Negotiations

Several challenges occur at both the cognitive (mind) and the emotional (heart) level, and can crop up in multiparty negotiations. We present four key challenges of multiparty negotiations and follow with some practical advice.

Dealing with Coalitions

A key difference between two-party and group negotiations is the potential for two or more parties within a group to form a coalition to pool their resources and exert greater influence on outcomes (for a review, see Komorita & Parks, 1995). A **coalition** is a (sub)group of two of more individuals who join together in using their resources to affect the outcome of a decision in a mixed-motive situation (see Komorita & Parks, 1995; Murnighan, 1978) involving at least three parties (Gamson, 1964). For example, parties may seek to maximize control over other members, maximize their status in the group, maximize similarity of attitudes and values, or minimize conflict among members. Coalition formation is one way that otherwise weak group members may marshal a greater share of resources. Coalitions involve both cooperation and competition. Members of coalitions cooperate with one another in competition against other coalitions, but compete against one another regarding the allocation of rewards the coalition obtains. Coalitions are so important that we have a special section to discuss them.

Formulating Trade-Offs

Integrative agreements are more difficult to fashion in multiparty negotiations because the trade-offs are more complex. The issues may be linked, making trade-offs across issues difficult to construct. Moreover, in a multiparty negotiation, integrative trade-offs may be achieved either through circular or reciprocal logrolling (Palmer & Thompson, 1995). **Circular logrolling** involves trade-offs that require each group member to offer another member a concession on one issue while receiving a concession from yet another group member on a different issue. A circular trade-off is typified by the tradition of drawing names from a hat to give holiday gifts to people. People receive a gift from one person and give a gift to yet another person. Ideally, we give gifts that are more appreciated by the recipient than by the giver. In contrast, **reciprocal trade-offs** are fashioned between two members of a larger group. Reciprocal trade-offs are typified in the more traditional form of exchanging presents. Circular trade-offs are more risky than reciprocal trade-offs because they involve the cooperation of more than two group members.

Voting and Majority Rule

Groups often simplify the negotiation of multiple issues among multiple parties through voting and decision rules. However, if not used wisely, decision rules can thwart effective negotiation, both in terms of pie-expansion and pie-slicing. A number of problems are associated with voting and majority rule (for an overview, see Bottom, Eavey, Miller, & Victor, 2000; Bottom, Handlin, King, & Miller, in press).

Problems with Voting and Majority Rule   **Voting** is the procedure of collecting individuals' preferences for alternatives on issues and selecting the most popular alternative as the group choice. The most common procedure used to aggregate preferences of team members is **majority rule.** However, majority rule presents several problems in the attainment of efficient negotiation settlements. Despite its democratic appeal, majority rule fails to recognize the strength of individual preferences. One person in a group may feel very strongly about an issue, but his or her vote counts the same as the vote of someone who does not have a strong opinion about the issue. Consequently, majority rule does not promote integrative trade-offs among issues. In fact, groups negotiating under unanimous rule reach more efficient outcomes than groups operating under majority rule (Beersma & De Dreu, 2002; Mannix, Thompson, & Bazerman, 1989; Thompson, Mannix, & Bazerman, 1988).

Although unanimity rule is time-consuming, it encourages group members to consider creative alternatives to expand the size of the pie and satisfy the interests of all group members. Because strength of preference is a key component in the fashioning of integrative agreements, majority rule hinders the development of mutually beneficial trade-offs. Voting in combination with other decision aids, such as agendas, may be especially detrimental to the attainment of efficient outcomes because it prevents logrolling (Mannix, Thompson, & Bazerman, 1989; Thompson, Mannix, & Bazerman, 1988).

Other problems arise with voting. Within groups that demonstrate "egoistic" motives (as opposed to prosocial motives), majority rule leads to more distributive and less integrative behavior (Beersma & De Dreu, 2002). Group members may not agree upon a method for voting; for example, some members may insist upon unanimity, others may argue for a simple majority rule, and still others may advocate a weighted majority rule. Even if a voting method is agreed upon, it may not yield a choice. For example, a group may not find a majority if the group is evenly split. Voting does not eliminate conflicts of interest, but instead, provides a way for group members to live with conflicts of interest; for this reason, majority rule decisions may not be stable. In this sense, voting hides disagreement within groups, which threatens long-term group and organizational effectiveness.

Voting Paradoxes   Consider a three-person (Raines, Warner, and Lassiter) product development team. The three are in conflict over which design to use—*A*, *B*, or *C*. The preference ordering is depicted in Table 9-1. Everyone is frustrated, and the group has argued for hours. As a way of resolving the conflict, Warner suggests voting between designs *A* and *B*. In that vote *A* wins, and *B* is discarded. Warner then proposes that the

TABLE 9-1	Managers' Preferences for Product Designs		
Manager	*Design A*	*Design B*	*Design C*
Raines	1	2	3
Warner	2	3	1
Lassiter	3	1	2

group vote between *A* and *C*. In that vote, *C* wins. Warner then declares that design *C* be implemented. Lassiter concludes that the group vote was fair and agrees to develop design *C*. However, Raines is perplexed and suggests taking another vote. Warner laughs and says, "We just took a vote and you lost—so just accept the outcome!" Raines glares at Warner and says, "Let's do the vote again, and I will agree to accept the outcome. However, this time I want us to vote between *B* and *C* first." Warner has no choice but to go along. In this vote *B* is the clear winner, and *C* is eliminated. Next, the vote is between *A* and *B*, and *A* beats *B*. Raines happily declares *A* the winner. Lassiter then jumps up and declares that the whole voting process was fraudulent, but cannot explain why.

Raines, Warner, and Lassiter are victims of the **Condorcet paradox.** The Condorcet paradox demonstrates that the winners of majority rule elections will change as a function of the *order* in which alternatives are proposed. Alternatives that are proposed later, as opposed to earlier, are more likely to survive sequential voting (May, 1982). Thus, clever negotiators arrange to have their preferred alternatives entered at later stages of a sequential voting process.

The unstable voting outcomes of the product development team point to a larger concern known as the **impossibility theorem** (Arrow, 1963). This theorem states that the derivation of group preference from individual preference is indeterminate. Simply put, no method can combine group members' preferences in a way that guarantees group preference is maximized when groups contain three or more members and are facing three or more options. In other words, even though each manager's preferences are transitive, the group-level preference is intransitive.

Strategic Voting   The problem of indeterminate group choice is further compounded by the temptation for members to **strategically misrepresent** their true preferences so that a preferred option is more likely to be favored by the group (Chechile, 1984; Ordeshook, 1986; Plott, 1976; Plott & Levine, 1978). For example, a group member may vote for his least-preferred option to ensure that the second choice option is killed. Raines could have voted strategically in the first election to ensure that his preferred strategy was not eliminated in the first round.

Consensus Decisions   Consensus agreements require the consent of all parties to the negotiation before an agreement is binding. However, consensus agreements do not imply unanimity. For an agreement to be unanimous, parties must agree inwardly as well as outwardly. Consensus agreements imply that parties agree *publicly* to a particular settlement, even though their *private* views about the situation may be in conflict.

Although consensus agreements are desirable, they precipitate several problems. They are time-consuming because they require the consent of all members, who are often not in agreement. Second, they often lead to compromise, in which parties identify a lowest common denominator acceptable to all. Compromise agreements are an extremely easy method of reaching agreement and are compelling because they appear to be fair, but they are usually inefficient because they fail to exploit potential Pareto-improving trade-offs. (See Mnookin, 2003, for a discussion of "the sufficient consensus standard" applied to negotiations in South Africa and Northern Ireland.)

Communication Breakdowns

Most people take communication for granted in their interactions with multiple parties. In a perfect communication system, a sender transmits or sends a message that is accurately received by a recipient. Errors are possible at three different points: The sender may fail to send a message; the message may be sent, but is inaccurate or distorted; or, an accurate message is sent, but is distorted or not received by the recipient. In a multiparty environment, the complexity grows when several people are simultaneously sending and receiving messages. The extent to which communication is restricted influences how the pie is divided. For example, parties with weaker BATNAs benefit from a more constrained communication structure, especially if they are the conduit of communication (Bolton, Chatterjee, & McGinn, 2003). In contrast, negotiators with stronger BATNAs benefit from a more public communication structure that promotes competitive bidding (Bolton, Chatterjee, & McGinn 2003).

Private Caucusing When groups grow large, communication among all parties is difficult. One way of simplifying negotiations is for negotiators to communicate in smaller groups, thereby avoiding full-group communication. Group members often form private caucuses for strategic purposes. However, private caucusing may cause problems. Full-group communication is more time-consuming but enhances equality of group members' outcomes, increases joint profitability, and minimizes perceptions of competition (Palmer & Thompson, 1995). However, a caveat comes with the benefits of full communication. When the task structure requires group members to logroll in a reciprocal fashion (as opposed to a circular fashion), restricted communication leads to higher joint outcomes than full communication. Private caucusing can take many different forms. For example, in 2003, China proposed a caucusing arrangement for restarting multiparty negotiations between the United States and Korea to end the standoff over North Korea's nuclear weapons program (*Seattle Post-Intelligencer*, July 16, 2003). The proposed arrangement called for a multilateral meeting in which bilateral talks would take place on the sidelines. This arrangement addresses North Korea's demand for individual, face-to-face negotiations with the United States, while also addressing U.S. insistence that any new talks involve Japan, South Korea, and China.

Biased Interpretation People often hear what they want to hear when receiving messages, especially ambiguous ones. For example, when people are given neutral information about a product, they interpret it in a way that is favorable toward their own position. Furthermore, they selectively pay attention to information in a report that favors their initial point of view and ignore or misinterpret information that contradicts their position.

Perspective-Taking Failures People are remarkably poor at taking the perspective of others. For example, people who are privy to information and knowledge that they know others are not aware of nevertheless act as if others are aware of it, even though it would be impossible for the receiver to have this knowledge (Keysar, 1998). This problem is known as the **curse of knowledge** (Camerer, Loewenstein, & Weber, 1989). For example, in a simulation, traders who possessed privileged information that could have been used to their advantage behaved as if their trading partners also had access to the privileged information. Perspective-taking deficiencies also explain why some instructors who understand an idea perfectly are unable to teach students the same idea. They are unable to put themselves in their students' shoes to explain the idea in a way the students can understand.

Indirect Speech Acts   Each statement one person makes to another has an intended meaning that is couched in casual conversation. **Indirect speech acts** are the ways in which people ask others to do things—but in indirect ways. For example, consider the various ways of requesting that a person shut a door (see Table 9-2). Each statement can serve as a request to perform that act even though (except for "close the door") the sentence forms are not requests but assertions and questions. Thus, statements 2 through 9 are indirect speech acts; a listener's understanding of the intention behind a communicator's intention requires an extra cognitive step or two, which can often fail, especially in cases of stress.

Indirect speech acts are a function of the magnitude of the request being made (i.e., trivial requests, such as asking someone for the time of day, are easy to accommodate; asking someone if you can have a job is much more difficult to accommodate), the power the recipient has over the sender, and the social distance in the culture (Brown & Levinson, 1987). Thus, as the magnitude of requests increases, the power distance increases, and as the social distance increases, requests made by negotiators will become more indirect. Of course, indirectness can be disastrous for effective communication.

Multiple Audience Problem   In some negotiation situations, negotiators need to communicate with another person in the presence of someone who should not understand the message. For example, consider a couple selling a house having a face-to-face discussion with a potential buyer. Ideally, the couple wants to communicate information

---

TABLE 9-2   Different Ways to Make a Request that Require Progressively More Inferences and Assumed Common Knowledge on the Part of the Receiver

1. Close the door.
2. Can you close the door?
3. Would you close the door?
4. It might help to close the door.
5. Would you mind awfully if I asked you to close the door?
6. Did you forget the door?
7. How about a little less breeze?
8. It's getting cold in here.
9. I really don't want the cats to get out of the house.

Sources: Adapted from Krauss, R. M., and Fussell, S. R. (1996). Social psychological models of interpersonal communication. In E. T. Higgins and A. W. Kruglanski (Eds.), *Social Psychology: Handbook of Basic Principles* (pp. 655–701). New York: Guilford; Levinson, S. C. (1983). *Pragmatics* (p. 264). Cambridge, England: Cambridge University Press.

to one another in a way that the spouse understands but the buyer does not—better yet, in such a way that the buyer is not even aware that a surreptitious communication is taking place. Fleming and Darley (1991) call this issue the **multiple audience problem.**

As it turns out, people are quite skilled at communicating information to the intended recipient in a way that the other party is unaware of (Fleming & Darley, 1991). People are able to "tune" their messages to specific audiences. For example, former president Ronald Reagan was gifted in his ability to send different messages to different audiences all within the same speech. Reagan's "evil empire" speech of March 8, 1983, to the National Association of Evangelicals (and, indirectly, the whole world) is a case in point. In the early sections of this speech, Reagan established identification with the evangelical audience through an ethos that exemplified their ideals, even using their technical vocabulary (e.g., "I believe in intercessionary prayer"). The section of his speech dealing with foreign policy was addressed to a complex array of audiences, foreign as well as domestic. The "evil empire" phrase had strong resonance not only with evangelicals, but with opponents of the Soviet Union everywhere, including elements within Poland and Czechoslovakia. For the benefit of his diplomatic audiences, however, Reagan carefully avoided specific references to evil actions of the Soviet Union, personally deleting from early drafts all references to chemical warfare in Afghanistan. And the speech's attack on the nuclear freeze movement of that time was balanced with a call for "an honest freeze," a term that created "presence" for his proposal for "extensive prior negotiations on the systems and numbers to be limited and on the measures to ensure effective verification and compliance" (Myers, 1999, p. 65). To his audience in the international and diplomatic and arms control communities, including those within the Soviet Union, such praise alluded to extratextual facts that gave this part of the message a pragmatic connotation (Myers, 1999).

Key Strategies for Multiparty Negotiations

Given that multiparty negotiations are complex and present special challenges, what strategies and practices should negotiators put into place to enhance their ability to expand the pie and slice it in a multiparty context? Consider the following strategies.

Know Who Will Be at the Table

Moreover, understand the interests of constituencies they represent (the hidden table).

Manage the Information and Systematize Proposal Making

People experience "information overload" when dealing with multiple parties and multiple issues. It is nearly impossible to keep track of the issues, alternatives, and preferences of each party without some kind of information management device. We strongly suggest that negotiators develop a matrix that lists each party (along the rows) and each issue along the columns, and then track each person's preferences for each issue. To the extent that this information can be publicly created and displayed, it can greatly enhance the ability of the group to find true win-win agreements.

Observations of multiparty negotiations suggest that negotiating groups severely mismanage their time. For example, negotiating groups begin by engaging in distributive bargaining and then transition into integrative bargaining (Olekalns, Brett, & Weingart, 2003). Groups tend not to make proposals and explore options and alternatives in a systematic fashion. This behavior can lead to **tunnel vision,** which is the tendency for people in group negotiations to underestimate the number of feasible options available. For example, in one of our investigations, we asked people who had just completed a multiparty negotiation how many feasible agreements they thought were possible (the negotiation contained five issues and four to five alternatives within each issue). The modal response was one. On average, people estimated approximately four feasible outcomes for the group (the highest estimate was 12). In fact, feasible outcomes numbered 55! This example illustrates the tunnel vision (and ensuing desperation) that can overtake a group if they fail to systematize their proposal making. We strongly encourage members to make several multi-issue proposals and to keep a record of which proposals have been considered.

Use Brainstorming Wisely

We also encourage groups to use brainstorming wisely. Most groups suggest fewer and lower-quality ideas than do individuals thinking independently (Diehl & Stroebe, 1987). We suggest instructing parties to group negotiation to engage in **brainwriting** prior to meeting face to face (Paulus, 1998). Brainwriting, or solitary writing, is a strategy whereby group members independently write down ideas for resolving negotiations and then, later, when the group meets, they share those ideas. Brainwriting capitalizes on the fact that individuals are better at generating ideas but groups are superior in terms of evaluating ideas.

Develop and Assign Process Roles

Multiparty negotiations need, at the very least, a timekeeper, a process manager, and a recorder of information. We encourage groups to assign these roles to group members, then consider what additional process roles will be helpful prior to negotiating and assign these roles to other parties in the group. These roles can be rotated, so as not to give any particular member an advantage or disadvantage.

Stay at the Table

It is unwise for group members to break away from the table when all parties need to reach agreement (Palmer & Thompson, 1995). When groups break away from the table, coalitions are more likely to form, which can be detrimental for the group (Mannix, 1993).

Strive for Equal Participation

The problem of "uneven" participation, wherein one or two people do all the talking, thwarts information exchange in groups. As the group grows larger, the "uneven participation" problem is more of an issue.

Allow for Some Points of Agreement, Even If Only on Process

Sometimes group negotiations can get bogged down because it takes longer for parties to reach agreements—even on a single issue. Failure to reach agreement on negotiation issues can make group members feel that they are not making progress and that negotiations are stalemated. Further, it can create a combative atmosphere. For example, the more persistent cooperative negotiators are in their use of integrative strategies, the better they do for themselves (Kern, Brett, & Weingart, 2003). A good strategy at this point is not to reach agreement just for the sake of reaching settlement, but instead, to agree on the process of reaching settlement. For example, a group member may suggest something like the following:

> I know that we have been working for over two hours and have not been able to agree on a single issue. We could take this as a sign of failure or ill will, but I do not think that would be wise. I suggest that we take 10 minutes as a group to list all of the settlements that we have considered and then independently rank them in terms of their favorability. This ranking may give us some sense of where and how to look for possible agreements.

Avoid the "Equal Shares" Bias

A tendency often emerges in group negotiations to divide things equally amongst the parties involved (see also Chapter 3, on pie slicing). This bias is problematic for several reasons. First and foremost, as we saw in Chapter 3, no fair method of allocation is universally acceptable. Multiple criteria of fairness can be justified as "fair" in some sense, and none are necessarily superior to others. Second, pressure is strong in many groups to behave in an egalitarian fashion, but privately, people are not inclined to be egalitarian.

Avoid the Agreement Bias

We caution negotiators against the agreement bias, which we described in a previous chapter. Specifically, this behavior occurs when negotiators focus on reaching common ground with the other party and are reluctant to accept differences of interest, even when such acceptance might create viable options for joint gain.

Another word of warning: Don't assume everyone wants to "get to yes." In some negotiation situations, people are paid to break deals and stall agreement. Some parties at the table may not desire to reach settlement, but rather, have an incentive to forestall reaching settlement. For example, Crowne Plaza Hotel owner Steve Cohn went to incredible lengths to kill a deal that would bring a new Marriott Hotel to the Phoenix, Arizona, area. Cohn said that the Marriott hotel would kill his business and launched an attack to stop the negotiations. First he funded a petition drive to put the issue on the ballot. Council members, faced with the delay and uncertain outcome of a referendum vote, killed the Marriott deal. City officials quickly completed a second deal with an emergency clause, which prevented a public vote. In response, Cohn sued to block the hotels and then announced a petition drive for a ballot initiative requiring a public vote on the hotel deals. Cohn knows that Marriott will not wait the time needed to settle a lawsuit. Phoenix mayor Skip Rimsza said, "The delay continues to raise the cost and Cohn controls the delay" (*The Arizona Republic*, Dec. 7, 1999).

Avoid Sequential Bargaining

Groups often use sequential bargaining (and discuss one issue at a time) rather than simultaneous bargaining (where several issues are under consideration at any given time). By independently discussing and voting on each issue, negotiators cannot fashion win-win trade-offs among issues (Mannix, Thompson, & Bazerman, 1989; Thompson, Mannix, & Bazerman, 1988).

COALITIONS

Coalitions face three sets of challenges: (1) the formation of the coalition, (2) coalition maintenance, and (3) the distribution of resources among coalition members. Next, we take up these challenges and provide strategies for maximizing coalition effectiveness.

Key Challenges of Coalitions

Optimal Coalition Size

Ideally, coalitions should contain the minimum number of people sufficient to achieve a desired goal. Coalitions are difficult to maintain because members are tempted by other members to join other coalitions, and agreements are not enforceable (Mannix & Loewenstein, 1993).

Trust and Temptation in Coalitions

Coalitional integrity is a function of the costs and rewards of coalitional membership; when coalitions are no longer rewarding, people will leave them. Nevertheless, members of coalitions experience a strong pull to remain intact even when it is not rational to do so (Bottom, Eavey, & Miller, 1996). According to the **status quo bias,** even when a new coalition structure that offers greater gain is possible, members are influenced by a norm of **coalitional integrity,** such that they stick with their current coalition (Bottom, Eavey, & Miller, 1996). Negotiators should form coalitions early so as to not be left without coalitional partners.

Dividing the Pie

The distribution of resources among members of coalitions is complex because a normative method of fair allocation does not exist (Raiffa, 1982). Experience and risk tolerance influence the size of the pie that coalition negotiators get (Bottom, Holloway, McClurg, & Miller, 2000). For example, Bottom and colleagues (2000) found that novice negotiators often settled for "equal division," but experienced negotiators never did so. Experienced negotiators were much more willing and able to exploit differences in their relative bargaining power. Bottom and colleagues (2000) noted that veteran politicians such as Sam Rayburn, Lyndon Johnson, and Dan Rostenkowski are known for their ability to exploit their sources of power and build winning coalitions around policy initiatives. To illustrate this observation, consider the following example. Lindholm, Tepe, and Clauson are three small firms producing specialized products, equipment, and research for the rehabilitation medicine community.[1] This area has become a critical, high-growth industry, and each firm is exploring ways to expand and improve its technologies through innovations in the research and development (R&D) divisions. Each firm recently applied for R&D funding from the National Rehabilitation Medicine Research Council (NRMR).

The NRMR is a government agency dedicated to funding research in rehabilitation medicine and treatment. The NRMR is willing to provide funds for the proposed research, but because the firms' requests are so similar, they will fund only a **consortium** of two or three firms. The NRMR will not grant funding to Lindholm, Tepe, or Clauson alone.

---

[1]This example is based on the case Federated Science Fund, written by Elizabeth Mannix, available through the Dispute Resolution Research Center, Kellogg School of Management, Northwestern University (e-mail: drrc@kellogg.northwestern.edu); and the Social Services case, by Howard Raiffa (1982), *The Art and Science of Negotiation.*

Thus, if we had a total of $280,000, we could solve each equation. But, the harsh reality is that we do not. So, the second step is to get the total down to $240,000 by deducting $40,000 from somewhere. In the absence of any particular argument as to why one party's share should be cut, we deduct an equal amount, $13,333, from each party's share. In the final step, we compute the "core" shares as follows:

Lindholm: $116,670
Tepe: $76,670
Clauson: $46,670

As Lindholm, you are delighted. Tepe agrees, but Clauson is not happy. Clauson thinks that $46,670 is too little and hires a consultant to evaluate the situation. The consultant proposes a different method, called the Shapley model.

The Shapley model.   Consider a coalition formation in which one player starts out alone and then is joined by a second and third player. The Shapley model determines the overall payoff a player can expect on the basis of his or her **pivotal power,** or the ability to change a losing coalition into a winning coalition. The consultant considers all possible permutations of players joining coalitions one at a time. The marginal value added to each coalition's outcome is attributed to the pivotal player. The Shapley value is the mean of a player's added value (see Table 9-4). When all players bring equal resources, the Shapley value is the total amount of resources divided by the total number of people. This outcome, of course, is the "equal division" principle, as well as the "equity principle."

When Clauson's consultant presents this report, Clauson is delighted with a share that increased by almost $20,000. Lindholm is nonplussed with a share that decreased. Tepe is tired of all the bickering and proposes that they settle for something in between the two proposed solutions.

Raiffa's hybrid model.   We have presented two models to solve for shares in coalition situations. The medium-power player's share in both models is identical, but the high- and low-power player's shares fluctuate quite dramatically. It is possible that an egocentric argument could ensue between Lindholm and Clauson as to which model to employ. One solution is a hybrid model in which the mean of the

TABLE 9-4 Analysis of Pivotal Power in the Shapley Model			
Order of Joining	***Lindholm Added Value***	***Tepe Added Value***	***Clauson Added Value***
LTC	0	$220,000	$ 20,000
LCT	0	50,000	190,000
TLC	$220,000	0	20,000
TCL	90,000	0	150,000
CLT	190,000	50,000	0
CTL	90,000	150,000	0
Shapley (average)[2]	98,333	78,333	63,333

[2]These figures are rounded slightly.

that initially, agents show greater loyalty to their principals, but over time, their loyalty to the other agent is greater. Moreover, to the extent that the across-the-table relationship among agents was strong, the likelihood of agreement was greater and settlements occurred in the middle of the bargaining zone. Most notably, to the extent that the agents were socially similar (i.e., graduated from same school, etc.) and familiar with each other, they were more likely to forge a bond.

Communication Distortion

Because it is often the agent doing the negotiating (rather than the principal), more opportunity is present for communication distortion to occur. Any one message can be sent in an infinite number of ways. **Message tuning** refers to how senders tailor messages for specific recipients. People who send messages (e.g., "I have no fuel"; "I did not receive the attached file") will edit their messages in a way that they think best suits the recipient. For example, people give longer and more elaborate street directions and instructions to people whom they presume to be nonnatives or unfamiliar with a city (Krauss & Fussell, 1991). Also, senders capitalize on the knowledge that they believe the recipient to already hold (e.g., "Turn right when you see that big tree that the city pruned last week"). For this reason, negotiators may send shorter, less complete messages to one another because they believe that they can capitalize on an existing shared knowledge base. However, negotiators often overestimate the commonality of information they share with others. Consequently, the messages they send become less clear (e.g., in the previous example, the other person may not know the location of the tree that was pruned by the city last week).

Message senders have a bias to present information that they believe will be favorably received by the recipient, and therefore they will distort messages (Higgins, 1999). For example, when people present a message to an audience they believe is either for or against a particular topic, they err in the direction of adopting the audience's point of view. It is as if they know that the messenger who brings unwelcome news is endangered—so one way of dealing with this factor is to modify the news. Unfortunately, message distortion can play havoc with effective teamwork.

Loss of Control

Because an agent is negotiating in your stead, you are giving up control over the process of negotiation and, ultimately, the outcome. Indeed, agents are more active in a negotiation and initiate interactions more than either of the principals (Valley, White, & Iacobucci, 1992).

Agreement at Any Cost

Because agents have an incentive to reach agreement, they may fall prey to the "getting to yes" bias in which agreement becomes more important than the contents of the deal (Gibson, Thompson, & Bazerman, 1994). Simply stated, the desire to reach agreement quickly and efficiently may lead agents to withhold information from principals that might impede a deal.

Strategies for Working Effectively with Agents

Shop Around

Do not assume that the first agent you meet is uniquely qualified to represent you. Ask the agent how he or she will successfully represent your interests. Ask the agent about what is expected of you. Ask the agent about the nature of your relationship and what obligations, if any, you have to one another. For example, many real estate agents have easy-exit clauses that allow principals to remove agents without difficulty; in the absence of this clause, a principal might be committed to an agent for a lengthy period of time. For example, Darcy Bouzeous is one of the few women in the world who negotiates talent contracts for sports stars and media personalities. Says Bouzeous, "I do not believe in having a retention agreement. If they do not like what I've done, I do not think they have to be stuck with me" (*Chicago Sun-Times*, Oct. 22, 1990). Ask agents about their negotiation training and strategies. (See Table 9-6 for some suggestions about questions to ask an agent.)

Know Your BATNA Before Meeting with Your Agent

Do your homework before meeting with your agent. Know your own BATNA. Prepare questions to ask your agent that will allow you to test the soundness of your BATNA, but do not give away your BATNA. For example, a home seller might say, "I would like to find out from you what average sales prices are for this type of home."

Communicate Your Interests to Your Agent Without Giving Away Your BATNA

One of the most challenging tasks for a negotiator is to communicate his or her interests, priorities, and preferences, but not reveal his or her BATNA. You can help your agent to help you most effectively by listing, in order of priority, your key interests and what you perceive to be the alternatives within each of those areas of interest. Anticipate that your agent will, in so many words, ask you about your BATNA. When this question comes up (and it will!), focus the conversation onto your priorities (e.g., "I am not sure how helpful it is to tell you the most money I am willing to pay for the house you showed me today. However, I am really interested in a home within this school district area and a double garage. In fact, I would be willing to pay more for those features than a master suite and an updated kitchen").

Capitalize on the Agent's Expertise

Good agents will have a wealth of expertise in their particular area. Ask them about what they perceive to be their key strategies for targeting opportunities for you and closing deals.

TABLE 9-6   Questions that Potential Home Buyers Should Ask Real-Estate Agents

1. Can you represent me as a buyer's agent?
2. How will you find me homes?
3. How can you leverage my down payment, interest rate, and monthly payment?
4. What different points will you be able to negotiate on my behalf?
5. How long have you been selling real estate full time?
6. What can I expect in terms of communication?
7. Does your contract have an "easy exit" clause in it?
8. Under what conditions will you cut your commission?

Source: Ron Holdridge, Re/Max Metro Realty, Seattle, Washington.

Tap into Your Agent's Sources of Information

Agents, by virtue of their professional affiliations and networks, have access to a lot of information. However, you should not expect that passivity on your part will lead your agent to provide you with information. Rather, you need to ask your agent to provide key information for you. If your agent is unwilling or unable to do so, interview another agent and see whether he or she can provide the information.

Discuss Ratification

By nature of the principal-agent relationship, an agent's authority is limited with respect to making certain concessions or types of agreements (i.e., your agent cannot lower or increase your offer without explicit direction from you). Thus, agents may effectively resist making too many and too deep concessions that you might impulsively make in the heat of negotiation. In this sense, your agent provides a buffer zone between yourself and the other party.

Use Your Agent to Help Save Face

Sometimes, negotiators make what they regard to be perfectly reasonable proposals that are insulting to the other party. When this situation happens (and if your opponent is an emotional type), negotiations may start on a losing course. In an agent-mediated negotiation, you can attempt to salvage damaged egos and relationships by blaming your agent.

Use Your Agent to Buffer Emotions

In keeping with this point about saving face, agents can be an effective emotional buffer between parties who may either dislike one another or are irrational (see Chapter 5 on bargaining styles). Effective agents will put a positive "spin" on the communications by each party and effectively "tune into" their principal's needs.

CONSTITUENT RELATIONSHIPS

When a negotiating party is embedded within an organization, several peripheral players may have an indirect stake in the outcome and influence the negotiation process. A **constituent** is ostensibly on the "same side" as a principal, but exerts an independent influence on the outcome through the principal. Constituents can be used to exert pressure on the other side of the table. For example, consider the constituents involved in the 2002 dispute between a powerful women's organization and the men-only Augusta National Golf Club (*BusinessWeek,* Aug. 12, 2002, p. 75). The dispute began when Martha Burke, the chairwoman of the National Council of Women's Organizations, sent a letter to the chairman of Augusta, William W. "Hootie" Johnson, urging him to open the club to female membership. After being rebuffed by Johnson, Burke went after his constituents, including Masters Tournament sponsors such as Coca-Cola, IBM, GM, and Citigroup, whose chairman, Sanford Weill, is a member of Augusta.

By the same token, constituencies can also exert pressure on negotiators. For example, in the United States–North Korea dispute over nuclear weapon proliferation, China is an involved constituent. China sent an envoy to the North Korean capital and proposed a formula for restarting negotiations. Moreover, China exerted pressure on both sides to find a diplomatic solution (*New York Times*, July 16, 2003b).

We distinguish three types of constituencies: superiors, who have authority over principals; subordinates, who are under the authority of principals; and constituencies, the party whom the principal represents—that is, for whom the principal is responsible and to whom the principal is accountable (collateral parties are represented by *C* in Figure 9-2). In the opening example, IBM is accountable to its major shareholders and customers, who are ostensibly on their side, but may have interests of their own. Further, the SCO group has dual accountability to the Canopy Group (as 43% owners, as well as its investor BayStar Capital, and ultimately to Noorda as the parent company of Canopy).

Challenges for Constituent Relationships

Accountability

Negotiators at the bargaining table comprise the primary relationship in negotiation. The relationship that parties share with their constituents is the **second table** (Ancona, Friedman, & Kolb, 1991). Constituents do not have to be physically present at the negotiation table for their presence to be strongly felt (Kramer, Pommerenke, & Newton, 1993; Pruitt & Carnevale, 1993; Tetlock, 1985). Negotiators who are accountable to their constituents make higher demands and are less willing to compromise in negotiation than those not accountable to constituents (Ben-Yoav & Pruitt, 1984; Carnevale, Pruitt, & Britton, 1979; O'Connor, 1994).

The second table has a paradoxical effect on the primary table. Representatives of constituents are not often given power to enact agreements; that is, the representative is not monolithic (Raiffa, 1982). In some cases, this restriction would seem to reduce his or her power at the bargaining table, but the opposite can be true. The negotiator whose "hands are tied" is often more effective than is the negotiator who has the power to ratify agreements. Anyone who has ever negotiated a deal on a new car has probably experienced the "my hands are tied" or "let me take it to the boss" ploy, in which the salesperson induces the customer to commit to a price that requires approval before a deal is finalized.

Accountability to collateral actors is an inevitable aspect of organizational life (Tetlock, 1985, 1992). At least two motivational processes are triggered by accountability: decision-making vigilance and evaluation apprehension.

Decision-Making Vigilance   Decision makers who are accountable for their actions consider relevant information and alternatives more carefully (Tetlock, 1985, 1992). Accountability increases thoughtful, deliberate processing of information and decreases automatic, heuristic processing (see also Chaiken, 1980; Fiske & Neuberg, 1990). Accountability would seem to uniformly improve the quality of decisions made by negotiators and increase the likelihood of integrative agreements.

However, decision accountability may not always promote more thorough and unbiased processing of information if organizational actors are partisan to a particular view (Thompson, 1995b). Imagine a situation in which an observer watches a videotape of people negotiating. Some observers are told to take an objective and impartial view of the situation; other observers are instructed to take the perspective of one of the parties. Further, some observers are told that they will be accountable for their actions and behaviors (e.g., they must justify their decisions to others who will question them), whereas others are not accountable. After watching the tape, observers indicate what they think each negotiator wanted. Accountable partisans fall prey to the fixed-pie assumption because they are motivated to reach a particular conclusion. However, nonpartisan observers are willing to reach whatever conclusion the data will allow, and their judgments are therefore driven by the evidence, not their desires.

Evaluation Apprehension and Face-Saving Negotiators who are accountable for their behaviors are concerned with how they are viewed by others. When people are concerned what others will think, they use face-saving strategies and make their actions appear more favorable to relevant others. Negotiators who want to save face will be more aggressive and uncompromising so that they will not be viewed as suckers or pushovers. Negotiators who are accountable to constituents are more likely to maintain a tough bargaining stance, make fewer concessions, and hold out for more favorable agreements compared to those who are not accountable (see Carnevale & Pruitt, 1992).

However, an interesting twist happens when teams are accountable for their actions at the bargaining table. A **diffusion of responsibility** occurs across members of the team (O'Connor, 1997). Teams respond differently than solo negotiators to accountability pressure.

Conflicts of Interest

Negotiators often face a conflict between their goals and those of their constituency. For the manager interested in effective dispute resolution, it is not only important to understand the relationships negotiators share across the bargaining table, it is important to understand the hidden table of constituent relationships (see Kolb, 1983). Consider a negotiation involving teams of two people who are either personally acquainted or strangers to one another. Each team reports to a manager. Some teams report to a "profit-oriented" manager who instructs the team to "serve the interests of the group at all costs." Some teams report to a "people-oriented" manager who instructs the team to maximize interests while maintaining harmonious intergroup relations. Teams who report to the "profit" supervisor claim a greater share of the resources than do teams who report to the "people" supervisor and teams not accountable to a manager (Peterson & Thompson, 1997). When team members are acquainted, no differences occur in relative profitability. Why? Negotiators are better able to maximize profit when the goal is clear and they do not share a previous relationship.

Strategies for Improving Constituent Relationships

Communicate with Your Constituents

Representatives need to understand their constituents' real needs and interests, not just their positions. Moreover, when constituents feel heard, they are less likely to take extreme action. In many cases, representatives act too early—before they understand their constituency's real needs—so as to demonstrate their competence. Riddle

Memorial Hospital took the step of actually creating a "hot line" for its consumers and patients to call when the hospital was involved in negotiations with Blue Cross. The hospital's CFO, Ron Eyler explained, "We thought it was important that the community wasn't put in the middle, and I think Blue Cross shared the sentiment. The phone line was there to help provide information to our community so they wouldn't panic" (*Bestwire*, July 3, 2002, para. 10).

Do Not Expect Homogeneity of Constituent Views

Constituencies are often composed of individuals and subgroups with different needs and interests. On some level, they realize that they can achieve more through collective action and representation, but be aware of heterogeneity of views within the constituency. For example, consider the negotiations between David Trimble and Gerry Adams of the Unionist and Republican parties in Ireland. Both leaders were personally anxious to make progress during March 1999; however, their freedom of movement was severely limited due to constituency pressures. Trimble leads a sharply divided union, which is structurally fragmented into several parties and often confused in its aims (*The Independent*, Mar. 10, 1999).

Educate Your Constituents on Your Role and Your Limitations

Constituents, like other people, suffer from egocentric bias, meaning that they view the world from their own perspective in a self-serving fashion. From their point of view, they often see your role as one of educating the other side about the reality of the situation. They may often believe your task is easier than it really is. It is important to clearly define your role to your constituents early on in the process. Set realistic expectations. Do not characterize yourself as an "evangelist" for their "crusade." Share with your constituents all possible outcomes, not just the favorable ones they think will occur.

Help Your Constituents Do Horizon Thinking

Horizon thinking involves making projections about future outcomes. People have a difficult time thinking about future events (Gilbert & Wilson, 2000), tend to under- or overestimate the duration of future emotional states (Gilbert, Pinel, Wilson, Blumberg, & Wheatley, 1998), and fail to account for positive or negative circumstances that could arise (Loewenstein & Schkade, 1999; Schkade & Kahneman, 1998; Wilson et al., 1998). You can help your constituents develop a sound BATNA and realistic aspirations by helping them to engage in horizon thinking.

TEAM NEGOTIATION

Consider the following situations:

- A husband and wife negotiate with a salesperson on the price of a new car.
- A group of disgruntled employees approach management about wages and working conditions.
- A large software company approaches a small software company about an aquisition.

In all these examples, people join together on one side of the bargaining table as a team. Presumably, in each of these cases, one member could do all the negotiating for the team, but teams believe that they will be more effective if they are both at the bargaining table. Unlike solo negotiators, members of negotiating teams may play different roles for strategic reasons, such as "good cop–bad cop" (Brodt & Tuchinsky, 2000). Are teams effective at exploiting integrative potential at the bargaining table? To answer the question of whether two heads are better than one, Thompson, Peterson, and Brodt (1996) compared three types of negotiation configurations: team vs. team, team vs. solo, and solo vs. solo negotiations. The presence of at least one team at the bargaining table dramatically increased the incidence of integrative agreement (see also Morgan & Tindale, 2002).

Why are teams so effective? Negotiators exchange much more information about their interests and priorities when at least one team is at the bargaining table than when two individuals negotiate (O'Connor, 1994; Rand & Carnevale, 1994; Thompson, Peterson, & Brodt, 1996). Information exchange leads to greater judgment accuracy about parties' interests (O'Connor, 1994; Rand & Carnevale, 1994; Thompson, Peterson, & Brodt, 1996), which promotes integrative agreement (Thompson, 1991). The **team effect** is quite robust: It is not even necessary that members of teams privately caucus with one another to be effective (Thompson, Peterson, & Brodt, 1996). In negotiations with integrative potential, teams outperform solos; however, in extremely competitive tasks, teams are more likely to behave in a competitive fashion (Morgan & Tindale, 2002).

The presence of a team at the bargaining table increases the integrativeness of joint agreements (Morgan & Tindale, 2002; O'Connor, 1994; Rand & Carnevale, 1994), but what about the distributive component? Do teams outperform their solo counterparts? Not necessarily. Nevertheless, both teams and solo players believe that teams have an advantage—a **team efficacy effect** (O'Connor, 1994; Rand & Carnevale, 1994, Thompson, Peterson, & Brodt, 1996). Even in situations in which teams reap greater shares of profit than their solo counterparts, solos are still better off negotiating with a team than with another solo player. The solo negotiator earns less than the team, but the amount of jointly available resources is greater in the team-solo negotiation than in the solo-solo negotiation.

Challenges That Face Negotiating Teams
For a comprehensive review, see Brodt and Thompson (2001).

Picking Your Teammates
We cannot tell you who to select for your negotiating team, but we can help you figure out what to look for. Consider the following three skills as criteria for choosing and evaluating teammates:

1. **Negotiation expertise**: People with good negotiation skills may be worth their weight in gold if, for example, they are able to devise an integrative solution to a complex conflict situation. A negotiation expert can streamline preparation, make sure that the team avoids the four major sandtraps of negotiation (see Chapter 1), avoids destructive conflict strategies, and instigates a creative problem-solving process.

2. **Technical expertise**: It helps to have someone with technical expertise in the domain of interest. For example, when house buying, it is wonderful to have someone who is skilled in architecture, plumbing, electricity, and so on. Furthermore, by tapping into technical expertise of our teammates, we can better prioritize our own interests.

3. **Interpersonal skills**: It often helps to have people with good interpersonal skills on a negotiating team, even if they are not specifically trained in negotiation. Negotiation involves many interpersonal skills, such as the ability to establish rapport, communicate effectively, and redirect a power- or rights-based argument to one focusing on interests (Ury, Brett, & Goldberg, 1988).

How Many on the Team?

Two or three heads can be better than one, but at some point, conformity pressures increase with group size, peaking at about five and then leveling off (Latané, 1981). As teams grow in size, coordination problems increase.

Communication on the Team

Communication, or **information pooling,** is facilitated if members are acquaintances or share a relationship. For example, when the clues for solving a murder mystery game are distributed among group members, groups of friends are more likely to pool their diverse information than are groups of strangers (Gruenfeld, Mannix, Williams, & Neale, 1996).

Team Cohesion

Cohesion is the strength of positive relations within a team (Evans & Dion, 1991), the sum of pressures acting to keep individuals in a group (Back, 1951), and the result of all forces acting on members to remain in a group (Festinger, 1950). Cohesive groups perform better than less cohesive groups (Evans & Dion, 1991). The three sources of cohesion are (1) attraction to the group or resistance to leaving the group, (2) morale and motivation, and (3) coordination of efforts.

Different kinds of bonds keep teams together. **Common-identity groups** are composed of members who are attracted to the group; the individual members may come and go. For example, Joe is a member of a gay students' organization. He has several friends in the group, but the basis of his attraction to the group is its mission and purpose. **Common-bond groups** are composed of members who are attracted to particular members in the group (Prentice, Miller, & Lightdale, 1994). For example, take the negotiating team of George Madison, director of the Governor's Office of Employee Relations in New York, and John Currier, the executive deputy director. On the surface, they seem as different as night and day: Madison dresses in custom, pin-striped suits, monogrammed dress shirts, and gold cuff links, exuding a Gucci kind of elegance as he sips from silver-rimmed martini glasses. In contrast, Currier wears a work shirt and hiking shoes and says, "I'm a bricklayer at heart" (*Times Union-Albany*, Mar. 2, 2003, p. B1). Yet, they have a common bond as the basis of their teamwork: They both lost their fathers at an early age and were raised by strong women who instilled a "fierce work ethic" in them. They work from adjoining offices in a suite connected by an open doorway. And they seem joined at the hip when they walk to the Capitol for meetings.

Information Processing

Often organizational members negotiate as a team or a group because no single person has the requisite knowledge and expertise required to negotiate effectively. Thus, knowledge is distributed among team members. How effective are teams at utilizing knowledge that is distributed among members?

The issue of how teams decide who is responsible for storing and retaining information is crucial to the effectiveness of the team. Trade-offs are involved in the storage of information. It is more efficient for each team member to be responsible for a particular piece of information so that each member is not overwhelmed by too much data. However, as the redundancy of storage is minimized, so are the chances of successfully retrieving the desired information. Furthermore, groups are less likely to consider and discuss information that is shared only by a subset of its members. They suffer from the **common information bias** (Gigone & Hastie, 1993; Stasser, 1992).

It cannot and should not be assumed that members of a group are privy to the same facts and information. People rely on others for information. In fact, members of product development teams rely on informal social exchanges more than technical reports for information. Teams of individuals can be more efficient by dividing the labor. However, distributed cognition is risky because if a team loses one of its members, information may be lost to the entire group. Thus, groups face a dilemma: divide responsibility, which increases their dependence upon each individual member; or share information, which is clumsy and redundant.

Strategies for Improving Team Negotiations

Prepare Together

Preparing for a negotiation as a team is much more effective than if all members prepare separately. Team preparation is so important that we developed a worksheet for effective team preparation (see Box 9-1). Preparing together creates a transactive memory system in which group members understand the information that others have and how and when to access it. For example, in one investigation, groups were given instructions on how to assemble a transistor radio. Some groups trained together; in other groups, individuals trained individually (or with a different group). When it came to actual performance, groups who had trained together outperformed those who had trained individually or with different groups (Moreland, Argote, & Krishnan, 1996).

Plan Scheduled Breaks

Make sure that you schedule breaks into your negotiation to allow team members to meet privately. However, a word of caution: Many teams spend too much time in private caucus and not enough time at the table. This behavior is ultimately not effective for negotiation.

Assess Accountability

It is important to assess the extent to which team members are accountable to others outside of the team. For example, when teams are accountable to a supervisor, they are more effective than when they negotiate strictly on their own behalf (Peterson & Thompson, 1997).

BOX 9-1

PREPARING FOR YOUR TEAM-ON-TEAM NEGOTIATION

Team-on-team Negotiation can be an advantage over solo negotiation if the team prepares properly. Here are some guidelines:

Step 1:   Individual Preparation

- Identify the issues.
- Identify your BATNA.
- Determine what *you* believe to be your team's "worst-case" scenario.
- Determine what *you* believe to be your team's "best-case" scenario.
- Write these scenarios down and be prepared to share them with the members of your team.

Step 2:   As a Team, Decide on Your Procedures for Running the Preparation Meeting

- Who is going to run the meeting (i.e., who is going to summarize, synthesize, etc.)?
- What materials do you need to be effective (calculator, flipcharts, computer, etc.), and who is bringing them?
- What is your time line, and who will enforce it so that the team arrives at the negotiation table prepared and refreshed?

Step 3:   As a Team, Clarify Facts and Information (*Note:* You are not discussing strategy yet!)

- Develop a "Positions and Interests" chart.
- Prioritize your issues. Understand the reasons for your priorities.
- Identify what you think the other party's priorities are.

- Identify what information you need from the other party.
- Determine your BATNA.
- What do you know about the other party's BATNA?
- Identify your worst-case scenario (reservation price).
- Identify your best-case scenario (target).
- As you complete the preceding tasks, make a list of questions to research.
- Identify information that is too sensitive to reveal at any point under any condition (get clarification and closure within the team on this point).
- Identify information that you are willing to share with the other team if they inquire (get clarification and closure within the team on this point).

Step 4:   Strategy

- As a team, plan your OPENING OFFER. (*Note*: It is not advisable to simply want the "other party" to open; you need to be able to put something on the table at some point.)
- Choose a *lead negotiator* (speaker).
- Choose a *lead strategist* (listener and strategic watchdog).
- Choose an *accountant* to run the numbers.
- Choose a *scribe* to keep track of offers. Decide on a signal to adjourn for a private caucus.

INTERGROUP NEGOTIATION

Individuals who represent different social groups often negotiate with members of other groups (see Deutsch, 1973; Klar, Bar-Tal, & Kruglanski, 1988; Sherif, 1936). For example, members of a student council and university administrators, union and management negotiators, and groups of students from rival universities are all examples of intergroup negotiators. On a larger scale, nations negotiate with other nations. The toll in death, suffering, and displacement caused by intergroup conflict has reached staggering proportions in the past decade. It is estimated that armed conflicts have claimed the lives of 30 million people and moved 45 million people from their homes (McGuire, 1998).

Challenges of Intergroup Negotiations

Stereotyping

In intergroup negotiations, parties identify with their organization and often hold negative impressions about members of the other organizations (Kramer, 1991; for reviews, see Stroebe, Kruglanski, Bar-Tal, & Hewstone, 1988; Worchel & Austin, 1986). For example, SCO may consider IBM to represent "big business"; IBM may consider SCO to be attempting to unfairly profit from open-source software. These disparate and possibly exaggerated perceptions influence both companies' willingness to collaborate.

Changing Identities

People identify with many different social groups (Kramer, 1991). For example, a student might consider a relevant group to be the other students in his or her study group, the class as a whole, marketing majors in general, or the entire student body. At any given time, one group might be more or less salient to the student: At a football game, students might identify most strongly with the entire student body; in a dining hall, students might identify most strongly with a particular dorm or floor.

Imagine that you are in an organization in which marketing and finance are distinct subgroups located on different floors of a building. Contrast that arrangement to a situation in which marketing and finance are not separate functional units, but instead, part of the same product team. What happens in the case in which a marketing manager negotiates with a financial manager? Negotiations among individuals representing different social groups are less mutually beneficial than negotiations among individuals who perceive themselves as belonging to a larger social organization—one that encompasses all those present at the bargaining table (Kramer, 1991). When people define their social identity at the level of the organization, they are more likely to make more organizationally beneficial choices than when social identity is defined at an individual or subgroup level. For example, when group members are instructed to consider features they have in common with another group, behavior toward outgroups is much more generous than when they consider features that are distinct (Kramer & Brewer, 1984).

In-Group Bias

According to Eidelson and Eidelson (2003), five beliefs propel groups toward conflict: superiority, injustice, vulnerability, distrust, and helplessness. These deeply entrenched beliefs can trigger destructive action. Moreover, to the extent that groups receive social support from their fellow in-group members, such beliefs can lead to even greater intergroup conflict (Wildschut, Insko, & Gaertner, 2002). Group distinctions and social boundaries may be created on the basis of completely arbitrary distinctions (Tajfel, 1970). For example, Thompson (1993) divided participants into two groups on the basis of an arbitrary procedure (random draws from a box). Then, individuals negotiated with either a member of their "own group" or the "other group." Even though the information concerning the negotiation situation was identical in both respects, negotiations with members of out-groups were anticipated to be more contentious than negotiations with members of in-groups; further, the mere anticipation of negotiation with an out-group member led to increased **in-group bias,** or positive evaluations of one's own group relative to the out-group.

When we anticipate negotiations with out-group members, we are more likely to engage in **downward social comparison** (Wills, 1981). We evaluate the competitor to be less attractive on a number of organizationally relevant dimensions (such as intelligence, competence, and trustworthiness) than members of our group. However, after successful negotiation with out-groups, intergroup relations improve, and downward social comparison virtually disappears (Thompson, 1993). Negotiation with out-group members is threatening to organizational actors, but to the extent that integrative agreements are feasible, negotiation has remarkable potential for improving intergroup relations. Although our initial expectations may be quite pessimistic, interactions with members of opposing groups often have a beneficial impact on intergroup relations if several key conditions are met, such as mutual dependence for goal attainment (see Aronson & Bridgeman, 1979).

People of high status, those of low status who have few alternatives, and members of groups who have an opportunity to improve their group are most likely to identify with their group. Members of groups with lower perceived status display more in-group bias than members of groups with higher perceived status (Ellemers, Van Rijswijk, Roefs, & Simons, 1997). However, high-status group members show more in-group bias on group status-related dimensions, whereas low-status group members consider the in-group superior on alternative dimensions (Ellemers & Van Rijswijk, 1997).

Extremism

Groups in conflict often misperceive each other's beliefs. Parties in conflict do not have an accurate understanding of the views of the other party and exaggerate the position of the other side in a way that promotes the perception of conflict (Robinson, Keltner, Ward, & Ross, 1994; Ross & Ward, 1996). Each side views the other as holding more extreme and opposing views than is really the case. Consider the 1986 Howard Beach incident involving the death of a young African-American man who was struck by a passing car as he attempted to escape from a group of white pursuers in the Howard Beach neighborhood of New York City. A trial ultimately led to the conviction of some (but not all) of the young man's pursuers. Many details of the case were ambiguous and controversial, leading each party to take exaggerated perceptions of the views of the other parties, thereby exacerbating the perception of differences in opinion. Partisans on either side of the affirmative action debate greatly overestimate the liberalism of proponents and the conservatism of opponents (Sherman, Nelson, & Ross, 2003). The same polarization effect is found for other policy issues, such as abortion and immigration.

Why does this extremism occur? According to the **naïve realism** principle (Ross & Ward, 1996), people expect others to hold views of the world similar to their own.

When conflict erupts, people are initially inclined to sway the other party with evidence. When this tactic fails to bridge interests, people regard dissenters as extremists who are out of touch with reality.

Strategies for Optimizing Intergroup Negotiations

Separate Conflict of Interest from Symbolic Conflict

Conflict between groups does not always arise from competition over scarce resources. Many conflicts between groups do not have their roots in resource scarcity, but rather in fundamental differences in values (Bobo, 1983). Consider for example, the strong protests made against busing by people whose lives are not affected by it (Sears & Allen, 1984). Presumably, people who do not have children or grandchildren are not affected by busing. However, they tend to have strong feelings about it. Busing does not represent an economic issue to them, but rather a symbolic issue. It is important to understand which issues are symbolic and which are economic.

Moreover, adversaries are more optimistic about intergroup negotiation when they are exposed to the actual, rather than assumed, views of their counterparts (Sherman, Nelson, & Ross, 2003).

Search for Common Identity

To the extent groups in conflict can share a common identity, conflict and competition can decrease dramatically (Kramer & Brewer, 1986). Kramer notes that people in organizations can identify at different levels within their organization (e.g., person, group, department, unit, organization as a whole, etc.). For example, in one investigation, groups were told to focus on their group identities. Other groups who were involved in an objectively identical conflict were told to focus on the collective organization. Cooperation was greatly increased when groups focused on the collective, rather than their group identities.

Avoid the Out-Group Homogeneity Bias

Suppose that three white managers watch a videotape of a discussion among members of a mixed-race group, composed of three African-American men and three Caucasian men. After watching the videotape, the managers are presented with the actual text of the conversation and asked to indicate who said what. They are very good at remembering whether an African-American or Caucasian person made a particular comment, but their accuracy in terms of differentiating which African-American male said what is abysmal (Linville, Fischer, & Salovey, 1989). Thus, within-race (or within-group) errors are more prevalent than between-race errors, because people categorize members of out-groups not as individuals, but simply as "black Americans." Thus, it is important for people to treat members of out-groups as individuals.

Contact

The "mere contact" strategy is based on the principle that greater contact among members of diverse groups increases cooperation among group members. Unfortunately, contact in and of itself does not lead to better intergroup relations, and in some cases may even exacerbate negative relations among groups. For example, contact between African-Americans and Caucasians in desegregated schools does not reduce racial prejudice (Gerard, 1983; Schofield, 1986); little relationship is noted between interdepartmental contact and conflict in organizations (Brown et al., 1986); and college students studying in foreign countries become increasingly negative toward their host countries the longer they remain in them (Stroebe, Lenkert, & Jonas, 1988).

Several conditions need to be in place before contact can have its desired effects of reducing prejudice.

- **Social and institutional support**: For contact to work, a framework of social and institutional support is needed. That is, people in positions of authority should be unambiguous in their endorsement of the goals of the integration policies. This support fosters the development of a new social climate in which more tolerant norms can emerge.
- **Acquaintance potential**: A second condition for successful contact is that it be of sufficient frequency, duration, and closeness to permit the development of meaningful relationships between members of the groups concerned. Infrequent, short, and casual interaction will do little to foster more favorable attitudes and may even make them worse (Brewer & Brown, 1998). This type of close interaction will lead to the discovery of similarities and disconfirm negative stereotypes.
- **Equal status**: The third condition necessary for contact to be successful is that participants have equal status. Many stereotypes of out-groups comprise beliefs about the inferior ability of out-group members to perform various tasks. If the contact situation involves an unequal-status relationship between men and women, for example, with women in the subordinate role (e.g., taking notes, acting as secretaries), stereotypes are likely to be reinforced rather than weakened (Bradford & Cohen, 1984). If, however, the group members work on equal footing, prejudiced beliefs become hard to sustain in the face of repeated experience of task competence by the out-group member.
- **Shared goal**: When members of different groups depend on each other for the achievement of a jointly desired objective, they have instrumental reasons to develop better relationships. The importance of an overriding, clear, shared group goal is a key determinant of intergroup relations. Sometimes a common enemy is a catalyst for bonding among diverse people and groups. For example, by "waging a war against cancer," members of different medical groups and laboratories can work together.
- **Cross-group friendships**: Sometimes it is not necessary for groups to have real contact with one another to improve intergroup relations. If group members know that another member of their own group has a friendship or relationship with a member of the out-group, or a cross-group friendship, in-group members have less negative attitudes toward the out-group (Wright, Aron, McLaughlin-Volpe, & Ropp, 1997). It is not necessary that all members of a group have cross-group friendships; merely knowing that one member of the group does can go a long way toward reducing negative out-group attitudes.

Many of these strategies are preventative in their approach and can help ward off unhealthy, destructive competition between groups. What steps can a manager take to deal with conflict after it has erupted?

The GRIT Strategy

The **G**raduated and **R**eciprocal **I**nitiative in **T**ension Reduction, or **GRIT model,** is a model of conflict reduction for warring groups. Originally developed as a program for international disarmament negotiations, it can be used to deescalate intergroup problems on a smaller, domestic scale as well (Osgood, 1979). The goals of this strategy are to increase communication and reciprocity between groups while reducing mistrust, thereby allowing for deescalation of hostility and creation of a greater array of possible outcomes. The model prescribes a series of steps that call for specific communication between groups in the hope of establishing the "rules of the game." Other stages are designed to increase trust between the two groups as the consistency in each group's responses demonstrates credibility and honesty. Some steps are necessary only in extremely intense conflict situations in which the breakdown of intergroup relations implies a danger for the group members.

Mikhail Gorbachev's decisions in the period from 1986 to 1989 closely resemble the GRIT model (Barron, Kerr, & Miller, 1992). Gorbachev made a number of unilateral concessions that resulted in serious deescalation of world tensions in this period. On two occasions, the Soviets stalled resumption of atmospheric nuclear testing despite their inability to extend the prior treaty with the Reagan administration. They then agreed twice to summit meetings despite the Reagan administration's refusal to discuss the Star Wars defense system. They then agreed to the Intermediate and Strategic Range Nuclear Missile (INF) Treaty (exceeding the United States' requests for verification) with continued refusal by the United States to bargain about Star Wars. Next came agreements on the Berlin Wall and the unification of Germany. Eventually, even the staunchly anti-Communist/anti-Soviet Reagan-Bush regime had to take notice. These events led to a period of mellowing tensions between these two superpowers (see Table 9-7).

Although the GRIT model may seem overly elaborate and therefore inapplicable to most organizational conflicts, the model clarifies the difficulties inherent in establishing mutual trust between parties that have been involved in prolonged conflict. Although some of the stages are not applicable to all conflicts, the importance of clearly announcing intentions, making promised concessions, and matching reciprocation are relevant to all but the most transitory conflicts.

TABLE 9-7   GRIT Strategy

1. Announce your general intentions to deescalate tensions and your specific intention to make an initial concession.
2. Execute the initial concession unilaterally, completely, and, of course, publicly. Provide as much verification as possible.
3. Invite reciprocity from the out-group. Expect the out-group to react to these steps with mistrust and skepticism. To overcome this, continued concessions should be made.
4. Match any reciprocal concessions made by the out-group and invite more.
5. Diversify the nature of your concessions.
6. Maintain your ability to retaliate if the out-group escalates tension. Any such retaliation should be carefully calibrated to match the intensity of the out-group's transgression.

Source: Barron, R. S., Kerr, N. L., and Miller, N. (1992). *Group Process, Group Decision, Group Action* (p. 151). Pacific Grove, CA: Brooks/Cole.

CONCLUSION

Multiparty negotiations require all of the pie-slicing and pie-expanding skills of two-party negotiations, and then some. The key challenges of multiparty negotiations are the development and management of coalitions, the complexity of information management, voting rules, and communication breakdowns. We discussed several different levels of analysis involved in multiparty negotiations and key strategies to finesse each situation, including coalition management, principal-agent relationships, team negotiation, intergroup negotiation, and dealing with constituencies. Having explored a few features of the SCO-IBM negotiation at each level of analysis, it is clear that all levels are necessary to fully understand and capitalize on the dynamics of multiparty negotiations. For example, had we restricted our analysis merely to the level of the interaction between the principals, we would have failed to detect the second table that includes IBM customers, BayStar Capital, Microsoft, SCO owners, and shareholders. Moreover, we would have failed to appreciate how agents, as coming to the table with their own reputations (e.g., anti-Microsoft), influence the course of negotiations. Table 9-8 summarizes the six levels of analysis, the key challenges facing the negotiator at each level, and the best strategies to surmount these challenges.

TABLE 9-8 Summary of Challenges and Strategies for Each Level of Multiparty Analysis

Level of Analysis	Challenges	Strategies
Multiparty negotiation	Coalition formation Difficulty formulating trade-offs Voting paradoxes • Strategic voting Majority rule suppresses strength of preference Communication breakdowns • Private caucusing • Biased interpretation • Perspective taking failures • Indirect speech acts • Multiple audience problem	Information management Systematize proposal making Use brainstorming wisely Develop and assign process roles Stay at the table Strive for equal participation Avoid the "equal shares" bias Avoid the "agreement bias" Avoid agendas
Coalitions	Optimal coalition size? Trust and temptation Dividing the pie	Core solution Shapley model Raiffa's (1982) hybrid model Make contacts early Seek verbal commitments Allocate resources fairly

Principal-agent relationships	Conflicting incentives
	Shrinking bargaining zone
	Communication distortion
	Loss of control
	Agreement at any cost
		Shop around
		Know your BATNA before
		    meeting your agent
		Communicate interests, but do not
		    reveal your BATNA
		Capitalize on agent's expertise
		Tap into agent's sources of information
		Discuss ratification
		Use agent for saving face
		Use agent to buffer emotions

Principal-constituency relationships	Accountability
	• Evaluation apprehension
	• Face saving
	Conflict of interest
		Understand constituents' interest
		Do not expect homogeneity
		    within constituencies
		Educate constituents on your role
		    and limitations
		Help constituents do horizon thinking

Team negotiation	Choosing team mates How many on the team? Communication within the team Team cohesion Information processing	Prepare as a team (not separately) Plan scheduled breaks (to regroup) Role-play with each other Determine accountability
Intergroup negotiation	Stereotyping Changing identities In-group bias Extremism	Separate conflict of interest from symbolic conflict Search for common identity Avoid outgroup homogeneity bias Contact GRIT strategy

10 CROSS-CULTURAL NEGOTIATION

"After we acquired the company that made Koosh Ball, it was my job to ensure that sales and profit would go up. We flew to Hong Kong to meet with key vendors to see if there was an opportunity to improve pricing, and we tested the integrity of the current vendor's price with a second manufacturer and found we could get the balls for 3¢ less per ball. Then we had a very elaborate dinner with the current manufacturer and his whole family to find out whether it was possible to get his price down. . . . We're sitting in this room, 16 people at the table, and we're trying to accomplish three things. First, we want to have a good relationship. Especially in China, your word really matters and the honor you give your partner means everything. If we had walked in and said, 'I've second-sourced your product and can make it for 3¢ less,' he might have walked away because we would've embarrassed him. Second, we wanted to let him know we were growing the business and there was an opportunity for him to make more products for us. Third, we had to ask for his help. We never told him he needed to lower his price; we asked, was there anything he could do to help us? He understood what that meant, and he came back with a price that was a penny below the second source" (*Inc.*, Aug. 1, 2003a, p. 77).

This example reveals a key cultural difference between Western-style negotiation and Eastern-style communication. The Western negotiator resisted the instinct to directly discuss price; instead, subtly signaling the issue allowed the other party to maintain dignity. Negotiations across cultures are commonplace and, in many cases, a requirement for effective management in multinational and international companies. Often cross-cultural negotiations do not always go smoothly (see Box 10-1 for some examples of failed cross-cultural negotiation). Most managers cannot expect to negotiate only with people of their own country or culture throughout their career. In fact, North Americans are a minority—about 7 percent of the world's population. To get a better sense of the world's composition, imagine that the world's population is only 100 people. In this case, the population would include 55 Asians, 21 Europeans, 9 Africans, 8 South Americans, and 7 North Americans (Triandis, 1994).

BOX 10-1

FAILED CROSS-CULTURAL NEGOTIATION

Jayant J., representing an Indian software company, waited impatiently for a local manufacturer in Sao Paulo, Brazil, to clinch a business deal. After waiting almost one-and-a-half hours, it took all his effort to welcome the relaxed Brazilian, who barged into the lounge without even an apology and started the conversation with a joke. The Brazilian's habit of communicating by standing very close and touching Jayant frequently made Jayant, a stickler for etiquette, very uncomfortable and irritated. At the close of the deal, the Brazilian's reply for a firm commitment, "si Deus quizer" ("if God wishes"), was the final straw for Jayant, who thought the Brazilian was being vague. The meeting was a failure and they never met again (*Economic Times*, Nov. 8, 1999).

A Japanese manager wanted to study a multimillion-dollar business proposal before he gave his American counterpart an answer. "Give me five minutes," he said. The American smiled back and waited. A few seconds later, the American's mouth twitched. Then he fidgeted a bit more. A whole 18 seconds later, the American interrupted the silence, startling the Japanese businessman, who was much more accustomed to the silence (*The Star-Ledger*, Apr. 27, 1995).

As we have seen, even negotiators from the same culture often fail to reach integrative outcomes. When people from *different* cultures get together to negotiate, they may leave even more money on the table unless they are prepared (Brett, 2001). Failure to expand the pie has a number of undesirable ripple effects, including (but not limited to) feelings of exploitation, souring of a potentially rewarding relationship, and the destruction of potential global relationships.

Often, value is left on the table because people are not prepared for the challenges of cross-cultural negotiation. This chapter provides a business plan for effective cross-cultural negotiation. We begin by defining culture; then we identify the key dimensions by which culture affects judgment, motivation, and behavior at the bargaining table. Next, we identify the biggest barriers to effective intercultural negotiation and provide strategies for effective cross-cultural negotiation.

LEARNING ABOUT CULTURES

We need to make one thing perfectly clear up front: This chapter does not provide a crash course of how to negotiate with people of different cultures. Thus, we do not offer different advice on a country-by-country basis for two reasons. First, it would be contrary to the book's focus, which is to provide negotiation skills that work across contexts. In addition, we do not want to promote cultural stereotypes. By making a generic list of characteristics for cultures, we magnify the stereotypes, which is neither practical nor informative. Most people prefer to be considered as unique individuals, yet we are often too quick to lump people from different countries together as being "all the same."

A more useful approach is to develop a framework for thinking about culture. Jeanne Brett (2001) describes the difference between "stereotypes" and "prototypes," such that the latter recognizes that substantial variation is likely even within a culture. Using a prototype approach provides several advantages. First, a great deal of diversity can be found among people in any culture. A cultural framework is sensitive to heterogeneity within cultural groups. Second, most cultures are different today than they were 10 years ago—stereotypes in place today will be outdated tomorrow. We need a dynamic framework that allows us to learn how cultures change and grow. This chapter provides a means by which to expose our own cultural beliefs and those of others, how to avoid mistakes, and how to profit from intercultural negotiations (for an extensive treatment, see Brett, 2001).

Defining Culture

Many people conceive of culture strictly in terms of geography; however, culture does not just pertain to nations and countries. Rather, culture is the unique character of a social group; the values and norms shared by its members set it apart from other social groups (Lytle, Brett, & Shapiro, 1999). Culture concerns economic, social, political, and religious institutions. It also concerns the unique products produced by these groups—art, architecture, music, theatre, and literature (Brett, 2001). Cultural institutions preserve and promote a culture's ideologies. Culture influences mental models of how things work, behavior, and cause-and-effect relationships. To broaden our thinking about culture, consider that possible cultural differences are contained in all of the following:

- Families
- Social groups and departments in an organization
- Organizations
- Industries
- States
- Regions
- Countries
- Societies (e.g., foraging, horticultural, pastoral, agrarian, industrial, service, information)
- Continents
- Hemispheres

Nations, occupational groups, social classes, genders, races, tribes, corporations, clubs, and social movements may become the bases of specific subcultures. When thinking about culture and diversity, avoid the temptation to think of it as a single dimension (e.g., country of origin); culture is a complex whole, and it is best to use many criteria to discern one culture from another.

Culture as an Iceberg

We use Schneider's (1997) model of culture as an iceberg (see also Brett, 2001, for an extensive treatment). Typically, about one-ninth of an iceberg is visible; the rest is submerged. As Figure 10-1 indicates, the top (visible) part of the cultural iceberg is the behaviors, artifacts, and institutions that characterize a culture. This portion includes things such as traditions, customs, habits, and the like. These obvious behaviors and artifacts are an expression of deeper-held values, beliefs, and norms. Driving these values and norms are fundamental assumptions about the world and humanity, at the cultural iceberg's "base."

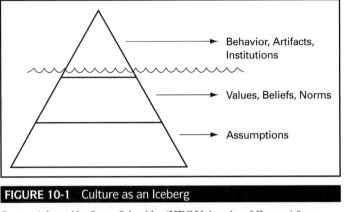

FIGURE 10-1   Culture as an Iceberg

Source: Adapted by Susan Schneider (HEC University of Geneva) from Schein, E. H. 1985. *Organizational Culture and Leadership,* p. 14. San Francisco: Jossey-Bass.

The artifacts and customs that characterize a culture are not arbitrary; rather, they are manifestations about fundamental values and beliefs about the world. Thus, to change such expressions and customs would be to challenge centuries-old beliefs and values.

CULTURAL VALUES AND NEGOTIATION NORMS

Cultures can differ in many dramatic ways. Next, we identify three dimensions of culture, following Brett (2001; see Table 10-1; Gelfand & Brett, 2004):

- Individualism versus collectivism
- Egalitarianism versus hierarchy
- Direct versus indirect communication

These three dimensions refer to motivation, influence, and information, respectively (Brett, 2001). Specifically, as we will discuss, *individualism-collectivism* refers to the basic human motive concerning preservation of the self versus the collective. The dimension of *egalitarianism-hierarchy* refers to the means by which people influence others, either laterally or hierarchically. Finally, *direct-indirect communication* refers to the manner in which people exchange information and messages.

Individualism Versus Collectivism

A key way in which many cultures differ is in terms of individualism and collectivism (Triandis, 1994; Hofstede, 1980; Schwartz, 1994; see Gelfand, Bhawuk, Nishii, & Bechtold, 2004, for a review). Next, we describe individualistic and collectivist cultural values, then identify negotiation strategy issues.

Individualism

In the discussion in Chapter 5 on bargaining style, we outlined three motivational orientations: individualistic, competitive, and cooperative. Individualism, as a cultural style, epitomizes the individualistic motivational orientation.[1] In individualistic cultures, the

---

[1]For simplicity, we include competitive style with individual style.

TABLE 10-1 Dimensions of Culture		
Cultural Dimension		
Goal: **Individual versus collective orientation**	*Individualists/Competitors:* Key goal is to maximize own gain (and perhaps the difference between oneself and others); source of identity is the self; people regard themselves as free agents and independent actors.	*Collectivists/Cooperators:* Key goal is to maximize the welfare of the group or collective; source of identity is the group; individuals regard themselves as group members; focus is on social relations.
Influence: **Egalitarianism versus hierarchy**	*Egalitarians:* Do not perceive many social obligations; often regard BATNA to be major source of bargaining power.	*Hierarchists:* Regard social order to be important in determining conflict management strategies; subordinates are expected to defer to superiors; superiors are expected to look out for subordinates.
Communication: **Direct versus indirect**	*Direct Communicators:* Engage in explicit, direct information exchange; ask direct questions; are not affected by situational constraints; face-saving issues likely to arise.	*Indirect Communicators:* Engage in tacit information exchange such as storytelling, inference-making; situational norms.

Source: Brett, J. M. (2001). *Negotiating Globally: How to Negotiate Deals, Resolve Disputes, and Make Decisions Across Cultural Boundaries.* San Francisco, CA: Jossey-Bass.

pursuit of happiness and regard for personal welfare are paramount. People in individualistic cultures give priority to their personal goals, even when these goals conflict with those of their family, work group, or country. Individual happiness and expression are valued more than collective and group needs. People from individualistic cultures enjoy having influence and control over their world and others. Consequently, individual accomplishments are rewarded by economic and social institutions. Furthermore, legal institutions in individualist cultures are designed to protect individual rights. One implication of individualism concerns the use of distributive tactics. People who are more self-interested are motivated to use more tactics that increase their bargaining power. Indeed, U.S. MBA students are more tolerant of certain kinds of ethically questionable tactics than are non-U.S. MBA students (Lewicki & Robinson, 1998). Specifically, U.S. MBA students are more accepting of competitive bargaining tactics and bluffing, which raises the possibility that U.S. negotiators may be perceived as less ethical by their international counterparts (see Lewicki & Robinson, 1998). On the other hand, U.S. negotiators are significantly less accepting of misrepresentation to an opponent's network. The norm in the United States of not spreading stories, particularly to the network of friends, is well entrenched.

Collectivism

Collectivist cultures are rooted in social groups, and individuals are viewed as members of groups. People in collectivist cultures give priority to in-group goals. The dominant motive is concern for, and belonging to, the group. People of collectivist cultures view their work groups and organizations as fundamental parts of themselves. Collectivists are concerned about how the results of their actions affect members of their in-group; they share resources with in-group members, feel interdependent with in-group members, and feel involved in the lives of in-group members (Billings, 1989; Hui & Triandis, 1986). In contrast to individualistic cultures that focus on influence and control, people from collectivist cultures emphasize the importance of adjustment. Not surprisingly, collectivist cultures are more concerned with maintaining harmony in interpersonal relationships with the in-group than are individualistic cultures. Social norms and institutions promote the interdependence of individuals through emphasis on social obligations and the sacrifice of personal needs for the greater good. Legal institutions place the greater good of the collective above the rights of the individual, and political and economic institutions reward classes of people as opposed to individuals (Brett, 2001).

Whereas individualists want to save face and are concerned with their personal outcomes, collectivists are concerned with others' outcomes as well. An analysis of U.S. and Hong Kong negotiations reveal that U.S. negotiators are more likely to subscribe to self-interest and joint problem-solving norms, whereas Hong Kong Chinese negotiators are more likely to subscribe to an equality norm (Tinsley & Pillutla, 1998). Further, U.S. negotiators are more satisfied when they maximize joint gain, and Hong Kong Chinese negotiators are happier when they achieve outcome parity. The tendency of North Americans to engage in self-enhancement, an individualistic trait, is more than skin-deep. In one investigation of Canadians (individualists) and Japanese (collectivists), behaviors were covertly measured (Heine, Takata, & Lehman, 2000). Canadians were reluctant to conclude that they had performed worse than their average classmate (self-enhancement); in contrast, Japanese were hesitant to conclude that they had performed better—in short, they self-criticized. Individualism and collectivism represent a continuum with substantial within-culture variation. One factor that can push people toward behaving more in line with their native cultural values is accountability pressure—simply the extent to which they are answerable for conducting themselves in a certain manner (Gelfand & Realo, 1999).

Implications for Negotiation

Individualism-collectivism involves a variety of implications for the conduct of negotiation. We will outline seven of them:

1. Social networks
2. Cooperation
3. In-group favoritism
4. Social loafing versus social striving
5. Endowment
6. Dispositionalism versus situationalism
7. Preferences for dispute resolution

Social Networks Cultures differ dramatically in terms of their social networks (Morris, Podolny, & Ariel, 1999). Specifically, members of different cultures differ in terms of the density of their work friendships (i.e., how many friendships they share at work), the overlap of instrumental and socioemotional ties (i.e., whether the people they seek for information are also the ones whom they seek for comfort and emotional support), the closeness of the tie, the longevity of the tie, and whether the network relationships are directed upward, lateral, or downward. In one study, U.S. and Hong Kong students negotiated with someone whom they believed to be a friend or a stranger from their own culture. As expected based upon their collectivist orientation, the Hong Kong students changed their behavior more when interacting with a friend than did the U.S. students (Chan et al., 1994). Similarly, whereas U.S. managers are equally likely to trust and reciprocate with a partner as well as with someone in the network (whom they don't know directly), collectivist managers only trust and reciprocate when interacting with the relationship (Buchan, Croson, & Dawes, 2002). Perhaps this factor is why many realty agents report that Hispanics are often perplexed at the U.S. culture's habit of not meeting the seller of a home they are buying (*Star-Tribune*, June 14, 2003). Similarly, agents with whom the Hispanic principal works are often treated as part of the extended family, with invitations to life cycle events.

Morris, Podolny, and Ariel (1999) examined four cultures—North American, Chinese, German, and Spanish—and proposed that each culture developed social networks within the organization according to a different set of norms (see Table 10-2). North American business relationships are characterized by a market orientation in which people form relationships according to the market standard of whether it is profitable. Practically, this tendency means that North Americans form ties without the prior basis of friendship, paying attention only to instrumentality. Chinese business relationships are characterized by a familial orientation, in which employees make sacrifices for the welfare of the organization. Sharing resources within the in-group, loyalty, and deference to superiors characterize network relationships. German business relationships are characterized by legal-bureaucratic orientation, formal categories, and rules. Finally, Spanish business relationships are characterized by affiliative orientations, such as sociability and friendliness. A controlled cross-national comparison of network relationships in Citibank supported these network norms (Morris, Podolny, & Ariel, 1999).

TABLE 10-2 Dominant Norms of Business Relations		
Culture	*Dominant Attitude*	*Business Relationships*
North American: *Market norms*	Economic individualism	Short-lived Low-multiplexity
Chinese: *Familial norms*	Filial loyalty Economic collectivism	Directed upward to powerful
German: *Legal-bureaucratic norms*	Economic collectivism	Bounded by formal rules Low affectivity
Spanish: *Affiliative norms*	Self-expressive collectivism	Long-lived High affectivity

Source: Morris, M. W., Podolny, J. M., and Ariel, S. (1999). *Missing Relations: Incorporating Relational Constructs into Models of Culture.* Paper presented at 1998 SESP conference, Lexington, Kentucky.

Cooperation   People from collectivist cultural traditions engage in more cooperative behavior in mixed-motive interactions than do people from individualistic cultures (Cox, Lobel, & McLeod, 1991). For example, Japanese negotiators are more cooperative (and, in turn, expect others to be more cooperative) than are U.S. negotiators (Wade-Benzoni, Okumura, Brett, Moore, Tenbrunsel, & Bazerman, 2002). Greater cooperation in the face of uncertainty and the potential for exploitation imply that people from collectivist cultures place greater emphasis on the needs and goals of their group and are more likely to be willing to sacrifice personal interests for the attainment of group goals. Indeed, Americans are more likely to remember situations in which they *influenced* others; in contrast, Japanese people are more likely to remember situations in which they *adjusted* to others (a form of cooperation; Morling, Kitayama, & Miyamoto, 2002). An examination of Japanese and U.S. newspaper stories on conflict revealed that Japanese newspapers more frequently make reference to mutual blame than do U.S. newspapers, presumably because ascribing blame to both parties affords the maintenance of the social unit and is less threatening to the collective (Gelfand, Nishii, Holcombe, Dyer, Ohbuchi, & Fukuno, 2001). Moreover, Americans who successfully influenced others reported feeling very *efficacious* (a typical individualistic emotion); whereas Japanese people who adjusted reported feeling *related* (a collectivist emotion).

Awareness of different cultural norms can be a powerful bargaining strategy. For example, consider the negotiations that took place in Kyoto in 1997 to reach a pact on global warming. For more than a week, the negotiators at the Kyoto climate-change conference had been haggling over the terms of a treaty that would go a long way toward dealing productively with global warming. In the last hours of the negotiation, all of the world's industrialized nations had agreed to firm targets for reducing six different greenhouse gases. All but Japan, that is. The Japanese had been assigned the most modest goal: cut emission 6 percent below 1990 levels by the year 2012, compared with 7 percent for the United States and 8 percent for the 15 nations of the European Union. The Japanese would not budge. Five percent was their limit. So the U.S. delegation called Washington to report the impasse, and at 2 A.M., an exhausted Vice President Al Gore got on the phone with Japanese Prime Minister Ryutaro Hashimoto. Gore's cross-cultural skills were sharp: He first praised Hashimoto for Japan's leadership in playing host to the conference (focusing on hierarchical cultural norms) and then he pointed out how bad it would look for the host country to derail the agreement over a measly percentage point (focusing on collective well-being). It worked (*Time*, Dec. 22, 1997).

In-Group Favoritism   In-group favoritism is the strong tendency to favor the members of one's own group more than those in other groups, even when one has no logical basis for doing so. The in-group bias is so powerful that even when groups are formed on the basis of an arbitrary procedure, such as by drawing lots or random assignment, people tend to evaluate their group members more positively and reward them with more resources than members of the out-group (Tajfel, 1982). As might be expected, members of collectivist cultures display more in-group favoritism than members of individualistic cultures. For example, making group boundaries salient creates more competitive behavior among members of collectivist cultures than members of individualistic cultures (Espinoza & Garza, 1985). Moreover, members of collectivistic cultures become more competitive when they perceive their group to be in the minority (Espinoza & Garza, 1985). In-group favoritism often has positive effects for members of in-groups, but it can be deleterious for members of out-groups and for intergroup relations (see Chapter 9 for more on inter-group negotiation). However, according to Gabriel and Gardner (1999), you don't have to be from a collectivist culture to show collectivist behavior, such as in-group favoritism; rather, everyone has an "interdependent" and an "independent" self, which can be "triggered" (see Box 10-2 for an example).

Social Loafing Versus Social Striving   **Social loafing** is the tendency for people to work less hard and contribute less effort and resources in a group context than when working alone. For example, people clap less loudly, work less hard, and contribute less when

BOX 10-2

PRIMING INDIVIDUALISM AND COLLECTIVISM

Everyone needs to be individualistic at times and more collectivistic, or group-focused, at times. In a series of investigations, we "primed" U.S. managers to be either individualistic (focused on the self) or relational (focused on others). To create this focus, we had the U.S. managers read a story about a leader who had an important decision to make—choosing a successor. In one version of the story, the leader chooses someone on the basis of personal talent and merit (individualistic value); in the other version of the story, the leader chooses someone on the basis of his relationship to him (collectivistic value). Then, we watched how the U.S. managers resolved a dispute. The U.S. managers who were in a position of power in a dispute were significantly more generous and cooperative if they had previously read the collectivistic story. In contrast, the U.S. managers who had read the individualistic story were significantly more self-interested (Seeley, Thompson, & Gardner, 2003).

In another twist, we then had teams of managers negotiate against other teams. We hypothesized that if we used the same collectivistic prime, it would increase the negotiator's loyalty to his or her team and lead to significantly more in-group favoritism and less generosity across the table. The results confirmed the expectations (panel A). In panel A, we see that

negotiators are more generous when they have been "primed" with interdependence (rather than independence) in a one-on-one (dyadic negotiation). However, the tables turn when the priming occurs in a group setting: Here the negotiator who is primed with interdependence is less generous. In panel B, we see that the likelihood of impasse follows the same pattern: With interdependent negotiators, they are *least* likely to impasse when they are one-on-one and *most* likely to impasse when they are team-on-team.

The message? Self-interested or other-focused behavior can be triggered in negotiations with subtle primes. Triggering collectivism in a two-party situation will lead the powerful person to be more generous across the table; however, in a team situation, collectivism leads to greater in-group favoritism (to the tune of more than $80,000). Groups primed for collectivism were more successful in avoiding costly court action than were those who were primed to be independent—even though the facts in the situation, their bargaining reservation prices, and other details were objectively identical (Seeley, Thompson, & Gardner, 2003). In fact, no one who was primed with interdependence escalated to court action, but 20 percent of those with an independent focus did.

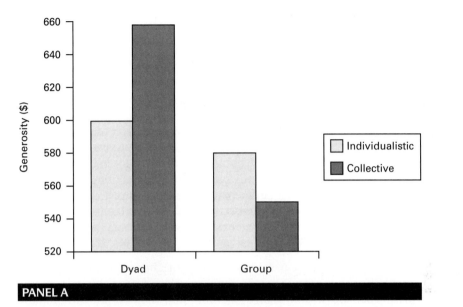

PANEL A

Source: Seeley, E., Thompson, L., and Garnder, W. (2003). *Power and Exploitation in Groups: Effects of Construal and Group Size.* Paper presented at the meetings of the Academy of Management. Seattle, Washington.

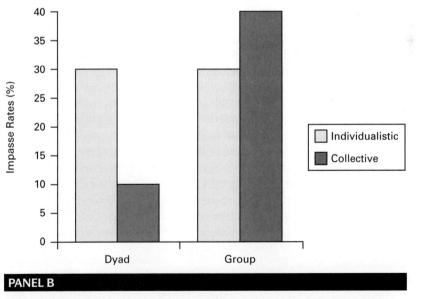

PANEL B

Source: Seeley, E., Thompson, L., and Garnder, W. (2003). *Power and Exploitation in Groups: Effects of Construal and Group Size.* Paper presented at the meetings of the Academy of Management. Seattle, Washington.

working in a group, as opposed to working alone (Kerr, 1983). Social loafing should occur less in collectivist cultures than individualist cultures, presumably because individualist cultures do not reward group effort, but collectivist cultures do. In a study of social loafing among management trainees in the United States and the People's Republic of China, Americans students loafed (individual performance declined in a group setting), but Chinese students did not (Earley, 1989). In fact, among Japanese participants, the opposite pattern occurred in the group: Social striving—collectivist concerns for the welfare of the group—increased people's motivation and performance (Shirakashi, 1985; Yamaguchi, Okamoto, & Oka, 1985). Self-serving biases, such as egocentrism (as discussed in Chapter 3) are more prevalent in individualistic cultures, such as the United States, in which the self is served by focusing on positive attributes and desire to stand out and be better than others. In contrast, members of collectivist cultures are less likely to hold a biased, self-serving view of themselves; rather, the self is served by focusing on negative characteristics in order to "blend in" (Gelfand, Higgins, Nishii, Raver, Dominguez, Murakami, Yamaguchi, & Toyama, 2002).

Endowment   Collectivism has implications for the ownership of resources. The endowment effect is the tendency for people to place more value on something that is currently in their possession than something that they do not own, independent of the value of the good itself. In Chapter 2, we noted that students who are given a coffee mug or a ballpoint pen demand a higher price to sell it than students who are asked to make an offer to buy the coffee mug or ballpoint pen are willing to pay (Kahneman, Knetsch, & Thaler, 1990). Individualist cultures show a strong endowment effect; however, members of collectivist cultures do not (Carnevale & Radhakrishnan, 1994). People from collectivist cultures show a group endowment effect—they value a good or resource more in contexts where they believe others can share it (Carnevale & Radhakrishnan, 1994, experiment 2).

Dispositionalism Versus Situationalism   **Dispositionalism** is the tendency to ascribe the cause of a person's behavior to his or her character or underlying personality. **Situationalism** is the tendency to ascribe the cause of a person's behavior to factors and forces outside of a person's control. For example, suppose that you are in the midst of a high-stakes negotiation, and you place an urgent call to your negotiation partner. Your partner does not return your call; yet, you know your partner is in town because you contacted the office secretary. What is causing your partner's behavior? It is possible that your partner is irresponsible (dispositionalism); similarly, it is possible that your partner never got your message (situationalism). Depending upon what you think is the true cause, your behavior toward your partner will be different—anger versus forgiveness, perhaps (Rosette, Brett, Barsness, & Lytle, 2000).

People from individualistic cultures view causality differently than do members of collectivist cultures. Dispositionalism is more widespread in individualistic than in collectivist cultures. To see how deep-seated these cultural differences are, look at Figure 10-2, panels A and B.

In Figure 10-2, panels A and B, the blue fish swims on a trajectory that deviates from that of others (indicated by darkest arrows). When asked to describe what was going on in videotapes of swimming fish whose movements were similar to those illustrated in Figure 10-2, members of individualistic cultures (Americans) perceived more influence of internal factors (dispositionalism), whereas members of collectivist cultures (Chinese)

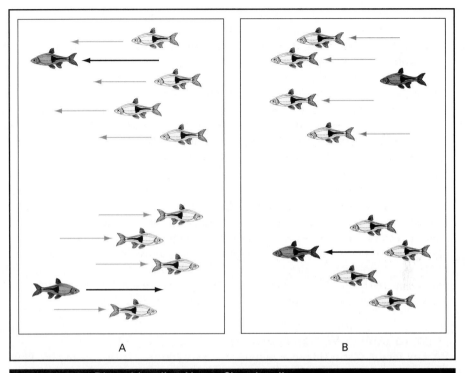

FIGURE 10-2   Dispositionalism Versus Situationalism

Diagrams showing trajectories of fish. The blue fishes have the darkest arrows in these diagrams. In A, the group joins the individual (top), and the individual joins the group (bottom); In B, the group leaves the individual (top), and the individual leaves the group (bottom).

Source: Adapted from Morris, M. W., and Peng, K. (1994). "Culture and Cause: American and Chinese Attributions for Social and Physical Events." *Journal of Personality and Social Psychology, 67*(6), 949–971.

perceived more external influence (situationalism) on the blue fish's motions (Morris & Peng, 1994). Specifically, Chinese people were more likely to view the fish as wanting to achieve harmony, whereas Americans were more likely to view the blue fish as striking out on its own. Similarly, an investigation of stories in American and Chinese newspapers reveals that English-language newspapers are more dispositional and Chinese-language newspapers are more situational when explaining the same crime stories (Morris & Peng, 1994). Specifically, when newspaper articles about "rogue trader" scandals were analyzed, U.S. papers made more mention of the individual trader involved, whereas Japanese papers referred more to the organization (Menon, Morris, Chiu, & Hong, 1999). Similarly, when a team member behaves in a maladjusted way, U.S. participants are more likely to focus on the member's traits, whereas the Hong Kong participants focus on situational factors. Dispositionalism also affects biases. People from individualistic cultures, such as the United States, are more likely to fall prey to the fixed-pie bias than are people from collectivistic cultures, such as Greece (Gelfand & Christakopolou, 1999).

Preferences for Dispute Resolution   Morris, Leung, and Sethi (1999) note four types of dispute resolution procedures that members of different cultures can use to resolve disputes: bargaining, mediation, adversarial adjudication, and inquisitorial adjudication. In *bargaining*, or negotiation, two disputants retain full control over the discussion process and settlement outcome. In *mediation*, disputants retain control over the final decision, but a third party guides the process. In *adversarial adjudication*, a judge makes a binding settlement decision, but disputants retain control of the process. Finally, in *inquisitorial adjudication*, disputants yield control over both the process and the final decision to a third party. Collectivist cultures such as China differ from individualistic cultures such as the United States in terms of preferences for dispute resolution (Leung, 1987; Morris, Leung, & Sethi, 1999). For example, when it comes to resolving conflict, Japanese managers prefer to defer to a higher status person, Germans prefer to regulate behavior via rules, and Americans prefer an interests model that relies on resolving underlying interests (Tinsley, 1998, 2001). Furthermore, cultural differences in attributional tendencies (i.e., collectivists view behavior as a function of situation; individualists view behavior as a function of disposition) create even more of a gap between preferences. Specifically, when negotiators encounter a disagreeable person across the bargaining table, individualists attribute that person's behavior to underlying disposition and desire more formal dispute resolution procedures; in contrast, collectivists are more likely to ascribe behavior to situational factors and prefer informal procedures (Morris, Leung, & Sethi, 1999).

Egalitarianism Versus Hierarchy

A key factor that influences behavior across cultures is the means by which people influence others and the basis of power in relationships. Some cultures have relatively permeable status boundaries and are egalitarian. Other cultures have relatively fixed status boundaries and influence is determined by existing hierarchical relationships. We describe these relationships in greater detail now.

Egalitarian Power Relationships

In egalitarian power relationships, everyone expects to be treated equally. Egalitarian power relationships do not mean that everyone is of equal status, but rather, status differences are easily permeated. Social boundaries that exist within organizations are permeable, and superior social status may be short-lived. Egalitarian cultures empower members to resolve conflict themselves. Furthermore, the base of power in negotiations may differ; in egalitarian cultures, one's BATNA and information are key sources of power (and status and rank are irrelevant). This same power base is not necessarily true in hierarchical cultures.

Hierarchical Power Relationships

In some cultures, great deference is paid to status; status implies social power and is not easily permeated or changed. Social inferiors are expected to defer to social superiors who, in return for privilege, are obligated to look out for the needs of social inferiors (Leung, 1987). Conflict threatens the stability of a hierarchical society; it implies either that social inferiors have not met expectation or that social superiors have not met the needs of social inferiors (Brett, 2001). The norm in hierarchical cultures is not to challenge high-status members; thus, conflict is less frequent between members of different social ranks than in egalitarian cultures (Brett, 2001). Furthermore, conflict between members of the same social rank in hierarchical cultures is more likely to be handled by deference to a superior than by direct confrontation between social equals (Leung, 1987). In cultures, just like organizations, hierarchy reduces conflict by providing norms for interaction. The key source of power in negotiation is status, rather than one's BATNA (although status and BATNA power are often correlated).

To examine which countries were collectivist and which were hierarchical, Hofstede (1980) analyzed the responses that IBM employees gave to a values questionnaire. The respondents were diverse in nationality, occupation within IBM, age, and sex. Figure 10-3 presents a grid of where different countries fall in terms of individualism and power distance. Power distance reflects the tendency to see a large distance between those in the upper part of a social structure and those in the lower part of that structure.

FIGURE 10-3   Position of Countries on Power Distance and Individualism

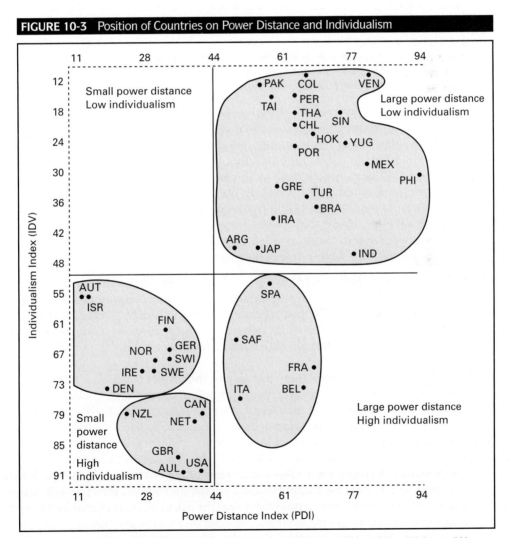

Source: G. Hofstede, *Culture's Consequences: International Differences in Work-Related Values,* p. 223, copyright © 1980 by Sage Publications, Inc. Reprinted by permission of Sage Publications, Inc.

It is clear from Figure 10-3 that individualism and power distance are highly correlated: Countries high in collectivism are also high in power distance. The most collectivist high-power countries are Venezuela, several other Latin American countries, the Philippines, and Yugoslavia. The most individualistic, low-power-distance countries were Austria and Israel.

Implications for Negotiation

Choose Your Representative   Cultural differences in power sources and power displays can be dramatic and unsettling because power is the basis for pie slicing. One of the first issues that negotiators must consider prior to intercultural negotiations is who will do the negotiating. In egalitarian cultures, power is usually determined by one's BATNA and thus, it is not unusual for different-status persons to find themselves at the bargaining table. In contrast, in hierarchical cultures, power is associated with one's position and rank, and it is insulting to send a lower-rank employee to meet with a CEO. For example, in China, relationships follow people, not organizations. The ideal negotiator is an "old friend of China" with whom the Chinese have had positive experiences or owe favors (*International Business*, July 1, 1998).

Understand the Network of Relationships   In cultures that have hierarchical power relationships, negotiations often require several levels of approval, all the way to the top. For example, in one failed negotiation, the central government of China voided McDonalds' long-standing agreement with the Beijing city government because leases of longer than 10 years require central government approval (*International Business*, July 1, 1998). In the centralized Chinese authority structure, negotiators seldom have the authority to approve the final deal. One by-product of this authority structure is that Chinese negotiators will attempt to secure a deal that is clearly weighted in their favor, so that it will be easier to persuade the higher authorities that the Chinese "won" the negotiation.

Face Concerns   Saving and giving face are important in hierarchical cultures. Negotiators need to know how to give face to others. This behavior raises the esteem of the negotiator in the eyes of their superiors and will in turn help them give face to their stakeholders. For example, flattery is a common form of Chinese face-saving (*International Business*, July 1, 1998). Pachtman cautions:

> Be aware of the effect flattery has on you; the proper response is not "thank you," but a denial and an even bigger compliment in return. Apologies are another powerful way to give face, but can obligate the apologizer; be prepared with a token concession in case the Chinese decide to "cash in" on your apology. (p. 25)

The Conduct of Negotiation   A Western view of negotiation holds that each party is expected to voice its own interests, and a back-and-forth exchange will occur. An Eastern view of negotiation is quite different. For example, negotiation among Japanese persons is similar to that of father and son, according to Adler (1991). The status relationship is explicit and important. The son (seller) carefully explains his situation and asks for as much as possible because he will have no chance to bicker once the father (buyer) decides. The son (seller) accepts the decision because it would hurt the relationship to argue and because he trusts the father (buyer) to care for his needs.

Direct Versus Indirect Communications

Cultures have distinctly different ways of communicating the same message. Direct versus indirect information sharing is a cultural dimension that refers to the amount of information contained in an explicit message versus implicit contextual cues (Hall, 1976). For example, different cultures have different norms about information-sharing strategies in negotiation (Hall, 1976). Broadly speaking, in some cultures the norms favor direct communication, whereas in other cultures, people communicate in an indirect, discreet fashion. The indirect-direct communication dimension has a direct implication for how much people should rely on contextual cues (Hall & Hall, 1990; Cohen, 1991).

Direct Communication

In a direct communication culture, such as the United States, messages are transmitted explicitly and directly, and communications are action-oriented and solution-minded (Ting-Toomey, 1985). In direct communication cultures, people step right up and tell you to your face what you did wrong, favoring direct confrontation and discussing problems freely. In a direct communication culture, the meaning is contained in the message; information is provided explicitly, without nuance (Brett, 2001). Furthermore, information is *context-free*, meaning that where and under what conditions the information is provided is pretty much irrelevant. In negotiations, these factors mean that parties will often ask direct questions about interests and alternatives.

Indirect Communication

In some cultures, people avoid direct confrontation when conflict occurs. This observation is not to say they do not address conflict; rather, it is done indirectly. The meaning of communication is inferred rather than directly interpreted; the context of the message stimulates preexisting knowledge that is then used to gain understanding (Brett, 2001). In negotiations, asking direct questions is not normative; rather, making a lot of proposals is a matter of indirect communication (Brett et al., 1998). The pattern of proposals allows inferences to be made about what is important to each party and where points of concession might be. In contrast to direct cultures, indirect cultures (such as Japan) transmit messages indirectly and implicitly, and communication is elusive (Ting-Toomey, 1985). For example, Japanese negotiators are less likely to say no and more likely to remain silent than U.S. negotiators when confronted with an option that is not favorable (Graham & Sano, 1984; March, 1990). (For a classification of direct and indirect communication cultures, see Table 10-3.)

The key point concerning direct versus indirect communication is that culture affects how negotiators share information. Negotiators from direct cultures prefer sharing information directly, asking questions, and getting—in return for giving—answers. In contrast, negotiators from indirect cultures prefer sharing information indirectly, telling stories in an attempt to influence their opponents, and gleaning information from proposals (Brett, Adair, Lempereur, Okumura, Shikhirev, Tinsley, & Lytle, 1998). Cultural norms and values have implications for the reciprocity principle in negotiation. For example, Adair (1999a) investigated intracultural and intercultural negotiation between the United States and Japan. Negotiators reciprocated culturally normative behaviors. Specifically,

TABLE 10-3 Direct and Indirect Communication Cultures	
Direct Communication Cultures	*Indirect Communication Cultures*
Germany	Japan
United States	Russia
Switzerland	France
Scandinavian cultures	Arabs
	Mediterranean peoples
	In general, cultures in which people have extensive information networks among family, friends, colleagues, and clients, and who are involved in close, personal relationships

Source: Brett, J. M. (2001). *Negotiating Globally: How to Negotiate Deals, Resolve Disputes, and Make Decisions Across Cultural Boundaries.* San Francisco, CA: Jossey-Bass.

U.S. negotiators were more likely to reciprocate direct information exchange; in contrast, Japanese negotiators were more likely to reciprocate indirect information exchange.

Implications for Negotiation

Information Necessary to Reach Integrative Agreements   Getting information out on the table is critical for expanding the pie; relying on context alone to convey information necessary to craft integrative agreements is not enough (Brett et al., 1998). Adair (2003) examined integrative sequences in same and mixed-culture negotiations. Managers from Hong Kong, Japan, Russia, and Thailand used more indirect integrative strategies (e.g., making multiple offers at same time); in contrast, managers from Israel, Germany, Sweden, and the United States used direct integrative strategies (e.g., asking for priority information). Moreover, because indirect communication is technically more complex, people from direct communication cultures cannot readily do it; in contrast, because direct communication is technically more simple, people from indirect cultures can do it. This situation then creates an asymmetry such that people from indirect cultures are skilled in both direct and indirect forms of communication, but the reverse is not true (Hall, 1976). In contrast, people from indirect cultures seamlessly enter into a "dance" of complementary, indirect information exchange (Adair & Brett, 2003). For example, by complementing priority information and offers, negotiators from indirect cultures supplement the information that may have not been sufficiently conveyed through reciprocal offers.

Brett and colleagues (1998) investigated negotiation strategies in six cultures: France, Russia, Japan, Hong Kong, Brazil, and the United States. Cultures that used direct (as opposed to indirect) information-sharing strategies or a combination of direct and indirect strategies reached the most integrative, pie-expanding agreements. Furthermore, exchanging information about preferences and priorities was insufficient. For example, in the same study of intracultural negotiations involving the United States, Japan, Brazil, France, Russia, and Hong Kong, negotiators from Russia and Hong Kong generated the lowest joint gains, or integrative agreements (Brett, Adair, Lempereur, Okumura, Shikhirev, Tinsley, & Lytle, 1998). Russia and Hong Kong are indirect communication countries. However, Japanese negotiators had high joint gains, even though they are an indirect communication culture as well. Why? The difference is that Japanese negotiators engaged in more direct information exchange (i.e., asking questions) than the negotiators from Russia or Hong Kong. Thus, making comparisons and contrasts to identify trade-offs and direct reactions appears to be essential (Brett, Adair, Lempereur, Okumura, Shikhirev, Tinsley, & Lytle, 1998).

One of the implications of indirect communication is that relationships often come before the mechanics of deal making. In direct cultures, the process of deal making comes first; in other cultures, the relationship comes first and provides a context for making deals. As a case in point, Vinita Kennedy, director of consulting services for the Lacek Group, a Minneapolis marketing firm, learned that lesson when she took an assignment in Tokyo in 1997. One of Kennedy's jobs was to help All Nippon Airways create a rewards program with local hotel chains. "You need to develop a relationship with people before you can get your business done," she says (Kiser, 1999, p. 117). Consequently, decisions are not made as quickly as they are in the United States. "Everyone has to go back and talk to their whole department and get full buy-in before they can move to the next step," she says (p. 117). And if a Japanese customer does not like the terms of the deal, he will not come out and say so. "It's rare that a Japanese person will tell you 'no,'" she says. "You need to read between the lines" (p. 117).

Dispute Resolution Preferences   U.S. managers often feel satisfied with their outcomes following such an interests-based procedure (Tinsley, 2001). However, other cultures use different dispute resolution strategies, often with equally satisfying results (Tinsley, 2001). For example, U.S. managers prefer to use interests-based methods, such as discussing parties' interests and synthesizing multiple issues (Tinsley & Brett, 2001). In one investigation, U.S. managers were more likely than Hong Kong Chinese managers to resolve a greater number of issues and reach more integrative outcomes; in contrast, Hong Kong Chinese managers were more likely to involve higher management in conflict resolution (Tinsley & Brett, 2001). One way that people from indirect cultures communicate their disapproval is by shaming others. For example, Chinese managers show a stronger desire to shame and teach moral lessons compared to U.S. managers (Tinsley & Weldon, 2003). In collectivist cultures, shaming is a common form of social control (Creighton, 1990; Demos, 1996). In contrast, U.S. managers are more likely to choose a direct approach in response to conflict.

KEY CHALLENGES OF INTERCULTURAL NEGOTIATION

What are the key challenges facing negotiators when negotiating across cultures? We identify eight common intercultural challenges now.

Expanding the Pie

Negotiators have more difficulty expanding the pie when negotiating across cultures than within a culture. In a landmark study of five countries (Japan, Hong Kong, Germany, Israel, and the United States), Brett (2001) examined intracultural (within the same culture) negotiations versus intercultural (across cultures) negotiations, and found that negotiations between Japan and the United States resulted in a smaller expansion of the pie than did intracultural negotiations (Japan–Japan and U.S.–U.S. negotiations). In another study, Brett and Okumura (1998) examined joint gains in intra- and intercultural negotiations between Japanese and U.S. negotiators and found that joint gains were significantly lower in intercultural negotiations, as opposed to intracultural negotiations. The key reason appeared to be the degree to which parties understood the priorities of the opponents and the opportunity for exploiting compatible issues. In cross-cultural negotiations, negotiators' bargaining styles did not match, meaning that they had less understanding of the opponent's priorities and consequently did not create as much value. Each culture expected the other culture to adopt its own style of negotiating—for example, North Americans expected others to talk directly, whereas people from indirect cultures expected to use other, implicit forms of communication, such as heuristic trial and error. U.S. negotiators exchange information directly and avoid using influence strategies when negotiating intra- and interculturally. In contrast, Japanese negotiators exchange information indirectly and use influence when negotiating intraculturally, but adapt their behaviors when negotiating interculturally (Adair, 1999b; Adair, Okumura, & Brett, 2001).

Dividing the Pie

We previously made the point that it is always in everyone's interest to expand the pie because it means more value for everyone. Hence, pie-expansion is the collaborative, or cooperative, aspect of negotiation. In contrast, dividing the pie is the competitive aspect, and we noted that feelings about fairness run deep. We pointed to a number of biases when it comes to thinking about fairness and these biases are even more magnified when people of different cultures sit down to negotiate.

As compared to other cultures, people from the United States are more unabashedly self-interested and, consequently, often have higher aspirations. We pointed out that aspirations manifest themselves in first offers that negotiators make and that aspirations are strongly predictive of the ultimate slice of the pie negotiators receive. Indeed, U.S. negotiators who have higher aspirations than their opponents achieve greater profit than managers from China and Japan, primarily because these collectivist cultures are not as self-interested (Chen, Mannix, & Okumura, 2003).

Sacred Values and Taboo Trade-Offs

Sacred values, or protected values, are the beliefs, customs, and assumptions that form the basis of a group or culture's belief system (Baron & Spranca, 1997; Tetlock, Peterson, & Lerner, 1996). Sacred values are, by definition, those values and beliefs that people regard to be so fundamental that they are not discussible nor debatable. Sacred values resist trade-offs with other values, particularly economic values. Most people are concerned about their participation in transactions of sacred values, rather than just the consequences that result. For example, consider the debate about forests in the western United States. In 2003, President Bush promoted a "healthy forest initiative" that would speed up the clearing of forests, overloaded with underbrush fuel, to prevent more massive wildfires. However, critics were appalled at the plan, which they argued would allow logging that goes beyond simple thinning (National Public Radio, Aug. 12, 2003). Most people experience anger at the thought of making trade-offs with sacred values and engage in denial of the need for trade-offs through wishful thinking. For example, consider the reaction that John Poindexter, a retired rear admiral, received in 2003 when he put forth a plan for the Pentagon to run a "terrorist futures-trading market"—an online trading parlor that would reward investors who accurately forecast terrorist attacks, assassinations, and coups (*New York Times*, Aug. 1, 2003). The day after the plan was announced, Poindexter was forced to resign from his position because several people, including democratic senators Byron Dorgan (North Dakota) and Ron Wyden (Oregon) called it "morally repugnant." (For an example of how to assess sacred or protected values, see Box 10-3). "Yes" or "Not Sure" answers imply that the value is secular (tradeable); "No" answers imply the value is sacred.

Sacred values are the opposite of secular values, which are issues and resources that can be traded and exchanged. Within a culture, a near-universal ascription to sacred values generally exists, with some notable exceptions. However, between cultures, extreme conflict may occur when one culture regards an issue to be sacred and another treats it as secular. Taboo trade-offs take place when sacred values are proposed for exchange or trade (Tetlock, Peterson, & Lerner, 1996).

Most people are horrified and shocked when parents offer to sell their children, citizens sell their right to a jury trial, and immigrants buy voting privileges. However, consider O. Henry's famous story *The Gift of the Magi*, in which a woman sells her hair to buy her husband a watch fob for Christmas. It is a tender and acceptable trade-off.

BOX 10-3

SACRED VALUES

Instructions: The following list contains actions that some people oppose. Some of these activities are happening right now, and others are not. Suppose that those in favor of each were willing to pay a great deal of money to see the action carried out. Please answer these questions with a "Yes," "No," or "Not Sure," answer according to whether you would accept money to perform these actions. (Adapted from Baron & Spranea, 1997.)

Actions:

1. Destruction of natural forests by human activity, resulting in the extinction of plant and animal species forever

2. Raising the IQ of normal children by giving them (completely safe) drugs

3. Using genetic engineering to make people more intelligent

4. Performing abortions of normal fetuses in the early stages of pregnancy

5. Performing abortions of normal fetuses in the second trimester of pregnancy

6. Fishing in a way that leads to the painful death of dolphins

7. Forcing women to be sterilized because they are retarded

8. Forcing women to have abortions when they have had too many children, for the purposes of population control

9. Putting people in jail for expressing non-violent political views

10. Letting people sell their organs (for example, a kidney or an eye) for whatever price they can command

11. Refusing to treat someone who needs a kidney transplant because he or she cannot afford it

12. Letting a doctor assist in the suicide of a consenting terminally ill patient

13. Letting a family sell their daughter in a bride auction (i.e., the daughter becomes the bride of the highest bidder)

14. Punishing people for expressing non-violent political opinions

Clearly, a very thin line separates acceptable from taboo trade-offs. On a purely rational level, these exchanges simply reflect the powerful **trade-off principle** we discussed in Chapter 4 on integrative bargaining.

The trade-off principle is ideal for handling scarce resource conflicts containing issues that are fungible. Principles of rationality (see Appendix 1) assume that people can compare resources and make apple-and-orange comparisons among resources and trade them in a way that maximizes their outcomes. Rational bargaining theory assumes that everything is comparable and has a price (see Appendix 1). However, the notion of trading becomes unconscionable in some conflict situations (Tetlock, Peterson, &Lerner, 1996). People sometimes refuse to place a monetary value on a good or even think of trading it. To even suggest a trade is cause for moral outrage and can sour negotiations. Attaching a monetary value to a bottle of wine, a house, or the services of a gardener can be a cognitively demanding task but raises no questions about the morality of the individual who proposes the sale or trade. In contrast, attaching monetary value to human life, familial obligations, national honor, and the ecosystem seriously undermine one's social identity or standing in the eyes of others (Schlenker, 1980). In a dispute concerning the construction of a dam that would remove native Indians from their ancestral land, a Yavapia teenager said, "The land is our mother. You don't sell your mother" (Espeland, 1994).

Proposals to exchange sacred values (e.g., body organs) for secular ones (e.g., money, time, or convenience) constitute taboo trade-offs. Given the inherently sacred values that operate in many countries, the familiar notions of trading and logrolling, so important to interests-based negotiation, are likely to be considered unacceptable and reprehensible to members of different cultures.

Sacred and secular issues are culturally defined, with no absolutes (Tetlock, Peterson, & Lerner, 1996). Sociocultural norms affect the sacredness of certain positions, such as smoking, which is now generally considered baneful but in the recent past was completely acceptable. The sanctity of issues is also influenced by the labels and names used to define conflicts. For example, in 1994, all three members of Alaska's congressional delegation began referring to the part of the Arctic National Wildlife Refuge (ANWR) that would be subject to oil exploration as the "Arctic Oil Reserve." The group believed that this term was more accurate because that part of the refuge was not officially classified as either wilderness or refuge. Environmentalists, on the other hand, objected to this term and did not even like the use of the acronym ANWR because they worried that unless the words *wildlife refuge* were clearly stated, the public would not understand the value of the land.

Truly sacred values cannot exist because we make value trade-offs every day, meaning that everyone "has their price." The implication is that with sufficient compensation, people are willing to trade off a "sacred" value. The critical issue is not how much it takes to compensate someone for a sacred issue but, instead, what factors allow trade-offs to occur on sacred issues.

The term *sacred* describes people's preferences on issues on which they view themselves as uncompromising. It immediately becomes obvious, however, that labeling an issue as sacred may be a negotiation ploy, rather than a reflection of heartfelt value. By anointing certain issues as sacred, and removing them from bargaining consideration, a negotiator increases the likelihood of a favorable settlement. The strategy is similar to the irrevocable commitment strategy (Schelling, 1960). We refer to issues that are not really sacred, but positioned as such, as **pseudosacred**[2] (Thompson & Gonzalez, 1997; Wade-Benzoni, Okumura, Brett, Moore, Tenbrunsel, & Bazerman, 2002). Thus, for example, if the Yavapia Indians would trade one acre of land for a hospital, new school, or money, then the land is not truly sacred but pseudosacred.

Biased Punctuation of Conflict

The biased punctuation of conflict occurs when people interpret interactions with their adversaries in self-serving and other-derogating terms (Kahn & Kramer, 1990). An actor, *A*, perceives the history of conflict with another actor, *B*, as a sequence of *B-A*, *B-A*, *B-A* in which the initial hostile or aggressive move was made by *B*, causing *A* to engage in defensive and legitimate retaliatory actions. Actor *B* punctuates the same history of interaction as *A-B*, *A-B*, *A-B*, however, reversing the roles of aggressor and defender. The biased punctuation of conflict is a frequent cause of warfare. Consider the long, sad history of international conflict between the Arabs and Israelis. Each country chooses different historical moments of origin in order to justify its own claims to land, and thus casts the other country in the role of the invader.

Negotiation behaviors are a continuous stream of cause-and-effect relationships where each person's actions influence the actions of others (Jones & Gerard, 1967). To an outside observer, their interaction is an uninterrupted sequence of interchanges. However, people who are actively engaged in conflict do not always see things this way. Instead, they organize their interactions into a series of discrete causal chunks (Swann, Pelham, & Roberts, 1987), a process known as **causal chunking** or **punctuation** (Whorf, 1956). Causal chunks influence the extent to which people are aware of their influence on others, as well as their impressions of others. Two kinds of chunking patterns are self-causal and other-causal. People form self-causal chunks (e.g., "My action causes my partner's action") when they possess an offensive set, and other-causal chunks when they possess a defensive set.

Disagreement about how to punctuate a sequence of events and a conflict relationship is at the root of many cross-cultural disputes. Consider the Wind River water dispute between the Shoshone and Arapaho tribes and the State of Wyoming (representing non-Indian farmers). The dispute boils down to whether Indian law or state law applies within Indian country. The Indian tribes see their action to literally turn off the water as a reasonable response to aggressive actions taken by non-Indians, "reclaiming some of what was wrongfully taken away." However, the non-Indians view the actions taken by the tribes as unprovoked ("aggressive Indian tribes demanding . . .") (*Toronto Star*, July 14, 1990).

Ethnocentrism

If egocentrism refers to unwarranted positive beliefs about oneself relative to others, then **ethnocentrism** refers to unwarranted positive beliefs about one's own group relative to other groups (LeVine & Campbell, 1972). We noted in Chapter 9 that most people display an in-group bias by evaluating members of their own group more favorably than members of out-groups and reward members of their own group more resources than members of out-groups, even when allocations of resources do not affect their own welfare (Doise, 1978). A nearly universal tendency is to rate one's own

---

[2]We are indebted to Max Bazerman for this term.

group as superior to other groups, even on the basis of little or no information. Ethnocentrism, or the universal strong liking of one's own group and the simultaneous negative evaluation of out-groups, generates a set of universal reciprocal stereotypes in which each culture sees itself as good and the other culture as bad, even when both groups engage in the same behaviors. The behavior may be similar, but the interpretation is not: "We are loyal, they are clannish; we are brave and willing to defend our rights, they are hostile and arrogant."

Even when members of groups do not know one another and never interact, people show in-group favoritism (Brewer, 1979; Tajfel, 1982; Tajfel & Turner, 1986). However, conflict between groups and intergroup bias do not always arise from competition over scarce resources. Much intergroup bias stems from fundamental differences in cultural values. Symbolic conflict can occur between cultural groups due to clashes of values and fundamental beliefs.

One unfortunate by-product of in-group favoritism is the tendency to view people from different cultures as more alike than they really are. Thus, the phrase "they all look alike" means that within-race and within-culture errors are more prevalent than between-race or between-cultural errors, because people categorize members of other cultures not as individuals, but as part of a group. As an example, consider the long-standing conflict between pro-choice and pro-life activists on the abortion issue (see Sidebar 10-1).

Sidebar 10-1. Stereotyping the Other Party

As an example of how members of groups tend to stereotype the other party, consider the conversation that occurred between Naomi Wolf, author of the best-seller *The Beauty Myth*, and Frederica Mathewes-Green, a syndicated religion columnist and author of a book called *Right Choices*. Try to figure out which woman made which of the following comments during a discussion in 1996:

> Where the pro-life movement has made its mistake is to focus only on the baby, and not the woman . . . You can boil 25 years of the pro-life rhetoric down to three words: "It's a baby."
>
> There's a whole industry to promote bonding with the wanted fetus, yet unwanted fetuses are treated as though they are unwanted lumps of batter.

The criticism of the pro-life movement's "it's a baby" focus came from Mathewes-Green, one of the movement's own. The criticism of the pro-choice movement's "unwanted lumps of batter" rhetoric came from Wolf, a staunch abortion-rights supporter.

When Wolf and Mathewes-Green met to talk, Wolf said that it was the first time that she had ever "knowingly been in the presence of a pro-lifer" (*St. Louis Post-Dispatch*, June 10, 1996, p. 11B). To her surprise, the other side was willing to have a conversation. And Mathewes-Green acknowledged that the pro-life movement had invited being stereotyped by "focusing only on the baby and not the woman" (p. 11B).

Stereotypes are another manifestation of ethnocentrism. Stereotypes of cultural groups are common; however, they often do not have a basis in reality. The problem is that if people act as if stereotypes are true, they are likely to create a self-fulfilling prophecy, whereby the stereotypes affect behavior. For example, Americans described their Japanese counterparts as being "poker-faced" or as displaying no facial expressions in a negotiation simulation. However, in the laboratory, a camera that was focused on each person's face during an intercultural negotiation recorded all facial expressions and revealed no differences in the number of facial expressions (smiles and frowns) between the Americans and Japanese. What's going on? Americans are not able to "read" Japanese expressions, and they wrongly describe them as "expressionless" (Graham, 1993).

Affiliation Bias

The **affiliation bias** occurs when people evaluate a person's actions on the basis of his or her affiliations rather than on the merits of the behavior itself. For example, when football fans watch a game, they believe the other side commits more infractions than does their own team (Hastorf & Cantril, 1954). Consider the following actions that a country could take: establishing a rocket base close to the borders of a country with whom it has strained relations; testing a new assault weapon; or establishing trade relations with a powerful country. People's perceptions of the acceptability of these actions differ dramatically as a function of the perceived agent. For example, during the time of the Cold War, U.S. citizens regarded the preceding actions to be much more beneficial when the United States was the one responsible than when the then-U.S.S.R. engaged in the same actions (Oskamp, 1965). People perceive the same objective behavior as either sinister or benign, merely as a consequence of the agent's affiliation.

Faulty Perceptions of Conciliation and Coercion

During World War II, the American journalist Edward R. Murrow broadcasted nightly from London, reporting on the psychological and physical consequences of the Nazi bombing of British cities (Rothbart & Hallmark, 1988). Contrary to Nazi intent, the bombing did not move the British toward surrender. It had quite the opposite effect, strengthening rather than diminishing British resolve to resist German domination. Shortly after the United States entered World War II, the Americans joined the British in launching costly bombing raids over Germany. In part, the intent was to decrease the German people's will to resist. Later research reported by the Office of Strategic Services that compared lightly and heavily bombed areas found only minimal differences in civilians' will to resist.

Several other conflicts follow the same psychological pattern, such as Pearl Harbor, South Africa, and North Vietnam. Each of these instances point to important differences in countries' perceptions of what will be effective in motivating an enemy and what will be effective in motivating themselves or their allies. Coercion is viewed as more effective with our enemies than with ourselves, whereas conciliation is viewed as more effective with ourselves than with our enemies. The unfortunate consequence, of course, is that this perception encourages aggressive rather than constructive action.

Three key reasons explain why this behavior occurs (Rothbart & Hallmark, 1988). A preference for punitive strategies with one's enemies may reflect a desire to inflict injury or pain, as well as a desire to influence behavior in a desired direction. The relative preference for punishment is based on an incompatible desire to both injure and modify the behavior of the enemy. Alternatively, people may be inclined to use more coercive strategies with an opponent because the appearance of toughness conveys information about their motives and intentions, which, in the long run, may bring about the desired result. Finally, the mere creation of mutually exclusive, exhaustive social categories (e.g., "them" and "us") leads to different assumptions about members of such groups: More favorable attributes are assigned to in-group than to out-group members (Brewer, 1979; Tajfel, 1970). Social categorization processes may be particularly powerful in cross-cultural disputes because of stereotypes.

Naïve Realism

A heated debate among English teachers concerns which books should be on the required reading list for American high school students. The Western Canon Debate features traditionalists, who prefer to have classics on the reading list, and revisionists, who believe that the reading list should be more racially, ethnically, and sexually diversified. In a recent analysis, traditionalists and revisionists were interviewed about their own and the other party's preferred books (Robinson & Keltner, 1996). Most strikingly, each party exaggerated the views of the other side in a way that made their differences bigger rather than smaller. Traditionalists viewed revisionists to be much more extreme than they really were; revisionists viewed traditionalists to be much more conservative. In fact, the groups agreed on 7 out of the 15 books on the reading list! Nevertheless, each group greatly exaggerated the difference between their own and the other's belief systems in a way that exacerbated the conflict. Further, people perceived the other side to be more uniform in their views, whereas they perceived their own views to be more varied and heterogeneous (Linville, Fischer, & Salovey, 1989). This faulty perception, of course, leads to beliefs such as "They're all alike." Ideological conflict is often exacerbated unnecessarily as partisans construe the other person's values to be more extremist and unbending than they really are.

For example, in 1995, Republican Congressman George Gekas of Pennsylvania was accused by the opposing party of espousing anti-environmental attitudes. The angered Gekas mocked the accusation: "Mr. Speaker and members of the House, I hate clean air. I don't want to breathe clean air. I want the dirtiest air possible for me and my household and my constituents. That's what the supporters of this motion want people to believe about our position on these riders. Now, you know that's absolutely untenable" (National Public Radio, Nov. 3, 1995).

The **fundamental attribution error** occurs when people explain the causes of the behavior of others in terms of their underlying dispositions and discount the role of situational factors (Ross, 1977). Many environmental disputes involve a group that is believed to be interested in the economic development of the environment and an opposing group that represents the interests of the ecosystem. According to the fundamental attribution error, when each group is asked to name the cause of the dispute, each will attribute the negative aspects of conflict to the dispositions of the other party. Specifically, developers regard environmentalists to be fanatic lunatics; environmentalists regard developers to be sinister and greedy.

PREDICTORS OF SUCCESS IN INTERCULTURAL INTERACTIONS

Your pharmaceutical company wants to expand its international base. You are charged with the task of selecting a few managers to participate in a special global initiatives assignment in various countries. You know that failure rates as high as 70 percent can be avoided (Copeland & Griggs, 1985). These costs include not only the lost salary of an executive, the cost of transporting the family, and the cost of setting up an office abroad, but also include damage to your organization, lost sales, on-the-job mistakes, and loss of goodwill. Unfortunately, ready-made personality measures are not good predictors of success abroad. The following characteristics have some value in predicting success (Martin, 1989; Triandis, 1994):

- Conceptual complexity: People who are conceptually complex (think in terms of shades of gray, rather than black and white) show less social distance to different others (Gardiner, 1972)
- Broad categorization: People who use broad categories adjust to new environments better than do narrow categorizers (Detweiler, 1980)
- Empathy
- Sociability
- Critical acceptance of stereotypes
- Openness to different points of view
- Interest in the host culture
- Task orientation
- Cultural flexibility (the ability to substitute activities in the host culture for own culture-valued activities)
- Social orientation (the ability to establish new intercultural relationships)
- Willingness to communicate (e.g., use the host language without fear of making mistakes)
- Patience (suspend judgment)
- Intercultural sensitivity
- Tolerance for differences among people
- Sense of humor
- Skills in collaborative conflict resolution

ADVICE FOR CROSS-CULTURAL NEGOTIATIONS

Global negotiations are characterized by differences that emerge at interpersonal behavioral levels and are manifestations of more deep-seated societal and institutional differences (Tinsley, Curhan, & Kwak, 1999). According to Tinsley and colleagues, negotiators should avoid arguing about the inherent legitimacy of a social system and instead focus on understanding at the interpersonal level. Brett (2001) researched and proposed several strategies that can improve cross-cultural effectiveness (see Box 10-4 for Tinsley's similar suggestions). A discussion of Brett's (2001) prescriptive advice appears in the following sections.

BOX 10-4

ADVICE FOR INTERNATIONAL NEGOTIATORS

1. Acknowledge differences at the individual and societal levels.

2. Trade off differences in preferences and abilities.

3. Ask questions to ensure understanding of the other party's perspective.

4. Understand the norms and the meaning underlying them.

5. Avoid arguing the inherent legitimacy of a social system.

6. Be prepared to manage bureaucratic interactions with governments.

Source: Tinsley, Curhan, & Kwak (1999).

Anticipate Differences in Strategy and Tactics That May Cause Misunderstandings

Negotiators from different cultures differ in terms of three major dimensions that affect their negotiation behavior and style: individualism-collectivism, hierarchy-egalitarianism, and direct-indirect communications. The negotiator who is able to anticipate differences in terms of these three dimensions is going to be at a pie-expanding and pie-slicing advantage in intercultural negotiations. Further, when encountering differences, the negotiator who is aware of cultural differences will not make negative attributions about her opponent, but instead, view discomfort as a natural consequence of different cultural styles.

Analyze Cultural Differences to Identify Differences in Values That Expand the Pie

We noted in Chapter 4 (integrative negotiation) and Chapter 8 (creativity in negotiation) that it is differences, rather than similarities, between negotiators that can open up windows for expanding the pie and creating joint gain. Presumably, more degrees of difference are present between members of different cultures than members of the same culture. The level of differences means that the amount of integrative, or win-win, potential is higher in intercultural negotiations, as opposed to intracultural negotiations. The culturally enlightened negotiator will search for differences in beliefs, values, risk profiles, expectations, and abilities that can be used to leverage opportunities for joint gain, such as through the creation of value-added trade-offs (logrolling) and the construction of contingency contracts.

Recognize That the Other Party May Not Share Your View of What Constitutes Power

The other party's estimate of his or her power may be based on factors that you think are irrelevant to the negotiation. Negotiators from egalitarian cultures should be prepared to present information about their company and products, even when they think such information should have no bearing on the outcome. In failing to make a presentation comparable to the one made by the negotiator from the hierarchical culture, negotiators from egalitarian cultures risk appearing weak. By the same token, negotiators from hierarchical cultures should be aware that power-based persuasion, although normative in deal-making negotiations in their own cultures, is not normative in egalitarian cultures. Furthermore, in egalitarian cultures, power-based persuasion is likely to be reciprocated directly with power-based persuasion and may lead to impasse (Brett & Okumura, 1998). One American businessperson suffered due to a lack of understanding about cultural behavioral styles. After long, hard bargaining, a U.S. firm landed a large contract with a Japanese firm. At the signing ceremony, however, the Japanese executive began reading the contract intently. His scrutiny seemed endless. The American panicked and offered to take $100 off of each item. What the U.S. executive did not know was that the Japanese president was merely demonstrating authority, not backing out (*Chicago Sun-Times*, Feb. 10, 1986).

Avoid Attribution Errors

An attribution error is the tendency to ascribe someone's behavior or the occurrence of an event to the wrong cause. For example, people often attribute behaviors of others to their underlying personality (e.g., a smile from another person is often attributed to a "good" disposition; similarly, a frown is presumed to be a manifestation of a grouchy personality; Ross, 1987). However, the behavior of others is more often a reflection of particular features of the situation, rather than enduring personality traits. Negotiators who are interculturally naïve are more likely to fall prey to the fundamental attribution error than are people who are interculturally sensitive, who are more likely to view behavior as a manifestation of cultural and situational norms.

Find Out How to Show Respect in the Other Culture

One of the most important preparatory steps a negotiator can take when commencing intercultural negotiation is to find out how to show respect in the other culture. It is a fallacy to assume that the other culture will have the same customs as one's own culture and that ignorance of customs will be forgiven. In one simulation, parties on opposite sides of the table attempted to show respect by studying the cultural style of the other and adapting to it (see Sidebar 10-2). For an example of a failure to show respect in another culture, see Sidebar 10-3.

Sidebar 10-2. An Experiment in Cultural Perspective-Taking

Two professors—Shyam Kamath and Martin Desmaras—arranged for a realistic mock negotiation between U.S. managers and Brazilians (*Ascribe News*, June 5, 2003). Most of the time, executives from different cultures are not prepared for one another, but the managers in this situation went overboard: Each party carefully researched the other party's cultural style and decided to adapt its own bargaining style to it. The strange result was a situation in which the Brazilians wanted to get down to business immediately and the Americans avoided negotiations while attempting to establish relationships before talking about any contract details. Said one American, "What really surprised us was that they wanted to get down to business right away. We knew better than to push them into a decision at the start, but they came in with their price offer

continued

right away" (para. 3). Said the Brazilians, "They [the Americans] seemed to want to take more time at the start. Our side acted more like Americans" (para. 4). Kim Smith, business development manager for Hertz Corp., said, "I began to worry that if their side acted like Americans and we acted like Brazilians, we wouldn't get anything done" (para. 5).

Sidebar 10-3. Failing to Show Respect in Another Culture Can Lead to Conflict

In 1992, the Walt Disney Company undertook a $5 billion EuroDisney theme park project in Paris. It began with great visions of a united workforce wearing Disney dress and adopting American grooming. Behavioral codes banned alcohol in the park, and meetings were conducted in English. The French perceived these requirements and restrictions as an unnecessary cultural imposition. They retaliated with insults, storming out of training meetings, and initiating lawsuits. The French press joined in by launching an anti-Disney campaign, and French railroad workers regularly initiated strikes from the Paris-EuroDisney train for months. The annual employee turnover hit a crippling 25 percent, pushing up labor costs by 40 percent. Disney paid a heavy price before making amends (*Economic Times*, Nov. 8, 1999).

Know Your Options for Change

Succeeding in international business requires that people gain international competence as well as business competence (Matsumoto, 1996). You have done your homework, researched your negotiation opponent's culture, and have a good idea of what to expect during the meeting and which customs are important. You have also uncovered an unsettling fact: In your client's culture, women are regarded as property and second-class citizens. They are not supposed to be opinionated or hold jobs with decision-making importance. Imagine that you are a man, and your key business associate is a woman, trained at an Ivy League university, well-versed in cultural issues and your client's strategic situation. For you both to sit at the bargaining table would be an insult to your client. Your supervisor is pressing you to open the door to this client's company. What do you do?

This situation is unenviable. It is difficult to imagine leaving our colleague behind; you need her skills and, moreover, you do not want to break up your partnership. Yet, bringing her involves an inevitable culture clash. Further, shutting the door on this client shuts the door on the entire country. You have thoughts about enlightening your client, but wonder whether a five-minute lesson from you can overcome centuries of discrimination sewn into the fabric of a country.

It is a dilemma without any best answer. However, the manager who identifies this situation early on is in a better situation to positively address it than is the manager who naïvely steps off the plane with the issue unresolved.

Sometimes, options for change are driven by skill sets—or lack thereof. Most Americans are monolingual, compared to other cultures. Furthermore, members of other cultures know that Americans are monolingual, and so, adapt accordingly. For example, Lindsley (1999) observed interactions between North Americans and Mexicans and observed that Mexican bilingual managers immediately switched to English when interacting with North Americans; however, North American linguistic accommodation was a rare occurrence.

Before reading further, think about what courses of action you might take. Berry (1980) described four ways for two cultures to relate to each other (see Figure 10-4). The first issue is whether the individual (or group) finds it valuable to maintain distinct cultural identity and characteristics. The second issue is whether the individual (or group) desires to maintain relationships with other (cultural) groups.

- **Integration** is a type of acculturation whereby each group maintains its own culture and also maintains contact with the other culture. Thus, you bring your associate to the meetings, and clearly uphold your firm's egalitarian attitudes, yet also make it clear that you have a strong desire to build relationships with the other group.
- **Assimilation** occurs when a group or person does not maintain its culture but does maintain contact with the other culture. You leave your associate at home and try to follow the mores of the other party's culture.
- **Separation** occurs when a group or individual maintains its culture but does not maintain contact with the other culture. You bring your associate to the meetings and remain oblivious to the other group's culture, or you tell your supervisor you do not want this assignment.
- **Marginalization** occurs when neither maintenance of the group's own culture nor contact with the other culture is attempted. You leave your associate at

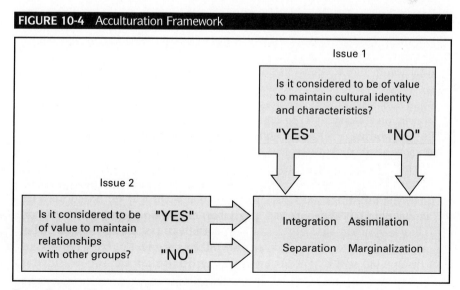

FIGURE 10-4 Acculturation Framework

Issue 1

Is it considered to be of value to maintain cultural identity and characteristics?

"YES"   "NO"

Issue 2

Is it considered to be of value to maintain relationships with other groups?

"YES"

"NO"

Integration   Assimilation

Separation   Marginalization

Source: Reprinted by permission of John W. Berry.

home and do not attempt to understand the cultural values of the other firm. Marginalization is the most unfavorable condition (Berry, Poortinga, Segall, & Dasen, 1992).

CONCLUSION

Negotiating across cultures is a necessity for success in the business world because globalization is a major objective of most companies. Unfortunately, cross-cultural negotiations frequently result in less effective pie expansion than do intracultural negotiations. Part of the problem is a lack of understanding cultural differences. We used Brett's (2001) tripartite model of culture and identified individualism-collectivism, egalitarianism-hierarchy, and direct-indirect communication as key dimensions of cultural differences. Key challenges of intercultural negotiation are expanding the pie, dividing the pie, dealing with sacred values and taboo trade-offs, biased punctuation of conflict, ethnocentrism, the affiliation bias, faulty perceptions of conciliation and coercion, and naïve realism. We suggested that negotiators learn to analyze cultural differences to identify differences in values that could expand the pie, recognize different conceptions of power, avoid attribution errors, find out how to show respect in other cultures, and assess options for change, including integration, assimilation, separation, and marginalization.

11

TACIT NEGOTIATIONS AND SOCIAL DILEMMAS

"On December 5, 1994, the U.S. Federal Communication Commission began to accept bids for 99 licenses that would permit licensees to offer [wireless] broadband personal communications services (PCS) in regions covering the United States and its territories. The auction continued for more than three months, and at its conclusion, the total of the winning bids stood in excess of $7 billion. Thirty bidders were involved in the early rounds of the auction, and 18 of them eventually acquired licenses. . . . Within the FCC, Evan Kwerel suggested that licenses be allocated by auction, and [the U.S.] Congress gave the FCC a mandate to do so. However, the congressional mandate was written in broad terms and left the FCC to decide what particular type of auction process to use. . . . The most obvious way of communicating one's interest is by bidding on desired items. The format of the FCC auction provided several other ways for bidders to communicate [tacitly] with one another. Perhaps the most blatant means of communication would be to encode messages using the lower-order digits of one's bids. . . . To use the lowest three or four digits of a bid to send a signal would be of negligible cost. For example, assume that one bidder is competing with another on a particular license, and the second bidder is standing as the highest bidder, at an attractive price, on some other license. Then a bid by the first bidder on the license in contention, with trailing digits equal to the identification number of the other license, could serve as a threat: 'Top my bid here, and I'll raise the price on your license next round.' . . . As long as the bidders have some idea of one another's general interests, either message would be easy to read." In the auction, prices were well below expectations of final settlement prices. A careful examination of the "trailing digits" contained in the bids of companies such as WirelessCo (a consortium of Sprint and three cable television companies), PCS PrimeCo (a consortium of four regional Bell operating companies), and American Portable Telecommunications suggests that the companies were tacitly signaling to one another so as to drive the prices down (Weber, 1997, pp. 529–533, 545).

The FCC's first broadband auction suggests that even the fiercest competitors can find ways to collude so as to meet each other's interests even when they cannot communicate directly. The fact that they could read and interpret information about each other's intentions through the trailing digits of their bids facilitated strategic demand reduction. Behavior in the broadband auction stands in sharp contrast to the price wars that many companies participate in.

So far, we focused on negotiation situations in which people seek to reach mutual agreement in terms of a binding contract, called **explicit negotiations.** In contrast, many negotiations that occur within and between organizations are conducted without contracts and explicit agreements, such as the FCC's broadband auctions. We call these situations **tacit negotiations** (Schelling, 1960). In tacit negotiations, negotiators are interdependent with respect to outcomes, but they make independent decisions. Unlike traditional negotiations, parties do not need to meet and talk for an outcome to be reached. Rather, their fate is determined by the actions they take and the actions taken by others. People can either behave in a cooperative fashion (e.g., not bidding for certain licenses; an employee makes a modest request for company resources) or in a competitive fashion (e.g., bidding aggressively for licenses; an employee "pads" a request or perhaps shirks teamwork in favor of advancing his or her own career). Another example: A company engages in a negative advertising campaign. The company's main competitor then starts to advertise negatively. Consider, for example, how the founder, chairman, and president of Commerce Bancorp, Vernon W. Hill II, approaches competition: He gives his managers $5,000 if they can shut down a rival branch (*BusinessWeek*, Aug. 11, 2003e). In the case of the FCC's broadband auctions, tacit cooperation among the competitors hurts the general consumer (as in the case of price-fixing); and in the case of negative campaigning, extreme competition also hurts the consumer. Thus, the effects of extreme cooperation or competition depend upon one's vantage point.

The distinction between these two different types of negotiation situations was first articulated by the famous mathematician John Nash (1951, 1953), who referred to one branch of negotiations as "cooperative games" and the other as "noncooperative games." In using the terms *cooperative* and *noncooperative,* Nash was not referring to the motivations or behaviors of the parties involved, but rather how the underlying situation was structured (see Table 11-1 for the difference between the two main types of negotiations).

In business, our welfare depends on the actions of others. The situation that results when people engage in behaviors that maximize self-interest but lead to collective disaster, such as a bidding war or negative campaigning, is a **social dilemma.** In this chapter, we discuss two kinds of social dilemmas: two-person dilemmas and multiperson dilemmas. The two-person dilemma is the **prisoner's dilemma;** the multiperson dilemma is a social dilemma. They are dilemmas because the choices available to negotiators are risky. Some choices risk exploitation; others risk antagonizing others. We discuss how dilemmas may be effectively handled.

TABLE 11-1 Two Major Types of Negotiation Situations	
Cooperative Negotiations	*Noncooperative Negotiations*
• Contract is explicit	• Contract is tacit
• Mutual understanding (people know what they are getting before they agree)	• People often do not know what others will do
• People negotiate via proposals and counterproposals and can use words to explain and justify their offers	• People negotiate through their behaviors and actions (rather than their promises of what they will do)
• People usually come to the table voluntarily	• People are often pulled into negotiations without wanting to be

Sources: Nash, J. (1951). Non-cooperative games. *Annals of Mathematics,* 54(2), 286–295; and Nash, J. (1953). Two person cooperative games. *Econometrica,* 21, 129–140.

BUSINESS AS A SOCIAL DILEMMA

At least four challenges of the future suggest that people will have to learn how to engage in effective tacit negotiation and intelligently navigate social dilemmas, both inside their own companies as well as with other companies.

Decentralization

Many companies are moving away from top-down, hierarchical management systems to decentralized management systems, where managers are empowered to make decisions, broker deals, and capitalize on opportunities. However, decentralization of business units often leads to conflicts of interest—meaning that the parties involved have their own interests in mind, which are not necessarily aligned with those of others. In these situations, managers face a choice between acting in ways that further their own interests or in ways that further the interests of the other party (perhaps with some expense to their own interests).

Strategic Alliances

In many industries and across industries, companies are forming strategic alliances. Alliances are crucial for companies who are in battle for market share. Increasing competitive pressures make it imperative that companies develop new strengths and deliver products and services quickly and at a lower cost. Strategic alliances allow companies to develop products and rapidly expand their markets while managing risk and costs through resource sharing. However, the majority of alliances are unsuccessful (Segil, 1999). Fifty-five percent of alliances and 78 percent of mergers and acquisitions fall apart within three years and only 23 percent recover the costs. Key factors in the development of strategic alliances include the management of competition. Whereas some companies refuse to consider alliances with competitors, others find ways to transform the relationship into profitable partnerships (Segil, 1999). For example, in 2003, several "Baby Bells"—SBC, BellSouth, and Qwest—forged alliances with EchoStar and DirectTV to market alternatives to cable (*San Antonio Express-News*, Sept. 1, 2003). Similarly, in 2003, the SkyTeam alliance led by Air France and Delta Air Lines invited KLM into the alliance along with U.S. partners Continental and Northwest (*Wall Street Journal Europe*, Dec. 11, 2003).

Specialization

The extent to which business units and companies are highly specialized dictates their dependence on others. For example, General Motors has several plants that specialize in only one area of manufacturing (e.g., brakes, etc.). However, to assemble a complete automobile, it is necessary for each of the plants to cooperate with one another. If employees at one plant go on strike, they can create havoc in other plants and halt the production of automobiles. The members of each plant have an incentive to further their own interests (e.g., increasing their wages), but often, these actions come at the expense of other plants and the company as a whole.

Competition

Competitors routinely face social dilemmas. Some industries seem particularly vicious, such as telephone companies. For example, Ivan Seidenberg, the CEO of Verizon, is ruthless when it comes to competitors: In March of 2003, Verizon became the first Bell to slice its broadband Internet service by 30 percent—as much as 20 percent cheaper than its competitors, AOL and Comcast. One competitor, SBC Communications Inc., responded by saying, "We'll watch them [Verizon] closely and go to school on them if they have found something economic" (*BusinessWeek*, Aug. 4, 2003b, p. 53). Comcast and other cable companies are hell-bent on torpedoing Seidenberg's plans by destroying Verizon's profits before it can use them to get into the video business.

In contrast, other industries have attempted to find points of cooperation that can align their competitive goals. For example, in 1998, two national dairy companies using separate advertising campaigns agreed to create a single marketing plan to increase milk sales in the United States. Dairy Management, Inc., which used the "Got Milk?" campaign, and the National Fluid Milk Processor Promotion Board, which used a popular collection of advertisements in which celebrities wear milk mustaches, coordinated campaigns to increase total fluid milk sales by 4 percent by the year 2000 (*New York Times*, Feb. 6, 1998). Willingness to engage in generic advertising (e.g., advertising the local mall instead of one's own store) is a common form of interfirm cooperation. A simulation of generic advertising revealed that companies confronting a declining trend contributed significantly more dollars to generic advertising; moreover, it positively influenced their expectations that others would contribute as well (Krishnamurthy, Bottom, & Rao, 2003).

COMMON MYTHS ABOUT INTERDEPENDENT DECISION MAKING

In approaching social dilemmas and tacit negotiation, people are often guilty of mythological thinking. We expose the three leading myths that impair decision making before presenting what we believe is an effective decision-making strategy.

Myth 1: "It's a Game of Wits: I Can Outsmart Them"

Many people believe that they can stay one move ahead of the "other guy." However, effective decision making in noncooperative situations is not about outsmarting people. It is unrealistic to believe we can consistently outwit others—an egocentric illusion.

A better and more realistic goal is to understand the incentive structure in the situation and take the perspective of the other party. In the fraternal twin model, we need to imagine that the person we are dealing with is every bit as intelligent and motivated as we are—it is pretty hard to outwit ourselves!

Myth 2: "It's a Game of Strength: Show 'em You're Tough"

This negotiator goes into battle fighting fire with fire. The problem is that this behavior can unnecessarily escalate conflict situations, especially if people have a false sense of uniqueness. For example, hours after Carly Fiorina, CEO of Hewlett Packard, promised in an August 2003 conference call to be less aggressive in PC pricing to bolster margins, Dell announced a broad swath of price cuts as large as 22 percent on PCs and servers. "The unspoken taunt is clear" (*BusinessWeek*, Sept. 1, 2003, p. 80).

Myth 3: "It's a Game of Chance: Hope for the Best"

This negotiator believes that outcomes are not predictable and depend on ever-changing aspects of the situation: personality, mood, time of day, and so on. This person erroneously believes that either it takes a long time to figure out a good strategy or it is just downright impossible.

In this chapter, we suggest that tacit negotiation and dilemmas are neither games of wits, strength, or chance, but decision opportunities. We use principles of logic and psychology to optimally deal with social dilemmas in business.

THE PRISONER'S DILEMMA

Thelma and Louise are common criminals who have just been arrested on suspicion of burglary. Law enforcement has enough evidence to convict each suspect of a minor breaking-and-entering crime, but insufficient evidence to convict the suspects on a more serious felony charge of burglary and assault. The district attorney immediately separates Thelma and Louise after their arrest. Each suspect is approached separately and presented with two options: confess to the serious burglary charge or remain silent (not confess). The consequences of each course of action depend on what the other decides to do. The catch is that Thelma and Louise must make their choices independently. They cannot communicate with each other in any way prior to making an independent, irrevocable decision. The decision situation that each suspect faces is illustrated in Figure 11-1, which indicates that Thelma and Louise will go to prison for as many as 15 years, depending upon what the other partner chooses. Obviously, it is an important decision. Imagine that you are an advisor to Thelma. Your concern is not morality or ethics; you are simply trying to get her a shorter sentence. What do you advise her to do?

Ideally, it is desirable for both suspects to not confess, thereby minimizing the prison sentence to one year for each (cell A). This option is risky, however. If one confesses, then the suspect who does not confess goes to prison for the maximum sentence of 15 years—an extremely undesirable outcome (cell B or C). In fact, the most desirable situation from the standpoint of each suspect would be to confess and have the other person not confess. Then, the confessing suspect would be released, and his or her partner would go to prison for the maximum sentence of 15 years. Given these contingencies, what should

	Thelma	
	Do not confess (remain silent)	**Confess**
Do not confess (remain silent)	A T = 1 yr L = 1 yr	B T = 0 yrs L = 15 yrs
Confess	C T = 15 yrs L = 0 yrs	D T = 10 yrs L = 10 yrs

Louise

FIGURE 11-1
Consequences of Thelma and Louise's Behaviors

Note: Entries represent prison term length. T = Thelma's term length; L = Louise's term length.

Thelma do? Before reading further, stop and think about what you think is her best course of action.

The answer is not easy, which is why the situation is a dilemma. It will soon be demonstrated that when each person pursues the course of action that is most rational from her point of view, the result is mutual disaster. That is, both Thelma and Louise go to prison for 10 years (cell D). The paradox of the prisoner's dilemma is that the pursuit of individual self-interest leads to collective disaster. The conflict between individual and collective well-being derives from rational analysis. It is easy for Thelma and Louise to see that each could do better by cooperating, but it is not easy to know *how* to implement this behavior. The players can get there only with coordinated effort.

Cooperation and Defection as Unilateral Choices

We will use the prisoner's dilemma situation depicted in Figure 11-1 to analyze decision making. We will refer to the choices that players make in this game as **cooperation** and **defection,** depending upon whether they remain silent or confess. The language of cooperation and defection allows the prisoner's dilemma game structure to be meaningfully extended to other situations that do not involve criminals, but nevertheless have the same underlying structure, such as whether an airline company should bid for a smaller company, or whether a cola company or politician should engage in negative advertising. However, prisoner's dilemmas don't just describe criminals and business strategy; in fact, the prisoner's dilemma was initially developed to provide a compelling analysis of the negotiations between the United States and the Soviet Union. The United States and the Soviet Union each sought to develop and deploy arsenals of nuclear arms they thought necessary for military defense. In the 1960s, public concern increased over the nuclear arms race.

Rational Analysis

We use the logic of game theory to provide a rational analysis of this situation. In our analysis, we consider three different cases: (1) one-shot, nonrepeated play situations (as in the case of Thelma and Louise); (2) the case in which the decision is repeated for a finite number of terms (such as might occur in a yearly election for a position on a five-year task force); and (3) the case in which the decision is repeated for a potentially infinite number of trials or the end is unknown (such as might occur in financial companies, airlines, hotels, and cola companies).

Case 1: One-Shot Decision

Game theoretic analysis relies on the principle of dominance detection; a dominant strategy results in a better outcome for player 1 no matter what player 2 does.

To illustrate the dominance principle, suppose that you are Thelma and your partner in crime is Louise. First, consider what happens if Louise remains silent (does not confess). Thus, we are focusing on the first row in Figure 11-1. Remaining silent puts you in cell A: You both get one year. This outcome is not too bad, but maybe you could do better. Suppose that you decide to confess. In cell B, you get 0 years and Louise gets 15 years. Certainly no prison sentence is much better than a one-year sentence, so confession seems like the optimal choice for you to make, given that Louise does not confess.

Now, what happens if Louise confesses? In this situation, we focus on row 2. Remaining silent puts you in cell C: You get 15 years, and Louise gets 0 years, which is not very good for you. Now, suppose that you confess. In cell D, you both get 10 years. Neither outcome is splendid, but 10 years is certainly better than 15 years. Given that Louise confesses, what do you want to do? The choice amounts to whether you want to go to prison for 15 years or 10 years. Again, confession is the optimal choice for you.

We just illustrated the principle of **dominance detection.** No matter what Louise does (remains silent or confesses), it is better for Thelma to confess. Confession is a dominant strategy; under all possible states of the world, players in this game should choose to confess. We know that Louise is smart and has looked at the situation the same way as Thelma and has reached the same conclusion. In this sense, mutual defection is an **equilibrium outcome,** meaning that no player can unilaterally (single-handedly) improve her outcome by making a different choice.

Thus, both Thelma and Louise are led through rational analysis to confess, and they collectively end up in cell D, where they both go to prison for a long period of time. This outcome seems both unfortunate and avoidable. Certainly, both suspects would prefer to be in cell A than in cell D. Is escape possible from the tragic outcomes produced by the prisoner's dilemma? Are we doomed to collective disaster in such situations?

It would seem that players might extricate themselves from the dilemma if they could communicate, but we already noted that communication is outside of the bounds of the noncooperative game. Further, because the game structure is noncooperative, any deals that players might make with one another are nonbinding. For example, antitrust legislation prohibits companies from price fixing, which means that any communication that occurs between companies regarding price fixing is unenforceable, not to mention punishable by law.

What other mechanism might allow parties in such situations to avoid the disastrous outcome produced by mutual defection? One possibility is to have both parties make those decisions over **multiple trials.** Suppose that the parties did not make a single choice but instead made a choice, received feedback about the other player's choice, experienced the consequences, and then made another choice. Perhaps repeated interaction with the other person would provide a mechanism for parties to coordinate their actions. If the game is to be played more than once, players might reason that by cooperating on the first round, cooperation may be elicited in subsequent periods. We consider that situation next.

Case 2: Repeated Interaction over a Fixed Number of Trials

Instead of making a single choice and living with the consequence, suppose that Thelma and Louise were to play the game in Figure 11-1 a total of 10 times. It might seem strange to think about criminals repeating a particular interaction, so it may be useful to think about two political candidates deciding whether to engage in negative campaigning (hereafter referred to as campaigning). Term limits in their state dictate that they can run and hold office for a maximum of five years. An election is held every year. During each election period, each candidate makes an independent choice (to campaign or not), then learns of the other's choice (to campaign or not). After the election, the candidates consider the same alternatives once again and make an independent choice; this interaction continues for five separate elections.

We use the concept of dominance as applied previously to analyze this situation, but we need another tool that tells us how to analyze the repeated nature of the game. **Backward induction** is the mechanism by which a person decides what to do in a repeated game situation, by looking backward from the last stage of the game.

We begin by examining what players should do in election 5 (the last election). If the candidates are making their choices in the last election, the game is identical to that analyzed in the one-shot case from earlier. Thus, the logic of dominant strategies applies, and we are left with the conclusion that each candidate will choose to campaign. Now, given that we know that each candidate will campaign in the last election, what will they do in the fourth election?

From a candidate's standpoint, the only reason to cooperate (or to not campaign) is to influence the behavior of the other party in the subsequent election. In other words, a player might signal willingness to cooperate by making a cooperative choice in the period before. We have already determined that it is a foregone conclusion that both candidates will defect (choose to campaign) in the last election, so it is futile to choose the cooperative (no campaigning) strategy in the fourth election. So, what about the third election? Given that candidates will not cooperate in the last election, nor in the second-to-last election, they would find little point to cooperating in the third-to-last election for the same reason that cooperation was deemed to be ineffective in the second-to-last election. As it turns out, this logic can be applied to every election in such a backward fashion. Moreover, this reasoning is true in any situation with a finite number of elections. This realization leaves us with the conclusion that defection remains the dominant strategy even in the repeated trial case.[1]

This result is disappointing. It suggests that cooperation is not possible even in long-term relationships. It runs counter to intuition, observation, and logic, however. We must consider another case, arguably more realistic of the situations we want to study in most circumstances, in which repeated interaction continues for an infinite or indefinite amount of time.

---

[1]Formally, if the prisoner's dilemma is repeated finitely, all Nash equilibria of the resulting sequential games have the property that the noncooperative outcome, which is Pareto-inferior, occurs in each period, no matter how large the number of periods.

Case 3: Repeated Interaction for an Infinite or Indefinite Amount of Time

In the case in which parties interact with one another for an infinite or indefinite period of time, the logic of backward induction breaks down. No identifiable end point from which to reason backward exists. We are left with forward-thinking logic.

If we anticipate playing a prisoner's dilemma game with another person for an infinitely long or uncertain length of time, we reason that we might influence their behavior with our own behavior. We may signal a desire to cooperate on a mutual basis by making a cooperative choice in an early trial. Similarly, we can reward and punish their behavior through our actions.

Under such conditions, the game theoretic analysis indicates that cooperation in the first period is the optimal choice (Kreps, Milgrom, Roberts, & Wilson, 1982). Should our strategy be to cooperate no matter what? No! If a person adopted cooperation as a general strategy, it would surely lead to exploitation. So, what strategy would be optimal to adopt? Before reading further, stop and indicate what is a good strategy.

The Tournament of Champions

In 1981, Robert Axelrod, a leading game theorist, posed this question to readers in an article in *Science* magazine. Axelrod spelled out the contingencies of the prisoner's dilemma game and invited members of the scientific community to submit a strategy to play in a prisoner's dilemma tournament. To play in the tournament, a person had to submit a strategy (a plan that would tell a decision maker what to do in every trial under all possible conditions) in the form of a computer program written in FORTRAN code. Axelrod explained that each strategy would play all other strategies across 200 trials of a prisoner's dilemma game. He further explained that the strategies would be evaluated in terms of the maximization of gains across all opponents they faced. Hundreds of strategies were submitted by eminent scholars from around the world.

The Winner Is a Loser

The winner of the tournament was the simplest strategy submitted. The FORTRAN code was only four lines long. The strategy was called **tit-for-tat** and was submitted by Anatol Rapoport. Tit-for-tat accumulated the greatest number of points across all trials with all of its opponents. The basic principle for tit-for-tat is simple. Tit-for-tat always cooperates on the first trial, and on subsequent trials, it does whatever its opponent did on the previous trial. For example, suppose that tit-for-tat played against someone who cooperated on the first trial, defected on the second trial, and then cooperated on the third trial. Tit-for-tat would cooperate on the first trial and the second trial, defect on the third trial, and cooperate on the fourth trial.

Tit-for-tat never beat any of the strategies it played against. Because it cooperates on the first trial, it can never do better than its opponent. The most tit-for-tat can do is earn as much as its opponent. If it never wins (i.e., beats its opponent), how can tit-for-tat be so successful in maximizing its overall gains? The answer is that it induces cooperation from its opponents. How does it motivate this behavior? Several characteristics make tit-for-tat an especially effective strategy for inducing cooperation.

Psychological Analysis of Why Tit-for-Tat Is Effective

Not Envious   One reason why tit-for-tat is effective is that it is not an envious strategy. It does not care that it can never beat the opponent. Tit-for-tat can never earn more than any strategy it plays against. Rather, the tit-for-tat strategy is designed to maximize its own gain in the long run.

Nice   Tit-for-tat always begins the interaction by cooperating. Furthermore, it is never the first to defect. Thus, tit-for-tat is a nice strategy. This feature is important because it is difficult for people to recover from initial defections. Competitive, aggressive behavior often sours a relationship. Moreover, aggression often begets aggression. The tit-for-tat strategy neatly avoids the costly mutual escalation trap that can lead to the demise of both parties.

Tough   A strategy of solid cooperation would be easily exploitable by an opponent. Tit-for-tat can be provoked—it will defect if the opponent invites competition. Tit-for-tat reciprocates defection, an important feature of its strategy. By reciprocating defection, tit-for-tat conveys the message that it cannot be taken advantage of. Indeed, tit-for-tat players effectively move competitive players away from them, thus minimizing noncooperative interaction (Van Lange & Visser, 1999).

Forgiving   We noted that tit-for-tat is tough in that it reciprocates defection. It is also a forgiving strategy in the sense that it reciprocates cooperation, another important feature of the tit-for-tat strategy. It is often difficult for people in conflict to recover from defection and end an escalating spiral of aggression. Tit-for-tat's eye-for-an-eye strategy ensures that its responses to aggression from the other side will never be more than it receives.

Not Clever   Ironically, one reason why tit-for-tat is so effective is that it is not very clever. It is an extremely simple strategy, and other people can quickly figure out what to expect from a player who follows it. This predictability has important psychological properties. When people are uncertain or unclear about what to expect, they are more likely to engage in defensive behavior. When uncertainty is high, people often assume the worst about another person. Predictability increases interpersonal attraction.

In summary, tit-for-tat is an extremely stable strategy. Negotiators who follow it often induce their opponents to adopt the tit-for-tat strategy. However, few who play prisoner's dilemma games actually follow tit-for-tat. For example, in our analysis of more than 600 executives playing the prisoner's dilemma game, the defection rate is nearly 40 percent, and average profits are only one-tenth of the possible maximum! But tit-for-tat is not uniquely stable; other strategies are stable as well. For example, solid defection is a stable strategy. Two players who defect on every trial have little reason to do anything else. The message is that once someone has defected, it is difficult to renew cooperation.

Recovering from Defection

Suppose that you are the manager of a large HMO. The health care industry is highly competitive, with different companies vying to capture market share by touting low deductibles and so on. You have analyzed the situation with your competitors to be a noncooperative game. You have thought about how your competitor must view the situation, and you have decided to take a cooperative approach and *not* engage in negative advertising. Later that week, you learn that your opponent has taken out a full-page ad in *The Wall Street Journal* that denigrates your HMO by publicizing questionable statistics about your mortality rates, quotes from angry patients, and charges about negligent physicians. You counter with some negative TV spots. You are spending a lot of money and are angry. Can you stop this escalating spiral of defection? Probably so, if you consider the following strategies.

Make Situational Attributions   We often blame the incidence of escalating mutually destructive conflict on others' ill will and evil intentions. We fail to realize that we might have done the same thing as our competitor had we been in his or her shoes. Why? We punctuate events differently than do our opponents. We see our behavior as a defensive *response* to the other. In contrast, we view the other as engaging in unprovoked acts of aggression. The solution is to see the other side's behavior as a response to our own actions. In the preceding situation, your competitor's negative ad campaign may be a payback for your campaign a year ago.

One Step at a Time   Trust is not rebuilt in a day. We rebuild trust incrementally by taking a series of small steps that effectively "reward" the other party if they behave cooperatively. For example, the GRIT (graduated reduction in tension relations) strategy (reviewed in Chapter 9) calls for parties in conflict to offer small concessions (Osgood, 1979). This approach reduces the risk for the party making the concession.

Getting Even and Catching Up   As we saw in Chapter 3 on distributive negotiation (pie slicing), people are especially concerned with fairness. The perception of inequity is a major threat to the continuance of relationships. One way of rebuilding trust is to let the other party "get even" and catch up. The resurrection of a damaged relationship may depend on repentance on the part of the injurer and forgiveness on the part of the injured (Bottom, Gibson, Daniels, & Murnighan, 1996). Even more surprising is that it is the thought that counts: Small amends are as effective as large amends in generating future cooperation.

Make Your Decisions at the Same Time   Imagine that you are playing a prisoner's dilemma game like that described in the Thelma and Louise case. You are told about the contingencies and payoffs in the game and then asked to make a choice. The twist in the situation is that you are either told that your opponent: (1) has already made her choice earlier that day, (2) will make her choice later that day, or (3) will make her choice at the same time as you. In all cases, you will *not* know the other person's choice before making your own. When faced with this situation, people are more likely to cooperate when their opponent's decision is temporally contiguous with their own decision—that is, when the opponent makes her decision at the same time (Morris, Sim, & Girrotto, 1995). Temporal contiguity fosters a causal illusion: the idea that our behavior at a given time can influence the behavior of others. This logical impossibility is not permissible in the time-delayed decisions.

In the prisoner's dilemma game, people make choices simultaneously; therefore, one's choice cannot influence the choice that the other person makes on a given trial—only in subsequent trials. That is, when Thelma makes her decision to confess or not, it does not influence Louise, unless she is telepathic. However, people *act as if* their behavior influences the behavior of others, even though it logically cannot.

In an intriguing analysis of this perception, Douglas Hofstadter wrote a letter, published in *Scientific American*, to 20 friends (see Box 11-1). Hofstadter raised the question of whether one person's action in this situation can be taken as an indication of what all people will do. He concluded that if players are indeed rational, they will either all choose to defect or all choose to cooperate. Given that all players are going to submit the same answer, which choice would be more logical? It would seem that cooperation is best (each player gets $57 when all cooperate and only $19 when they all defect). At this point, the logic seems like magical thinking: A person's choice at a given time influences the behavior of others at the same time. Another example: People explain that they have decided to vote in an election so that others will, too. Of

---

BOX 11-1

LETTER FROM DOUGLAS HOFSTADTER TO 20 FRIENDS IN *SCIENTIFIC AMERICAN*

Dear____ :

I am sending this letter by special delivery to 20 of you (namely, various friends of mine around the country). I am proposing to all of you a one-round Prisoner's Dilemma game, the payoffs to be monetary (provided by *Scientific American*). It is very simple. Here is how it goes.

Each of you is to give me a single letter: *C* or *D*, standing for "cooperate" or "defect." This will be used as your move in a Prisoner's Dilemma with *each* of the 19 other players.

Thus, if everyone sends in *C*, everyone will get $57, whereas if everyone sends in *D*, everyone will get $19. You can't lose! And, of course, anyone who sends in *D* will get at least as much as everyone else. If, for example, 11 people send in *C* and nine send in *D*, then the 11 *C*-ers will get $3 a piece from each of the other *C*-ers (making $30) and will get nothing from the *D*-ers. Therefore, *C*-ers will get $30 each. The *D*-ers in contrast, will pick up $5 a piece from each of the *C*-ers (making $55) and will get $1 from each of the other *D*-ers (making $8), for a grand total of $63. No matter what the distribution is, *D*-ers always do better than *C*-ers. Of course, the more *C*-ers there are, the better *everyone* will do!

By the way, I should make it clear that in making your choice you should not aim to be the *winner* but simply to get as much *money* for yourself as possible. Thus, you should be happier to get $30 (say, as a result of saying *C* along with 10 others, even though the nine *D*-sayers get more than you) than to get $19 (by saying *D* along with everyone else, so that nobody "beats" you.) Furthermore, you are not supposed to think that at some later time you will meet with and be able to share the goods with your coparticipants. You are not aiming at maximizing the total number of dollars *Scientific American* shells out, only at maximizing the number of dollars that come to *you*!

Of course, your hope is to be the *unique* defector, thereby really cleaning up: with 19 *C*-ers, you will get $95 and they will each get 18 times $3, namely $54. But why am I doing the multiplication or any of this figuring for you? You are very bright. So are the others. All about equally bright, I would say. Therefore, all you need to do is tell me your choice. I want all answers by telephone (call collect, please) *the day you receive this letter*.

It is to be understood (it *almost* goes without saying, but not quite) that you are not to try to consult with others who you guess have been asked to participate. In fact, please consult with no one at all. The purpose is to see what people will do on their own, in isolation. Finally, I would appreciate a short statement to go along with your choice, telling me *why* you made this particular one.

Yours,

Doug H.

Source: Hofstadter, D. (1983). Metamagical thinking. *Scientific American, 248,* 14–28.

course, it is impossible that one person's voting behavior could affect others in a given election, but people act as if it does. Hofstadter argues that decision makers wrestling with such choices must give others credit for seeing the logic that oneself has seen. Thus, we need to believe that others are rational (like ourselves) and that they believe that everyone is rational. Hofstadter calls this rationality *superrationality*. For this reason, choosing to defect undermines the very reasons for choosing it. In Hofstadter's game, 14 people defected, and six cooperated. The defectors received $43; the cooperators received $15. Robert Axelrod was one of the participants who defected, remarking a one-shot game offers no reason to cooperate.

SOCIAL DILEMMAS

Sometimes, managers find themselves involved in a prisoner's dilemma that contains several people (e.g., in the opening example of the research group). In these types of situations, negotiators find themselves choosing between cooperative strategies and self-interested strategies. The multiperson prisoner's dilemma is known as a social dilemma. (See Sidebars 11-1 and 11-2 for other types of social dilemma—volunteer dilemmas and ultimatum dilemmas.) In general, people tend to behave more competitively (in a self-interested fashion) in social dilemmas as compared to prisoner's dilemmas. Why do they act this way?

Sidebar 11-1. Volunteer Dilemma

The **volunteer dilemma** is a situation in which at least one person in a group must sacrifice his or her own interests to better the group. An example is a group of friends who want to go out for an evening of drinking and celebration. The problem is that not all can drink if one person must safely drive everyone home. A "designated" driver is a volunteer for the group. Most organized entities would not function if no one volunteered. The act of volunteering strengthens group ties (Murnighan, Kim, & Metzger, 1993).

Sidebar 11-2. Ultimatum Dilemma

In an ultimatum bargaining situation, one person makes a final offer—an ultimatum—to another person. If the other person accepts the offer, then the first player receives the demand that he or she made, and the other player agrees to accept what was offered to him or her. If the offer is refused, then no settlement is reached—an impasse occurs—and negotiators receive their respective reservation points.

How should we negotiate in ultimatum situations? What kind of a final offer should we make to another person? When the tables are turned, on what basis should we accept or refuse a final offer someone makes to us?

Suppose someone with a $100 bill in hand comes to you and the person sitting on the bus beside you. This person explains that the $100 is yours to share with the other person if you can propose a split that the other person will agree to. The only hitch is that the division you propose is a once-and-for-all decision: You cannot discuss it with the other person, and you have to propose a take-it-or-leave-it split. If the other person accepts your proposal, the $100 will be allocated accordingly. If the other person rejects your proposal, no one gets any money, and you do not have the opportunity to propose another offer. Faced with this situation, what should you do? (Before reading further, indicate what you would do and why.)

It is useful for us to solve this problem using the principles of decision theory and then see whether the solution squares with our intuition. Once again, we use the concept of backward induction, working backward from the last period of the game. The last decision in this game is an ultimatum. In this game, player 2 (the person beside you on the bus) must decide whether to accept the proposal offered by you or reject the offer and receive nothing. From a rational standpoint, player 2 should accept any positive offer you make to him or her because, after all, something (even 1 cent) is better than nothing.

Now we can examine the next-to-last decision in the game and ask what proposal player 1 (you) should make. Because you know that player 2 should accept any positive offer greater than $0, the game theoretic solution is for you to offer $0.01 to player 2 and demand $99.99 for yourself. This proposal is a **subgame perfect equilibrium** (Selten, 1975) because it is rational within each period of the game. Said in a different way, even if the game had additional periods to be played in the future, your offer of $99.99 (to you) and $0.01 to the other person would still be rational at this point.

Contrary to game theoretic predictions, most people do not behave in this way. That is, most player 1s propose amounts substantially greater than $0.01 for player 2, often around the midpoint, or $50. Further, player 2s often reject offers that are not 50–50 splits (Pillutla & Murnighan, 1995). Thus, some player 2s choose to have $0 rather than $1 or $2—or even $49. Player 1s act nonrationally and so do player 2s. This response seems completely counter to one's interests, but as we saw in Chapter 2, people are often more concerned with how their outcomes compare to others than with the absolute value of their outcomes (see Loewenstein, Thompson, & Bazerman 1989; Messick & Sentis, 1979).

Croson (1996) also found that acceptance rates are driven by how much information the responder has about the size of the total pie. When the responder does not know the size of the pie and receives a dollar offer, she is much more likely to reject it.

First, the prisoner's dilemma involves two parties; the social dilemma involves several people. This size difference is important. People tend to behave more competitively in groups than in two-person situations (Insko et al., 1994).

Second, the *costs of defection are spread out*, rather than concentrated upon one person. Simply stated, when one person makes a self-interested choice and others choose to cooperate, everyone but the defector absorbs some (but not all) of the cost. Thus, the defecting person can say to himself or herself that everyone is suffering a little bit, rather than a lot. This mindset may lead people to be more inclined to serve their own interests.

Third, social dilemmas are *riskier* than prisoner's dilemmas. In the two-person dilemma, a certain minimal payoff to parties can be anticipated in advance. However, this outcome is not true in a social dilemma. The worst-case scenario is when the negotiator chooses to cooperate and everyone else defects. The costs of this situation are very great. Greater risk and more uncertainty lead people to behave in a more self-interested, competitive fashion.

Fourth, social dilemmas *provide anonymity* that prisoner's dilemmas do not. Whereas anonymity is impossible in two-party situations, in social dilemmas people can "hide among the group." When people feel less accountable, they are more inclined to behave in a self-interested, competitive fashion.

Finally, people in social dilemmas *have less control* over the situation. In a classic, two-party prisoner's dilemma, people can directly shape and modify the behavior of the other person. Specifically, by choosing defection, one person may punish the other; by choosing cooperation, he or she can reward the other. This logic is the beauty of the tit-for-tat strategy. However, in a social dilemma, if someone defects, one person cannot necessarily punish the other on the next round because others will also be affected and, as we have seen, the costs of defection are spread out. For example, consider a classic social dilemma—the OPEC group (see their official Web site at http://www.opec.org). OPEC is a group of mostly Middle Eastern oil companies that all agree to reduce their production of oil. Lowering the volume of available oil creates greater demand, and oil prices go up. Obviously, each company within OPEC has an incentive to increase its production of oil, thus creating greater profit for itself. However, if all companies violate the OPEC agreement and increase the production of oil, demand decreases, and so does the price of oil, thus driving down profits for the entire group.

The Tragedy of the Commons

Imagine that you are a farmer. You own several cows and share a grazing pasture known as a "commons" with other farmers. One hundred farmers share the pasture.

Each farmer is allowed to have one cow graze. Because the commons is not policed, it is tempting for you to add one more cow. By adding another cow, you can double your utility, and no one will really suffer. If everyone does the same thing, however, the commons will be overrun and the grazing area depleted. The cumulative result will be disastrous. What should you do in this situation if you want to keep your family alive?

The analysis of the "tragedy of the commons" (from Hardin, 1968) may be applied to many real-world problems, such as pollution, use of natural resources, and overpopulation. In these situations, people are tempted to maximize their own gain, reasoning that their pollution, failure to vote, and Styrofoam cups in the landfill will not have a measurable impact on others. However, if everyone engages in this behavior, the collective outcome is disastrous: Air will be unbreathable, not enough votes will support a particular candidate in an election, and landfills will be overrun. Thus, in the social dilemma, the rational pursuit of self-interest produces collective disaster.

In the social dilemma situation, each person makes behavioral choices similar to those in the prisoner's dilemma: to benefit oneself or the group. As in the prisoner's dilemma, the choices are referred to as cooperation and defection. The defecting choice always results in better personal outcomes, at least in the immediate future, but universal defection results in poorer outcomes for everyone than with universal cooperation.

A hallmark characteristic of social dilemmas is that the rational pursuit of self-interest is detrimental to collective welfare. This factor has serious and potentially disastrous implications. (In this sense, social dilemmas contradict the principle of hedonism and laissez-faire economics.) Unless some limits are placed on the pursuit of personal goals, the entire society may suffer.

Types of Social Dilemmas

The two major forms of the social dilemma are: **resource conservation dilemmas** (also known as **collective traps**) and **public goods dilemmas** (also known as **collective fences;** see Messick & Brewer, 1983). In the resource conservation dilemma, individuals take or harvest resources from a common pool (like the farmers in the commons). Examples of the detrimental effects of individual interest include pollution, harvesting (of fossil fuels), burning of fossil fuels, water shortages, and negative advertising (see Sidebar 11-3 and actual ads). The defecting choice occurs when people consume too much. The result of overconsumption is collective disaster. For groups to sustain themselves, the rate of consumption cannot exceed the rate of replenishment of resources.

> ### Sidebar 11-3. Comparative Advertising
> Since the 1970s, in a trend toward "comparative advertising," companies compare their product with competitors' products and point out the advantages of their own product and the disadvantages of the competitors' products. Hardly any industry has managed to avoid comparative advertising. Advertisers have

battled over milk quality, fish oil, beer taste, electric shavers, cola, coffee, magazines, cars, telephone service, banking, credit cards, and peanut butter. The ads attack the products and services of other companies. What is the effect of the attack ad? For the consumer, attack ads keep prices down and quality high. However, it can also lead to consumer resentment toward the industry. The effect is much more serious for the advertisers, who can effectively run each other out of business. (See examples of comparative advertising on subsequent pages.)

Sidebar 11-3   Example of Negative (Competitive) Advertising

Source: Courtesy of The Savin Corporation, Stanford, Connecticut.

Business Class Legroom	
Delta BusinessElite	36.5"
Continental	31"
British Airways	24"
Lufthansa	23"
American Airlines	22"

Business Class Recline	
Delta BusinessElite	160°
Continental	152°
British Airways	140°
Lufthansa	135°
American Airlines	132°

Nonstop European Destinations	
Delta BusinessElite	23
Continental	17
American Airlines	12
British Airways	3
Lufthansa	3

Nonstop destinations from the U.S.

Concierge Service At Every Gateway	
Delta BusinessElite	Yes
Continental	No
British Airways	No
Lufthansa	No
American Airlines	No

Looks great on paper.
Feels even better in person.

Presenting Delta BusinessElite.™

There are a lot of reasons to fly Delta's new BusinessElite,

but don't take our word for it. Experience it for yourself.

With more personal space than other leading airlines' business

classes, and our convenient BusinessElite Concierge service at all

32 intercontinental destinations, we think you'll agree. BusinessElite

to Europe, Japan, India and Brazil simply outclasses business class.

BUSINESS*elite*˙

▲ **Delta Air Lines**

For reservations, visit us at www.bizelite.com or call Delta Air Lines at 1-800-241-4141. Or see your Travel Agent today.

Personal space is defined as the sum of legroom and recline. Legroom based on measurements taken from the foremost point of the bottom seat cushion to the back of the seat in front of it using non-bulkhead seats on a widebody aircraft of Continental (DC10-30), British Airways (747-200), Lufthansa (A340-300) and American Airlines (767-300). ©1999 Delta Air Lines, Inc.

Sidebar 11-3   Example of Explicit Comparative Advertising

Source: Courtesy of Delta Air Lines, Atlanta, Georgia.

In public goods dilemmas, people contribute or give resources to a common pool or community. Examples include donating to public radio and television, paying taxes, voting, doing committee work, and joining unions. The defecting choice is to not contribute. Those who fail to contribute are known as defectors or free riders. Those who pay while others free ride are affectionately known as suckers.

Think of resource conservation dilemmas as situations in which people *take* things; and think of public goods dilemmas as situations in which people must *contribute*. Moreover, both kinds of dilemmas—taking too much and failing to contribute—can occur within an organization or between different organizations (see Table 11-2 for examples).

How to Build Cooperation in Social Dilemmas

Most groups in organizations could be characterized as social dilemma situations (Kopelman, Weber, & Messick, 2002; Kramer, 1991; Mannix, 1993). Members are left to their own devices to decide how much to take or contribute for common benefit. Consider an organization in which access to supplies and equipment, such as computers, Xerox paper, stamps, and envelopes, is not regulated. Each member may be tempted to overuse or hoard resources, thereby contributing to a rapid depletion of supply.

Many individual characteristics of people have been studied, such as gender, race, Machiavellianism, status, age, and so on (for a review, see Kopelman, Weber, & Messick, 2002). Few, if any, reliable individual differences actually predict behavior in a prisoner's dilemma game. In fact, people cooperate more than rational analysis would predict. Many investigations use a single trial or fixed number of trials in which the rational strategy is solid defection. When the game is infinite or the number of trials is indefinite, however, people cooperate less than they should. What steps can the manager take to build greater cooperation and trust among organization members? Two major types of approaches for maximizing cooperation are structural strategies (which are often institutional changes) and psychological strategies (which are usually engaged in by the organizational actor; see Table 11-3).

Structural Strategies

Structural strategies involve fundamental changes in the way that social dilemmas are constructed. They are usually the result of thoughtful problem solving and often produce a change in incentives.

Align Incentives   Monetary incentives for cooperation, privatization of resources, and a monitoring system increase the incidence of cooperation. For example, by putting in "high-occupancy vehicle" lanes on major highways, single drivers

TABLE 11-2 Different Kinds of Social Dilemmas		
	Taking	*Contributing*
Internal (intraorganizational)	Resources (e.g., money, real estate, staffing) Budget fudging	Committee work Recognition
External (interorganizational)	Price competition Brand competition Overharvesting Pollution	Paying taxes Public television

TABLE 11-3	Summary of Strategies for Maximizing Cooperation in Social Dilemmas
Structural Strategies	*Psychological Strategies*
Align incentives	Psychological contracts
Monitor behavior	Superordinate goals
Regulation	Communication
Privatization	Personalize others
Tradable permits	Social sanctions
	Focus on benefits of cooperation

Source: Brett, J., & Thompson, L. (2003). Negotiation Strategies for Managers. Executive course, Kellogg School of Management, Northwestern University, Evanston, IL.

are more motivated to carpool. However, realignment of incentives can be time-consuming and expensive.

Often, defectors are reluctant to cooperate because the costs of cooperation seem exorbitantly high. For example, people often defect by not paying their parking tickets because the price is high and they have several tickets. In some cases, city officials have allowed for amnesty delays for delinquent parking tickets, whereby people can cooperate at a cost less than they expected. Cities have adopted similar policies to induce people to return borrowed library books. (For a description of New York City's parking ticket amnesty program, visit http://www.parkingticket.com/amnesty.)

Cooperation can also be induced through reward and recognition in organizations. Recognition awards, such as gold stars, employee-of-the-month awards, and the like, are designed to induce cooperation rather than defection in a variety of organizational social dilemmas.

In some instances, cooperation can be induced by increasing the risk associated with defection. For example, some people do not pay their state or federal income tax in the United States. This behavior is illegal and if a defector is caught, he or she can be convicted of a crime. The threat of spending years in jail often lessens the temptation of defection. However, most tacit negotiations in organizations are not policed in this fashion and therefore, defection is more tempting for would-be defectors.

Monitor Behavior   When we monitor people's behavior, they often conform to group norms. The same beneficial effects also occur when people monitor their own behavior. For example, when people meter their water consumption during a water shortage, they use less water (Van Vugt & Samuelson, 1999). Moreover, people who metered their water usage expressed greater concern with the collective costs of overconsumption during a drought.

One method of monitoring behavior is to elect a leader. For example, people often will be in favor of electing a leader when they receive feedback that their group has failed at restricting harvests from a collective resource (Messick et al., 1983; Rutte & Wilke, 1984). When a leader is introduced into a social dilemma situation, especially an autocratic leader (Van Vugt & De Cremer, 1999), individual group members might fear restriction of their freedom. In a direct test of people's willingness to elect a leader, van Dijk, Wilke, and Wit (2003) found that people are more reluctant to install leaders in public goods situations (contributing) than in common resource situations (taking), because it is more threatening to give up decision freedom over private property than over collective property.

Regulation   Regulation involves government intervention to correct market imperfections with the idea of improving social welfare. Examples include rationing, in which limits are placed on access to a common-pool resource (i.e., water use). Regulation also occurs in other markets, such as agriculture. The telephone industry in the United States is a heavily regulated industry; in 1934 Congress created the Federal Communications Commission (FCC) to oversee all wire and radio communication (e.g., radio, broadcast, telephone). Even though regulation does not always result in a system that encourages responsible behavior (cf. the moral hazard problem created by the federal deposit insurance system), the intent of regulation is to protect public (social) interests.

Privatization   The basic idea of privatization is to put public resources under the control of specific individuals or groups—public lands in private hands. The rationale is that public resources will be better protected if they are in the control of private groups or individuals. For example, protracted battles over public lands in New Mexico prompted the U.S. Congress to develop a national preserve that is not administered by federal land managers, but by a board of nine private trustees, appointed by the president (National Public Radio, Sept. 23, 2002). Valles Caldera, New Mexico, is a 90,000-acre volcanic bowl with scenic overlooks. The federal government bought the land two years ago for $100 million. The trustees, who include experts in ranching, forestry, government, and conservation, decide what activities to allow based upon their sense of what best serves the common good. For example, 700 cows graze in Caldera's grassy valleys—a temporary arrangement to help 40 local ranchers stricken by drought. Hikers are only allowed to enter by bus, at a cost of more than $40 each. Moreover, the region contains rich oil and gas reserves, timbering potential, and great hunting with thousands of elk.

Another example: Hawaii's Sea Grant, partnering with the Oceanic Institute, works with government and private organizations to examine biological, environmental, and economic feasibility of offshore aquaculture in the Pacific region. The *moi*, a fish grown by Hawaiian researchers, is highly valued by Hawaiians, but is currently depleted in local waters. Moi grow well in captivity and reach market size in only six to eight months. At the end of the first season, for example, the Hawaii Offshore Aquaculture Research Project (HOARP) harvested more than 19 tons of moi. In the second year, the stocking density of the fish doubled and the overall harvest was over 34 tons (SOBEL, 2004).

Tradable Permits   Tradable environmental allowance (TEA) governance structures are another way of navigating social dilemmas. In TEA arrangements, instead of competing for scarce resources (like the right to pollute), companies purchase the rights to pollute or to use scarce resources (Brett & Kopelman, 2004). The idea is that users will treat these rights as they would conventional property, and thus, conserve resources carefully (Ackerman & Stewart, 1988; Kriz, 1998; Tipton, 1995). Tradable permits have been successfully used for managing fisheries, water supply, and air and water pollution in many different countries (Tietenberg, 2002). For example, in the fishing industry, the total allowable catch (or TAC) is set by government agencies and subsequently allocated to associations or individual users. As in the case of pollution, these allocations can be traded by individuals or companies.

Psychological Strategies

In contrast to structural strategies, which often require an act of government or layers of bureaucracy to enact, psychological strategies are inexpensive and only require the wits of the influence agent.

Psychological Contracts Legal contracts involve paperwork and are similar to the deterrence-based trust mechanisms we discussed in Chapter 6. In contrast, psychological contracts are commonly known as "handshake deals." They are usually not binding in a court of law, but they create a psychological pressure to commit. People are more likely to cooperate when they promise to cooperate. Although any such promises are nonbinding and are therefore "cheap talk," people nevertheless act as if they are binding. The reason for this behavior, according to the **norm of commitment,** is that people feel psychologically committed to follow through with their word (Cialdini, 1993). The norm of commitment is so powerful that people often do things that are completely at odds with their preferences or that are highly inconvenient. For example, once people agree to let a salesperson demonstrate a product in their home, they are more likely to buy it. Homeowners are more likely to consent to have a large (over 10 feet tall), obtrusive sign in their front yard that says "Drive Carefully" when they agree to a small request made the week before (Freedman & Fraser, 1966).

Superordinate Goals Our behavior in social dilemmas is influenced by our perceptions about what kinds of behavior are appropriate and expected in a given context. In an intriguing examination of this idea, people engaged in a prisoner's dilemma task. The game was not described to participants as a "prisoner's dilemma," though. In one condition, the game was called the "Wall Street game," and in another condition, the game was called the "community game" (Ross & Samuels, 1993). Otherwise, the game, the payoffs, and the choices were identical. Although rational analysis predicts that defection is the optimal strategy no matter what the name, in fact, the incidence of cooperation was three times as high in the community game than in the Wall Street game, indicating that people are sensitive to situational cues as trivial as the name of the game. Indeed, people behave more competitively in social dilemmas involving economic decisions compared to those involving noneconomic decisions (Pillutla & Chen, 1999).

Communication A key determinant of cooperation is *communication* (Komorita & Parks, 1994; Liebrand, Messick, & Wilke, 1992; Messick & Brewer, 1983; Sally, 1995). If people are allowed to communicate with the members of the group prior to making their choices, the incidence and level of cooperation increase dramatically (Sally, 1995).

Two reasons explain this increase in cooperation (Dawes, van de Kragt, and Orbell, 1990). First, communication enhances group identity or solidarity. Second, communication allows the group members to make public commitments to cooperate. Verbal commitments in such situations indicate the willingness of others to cooperate. In this sense, they reduce the uncertainty that people have about others in such situations and provide a measure of reassurance to decision makers. Kerr and Kaufman-Gilliland (1994) found that of the two explanations, it was the commitment factor that was most important about communication.

In our investigations on the relative effectiveness of verbal face-to-face communication as compared to written-only or no communication, we find that people who communicate face-to-face are much more likely to reach a mutually profitable deal because they are able to coordinate on a price above each party's BATNA (Valley, Thompson, Gibbons, & Bazerman, 2002). Commitments also shape subsequent behavior. People are extremely reluctant to break their word, even when their words are nonbinding. If people are prevented from making verbal commitments, they attempt to make nonverbal ones.

The other reason why communication is effective in engendering cooperation is that it allows group members to develop a shared group identity. Communication allows people to get to know one another and feel more attracted to their group. People derive a sense of identity from their relationships to social groups (Tajfel, 1979). When our identity is traced to the relationships we have with others in groups, we seek to further the interests of these groups. This identification leads to more cooperative, or group-welfare, choices in social dilemmas.

Social identity is often built through relationships. For example, as a consequence of population growth, the politics of water distribution, and five years of drought, California had widespread shortages of water in 1991. Residents of many areas were encouraged to voluntarily conserve water and were subjected to regulations imposed by the Public Utilities Commission. A telephone survey of hundreds of residents of the San Francisco area revealed that people were more willing to support authorities when they had strong relational bonds to the authorities (Tyler & Degoey, 1995). The effectiveness of authorities in eliciting cooperation in water-shortage dilemmas is linked to the social bonds that they share with community members.

Personalize Others   People often behave as if they were interacting with an entity or organization rather than a person. For example, an embittered customer claims that the airline refused her a refund when in fact it was a representative of the airline who did not issue a refund. To the extent that others can be personalized, people are more motivated to cooperate than if they believe they are dealing with a dehumanized bureaucracy. Even more important is that people see you as a cooperator. People cooperate more when others have cooperated in a previous situation (Pillutla & Chen, 1999).

For example, Knez and Camerer (2000) created a simulation that resembled the transfer of cooperative norms in small firms (which are largely cooperative) as firms grow larger and become more like prisoner's dilemmas (which pit self-interest against cooperation). Some managers shared a history of coordinating their behavior; others did not. Those who had a history of coordinating their actions together were more likely to cooperate in a subsequent prisoner's dilemma situation. Further, the difference was dramatic—those who had a previous history cooperated in the prisoner's dilemma game about 71 percent of the time, whereas others without a history only cooperated 15–30 percent of the time.

Still another reason why people cooperate is that they want to believe that they are nice. For example, one person attributed his decision to make a cooperative choice in the 20-person prisoner's dilemma game to the fact that he did not want the readers of *Scientific American* to think that he was a defector (Hofstadter, 1983). This behavior is a type of impression management (Goffman, 1959). Impression management raises the question of whether people's behavior is different when it is anonymous than when it is public. The answer appears to be yes. However, it is not always the case that public behavior is more cooperative than private behavior. For example, negotiators who are accountable to a constituency often bargain harder and are more competitive than when they are accountable for their behavior (see Carnevale, Pruitt, & Seilheimmer, 1981).

Social Sanctions   In November 1995, USAir announced that it was putting its company up for sale (for a full treatment, see Diekmann, Tenbrunsel, & Bazerman, 1998). Financial analysts speculated that the sale of USAir would lead to a bidding war between the major airlines, because whichever airline acquired USAir would have a market advantage. None of the airlines wanted to be in the position of not acquiring USAir and seeing another airline buy the company.

Following the announcement of the sale of USAir, a strange series of events followed that was not forecast by financial analysts: No one bid for USAir. Analysts did not realize that the major airlines had learned an important principle through their experience in the 1980s with the frequent flyer and triple mile programs, which were designed to be competitive strategies to capture market share. However, the approach backfired in the airline industry when all of the major airlines developed frequent flyer programs, and a price war began, which resulted in the loss of millions of dollars among airlines.

Robert Crandall, the chair of American Airlines, was effective in averting a costly escalation war for USAir. How did he do it? Before reading further, stop and indicate what you would do if it was your company.

Robert Crandall wrote and published an open letter to the employees of American Airlines that appeared in the *Chicago Tribune* (see Box 11-2). The letter clearly indicated that American Airlines was interested in avoiding a costly bidding war with United Airlines for USAir. The letter clearly stated the *intentions* of American not to make an opening bid for USAir. The letter further indicated that American would bid competitively if United initiated bidding for USAir. The letter effectively signaled the intentions of American Airlines in a way that made bidding behavior seem too costly. Although the letter was addressed to the employees of American Airlines, it is obvious that the real targets of this message were the other airlines.

Focus on Benefits of Cooperation   According to Camerer and his colleagues (Anderson & Camerer, 2000; Camerer & Ho, 1998, 1999a, 1999b), the probability that a person will make a particular choice in a social dilemma is a function of the attraction of that choice in terms of its ability to return a desirable outcome immediately. Our attraction to a choice is usually a reflection of our ability to imagine or mentally

---

BOX 11-2

LETTER TO THE EMPLOYEES OF AMERICAN AIRLINES FROM ROBERT CRANDALL, CHAIRMAN

We continue to believe, as we always have, that the best way for American to increase its size and reach is by internal growth—not by consolidation. So we will not be the first to make a bid for USAir.

On the other hand, if United seeks to acquire USAir, we will be prepared to respond with a bid, or by other means as necessary, to protect American's competitive position.

Source: S. Ziemba. American to United: Avoid bidding war. *Chicago Tribune*, November 10, 1995.

simulate good outcomes (Parks, Sanna, & Posey, 2003). In a direct examination of people's ability to think positively in a prisoner's dilemma game, participants were instructed to think about some alternatives that were "worse" or "better" than what actually happened; then they played some more. The results were startling: Negotiators' subsequent cooperation with their partner was directly related to the number of best-case scenarios they generated; and negotiators who generated worst-case scenarios defected a lot (Parks, Sanna, and Posey, 2003). The message? Thinking about the how good we can be greatly increases cooperation. For example, Steve Ballmer, CEO of Microsoft, explains that he has reached out to archrival Larry Ellison (CEO of Oracle) in a gesture of cooperation: "I went down shortly after I became CEO to visit with Larry Ellison and talked about how we could work cooperatively on things that are important to our customers" (*BusinessWeek*, Dec. 1, 2003, p. 72).

How to Encourage Cooperation in Social Dilemmas When Parties Should Not Collude

In the examples thus far, we suggested ways that negotiators can entice others to cooperate so as to increase joint gain and, ultimately, individual gain. However, in many situations, it is illegal for parties to cooperate. Consider, for example, the problem of price-fixing among companies within an industry. Our opening example of the broadband auctions is a good illustration on how companies signal their desire to cooperate with one another. Another example concerns how a pharmaceutical company might respond to the entry of a new competitor in a particular class of a drug. Another example would include the manner in which Robert Crandall, previous CEO of American Airlines, effectively signaled his intentions regarding the sale of USAir (Box 11-2). Brett (2001) suggests the following principles to encourage cooperation in social dilemmas when companies should not privately collude:

- **Keep your strategy simple**: The simpler your strategy, the easier it is for your competitors to predict your behavior. The correspondence is nearly one-to-one between uncertainty and competitive behavior: Greater uncertainty leads to more competitive behavior (see Kopelman, Weber, & Messick, 2002); thus, help to minimize uncertainty for your competitors.
- **Signal via actions**: The adage that behaviors speak louder than words is important. Competitive others focus on your actions, not on your words.
- **Do not be the first to defect**: As we have seen, it is difficult to recover from escalating spirals of defection. Thus, do not be the first to defect.
- **Focus on your own payoffs, not your payoffs relative to others**: Often, it is the case that social dilemmas trigger competitive motives (as discussed in Chapter 5). As you recall, the competitive motive is a desire to "beat" the other party. A better bet is to stay focused on your profits.
- **Be sensitive to egocentric bias**: As we discussed, most people view their own behavior as more cooperative than that of others. We see ourselves as more virtuous, more ethical, and less competitive than others see us. When planning your strategy, consider the fact that your competitors will see you more negatively than you perceive yourself. Steve Ballmer, of Microsoft, is well aware of the egocentric bias, "It doesn't matter how we may have seen ourselves, we have to see ourselves as others see us. That, by far, is the biggest lesson" (*BusinessWeek*, Dec. 1, 2003, p. 72).

ESCALATION OF COMMITMENT

Suppose you make a small investment in a start-up Internet company that seems to have great potential. After the first quarter, you learn that the company suffered an operating loss. You cannot recover your investment; your goal is to maximize your long-term wealth. Should you continue to invest in the company? Consider two possible ways to look at this situation: If you consider the performance of the company during the first quarter to be a loss, and if you view continued investment as a choice between

1. Losing the small amount of money you have already invested, or
2. Taking additional risk by investing more money in the company, which could turn around and make a large profit or plummet even further.

The reference point effect described in Chapter 2 would predict that most negotiators would continue to invest in the company because they have already adopted a "loss frame" based upon their initial investment. Suppose that you recognize that the Internet company did not perform well in the first period and consider your initial investment to be a sunk cost—that is, water under the bridge. In short, you adapt your reference point. Now, ask yourself whether it would be wiser to

1. Not invest in the company at this point (a sure outcome of $0), or
2. Take a gamble and invest more money in a company that has not shown good performance in the recent past.

Under these circumstances, most people choose not to invest in the company because they would rather have a sure thing than a loss. A negotiator's psychological reference point also influences the tendency to fall into the escalation trap. Recall that negotiators are risk-seeking when it comes to losses and risk-averse for gains. When negotiators see themselves as trying to recover from a losing position, chances are they will engage in greater risk than if they see themselves as starting with a clean slate. Like the gambler in Las Vegas, negotiators who are hoping to hold out longer than their opponent (as in a strike) have fallen into the escalation trap. Most decision makers and negotiators do not readjust their reference point. Rather, they fail to adapt their reference point and continue to make risky decisions, which often prove unprofitable.

The **escalation of commitment** refers to the unfortunate tendency of negotiators to persist with a losing course of action, even in the face of clear evidence that their behaviors are not working and the negotiation situation is quickly deteriorating. The two types of escalation dilemmas are personal and interpersonal. In both cases, the dilemma is revealed when a person would do something different if they had not already been involved in the situation.

Personal escalation dilemmas involve only one person, and the dilemma concerns whether to continue with what appears to be a losing course of action or to cut one's losses. Continuing to gamble after losing a lot of money, pouring money into a car or house that continues to malfunction or deteriorate, and waiting in long lines that are not moving are examples of personal escalation dilemmas. To stop is to in some sense admit failure and accept a sure loss. Continuing to invest holds the possibility of recouping losses. Consider, for example, the case of John R. Silber, previous president of Boston University, who decided to invest in Seragen, a biotechnology company with a promising cancer drug. After investing $1.7 million over six years, the value of the company in 1998 was $43,000 (*New York Times*, Sept. 20, 1998).

Interpersonal escalation dilemmas involve two or more people, often in a competitive relationship, such as negotiation. Union strikes are often escalation dilemmas, and so is war. Consider the situation faced by Lyndon Johnson during the early stage of the Vietnam War. Johnson received the following memo from George Ball, then undersecretary of state:

> The decision you face now is crucial. Once large numbers of U.S. troops are committed to direct combat, they will begin to take heavy casualties in a war they are ill-equipped to fight in a noncooperative if not downright hostile countryside. Once we suffer large casualties, we will have started a well-nigh irreversible process. Our involvement will be so great that we cannot—without national humiliation—stop short of achieving our complete objectives. Of the two possibilities I think humiliation will be more likely than the achievement of our objectives—even after we have paid terrible costs (*The Pentagon Papers*, 1971, p. 450).

In escalation dilemmas, negotiators commit further resources to what appears to unbiased observers to be a failing course of action. In most cases, people fall into escalation traps because initially, the situation does not appear to be a losing enterprise. The situation becomes an escalation dilemma when the persons involved in the decision would make a different decision if they had not been involved up until that point, or when other objective persons would not choose that course of action. Often, in escalation situations, a decision is made to commit further resources to "turn the situation around," such as in the case of gambling (personal dilemma) or making a final offer (interpersonal dilemma). This process may repeat and escalate several times as additional resources are invested. The bigger the investment and the more severe the possible loss, the more prone people are to try to turn things around.

The escalation of commitment process is illustrated in Figure 11-2 (Ross & Staw, 1993). In the first stage of the escalation of commitment, a person is confronted with questionable or negative outcomes (e.g., a rejection of one's offer by a negotiation opponent, decrease in market share, poor performance evaluation, a malfunction, or hostile behavior from a competitor). This external event prompts a reexamination of the negotiator's current course of action, in which the utility of continuing is weighted against the utility of withdrawing or changing course. This decision determines the negotiator's commitment to his or her current course of action. If this commitment is low, the negotiator may make a concession, engage in integrative negotiations (rather than distributive negotiations), or possibly revert to his or her BATNA. If this commitment is high, however, the negotiator will continue commitment and continue to cycle through the decision stages.

When negotiators receive indication that the outcomes of a negotiation may be negative, they should ask themselves: *What are the personal rewards for me in this situation?* In many cases, the *process* of the negotiation itself, rather than the *outcome* of the negotiation, becomes the reason for commencing or continuing negotiations. This reasoning leads to a self-perpetuating reinforcement trap, wherein the rewards for continuing are not aligned with the actual objectives of the negotiator. Ironically, people who have high, rather than low, self-esteem are more

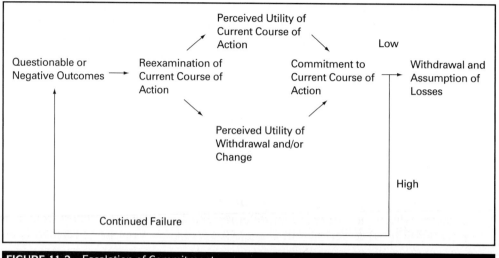

FIGURE 11-2   Escalation of Commitment

Source: Adapted from Ross, J., and Staw, B.M. (August 1993). Organizational escalation and exit: Lessons from the Shoreham Nuclear Power Plant. *Academy of Management Journal,* 701–732.

likely to become victimized by psychological forces—people with high self-esteem have much more invested in their ego and its maintenance than do those with low self-esteem (Taylor & Brown, 1988). Sometimes face-saving concerns lead negotiators to escalate commitment; some negotiators worry that they will look silly or stupid if they back down from an initial position. Ego protection often becomes a higher priority than the success of the negotiation.

Avoiding the Escalation of Commitment in Negotiations

Most negotiators do not realize that they are in an escalation dilemma until it is too late. Complicating matters is the fact that, in most escalation dilemmas, a negotiator (like a gambler) might have some early "wins" or good signs that reinforce their initial position. How can a negotiator best get out of an escalation dilemma?

The best advice is to adopt a policy of risk management: be aware of the risks involved in the situation; learn how to best manage these risks; and set limits, effectively capping losses at a tolerable level. It is also important to find ways to get information and feedback about the negotiation from a different perspective.

Set Limits

Ideally, a negotiator should have a clearly defined BATNA. At no point should a negotiator make or accept an offer that is worse than his or her BATNA.

Avoid Tunnel Vision

A negotiator should get several perspectives on the situation. Ask people who are not personally involved in the negotiation for their appraisal. Be careful not to bias their evaluation with your own views, hopes, expectations, or other details, such as the cost of extricating yourself from the situation, because that will only predispose them toward your point of view, which is not what you want—you want an honest, critical assessment.

Recognize Sunk Costs

Probably the most powerful way to escape escalation of commitment is to simply recognize and accept sunk costs. Sunk costs are basically water under the bridge: money (or other commitments) previously spent that cannot be recovered. It is often helpful for negotiators to consider removal of the project, product, or program. In this way, the situation is redefined as one in which a decision will be made immediately about whether to invest; that is, if you were making the initial decision today, would you make the investment currently under consideration (as a continuing investment), or would you choose another course of action? If the decision is not one that you would choose anew, you might want to start thinking about how to terminate the project and move on to the next one.

Diversify Responsibility and Authority

In some cases, it is necessary to remove or replace the original negotiators from deliberations precisely because they are biased. One way to carry out such a removal is with an external review or appointing someone who does not have a personal stake in the situation.

Redefine the Situation

Often, it helps to view the situation not as the "same old problem" but as a new problem to be dealt with. Furthermore, it often helps to change the decision criteria. For example, consider how Johns-Manville, the asbestos manufacturer, handled catastrophe. As a manager at Manville for more than 30 years, Bill Sells witnessed colossal examples of self-deception. Manville managers at every level were unwilling to acknowledge the evidence available in the 1940s about the hazards of asbestos, and their capacity for denial held steady through the following decades, despite mounting evidence of old and new hazards:

> The company developed a classic case of bunker mentality: refusing to accept facts; assuming that customers and employees were aware of the hazards and used asbestos at their own risk; denying the need for and the very possibility of change at a company that had successfully hidden its head in the sand for 100 years. Manville funded little medical research, made little effort to communicate what it already knew, and took little or no proactive responsibility for the damage asbestos might do . . . with tragic consequences for workers' health and decidedly negative effects on maintenance costs, productivity, and profit. Once when he raised objections, Sells was told by his boss, "Bill, you're not loyal," to which he replied, "No, no, you've got it wrong. I'm the one who *is* loyal." (Teal, 1996, p. 38)

In 1968, Sells successfully redefined the situation. He viewed it as one of business integrity, launching a $500,000 program to replace and rebuild nearly all the safety equipment at a troubled asbestos facility in Illinois. It was too late to save asbestos or its victims, but he put into practice important changes, such as funding arm's-length studies, immediate total disclosure, and the elimination of pro-company "spin" on any study results (Teal, 1996).

CONCLUSION

Most people are involved in tacit negotiations, wherein they communicate via behaviors. Prisoner's dilemmas and social dilemmas are characterized by the absence of contracts and enforcement mechanisms. In these dilemmas, people choose between acting in a self-interested fashion or in a cooperative fashion, which makes the negotiator vulnerable to exploitation. Optimal pie-expanding and pie-slicing strategies in the two-person prisoner's dilemma can be achieved via the tit-for-tat strategy, but tit-for-tat works only with two players in a repeated game. However, many tacit negotiations within and between organizations involve more than two players and are social dilemmas. The best way to ensure cooperation in social dilemmas is to align incentives, remove temptations to defect, seek verbal commitments, communicate with involved parties, build social identity, publicize commitments, personalize others, redefine the situation, and help manage impressions. Escalation dilemmas occur when people invest in what is (by any objective standards) a losing course of action. People can deescalate via setting limits, getting several perspectives, recognizing sunk costs, and diversifying responsibility.

12

NEGOTIATING VIA INFORMATION TECHNOLOGY

On November 8, 1999, the 107 *Calgary Herald* newsroom employees went on strike—the first time since the daily newspaper's founding in 1883. Two days before their strike notice took effect, they were locked out of the building, with no time to remove personal belongings. The computer security system was reprogrammed to deny access to nonmanagement employees, except those who had informed the company in advance they would cross the picket line. The conduct of the negotiations during that time was nearly unprecedented, from a technological standpoint. The strikers used technology extensively during the eight-month strike. In a province with relatively little or no unionization, strikers had few models of how to proceed. However, the picket line were a number of reporters and editors who were highly computer literate, photographers who knew how to use digital cameras (to photograph startling stacks of undelivered newspapers ready for incineration), and sophisticated computer programmers. A strike Web site was established as a tool for communicating with strikers, 75 percent of whom had Internet access at home, providing round-the-clock and up-to-the-minute updates on strike developments. At the same time, the company was using extremely sophisticated technology to pick up every word that people said on the picket line. The rumors that microphones were being used, and videotapes and sound recordings of strikers were being made proved true. Backing the high-tech Web site, the sophisticated techno-strikers used printers to create leaflets that provided Web addresses and self-mailers. The constant e-mails between the strike team provided a tremendous morale booster and emotional connection during what otherwise might have been a long, lonely fight. Among the most innovative uses of technology was the "cyber picket line;" cell phones as well became a major weapon for the strikers (Barnett, 2003).

The impact of technology on the course of negotiations in the *Calgary Herald* was dramatic and clearly suggests that technology can and does shape behavior at the bargaining table. This chapter examines the impact of information technology on negotiation, with a particular focus on e-mail negotiations (e-negotiations). We describe a simple model of social interaction called the place-time model and use it to evaluate the impact of information technology on negotiation. The model focuses on negotiators who either negotiate in the same or different physical location and at the same or different time. For each of these cases, we describe what to expect and ways to deal with the limitations of that communication mode. We follow this discussion with a section on how information technology affects negotiation behavior. We then describe strategies to help negotiators expand and divide the pie effectively.

PLACE-TIME MODEL OF SOCIAL INTERACTION

Any negotiation, broadly speaking, has four possibilities as depicted in the **place-time model** in Table 12-1 (see also Englebart, 1989; Johansen, 1988). The place-time model is based on the options that negotiators have when doing business across different locations and times. As might be suspected, negotiation behavior unfolds differently in face-to-face situations than in electronic forums.

Richness is the potential information-carrying capacity of the communication medium (Drolet & Morris, 2000). Communication media may be ordered on a continuum of richness, with face-to-face communication being at the relatively "rich" end, and formal, written messages, such as memos and business correspondence, being at the relatively "lean" or modality-restricted end (Daft & Lengel, 1984; Daft, Lengel, & Trevino, 1987; see Figure 12-1).

Face-to-face communication conveys the richest information because it allows for the simultaneous observation of multiple clues including body language, facial expression, and tone of voice, providing people with a greater awareness of context. In contrast, formal numerical documentation conveys the least-rich information, providing few clues about the context. In addition, geographical propinquity and time constraints affect negotiations.

Let's consider each of the four types of communications in the place-time model in greater detail.

Face-to-Face Communication

Face-to-face negotiation is the clear preference of most negotiators and rightly so. Face-to-face contact is crucial in the initiation of relationships and collaborations, and people are more cooperative when interacting face-to-face than via other forms of

TABLE 12-1 Place-Time Model of Interaction		
	Same Place	*Different Place*
Same Time	Face-to-face	Telephone
		Videoconference
Different Time	Single text editing	E-mail
	Shift work	Voice mail

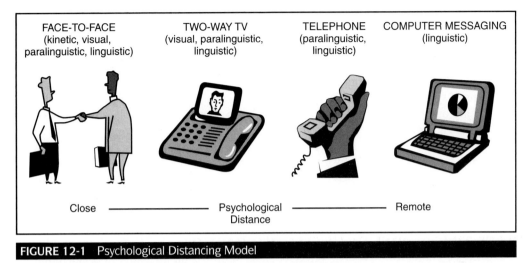

FIGURE 12-1 Psychological Distancing Model

Source: Adapted from Wellens, A. R. (1989). Effects of telecommunication media upon information sharing and team performance: Some theoretical and empirical findings. *IEEE AES Magazine,* September, p. 14.

communication. Personal, face-to-face contact is the lubricant of the business engine. Without it, things do not move as well, and relationships between people are often strained and contentious (see Sidebar 12-1 for an example).

Sidebar 12-1. The Importance of Face-to-Face Communication

A group of top managers at a progressive Silicon Valley company hated their weekly meetings, but enjoyed e-mail because it is quick, direct, and to the point. They thought meetings were "gassy, bloated, and a waste of time." So they decided to cancel their regular meetings and meet only when confronted with problems just too tough to handle over the network. Three months later, the same people resumed their regularly scheduled face-to-face meetings. They discovered that they had created a "morale-busting, network-generated nightmare." When the managers did get together, the meetings were unpleasant and unproductive. Precisely because they could use e-mail to reach consensus on easy issues, arguing the thorny issues face-to-face turned their "big problem" meetings into combat zones. E-mail interaction had eliminated the opportunity for casual agreement and social niceties that make meetings enjoyable. Even the e-mail communication became most hostile as participants maneuvered themselves in anticipation of the big-problem meeting (Schrage, 1995).

Face-to-face negotiations are particularly important when negotiators meet for the first time. This meeting is when norms of interaction are established and when misunderstandings should be resolved. Negotiators are more cooperative when interacting face-to-face rather than over the telephone (Drolet & Morris, 1995). Face-to-face communication (as opposed to using the telephone or more restricting forms) fosters the development of interpersonal synchrony and rapport, and thus leads to more trusting, cooperative behavior (Drolet & Morris, 1995). Face-to-face meetings are ideal for wrestling with complex negotiations. Valley, Moag, and Bazerman (1998) report that "Any mode of communication during bargaining increases the efficiency of outcomes over economic predictions" (p. 212). According to Valley and colleagues (1998), who investigated face-to-face versus writing-only and telephone negotiations, face-to-face negotiators reach more integrative (win-win) outcomes and more balanced distributions of surplus (even pie slicing) than writing-only or telephone negotiations. Further, writing-only negotiations had a higher incidence of impasse, and telephone negotiations increased the likelihood of losing buyers and highly profitable sellers.

In most companies, the incidence and frequency of face-to-face communication is nearly perfectly predicted by how closely people are located to one another: Employees who work in the same office or on the same floor communicate much more frequently than those located on different floors or in different buildings. The incidence of communication literally comes down to feet—a few paces can have a huge impact. For example, communication frequency between R&D researchers drops off logarithmically after only 5 to 10 meters of distance between offices (Allen, 1977). Workers in adjacent offices communicate twice as often as those in offices on the same floor, including via e-mail and telephone transmissions (Galegher, Kraut, & Egido, 1990).

Just what do people get out of face-to-face contact that makes it so important for smooth negotiations? First, face-to-face communication is easier and therefore more likely to occur than are other forms of communication. Simply stated, most people need a reason to walk up the stairs or to make a phone call. We underestimate how many negotiations occur from chance encounters, which virtually never happen in any mode but face-to-face because of perceived effort. Negotiations of opportunity are very important for long-term business success.

Second, although it is seldom consciously realized, people primarily rely on nonverbal signals to help them conduct social interactions. One estimate is that 93 percent of the meaning of messages is contained in the nonverbal part of communication, such as voice intonation (Meherabian, 1971; see also Appendix 2 on nonverbal communication). Perhaps this nonverbal factor is why business executives endure the inconvenience of travel across thousands of miles and several time zones so that they can negotiate face-to-face.

The emphasis on the human factor is not just old-fashioned business superstition. Important behavioral, cognitive, and emotional processes are set into motion when people meet face-to-face. However, unless people are trained, they do not know what exactly it is about face-to-face interaction that facilitates negotiation—they just know that negotiations are smoother and friendlier. Face-to-face negotiation allows people to develop rapport—the feeling of being "in sync" or "on the same wavelength" with another person—and rapport is a powerful determinant of whether they develop trust. Nonverbal (body orientation, gesture, eye contact, head nodding) and paraverbal (speech fluency, use of "uh-huhs," etc.) behaviors are key to building rapport. When the person we are negotiating with sits at a greater distance, has an indirect body orientation, backward lean, crossed arms, and avoids eye contact, we feel less rapport than when the same person sits with a forward lean and an open body posture and maintains steady eye contact.

However, we do not always have the luxury of meeting face-to-face. People often turn to the telephone, but even then, people do not always reach their party. Some estimates suggest that up to 70 percent of initial telephone attempts fail to reach the intended party (Philip & Young, 1987).

Same Time, Different Place

The same-time, different-place mode, in which people negotiate in real time but are not physically in the same place, is often the alternative to face-to-face negotiations. The most common means is via telephone (telephone tag is different time, different place); videoconferencing is another example.

In telephone conversations, people lack facial cues; in videoconferencing, they lack real-time social cues, such as pauses, mutual gaze, and another person's nonverbal response to what is being said (looking away, rolling their eyes, or shaking or nodding their head).

When technology tries to replace the dynamics of face-to-face interaction, it often falls short. As a case in point, consider an engineering work group, located in two offices 1,000 kilometers apart, that experimented with an omnipresent video wall and cameras in all offices to link the sites together (Abel, 1990). Generally, the engineers interacted across the distance as one cohesive group, but some disturbing incidents took place. Video links were not very effective in generating new relationships or in resolving divisive differences, and miscommunication was treated as rudeness. Members of a design team were unable to listen to each other's ideas until they met face-to-face for three days, where they reached consensus.

Next, we identify four key challenges to same-time, different-place negotiations.

Loss of Informal Communication

Probably the most limiting aspect of same-time, different-place negotiations is the inability to chat informally in the hall or inside offices. The impromptu and casual conversations that negotiators have in a restroom, by a water cooler, or walking back from lunch are often where the most difficult problems are solved and the most important interpersonal issues are addressed. Often, stalemated negotiations get resolved outside of the official bargaining forum. Beyond a short distance, people do not benefit from the spontaneous exchanges that occur outside of formal meetings. Many companies clearly realize that the informal communication that occurs in their organizations is what is most important and most critical, and they are doing something about it. For example, instant messaging is used on an increasing basis among employees in companies. Written as short, rapid responses, instant messages are used to schedule one-on-one meetings and for "back channel" communications during sales calls (*Investors' Business Daily*, Nov. 12, 2003). However, they can be more prone to spontaneous emotion than e-mail.

Lost Opportunity

Negotiations do not just occur when people are in disagreement and haggling over scarce resources. In fact, many negotiations are negotiations of opportunity—kind of like entrepreneurial joint ventures. Negotiations of opportunity, because they are not planned, usually occur during informal, chance encounters.

Separation of Feedback

Another negative impact of physical separation is the absence of feedback. Greater distance tends to block the corrective feedback loops provided in face-to-face negotiations. One manager contrasted how employees who worked in his home office negotiated with him, compared to employees 15 kilometers away (Armstrong & Cole, 1995). Engineers in the home office would drop by and catch him in the hall or at lunch: "I heard you were planning to change project X," they would say. "Let me tell you why that would be stupid." The manager would listen to their points, clarify some details, and all would part better informed. In contrast, employees at the remote site would greet his weekly visit with formally prepared objections, which took much longer to discuss and were rarely resolved as completely as the more informal hallway discussions. In short, negotiators interacting remotely do not get the coincidental chances to detect and correct problems on a casual basis.

Negotiation Timing

Conflicts are expressed, recognized, and addressed more quickly if negotiators work in close proximity. A manager can spot a problem and "nip it in the bud" if he or she works near his or her employees. When people are physically separated, the issues are more likely to go unresolved; this tendency contributes to an escalating cycle of destructive negotiation behavior.

Although many disadvantages of distance can be listed when it comes to negotiation, it is not always a liability for negotiators. The formality of a scheduled phone meeting can compel each party to better prepare for the negotiation and to address the issues more efficiently. Also, it can create a "buffer zone" between parties, meaning that it might be a good thing if one party does not see the other rolling his or her eyes.

Different Time, Same Place

In the different-time, same-place mode, negotiators interact asynchronously, but have access to the same physical document or space. An example might be shift workers who pick up the task left for them by the previous shift; another example would be two collaborators working on the same electronic document. One colleague finishes and then gives the text to a partner, who further edits and develops it. Although people seldom realize it, they negotiate quite frequently in an asynchronous fashion. Take the example of a distributed team of software engineers located in Bangalore, Palo Alto, and London, working on the development of a piece of software. Their "24-hour laboratory" makes active use of global time differences. At the end of the working day, the Bangalore group downloads its work to the London team, which contributes its bit; this work is in turn picked up by the Palo Alto team (*Australian Financial Review*, Sept. 30, 1998).

Different Place, Different Time

In the different-place, different-time model, negotiators communicate asynchronously in different places. *Training* (Oct. 1, 1999) notes that, just as the telephone became an important medium for working out deals, the Internet is rapidly becoming the medium of choice for many "technobargainers." The most common example is electronic mail (e-mail): Jerry, who is in Seattle, sends a message to Sally, who is in Japan. With e-mail, parties do not have to be available simultaneously for negotiation to occur. For an overview of the dynamics of e-mail negotiation, see Thompson and Nadler (2002). We identify five key biases that affect the ability of people to negotiate via e-mail.

Temporal Synchrony Bias

The **temporal synchrony bias** is the tendency for negotiators to behave as if they are communicating synchronously when in fact they are not. Certainly e-negotiators are aware that e-mail is, in fact, asynchronous communication, but they often discount this or ignore some of its implications. One of the things that negotiators like about negotiation is the ability to make proposals and counteroffers, almost in a tennis-game-like fashion. Howard Raiffa (1982) refers to this interaction as the "negotiation dance." However, e-negotiations disrupt the natural dance face-to-face negotiation. In our research, we found less turn-taking behavior in negotiations conducted via e-mail than in face-to-face negotiations (Morris, Nadler, Kurtzberg, & Thompson, 2002). Moreover, it is the volume of turn-taking or "dancing" within negotiations that predicts schmoozing behavior (e.g., small talk) and facilitates trust and rapport (Morris et al., 2002).

Conversational turn-taking does not just make the process of negotiation seem smoother and more natural, it also serves an important informational function: It allows people to engage in a natural process of immediate correction, which is somewhat similar to the double-loop learning idea (Chapter 1). In face-to-face interactions, receivers and senders typically engage in a process of rapid correction of information (e.g., Higgins, 1999; Krauss & Chiu, 1998). However, in e-negotiations, negotiators are faced with the mysterious task of interpreting impoverished communication without the opportunity for clarification. Thus, e-negotiators are forced to make more assumptions than face-to-face negotiators. Indeed, our investigations of e-negotiations reveal that e-negotiators ask fewer clarifying questions than do face-to-face negotiators (Morris et al., 2002).

Burned Bridge Bias
The **burned bridge bias** is the tendency for e-negotiators to engage in more risky interpersonal behaviors (e.g., making threats and demands and ultimatums) in an impoverished medium than they would face-to-face. When people are communicating face-to-face, they conform to what psychologists call a "politeness ritual," in which they nod, smile, make direct eye contact, and make verbalizations ("uh-huh," etc.) that serve to affirm the other person and strengthen the relationship between negotiators. Thus, the politeness ritual sets the stage for trust and rapport between negotiators who are navigating a mixed-motive relationship. Indeed, negotiators who are successful in building positive rapport are more likely to build trust (Morris et al., 2002).

Several reasons explain why e-negotiators may burn relationship bridges. First, they experience less personal accountability for the relationship. E-negotiations occur in a social vacuum. In contrast, face-to-face negotiations often take place in a richly grounded social network; in this sense, individuals feel greater accountability for their behaviors (Wicklund & Gollwitzer, 1982). Indeed, observers of face-to-face interactions are able to immediately assess the "felt rapport" between interactants. Further, observers appear to pay attention to the right cues: The greater the synchrony of the nonverbal displays, the more likely an outsider will judge that a high level of rapport is present in the interaction (Bernieri, 1991; Bernieri, Davis, Rosenthal, & Knee, 1994).

Second, negotiators often use more aggressive strategies because they don't think about the future of their relationship. Again, the accountability factor plays a role with many e-communicators failing to recognize that their e-communications have a permanence to them. Even though e-mails can be "deleted," they are actually retrievable from most computer systems. Yet people act as if the messages are ephemeral (Sproull & Keisler, 1991). For example, in his congressional hearing, Oliver North was extremely careful in his spoken interviews (presumably aware that the camera was on him, indelibly recording every utterance); however, he was obviously much more lax in his computer mail (Sproull & Keisler, 1991).

Squeaky Wheel Bias

The **squeaky wheel bias** is the tendency for negotiators to adopt an adversarial negotiation style (similar to the demanding, negative emotional style described in Chapter 5) when communicating via e-mail—whereas the same negotiator might use a positive emotional style in a face-to-face interaction. Indeed, people are more likely to engage in counternormative social behavior when interacting via e-mail (Keisler & Sproull, 1992). They focus more on the content of the task and less on the etiquette of the situation. For example, bad news is conveyed to superiors with less delay through e-mail than in face-to-face encounters (Sproull & Keisler, 1991). In a direct comparison of face-to-face negotiations versus e-negotiations, people negotiating via e-mail were more likely to negatively confront one other (Morris, Nadler, Kurtzberg, & Thompson, 2002). Rude, impulsive behavior, such as "flaming," increases when people interact through e-mail, in part because people pay more attention to the content of the message and less attention to the style of their message. One investigation of flaming suggests that people are eight times more likely to flame in e-communication than in face-to-face communication (Dubrovsky, Keisler, & Sethna, 1991). Conflict escalates more quickly and frequently, which serves as a roadblock to effective integrative negotiation.

When social context cues are missing or weak, people feel distant from others and somewhat anonymous. They are less concerned about making a good appearance, and humor tends to fall apart or to be misinterpreted. The expression of negative emotion is no longer minimized because factors that keep people from expressing negative emotion are not in place when they communicate via information technology. Simply, in the absence of social norms that prescribe the expression of positive emotion, people are more likely to express negative emotion. One MBA student lost a job when he sent his supervisor an e-mail message that was perceived as insensitive. The student was using e-mail to renegotiate his job responsibilities and proceeded to outline what he saw as problems within the organization and the people who were running it. Shortly thereafter, he was called into a meeting with the senior staff, and everyone was holding a copy of his e-mail (*Training*, Oct. 1, 1999).

Not surprisingly, the tendency for people to "flame" one another via e-mail has led some to attempt to humanize e-communication. The use of symbols is one way of adding more of a human touch to otherwise stark communication. (Table 12-2 illustrates the most common emotional expressions in e-mail exchange.)

Sinister Attribution Bias

People often misattribute the behavior of others to their underlying character traits while ignoring the influence of temporary, situational factors (Ross, 1977). The **sinister attribution bias** refers to the tendency for e-communicators to ascribe diabolical intentions to the other party (Thompson & Nadler, 2002). Kramer (1995) coined the term *sinister attribution error* to refer to the tendency of people to attribute malevolent motives to people whom we don't know or who represent the out-group. Attributing sinister motives to out-group members is especially prevalent in e-communication in which the absence of social cues leads to feelings of social isolation and distance. Indeed, Fortune and Brodt (2000) found that e-negotiators were more likely to mistrust and suspect the other party of lying or deceiving them, relative to negotiators interacting face-to-face. Yet e-negotiators were, in fact, no more likely than face-to-face

TABLE 12-2	Emoticons in e-mail communication used to express emotion
Emoticans	*Definition*
:)	The basic smiley. This smiley is used to inflect a sarcastic joking statement because we can't hear voice inflection over e-mail.
;-)	Winky smiley. User just made a flirtatious and/or sarcastic remark. More of a "don't hit me for what I just said" smiley.
:-(	Frowning smiley. User did not like the last statement or is upset or depressed about something.
:-T	Indifferent smiley. Better than a :-(but not quite as good as a :-).
:->	User just made a really biting sarcastic remark. Worse than a ;-).
>:->	User just made a really devilish remark.
>;->	Winky and devil combined. A very lewd remark was just made.
|-)	hee hee
|-D	ho ho
:-o	oops
:-P	nyahhh!

negotiators to deceive the other party. In short, the situation provided no factual basis to fuel the increased suspicion of the other party.

A key question concerns how information technology affects negotiation performance. Table 12-3 summarizes the main findings concerning how information technology—and in particular, e-negotiations—affects economic measures of performance (level 1 integrative agreements, distributive outcomes) and social measures of performance (e.g., trust, respect, etc.; see also McGinn & Croson, 2004). Negotiators who communicate face-to-face are more likely to reach deals and avoid impasses than are e-negotiators. Further, the likelihood of reaching a mutually profitable negotiation (and avoiding impasse) is a function of the richness of the communication. For example, when negotiators are allowed to communicate in writing or face-to-face, they are more likely to settle in the ZOPA as compared to negotiators who do not interact and just make offers (McGinn, Thompson, & Bazerman, 2003). Considerable debate continues to surround the question of whether information technology hurts or hinders the ability of negotiators to expand the pie. Croson (1999) compared face-to-face negotiated outcomes with computer-mediated negotiation outcomes and found that computer-mediated outcomes were equally or more integrative than were face-to-face outcomes. Croson (1999) also reported that computer-mediated negotiations resulted in outcomes that were more fair, as judged in terms of being more equal in value.

INFORMATION TECHNOLOGY AND ITS EFFECTS ON SOCIAL BEHAVIOR

In addition to affecting negotiated outcomes, information technology has an extremely powerful effect on social behavior in general (Keisler & Sproull, 1992). Many people are surprised at how they find themselves behaving when communicating via e-mail. To be successful, negotiators must understand how their own behavior is affected by technology.

TABLE 12-3   Information Technology's Effect on Negotiator Performance

	E-negotiations vs. Face-to-Face	*Enhanced E-negotiations (via schmoozing, in-group status, etc.) vs. Nonenhanced E-negotiations*
Impasse rates (finding the ZOPA)		Brief personal disclosure over e-mail reduces likelihood of impasse Out-group negotiations result in more impasses than in-group negotiations
Integrative behavior (e.g., multi-issue offers)	E-negotiators make more multi-issue offers	
Pie size (expanding the pie)	Mixed results, with some investigations finding that face-to-face results in better joint profits; other studies indicating no difference	Brief telephone call prior to e-negotiations improves joint outcomes
Distributive behaviors (e.g., threats, etc.)		Negotiators concerned about group's reputation use more aggressive strategies, leading to lower outcomes than negotiators focused on own reputation
Pie slicing (distributive outcomes)	Computer-mediated negotiations result in more equal pie-slices than do face-to-face	
Trust and rapport	Less rapport in e-negotiations	Brief telephone call prior to e-negotiation increases cooperation and relationship quality Negotiators who attempt to build rapport build more trust than those who try to dominate

Source: Table partially adapted from Thompson, L., & Nadler, J. (2002). Negotiating via information technology: Theory and application. *Journal of Social Issues, 58*(1), 109–124.

Status and Power: The "Weak Get Strong" Effect

In face-to-face interactions, people do not contribute to conversation equally. Walk into any classroom, lunch discussion, or business meeting, and it will be immediately obvious that one person in a two-party group does most of the talking, and a handful of people do more than 75 percent of the talking in a larger group. For example, in a typical four-person group, two people do more than 70 percent of the talking; in a six-person group, three people do over 85 percent of the talking, and in a group of eight, three people do 77 percent of the talking (Shaw, 1981). Even when performance depends on contributions, participation is not equal.

So who dominates most face-to-face discussions and negotiations? Almost without exception, status predicts domination. Higher-status people talk more, even if they are not experts on the subject. Not surprisingly, managers speak more than subordinates, and men speak more than women. If no inherent organizational status system is obvious, negotiators rely on superficial symbols of status, such as gender, age, and race. Situational factors also affect perceived status. The person who sits at the head of the table talks more than those on the sides, even if seating arrangement is arbitrary (Strodtbeck & Hook, 1961). Appearance can affect status: Those in business suits talk more than others. Dynamic cues can define status, such as nodding in approval, touching (high-status people touch those of lower status, but not vice versa), hesitating, and frowning.

What happens when negotiators interact via technology, such as electronic mail? The traditional status cues are missing, and the dynamic cues are distinctly less impactive, which has a dramatic effect on negotiation behavior. Power and status differences are minimized. People in traditionally weak positions in face-to-face negotiations become more powerful when communicating via information technology because status cues are harder to read (Sproull & Keisler, 1991). In a direct test of this idea, we had managers negotiate via e-mail and some negotiate via instant messaging (Chakravarti, Loewenstein, Morris, Thompson, & Kopelman, 2004). We reasoned that instant messaging is much more like face-to-face interaction because negotiators need to respond quickly and in real time. For example, when someone is asked a question about the quality of a product in instant message mode, the seller needs to provide an answer quickly and assuredly. We hypothesized that the instant messaging medium would be an advantage when negotiators had a strong bargaining position, but backfire when negotiators had a weak bargaining position, because they would be "exposed" and could not easily run for cover. It was exactly the result we found: Sellers who had strong arguments for their product fared particularly well in instant messaging because they could, in a sense, verbally bamboozle the buyers; however, sellers who had weaker arguments were not able to hold their own in instant messaging and did much better negotiating via traditional e-mail. The message: If you have a strong bargaining position, impoverished media can help you; if you have a weak bargaining position, insist on face-to-face or otherwise immediate communication.

The very nature of e-mail hides traditional status cues. When people receive e-mail from others, they often do not know the sender's status or, for that matter, where the person works or if they are at a company. People who would normally not approach others in person are much more likely to initiate e-mail exchange. Traditional, static cues such as position and title are not as obvious on e-mail. It is often impossible to tell whether you are communicating with a president or clerk on e-mail because traditional e-mail simply lists the person's name, not title. Addresses are often shortened and may be difficult to comprehend. Even when they can be deciphered, e-mail addresses identify the organization, but not the subunit, job title, social importance, or level in the organization of the sender. Dynamic status cues, such as dress, mannerisms, age, and gender, are also missing in e-mail. In this sense, e-mail acts as an equalizer because it is difficult for high-status people to dominate discussion. The absence of these cues leads people to respond more openly and less hesitatingly than in face-to-face interaction. People are less likely to conform to social norms and other people when interacting via electronic communication.

Overall, the amount of participation will be less in electronic versus face-to-face communication, but the contributions of members will be more equal (for a review, see McGrath & Hollingshead, 1994). For example, when groups of executives meet face-to-face, men are five times more likely than women to make the first decision proposal.

When those same groups meet via computer, women make the first proposal as often as men do (McGuire, Keisler, & Siegel, 1987). Furthermore, the time to complete a task is longer on e-mail than in face-to-face interaction, probably because people talk much faster than they write.

Social Networks

In traditional organizations, social networks are determined by who talks to whom; in the new organization, social networks are determined by who communicates with whom via technology. Peripheral people who communicate electronically become better integrated into their organization (Eveland & Bikson, 1988). Computerized interaction increases the resources of low-network people.

The nature of social networks that shape negotiation behavior changes dramatically when information technology enters the picture as a form of communication. E-mail networks, or connection between people who communicate via electronic e-mail, increase the information resources of low-network people. When people need assistance (e.g., information or resources), they often turn to their immediate social network. When such help is not available, they use weak ties, such as relationships with acquaintances or strangers, to seek help that is unavailable from friends or colleagues. However, a problem arises: In the absence of personal relationships or the expectation of direct reciprocity, help from weak ties might not be forthcoming or could be of low quality.

Some companies, particularly global companies and those in the fields of information technology and communications, need to rely on e-mail and employees within the company forming connections with each other on the basis of no physical contact. The incentives for taking the time to assist someone who is dealing with a problem and is located in a different part of the world are pretty minuscule.

Tandem Corporation is a global computer manufacturer that has a highly geographically dispersed organization (Sproull & Keisler, 1991). Managers in the Tandem Corporation need technical advice to solve problems, but they cannot always get useful advice from their local colleagues. Simply stated, the local social networks are often not sufficient to solve problems. What can be done?

An investigation of Tandem's e-mail revealed some startling and encouraging findings (Sproull & Keisler, 1991): Managers who put out a request for technical assistance received an average of 7.8 replies per request. All of the replies were serious, and respondents spent 9 minutes per reply. The replies solved the problem 50 percent of the time. Information providers gave useful advice and solved the problems of information seekers, despite their lack of a personal connection with the person requesting information.

Another possibility is to catalog or store information in some easily accessible database. In a technical company, this database would include published reports and scientific manuals. However, engineers and managers do not like to consult technical reports to obtain needed information; most of the information they use to solve their problems is obtained through face-to-face discussions. People in organizations usually prefer to exchange help through strong collegial ties, which develop through physical proximity, similarity, and familiarity. Back in the late 1990s, several industries predicted that buyers and sellers would use Web sites to find one another, and thereby disrupt traditional distribution channels and drive down prices. Yet, of the 1,500 B2B (business-to-business) exchanges started, only 43 percent remain (*Inc.*, Aug. 1, 2003c). Buyers place a premium on long-term relationships with vendors.

Is it sending or receiving messages that expands one's social network and ultimate organizational commitment? The amount of e-mail a person sends (but not receives) predicts commitment (Sproull & Keisler, 1991). Thus, e-mail can provide an alternate route to letting people have a voice if they are low contributors in face-to-face meetings.

Risk Taking

Consider the following choices:

1. $20,000 return over two years
2. 50 percent chance of $40,000 return; 50 percent chance of nothing

Obviously, option 1 is the "safe" (riskless) choice; option 2 is the risky choice. However, these two options are mathematically identical, meaning that in an objective sense, people should not favor one option over the other (see also Appendix 1). When posed with these choices, most people are risk-averse, meaning that they select the option that has the sure payoff as opposed to holding out for the chance to win big (or, equally as likely, not win at all). Consider what happens when the following choice is proposed:

1. Sure loss of $20,000 over two years
2. 50 percent chance of losing $40,000; 50 percent of losing nothing

Most managers are risk-seeking and choose option 2. Why? According to the **framing effect** (Chapter 2; Kahneman & Tversky, 1979), people are risk-averse for gains and risk-seeking for losses. This tendency can lead to self-contradictory, quirky behavior. By manipulating the reference point, a person's fiscal policy choices can change.

Groups tend to make riskier decisions than do individuals given the same choice. Thus, risk-seeking is greatly exaggerated in groups who meet face-to-face. Paradoxically, groups who make decisions via electronic communication are risk-seeking for both gains and losses (McGuire, Keisler, & Siegel, 1987). Furthermore, executives are just as confident of their decisions whether they are made through electronic communication or face-to-face communication. For example, in comparisons of people negotiating face-to-face, by e-mail, or through a combination of both (Shell, 1999), people who use only e-mail reach more impasses. According to Shell, "People tend to escalate disagreement when they focus on the issues and position without the benefit of the contextual, personal information that comes across when we speak or go face to face with our counterpart" (p. 106).

Rapport and Social Norms

Building trust and rapport is critical for negotiation success. The greater the face-to-face contact between negotiators and the greater the rapport, the more integrative the outcomes are likely to be. Rapport is more difficult to establish with impoverished mediums of communication (Drolet & Morris, 2000). For example, Drolet and Morris (2000) tested the hypothesis that visual access between negotiators fosters rapport and thus facilitates cooperation and pie expansion. They instructed some negotiators to stand face-to-face or side-by-side (unable to see each other) in a simulated strike negotiation. Face-to-face negotiators were more likely to coordinate on a settlement early in the strike, resulting in higher joint gains. Further, rapport was higher between face-to-face negotiators than between side-by-side negotiators. In a different investigation (Drolet & Morris, 1995), comparisons were made between face-to-face, videoconference, and audio-only negotiation interactions. Face-to-face negotiators felt a greater amount of rapport than did negotiators in the videoconference and audio-only conditions. Further, independent observers judged face-to-face negotiators to be more "in sync" with each other. Face-to-face negotiators had more trust in each other and were more successful at coordinating their decisions.

Paranoia

On the TV show *Saturday Night Live*, Pat (Julia Sweeney) was a character whose sex was unknown. Pat had an androgynous name, wore baggy clothes, and did not display any stereotypical male or female characteristics or preferences. Most people found it maddening to interact with Pat without knowing his or her gender. Gender ambiguity also happens when interacting via technology. It is generally impolite to ask someone whether he or she is a man or woman. Therefore, we are left feeling uncertain. Uncertainty, consequently, increases paranoia. Paranoid people are more likely to assume the worst about another person or situation (Kramer, 1995).

When technological change creates new social situations, traditional expectations and norms lose their power. People invent new ways of behaving. Today's electronic technology is impoverished in social cues and shared experience. People "talk" to other people, but they do so alone (Sproull & Keisler, 1991). As a result, their messages are likely to display less social awareness. The advantage is that social posturing and sycophancy decline. The disadvantage is that politeness and concern for others also decline. Two characteristics of computer-based communication, the plain text and perceived ephemerality of messages, make it relatively easy for a person to forget or ignore his or her audience and consequently send messages that ignore social boundaries, disclose the self, and are too blunt (Sproull & Keisler, 1991).

Did the following exchange occur in a meeting room or via the internet?

NEGOTIATOR A: If I do not get your answer by tomorrow, then I assume that you agree with my proposal.
NEGOTIATOR B: From my perspective, I do not see any rationale or any incentive to transfer this revolutionary technology to your division.
NEGOTIATOR A: I do not have to remind you how pushing the issue up the corporate ladder can prejudice both our careers.
NEGOTIATOR B: Your offer is ridiculous.
NEGOTIATOR A: It is my final offer.

Most people correctly note that this exchange occurred on the Internet. The phenomenon of flaming suggests that through electronic mail, actions and decisions (not just messages) might become more extreme and impulsive (Sproull & Keisler, 1991).

STRATEGIES FOR ENHANCING TECHNOLOGY-MEDIATED NEGOTIATIONS

Often, negotiators do not have the luxury of face-to-face meetings for the duration of their negotiations. Under such circumstances, what strategies can be taken to enhance successful pie expansion and pie slicing? Consider the following tactics.

Initial Face-to-Face Experience

Alge, Wiethoff, and Klein (2003) compared the effectiveness of virtual and face-to-face teams working on a brainstorming exercise and a negotiation exercise. Virtual teams worked better on the brainstorming exercise, but face-to-face teams did better on the negotiation exercise. Moreover, Alge and colleagues (2003) found that even though the face-to-face teams communicated better initially (during the early stages of a project), as virtual teams gained experience they communicated as openly and shared information as effectively as face-to-face teams. According to Alge, "A manager who wants to put a working group together for a long, complex project should choose a team whose members are in the same location or initially invest the resources to give the team members an opportunity to get to know each other. Then, as teams become more experienced and familiar with each other and the technology, they can exchange ideas more effectively using 'lean' Internet media that lack the nonverbal communication, social cues, and nuances that exist in face-to-face interactions" (Associated Press, Apr. 23, 2003).

Oftentimes, people can develop rapport on the basis of a short face-to-face meeting, which can reduce uncertainty and build trust. Face-to-face contact humanizes people and creates expectation for negotiators to use in their subsequent long-distance work together. For example, Christopher H. Browne, managing director of Tweedy Browne Company, a New York based investment-management firm, is a self-professed "e-mail junkie." When he presented the University of Pennsylvania with a gift of $10 million, it was his suggestion that they hammer out the details about payment and purpose of the gift online. However, he was careful to make this suggestion after an initial face-to-face meeting about the gift with university officials. Four days and several e-messages later, the deal was completed. Both Browne and university officials said that the process could have taken weeks, had they relied on telephone calls and faxes. University officials said that they were going to make a personal trip to New York to thank Browne: "Even though this [the deal] was done in cyberspace, we don't want to lose sight of the fact that there are real people involved" (*Chronicle of Higher Education*, Feb. 9, 2000, p. 2).

One-Day Videoconference/Teleconference

If an initial, face-to-face meeting is out of the question, an alternative may be to at least get everyone online so that people can attach a name to a face. Depending upon the size of the team and locations of different members, this alternative may be more feasible than a face-to-face meeting. For example, in one investigation, negotiators who had never met one another were instructed to have a short phone call prior to commencing e-mail-only negotiations (Morris, Nadler, Kurtzberg, & Thompson, 2002). Another group did not have an initial phone call with their opponent. The sole purpose of the phone call was to get to know the other person. The simple act of chatting and exchanging personal information built rapport and overcame some of the communication difficulties associated with the impoverished medium of e-mail. Negotiators who engaged in the initial phone conversation found that their attitudes toward their opponents changed; negotiators who had chatted with their opponent felt less competitive and more cooperative before the negotiation began, compared with negotiators who had not chatted with their opponent. In the end, negotiators who had made personal contact with their opponent felt more confident that future interaction with the same person would go smoothly. A relationship of trust was thus developed through the rapport-building phone call prior to the negotiation. Not surprisingly, negotiators who had had an initial phone call were less likely to reach impasse, and achieved higher joint gains compared to those who did not have the initial phone call. The simple act of making an effort to establish a personal relationship through telephone contact before engaging in e-mail negotiations can have dramatic positive consequences.

Schmoozing

Schmoozing (as described in Chapter 6) is our name for non-task-related contact between people, which has the psychological effect of having established a relationship with someone (Moore, Kurtzberg, Thompson, & Morris, 1999; Morris et al., 2002). The effectiveness of electronic schmoozing has been put to the test, and the results are dramatic: Schmoozing increases liking and rapport and results in more profitable business deals than when people simply "get down to business" (Moore et al., 1999). Negotiators who schmoozed (on the phone) developed more realistic goals, resulting in a larger range of possible outcomes, and were less likely to impasse compared to nonschmoozers. The key mediating factor was rapport. Moreover, the negotiators who schmoozed on the phone prior to getting down to the business of e-negotiation expressed greater optimism about a future working relationship with the other party, compared to negotiators who did not schmooze (Morris et al., 2002).

Another route to building trust and rapport is to build a shared social identity. For example, e-negotiations between managers at the same university (company) versus negotiations between competitor universities (companies) reveals that membership in the same university (company) reduces the likelihood of impasse in e-negotiations (Moore et al., 1999). In contrast, negotiators who do not share social ties with their counterpart consistently underperform on the key measures of negotiator performance.

Perhaps the most attractive aspect of schmoozing is that it is relatively low-cost and efficient. Merely exchanging a few short e-mails describing yourself can lead to better business relations. However, you should not expect people to naturally schmooze—at least at the outset of a business relationship. Team members working remotely have a tendency to get down to business. As a start toward schmoozing, tell the other person something about yourself that does not necessarily relate to the business at hand (e.g., "I really enjoy sea kayaking"); also, provide a context for your own work space (e.g., "It is very late in the day, and there are 20 people at my door, so I do not have time to write a long message"). Furthermore, ask questions that show you are interested in the other party as a person; this approach is an excellent way to search for points of similarity. Finally, provide the link for the next e-mail or exchange (e.g., "I will look forward to hearing your reactions on the preliminary report, and I will also send you the tapes you requested").

CONCLUSION

We used the place-time model of social interaction to examine how the medium of communication affects negotiation. We examined how the use of information technology affects social behavior. In particular, we focused on how non–face-to-face interaction results in more actual airtime than does the same group meeting face-to-face. Part of the reason is that cues about someone's status and authority are not as evident when not face-to-face. We discussed social networks and how information technology effectively expands the potential reach and influence of managers. We noted that people are more likely to display risk-seeking behavior (i.e., choosing gambles over sure things) when interacting via information technology, as opposed to face-to-face. Probably the biggest threat to effective negotiation in non–face-to-face settings is the loss of rapport and the tendency for people to be less conscious of social norms, such as politeness rituals. We discussed several methods for enhancing technology-mediated negotiations, including an initial face-to-face experience so that negotiators can establish social norms, a one-day videoconference, and schmoozing, especially given that most people tend to get down to business on e-mail as opposed to socializing.

Appendix 1

ARE YOU A RATIONAL PERSON? CHECK YOURSELF

The purpose of this appendix is to introduce the key principles of rational behavior and to help you assess your own rationality. First, we present the key principles of *individual rationality*, which focuses on how people make independent decisions. Then we present and discuss *game theoretic rationality*, which focuses on how people make interdependent decisions.

Why Is It Important to Be Rational?

Let's first consider why it is important for a negotiator to be rational. Perhaps if we behave irrationally, we might confuse our opponent and reap greater surplus for ourselves, or we might simply profit from following intuition rather than logic. Rational models of negotiation behavior offer a number of important advantages for the negotiator:

- *Pie expansion and pie slicing.* Models of rational behavior are based upon the principle of maximization such that the course of action followed guarantees that the negotiator will maximize his or her interests (whether that interest is monetary gain, career advancement, prestige, etc.). In short, the best way to maximize one's interests is to follow the prescriptions of a rational model.
- *Stop kidding yourself.* The rational models that we present in this appendix make clear and definitive statements regarding the superiority of some decisions over others. Thus, they do not allow you to justify or

rationalize your behavior. The truth may hurt sometimes, but it is a great learning experience.

- *Measure of perfection.* Rational models provide a measure of perfection or optimality. If rational models did not exist, we would have no way of evaluating how well people perform in negotiations nor what they should strive to do. We would not be able to offer advice to negotiators because we would not have consensus about what is a "good" outcome. Rational models provide an ideal.
- *Diagnosis.* Rational models serve a useful diagnostic purpose because they often reveal where negotiators make mistakes. Because rational models are built on a well-constructed theory of decision making, they offer insight about the mind of the negotiator.
- *Dealing with irrational people.* As we have seen, it is not an effective bargaining strategy to attempt to outsmart or trick your opponent. We have further seen that people often follow the norm of reciprocity—even for negative and ineffective behaviors. A negotiator who is well-versed in rational behavior can often deal more effectively with irrational people.
- *Being consistent.* Another advantage of rational models is that they can help us be consistent. Consistency is important for several reasons. Inconsistency in our behavior can inhibit learning. Furthermore, it can send our opponent ambiguous

messages. When people are confused or uncertain, they are more defensive, and trust diminishes.

- ***Making decisions.*** Rational models provide a straightforward method for thinking about decisions and a way of choosing among options, which, if followed correctly, will produce the "best" outcome for the chooser, maximizing his or her own preferences (as we will see in this appendix).

As the cartoon (Figure A1-1) suggests, people's behavior is not always rational. Even so, principles and assumptions derived from rational models are still a fundamental part of our "mix" for understanding human behavior.

Individual Decision Making

Negotiation is ultimately about making decisions. If we cannot make good decisions on our own, joint decision making will be even more difficult. Let's examine individual rationality. Sometimes our decisions are trivial, such as whether to have chocolate cake or cherry pie for dessert. Other times, our decisions are of great consequence, such as when we choose a career or a spouse. Our decisions about how to spend the weekend may seem fundamentally different from deciding what to do with our entire life, but some generalities cut across domains. Rational decision-making models provide the tools necessary for analyzing trivial decisions as well as those of monumental importance. The three main types of decisions are riskless choice, decision making under uncertainty, and risky choice.

Riskless Choice

Riskless choice, or decision making under certainty, involves choosing between two or more readily available options. For example, a choice between two apartments is a riskless

FIGURE A1-1

It's two and one

ECONOMIX

RATIONAL BEHAVIOUR

CHARACTER DEFECT

choice, as is choosing among 31 flavors of ice cream or selecting a book to read. Often, we do not consider these events to be decisions because they are so simple and easy. However, at other times, we struggle when choosing among jobs or careers, and we find ourselves in a state of indecision.

Imagine that you have been accepted into the MBA program at your top two choices: university X and university Y. This enviable situation is an **approach-approach conflict,** meaning that in some sense, you cannot lose—both options are attractive; you need only to decide which alternative is best for you. You have to make your final choice by next week. In front of you is a large stack of brochures, descriptions, and information about the schools. How should you begin to analyze the situation?

To analyze this decision situation, we will employ a method known as **multiattribute utility technique** (or **MAUT,** see Baron, 1988, for an overview). According to MAUT, a decision maker faces five main tasks: (1) identify the alternatives, (2) identify dimensions or attributes of the alternatives, (3) evaluate the utility associated with each dimension, (4) weight or prioritize each dimension in terms of importance, and (5) make a final choice.

Identification of Alternatives   The first step is usually quite straightforward. The decision maker simply identifies the relevant alternatives. For example, you would identify the schools to which you had been accepted. In other situations, the alternatives may not be as obvious. For example, in many situations, the identification of alternatives often requires complex problem solving. In the case that you did not get any acceptance letters, you must brainstorm about what to do with your life.

Identification of Attributes   The second step is more complex and involves identifying the key attributes associated with the

alternatives. The attributes are the features of an alternative that make it appealing or unappealing. For example, when choosing among schools, relevant attributes might include the cost of tuition, reputation of the program, course requirements, placement options, weather, cultural aspects, family, and faculty. The number of attributes that you may identify as relevant to your decision is not limited.

Utility   The next step is to evaluate the relative utility or value of each alternative for each attribute. For example, you might use a 1-to-5 scale to rate how each school fares on each of the identified attributes. You might evaluate the reputation of university X very highly (5) but the weather as very unattractive (1); you might evaluate university Y's reputation to be moderately high (3) but the weather to be fabulous (5). MAUT assumes preferential independence of attributes (i.e., the value of one attribute is independent of the value of others).

Weight   In addition to determining the evaluation of each attribute, the decision maker also evaluates how important that attribute is to him or her. The importance of each attribute is referred to as weight in the decision process. Again, we can use a simple numbering system, with 1 representing relatively unimportant attributes and 5 representing very important attributes. For example, you might consider the reputation of the school to be very important (5) but the cultural attributes of the city to be insignificant (1).

Making a Decision   The final step in the MAUT procedure is to compute a single, overall evaluation of each alternative. For this task, first multiply the utility evaluation of each attribute by its corresponding weight, and then sum the weighted scores across each attribute. Finally, select the option that has the highest overall score.

TABLE A1-1 Multi-Attribute Decision Making

Attribute (weight)	University Y (evaluation)	University X (evaluation)
Tuition cost (4)	Inexpensive (5)	Expensive (1)
Reputation (5)	Medium (3)	High (5)
Climate (3)	Lousy (1)	Great (5)
Culture (1)	Good (4)	Poor (1)

Utility of University (Y) = (4*5) + (5*3) + (3*1) + (1*4) = 42
Utility of University (X) = (4*1) + (5*5) + (3*5) + (1*1) = 45

An example of this procedure is illustrated in Table A1-1.

We can see from the hypothetical example in Table A1-1 that university X is a better choice for the student compared to university Y. However, it is a close decision. If the importance of any of the attributes were to change (e.g., tuition cost, reputation, climate, or culture), then the overall decision could change. Similarly, if the evaluation of any attributes changes, then the final choice may change. Decision theory can tell us how to *choose*, but it cannot tell us how to weight the attributes that go into making choices.

According to the **dominance principle,** one alternative dominates another if it is strictly better on at least one dimension and at least as good on all others. For example, imagine that university Y had been evaluated as a 5 in terms of tuition cost, a 5 in reputation a 4 in climate, and a 4 in culture; and university X had been evaluated as a 1, 5, 4, and 3, respectively. In this case, we can quickly see that university Y is just as good as university X on two dimensions (reputation and climate) and better on the two remaining dimensions (tuition cost and culture). Thus, university Y dominates university X. Identifying a dominant alternative greatly simplifies decision making: If one alternative dominates the other, we should select the dominating option.

The example seems simple enough. In many situations, however, we are faced with considering many more alternatives, each having different dimensions. It may not be easy for us to spot a dominant alternative when we see one. What should we do in this case? The first step is to eliminate from consideration all options dominated by others, and choose among only the nondominated alternatives that remain.

The dominance principle as a method of choice seems quite compelling, but it applies only to situations in which one alternative is clearly superior to others. It does not help us with the agonizing task of choosing among options that involve trade-offs among highly valued aspects. We now turn to situations that defy MAUT and dominance detection.

Decision Making Under Uncertainty

Sometimes we must make decisions when the alternatives are uncertain or unknown. These situations are known as decision making under uncertainty or decision making in ignorance (Yates, 1990). In such situations, the decision maker has no idea about the likelihood of events. Consider, for example, a decision to plan a social event outdoors or indoors. If the weather is sunny and warm, it would be better to hold the event outdoors; if it is rainy and cold, it is better to plan the event indoors. The plans must be made a month in advance, but the weather cannot be predicted a month in advance. The distinction between risk and uncertainty hinges upon whether probabilities are known exactly (e.g., as in games of chance) or whether they must be judged by the decision maker with some degree of imprecision (e.g., almost everything else). Hence, "ignorance" might be viewed merely as an extreme degree of uncertainty where the decision maker has no clue (e.g., probability that the closing price of Dai Ichi stock tomorrow on the Tokyo stock exchange is above 1,600 yen).

Risky Choice

In decision making under uncertainty, the likelihood of events is unknown; in risky choice situations, the probabilities are known. Most theories of decision making are based on an assessment of the probability that some event will take place. Because the outcomes of risky choice situations are not fully known, outcomes are often referred to as "prospects." Many people are not accurate at computing risk, even when the odds are perfectly known, as in the case of gambling (see Box A1-1 for some odds associated with winning the lottery).

Negotiation is a risky choice situation because parties cannot be completely certain about the occurrence of a particular event.

For instance, a negotiator cannot be certain that mutual settlement will be reached because negotiations could break off as each party opts for his or her BATNA. To understand risky choice decision making in negotiations, we need to understand expected utility theory.

Expected Utility Theory   Expected utility theory (EU) has a long history, dating back to the sixteenth century when French noblemen commissioned their court mathematicians to help them gamble. Modern utility theory is expressed in the form of gambles, probabilities, and payoffs. Why do we need to know about gambling to be effective negotiators? Virtually all negotiations involve choices, and many choices involve uncertainty, which makes them gambles. Before we can negotiate effectively, we need to be clear about our own preferences. Utility theory helps us do that.

EU is a theory of choices made by an individual actor (von Neumann & Morgenstern, 1947). It prescribes a theory of "rational behavior." Behavior is rational if a

---

BOX A1-1

UNDERSTANDING RISK AND PROBABILITY

Millions of people purchase lottery tickets and gamble—every week and every day. But do they really understand the stakes? Consider these statistics:

- If you toss a coin 26 times, your odds of getting 26 heads in a row are greater than the chance that your Powerball ticket will win you the jackpot.

- To have a reasonable chance of winning the Massachusetts lottery by purchasing a lottery ticket each

week, you would need to persist for 1.6 million years.

- If you drive 10 miles to buy a Powerball ticket, you are 16 times more likely to die en route in a car crash than to win.

- If you are an average British citizen who buys a ticket in Britain's National Lottery on Monday, you are 2,500 times more likely to die before the Saturday draw than to win the jackpot. Viewers of the lottery draw are 3 times more likely to die during the 20-minute program than to win.

Source: Myers, D. (2003). The odds on the odds. *Across the Board, 40*(6), 6.

person acts in a way that maximizes his or her decision utility or the anticipated satisfaction from a particular outcome. The maximization of utility is often equated with the maximization of monetary gain. But satisfaction can come in many nonmonetary forms as well. Obviously, people care about things other than money. For example, weather, culture, quality of life, and personal esteem are all factors that bear on a job decision, in addition to salary.

EU is based on revealed preferences. People's preferences or utilities are not directly observable but must be inferred from their choices and willful behavior. To understand what a person really wants and values, we have to see what choices he or she makes. Actions speak louder than words. In this sense, utility maximization is a tautological statement: A person's choices reflect personal utilities; therefore, all behaviors may be represented by the maximization of this hypothetical utility scale.

EU is based on a set of axioms about preferences among gambles. The basic result of the theory is summarized by a theorem stating that if a person's preferences satisfy the specified axioms, then the person's behavior maximizes the expected utility. Before we can talk about what rational behavior is, we need to understand what a utility function is.

Utility Function A **utility function** is the quantification of a person's preferences with respect to certain objects such as jobs, potential mates, and ice cream flavors. Utility functions assign numbers to objects and gambles that have objects as their prizes (e.g., flip a coin and win a trip to Hawaii or free groceries). For example, a manager's choice to stay at her current company could be assigned an overall value, say a 7 on a 10 point scale. Her option to take a new job might be assigned a value of either 10 or 2, depending on how things work out for her at the new job. One's current job is the sure

thing; the alternative job, because of its uncertainty, is a gamble. How should we rationally make a decision between the two?

We first need to examine our utility function. The following seven axioms guarantee the existence of a utility function. The axioms are formulated in terms of preference-or-indifference relations defined over a set of outcomes (see also Coombs, Dawes, & Tversky, 1970). As will become clear, the following axioms provide the foundation for individual decision making as well as negotiation, or joint decision making.

Comparability A key assumption of EU is that everything is comparable. That is, given any two objects, a person must prefer one to the other or be indifferent to both; no two objects are incomparable. For example, a person may compare a dime and a nickel or a cheeseburger and a dime. We might compare a job offer in the Midwest to a job on the West Coast. Utility theory implies a single, underlying dimension of "satisfaction" associated with everything. We can recall instances in which we refused to make comparisons, however, which often happens in the case of social or emotional issues such as marriage and children. However, according to utility theory, we need to be able to compare everything to be truly rational. Many people are uncomfortable with this idea, just as people can be in conflict about what is negotiable.

Closure The closure property states that if x and y are available alternatives, then so are all the gambles of the form (x, p, y) that can be formed with x and y as outcomes. In this formulation, x and y refer to available alternatives; p refers to the probability that x will occur. Therefore (x, p, y) states that x will occur with probability p, otherwise y will occur. The converse must also be true: $(x, p, y) = (y, 1 - p, x)$, or y will occur with probability $(1 - p)$, otherwise x will occur.

As an example, imagine that you assess the probability of receiving a raise from your current employer to be about 30 percent. The closure property states that the situation expressed as a 30 percent chance of receiving a raise (otherwise, no raise) is identical to the statement that you have a 70 percent chance of not receiving a raise (otherwise, receiving a raise).

So far, utility theory may seem to be so obvious and simple that it is absurd to spell it out in any detail. However, we will soon see how people violate basic "common sense" all the time, and hence, behave irrationally.

Transitivity   Transitivity means that if we prefer x to y and y to z, then we should prefer x to z. Similarly, if we are indifferent between x and y and y and z, then we will be indifferent between x and z.

Suppose your employer offers you one of three options: a transfer to Seattle, a transfer to Pittsburgh, or a raise of $5,000. You prefer a raise of $5,000 over a move to Pittsburgh, and you prefer to move to Seattle more than a $5,000 raise. The **transitivity property** states that you should therefore prefer a move to Seattle over a move to Pittsburgh. If your preferences were not transitive, you would always want to move somewhere else. Further, a third party could become rich by continuously "selling" your preferred options to you.

Reducibility   The **reducibility axiom** refers to a person's attitude toward a compound lottery, in which the prizes may be tickets to other lotteries. According to the reducibility axiom, a person's attitude toward a compound lottery depends only on the ultimate prizes and the chance of getting them as determined by the laws of probability; the actual gambling mechanism is irrelevant:

$$(x, pq, y) = [(x, p, y), q, y]$$

Suppose that the dean of admissions at your first-choice university tells you that you have a 25 percent chance of getting accepted to the MBA program. How do you feel about the situation? Now, suppose the dean tells you that there is a 50 percent chance that you will not get accepted and a 50 percent chance that you will face a lottery-type admission procedure, wherein half the applicants will get accepted and half will not. Which situation do you prefer to be in? According to the reducibility axiom, both situations are identical. Your chances of getting admitted into graduate school are the same in each case: exactly 25 percent. The difference between the two situations is that one involves a **compound gamble** and the other does not.

Compound gambles differ from simple ones in that their outcomes are themselves gambles rather than pure outcomes. Furthermore, probabilities are the same in both gambles. If people have an aversion or attraction to gambling, however, these outcomes may not seem the same. This axiom has important implications for negotiation; the format by which alternatives are presented to negotiators—in other words, in terms of gambles or compound gambles—strongly affects our behavior.

Substitutability   The **substitutability axiom** states that gambles that have prizes about which people are indifferent are interchangeable. For example, suppose one prize is substituted for another in a lottery but the lottery is left otherwise unchanged. If you are indifferent between the old and the new prizes, you should be indifferent between the lotteries. If you prefer one prize to the other, you will prefer the lottery that offers the preferred prize.

As an illustration, imagine you work in the finance division of a company, and your supervisor asks you how you feel about transferring to either the marketing or sales division in your company. You respond that you are indifferent between the two. Then your supervisor presents you with a choice: Either you can be transferred to the sales division, or you can move to a finance position in an out-of-state parent branch of the company. After wrestling with the decision, you decide that you prefer to move out of state rather than transfer to the sales division. A few days later, your supervisor surprises you by asking whether you prefer to be transferred to marketing or to be transferred out of the state. According to the substitutability axiom, you should prefer to transfer because, as you previously indicated, you are indifferent to marketing and sales; they are substitutable choices.

Betweenness   The **betweenness axiom** asserts that if x is preferred to y, then x must be preferred to any probability mixture of x and y, which in turn must be preferred to y. This principle is certainly not objectionable for monetary outcomes. For example, most of us would rather have a dime than a nickel and would rather have a probability of either a dime or a nickel than the nickel itself. But consider nonmonetary outcomes, such as skydiving, Russian roulette, and bungee jumping. To an outside observer, people who skydive apparently prefer a probability mixture of living and dying over either one of them alone; otherwise, one can easily either stay alive or kill oneself without ever skydiving. People who like to risk their lives appear to contradict the betweenness axiom. A more careful analysis reveals, however, that this situation, strange as it may be, is not incompatible with the betweenness axiom. The actual outcomes involved in skydiving are (1) staying alive after skydiving, (2) staying alive without skydiving, or (3) dying while skydiving. In choosing to skydive, therefore, a person prefers a probability mix of (1) and (3) over (2). This analysis reveals that "experience" has a utility.

Continuity or Solvability   Suppose that of three objects, A, B, and C, you prefer A to B and B to C. Now, consider a lottery in which

there is a probability, p, of getting A and a probability of $1 - p$ of getting C. If $p = 0$, the lottery is equivalent to C; if $p = 1$, the lottery is equivalent to A. In the first case, you prefer B to the lottery; in the second case, you prefer the lottery to B. According to the **continuity axiom,** a value, p, that falls between 0 and 1 indicates your indifference between B and the lottery. Sounds reasonable enough.

Now consider the following example from von Neumann and Morgenstern (1947) involving three outcomes: receiving a dime, receiving a nickel, and being shot at dawn. Certainly, most of us prefer a dime to a nickel and a nickel to being shot. The continuity axiom, however, states that at some point of inversion, some probability mixture involving receiving a dime and being shot at dawn is equivalent to receiving a nickel. This derivation seems particularly disdainful for most people because no price is equal to risking one's life. However, the counterintuitive nature of this example stems from an inability to understand very small probabilities. In the abstract, people believe they would never choose to risk their life but, in reality, people do so all the time. For example, we cross the street to buy some product for a nickel less, although by doing so we risk getting hit by a car and being killed.

In summary, whenever these axioms hold, a utility function exists that (1) preserves a person's preferences among options and gambles, and (2) satisfies the expectation principle: The utility of a gamble equals the expected utility of its outcomes. This utility scale is uniquely determined except for an origin and a unit of measurement.

Expected Value Principle   Imagine that you have a rare opportunity to invest in a highly innovative start-up company. The company has developed a new technology that allows cars to run without gasoline. The cars are fuel efficient, environmentally clean, and less expensive to maintain than regular gasoline-fueled cars. On the other hand, the technology is new and unproven. Further, the company does not have the resources to compete with the major automakers. Nevertheless, if this technology is successful, an investment in the company at this point will have a 30-fold return. Suppose you just inherited $5,000 from your aunt. You could invest the money in the company and possibly earn $150,000 — a risky choice. Or you could keep the money and pass up the investment opportunity. You assess the probability of success to be about 20 percent. (A minimum investment of $5,000 is required.) What do you do?

The dominance principle does not offer a solution to this decision situation because it provides no clearly dominant alternatives. But the situation contains the necessary elements to use the **expected value principle,** which applies when a decision maker must choose among two or more prospects, as in the previous example. The "expectation" or "expected value" of a prospect is the sum of the objective values of the outcomes multiplied by the probability of their occurrence.

For a variety of reasons, you believe there is a 20 percent chance that the investment could result in a return of $150,000, which mathematically is $0.2 \times \$150,000 = \$30,000$. There is an 80 percent chance that the investment will not yield a return, or $0.8 \times \$0 = \$0$. Thus, the expected value of this gamble is $30,000 minus the cost, or $-\$5,000 = \$25,000$.

The expected value principle dictates that the decision maker should select the prospect with the greatest expected value. In this case, the risky option (with an expected value = $30,000) has a greater expected value than the sure option (expected value = $0).

A related principle applies to evaluation decisions, or situations in which decision makers must state, and be willing to act upon, the subjective worth of a given alternative. Suppose you could choose to "sell" your opportunity to invest to another person. What would you consider to be a fair price to do so? According to the expected-value evaluation principle, the evaluation of a prospect should be equal to its expected value. That is, the "fair price" for such a gamble would be $25,000. Similarly, the opposite holds: Suppose that your next-door neighbor held the opportunity but was willing to sell the option to you. According to the expected value principle, people would pay up to $25,000 for the opportunity to gamble.

The expected value principle is intuitively appealing, but should we use it to make decisions? To answer this question, it is helpful to examine the rationale for using expected value as a prescription. Let's consider the short-term and long-term consequences (Yates, 1990). Imagine that you will inherit $5,000 every year for the next 50 years. Each year, you must decide whether to invest the inheritance in a start-up company (risky choice) or keep the money (the sure choice). The expected value of a prospect is its long-run average value. This principle is derived from a fundamental principle: the **law of large numbers** (Feller, 1968; Woodroofe, 1975). The law of large numbers states that the mean return will get closer and closer to its expected value the more times a gamble is repeated. Thus, we can be fairly sure that after 50 years of investing your money, the average return would be about $25,000. Some years you would lose, others you would make money, but on average, your return would be $25,000. When you look at the gamble this way, it seems reasonable to invest.

Now imagine that the investment decision is a once-in-a-lifetime opportunity. In this case, the law of large numbers does not apply to expected value decision principle. You will either make $150,000, make nothing, or keep $5,000. No in-between options are possible. Under such circumstances, you can often find good reasons to reject the guidance of the expected value principle (Yates, 1990). For example, suppose that you need a new car. If the gamble is successful, buying a car is no problem. But if the gamble is unsuccessful, you will have no money at all. Therefore, you may decide that buying a used car at or under $5,000 is a more sensible choice.

Risk Attitudes   The expected value concept is the basis for a standard way of labeling risk-taking behavior. For example, in the previous situation you could either take the investment gamble or receive $25,000 from selling the opportunity to someone else. In this case, the "value" of the sure thing (i.e., receiving $25,000) is identical to the expected value of the gamble. Therefore, the "objective worth" of both alternatives is identical. What would you rather do? Your choice reveals your **risk attitude.** If you are indifferent to the two choices and are content to decide on the basis of a coin flip, you are **risk-neutral** or **risk-indifferent.** If you prefer the sure thing, then your behavior may be described as **risk-averse.** If you choose to gamble, your behavior is classified as **risk-seeking.**

Although some individual differences occur in people's risk attitudes, people do not tend to exhibit consistent risk-seeking or risk-averse behavior (Slovic, 1962, 1964). Rather, risk attitudes are highly context dependent. The fourfold pattern of risk attitudes predicts that people will be risk-averse for moderate to high probability gains and low-probability losses, and risk-seeking for low-probability gains and moderate- to high-probability losses (Tversky & Kahneman, 1992; Tversky & Fox, 1995).

Expected Utility Principle   How much money would you be willing to pay to play a game with the following two rules: (1) An unbiased coin is tossed until it lands on heads. (2) The player of the game is paid $2 if heads

appears on the opening toss, $4 if heads first appears on the second toss, $8 on the third toss, $16 on the fourth toss, and so on. Before reading further, indicate how much you would be willing to pay to play the game.

To make a decision based upon rational analysis, let's calculate the expected value of the game by multiplying the payoff for each possible outcome by the probability of its occurring. Although the probability of the first head appearing on toss n becomes progressively smaller as n increases, the probability never becomes zero. In this case, note that the probability of heads for the first time on any given toss is $(1/2)^n$, and the payoff in each case is (2^n); hence, each term of the infinite series has an expected value of $1. The implication is that the value of the game is infinite (Lee, 1971). Even though the value of this game is infinite, most people are seldom willing to pay more than a few dollars to play it. Most people believe that the expected value principle in this case produces an absurd conclusion. The observed reluctance to pay to play the game, despite its objective attractiveness, is known as the **St. Petersburg paradox** (Bernoulli, 1738/1954).

How can we explain such an enigma? We might argue that expected value is an undefined quantity when the variance of outcomes is infinite. Because, in practice, the person or organization offering the game could not guarantee a payoff greater than its total assets, the game was unimaginable, except in truncated and therefore finite form (Shapley, 1977). So what do we do when offered such a choice? We have decided that to regard it as "priceless" or even to pay hundreds of thousands of dollars would be absurd. So, how should managers reason about such situations?

Diminishing Marginal Utility   The reactions people have to the St. Petersburg game are consistent with the proposition that people decide among prospects not according to their expected objective values, but rather according to their expected subjective values. In other words, the psychological value of money does not increase proportionally as the objective amount increases. To be sure, virtually all of us like more money rather than less money, but we do not necessarily like $20 twice as much as $10. And the difference in our happiness when our $20,000 salary is raised to $50,000 is not the same as when our $600,000 salary is raised to $630,000. Bernoulli proposed a logarithmic function relating the utility of money, u, to the amount of money, x. This function is **concave,** meaning that the utility of money decreases marginally. Constant additions to monetary amounts result in less and less increased utility. The principle of **diminishing marginal utility** is related to a fundamental principle of psychophysics, wherein good things satiate and bad things escalate. The first bite of a pizza is the best; as we get full, each bite brings less and less utility.

The principle of diminishing marginal utility is simple, yet profound. It is known as the "everyman's utility function" (Bernoulli, 1738/1954). According to Bernoulli, a fair price for a gamble should not be determined by its expected (monetary) value, but rather by its expected utility (see Figure A1-2). Thus,

the logarithmic utility function in Figure A1-2 yields a finite price for the gamble.

According to EU, each of the possible outcomes of a prospect has a utility (subjective value) that is represented numerically. The more appealing an outcome is, the higher its utility. The expected utility of a prospect is the sum of the utilities of the potential outcomes, each weighted by its probability. According to EU, when choosing among two or more prospects, people should select the option with the highest expected utility. Further, in evaluation situations, risky prospects should have an expected utility equal to the corresponding "sure choice" alternative.

Expected utility (EU) principles have essentially the same form as expected value (EV) principles. The difference is that expectations are computed using objective (dollar) values in EV models as opposed to subjective values (utility) in EU models.

Risk Taking   A person's utility function for various prospects reveals something about his or her risk-taking tendencies. If a utility function is concave, a decision maker will always choose a sure thing over a prospect whose expected value is identical to that sure thing. The decision maker's behavior is risk-averse (Figure A1-3, Panel A).

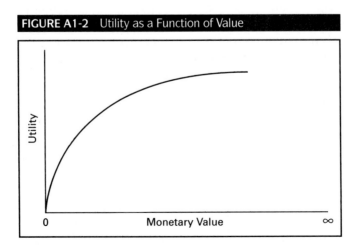

FIGURE A1-2   Utility as a Function of Value

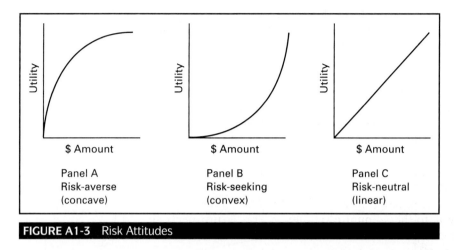

Panel A
Risk-averse
(concave)

Panel B
Risk-seeking
(convex)

Panel C
Risk-neutral
(linear)

FIGURE A1-3 Risk Attitudes

The risk-averse decision maker would prefer a sure $5 over a 50–50 chance of winning $10 or nothing—even though the expected value of the gamble [0.5($10) + 0.5($0) = $5] is equal to that of the sure thing. If a person's utility function is convex, he or she will choose the risky option (Figure A1-3, Panel B). If the utility function is linear, his or her decisions will be risk-neutral and, of course, identical to that predicted by expected value maximization (Figure A1-3, Panel C).

If most managers' utility for gains are concave (i.e., risk-averse), then why would people ever choose to gamble? Bets that offer small probabilities of winning large sums of money (e.g., lotteries, roulette wheels) ought to be especially unattractive, given that the concave utility function that drives the worth of the large prize is considerably lower than the value warranting a very small probability of obtaining the prize.

Imagine that, as a manager, one of your subordinates comes to you with the following prospects based upon the consequences of a particular marketing strategy:

Strategy A: 80 percent probability of earning $40,000, otherwise $0
Strategy B: Earn $30,000 for sure

Which do you choose? Only a small minority of managers (20 percent) choose strategy A over strategy B. Meanwhile, suppose that another associate on a different project presents you with the following two plans:

Strategy C: 20 percent probability of earning $40,000, otherwise $0
Strategy D: 25 percent probability of earning $30,000, otherwise $0

Faced with this choice, a clear majority (65 percent) choose strategy C over strategy D (the smaller, more likely payoff) (adapted from Kahneman & Tversky, 1979).

However, in this example, the manager's choice behavior violates EU, which requires consistency between the A versus B choice and the C versus D choice. In Figure A1-4, Branch 1 depicts the C versus D choice [i.e., 25% chance of making $3,000 (otherwise $0) or 20% chance of making $4,000 (otherwise $0)]. In Branch 2 of Figure A1-4, another stage has been added to the gamble between A and B, which effectively makes the two-stage gamble in Branch 2 identical to the one-stage gamble in Branch 1. Because Branch 1 is objectively identical to Branch 2, then a manager should not make different choices when faced with each decision. Stated

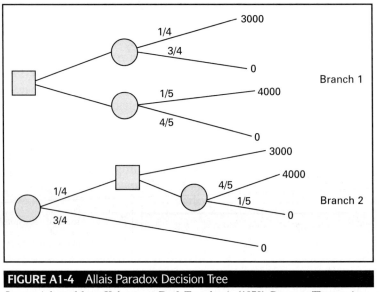

FIGURE A1-4   Allais Paradox Decision Tree

Source: Adapted from Kahneman, D., & Tversky, A. (1979). Prospect Theory: An Analysis of Decision Under Risk. *Econometrica, 47,* 263–291. Copyright © by The Econometric Society.

another way, in the A versus B and C versus D choices, the ratio is the same: (0.8/1) = (0.20/0.25). However, managers' preferences usually reverse. According to the **certainty effect,** people have a tendency to overweight certain outcomes relative to outcomes that are merely probable. The reduction in probability from certainty (1) to a degree of uncertainty (0.8) produces a more pronounced loss in attractiveness than a corresponding reduction from one level of uncertainty (0.2) to another (0.25). Managers do not think rationally about probabilities. Those close to 1 are often (mistakenly) considered sure things. On the flip side is the possibility effect: the tendency to overweight outcomes that are possible relative to outcomes that are impossible.

Decision Weights   Decision makers transform probabilities into psychological decision weights. The decision weights are then applied to the subjective values. Prospect theory proposes a relationship between the probabilities' potential outcomes and the

weights those probabilities have in the decision process.

Figure A1-5 illustrates the probability weighting function proposed by cumulative prospect theory. It is an inverted-S function that is concave near 0 and convex near 1. The probability-weighting function offers several noteworthy features.

Extremity Effect   People tend to overweight low probabilities and under-weight high probabilities.

Crossover Point   The **crossover probability** is the point at which objective probabilities and subjective weights coincide. Prospect theory (Kahneman & Tversky, 1979) does not pinpoint where the crossover occurs, but it is definitely lower than 50 percent.

Subadditivity   Adding two probabilities, p_1 and p_2, should yield a probability $p_3 = p_1 + p_2$. For example, suppose you are an investor considering three stocks, A, B, and C. You assess the probability that stock A will close two points higher today than yesterday to be

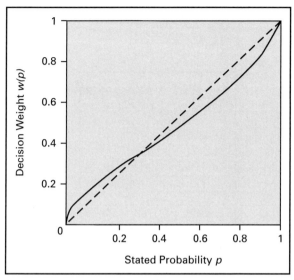

FIGURE A1-5 A Weighting Function for Decision Under Risk

Source: Fox, C. R. (1998). A Belief-Based Model of Decision Under Uncertainty. *Management Science, 44,* 879–896. Copyright © by The Econometric Society.

20 percent, and you assess the probability that stock B will close two points higher today than yesterday to be 15 percent. The stocks are two different companies in two different industries and are completely independent. Now consider the price of stock C, which you believe has a 35 percent probability of closing two points higher today. The likelihood of a two-point increase in either stock A or B should be identical to the likelihood of a two-point increase in stock C. The probability-weighting relationship, however, does not exhibit additivity. That is, for small probabilities, weights are subadditive, as we see from the extreme flatness at the lower end of the curve. It means that most decision makers consider the likely increase of either stocks A or B to be less likely than an increase in stock C.

Subcertainty Except for guaranteed or impossible events, weights for complementary events do not sum to 1. One implication of the **subcertainty** feature of the probability-weight relationship is that for all probabilities, p, with $0 < p < 1$, $p(p) + p(1 - p) < 1$.

Regressiveness According to the **regressiveness principle,** extreme values of some

quantity do not deviate very much from the average value of that quantity. The relative flatness of the probability-weighting curve is a special type of regressiveness suggesting that people's decisions are not as responsive to changes in uncertainty as are the associated probabilities. Another aspect is that nonextreme high probabilities are underweighted, and low ones are overweighted.

The subjective value associated with a prospect depends on the decision weights and the subjective values of potential outcomes. Prospect theory (Kahneman & Tversky, 1979) makes specific claims about the form of the relationship between various amounts of an outcome and their subjective values. Figure A1-6 illustrates the generic prospect theory value function.

Three characteristics of the value function are noteworthy. The first pertains to the decision maker's **reference point.** At some focal amount of the pertinent outcome, smaller amounts are considered losses and larger amounts gains. That focal amount is the negotiator's reference point. People are sensitive to *changes in wealth.*

A second feature is that the shape of the function changes markedly at the reference

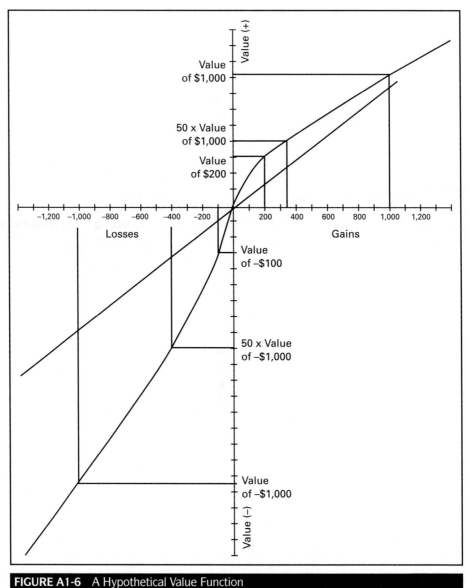

FIGURE A1-6 A Hypothetical Value Function

Source: Reprinted by permission of The Econometric Society.

point. For gains, the value function is concave, exhibiting diminishing marginal value. As the starting point for increases in gains becomes larger, the significance of a constant increase lessens. A complementary phenomenon occurs in the domain of losses: Constant changes in the negative direction away from the reference

point also assume diminishing significance the farther from the reference point the starting point happens to be.

Finally, the value function is noticeably steeper for losses than for gains. Stated another way, gains and losses of identical magnitude have different significance for people; losses are considered more important. We are much more disappointed about losing $75 than we are happy about making $75.

Combination Rules How do decision weights and outcome values combine to determine the subjective value of a prospect? The amounts that are effective for the decision maker are not the *actual* sums that would be awarded or taken away, but are instead the *differences* between those sums and the decision maker's reference point.

Summing Up: Individual Decision Making

Decisions may sometimes be faulty or irrational if probabilities are not carefully considered. A negotiator's assessment of probabilities affects how he or she negotiates. Clever negotiators are aware of how their *own* decisions may be biased, as well as how the decisions of others may be manipulated to their own advantage. Now that we know about how individuals make decisions, we are ready to explore multiparty, or interdependent, decision making.

Game Theoretic Rationality

Each outcome in a negotiation situation may be identified in terms of its utility for each party. In Figure A1-7, for example, party 1's utility function is represented as u_1; party 2's utility function is represented as u_2. Remember that utility payoffs represent the satisfaction parties derive from particular commodities or outcomes, not the actual monetary outcomes or payoffs themselves. A bargaining situation like the one in Figure A1-7 has a feasible set of utility outcomes, or F, defined as the set of all its possible utility outcomes for party 1 and party 2 and by its conflict point, c, where $c = (c_1, c_2)$. c represents the point at which both parties would prefer not to reach agreement—the reservation points of both parties.

Two key issues concern rationality at the negotiation table: one pertains to pie slicing and one pertains to pie expansion. First, people should not agree to a utility payoff smaller than their reservation point; and second, negotiators should not agree on an outcome if another outcome exists that is Pareto-superior, that is, an outcome more preferable to one party and does not decrease utility for the other party (e.g., level 3 integrative agreements in Chapter 4).

For example, in Figure A1-7, the area F is the feasible set of alternative outcomes expressed in terms of each negotiator's utility function. The triangular area bcd is the set of all points satisfying the individual rationality requirement. The upper-right boundary $abde$ of F is the set of all points that satisfy the joint rationality requirement. The intersection of the area bcd and of the boundary line $abde$ is the arc bd: It is the set of all points satisfying both rationality requirements. As we can see, b is the least favorable outcome party 1 will accept; d is the least favorable outcome party 2 will accept.

The individual rationality and joint rationality assumptions do not tell us how negotiators should divide the pie. Rather, they tell us only that negotiators should make the pie as big as possible before dividing it. How much of the pie should you have?

Nash Bargaining Theory

Nash's (1950, 1953) bargaining theory specifies how negotiators should divide the pie, which involves "a determination of the amount of satisfaction each individual should expect to get from the situation or, rather, a determination of how much it should be worth to each of these individuals to have this opportunity to bargain" (p. 155). Nash's theory makes a *specific* point prediction of the outcome of negotiation, the **Nash solution,** which specifies the outcome of a negotiation if negotiators behave rationally.

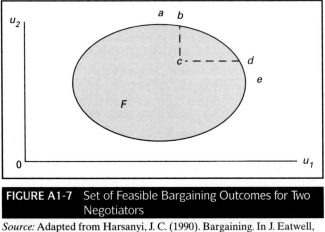

FIGURE A1-7 Set of Feasible Bargaining Outcomes for Two Negotiators

Source: Adapted from Harsanyi, J. C. (1990). Bargaining. In J. Eatwell, M. Milgate, & P. Newman (Eds.) *The New Palgrave: A Dictionary of Economics.* New York: Norton, 54–67.

Nash's theory makes several important assumptions: Negotiators are rational; that is, they act to maximize their utility. The only significant differences between negotiators are those included in the mathematical description of the game. Further, negotiators have full knowledge of the tastes and preferences of each other.

Nash's theory builds on the axioms named in EU by specifying additional axioms. By specifying enough properties, we exclude all possible settlements in a negotiation, except one. Nash postulates that the agreement point, u, of a negotiation, known as the Nash solution, will satisfy the following five axioms: uniqueness, Pareto-optimality, symmetry, independence of equivalent utility representations, and independence of irrelevant alternatives.

Uniqueness The **uniqueness axiom** states that a unique solution exists for each bargaining situation. Simply stated, one and only one best solution exists for a given bargaining situation or game. In Figure A1-8, the unique solution is denoted as u.

Pareto-Optimality The bargaining process should not yield any outcome that both people find less desirable than some other feasible outcome. The Pareto-optimality (or efficiency) axiom is simply the joint rationality assumption made by von Neumann and Morgenstern (1947) and the level 3 integrative agreement discussed in Chapter 4. The **Pareto-efficient frontier** is the set of outcomes corresponding to the entire set of agreements that leaves no portion of the total amount of resources unallocated. A given option, x, is a member of the Pareto frontier if, and only if, no option y exists such that y is preferred to x by at least one party and is at least as good as x for the other party.

Consider Figure A1-8: Both people prefer settlement point u (u_1, u_2), which eliminates c (c_1, c_2) from the frontier. Therefore, settlement points that lie on the interior of the arc bd are Pareto-inefficient. Options that are not on the Pareto frontier are dominated; settlements that are dominated clearly violate the utility principle of maximization. The resolution of any negotiation should be an option from the Pareto-efficient set because any other option unnecessarily requires more concession on the part of one or both negotiators.

Another way of thinking about importance of Pareto-optimality is to imagine that

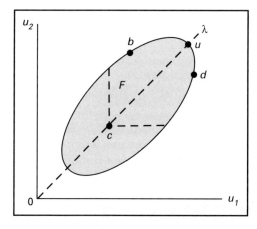

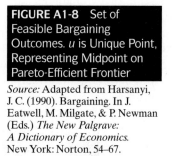

FIGURE A1-8 Set of Feasible Bargaining Outcomes. u is Unique Point, Representing Midpoint on Pareto-Efficient Frontier

Source: Adapted from Harsanyi, J. C. (1990). Bargaining. In J. Eatwell, M. Milgate, & P. Newman (Eds.) *The New Palgrave: A Dictionary of Economics.* New York: Norton, 54–67.

in *every* negotiation, whether it be for a car, a job, a house, a merger, or some other situation, a table sits with hundreds, thousands, and in some cases, millions of dollars on it. The money is yours to keep, provided that you and the other party (e.g., a car dealer, employer, seller, business associate, etc.) agree how to divide it. Obviously, you want to get as much money as you can, which is the distributive aspect of negotiation. Imagine for a moment that you and the other negotiator settle upon a division of the money that both of you find acceptable. However, imagine that you leave half or one-third or some amount of money on the table. A fire starts in the building, and the money burns. This scenario is equivalent to failing to reach a Pareto-optimal agreement. Most of us would never imagine allowing such an unfortunate event to happen. However, in many negotiation situations, people do just that—they leave money to burn.

Symmetry In a symmetric bargaining situation, the two players have exactly the same strategic possibilities and bargaining power. Therefore, neither player has any reason to accept an agreement that yields a lower payoff than that of the opponent.

Another way of thinking about symmetry is to imagine interchanging the two players.

This alteration should not change the outcome. In Figure A1-8, symmetry means that u_1 will be equal to u_2. The feasible set of outcomes must be symmetrical with respect to a hypothetical 45-degree line, 1, which begins at the origin 0 and passes through the point c, thereby implying that $c_1 = c_2$. Extending this line out to the farthest feasible point, u, gives us the *Nash point*, wherein parties' utilities are symmetric.

The symmetry principle is often considered to be the fundamental postulate of bargaining theory (Harsanyi, 1962). When parties' utilities are known, the solution to the game is straightforward (Nash, 1950). As we already noted, however, players' utilities are usually not known. This uncertainty reduces the usefulness of the symmetry principle. That is, symmetry cannot be achieved if a negotiator has only half of the information (Schelling, 1960).

The Pareto-optimality and symmetry axioms uniquely define the agreement points of a symmetrical game. The remaining two axioms extend the theory to asymmetrical games in which the bargaining power is asymmetric.

Independence of Equivalent Utility Representations Many utility functions can represent the same preference. Utility functions are behaviorally equivalent if one can be obtained from the other by an order-preserving linear transformation — for example, by shifting the zero point of the utility scale or by changing the utility unit. A distinguishing feature of the Nash solution outcome is that it is independent of the exchange rate between two players' utility scales; it is invariant with respect to any fixed weights we might attach to their respective utilities.

The solution to the bargaining game is not sensitive to positive linear transformations of parties' payoffs because utility is defined on an interval scale. Interval scales such as temperature preserve units of measurement but have an arbitrary origin (i.e., zero point) and unit of measurement. The utility scales for player 1 and player 2 in Figure A1-8 have an arbitrary origin and unit of measurement.

For example, suppose that you and a friend are negotiating to divide 100 poker chips. The poker chips are worth $1 each if redeemed by you and worth $1 each if redeemed by your friend. The question is: How should the two of you divide the poker chips? The Nash solution predicts that the two of you should divide all of the chips and not leave any on the table (Pareto-optimality principle). Further, the Nash solution predicts that you should receive 50 chips, and your friend should receive 50 chips (symmetry principle). So far, the Nash solution probably sounds fine. Now, suppose that the situation is slightly changed. Imagine that the chips are worth $1 each if redeemed by you, but they are worth $5 each if redeemed by your friend. (The rules of the game do not permit any kind of side payments or renegotiation of redemption values.) Now, how should the chips be divided? All we have done is transform your friend's utilities using an order-preserving linear transformation (multiply all her values by 5) while keeping your utilities the same. The Nash solution states that you should still divide the chips 50–50 because your friend's utilities have not

changed; rather, they are represented by a different, but nevertheless equivalent, linear transformation.

Some people have a hard time with this axiom. After all, if you and your friend are really "symmetric," one of you should not come out richer in the deal. But consider the arguments that could be made for one of you receiving a greater share of the chips. One of you could have a seriously ill parent and need the money for an operation; one of you might be independently wealthy and not need the money; or one of you could be a foolish spendthrift and not deserve the money. Moreover, there could be a disagreement: One of you regards yourself to be thoughtful and prudent but is regarded as silly and imprudent by the other person. All of these arguments are outside the realm of Nash's theory because they are **indeterminate**. Dividing resources to achieve *monetary* equality is as arbitrary as flipping a coin.

But wait a minute. In negotiation, doesn't everything really boil down to dollars? No. In Nash's theory, each person's utility function may be normalized on a scale of 0 to 1 so that his or her "best outcome" = 1 and "worst outcome" = 0. Therefore, because the choices of origin and scale for each person's utility function are unrelated to one another, actual numerical levels have no standing in theory, and no comparisons of numerical levels can affect the outcome.

This axiom has serious implications. By permitting the transformation of one player's utilities without any transformation of the other player's utilities destroys the possibility that the outcome should depend on interpersonal utility comparisons. Stated simply, it is meaningless for people to compare their utility with another. The same logic applies for comparing salaries, the size of offices, or anything else.

However, people do engage in interpersonal comparisons of utility (Chapter 3). The important point is that interpersonal comparisons and arguments based on "fairness" are inherently subjective, which leaves no rational method for fair division.

Independence of Irrelevant Alternatives
The **independence of irrelevant alternatives** axiom states that the best outcome in a feasible set of outcomes will also be the best outcome in any smaller subset of feasible outcomes that still contains that outcome. For example, a subset of a bargaining game may be obtained by excluding some of the irrelevant alternatives from the original game, without excluding the original agreement point itself. The exclusion of irrelevant alternatives does not change the settlement.

Consider Figure A1-8: The Nash solution is point *u*. Imagine that the settlement options in the half-ellipse below the 45-degree line are eliminated. According to the independence of irrelevant alternatives axiom, this change should not affect the settlement outcome, which should still be *u*.

This axiom allows a point prediction to be made in asymmetric games by allowing them to be enlarged to be symmetric. For example, imagine that the game parties play is an asymmetric one like that just described (that is, the half-ellipse below the 45-degree line is eliminated). Such a bargaining problem would be asymmetric, perhaps with player 2 having an advantage. According to Nash, it is useful to expand the asymmetric game to be one that is symmetric—for example, by including the points in the lower half of the ellipse that mirrors the half-ellipse above the 45-degree line. Once these points are included, the game is symmetric, and the Nash solution may be identified. Of course, the settlement outcome yielded by the new, expanded game must also be present in the original game.

The independence of irrelevant alternatives axiom is motivated by the way negotiation unfolds (Harsanyi, 1990). Through a process of voluntary mutual concessions, the set of possible outcomes under consideration gradually decreases to just those around the eventual agreement point. This axiom asserts that the winnowing process does not change the agreement point.

In summary, Nash's theorem states that the unique solution possesses these properties. Nash's solution selects the unique point that maximizes the geometric average (i.e., the product) of the gains available to people as measured against their reservation points. For this reason, the Nash solution is also known as the Nash product. If all possible outcomes are plotted on a graph whose rectangular coordinates measure the utilities that the two players derive from them, as in Figures A1-7 and A1-8, the solution is a unique point on the upper-right boundary of the region. The point is unique because two solution points could be joined by a straight line representing available alternative outcomes achievable by mixing, with various odds, the probabilities of the original two outcomes, and the points on the line connecting them would yield higher products of the two players' utilities. In other words, the region is presumed convex by reason of the possibility of probability mixtures, and the convex region has a single maximum-utility-product point, or Nash point.

Appendix 2

NONVERBAL COMMUNICATION AND LIE DETECTION

The purpose of this appendix is to help you (1) be a better reader of nonverbal communication, and (2) be a better sender of nonverbal communication.

What Are We Looking for in Nonverbal Communication?

What exactly do we mean by nonverbal communication? Nonverbal communication is anything that is "not words." Specifically, it includes the following:

- *Vocal cues or paralinguistic cues.* Paralinguistic cues include pauses, intonation, and fluency. Vocal cues, such as tone and inflection, are nonverbal; they include speech volume, pace, and pitch.
- *Facial expressions.* Smiling, frowning, or expressing surprise. "Facial expressions are books without covers" (DePaulo & Friedman, 1998).
- *Eye contact.* Often, a high level of held gazing can be interpreted as sign of liking or friendliness. However, in other cultures, prolonged eye contact is a sign of dominance or aggression (Ellsworth & Carlsmith, 1973).
- *Interpersonal spacing.* The distance between people when they talk or communicate.
- *Posture.*
- *Body movements.* When people are experiencing greater arousal, or nervousness, they tend to make more movements.
- *Gesture.* The three basic kinds of gestures are (1) *emblems,* which symbolize certain messages, such as

the North American thumbs-up for "OK," and the finger on the lips for "quiet;" (2) *illustrators,* which embellish a verbal message, such as the widening of hands and arms when talking about something that is large; and (3) *adaptors,* which include things like touching one's nose or twitching in such a way that does not embellish or illustrate a particular point.
- *Touching.* Touching another person (in an appropriate way) often leads to positive reactions.

Nonverbal communication is informative because it is relatively irrepressible in that people cannot control it. What nonverbal signals do negotiators look for, and what do they reveal? To address this question, we conducted a survey of 50 MBA students who had recently completed a multiparty negotiation. The majority of students relied on three nonverbal cues as a window into other party's true feelings and intentions: (1) eye contact (people who are lying avoid looking the other party straight in the eyes); (2) closed body posture ("When he leans toward me while he talks, I tend to trust him more"); and (3) nervousness, twitching, and fidgeting (if people play with their shoestrings, tap their pen, bite their lip, or indicate any other nervous tension, it usually signals anxiety and nervousness). Other indicators mentioned, although much less frequently included, are lack of gestures (too much stillness), emotional outbursts, and autonomic responses, such as sweating and blushing.

NONVERBAL BEHAVIORS

What nonverbal behaviors mean you should not trust someone?

- Fidgeting
- Excessive smiling; sheepish smiles
- Overly serious tone; lack of emotion
- Averting eyes; lack of eye contact
- Being too quiet

What nonverbal behaviors mean you can trust someone?

- Direct speech
- Open gestures and behavior
- Smiling
- Pointing

Note: These are behaviors that are perceived to be linked to trust; they are not actually indicative of trust.

What particular nonverbal behaviors do negotiators notice that lead them to distrust someone? (See Box A2-1 for a list of such behaviors.)

Next, we consider three aspects of nonverbal communication of interest to anyone in the corporate world: (1) gender differences, in terms of ability and accuracy, (2) nonverbal abilities of powerful and dominant people, and (3) nonverbal abilities of charismatic people (DePaulo & Friedman, 1998). Obviously, power and charisma have implications for success at the bargaining table.

Are Women More "Nonverbally Gifted" Than Men?

Popular culture has it that women are more nonverbally sensitive than are men. And scientific evidence backs up this claim: Women *are* more skilled in terms of **nonverbal expression** (DePaulo & Friedman, 1998; Hall, 1984). In general, women are more open, expressive, approachable, and actively involved in social interaction than are men. Their faces are more readable than men's, and they smile and gaze at other people and approach them more closely than do men. Women are also gazed at more, and approached more closely

than are men (Hall, 1984). During interactions, women seem more focused on the other person, and they also elicit more warmth and less anxiety from others (Abramowitz, Abramowitz, & Weitz, 1976). It is worth pointing out, however, that the sexes are held to different standards of appropriate expressivity; women are typically considered more expressive, and men are viewed as more composed (Hall, 1984). Women anticipate greater costs and fewer rewards than men if they fail to express positive emotion in response to someone else's good news (Stoppard & Gun-Gruchy, 1993).

Nonverbal expressiveness is linked with social power. Greater expressivity is required by those of lower social status and power (Henley, 1977); women traditionally have lower social status than men. Indeed, in studies of visual dominance (measured as the ratio of time a person spends looking at his or her partner while speaking relative to the time spent looking while listening), women are often less dominant. As a general rule, high-power people are more visually dominant than low-power people (Dovidio & Ellyson, 1982). When women have uncertain support in a leadership position, men express more visual dominance than women (Brown,

Dovidio, & Ellyson, 1990). When people show more visual dominance, they are perceived as more powerful. Furthermore, when women and men are assigned to different power roles, low-power people (regardless of gender) are better able to read their partner's cues (Snodgrass, 1985, 1992).

In terms of **nonverbal reception,** women are no better than men at recognizing covert messages, such as discrepant or deceptive communication (which we will discuss later). However, when people are being truthful, women are more accurate than men; however, when people are being deceptive (i.e., when the negotiator is pretending to like someone), women are less accurate than men (DePaulo, Epstein, & Wyer, 1993; Rosenthal & DePaulo, 1979a, 1979b).

In short, women are better at detecting feelings, but are not necessarily better at detecting deception, because anyone who is inferior in status is more sensitive to states of mind of superiors. For example, when women and men are assigned to be supervisors or subordinates in organizational simulations, no differences are evident in emotional sensitivity between genders: Subordinates, regardless of gender, are more sensitive than their superiors.

Dominance

Human beings often assert dominance and power through nonverbal cues. Dominant people sit higher, stand taller, talk louder, and have more space and more resources than nondominant people. Dominant people are more likely to invade others' space (e.g., putting their feet up on their own or someone else's desk), make more expansive gestures, walk in front of others, sit in front of others or sit at the head of a table, interrupt more often, control time, and stare the other party down more, but tend to look away more often when the other party is speaking (DePaulo & Friedman, 1998).

High social power is reliably indicated by patterns of looking while speaking and

listening. People with less power look more when listening than when speaking. In contrast, more powerful people look about the same amount when listening as when speaking (Exline, Ellyson, & Long, 1975). When people interact with a dominant person, they often respond by decreasing their postural stance (i.e., they often behave more submissively); in contrast, people who interact with a submissive person often increase their stance (i.e., they behave more assertively; Tiedens & Fragale, 2003). Interestingly, liking between people is greater when the interaction is complementary as opposed to reciprocal, meaning that dominance in response to submission and submission in response to dominance results in greater liking between people than dominance in response to dominance and submission in response to submissiveness. In short, people—whether they are dominant or submissive—are more comfortable and like each other more when interacting with people who are not like themselves (Tiedens & Fragale, 2003).

When men and women have equal knowledge, power, and expertise (or when men have more), men behave *visually* as though they really are more powerful. However, when women have the advantage, they "look" like powerful people more often than men (Dovidio, Brown, et al., 1988; Dovidio, Ellyson, et al., 1988).

Personal Charisma

Charisma is a social skill having to do with verbal and nonverbal expressiveness. People vary strikingly in the intensity, expansiveness, animation, and dynamism of their nonverbal (and verbal) behaviors (Friedman, Prince, Riggo, & DiMatteo, 1980; Halberstadt, 1991; Manstead, 1991). Differences in expressiveness are linked directly to affection, empathy, influence, and professional success, as well as to interpersonal experiences, such as the regulation of one's own emotional experiences and physical and mental health.

Expressiveness, or "spontaneous sending," is the ease with which people's feelings can be read from their nonverbal expressive behaviors when they are not trying to deliberately communicate their feelings to others (Buck, 1984; Notarius & Levenson, 1979). Expressiveness instantly makes a difference in setting the tone of social interactions. Even commonplace interpersonal behaviors, such as walking into a room and initiating a conversation (Friedman, Riggio, & Casella, 1988) or greeting someone who is approaching (DiMatteo, Friedman, & Taranta, 1979) suggest this social skill is immediately influential. Why? Expressive people make better first impressions and, even over time, they are better liked than unexpressive people (Cunningham, 1986). Expressive people are considered to be more attractive than unexpressive people (DePaulo, Blank, Swaim, & Hairfield, 1992). Furthermore, expressive people capture people's attention (Sullins, 1989) and then "turn on" the expressive behavior of other people (Buck, 1984). Expressive people are good actors, feigning convincing expressions of feelings that they are not actually experiencing (Buck, 1975). It follows that they are also good liars (DePaulo, Blank, Swaim, & Hairfield, 1992).

The most interpersonally successful communicators are nonverbally sensitive, nonverbally expressive, nonverbally self-controlled, and motivated to perform for their "audiences" (DePaulo & Friedman, 1998). In social interactions, expressive people can "set the tone and frame the field" (DePaulo & Friedman, 1998, p. 14).

Detecting Deception

Nonverbal sensitivity (in terms of accuracy) is a plus in negotiation, as it is in most social interaction. For instance, doctors who are good at reading body language have more satisfied patients (DiMatteo, Hays, & Prince, 1986). Students who are nonverbally sensitive learn more than less sensitive students (Bernieri, 1991). However, nonverbal

sensitivity is difficult to achieve. As a skill, it is not correlated with intelligence, and it is very "channel-specific": Skill at understanding facial expression and body movements is measurably different from skill at understanding tone of voice (DePaulo & Rosenthal, 1979). The good news is that nonverbal sensitivity improves with age (Buck, 1984; Zuckerman, Blanck, DePaulo, & Rosenthal, 1980). See Table A2-1 for a list of the cues that are relevant when detecting lies.

Reading and sending nonverbal messages in negotiation is one thing; detecting deception (and pulling off deception) is another (for reviews, see Croson, in press; Schweitzer, 2001). Obviously, it is to a negotiator's advantage to accurately detect deception at the negotiation table. Perhaps this skill might have been able to help Corina Galindo, a teacher's assistant when she entered into a bait-and-switch scheme for a home refinance (*Forbes*, Sept. 2, 2002a, p. 63). At the closing, on a Saturday, Galindo says that her loan officer sprung a second mortgage on her with a rate of 23.9 percent. She protested, but the loan officer pressured her and said that his family was waiting for him and she must hurry. In fact, relying on nonverbal cues may be our only hope of detecting deception. People believe that either liars cannot control their nonverbal behaviors and therefore these behaviors will "leak out" and betray the liar's true feelings; or liars simply will not control all of their nonverbal cues (Ekman & Friesen, 1969).

Unfortunately, no fool-proof nonverbal indicators of deception have been discovered. In fact, most people cannot tell from demeanor when others are lying (Ekman, O'Sullivan, & Frank, 1999). In fact, accuracy rates are close to chance levels (see DePaulo, 1994; DePaulo, Lassiter, & Stone, 1982; Zuckerman, Koestner, & Driver, 1981). People who have been professionally trained (e.g., law enforcement groups) can be more

TABLE A2-1	Cues for Detecting Lies	
Cue	**Perceived**	**Actual**
Facial movements	yes	**no**
Speech hesitation	yes	yes
Changes in pitch	yes	yes
Speech errors	yes	yes
Speech rate	yes	**no**
Response length	no	yes (short for liars)
Blinking	(no data)	yes (more for liars)
Pupil dilation	(no data)	yes
Touching self	no	yes
Postural shifts	yes	**no**
Gaze	yes	**no**

Perceived: what people think are cues that indicate deception.

Actual: whether cues truly indicate deception.

Source: Ekman, P. (2001). *Telling Lies: Clues to Deceit in the Marketplace, Politics, and Marriage,* 3rd ed. New York: Norton.

accurate (Ekman et al., 1999). For example, law enforcement officers and clinical psychologists are very accurate in judging videotapes of people who are lying or telling the truth (Ekman, O'Sullivan, & Frank, 1999).

There are many things to lie about in negotiation. Some lies may be complete falsifications (such as falsifying an inspection report or pretending that another buyer will be calling at any moment with an offer); other lies may be exaggerations (exaggerating the appraised value of a property, exaggerating the attractiveness of one's BATNA). It is more difficult for liars to successfully carry off hard lies (i.e., complete falsifications of information) than to carry off easy lies (exaggerations). Consequently, it is easier for negotiators to detect complete falsifications.

What should you do to maximize the chances of catching a lie in negotiation? It is generally not an effective lie detection strategy to ask people whether they are lying. Usually, they will say no. So what can you do? Several direct methods, as well as some indirect methods, may be helpful (see also Schweitzer, 2001).

Direct Methods

Triangulation   One of the best methods of lie detection is questioning. The process of asking several questions, all designed as cross-checks on one another, is known as **triangulation.** For example, if a person wants to accurately assess the time of day, relying on only one clock can be risky. A better method is to use two or three clocks or different timepieces. Similarly, if a person wants to "catch" a liar, a good strategy is to examine nonverbal cues, verbal cues, and perhaps outside evidence as well.

Direct questions are particularly effective in curtailing lies of omission; however, they may actually increase lies of commission (Schweitzer & Croson, 1999). Detectives and lawyers ask several questions of people they think might be lying. Their questions are designed so that inconsistencies emerge if a person is lying. It is very difficult for even the best of liars to be perfectly consistent in all aspects of a lie.

Objective Evidence   Another direct fashion is to focus on inconsistencies and vagueness. And, in the case of inconsistency, ask for evidence; if appropriate, suggest contingencies. When people buy a used car, they often don't simply rely on the owner's claims of its reliability; rather, they seek an objective, expert opinion. For example, they often have an experienced mechanic inspect the car. This additional assessment is what we mean by *objective evidence*.

Linguistic Style   Telling lies often requires creating a story about an experience or attitude that does not exist. Consequently, false stories are qualitatively different from true stories. Compared to truth-tellers, liars have less cognitive complexity (shades of gray) in their stories, use fewer self-references and fewer other-references, and use more negative-emotion words (Newman, Pennebaker, Berry, & Richards, 2003). Liars hesitate more and have more speech errors. Further, their response length to questions is shorter.

Indirect Methods
Enrich the Mode of Communication   It is usually easier to catch a liar when communicating face-to-face rather than communicating via telephone or e-mail. If negotiations have been proceeding by phone, written correspondence, or e-mail, the negotiator who wants to catch a lie should insist on a face-to-face interaction. First, people are less likely to lie face-to-face than they are when on the telephone or e-mail. Second, it is easier to detect a lie in a face-to-face interaction partly because it is much more difficult for liars to monitor themselves when the communication modality is multichanneled (as it is in face-to-face negotiations). Telltale signs of lying are often found in nonverbal "leakage," such as in the hands or body, rather than the face or words, which liars usually carefully monitor (Ekman, 1984). For example, liars tend to touch themselves more and blink more than truth-tellers.

Do Not Rely on a Person's Face   Most people look at a person's face when they want

to detect deception, but this focus is not always effective. Perceivers are able to detect deception at greater-than-chance levels from every individual channel or combination of channels with the exception of one—the face (Zuckerman, DePaulo, & Rosenthal, 1981). In fact, people are better off when they cannot see another's face. Facial expressions are misleading at worst and, at best, are of qualified use as cues to deceit. Gaze is not diagnostic in detecting a liar.

Tone of Voice   Paying attention to tone of voice is a better indicator of deception than is facial expression (DePaulo, Lassiter, & Stone, 1982). Useful information can come through the voice, which people do not often look for or detect. People's pitch is higher when they are lying than when they are telling the truth; they speak more slowly and with less fluency and engage in more sentence repairs (Ekman, 1992).

Microexpressions   Deception can be detected in the face if you are specially trained to look for microexpressions (or if you have a video-tape that you can play back to look for microexpressions). **Microexpressions** are expressions that people show on their face for about one-tenth of a second. These expressions reveal how a person is truly feeling, but because of social pressure and self-presentation, they are quickly wiped away by the person feeling them. As an example, consider an investigation in which the facial expressions of men and women participants were secretly observed while they were interacting with male and female assistants specially trained to act as leaders during a group discussion (Butler & Geis, 1990). The results were clear: Female leaders received more negative nonverbal cues (microexpressions) from other members of the group than did male leaders. Moreover, male leaders also received more positive nonverbal cues per minute than did female leaders. Disturbingly, these findings emerged even though participants strongly denied any bias against females.

Interchannel Discrepancies To detect deception, look for inconsistencies among these channels, such as tone of voice, body movements, gestures, and so on. As a general rule, watch the body, not the face, and look for clusters of clues. *Illustrators* are another type of body movement that can provide clues about deception (Ekman, 1992). Illustrators depict speech as it is spoken. It is the hands that usually illustrate speech—giving emphasis to a word or phrase, tracing the flow of thought in the air, drawing a picture in space, or showing an action can repeat or amplify what is being said. Eyebrow and upper eyelid movements can also provide emphasis illustrators, as can the entire body or upper torso. Illustrators are used to help explain ideas that are difficult to put into words. For example, people are more likely to illustrate when asked to define the word *zigzag* than the word *chair*. Illustrators increase with involvement with what is being said; people illustrate less than usual when they are uninvolved, bored, disinterested, or deeply saddened. Illustrators are often confused with emblems, but it is important to distinguish them because these two kinds of body movements may change in opposite ways when people lie: emblematic slips may increase, whereas illustrators will usually decrease. People who feign concern or enthusiasm can be betrayed by the failure to accompany their speech with increased illustrators, and illustrators decrease when a person does not know exactly what to say. For example, if a liar has not adequately worked out a lie in advance, the liar will have to be cautious and carefully consider each word before it is spoken.

Eye Contact People who are lying blink more often, have dilated pupils, and have lower eye contact than truth-tellers. However, blinking rates and dilation of pupils are almost impossible to detect with the naked eye (which is why "gaze" is listed as not diagnostic in Table A2-1). Although eye contact is the primary cue used by MBA students to detect deceit, it is not reliable; often, it is irrelevant, primarily because it is something that people can control too readily.

Be Aware of Egocentric Biases Most negotiators regard themselves as truthful and honest and their opponents as dishonest, indicating an egocentric bias. For example, in our investigation, MBA students thought they deceived others in a 10-week negotiation course 40 percent of the time, whereas they thought that they had been deceived by others 22 percent of the time.

How Motivation and Temptation Affects Lying and Deception

People are more likely to be deceptive when they are likely to get away with it and especially when their potential gain from deception is highest. As a case in point, Boles, Croson, and Murnighan (2000) watched how people behaved in an ultimatum situation when they had enticing prospects for large monetary gain if they deceived. Although "proposers" and "responders" chose deceptive strategies almost equally, proposers told more outright lies (Boles et al., 2000). Moreover, proposers were more deceptive when their potential profits were highest. Croson (2002) reports that proposers deceive about 13.6 percent of the time and responders deceive about 13.9 percent of the time. Moreover, at least in the short term, negotiators who deceive benefit from their deception. However, "motivated communication" is not purely opportunistic: If liars feel that they can "justify" a lie (such as when some uncertainty is involved), they are more likely to lie, even when the costs and benefits for misrepresentation are held constant (Schweitzer & Hsee, 2002).

Schweitzer, Brodt, and Croson (in press) distinguish two types of lies: monitoring-dependent and monitoring-independent. Monitoring-dependent lies require that the liar monitor the reaction of the target in order for the lie to be effective; conversely, monitoring-independent lies do not require the liar to monitor. As a case in point, if someone wants to lie about a closing date, it would be important to determine what kind of closing date is preferred by the target (one cannot assume early or late). Conversely, if one is attempting to lie about interest rates, it is safe to assume that mortgage holders would uniformly want lower rates; and thus, it is not as important to monitor their reaction to this type of statement. Consequently, liars are more likely to tell monitoring-dependent lies when they have visual access (than when they don't). The use of monitoring-independent lies is the same, with or without visual access. In this sense, visual access can actually harm potential targets of deception by increasing their risk of being deceived.

As far as people's ability to detect deception, when potential deceivers have high incentives to deceive, they are more emotional (DePaulo & Kirkendol, 1989). It is hard to conceal these feelings. An exception might be people who have great practice at lying and few qualms about the appropriateness of stretching the truth in a selling context, such as experienced salespersons (DePaulo & DePaulo, 1989).

Deception and Secrecy Can Create a Life of Their Own

People who are told to keep a secret can become preoccupied with the secret (Wegner, 1994). The secret becomes more accessible in their memory and absorbs their consciousness (as judged by word association and reaction times). Why? Keeping a secret takes mental control. Often, secrecy is linked to obsession and attraction (Wegner, Lane, & Dimitri, 1994). For example, in a card-playing game, some pairs were told to engage in "nonverbal communication" with their feet to try to influence the game. They were told to either keep it a secret from the other couple or let it be known. After the game, those players who engaged in more nonverbal, secret communication reported more attraction to the other party than those who did not engage in the secretive behavior (Wegner, Shortt, Blake, & Page, 1990).

Appendix 3

THIRD-PARTY INTERVENTION

Sometimes, despite the best of intentions, the bargaining process breaks down, and negotiators are unable to reach an agreement on their own. In such instances, parties may pursue legal action. Sometimes, on the way to court, parties try third-party intervention. Third-party intervention can be an excellent means of reaching settlement when the costs of disagreement are high.

Some negotiators make mediation-arbitration contingencies in the event of disagreement, thereby promising in advance to avoid legal action. For example, as the first wave of Y2K-inspired lawsuits began to emerge, a group of the largest companies vowed not to let the litigation grow into a torrent. A dozen multinational corporations, including General Mills, McDonald's Corp., Philip Morris, and Bank of America, signed a commitment to use mediation, not litigation, for Y2K disputes with supply-chain partners and vendors (McKendrick, 1999).

Next, we review the roles of third parties, key challenges facing third parties, and strategies for enhancing the effectiveness of third-party intervention.

Common Third-Party Roles

A third party may intervene in a dispute in a number of ways (see Rubin, Pruitt, & Kim, 1994, for a more complete discussion).

Mediation

Mediation is a procedure whereby a third party assists disputants in achieving a voluntary settlement (i.e., the mediator cannot impose a settlement on the disputants). Mediation offers the possibility of discovering underlying issues and promoting integrative agreements (McEwen & Maiman, 1984; McGrath, 1966). Mediation produces a high

settlement rate (typically 60–80 percent), though settlement is not guaranteed (Hoh, 1984; Kochan, 1979; Kressel & Pruitt, 1989). According to Ross and Conlon (2000), mediation can also serve an important face-saving function: Each party can make concessions without appearing weak. Finally, disputants often see mediation procedures as fair (Karambayya & Brett, 1989; Pierce, Pruitt, & Czaja, 1993; Ross, Conlon, & Lind, 1990).

Arbitration

Arbitration is a procedure whereby a third party holds a hearing, at which time disputants state their position on the issues, call witnesses, and offer supporting evidence for their respective positions (Ross & Conlon, 2000). After the hearing, the arbitrator issues a binding settlement. The greatest advantage of arbitration is that it always produces a settlement. Moreover, the mere threat of arbitration often motivates parties to settle voluntarily (Farber & Katz, 1979). And, similar to mediation, arbitration allows disputants to "save face" with their constituents because they can always blame the arbitrator if the imposed settlement is unsatisfactory (Marmo, 1995; Rose & Manuel, 1996). The two major types of arbitration are traditional arbitration and final-offer arbitration.

Traditional Arbitration In traditional arbitration, each side submits a proposed settlement to the arbitrator who is at liberty to come up with settlement terms that both sides must agree to. Oftentimes, the final settlement may be a midpoint between the settlement terms submitted by either party. For example, on Cybersettle.com, the online out-of-court settlement service, the algorithm immediately imposes a final settlement outcome that is midway between the last two offers submitted by either party. Thus, each side has an incentive to shape the arbitrator's final judgment by submitting an offer that is self-serving.

An obvious disadvantage of traditional arbitration is that parties may reason that the third party will impose a settlement midway between the two final proposals submitted. This expectation would of course lead the parties to submit extreme final proposals. The tendency for disputants to exaggerate their demands and reduce their level of concession making is known as the "chilling effect" (Notz & Starke, 1987).

Final-Offer Arbitration   Final-offer arbitration was developed in response to the chilling effect problem of traditional arbitration (Farber, 1981). In final-offer arbitration, the disputants submit final proposals to the arbitrator who then chooses one of the two final settlements to impose. Thus, the incentive of the parties involved is to submit a settlement that will be viewed as most fair in the eyes of the arbitrator.

Med-Arb   Recognizing the strengths (and weaknesses) of mediation and arbitration, some scholars and practitioners have advocated the adoption of hybrid procedures: mediation-arbitration and arbitration-mediation (see Ross & Conlon, 2000, for a review). Mediation-arbitration (hereafter med-arb) consists of two phases: (1) mediation, followed by (2) arbitration, if mediation fails to secure an agreement by a predetermined deadline. The same third party serves as both mediator and arbitrator (Kagel, 1976). Thus, arbitration is only engaged if mediation fails.

Arb-Med   Arbitration-mediation (hereafter arb-med) consists of three phases (see Ross & Conlon, 2000, for a review). In phase one, the third party holds an arbitration hearing. At the end of this phase, the third party makes a decision, which is placed in a sealed envelope and is not revealed to the parties. The second phase consists of mediation. The sealed envelope containing the third party's decision is displayed prominently during the mediation phase. Only if mediation fails to produce a voluntary agreement by a specified deadline, do the parties enter the third phase, called the ruling phase. Here, the third party removes the ruling from the envelope and reveals the binding ruling to the disputants (Cobbledick, 1992; Sander, 1993). To ensure that the envelope contains the original ruling and not a later decision (e.g., a ruling created after the mediation phase), the third party can ask a disputant from each side to sign the envelope across the seal at the beginning of mediation. According to Ross and Conlon (2000), the greatest benefit of arb-med is that it encourages disputants to settle their differences themselves.

In a direct test of the effectiveness of med-arb and arb-med, Conlon, Moon, and Ng (2002) pitted the two procedures against one another. Disputants in the arb-med procedures settled in the mediation phase of their procedure more frequently and achieved settlements of higher joint benefit than did disputants in the med-arb procedure.

Key Choice Points Among Third-Party Intervention

We described four key types of third-party intervention. Although each of them represents formal types of third-party intervention, more informal types of intervention are also possible. We now consider the key points of distinction—something we call choice points—involved in third-party intervention.

Outcome Versus Process Control

The key aspect in any type of third-party intervention involves the control held by the third party. The ability to control the outcome is the key distinction between mediation and arbitration. Outcome control refers to the ability of the third party to impose a final, binding settlement on the parties. In contrast, process control refers to the ability of the third party to control the discussions, questions, and process of communication.

The mediator has process control, but does not have outcome control (i.e., the power to impose a settlement). In arbitration, third parties have process and outcome control. It should be noted that arbitration may be passive or inquisitive, and the arbitrator can have full discretion to impose any kind of settlement or have constraints such as the requirement to choose one side's final offer.

Formal Versus Informal

The roles of many, perhaps most, third parties are defined on the basis of some formal understanding among the disputants, or on the basis of legal precedents or licensing and certification procedures. Third-party roles are effective to the extent that they are acknowledged by the disputants as implying a legitimate right to be in the business of resolving conflicts. Formal roles include professional mediator, arbitrator, or ombudsperson. However, a variety of informal third-party roles include those such as a friend who intervenes in a marriage dispute.

Invited Versus Uninvited

Most commonly, a third party intervenes at the request of one or both of the principals. For example, a divorcing couple may seek the services of a divorce mediator. Such invited roles are effective for two reasons: First, the invitation to intervene suggests that at least one of the parties is motivated to address the dispute in question. Second, the invitation makes the third party appropriate, acceptable, and desirable, thereby increasing clout and legitimacy. Uninvited roles may include that of a customer in an airport witnessing a conflict between a flight agent and a passenger.

Interpersonal Versus Intergroup

Third parties typically intervene in disputes between individuals. In more complex situations, third-party intervention can occur in disputes between groups or nations.

Content Versus Process Orientation

Some third-party roles focus primarily on the content of a dispute, such as the issues or substance under consideration. Others focus more on the process of decision making and on the way in which decisions are taking place. Arbitrators (and to a lesser extent, mediators) are typically content-oriented. In contrast, marriage counselors are more process-focused (i.e., trying to get each party to listen to one another, etc.).

Challenges Facing Third Parties

A number of challenges face the third party. We now outline some of the more important challenges (see Bazerman & Neale, 1992).

Increasing the Likelihood That Parties Reach an Agreement If a Positive Bargaining Zone Exists

Effective third-party intervention not only assesses whether a positive bargaining zone exists, but it helps parties reach agreement if it does. If settlement is not likely, it is to both parties' advantage to realize this issue quickly and resort to their BATNAs. For example, an increasing number of divorcing couples are settling their financial disputes through face-to-face cooperation rather than courtroom confrontations (*The Pantagraph*, June 22, 2003). The benefit of mediation, as opposed to the courtroom, is that the parties can talk back and forth and they can often reach settlement quicker. One man estimated that he saved more than $10,000 in attorney fees by settling the financial issues with his wife during a pair of two-hour mediation sessions. Moreover, rather than focusing on their "legal rights" they focus on their "future needs" (i.e., interests rather than rights focus;

see Chapter 5). However, if the divorcing couple is emotional, it may not work.

Promoting a Pareto-Efficient Outcome

It is not enough for third parties to help negotiators reach agreement. Ideally, third parties should strive for Pareto-optimal win-win agreements. Obviously, this type of agreement will not happen if the third party is not properly trained in integrative bargaining strategies or places a higher premium on reaching agreement over reaching a win-win agreement. Third parties should not let the desperation of the negotiators narrow their own view of the possibilities for integrative agreement.

Promoting Outcomes That Are Perceived as Fair in the Eyes of Disputants

When people feel that a deal is fair, they are more likely to agree to it, less likely to renege on it, and more likely to come to the table in the future. For example, take Martin Scheinman, who makes his living as a labor arbitrator. Union leaders who do not trust one another trust Scheinman. Appointed to a second presidential mediation board after the original one could not settle the LIRR dispute, Scheinman engineered a settlement with one union when all seemed hopeless. One of his keys is proposing settlements that seem fair in the eyes of disputing parties, and one of the ways that he appeals to this sense of fairness is by making parties look good (*Newsday*, Feb. 2, 1987). However, third parties can be (negatively) affected by an acrimonious relationship among disputants. For example, Thompson and Kim (2000) examined how effective mediators were in proposing solutions depending upon whether the disputants had a positive or negative relationship and whether their feelings were genuine or contrived. Mediators' suggestions were most likely to be win-win when the relationship among the negotiators

was positive and genuine. Conversely, mediators were most likely to propose fixed-pie solutions when the negotiators' relationship was negative and not genuine.

Improving the Relationship Between Parties

Ideally, effective third-party intervention should increase the level of trust and rapport between parties.

Empowering Parties in the Negotiation Process

It has been said that good therapists are those who work themselves out of a job. The same can be said of mediators. An excellent mediator not only helps parties reach integrative settlements, but improves the ability of parties to reach settlements on their own. Ideally, the ability of negotiators to effectively resolve conflict and reach effective outcomes should be enhanced via the influence of a third party.

Debiasing Negotiators

Biased perceptions run rampant among negotiators, even in the best of circumstances. When conflict has escalated and parties are emotional, biased perceptions further escalate. Third parties should attempt, whenever possible, to debias negotiations. Unfortunately, a number of biases lurk in the jungle of conflict, including the following biases.

Exaggeration of Conflict Bias   One pervasive bias exaggerates differences between oneself and the opposite party (in negotiation) and even in third parties (in mediation; Morris, 1995). For example, when students from rival universities watch the same videotape of a football game, they perceive their own team as committing fewer infractions than those attributed to their team by the opposing side (Hastorf & Cantril, 1954). The problem is that people generally underestimate the extent to which their beliefs are shaped by subjective construal rather than by direct perception of objective reality (Griffin & Ross, 1991).

Examination of partisans of both sides of contemporary social conflict (e.g., liberal versus conservative groups, pro-life versus pro-choice groups) reveal that partisans overestimate the extremity and consistency of the view of the other side (Robinson, Keltner, Ward, & Ross, 1994). For example, Allred, Hong, and Kalt (2002) examined a deep-rooted conflict between the Nez Perce Tribe and local nontribal governments that operate within the boundaries of the Nez Perce Reservation. Allred, Hong, and Kalt (2002) distinguished between "offensiveness" (attempting actions that benefit one's own side relative to the other side) and "defensiveness" (antipathy toward actions that harm one's own side to the other side's benefit). Overall, disputants were more defensive than offensive. However, disputants consistently exaggerated the offensiveness of the other side, and at the same time, underestimated the defensiveness of the other side.

Hostile Media Bias   Sometimes, parties on both sides of a conflict will view an even-handed media report to be partial to the other side. For example, news accounts of the 1982 Beirut Massacre were judged by partisans on both sides of the Arab-Israeli conflict to be partial to the other side (Vallone, Ross, & Lepper, 1985). Similarly, in another investigation, negotiators role-played an organizational mediation. Both sides to the conflict perceived the mediator to be partial to the opponent. Even when a mediator is partial to a particular side, that party often fails to realize this partiality and assumes the mediator is biased against it.

Overconfidence Bias   In general, disputants overestimate the extent to which their beliefs are shared by a third party. For example,

when negotiators are asked to estimate their likelihood of prevailing in final-offer arbitration, they are overconfident that the third party will favor their proposal (Bazerman & Neale, 1982; Neale & Bazerman, 1983). The evidence for bias in judgment is the finding that parties on both sides of the dispute estimate a greater than 50 percent chance of prevailing. Obviously, they cannot both be right.

The hostile media bias and the overconfidence bias seem to be contradictory. That is, it just cannot be that people feel that the mediator is simultaneously taking the view of the other side yet also more likely to agree with their own position. The apparent inconsistency stems from the nature of the judgment made by negotiators (Morris & Su, 1995). In a direct test of this question, Morris and Su examined negotiators' perceptions of mediator behavior in a realistic simulation of a conflict in an organization. It was revealed that each negotiator simultaneously displayed an egocentric (overconfidence) bias, evaluating his or her behavior as more successful than that of the counterparts'. However, when asked about the amount and content of the mediator's attention to disputants, they saw themselves as coming up short. Each party perceived that the mediator spent more time talking and listening to the opponent, allowing more faulty arguments from the opponent and showing less resistance to the opponent's persuasion attempts. Also, both sides perceived the mediator as less receptive to their concerns and less active in exploring their interests than those of the opponent.

Maintaining Neutrality

Nothing guarantees that third parties are neutral (Gibson, Thompson, & Bazerman, 1994). In fact, third parties evince many of the biases that plague principals, such as framing effects (Carnevale, 1995). Even a neutral mediator may be mistakenly viewed as partial to one's adversary (Morris & Su, 1995). Also, third parties may have a bias to broker an agreement at any cost, which may be disadvantageous to the principals—if no positive bargaining zone exists. Finally, the threat of third-party intervention may inhibit settlement if principals believe that an arbitrator is inclined to impose a compromise settlement. For this reason, final-offer arbitration may be more effective than traditional arbitration (Farber, 1981; see also Chelius & Dworkin, 1980; cited in Raiffa, 1982, table 4).

Managers are often called on to resolve disputes in organizations (Tornow & Pinto, 1976). In contrast to traditional arbitrators and mediators, managers may have a direct stake in the outcome and an ongoing relationship with the disputants. In addition, managers are more likely to have technical expertise and background knowledge about the dispute. Although several intervention techniques are available to managers, they often choose techniques that maximize their own control over the outcome (Karambayya & Brett, 1989; Sheppard, 1984).

Strategies for Enhancing Effectiveness of Third-Party Intervention

What steps can negotiators take to maximize the effectiveness of third-party intervention or, ideally, avoid it altogether? Consider the following steps.

Test Your Own Position

A good scientist will set up an experiment that includes "blinds." For example, in testing the effectiveness of a particular drug, some patients might be given the drug and the other group a placebo or sugar pill. The experimenters further blind themselves to which group was given what and assesses the outcome. The same should be true for your own negotiation position. For example, if you find yourself in a terrible struggle with a merchant or neighbor, describe the situation in such a way to the third party so as not to indicate what role you are playing in the struggle. Then ask the third party for an honest opinion.

Role-Play a Third Party in Your Own Dispute

Describe the negotiation situation you are in to some colleagues who might be willing to play the roles involved. Then take on the role of a third party in the situation. Try to come up with a solution to which both parties feel comfortable agreeing.

Training in Win-Win Negotiation

Perhaps no other skill is as important as the ability to focus on expanding the size of the bargaining zone through the discovery of interests and then fashioning value-added trade-offs.

NEGOTIATING A JOB OFFER

When negotiating a job, you need all the essential skills covered in Part I (Chapters 1, 2, 3, and 4). In addition, you should be comfortable with your own bargaining style (and know its limits; see Chapter 5). You should be well versed in building trust and rapport (Chapter 6) and know the ins and outs of power (Chapter 7) and how to kindle creativity (Chapter 8). This appendix is designed to provide you with even more skills for this all-important negotiation that will reoccur throughout your life. We organized this appendix into three phases: preparation, in-vivo process, and postoffer.

Preparation

Salary negotiations are extremely important negotiations because they affect your livelihood and welfare for years to come. A misassumption at this point can have dramatic effects on your quality of life.

Step 1: Figure Out What You Really Want

This step sounds easy enough, but for a 28-year-old, it means an ability to project forward in time and to be concerned with things such as retirement and benefits. Karen Cates of the Kellogg School (1997) recommends working through a checklist of needs and wants (see Box A4-1). Cates further suggests a practical, step-by-step approach to compensation and benefits (see Table A4-1).

Step 2: Do Your Homework

Research the company and the industry. Fortunately, the Internet is dramatically changing the ability of people to get information quickly and easily, especially when it comes to salaries. Several Web sites offer salary surveys, job listings with specified pay levels, and even customized compensation analyses. For example, JobStar, run by a regional public library agency in California, offers links to more than 300 free salary surveys on the Web. ExecuNet, a for-profit job search network, divulges information about the salary, bonus, and stock options offered for the thousands of upper-management positions in their online database. However, for many jobs, cyberspace pay information represents only a starting point. In other words, these Web sites can only tell you if you are in the ballpark and can stop you from underbidding yourself (see Sidebar A4-1).

It is important to do your homework so that you don't ask for something that has already been institutionalized. For example, many companies have on-site chefs because they realized that it just does not make sense to break at noon, have everyone get in cars, and go and get lunch.

Step 3: Determine Your BATNA and Your Aspiration

A negotiator always has a BATNA. Some students who are beginning to negotiate with firms will agitatedly claim that they do not have a BATNA because they do not have any job offers in hand. They may not have an *attractive* BATNA, but they inevitably will do something with their lives if they do not get a job offer. Perhaps they will simply "extend" their job search indefinitely; perhaps they will travel abroad; perhaps they will do freelance or volunteer work, take a research assistantship at a university, or search for a nonprofessional job while they continue their career search. All of these options are possible BATNAs; they should be assessed and the best one focused upon and evaluated carefully.

BOX A4-1

CHECKLIST OF NEEDS AND WANTS

Necessary Living Expenses	*Additional Living Expenses*
Housing (including utilities)	Recreation and entertainment (vacations, events, activities, books, etc.)
Auto	
Computer	Services (professional and household)
Child care	Continuing education
Insurance (auto, home, life, professional)	Children's expenses (lessons, schooling)
Personal (food, medical, clothing, household)	Gifts, charity
Student loan debt service	
Taxes (income, property, etc.)	

Source: Cates, K. (1997). Tips for negotiating a job offer. Unpublished manuscript, Kellogg School of Management, Northwestern University, Evanston, IL.

TABLE A4-1 Compensation and Benefits (Cates, 1997)			
Compensation	*Retirement*	*Paid Leave*	*Protection*
Salary	Pension/401K	Vacation, sick, and personal days	Insurance (life, disability, health, other)
Bonus	Guaranteed pay plans (supplemental unemployment)	Training time	
Other variable pay		Holidays and special travel considerations	Care plans (child, elder)
Stock/equity interest	Savings plans		Wellness programs

Our BATNAs are never as attractive as we would like them to be. The rare times when we have two or more fabulous job offers in hand, two bids on our house, and lucrative investment opportunities, we can afford to push for a lot more in negotiations. Obviously, you are in a much better position to successfully negotiate an attractive compensation package if your BATNA is attractive. As we stated in Chapter 2, your BATNA is dynamic, and it is important to not be passive about it.

It is important to think about how we might improve upon our BATNA. Most negotiators do not spend adequate time attempting to improve their current situa-tion. As a result, they approach negotiations feeling more desperate than they need to be.

Step 4: Research the Employer's BATNA
Developing your BATNA is only half of the work that needs to be done before the nego-tiation. The next step is to determine the other party's BATNA, which requires tap-ping into multiple sources of information.

Step 5: Determine the Issue Mix
You have made your best assessment of the employer's BATNA. The negotiation is fast approaching. Now what? The next step is to determine the issues that are important

to you in this negotiation. Do not make the mistake of letting the employer define the issues for you. Be ready to talk about your interests and needs.

Sidebar A4-1. How the Internet Can Help You Obtain a Better Salary

Executive recruiter Korn/Ferry International unexpectedly got a firsthand lesson in salary information on cyberspace when they created an electronic job-search venture called Futurestep with *The Wall Street Journal*. To compile an internal database of possible applicants for midlevel managerial vacancies, Futurestep offers people a free analysis of their salary and bonus potential, among other things. Unexpectedly, several Korn/Ferry recruiters signed up for Futurestep and found that they were underpaid. For example, Peter Reed, a 28-year-old recruiter in Korn/Ferry's Chicago office, says that he found out he was 18 percent below prevailing rates. Reed says that Futurestep analysis will be part of his action plan when it comes to review time. The result: Korn/Ferry increased Reed's base salary 10 percent (*The Wall Street Journal*, Sept. 22, 1998).

After you determine which issues are important from your perspective, go back through your list and attempt to create an even more detailed list, breaking down each of the issues into smaller and smaller subsets. Breaking up the issues into smaller subsets does two things. First, it allows the negotiator to be much more specific about what is important (e.g., the paid aspect of a vacation or the number of days allowed off). Second, it provides much greater opportunity for creative agreements.

In addition to focusing on the issues and concerns of importance to you, anticipate the other party's perspective. Again, information and research can help here.

Step 6: Prepare Several Scenarios

Most likely, the negotiations will not go at all as planned. Rather than being caught off guard, prepare your response to several different scenarios, including the following:

- The employer agrees immediately to your counteroffer.
- The employer makes a low-ball offer (in your eyes) and flatly states, "This is our final offer."
- The employer makes one small concession.
- The employer asks you to make a reasonable offer.

Step 7: Consider Getting a "Coach"

A job coach is someone who can help people advance their careers and achieve their compensation goals. Job coaches are people who help managers plan their future. The way that Peter Goodman, CEO of MyJobCoach, puts it, "If you have a legal issue, you go to a lawyer for advice. When doing financial planning, you go to an accountant. So why would you not go to a career coach when planning your career, the area where you spend over 70% of your waking life?" The number of "job coaches" has grown from 5,300 nationwide in 1998 to more than 10,000 in 2001 (*Business Wire*, July 30, 2001). CEOs have always taken coaching seriously, at least when it comes to negotiating their compensation packages. For example, Joseph Bachelder has negotiated job contracts for top corporate executives for 23 years (*The Wall Street Journal*, June 25, 2003). His hourly rate of $975 does not deter George Fisher (Eastman Kodak), Patricia Russo (Lucent), Lou Gerstner, Jamie Dimon (Bank One), and executives at Allied Signal and IBM. He also negotiates severance for departures, including that of Jack Grubman, former Salomon Smith Barney telecom analyst. In his typical role, he invites CEOs to talk about their financial goals. Bachelder employs a Ph.D. mathematician, B. Roslyn Abramov, to help leverage the number-crunching showdowns. He is not reluctant to remind companies that terminated executives can be important witnesses in continuing litigation. Moreover, savvy companies often suggest that their employees use Bachelder. For example, Lucent suggested that Richard McGinn, dismissed as CEO in October 2000, use Bachelder because they reasoned that his expertise in wrapping up matters ultimately would serve Lucent well. In other cases, ousted executives want to restart their careers quickly and be freed from a thicket of noncompete clauses. One such client, Jamie Dimon (previously Citigroup), hired Bachelder to ensure that he could take helm of Bank One and take six of his former colleagues with him.

In Vivo: During the Negotiation Itself

You have done your preparation. Now it is time for the actual negotiation.

Think About the Best Way to Position and Present Your Opening Offer

Remember to back up your offer with a compelling rationale. Use objective standards. Focus and select those standards that are favorable to you, and be prepared to indicate why standards unfavorable to you are inappropriate.

Assume That Their Offer Is Negotiable

Do not ask, "Can we negotiate this offer you have made?" because a negative response can put you in a weak position. Rather, assume that the offer is negotiable and begin by articulating your needs and interests. Cates (1997) advises saying the following: "I have

some questions about the insurance coverage that I would like to talk about if we can," or "I have some concerns about your moving allowance, and I need to talk to you about it." A survey conducted by the Society for Human Resource Management found that 8 out of 10 recruiters were willing to negotiate pay and benefits with job applicants, but only one-third of the job applicants surveyed said they felt comfortable negotiating (*U.S. News and World Report*, Nov. 1, 1999). Most job applicants do not push employers at the negotiating table. The failure to negotiate a first offer from an employer can cost workers a lot of money. "A 22-year-old who secures a $2,000 increase in annual salary at his or her first job will, because of the compounding effects of years of raises to follow, most likely generate roughly $150,000 in extra income over the course of a 40-year career" (*U.S. News and World Report*, Nov. 1, 1999). The effect is even more dramatic for an MBA student negotiating a $90,000 job offer. What's more, if you do not negotiate for what you want in that brief window between your receipt of a job offer and your acceptance of it, you may never get it. You are never more powerful than when you are responding to "their offer" because it is the one time the employer may want you more than you want them (*U.S. News and World Report*, Nov. 1, 1999). What are some things to ask for in your negotiation? (For a list of possibilities, see Sidebar A4-2.)

Sidebar A4-2. Things to Ask for When Negotiating an Offer

Some things to ask for when negotiating an offer (other than a higher salary, which is always worth asking for):

- Paid time off plans
- Free parking
- Season passes (ski lift, opera, whatever you fancy)

continued

- Money to move your hobbies (horses, motorcycles) to the new location
- Right to hire an assistant
- Right to take three-hour lunches (as long as the work gets done)
- Right to take off of work if the wind is blowing at a certain speed (if your hobby is windsurfing)
- Car
- Signing bonus (or bonus for achieving certain milestones)
- Severance pay
- Stock options or profit sharing
- Accelerated performance review (if you are confident that you need only six months to prove you deserve a raise)
- Clothing allowance (typical only in the fashion and entertainment industries)
- Computer, cell phone, laptop, or other home-office equipment (especially common at technology companies, but spreading quickly)
- Flexible scheduling (does not cost real cash)
- Memberships: dues for professional associations and athletic clubs
- Telecommuting: ask for this ahead of time, because most companies still handle this issue on a worker-by-worker basis
- Tuition reimbursement and coverage of books, fees, noncore courses
- Vacation: extra days and scheduling
- Pet health insurance
- Concierge and dry-cleaning services
- On-site fitness centers
- Prepared, take-home meals

Sources: *U.S. News and World Report*, Nov. 1, 1999; *Crain's Detroit Business*, May 7, 2001.

Immediately Reanchor Them by Reviewing Your Needs and Your Rationale

Indicate your interest in working for their company, and tell them how your needs (and wants) can be met in a variety of ways. Many candidates reach impasse because employers falsely assumed that the candidates did not want the job when they did. Thus, keep reiterating your heartfelt interest in their company. Cates (1997) advises to "get your requests on the table and keep them there." According to Cates, salary negotiations are really about candidates helping recruiters to solve their problems. In other words, let the employer know what they can do to make their offer more appealing. This offer of information may even come to sharing your own prioritization and MAUT analysis of the issues.

Do Not Reveal Your BATNA Nor Your Reservation Point

Negotiators have a million ways of asking people about their BATNAs. Asking a potential job recruit about his or her current salary and wage package is one of them. Remember that this information is your business, not the recruiter's. If you are currently employed, redirect the discussion by indicating what it is going to take to move you (e.g., a more exciting job and a wage package commensurate with the job). If you are not employed, respond by explaining what it will take to hire you. Again, ward off direct attacks about previous salary by explaining that whether you will accept a position depends on the nature of the job offer and wage package.

You should be prepared to take the initiative in the conversation. Practice by role-playing. If the employer attempts to get you to talk about why you are leaving a former job, avoid falling into the trap of trashing a former employer, even if you did have a miserable experience. It is a small world, and a relationship you do not immediately see may be involved. Even more important, the employer will probably get the wrong impression about you (e.g., regard you as a troublemaker or as overly critical).

If you have not yet been offered the job but sense that the employer wants to find out what you desire in a job offer, avoid talking about salary or specific terms until you have a job offer. You are in a much weaker position to negotiate before you have a job offer than after you are offered a position. If you have been told that "things will work out" or that "a job offer is coming," express appreciation and inquire when you will receive formal notice. After that, schedule a meeting to talk about the terms. While you are negotiating, you shou..d assume that everything is negotiable. If you are told that some aspect of the job is "not negotiable," ask questions, such as whether everyone (new hires and veterans) receives the same treatment.

Rehearse and Practice

It is important to plan for negotiation. According to Michael Chaffers, a senior consultant with CMI, a negotiation group in Cambridge, Massachusetts, "A pitch for a raise is no different than making a presentation on any subject: It helps to practice beforehand and even do some role playing. Tell an empty chair what you plan to say to your boss (though you might want to make sure no one's around to see you). If you can find a willing participant, have them play the boss, while acting cantankerous and giving you flack" (*Machine Design*, Feb. 11, 1999, p. 96).

Imagine That You Are Negotiating on Behalf of Someone Else (Not Just Yourself)

Many people are reluctant to negotiate their job offer because they feel greedy or have a hard time acting assertively. However, these same people are quite effective when negotiating for a company or for someone else. One solution is to approach a job negotiation as if you were negotiating on behalf of an important company: your own family. If we think about the direct effect that our salary will have on our ability to provide for our children, our spouse, and our parents, we can be much more effective. Even the unmarried student without children is well-advised to think about the family he or she will have or might have in the not-so-distant future and negotiate on the behalf of those people.

Postoffer: You Have the Offer, Now What?

Do Not Immediately Agree to the Offer

Do not start negotiating until you have a firm job offer and a salary figure from the employer. Do not prolong things, however; this approach only frustrates the employer. Instead, give the employer positive reinforcement. Cates (1997) suggests something like, "This looks great. I need to go over everything one last time before we make this official. I will call you at [a specific time]."

Get the Offer in Writing

If the employer says that it is not standard to make written offers, be sure to consult with others who would know this (e.g., the company's human resources division). At the very least, inform them that you will write down your understanding of the terms and put it in a letter or memo to them. Keep notes for yourself regarding the points agreed to during each meeting.

Be Enthusiastic and Gracious

Someone has just made you an offer. Thank them and show your appreciation, but do not accept immediately. Say, instead, "Let me go home and think about it." Make an appointment to return the following day and state your negotiating position in person.

Assess Their Power to Negotiate with You

Before you begin negotiating or contemplating a counteroffer, determine who in the company has the ability to negotiate. Generally, those persons higher up in the organization are the ones who negotiate and the ones who care most about hiring good people. You should be well-versed about the advantages and disadvantages of negotiating with an intermediary, such as a human resources manager (see Chapter 9 on multiple parties). If you sense that things are not going well in the negotiation, try to bring someone else into the loop. However, make this move in a gracious way, so as not to antagonize the person with whom you are dealing.

Tell Them Exactly What Needs to Be Done for You to Agree

A powerful negotiating strategy is to let the employer know exactly what it will take for you to agree. This technique is effective because the employer can put aside any fears about the negotiation dragging on forever and being nickel-and-dimed to death. When you make your demands, though, ground them in logic and clear rationale. Requesting something too far out of whack may lose you the job. Ross Gibson, vice president for human resources at American Superconductor in Boston, says he judges applicants by the way they negotiate—and withdraws offers from those who come across as immature or greedy (*U.S. News and World Report*, Nov. 1, 1999).

Do Not Negotiate If You Are Not or Could Not Be Interested

Suppose that you are the lucky person sitting on four job offers, all from consulting firms (A, B, C, and D). You have done enough research, cost-benefit analysis, and soul searching to determine that, in your mind, firms A and B are superior in all ways to firms C and D. The question is: Should you let firms C and D off the hook, or string them along so as to potentially improve your power position when negotiating with firms A and B? Our advice is to politely inform firms C and D that you will not be accepting their offers at this time. You still have a wonderful BATNA, and it saves everyone a lot of time.

Exploding Offers

Exploding offers are ones that have a "time bomb" element to them (e.g., "The offer is only good for 24 hours"). The question is how to deal with exploding offers. Consider the case of Carla, who has no less than six interviews scheduled, including one interview at company A. Company A interviews Carla and makes her an exploding offer, with a deadline of the following week. Carla's interviews extend into the next four weeks. What should she do? This situation obviously requires a gambling decision (see Appendix 1 on risky decision making). In our experience, firms usually do not rescind exploding offers once they have made them (unless it is for family, medical, and emergency reasons, as a matter of courtesy). Generally, we advise that job candidates who receive an exploding offer above their BATNA seriously consider the offer. It certainly cannot hurt to inform your other companies that you have an exploding offer and move up the time of the interview, if at all possible.

Do Not Try to Create a Bidding War

Bidding wars regularly occur on Wall Street, in professional athletics, and in the business world. We do not advise, however, that job candidates attempt to create bidding wars between companies. Rather, we advise that job candidates signal to potential employers that they have attractive BATNAs, that they do not want to start a bidding war, and that they tell their top-rated company what it would take to get them to work at the company.

Know When to Stop Pushing

According to Cates (1997), it is important to know when to stop negotiating. Cates suggests that negotiators stop when they see one or more of the following signals.

- The other side is not responsive.
- Reciprocal concessions are becoming miniscule.
- After some back and forth, they say "Enough!"

Use a Rational Strategy for Choosing Among Job Offers

If you find yourself in the lucky position of having multiple offers, you are then faced with a choice. First, you should recognize this enviable position as an approach-approach conflict. How should you weigh the choices?

The simplest way is to use MAUT by constructing a grid listing the choices along a row (e.g., firm A, firm B) and the relevant attributes along a column underneath (e.g., salary, fringe benefits, travel, vacation, bonus, etc.). Then, fill in the grid with the details of the offer and how they "stack up" compared to the others (on a scale of 1 to 5 or 1 to 10 in your mind). Next, you can simply add the columns to find a "winner." A more sophisticated version of this strategy is to multiply each grid value by how important it is before adding columns (with importance defined on a scale of 1 to 5). For example, for most people, salary is highly important (maybe a 5), whereas moving expenses are less important (maybe a 1 or 2). This distinction gives a more fine-grained assessment (see Appendix 1 for a step-by-step approach to the MAUT).

Academic References

Abel, M. J. (1990). Experiences in an exploratory distributed organization. In J. Galegher, R. E. Kraut, & C. Egido (Eds.), *Intellectual Teamwork: Social and Technological Foundations of Cooperative Work* (pp. 489–510). Hillsdale, NJ: Lawrence Erlbaum.

Abramowitz, C. V., Abramowitz, S. I., & Weitz, L. J. (1976). Are men therapists soft on empathy? Two studies in feminine understanding. *Journal of Clinical Psychology*, 32(2), 434–437.

Ackerman, B. A., & Stewart, R. B. (1988). Reforming environmental law: The democratic case for market incentives. *Columbia Journal of Environmental Law*, 13, 171–199.

Adair, W. (1999a). Exploring the norm of reciprocity in the global market: U.S. and Japanese intra- and intercultural negotiations. Working paper, J. L. Kellogg Graduate School of Management, Northwestern University, Evanston, IL.

Adair, W. (1999b). U. S. and Japanese mental models for negotiation. Working paper, J. L. Kellogg Graduate School of Management, Northwestern University, Evanston, IL.

Adair, W. (2003). Integrative sequences and negotiation outcome in same- and mixed-culture negotiations. Working paper, Northwestern University, Evanston, IL.

Adair, W., & Brett, J. M. (2003). The negotiation dance: Time, culture, and behavioral sequences in negotiation. Working paper, Dispute Resolution Research Center, Northwestern University, Evanston, IL.

Adair, W., Okumura, T., & Brett, J. M. (2001). Negotiation behavior when cultures collide: The U.S. and Japan. *Journal of Applied Psychology*, 86(3), 371–385.

Adams, S. (1965). Inequity in social exchange. In L. Berkowitz (Ed.), *Advances in Experimental Social Psychology*, vol. 2. New York: Academic Press.

Adamson, R. E., & Taylor, D. W. (1954). Functional fixedness as related to elapsed time and situation. *Journal of Experimental Psychology*, 47, 122–216.

Adler, N. J. (1991). *International Dimensions of Organizational Behavior*. Boston: PWK-Kent.

Akerlof, G. (1970). The market for lemons: Quality uncertainty and the market mechanism. *Quarterly Journal of Economics*, 84, 488–500.

Alge, B. J., Wiethoff, C., & Klein, H. J. (2003). When does the medium matter? Knowledge-building experiences and opportunities in decision-making teams. *Organizational Behavior and Human Decision Processes*, 91, 26–37.

Allen, T. J. (1977). *Managing the Flow of Technology: Technology Transfer and the Dissemination of Technological Information Within the R&D Organization*. Cambridge, MA: MIT Press.

Allison, S. T., & Messick, D. M. (1990). Social decision heuristics in the use of shared resources. *Journal of Behavioral Decision Making*, 3(3), 195–204.

Allred, K. G. (2000). Anger and retaliation in conflict: The role of attribution. In M. Deutsch & P. T. Coleman (Eds.), *The handbook of conflict resolution: Theory and Practice* (pp. 236–255). San Francisco: Jossey-Bass.

Allred, K. G., Hong, K., & Kalt, J. P. (2002). Partisan misperceptions and conflict escalation: Survey evidence from a tribal/local government conflict. Paper presented at the

International Association of Conflict Management, Park City, UT.

Allred, K. G., Mallozzi, J. S., Matsui, F., & Raia, C. P. (1997). The influence of anger and compassion on negotiation performance. *Organizational Behavior and Human Decision Processes*, 70(3), 175–187.

Ancona, D. G., Friedman, R. A., & Kolb, D. M. (1991). The group and what happens on the way to "yes." *Negotiation Journal*, 7(2), 155–173.

Anderson, C. M., & Camerer, C. (2000). Experience-weighted attraction learning in sender-receiver signaling games. *Economic Theory*, 16, 689–718.

Anderson, J. R. (1995). *Cognitive Psychology and Its Implications*, 4th ed. New York: Freeman.

Argyle, M., & Henderson, M. (1984). The rules of relationships. In S. Duck & D. Perlman (Eds.), *Understanding Personal Relationships: An Interdisciplinary Approach*. Beverly Hills, CA: Sage.

Argyris, C. (2002). Double-loop learning, teaching, and research. *Academy of Management Learning and Education*, 1(2), 206–218.

Armstrong, D. J., & Cole, P. (1995). Managing distances and differences in geographically distributed work groups. In S. E. Jackson & M. N. Ruderman (Eds.), *Diversity in Work Teams: Research Paradigms for a Changing Workplace* (pp. 187–215). Washington, DC: American Psychological Association.

Aronson, E., & Bridgeman, D. (1979). Jigsaw groups and the desegregated classroom: In pursuit of common goals. *Personality and Social Psychology Bulletin*, 5, 438–446.

Aronson, E., & Linder, D. (1965). Gain and loss of esteem as determinants of interpersonal attractiveness. *Journal of Experimental Social Psychology*, 1(2), 156–171.

Aronson, E., Willerman, B., & Floyd, J. (1966). The effect of a pratfall on increasing interpersonal attractiveness. *Psychonomic Science*, 4, 227–228.

Arrow, K. J. (1963). *Social Choice and Individual Values*. New Haven, CT: Yale University Press.

Aubert, V. (1963). Competition and dissensus: Two types of conflict and conflict resolution. *Conflict Resolution*, 7, 26–42.

Austin, W. (1980). Friendship and fairness: Effects of type of relationship and task performance on choice of distribution rules. *Personality and Social Psychology Bulletin*, 6, 402–408.

Axelrod, R. (1984). *The Evolution of Cooperation*. New York: Basic Books.

Babcock, L., Loewenstein, G., Issacharoff, S., & Camerer, C. (1995). Biased judgments of fairness in bargaining. *The American Economic Review*, 85(5), 1337–1343.

Back, K. W. (1951). Influence through social communication. *Journal of Abnormal Social Psychology*, 46, 9–23.

Balke, W. M., Hammond, K. R., & Meyer, G. D. (1973). An alternate approach to labor-management relations. *Administrative Science Quarterly*, 18(3), 311–327.

Bargh, J. A., Lombardi, W. J., & Higgins, E. T. (1988). Automaticity of chronically accessible constructs in person-situation effects on person perception: It's just a matter of time. *Journal of Personality and Social Psychology*, 55(4), 599–605.

Barnett, V. (2003). The use of information technology in a strike. *Journal of Labor Research*, 24(1), 55–72.

Baron, J. (1988). *Decision Analysis and Utility Measurement. Thinking and Deciding* (pp. 330–351). Boston: Cambridge University Press.

Baron, J., & Spranca, M. (1997). Protected values. *Organization Behavior and Human Decision Processes*, 70(1), 1–16.

Baron, R. A. (1990). Environmentally induced positive affect: Its impact on self-efficacy, task performance, negotiation, and conflict. *Journal of Applied Social Psychology*, 20(5), 368–384.

Barron, L. A. (2003). Ask and you shall receive? Gender differences in negotiators' beliefs about requests for a higher salary. *Human Relations*, 56(6), 635.

Barron, R. S., Kerr, N. L., & Miller, N. (1992). *Group Process, Group Decision, Group Action*. Pacific Grove, CA: Brooks/Cole.

Barry, B., & Oliver, R. L. (1996). Affect in dyadic negotiation: A model and propositions. *Organization Behavior and Human Decision Processes*, 67(2), 127–144.

Baumeister, R. F., Leith, K. P., Muraven, M., & Bratslavsky, E. (1998). Self-regulation as a key to success in life. In D. Pushkar & W. M. Bukowski (Eds.), *Improving Competence Across the Lifespan: Building Interventions Based and Theory and Research* (pp. 117–132). New York: Plenum Press.

Bazerman, M. H., Curhan, J. R., Moore, D. A., & Valley, K. L. (2000). Negotiation. *Annual Review of Psychology*, 51, 279–314.

Bazerman, M. H., Gibbons, R., Thompson, L., & Valley, K. L. (1998). Can negotiators outperform game theory? In J. Halpern & R. Stern (Eds.), *Debating Rationality: Nonrational Aspects of Organizational Decision Making* (pp. 78–98). Ithaca, NY: ILR Press.

Bazerman, M. H., & Gillespie, J. J. (1999). Betting on the future: The virtues of contingent contracts. *Harvard Business Review,* 77(4), 155–160.

Bazerman, M. H., Loewenstein, G, & White, S. (1992). Reversals of preference in allocating decisions: Judging an alternative versus choosing among alternatives. *Administrative Science Quarterly,* 37, 220–240.

Bazerman, M. H., Magliozzi, T., & Neale, M. A. (1985). Integrative bargaining in a competitive market. *Organizational Behavior and Human Decision Processes*, 35(3), 294–313.

Bazerman, M. H., Mannix, E., & Thompson, L. (1988). Groups as mixed-motive negotiations. In E. J. Lawler & B. Markovsky (Eds.), *Advances in Group Processes: Theory and Research,* vol. 5. Greenwich, CT: JAI Press.

Bazerman, M. H., & Neale, M. A. (1982). Improving negotiation effectiveness under final offer arbitration: The role of selection and training. *Journal of Applied Psychology,* 67(5), 543–548.

Bazerman, M. H., & Neale, M. A. (1983). Heuristics in negotiation: Limitations to effective dispute resolution. In M. Bazerman & R. Lewicki (Eds.), *Negotiating in Organizations* (pp. 51–67). Beverly Hills, CA: Sage.

Bazerman, M. H., & Neale, M. A. (1992). *Negotiating Rationally.* New York: Free Press.

Bazerman, M. H., Neale, M. A., Valley, K., Zajac, E., & Kim, P. (1992). The effect of agents and mediators on negotiation outcomes. *Organizational Behavior and Human Decision Processes*, 53, 55–73.

Bazerman, M. H., Russ, L. E., & Yakura, E. (1987). Post-settlement settlements in dyadic negotiations: The need for renegotiation in complex environments. *Negotiation Journal*, 3, 283–297.

Beaman, A. L., Cole, N., Preston, M., Glentz, B., & Steblay, N. M. (1983). Fifteen years of the foot-in-the-door research: A meta-analysis. *Personality and Social Psychology Bulletin*, 9, 181–186.

Beersma, B., & De Dreu, C. K. W. (2002). Integrative and distributive negotiation in small groups: Effects of task structure, decision rule, and social motive. *Organizational Behavior and Human Decision Processes*, 87(2), 227–252.

Benbow, C. P., & Stanley, J. C. (1980). Sex differences in mathematical ability: Fact or artifact? *Science*, 210(4475), 1262–1264.

Benson, P. L., Karabenick, S. A., & Lerner, R. M. (1976). Pretty pleases: The effects of physical attractiveness, race, and sex on receiving help. *Journal of Experimental Social Psychology*, 12(5), 409–415.

Ben-Yoav, O., & Pruitt, D. G. (1984). Accountability to constituents: A two-edged sword. *Organization Behavior and Human Processes,* 34, 282–295.

Berkowitz, L. (1972). Social norms, feelings and other factors affecting helping behavior and altruism. In L. Berkowitz (Ed.), *Advances in Experimental Social Psychology,* vol. 6 (pp. 63–108). New York: Academic Press.

Bernieri, F. J. (1991). Interpersonal sensitivity in teaching interactions. *Personality and Social Psychology Bulletin*, 17(1), 98–103.

Bernieri, F. J., Davis, J., Rosenthal, R., & Knee, C. (1994). Interactional synchrony and rapport: Measuring synchrony in displays devoid of sound and facial affect. *Personality and Social Psychology Bulletin*, 20, 303–311.

Bernoulli, D. (L. Sommer, trans.). (1954). Exposition of a new theory on the measurement of risk. (Original work published in 1738.) *Econometrica*, 22, 23–36.

Berry, J. W. (1980). Acculturation as varieties of adaptation. In A. Padilla (Ed.), *Acculturation:*

Theory, Models, and Some New Findings. Boulder, CO: Westview.

Berry, J. W., Poortinga, Y. H., Segall, M. H., & Dasen, P. R. (1992). *Cross-Cultural Psychology: Research and Applications.* New York: Cambridge University Press.

Bettenhausen, K., & Murnighan, J. K. (1985). The emergence of norms in competitive decision-making groups. *Administrative Science Quarterly*, 30, 350–372.

Bies, R. J., Shapiro, D. L., & Cummings, L. L. (1988). Causal accounts and managing organizational conflict: Is it enough to say it's not my fault? *Communication Research*, 15(4), 381–399.

Billings, D. K. (1989). Individualism and group orientation. In D. M. Keats, D. Munroe, & L. Mann (Eds.), *Heterogeneity in Cross-Cultural Psychology* (pp. 22–103). Lisse, The Netherlands: Swets and Zeitlinger.

Blau, P. M. (1964). *Exchange and Power in Social Life.* New York: Wiley.

Blount-White, S., Valley, K., Bazerman, M., Neale, M., & Peck, S. (1994). Alternative models of price behavior in dyadic negotiations: Market prices, reservation prices, and negotiator aspirations, *Organizational Behavior and Human Decision Processes*, 57(3), 430–447.

Bobo, L. (1983). Whites' opposition to busing: Symbolic racism or realistic group conflict? *Journal of Personality and Social Psychology*, 45(6), 1196–1210.

Boles, T., Croson, R., & Murnighan, J. K. (2000). Deception and retribution in repeated ultimatum bargaining. *Organizational Behavior and Human Decision Processes*, 83(2), 235–259.

Bolton, G. E., Chatterjee, K., & McGinn, K. L. (2003). How communication links influence coalition bargaining: A laboratory investigation. *Management Science,* 49(5), 583–598.

Bottom, W. P. (1996). Negotiating risks: Sources of uncertainty and the impact of reference points on concession-making and settlements. Unpublished manuscript, Washington University, St. Louis, MO.

Bottom, W. P. (1998). Negotiator risk: Sources of uncertainty and the impact of reference points on negotiated agreements. *Organizational Behavior and Human Decision Processes*, 76(2), 89–112.

Bottom, W. P., Eavey, C. L., & Miller, G. J. (1996). Getting to the core: Coalitional integrity as a constraint on the power of agenda setters. *Journal of Conflict Resolution*, 40(2), 298–319.

Bottom, W. P., Eavey, C. L., Miller, G. J., & Victor, J. N. (2000). The institutional effect on majority rule instability: Bicameralism in spatial policy decisions. *American Journal of Political Science*, 44(3), 523–540.

Bottom, W. P., Gibson, K., Daniels, S., & Murnighan, J. K. (1996). Rebuilding relationships: Defection, repentance, forgiveness and reconciliation. Working paper, Washington University, St. Louis, MO.

Bottom, W. P., Gibson, K., Daniels, S., & Murnighan, J. K. (2000). Resurrecting cooperation: The effects of explanations, penance, and relationships. Working paper, Washington University, St. Louis, MO.

Bottom, W. P., Gibson, K., Daniels, S., & Murnighan, J. K. (2002). When talk is not cheap: Substantive penance and expressions of intent in rebuilding cooperation. *Organization Science*, 13(5), 497–513.

Bottom, W. P., Handlin, L., King, R. R., & Miller, G. J. (in press). Institutional modifications of majority rule. Forthcoming in C. Plott & V. Smith (Eds.), *Handbook of Experimental Economics Results,* Amsterdam: Elsevier.

Bottom, W. P., Holloway, J., McClurg, S., & Miller, G. J. (2000). Negotiating a coalition: Risk, quota shaving, and learning to bargain. *Journal of Conflict Resolution*, 44(2), 147–169.

Bottom, W. P., Holloway, J., Miller, G. J., Mislin, A., & Whitford, A. (2003). Gift exchange and outcome based incentives in principal-agent negotiations. Working paper, Washington University, St. Louis, MO.

Bottom, W. P., Ladha, K., & Miller, G. J. (2002). Propagation of individual bias through group judgment: Error in the treatment of asymmetrically informative signals. *Journal of Risk and Uncertainty*, 25(2), 147–163.

Bottom, W. P., & Paese, P. W. (1999). Judgment accuracy and the asymmetric cost of errors in distributive bargaining. *Group Decision and Negotiation*, 8, 349–364.

Bottom, W. P., & Studt, A. (1993). Framing effects and the distributive aspect of integrative bargaining. *Organizational Behavior and Human Decision Processes*, 56(3), 459–474.

Bradford, D. L., & Cohen, A. R. (1984). *Managing for Excellence.* New York: John Wiley and Sons.

Brehm, S. S. (1983). Psychological reactance and social differentiation. *Bulletin de Psychologie*, 37(11–14), 471–474.

Brett, J. M. (2001). *Negotiating Globally: How to Negotiate Deals, Resolve Disputes, and Make Decisions Across Cultural Boundaries*. San Francisco, CA: Jossey-Bass.

Brett, J. M., Adair, W. A., Lempereur, A., Okumura, T., Shikhirev, P., Tinsley, C., & Lytle, A. (1998). Culture and joint gains in negotiation. *Negotiation Journal,* 14(1), 61–86.

Brett, J. M., & Kopelman, S. (2004). Cross-cultural perspectives on cooperation in social dilemmas. In M. Gelfand & J. Brett (Eds.), *The Handbook of Negotiation and Culture: Theoretical Advances and Cultural Perspectives.* (pp. 395–411). Palo Alto, CA: Stanford University Press.

Brett, J. M., & Okumura, T. (1998). Inter- and intracultural negotiation: U.S. and Japanese negotiators. *Academy of Management Journal,* 41(5), 495–510.

Brett, J. M., Shapiro, D. L., & Lytle, A. (1998). Breaking the bonds of reciprocity in negotiations. *Academy of Management Journal*, 41(4), 410–424.

Brewer, M. (1979). In-group bias in the minimal intergroup situation: A cognitive-motivational analysis. *Psychological Bulletin*, 86, 307–324.

Brewer, M. B., & Brown, R. J. (1998). Intergroup relations. In D. T. Gilbert, S. T. Fiske, & G. Lindzey (Eds.), *The Handbook of Social Psychology*, 4th ed., vol. 2 (pp. 554–594). New York: McGraw-Hill.

Brodt, S., & Thompson, L. (2001). Negotiating teams: A levels of analysis approach. *Group Dynamics: Theory, Research, and Practice*, 5(3), 208–219.

Brodt, S., & Tuchinsky, M. (2000). Working together but in opposition: An examination of the "good cop/bad cop" negotiating team tactic. *Organizational Behavior and Human Decision Processes*, 81(2), 155–177.

Brown, C. E., Dovidio, J. F., & Ellyson, S. L. (1990). Reducing sex differences in visual displays of dominance: Knowledge is power. *Personality and Social Psychology Bulletin*, 16(2), 358–368.

Brown, P., & Levinson, S. (1987). *Politeness: Some Universals in Language Use.* Cambridge, England: Cambridge University Press.

Brown, R. J., Condor, F., Mathew, A., Wade, G., & Williams, J. A. (1986). Explaining intergroup differentiation in an industrial organization. *Journal of Occupational Psychology*, 59, 273–286.

Buchan, N., Croson, R., & Dawes, R. M. (2002). Swift neighbors and persistent strangers: A cross-cultural investigation of trust and reciprocity in social exchange. *American Journal of Sociology*, 108(1), 168–206.

Buck, R. (1975). Nonverbal communication of affect in children. *Journal of Personality and Social Psychology,* 31(4), 644–653.

Buck, R. (1984). On the definition of emotion: Functional and structural considerations. *Cahiers de Psychologie Cognitive*, 4(1), 44–47.

Burger, J. M. (1986). Increasing compliance by improving the deal: The that's-not-all technique. *Journal of Personality and Social Psychology*, 51, 277–283.

Burt, R. S. (1992). *The Social Structure of Competition*. Cambridge, MA: Harvard University Press.

Burt, R. S. (1999). Entrepreneurs, distrust, and third parties: A strategic look at the dark side of dense networks. In L. L. Thompson, J. M. Levine, & D. M. Messick (Eds.), *Shared Cognition in Organizations: The Management of Knowledge* (pp. 213–244). Mahwah, NJ: Lawrence Erlbaum.

Butler, D., & Geis, F. L. (1990). Nonverbal affect responses to male and female leaders: Implications for leadership evaluations. *Journal of Personality and Social Psychology,* 58(1), 48–59.

Byrne, D. (1961). Interpersonal attraction and attitude similarity. *Journal of Abnormal and Social Psychology,* 62, 713–715.

Camerer, C., & Ho, T. –H. (1998). Experience-weighted attraction learning in coordination games: Probability rules, heterogeneity, and time-variation. *Journal of Mathematical Psychology*, 42, 305–326.

Camerer, C., & Ho, T. –H. (1999a). Experience-weighted attraction learning in games: Estimates from weak-link games. In D. V. Budescu, I. Erev, & R. Zwick (Eds.), *Games and Human Behavior* (pp. 31–51). Mahwah, NJ: Erlbaum.

Camerer, C., & Ho, T. –H. (1999b). Experience-weighted attraction learning in normal form games. *Econometrica*, 67, 827–874.

Camerer, C., & Loewenstein, G. (1993). In B. A. Mellers & J. Baron (Eds.), *Psychological Perspectives on Justice* (pp. 155–181). Boston: Cambridge University Press.

Camerer, C. F., Loewenstein, G., & Weber, M. (1989). The curse of knowledge in economic settings: An experimental analysis. *Journal of Political Economy*, 97, 1232–1254.

Cann, A., Sherman, S. J., & Elkes, R. (1975). Effects of initial request size and timing of a second request on compliance: The foot in the door and the door in the face. *Journal of Personality and Social Psychology*, 32(5), 774–782.

Carnevale, P. J. (1995). Property, culture, and negotiation. In R. M. Kramer & D. M. Messick (Eds.), *Negotiation as a Social Process: New Trends in Theory and Research* (pp. 309–323). Thousand Oaks, CA: Sage.

Carnevale, P. J., & Isen, A. (1986). The influence of positive affect and visual access on the discovery of integrative solutions in bilateral negotiations. *Organizational Behavior and Human Decision Processes*, 37, 1–13.

Carnevale, P. J., & Lawler, E. J. (1986). Time pressure and the development of integrative agreements in bilateral negotiations. Journal of Conflict Resolution, 30(4), 636–659.

Carnevale, P. J., & Pruitt, D. G. (1992). Negotiation and mediation. *Annual Review of Psychology*, 43, 531–582.

Carnevale, P. J., Pruitt, D. G., & Britton, S. (1979). Looking tough: The negotiator under constituent surveillance. *Personality and Social Psychology Bulletin*, 5, 118–121.

Carnevale, P. J., Pruitt, D. G., & Seilheimmer, S. (1981). Looking and competing: Accountability and visual access in integrative bargaining. *Journal of Personality and Social Psychology*, 40, 111–120.

Carnevale, P. J., & Radhakrishnan, S. (1994). Group endowment and the theory of collectivism. Unpublished manuscript, Department of Psychology, University of Illinois at Urbana–Champaign.

Cates, K. (1997). Tips for negotiating a job offer. Unpublished manuscript, J. L. Kellogg Graduate School of Management, Northwestern University, Evanston, IL.

Chaiken, S. (1979). Communicator physical attractiveness and persuasion. *Journal of Personality and Social Psychology*, 37(8), 1387–1397.

Chaiken, S. (1980). Heuristic versus systematic information processing and the use of source versus message cues in persuasion. *Journal of Personality and Social Psychology*, 39(5), 752–766.

Chaiken, S., Wood, W., & Eagly, A. H. (1996). Principles of persuasion. In Higgins, E. T., & Kruglanski, A. W. (Eds.), *Social Psychology: Handbook of Basic Principles* (pp. 702–742). New York: Guilford Press.

Chakravarti, A., Loewenstein, J., Morris, M., Thompson, L., & Kopelman, S. (2004). At a loss for words: Negotiators disadvantaged in technical knowledge are vulnerable to verbal domination and economic losses as a function of communication. Manuscript under review.

Chan, D. K. S., Triandis, H. C., Carnevale, P. J., Tam, A., & Bond, M. H. (1994). Comparing negotiation across cultures: Effects of collectivism, relationship between negotiators, and concession pattern on negotiation behavior. Unpublished manuscript, Department of Psychology, University of Illinois at Urbana–Champaign.

Chapman, L. J., & Chapman, J. P. (1967). Genesis of popular but erroneous diagnostic observations. *Journal of Abnormal Psychology*, 72, 193–204.

Chapman, L. J., & Chapman, J. P. (1969). Illusory correlation as an obstacle to the use of valid psychodiagnostic signs. *Journal of Abnormal Psychology*, 74(3), 271–280.

Chechile, R. (1984). Logical foundations for a fair and rational method of voting. In W. Swapp (Ed.), *Group Decision Making*. Beverly Hills, CA: Sage.

Chelius, J. R., & Dworkin, J. B. (1980). The economic analysis of final-offer arbitration as a conflict resolution device. *Journal of Conflict Resolution*, 24, 293–310.

Chen, Y., Mannix, E., & Okumura, T. (2003). The importance of who you meet: Effects of self- versus other-concerns among negotiators in the United States, the People's Republic of China, and Japan. *Journal of Experimental Social Psychology*, 39, 1–15.

Cialdini, R. B. (1975). Reciprocal concessions procedure for inducing compliance: The door-in-the-face technique. *Journal of Personality and Social Psychology*, 31(2), 206–215.

Cialdini, R. B. (1993). *Influence: Science and Practice*. New York: HarperCollins.

Clark, M., & Mills, J. (1979). Interpersonal attraction in exchange and communal relationships. *Journal of Personality and Social Psychology*, 37, 12–24.

Cobbledick, G. (1992). Arb-Med: An alternative approach to expediting settlement. Working paper, Harvard Program on Negotiation, Harvard University, Boston.

Cohen, H. (1980). *You Can Negotiate Anything*. Secausus, NJ: Lyle Stuart.

Cohen, R. (1991). *Negotiating Across Cultures: Communication Obstacles in International Diplomacy*. Washington, DC: United States Institute of Peace Press.

Conlon, D. E., Moon, H., & Ng, K. Y. (2002). Putting the cart before the horse: The benefits of arbitrating before mediating. *Journal of Applied Psychology*, 87(5), 978–984.

Coombs, C. H., Dawes, R. M., & Tversky, A. (1970). *Mathematical Psychology: An Elementary Introduction.* Upper Saddle River, NJ: Prentice Hall.

Copeland, L., & Griggs, L. (1985). *Going International*. New York: Random House.

Covey, S. R. (1999). Resolving differences. *Executive Excellence*, 16(4), 5–6.

Cox, T. H., Lobel, S. A., & McLeod, P. L. (1991). Effects of ethnic group cultural differences in cooperative and competitive behavior on a group task. *Academy of Management Journal*, 34(4), 827–847.

Craver, C. (1998). The impact of a pass/fail option on negotiation course performance. *Journal of Legal Education*, 48(2), 176–186.

Crawford, V. P., & Sobel, J. (1982). Strategic information transmission. *Econometrica*, 50, 1431–1451.

Creighton, M. R. (1990). Revisiting shame and guilt cultures: A forty-year pilgrimage. *Ethos*, 18, 279–307.

Croson, R. (1996). Information in ultimatum games: An experimental study. *Journal of Economic Behavior & Organization*, 30, 197–212.

Croson, R. (1999). Look at me when you say that: An electronic negotiation simulation. *Simulation and Gaming*, 30(1), 23–37.

Croson, R. (in press). Game-theoretic and experimental perceptions of deception. In C. Gerschlager (Ed.), *Modern Economic Analyses of Deception.*

Croson, R., Boles, T., & Murnighan, J. K. (2003). Cheap talk in bargaining experiments: Lying and threats in ultimatum games. *Journal of Economic Behavior & Organization*, 51(2), 143–159.

Csikszentmihalyi, M. (1997). *Finding Flow: The Psychology of Engagement with Everyday Life.* New York: Basicbooks.

Cunningham, M. R. (1986). Measuring the physical in physical attractiveness: Quasi-experiments on the sociobiology of female facial beauty. *Journal of Personality and Social Psychology*, 50, 925–935.

Curhan, J. R., Elfenbein, H. A., & Xu., A. (2004). What do people value when they negotiate? Establishing validity for the Subjective Value Inventory of negotiation performance. Working paper, Massachusetts Institute of Technology, Cambridge, MA.

Curhan, J. R., Neale, M. A., Ross, L., & Rosencranz-Engelmann, J. (2004). The O'Henry effect: The impact of relational norms on negotiation outcomes. Working paper, Massachusetts Institute of Technology, Cambridge, MA.

Daft, R. L., & Lengel, R. H. (1984). Information richness: A new approach to managerial behavior and organization design. *Research in Organization Behavior*, 6, 191–223.

Daft, R. L., Lengel, R. H., & Trevino, L. K. (1987). Message equivocality, media selection, and manager performance: Implications for information systems. *MIS Quarterly*, 11(3), 355–366.

Daly, J. P. (1995). Explaining changes to employees: The influence of justifications and change outcomes on employees' fairness judgments. *Journal of Applied Behavioral Science*, 31(4), 415–428.

Daly, J. P., & Geyer, P. D. (1994). The role of fairness in implementing large-scale change: Employee evaluations of process and outcome in seven facility relocations. *Journal of Organizational Behavior*, 15, 623–638.

Dawes, R. M., van de Kragt, A. J. C., & Orbell, J. M. (1990). Cooperation for the benefit of us— Not me, or my conscience. In J. Mansbridge (Ed.), *Beyond Self-Interest* (pp. 97–110). Chicago: University of Chicago Press.

De Dreu, C. K. W., Weingart, L. R., & Kwon, S. (2000). Influence of social motives on integrative negotiation: A meta-analytic review and test of two theories. *Journal of Personality and Social Psychology,* 78(5), 889–905.

Demos, J. (1996). Shame and guilt in early New England. In R. Harre & W. G. Parrott (Eds.), *The Emotions* (pp. 74–88). London: Sage.

DePaulo, B. M. (1994). Spotting lies: Can humans learn to do better? *Current Directions in Psychological Science*, 3(3), 83–86.

DePaulo, B. M., Blank, A. L., Swaim, G. W., & Hairfield, J. G. (1992). Expressiveness and expressive control. *Personality and Social Psychology Bulletin*, 18(3), 276–285.

DePaulo, B. M., Epstein, J. A., & Wyer, M. M. (1993). Sex differences in lying: How women and men deal with the dilemma of deceit. In M. Lewis & C. Saarni (Eds.), *Lying and Deception in Everyday Life* (pp. 126–147). New York: Guilford Press.

DePaulo, B. M., & Friedman, H. S. (1998). Nonverbal communication. In D. T. Gilbert, S. T. Fiske, & G. Lindzey (Eds.), *The Handbook of Social Psychology*, 4th ed. New York: McGraw-Hill.

DePaulo, B. M., & Kirkendol, S. E. (1989). The motivational impairment effect in the communication of deception. In J. C. Yuille (Ed.), *Credibility Assessment* (pp. 51–70). Dordrecht, The Netherlands: Kluwer.

DePaulo, B. M., Lassiter, G. D., & Stone, J. I. (1982). Attentional determinants of success at detecting deception and truth. *Personality and Social Psychology Bulletin*, 8(2), 273–279.

DePaulo, B. M., & Rosenthal, R. (1979). Telling lies. *Journal of Personality and Social Psychology*, 37(10), 1713–1722.

DePaulo, P. J., & DePaulo, B. M. (1989). Can deception by salespersons and customers be detected through nonverbal behavioral cues? *Journal of Applied Social Psychology*, 19(18, pt. 2), 1552–1577.

Detweiler, R. (1980). The categorization of the actions of people from another culture: A conceptual analysis and behavioral outcome. *International Journal of Intercultural Relations*, 4, 275–293.

Deutsch, M. (1953). The effects of cooperation and competition upon group processes. In D. Cartwright and A. Zander (Eds.), *Group Dynamics* (pp. 319–353). Evanston, IL: Row, Peterson.

Deutsch, M. (1960). The effect of motivational orientation upon trust and suspicion. *Human Relations*, 13, 122–139.

Deutsch, M. (1961). The face of bargaining. *Operations Research*, 9, 886–897.

Deutsch, M. (1973). *The Resolution of Conflict.* New Haven, CT: Yale University Press.

Deutsch, M. (1985). *Distributive Justice: A Social-Psychological Perspective.* New Haven, CT: Yale University Press.

Diehl, M., & Stroebe, W. (1987). Productivity loss in brainstorming groups: Toward the solution of a riddle. *Journal of Personality and Social Psychology*, 61, 392–403.

Diekmann, K. A., Samuels, S. M., Ross, L., & Bazerman, M. H. (1997). Self-interest and fairness in problems of resource allocation. *Journal of Personality and Social Psychology*, 72(5), 1061–1074.

Diekmann, K. A., Tenbrunsel, A., & Bazerman, M. H. (1998). Escalation and negotiation: Two central themes in the work of Jeffrey Z. Rubin. In D. Kolb & M. Aaron (Eds.), *Essays in Memory of Jeffrey Z. Rubin.* Cambridge, MA: Program on Negotiation.

Diekmann, K. A., Tenbrunsel, A. E., Shah, P. P., Schroth, H. A., & Bazerman, M. H. (1996). The descriptive and prescriptive use of previous purchase price in negotiations. *Organizational Behavior and Human Decision Processes,* 66(2), 179–191.

DiMatteo, M. R., Friedman, H. S., & Taranta, A. (1979). Sensitivity to bodily nonverbal communication as a factor in practitioner-patient rapport. *Journal of Nonverbal Behavior*, 4(1), 18–26.

DiMatteo, M. R., Hays, R. D., & Prince, L. M. (1986). Relationship of physicians' nonverbal communication skill to patient satisfaction, appointment noncompliance, and physician workload. *Health Psychology*, 5(6), 581–594.

Dion, K. L. (1972). Physical attractiveness and evaluations of children's transgressions. *Journal of Personality and Social Psychology*, 24(2), 207–213.

Dion, K. L., & Dion, K. K. (1987). Belief in a just world and physical attractiveness stereotyping. *Journal of Personality and Social Psychology*, 52(4), 775–780.

Doise, W. (1978). *Groups and Individuals: Explanations in Social Psychology*. Cambridge: Cambridge University Press.

Donohue, W. A. (1981). Analyzing negotiation tactics: Development of a negotiation interact system. *Human Communication Research*, 7(3), 273–287.

Dovidio, J. F., Brown, C. E., Heltman, K., Ellyson, S. L., et al. (1988). Power displays between women and men in discussions of gender-linked tasks: A multichannel study. *Journal of Personality and Social Psychology*, 55(4), 580–587.

Dovidio, J. F., & Ellyson, S. L. (1982). Decoding visual dominance: Attributions of power based on relative percentages of looking while speaking and looking while listening. *Social Psychology Quarterly*, 45(2), 106–113.

Dovidio, J. F., Ellyson, S. L., Keating, C. F., Heltman, K., et al. (1988). The relationship of social power to visual displays of dominance between men and women. *Journal of Personality and Social Psychology*, 54(2), 233–242.

Drolet, A. L., & Morris, M. W. (1995). Communication media and interpersonal trust in conflicts: The role of rapport and synchrony of nonverbal behavior. Unpublished manuscript, Stanford University, Palo Alto, CA.

Drolet, A. L., & Morris, M. W. (2000). Rapport in conflict resolution: Accounting for how nonverbal exchange fosters cooperation on mutually beneficial settlements to mixed-motive conflicts. *Journal of Experimental Social Psychology*, 36, 26–50.

Druckman, D., & Zechmeister, K. (1973). Conflict of interest and value dissensus: Propositions on the sociology of conflict. *Human Relations*, 26, 449–466.

Dubrovsky, V. J., Keisler, S., & Sethna, B. N. (1991). The equalization phenomenon: Status effects in computer-mediated and face-to-face decision-making groups. *Human-Computer Interaction*, 6(2), 119–146.

Duncker, K. (1945). On problem solving. *Psychological Monographs*, 58, 270.

Dunn, J., & Schweitzer, M. (2003). Feeling and believing: The influence of emotion on trust. Working paper, University of Pennsylvania, Philadelphia.

Dunning, D., Johnson, K., Ehrlinger, J., & Kruger, J. (2003). Why people fail to recognize their own incompetence. *Current Directions in Psychological Science*, 12(3), 83–87.

Dwyer, F. R., Schurr, P. H., & Oh, S. (1987). Developing buyer-seller relationships. *Journal of Marketing*, 51, 11–27.

Eagly, A. H., Ashmore, R. D., Makhijani, M. G., & Longo, L. C. (1991). What is beautiful is good, but . . . : A meta-analytic review of research on the physical attractiveness stereotype. *Psychological Bulletin*, 110(1), 109–128.

Earley, P. C. (1989). Social loafing and collectivism: A comparison of the United States and the People's Republic of China. *Administrative Science Quarterly*, 34, 565–581.

Ehrlinger, J., Johnson, K., Banner, M., Dunning, D., & Kruger, D. (2003). Why the unskilled are unaware: Further explorations of (absent) self-insight among the incompetent. Unpublished manuscript, Cornell University, Ithaca, NY.

Eidelson, R. J., & Eidelson, J. I. (2003). Dangerous ideas: Five beliefs that propel groups toward conflict. *American Psychologist*, 58(3), 182–192.

Eisenhardt, K. M., Kahwajy, J. L., & Bourgeois, L. J., III. (1997). How management teams can have a good fight. *Harvard Business Review*, 75(4), 77–85.

Ekman, P. (1984). The nature and function of the expression of emotion. In K. Scherer & P. Ekman (Eds.), *Approaches to Emotion*. Hillsdale, NJ: Erlbaum.

Ekman, P. (1992). *Telling Lies: Clues to Deceit in the Marketplace, Politics, and Marriage*, 2nd ed. New York: Norton.

Ekman, P. (2001). *Telling Lies: Clues to Deceit in the Marketplace, Politics, and Marriage*, 3rd ed. New York: Norton.

Ekman, P., & Friesen, W. V. (1969). Nonverbal leakage and clues to deception. *Psychiatry*, 32(1), 88–106.

Ekman, P., O'Sullivan, M. O., & Frank, M. G. (1999). A few can catch a liar. *Psychological Science*, 10(3), 263–266.

Ellemers, N., & Van Rijswijk, W. (1997). Identity needs versus social opportunities: The use of group level and individual level identity management strategies as a function of relative group size, status, and in-group identification. *Social Psychology Quarterly*, 60(1), 52–65.

Ellemers, N., Van Rijswijk, W., Roefs, M., & Simons, C. (1997). Bias in intergroup perceptions: Balancing group identity with social reality. *Personality and Social Psychology Bulletin*, 23(2), 186–198.

Ellsworth, P. C., & Carlsmith, J. M. (1973). Eye contact and gaze aversion in aggressive encounters. *Journal of Personality and Social Psychology*, 33, 117–122.

Elsbach, K. D. (1994). Managing organizational legitimacy in the California cattle industry: The construction and effectiveness of verbal accounts. *Administrative Science Quarterly*, 39(1), 57–88.

Englebart, D. (1989, November). Bootstrapping organizations into the 21st century. Paper presented at a seminar at the Software Engineering Institute, Pittsburgh, PA.

Enzle, M. E., & Anderson, S. C. (1993). Surveillant intentions and intrinsic motivation. *Journal of Personality and Social Psychology*, 64, 257–266.

Ertel, D. (1999). Turning negotiation into a corporate capability. *Harvard Business Review*, 77(3), 55–70.

Espeland, W. (1994). Legally mediated identity: The national environmental policy act and the bureaucratic construction of interests. *Law and Society Review*, 28(5), 1149–1179.

Espinoza, J. A., & Garza, R. T. (1985). Social group salience and interethnic cooperation. *Journal of Experimental Social Psychology*, 21, 380–392.

Etzkowitz, H., Kemelgor, C., & Uzzi, B. (1999). *Social Capital and Career Dynamics in Hard Science: Gender, Networks, and Advancement*. New York: Cambridge University Press.

Evans, C. R., & Dion, K. L. (1991). Group cohesion and performance: A meta-analysis. *Small Group Research*, 22, 175–186.

Eveland, J. D., & Bikson, T. K. (1988). Work group structures and computer support: A field experiment. *Transactions on Office Information Systems*, 6(4), 354–379.

Exline, R. V., Ellyson, S. L., & Long, B. (1975). Visual behavior as an aspect of power role relationships. In P. Pliner, L. Krames, & T. Alloway (Eds.), *Advances in the Study of Communication and Affect* (vol. 2: Nonverbal communication of aggression; pp. 21–52). New York: Plenum.

Farber, H. S. (1981). Splitting the difference in interest arbitration. *Industrial and Labor Relations Review*, 35, 70–77.

Farber, H. S., & Bazerman, M. H. (1986). The general basis of arbitrator behavior: An empirical analysis of conventional and final offer arbitration. *Econometrica*, 54, 1503–1528.

Farber, H. S., & Bazerman, M. H. (1989). Divergent expectations as a cause of disagreement in bargaining: Evidence from a comparison of arbitration schemes. *Quarterly Journal of Economics*, 104, 99–120.

Farber, H. S., & Katz, H. (1979). Why is there disagreement in bargaining? *American Economic Review*, 77, 347–352.

Farrell, J., & Gibbons, R. (1989). Cheap talk can matter in bargaining. *Journal of Economic Theory*, 48, 221–237.

Feingold, A. (1992). Good-looking people are not what we think. *Psychological Bulletin*, 111(2), 304–341.

Feller, W. (1968). *An Introduction to Probability Theory and Its Applications*, vol. 1, 3rd ed. New York: Wiley.

Festinger, L. (1950). Informal social communication. *Psychological Review, 57*, 271–282.

Fischhoff, B. (1975). Hindsight does not equal foresight: The effect of outcome knowledge on judgment under uncertainty. *Journal of Experimental Psychology: Human Perception and Performance, 1*, 288–299.

Fischhoff, B., Slovic, P., & Lichtenstein, S. (1977). Knowing with certainty: The appropriateness of extreme confidence. *Journal of Experimental Psychology: Human Perception and Performance, 3*(4), 552–564.

Fisher, R., & Ury. W. (1981). *Getting to Yes.* Boston: Houghton Mifflin.

Fisher, R., Ury, W., & Patton, B. (1991). *Getting to Yes,* 2nd ed. New York: Penguin.

Fiske, A. P. (1992). The four elementary forms of sociality: Framework for a unified theory of social relations. *Psychological Review, 99*(4), 689–723.

Fiske, S. T., & Dépret, E. (1996). Control, interdependence, and power: Understanding social cognition in its social context. In W. Stroebe & M. Hewstone (Eds.), *European Review of Social Psychology, 7*, 31–61.

Fiske, S. T., & Neuberg, S. L. (1990). A continuum of impression formation, from category-based to individuating processes: Influences of information and motivation on attention and interpretation. In M. P. Zanna (Ed.), *Advances in Experimental Social Psychology,* vol. 23 (pp. 1–74). New York: Academic Press.

Fleming, J. H., & Darley, J. M. (1991). Mixed messages: The multiple audience problem and strategic communication. *Social Cognition, 9*(1), 25–46.

Foa, U., & Foa, E. (1975). *Resource Theory of Social Exchange.* Morristown, NJ: General Learning Press.

Follett, M. (1994). *Prophet of Management: A Celebration of Writings from the 1920s* (P. Graham, Ed.). Boston: Harvard Business School Press.

Forbus, K. D., Gentner, D., & Law, K. (1995). MAC/FAC: A model of similarity-based retrieval. *Cognitive Science*, 19(2), 141–205.

Forgas, J. P. (1996). The role of emotion scripts and transient moods in relationships: Structural and functional perspectives. In

G. J. O. Fletcher & J. Fitness (Eds.), *Knowledge Structures in Close Relationships: A Social Psychological Approach* (pp. 275–296). Mahwah, NJ: Lawrence Erlbaum.

Forgas, J. P., & Moylan, S. J. (1996). On feeling good and getting your way: Mood effects on expected and actual negotiation strategies and outcomes. Unpublished manuscript, University of New South Wales.

Fortune, A., & Brodt, S. (2000). Face to face or virtually: The influence of task, past experience, and media on trust and deception in negotiation. Working paper, Duke University, Durham, NC.

Fox, C. R. (1998). A belief-based model of decision under uncertainty. *Management Science, 44*, 879–896.

Fox, G., & Nelson, J. *Sue the Bastards!: Everything You Need to Know to Go to—or Stay out of—Court.* Chicago: Contemporary Books.

Frank, R. H. (1988). *Passions Within Reason: The Strategic Role of the Emotions.* New York: Norton.

Frank, R. H., & Cook, P. J. (1995). *The Winner-Take-All Society.* New York: Penguin.

Fredrickson, B. L., & Kahneman, D. (1993). Duration neglect in retrospective evaluations of affective episodes. *Journal of Personality and Social Psychology, 65*(1), 45–55.

Freedman, J. L., & Fraser, S. C. (1966). Compliance without pressure: The foot-in-the-door technique. *Journal of Personality and Social Psychology, 4*, 195–203.

Friedman, H. S., Prince, L. M., Riggio, R. E., & DiMatteo, M. R. (1980). Understanding and assessing nonverbal expressiveness: The Affective Communication Test. *Journal of Personality and Social Psychology, 39*(2), 333–351.

Friedman, H. S., Riggio, R. E., & Casella, D. F. (1988). Nonverbal skill, personal charisma, and initial attraction. *Personality and Social Psychology Bulletin, 14*(1), 203–211.

Friedman, R. (1992). The culture of mediation: Private understandings in the context of public conflict. In D. Kolb and J. Bartunek (Eds.), *Hidden Conflict: Uncovering Behind-the-Scenes Disputes* (pp. 143–164). Beverly Hills, CA: Sage.

Froman, L. A., & Cohen, M. D. (1970). Compromise and logroll: Comparing the efficiency of two bargaining processes. *Behavioral Science,* 30, 180–183.

Fry, W. R., Firestone, I. J., & Williams, D. L. (1983). Negotiation process and outcome of stranger dyads and dating couples: Do lovers lose? *Basic and Applied Social Psychology,* 4, 1–16.

Gabriel, S., & Gardner, W. L. (1999). Are there "his" and "her" types of interdependence? The implications of gender differences in collective and relational interdependence for affect, behavior, and cognition. *Journal of Personality and Social Psychology,* 75, 642–655.

Galegher, J., Kraut, R. E., & Egido, C. (Eds.). (1990). *Intellectual Teamwork: Social and Technological Foundations of Cooperative Work.* Hillsdale, NJ: Erlbaum.

Galinsky, A., & Mussweiler, T. (2001). First offers as anchors: The role of perspective-taking and negotiator focus. *Journal of Personality and Social Psychology,* 81(4), 657–669.

Galinsky, A., Mussweiler, T., & Medvec, V. H. (2002). Disconnecting outcomes and evaluations: The role of negotiator focus. *Journal of Personality and Social Psychology,* 83(5), 1131–1140.

Galinsky, A., Seiden, V., Kim, P. H., & Medvec, V. H. (2002). The dissatisfaction of having your first offer accepted: The role of counterfactual thinking in negotiations. *Personality and Social Psychology Bulletin,* 28(2), 271–283.

Gamson, W. (1964). Experimental studies in coalition formation. In L. Berkowitz (Ed.), *Advances in Experimental Social Psychology,* vol. 1. New York: Academic Press.

Gardiner, G. S. (1972). *Aggression.* Morristown, NJ: General Learning Corp.

Gelfand, M. J., Bhawuk, D. P. S., Nishii, L. H., & Bechtold, D. (2004). Individualism and collectivism: Multilevel perspectives and implications for leadership. In R. J. House et al. (Eds.), *Culture, Leadership, and Organizations: The GLOBE Study of 62 Cultures.* Thousand Oaks, CA: Sage.

Gelfand, M. J., & Brett, J. M. (Eds.) (2004). *The Handbook of Negotiation and Culture: Theoretical Advances and Cultural Perspectives.* Palo Alto, CA: Stanford University Press.

Gelfand, M. J., & Christakopoulou, S. (1999). Culture and negotiator cognition: Judgment

accuracy and negotiation processes in individualistic and collectivistic cultures. *Organizational Behavior and Human Decision Processes,* 79(3), 248–269.

Gelfand, M. J., Higgins, M., Nishii, L. H., Raver, J. L., Dominguez, A., Murakami, F., Yamaguchi, S., & Toyama, M. (2002). Culture and egocentric perceptions of fairness in conflict and negotiation. *Journal of Applied Psychology,* 87(5), 833–845.

Gelfand, M. J., Nishii, L. H., Holcombe, K. M., Dyer, N., Ohbuchi, K–I., & Fukuno, M. (2001). Cultural influences on cognitive representations of conflict: Interpretations of conflict episodes in the United States and Japan. *Journal of Applied Psychology,* 86(6), 1059–1074.

Gelfand, M. J., & Realo, A. (1999). Individualism-collectivism and accountability in intergroup negotiations. *Journal of Applied Psychology,* 84(5), 721–736.

Gentner, D., Loewenstein, J. & Thompson, L. (2003). Learning and transfer: A general role for analogical encoding. *Journal of Educational Psychology,* 95(2), 393–408.

Gentner, D., Rattermann, M. J., & Forbus, K. D. (1993). The roles of similarity in transfer: Separating retrievability from inferential soundness. *Cognitive Psychology,* 25(4), 524–575.

Gerard, H. (1983). School desegregation: The social science role. *American Psychologist,* 38, 869–878.

Gerhart, B., & Rynes, S. (1991). Determinants and consequences of salary negotiations by male and female MBA graduates. *Journal of Applied Psychology,* 76(2), 256–262.

Getzels, J. W., & Jackson, P. W. (1962). *Creativity and Intelligence: Explorations with Gifted Students.* New York: Wiley.

Gibson, K., Thompson, L., & Bazerman, M. H. (1994). Biases and rationality in the mediation process. In L. Heath, F. Bryant, & J. Edwards (Eds.), *Application of Heuristics and Biases to Social Issues*, vol. 3. New York: Plenum.

Gick, M. L., & Holyoak, K. J. (1980). Analogical problem solving. *Cognitive Psychology,* 12, 306–355.

Gigone, D., & Hastie, R. (1993). The common knowledge effect: Information sharing and group judgment. *Journal of Personality and Social Psychology,* 65, 959–974.

Gilbert, D. T., Pinel, E. C., Wilson, T. D., Blumberg, S. J., & Wheatley, T. P. (1998). Immune neglect: A source of durability bias in affective forecasting. *Journal of Personality and Social Psychology,* 75(3), 617–638.

Gilbert, D. T., & Wilson, T. D. (2000). Miswanting: Some problems in the forecasting of future affective states. In J. P. Forgas (Ed.), *Feeling and Thinking: The Role of Affect in Social Cognition. Studies in Emotion and Social Interaction, Second Series* (pp. 178–197). New York: Cambridge University Press.

Gillespie, J. J., & Bazerman, M. H. (1998). Pre-settlement Settlement (PreSS): A simple technique for initiating complex negotiations. *Negotiation Journal,* 14(2), 149–159.

Gilovich, T., & Medvec, V. H. (1994). The temporal pattern to the experience of regret. *Journal of Personality and Social Psychology,* 67(3), 357–365.

Gilovich, T., Savitsky, K., & Medvec, V. H. (1998). The illusion of transparency: Biased assessments of others' ability to read one's emotional states. *Journal of Personality and Social Psychology,* 75(2), 332–346.

Glick, S., & Croson, R. (2001). Reputations in negotiation. In S. Hoch & H. Kunreuther (Eds.), *Wharton on Decision Making* (pp. 177–186). New York: Wiley.

Goffman, E. (1959). *The Presentation of Self in Everyday Life.* Garden City, NY: Doubleday.

Goldenberg, J., Nir, D., & Maoz, E. (in press). Structuring creativity: Bringing creative templates to negotiations. In L. Thompson & H–S. Choi (Eds.), *Creativity and Innovation in Organizational Teams.* Mahwah, NJ: Lawrence Erlbaum.

Gottman, J. M., & Levenson, R. W. (2000). The timing of divorce: Predicting when a couple will divorce over a 14-year period. *Journal of Marriage & the Family,* 62(3), 737–745.

Gouldner, A. W. (1960). The norm of reciprocity: A preliminary statement. *American Sociological Review,* 25, 161–179.

Graham, J. L. (1993). The Japanese negotiation style: Characteristics of a distinct approach. *Negotiation Journal,* 9(2), 123–140.

Graham, J. L., & Sano, Y. (1984). *Smart Bargaining: Doing Business with the Japanese.* Cambridge, MA: Ballinger.

Grandey, A. (2003). When "the show must go on": Surface acting and deep acting as determinants of emotional exhaustion and peer-rated service delivery. *Academy of Management Journal,* 46(1), 86–96.

Granovetter, M. (1973). The strength of weak ties. *American Journal of Sociology,* 78, 1360–1379.

Greenberg, J. (1988). Equity and workplace status: A field experiment. *Journal of Applied Psychology,* 73, 606–613.

Greenberg, J. (1990). Employee theft as a reaction to underpayment inequity: The hidden cost of pay cuts. *Journal of Applied Psychology,* 75, 561–568.

Griffin, D. W., & Ross, L. (1991). Subjective construal, social inference, and human misunderstanding. In M. P. Zanna (Ed.), *Advances in Experimental Social Psychology,* vol. 24 (pp. 319–359). San Diego, CA: Academic Press.

Griffin, E., & Sparks, G. G. (1990). Friends forever: A longitudinal exploration of intimacy in same-sex friends and platonic pairs. *Journal of Social and Personal Relations,* 7, 29–46.

Gruenfeld, D. H., Keltner, D. J., & Anderson, C. (1998). The effects of power on those who possess it. Working paper, J. L. Kellogg Graduate School of Management, Northwestern University, Evanston, IL.

Gruenfeld, D. H., Mannix, E. A., Williams, K., & Neale, M. A. (1996). Group composition and decision making: How member familiarity and information distribution affect process and performance. *Organizational Behavior and Human Decision Processes,* 67(1), 1–15.

Guetzkow, H., & Gyr, J. (1954). An analysis of conflict in decision-making groups. *Human Relations,* 7, 367–381.

Guilford, J. P. (1959). *Personality.* New York: McGraw-Hill.

Guilford, J. P. (1967). The nature of human intelligence. *Intelligence,* 1, 274–280.

Gulliver, M. P. (1979). The effect of the spatial visualization factor on achievement in operations with fractions. *Dissertation Abstracts International,* 39(9-A), 5381–5382.

Halberstadt, A. G. (1991). Toward an ecology of expressiveness: Family socialization in particular and a model in general. In R. S. Feldman & B. Rime (Eds.), *Fundamentals of Nonverbal Behavior: Studies in Emotion and Social Interaction* (pp. 106–160). New York: Cambridge University Press.

Hall, E. T. (1976). *Beyond Culture.* Garden City, NJ: Anchor Press.

Hall, E. T., & Hall, M. R. (1990). *Understanding Cultural Differences.* Yarmouth, ME: Intercultural Press.

Hall, J. A. (1984). *Nonverbal Sex Differences: Communication Accuracy and Expressive Style.* Baltimore, MD: Johns Hopkins University Press.

Hamermesh, D. S., & Biddle, J. E. (1994). Beauty and the labor market. *The American Economic Review,* 84(5), 1174.

Hamilton, D. L., & Gifford, R. K. (1976). Illusory correlation in interpersonal perception: A cognitive basis of sterotypic judgments. *Journal of Experimental Social Psychology,* 12, 392–407.

Hardin, G. (1968). The tragedy of the commons. *Science,* 162, 1243–1248.

Harinck, F., De Dreu, C. K. W., & Van Vianen, A. E. M. (2000). The impact of conflict issues on fixed-pie perceptions, problem-solving, and integrative outcomes in negotiation. *Organizational Behavior and Human Decision Processes,* 81(2), 329–358.

Harris, R. J., & Joyce, M. (1980). What's fair? It depends on how you ask the question. *Journal of Personality and Social Psychology,* 38, 165–170.

Harsanyi, J. (1962). Bargaining in ignorance of the opponent's utility function. *Journal of Conflict Resolution,* 6, 29–38.

Harsanyi, J. C. (1990). Bargaining. In J. Eatwell, M. Milgate, & P. Newman (Eds.), *The New Palgrave: A Dictionary of Economics* (pp. 54–67). New York: Norton.

Harvey, J. (1974). The Abilene Paradox: The management of agreement. *Organizational Dynamics,* 3(1), 63–80. © American Management Association International.

Hastorf, A., & Cantril, H. (1954). They saw a game: A case study. *Journal of Abnormal and Social Psychology,* 49, 129–134.

Hatfield, E., Caccioppo, J. T., & Rapson, R. L. (1992). Primitive emotional contagion. In M. S. Clark (Ed.), *Review of Personality and Social Pscyhology* (vol. 14: Emotion and Social Behavior, pp. 151–177). Newbury Park, CA: Sage.

Henley, N. M. (1977). *Body Politics: Power, Sex, and Non-Verbal Communication.* Upper Saddle River, NJ: Prentice Hall.

Heine, S. J., Takata, T., & Lehman, D. R. (2000). Beyond self-presentation: Evidence for self-criticism among Japanese. *Personality and Social Psychology Bulletin,* 26(1), 71–78.

Higgins, E. T. (1999). 'Saying is believing' effects: When sharing reality about something biases knowledge and evaluations. In L. Thompson, J. M. Levine, & D. M. Messick (Eds.), *Shared Cognition in Organizations: The Management of Knowledge.* Mahwah, NJ: Lawrence Erlbaum.

Hilty, J., & Carnevale, P. J. (1993). Black-hat/white-hat strategy in bilateral negotiation. *Organizational Behavior and Human Decision Processes,* 55(3), 444–469.

Hochschild, A. R. (1983). *The Managed Heart: Commercialization of Human Feeling.* Berkeley: University of California Press.

Hofstadter, D. (1983). Metamagical thinking. *Scientific American,* 248, 14–28.

Hofstede, G. (1980). *Culture's Consequences: International Differences in Work-Related Values.* Beverly Hills, CA: Sage.

Hoh, R. (1984). The effectiveness of mediation in public-sector arbitration systems: The Iowa experience. *Arbitration Journal,* 39(2), 30–40.

Homans, G. C. (1961). *Social Behavior: Its Elementary Forms.* New York: Harcourt, Brace, Jovanovich.

Huber, V., & Neale, M. A. (1986). Effects of cognitive heuristics and goals on negotiator performance and subsequent goal setting. *Organizational Behavior and Human Decision Processes,* 40, 342–365.

Huber, V., & Neale, M. A. (1987). Effects of self- and competitor goals on performance in an interdependent bargaining task. *Journal of Applied Psychology,* 72, 197–203.

Hui, C. H., & Triandis, H. C. (1986). Individualism-collectivism: A study of cross-cultural researchers. *Journal of Cultural Psychology, 17,* 225–248.

Hyder, E. B., Prietula, M. J., & Weingart, L. R. (2000). Getting to best: Efficiency versus optimality in negotiation. *Cognitive Science,* 24(2), 169–204.

Insko, C. A., Schopler, J., Graetz, K. A., Drigotas, S. M., et al. (1994). Interindividual-intergroup discontinuity in the prisoner's dilemma game. *Journal of Conflict Resolution,* 38(1), 87–116.

Isen, A. M. (1987). Positive affect, cognitive processes, and social behavior. In L. Berkowitz (Ed.), *Advances in Experimental Social Psychology,* vol. 20 (pp. 203–253). San Diego, CA: Academic Press, Inc.

Isen, A. M., & Baron, R. A. (1991). Affect and organizational behavior. In B. M. Staw & L. L. Cummings (Eds.), *Research in Organizational Behavior,* vol. 15 (pp. 1–53). Greenwich, CT: JAI Press.

Isen, A. M., Daubman, K. A., & Nowicki, G. P. (1987). Positive affect facilitates creative problem solving. *Journal of Personality and Social Psychology,* 52, 1122–1131.

Isen, A. M., Niedenthal, P. M., & Cantor, N. (1992). An influence of positive affect on social categorization. *Motivation and Emotion,* 16(1), 65–78.

Janis, I. L., & Mann, L. (1977). *Decision Making: A Psychological Analysis of Conflict, Choice, and Commitment.* New York: Free Press.

Jehn, K. A. (1997). A qualitative analysis of conflict types and dimensions in organizational groups. *Administrative Science Quarterly,* 42, 530–557.

Jehn, K. A. (2000). Benefits and detriments of workplace conflict. *The Public Manager,* 29(2), 24–26.

Jensen, M. C., & Meckling, W. H. (1976). Theory of the firm: Managerial behavior, agency costs, and ownership structure. *Journal of Financial Economics,* 3, 305–360.

Johansen, R. (1988). *Groupware: Computer Support for Business Teams.* New York: Free Press.

Jones, E. E., & Gerard, H. B. (1967). *Foundations of Social Psychology.* New York: Wiley.

Jones, E. E., Stires, L. K., Shaver, K. G., & Harris, V. A. (1968). Evaluation of an ingratiator by target persons and bystanders. *Journal of Personality,* 36(3), 349–385.

Kagel, J. (1976). Comment. In H. Anderson (Ed.), *New Techniques in Labor Dispute Resolution* (pp. 185–190). Washington, DC: BNA Books.

Kahn, R. L., & Kramer, R. M. (1990). *Untying the Knot: De-escalatory Processes in International Conflict.* San Francisco: Jossey-Bass.

Kahneman, D., Fredrickson, B. L., Schreiber, C. A., & Redelmeier, D. A. (1993). When more pain is preferred to less: Adding a better end. *Psychological Science,* 4(6), 401–405.

Kahneman, D., Knetsch, J. L., & Thaler, R. H. (1990). Experimental tests of the endowment effect and the Coase theorem. *Journal of Political Economy,* 98(6), 1325–1348.

Kahneman, D., & Miller, D. (1986). Norm theory: Comparing reality to its alternatives. *Psychological Review,* 93, 136–153.

Kahneman, D., & Tversky, A. (1979). Prospect theory: An analysis of decision under risk. *Econometrica,* 47, 263–291.

Kahneman, D., & Tversky, A. (1982). On the study of statistical intuitions. *Cognition,* 11(2), 123–141.

Kaplan, S., & Kaplan, R. (1982). *Cognition and Environment: Functioning in an Uncertain World.* New York: Praeger.

Karambayya, R., & Brett, J. M. (1989). Managers handling disputes: Third-party roles and perceptions of fairness. *Academy of Management Journal,* 32, 687–704.

Keenan, J., & Wilson, R. B. (1993). Bargaining with private information. *Journal of Economic Literature,* 31(1), 45–104.

Keisler, S., & Sproull, L. (1992). Group decision making and communication technology. *Organizational Behavior and Human Decision Processes,* 52, 96–123.

Kelley, H. H. (1966). A classroom study of dilemmas in interpersonal negotiations. In K. Archibald (Ed.), *Strategic Intervention and Conflict* (pp. 49–73). Berkeley, CA: University of California, Institute of International Studies.

Kelley, H. H., & Schenitzki, D. P. (1972). Bargaining. In C. G. McClintock (Ed.), *Experimental Social Psychology* (pp. 298–337). New York: Holt, Rinehart, and Winston.

Kelley, H. H., & Stahelski, A. J. (1970). Social interaction basis of cooperators' and competitors' beliefs about others. *Journal of Personality and Social Psychology,* 16(1), 66–91.

Kelley, H. H., & Thibaut, J. (1969). Group problem solving. In G. Lindzey & E. Aronson (Eds.), *Handbook of Social Psychology* (pp. 1–101). Reading, MA: Addison-Wesley.

Kelly, J. R. (1988). Entrainment in individual and group behavior. In J. E. McGrath (Ed.), *The Social Psychology of Time: New Perspectives* (Sage Focus Editions, vol. 91, pp. 89–110). Newbury Park, CA: Sage.

Kelman, H. C. (1991). Coalitions across conflict lines: The interplay of conflicts within and between the Israeli and Palestinian communities. Working paper series (no. 91–9), Harvard University, Center for International Affairs.

Kern, M. C., Brett, J. M., & Weingart, L. R. (2003). Getting the floor: Persistence, motives, strategy, and individual outcomes in multiparty negotiations. Working paper, Carnegie Mellon University, Pittsburgh, PA.

Kerr, N. L. (1983). Motivation losses in small groups: A social dilemma analysis. *Journal of Personality and Social Psychology,* 45, 819–828.

Kerr, N. L., & Kaufman-Gilliland, C. M. (1994). Communication, commitment, and cooperation in social dilemma. *Journal of Personality and Social Psychology,* 66(3), 513–529.

Keysar, B. (1998). Language users as problem solvers: Just what ambiguity problem do they solve? In S. R. Fussell & R. J. Kreuz (Eds.), *Social and Cognitive Approaches to Interpersonal Communication* (pp. 175–200). Mahwah, NJ: Lawrence Erlbaum.

Kiesler, C. A., & Kiesler, S. B. (1969). *Conformity.* Reading, MA: Addison-Wesley.

Kim, P. H., Diekmann, K. A., & Tenbrunsel, A. E. (2003). Flattery may get you somewhere: The strategic implications of providing positive vs. negative feedback about ability vs. ethicality in negotiation. *Organizational Behavior and Human Decision Processes,* 90, 225–243.

Kipnis, D. (1957). Interaction between bomber crews as a determinant of sociometric choice. *Human Relations,* 10, 263–270.

Kivisilta, P., Honkaniemi, L., & Sundvi, L. (1994, July 12). Female employees' physical appearance: A biasing factor in personnel assessment, or a success-producing factor in sales and marketing? Poster presented at the 23rd International Congress of Applied Psychology, Madrid, Spain.

Klar, Y., Bar-Tal, D., & Kruglanski, A. W. (1988). Conflict as a cognitive schema: Toward a social cognitive analysis of conflict and conflict termination. In W. Stroebe, A. Kruglanski, D. Bar-Tal, & M. Hewstone (Eds.), *The Social Psychology of Intergroup Conflict.* Berlin: Springer-Verlag.

Knez, M., & Camerer, C. (2000). Increasing cooperation in prisoner's dilemmas by establishing a precedent of efficiency in coordination games. *Organizational Behavior and Human Decision Processes,* 82(2), 194–216.

Kochan, T. A. (1979). Dynamics of dispute resolution in the public sector. In B. Aaron, J. R. Grodin, & J. L. Stern (Eds.), *Public-Sector Bargaining* (pp. 150–190). Washington, DC: BNA Books.

Kolb, D. (1983). *The Mediators.* Cambridge, MA: MIT Press.

Kollock, P. (1994). The emergence of exchange structures: An experimental study of uncertainty, commitment and trust. *American Journal of Sociology,* 100(2), 313–345.

Komorita, S. S., & Parks, C. D. (1994). *Social Dilemmas.* Madison, WI: Brown and Benchmark.

Komorita, S. S., & Parks, C. D. (1995). Interpersonal relations: Mixed-motive interaction. *Annual Review of Psychology,* 46, 183–207.

Kopelman, S., Rosette, A., & Thompson, L. (2004). The three faces of Eve: An examination of strategic positive, negative, and neutral emotion in negotiations. Manuscript under review.

Kopelman, S., Weber, J. M., & Messick, D. M. (2002). Factors influencing cooperation in commons dilemmas: A review of experimental psychological research. In E. Ostrom et al. (Eds.), *The Drama of the Commons* (pp. 113–156). Washington, DC: National Academy Press.

Kotter, J., & Schlesinger, L. (1979). Choosing strategies for change. *Harvard Business Review,* pp. 106–114.

Kramer, R. M. (1991). The more the merrier? Social psychological aspects of multiparty negotiations in organizations. In M. H. Bazerman, R. J. Lewicki, & B. H. Sheppard (Eds.), *Research on Negotiations in Organizations: Handbook of Negotiation Research,* vol. 3 (pp. 307–332). Greenwich, CT: JAI Press.

Kramer, R. M. (1995). Dubious battle: Heightened accountability, dysphoric cognition, and self-defeating bargaining behavior. In R. Kramer & D. Messick (Eds.), *Negotiation as a Social Process* (pp. 95–120). Thousand Oaks, CA: Sage.

Kramer, R. M. (1999). Trust and distrust in organizations: Emerging perspectives, enduring questions. *Annual Review of Psychology,* 50, 569–598.

Kramer, R. M., & Brewer, M. (1984). Effects of group identity on resource use in a simulated commons dilemma. *Journal of Personality and Social Psychology,* 46, 1044–1057.

Kramer, R. M., & Brewer, M. (1986). Social group identity and the emergence of cooperation in resource conservation dilemmas. In H. Wilke, C. Rutte, & D. Messick (Eds.), *Experimental Studies of Social Dilemmas.* Frankfurt: Peter Lang.

Kramer, R. M., Brewer, M. B., & Hanna, B. A. (1996). Collective trust and collective action: The decision to trust as a social decision. In R. M. Kramer & T. R. Tyler (Eds.), *Trust in Organizations* (pp. 357–389). Thousand Oaks, CA: Sage.

Kramer, R. M., & Hanna, B. A. (1988). Under the influence? Organizational paranoia and the misperception of others' influence behavior. In R. M. Kramer & M. A. Neale (Eds.), *Power and Influence in Organizations* (pp. 145–179). Thousand Oaks, CA: Sage.

Kramer, R., Pommerenke, P., & Newton, E. (1993). The social context of negotiation: Effects of social identity and accountability on negotiator judgment and decision making. *Journal of Conflict Resolution,* 37, 633–654.

Kramer, R. M., & Wei, J. (1999). Social uncertainty and the problem of trust in social groups: The social self in doubt. In T. R. Tyler & R. M. Kramer (Eds.), *The Psychology of the Social Self: Applied Social Research* (pp. 145–168). Mahwah, NJ: Lawrence Erlbaum.

Krauss, R. M., & Chiu, C. (1998). Language and social behavior. In D. T. Gilbert, S. T. Fiske, & G. Lindzey (Eds.), *The Handbook of Social Psychology,* 4th ed. (pp. 41–88). New York: McGraw-Hill.

Krauss, R. M., & Fussell, S. R. (1991). Perspective-taking in communication: Representations of others' knowledge in reference. *Social Cognition,* 9, 2–24.

Kray, L., Galinsky, A., & Thompson, L. (2002). Reversing the gender gap in negotiations: An exploration of stereotype regeneration. *Organizational Behavior and Human Decision Processes,* 87(2), 386–409.

Kray, L., Lind, A., & Thompson, L. (2004). It's a bet! How negotiator relationships and deal importance affect the resolution of differences. Manuscript under review.

Kray, L., Paddock, L., & Galinksy, A. (2003). Temporal framing: How a consideration of past successes and failures affects integrative negotiations. Manuscript under review.

Kray, L., Thompson, L., & Galinsky, A. (2001). Battle of the sexes: Gender stereotype confirmation and reactance in negotiations. *Journal of Personality and Social Psychology,* 80(6), 942–958.

Kreps, D. M., Milgrom, P., Roberts, J., & Wilson, R. (1982). Rational cooperation in the finitely repeated prisoner's dilemma. *Journal of Economic Theory,* 27, 245–252.

Kressel, K., & Pruitt, D. G. (1989). Conclusion: A research perspective on the mediation of social conflict. In K. Kressel & D. G. Pruitt (Eds.), *Mediation Research* (pp. 394–435). San Francisco: Jossey-Bass.

Krishnamurthy, S., Bottom, W. P., & Rao, A. G. (2003). Adaptive aspirations and contributions to a public good: Generic advertising as a response to decline. *Organizational Behavior and Human Decision Processes,* 92, 22–33.

Kriz, M. (1998). After Argentina. *National Journal,* 30(49), 2848–2853.

Kruger, J. (1999). Lake Wobegon be gone! The "below-average effect" and the egocentric nature of comparative ability judgments. *Journal of Personality and Social Psychology, 77,* 221–232.

Kruger, J., & Dunning, D. (1999). Unskilled and unaware of it: How difficulties in recognizing one's own incompetence lead to inflated self-assessments. *Journal of Personality and Social Psychology, 77,* 1121–1134.

Kuhlman, D. M., & Marshello, A. (1975). Individual differences in the game motives of own, relative, and joint gain. *Journal of Research in Personality, 9*(3), 240–251.

Kumar, R. (1997). The role of affect in negotiations: An integrative overview. *Journal of Applied Behavioral Science, 33*(1), 84–100.

Kurtzberg, T., Dunn-Jensen, L., & Matsibekker, C. (2003). When roles collide with reality: Novice attempts at agent-based negotiations. Paper presented at the Academy of Management Annual Meeting, Seattle, WA.

Kurtzberg, T., & Medvec, V. H. (1999). Can we negotiate and still be friends? *Negotiation Journal, 15*(4), 355–362.

Kwon, S., & Weingart, L. R. (2004). Unilateral concessions from the other party: Concession behavior, attributions, and negotiation judgments. *Journal of Applied Psychology, 89*(2), 263–278.

LaFrance, M. (1985). Postural mirroring and intergroup relations. *Personality and Social Psychology Bulletin, 11*(2), 207–217.

Lamm, H., & Kayser, E. (1978). An analysis of negotiation concerning the allocation of jointly produced profit or loss: The roles of justice norms, politeness, profit maximization, and tactics. *International Journal of Group Tensions, 8,* 64–80.

Landy, D., & Sigall, H. (1974). Beauty is talent: Task evaluation as a function of the performer's physical attractiveness. *Journal of Personality and Social Psychology, 29*(3), 299–304.

Langer, E. (1975). The illusion of control. *Journal of Personality and Social Psychology, 32,* 311–328.

Langer, E., Blank, A., & Chanowitz, B. (1978). The mindlessness of ostensibly thoughtful action: The role of placebic information in interpersonal interaction. *Journal of*

Personality and Social Psychology, 36, 635–642.

Langner, C., & Winter, D. (2001). The motivational basis of concessions and compromise: Archival and laboratory studies. *Journal of Personality and Social Psychology, 81*(4), 711–727.

Latané, B. (1981). The psychology of social impact. *American Psychologist, 36,* 343–356.

Lax, D. A., & Sebenius, J. K. (1986). *The Manager as Negotiator.* New York: Free Press.

Lax, D. A., & Sebenius, J. K. (1997, February 24). A better way to go on strike. *The Wall Street Journal,* Section A, p. 22.

Le Vine, R. A., & Campbell, D. T. (1972). *Ethnocentrism: Theories of Conflict, Ethnic Attitudes, and Group Behavior.* New York: Wiley.

Leavitt, H. (1989). Educating our MBAs: On teaching what we haven't taught. *California Management Review, 31*(3), 38–50.

Lee, W. (1971). *Decision Theory and Human Behavior.* New York: Wiley.

Lerner, H. G. (1985). *The Dance of Anger.* New York: Harper and Row.

Lerner, M. (1980). *The Belief in a Just World: The Fundamental Delusion.* New York: Plenum.

Leung, K. (1987). Some determinants of reactions to procedural models for conflict resolution: A cross-national study. *Journal of Personality and Social Psychology, 53*(5), 898–908.

Leventhal, H. (1976). The distribution of rewards and resources in groups and organizations. In L. Berkowitz & E. Walster (Eds.), *Advances in Experimental Social Psychology,* vol. 9 (pp. 92–133). New York: Academic Press.

Leventhal, H. (1980). What should be done with equity theory? New approaches to the study of fairness in social exchange. In K. Gergen, M. Greenberg, & R. Willis (Eds.), *Social Exchange: Advances in Theory and Research* (pp. 27–55). New York: Plenum Press.

Levine, J., & Moreland, R. L. (1994). Group socialization: Theory and research. In I. W. Stroebe & M. Hewstone (Eds.), *The European Review of Social Psychology,* vol. 5 (pp. 305–336). Chichester, England: Wiley.

Levine, J., & Thompson, L. (1996). Conflict in groups. In E. T. Higgins & A. Kruglanski (Eds.), *Social Psychology: Handbook of Basic Principles* (pp. 745–776). New York: Guilford.

LeVine, R. A. & Campbell, D. T. (1972). *Ethnocentrism: Theories of conflict, ethnic attitudes, and group behavior.* New York: Wiley.

Levinson, C., Smith, M., & Wilson, O. (1999). *Guerilla Negotiating: Unconventional Weapons and Tactics to Get What You Want.* New York: Wiley.

Lewicki, R. J. (1983). Lying and deception: A behavioral model. In M. H. Bazerman & R. J. Lewicki (Eds.), *Negotiating in Organizations.* Beverly Hills, CA: Sage.

Lewicki, R. J., & Bunker, B. B. (1996). Developing and maintaining trust in work relationships. In R. M. Kramer, & T. R. Tyler (Eds.), *Trust in Organizations: Frontiers of Theory and Research* (pp. 114–139). Thousand Oaks, CA: Sage.

Lewicki, R. J., & Robinson, R. J. (1998). Ethical and unethical bargaining tactics: An empirical study. *Journal of Business Ethics,* 17(6), 665–682.

Lewicki, R. J., & Stark, N. (1996). What's ethically appropriate in negotiations: An empirical examination of bargaining tactics. *Social Justice Research,* 9(1), 69–95.

Liebrand, W. B. G., Messick, D. M., & Wilke, H., Eds. (1992). *Social Dilemmas: Theoretical Issues and Research Findings.* Oxford, England: Pergamon Press.

Lim, S. G., & Murnighan, J. K. (1994). Phases, deadlines, and the bargaining process. *Organizational Behavior and Human Decision Processes,* 58, 153–171.

Lind, E. A., Kray, L., & Thompson, L. (1996). Adversity in organizations: Reactions to injustice. Paper presented at the Psychology of Adversity Conference, Amherst, MA.

Lind, E. A., & Tyler, T. R. (1988). *The Social Psychology of Procedural Justice.* New York: Plenum.

Lindsley, S. L. (1999, June). A layered model of problematic intercultural communication in U.S.-owned maquiladoras in Mexico. *Communication Monographs,* p. 145.

Linville, P. W., Fischer, G. W., & Salovey, P. (1989). Perceived distributions of the characteristics of in-group and out-group members: Empirical evidence and a computer simulation. *Journal of Personality and Social Psychology,* 57, 165–188.

Locke, K. D., & Horowitz, L. M. (1990). Satisfaction in interpersonal interactions as a function of similarity in level of dysphoria. *Journal of Personality and Social Psychology,* 58(5), 823–831.

Loewenstein, G. F., & Moore, D. A. (2004). When ignorance is bliss: Information exchange and inefficiency in bargaining. *Journal of Legal Studies,* 33(1), 37–58.

Loewenstein, G. F., & Schkade, D. (1999). Wouldn't it be nice? Predicting future feelings. In D. Kahneman & E. Diener (Eds.), *Well-Being: The Foundations of Hedonic Psychology* (pp. 85–105). New York: Russell Sage Foundation.

Loewenstein, G. F., Thompson, L., & Bazerman, M. H. (1989). Social utility and decision making in interpersonal contexts. *Journal of Personality and Social Psychology,* 57(3), 426–441.

Loewenstein, J., & Thompson, L. (2000). The challenge of learning. *Negotiation Journal,* 16(4), 399–408.

Loewenstein, J., Thompson, L., & Gentner, D. (1999). Analogical encoding facilitates transfer in negotiation. *Psychonomic Bulletin and Review,* 6(4), 586–597.

Loewenstein, J., Thompson, L., & Gentner, D. (2003). Analogical learning in negotiation teams: Comparing cases promotes learning and transfer. *Academy of Management Learning and Education,* 2(2), 119–127.

Lovallo, D., & Kahneman, D. (2003). Delusions of success: How optimism undermines executives' decisions. *Harvard Business Review,* 81(7), 56–63.

Lynn, M. (1997). Board games: Those who make it to the top are not usually shy, retiring types, and Cadbury only increases the likelihood of conflict. *Management Today,* pp. 30–34.

Lytle, A. L., Brett, J. M., & Shapiro, D. L. (1999). The strategic use of interests, rights and power to resolve disputes. *Negotiation Journal,* 15(1), 31–49.

Maisonneuve, J., Palmade, G., & Fourment, C. (1952). Selective choices and propinquity. *Sociometry,* 15, 135–140.

Mannix, E. (1993). Organizations as resource dilemmas: The effects of power balance on coalition formation in small groups. *Organizational Behavior and Human Decision Processes,* 55, 1–22.

Mannix, E., & Loewenstein, G. (1993). Managerial time horizons and inter-firm mobility: An experimental investigation. *Organizational Behavior and Human Decision Processes,* 56, 266–284.

Mannix, E. A., Thompson, L., & Bazerman, M. H. (1989). Negotiation in small groups. *Journal of Applied Psychology,* 74(3), 508–517.

Mannix, E. A., Tinsley, C. H., & Bazerman, M. H. (1995). Negotiating over time: Impediments to integrative solutions. *Organizational Behavior and Human Decision Processes,* 62(3), 241–251.

Manstead, A. S. R. (1991). Expressiveness as an individual difference. In R. S. Feldman & B. Rime (Eds.), *Fundamentals of Nonverbal Behavior: Studies in Emotion and Social Interaction* (pp. 285–328). New York: Cambridge University Press.

March, R. M. (1990). *The Japanese Negotiator: Subtlety and Strategy Beyond Western Logic,* 1st paperback ed. New York: Kodansha International.

Marlowe, D., Gergen, K., & Doob, A. (1966). Opponents' personality, expectation of social interaction and interpersonal bargaining. *Journal of Personality and Social Psychology,* 3, 206–213.

Marmo, M. (1995). The role of fact finding and interest arbitration in "selling" a settlement. *Journal of Collective Negotiations in the Public Sector,* 14, 77–97.

Martin, J. N. (1989). Intercultural communication competence. *International Journal of Intercultural Relations,* 13, 227–428.

Matsumoto, D. (1996). *Culture and Psychology.* Pacific Grove, CA: Brooks-Cole.

May, K. (1982). A set of independent, necessary and sufficient conditions for simple majority decisions. In B. Barry & R. Hardin (Eds.), *Rational Man and Irrational Society.* Beverly Hills, CA: Sage.

Mayer, J. D., Salovey, P., & Caruso, D. (2000). Models of emotional intelligence. In R. J. Sternberg (Ed.), The Handbook of Emotional Intelligence (pp. 396–420). New York: Cambridge University Press.

Mazur, A. (1985). A biosocial model of status in face-to-face groups. *Social Forces,* 64, 377–402.

McAlister, L., Bazerman, M. H., & Fader, P. (1986). Power and goal setting in channel negotiations. *Journal of Marketing Research,* 23, 238–263.

McClelland, G., & Rohrbaugh, J. (1978). Who accepts the Pareto axiom? The role of utility and equity in arbitration decisions. *Behavioral Science,* 23, 446–456.

McClintock, C. G., & Liebrand, W. B. (1988). Role of interdependence structure, individual value orientation, and another's strategy in social decision making: A transformational analysis. *Journal of Personality and Social Psychology,* 55(3), 396–409.

McClintock, C., Messick, D. M., Kuhlman, D., & Campos, F. (1973). Motivational bases of choice in three-choice decomposed games. *Journal of Experimental Social Psychology,* 9, 572–590.

McEwen, C. A., & Maiman, R. J. (1984). Mediation in small claims court: Achieving compliance through consent. *Law and Society Review,* 18, 11–49.

McGinn, K. L., & Croson, R. (2004). What do communication media mean for negotiations? A question of social awareness. In M. Gelfand & J. Brett (Eds.), *The Handbook of Negotiation and Culture: Theoretical Advances and Cultural Perspectives and Negotiation* (pp. 334–349). Palo Alto, CA: Stanford University Press.

McGinn, K. L., & Keros, A. T. (2002). Improvisation and the logic of exchange in socially embedded transactions. *Administrative Science Quarterly,* 47, 442–473.

McGinn, K. L., Thompson, L., & Bazerman, M. H. (2003). Dyadic processes of disclosure and reciprocity in bargaining with communication. *Journal of Behavorial Decision Making,* 16, 17–34.

McGrath, J. E. (1966). A social psychological approach to the study of negotiations. In R. V. Bowers (Ed.), *Studies on Behavior in*

Organizations (pp. 101–134). Athens, GA: University of Georgia Press.

McGrath, J. E., & Hollingshead, A. B. (1994). *Groups Interacting with Technology.* Thousand Oaks, CA: Sage.

McGrath, J. E., Kelly, J. R., & Machatka, D. E. (1984). The social psychology of time: Entrainment of behavior in social and organizational settings. *Applied Social Psychology Annual,* 5, 21–44.

McGuire, P. A. (1998, August). Historic conference focusing on creating a new discipline. *APA Monitor,* 29, 1, 15.

McGuire, T., Keisler, S., & Siegel, J. (1987). Group and computer-mediated discussion effects in risk decision-making. *Journal of Personality and Social Psychology,* 52(5), 917–930.

McKelvey, R. D., & Ordeshook, P. C. (1980). Vote trading: An experimental study. *Public Choice,* 35, 151–184.

McKendrick, J. (1999). The third way: Mitigate, not litigate Y2K beefs. *Midrange Systems,* 12(2), 52.

Medvec, V. H., & Galinsky, A. (2004). The strategic advantages of multiple equivalent offers. Working paper.

Medvec, V. H., Leonardelli, G., Claussen-Schulz, A., & Galinsky, A. (2004).Maximizing outcomes and maintaining relationships: Multiple equivalent offers in negotiations. Working paper.

Medvec, V. H., Madey, S. F., & Gilovich, T. (1995). When less is more: Counterfactual thinking and satisfaction among Olympic medalists. *Journal of Personality and Social Psychology,* 69(4), 603–610.

Meherabian, A. (1971). *Silent Messages.* Belmont, CA: Wadsworth.

Menon, T., Morris, M. W., Chiu, C., & Hong, Y. (1999). Culture and construal of agency: Attribution to individual versus group dispositions. *Journal of Personality and Social Psychology,* 76(5), 701–717.

Messick, D. M. (1993). Equality as a decision heuristic. In B. A. Mellers & J. Baron (Eds.), *Psychological Perspectives on Justice* (pp. 11–31). New York: Cambridge University Press.

Messick, D. M., & Bazerman, M. H. (1996). Ethical leadership and the psychology of decision making. *Sloan Management Review,* 37(2), 9–22.

Messick, D. M., & Brewer, M. (1983). Solving social dilemmas: A review. In L. Wheeler & P. Shaver (Eds.), *Review of Personality and Social Psychology,* vol. 4 (pp. 11–44). Beverly Hills, CA: Sage.

Messick, D. M., & Rutte, C. G. (1992). The provision of public goods by experts: The Groningen study. In W. B. G. Liebrand, D. M. Messick, & H. A. M. Wilke (Eds.), *Social Dilemmas: Theoretical Issues and Research Findings* (pp. 101–109). Oxford, England: Pergamon Press.

Messick, D. M., & Sentis, K. P. (1979). Fairness and preference. *Journal of Experimental Social Psychology,* 15(4), 418–434.

Messick, D. M., Wilke, H., Brewer, M. B., Kramer, R. M., Zemke, P. E., & Lui, L. (1983). Individual adaptations and structural change as solutions to social dilemmas. *Journal of Personality and Social Psychology,* 44(2), 294–309.

Meyerson, D., Weick, K. E., & Kramer, R. M. (1996). Swift trust and temporary groups. In R. M. Kramer & T. R. Tyler (Eds.), *Trust in Organizations: Frontiers of Theory and Research* (pp. 166–195). Thousand Oaks, CA: Sage.

Mikula, G. (1980). On the role of justice in allocation decisions. In G. Mikula (Ed.), *Justice and Social Interaction.* New York: Springer-Verlag.

Miller, G. A. (1956). The magical number seven plus or minus two: Some limits on our capacity for processing information. *Psychological Review,* 63, 81–97.

Mnookin, R. H. (2003). Strategic barriers to dispute resolution: A comparison of bilateral and multilateral negotiation. *Journal of Institutional and Theoretical Economics,* 159(1), 199–220.

Moore, D. A. (2004). The unexpected benefits of final deadlines in negotiation. *Journal of Experimental Social Psychology,* 40, 121–127.

Moore, D. A., & Kim, T. G. (2003). Myopic social prediction and the solo comparison effect. *Journal of Personality and Social Psychology,* 85(6), 1121–1135.

Moore, D. A., Kurtzberg, T., Thompson, L., & Morris, M. W. (1999). Long and short routes to success in electronically mediated negotiations:

Group affiliations and good vibrations. *Organization Behavior and Human Decision Processes,* 77(1), 22–43.

Moore, J. S., Graziano, W. G., & Millar, M. G. (1987). Physical attractiveness, sex role orientation, and the evaluation of adults and children. *Personality and Social Psychology Bulletin,* 13(1), 95–102.

Moreland, R. L., Argote, L., & Krishnan, R. (1996). Socially shared cognition at work. In J. L. Nye & A. M. Brower (Eds.), *What's Social About Social Cognition?* Thousand Oaks, CA: Sage.

Moreland, R. L., & Beach, S. R. (1992). Exposure effects in the classroom: The development of affinity among students. *Journal of Experimental Social Psychology,* 28(3), 255–276.

Morgan, P., & Tindale, R. S. (2002). Group vs. individual performance in mixed-motive situations: Exploring the inconsistency. *Organizational Behavior and Human Decision Processes,* 87(1), 44–65.

Morling, B., Kitayama, S., & Miyamoto, Y. (2002). Cultural practices emphasize influence in the United States and adjustment in Japan. *Personality and Social Psychology Bulletin,* 28(3), 311–323.

Morris, M. W. (1995). Through a glass darkly: Cognitive and motivational processes that obscure social perception in conflicts. Paper presented at the Academy of Management Meetings, Vancouver, BC.

Morris, M. W., Larrick, R. P., & Su, S. K. (1999). Misperceiving negotiation counterparties: When situationally determined bargaining behaviors are attributed to personality traits. *Journal of Personality and Social Psychology,* 77, 52–67.

Morris, M. W., Leung, K., & Sethi, S. (1999). Person perception in the heat of conflict: Perceptions of opponents' traits and conflict resolution in two cultures. Working paper no. 1360, Stanford University, Stanford, CA.

Morris, M. W., Nadler, J., Kurtzberg, T., and Thompson, L. (2002). Schmooze or lose: Social friction and lubrication in e-mail negotiations. *Group Dynamics: Theory, Research, and Practice,* 6(1), 89–100.

Morris, M. W., & Peng, K. (1994). Culture and cause: American and Chinese attributions for social and physical events. *Journal of Personality and Social Psychology,* 67(6), 949–971.

Morris, M. W., Podolny, J. M., & Ariel, S. (1999). Missing relations: Incorporating relational constructs into models of culture. Paper presented at 1998 SESP conference, Lexington, KY.

Morris, M. W., Sim, D. L. H., & Girotto, V. (1995). Time of decision, ethical obligation, and causal illusion: Temporal cues and social heuristics in the prisoner's dilemma. In R. Kramer & D. Messick (Eds.), *Negotiation as a Social Process* (pp. 209–239). Thousand Oaks, CA: Sage.

Morris, M. W., & Su, S. K. (1995). The hostile mediator phenomenon: When each side perceives the mediator to be partial to the other. Unpublished manuscript, Stanford University Graduate School of Business, Palo Alto, CA.

Mueller, J. S., & Curhan, J. R. (2004). Emotional intelligence and counterpart affect induction in the context of integrative negotiations. Working paper, Massachusetts Institute of Technology, Cambridge, MA.

Murnighan, J. K. (1978). Models of coalition behavior: Game theoretic, social psychological, and political perspectives. *Psychological Bulletin,* 85, 1130–1153.

Murnighan, J. K., Kim, J. W., & Metzger, A. R. (1993). The volunteer dilemma. *Administrative Science Quarterly,* 38(4), 515–538.

Myers, D. (2003). The odds on the odds. *Across the Board,* 40(6), 6.

Myers, F. (1999, February). Political argumentation and the composite audience: A case study. *Quarterly Journal of Speech,* pp. 55–65.

Nadler, J., Kurtzberg, T., Morris, M. W., & Thompson, L. (1999, February 15). Getting to know you: The effects of relationship-building and expectation on e-mail negotiations. Paper submitted to the 12th Conference of the International Association for Conflict Management, San Sebastián-Donostia, Spain.

Nadler, J., Thompson, L., & van Boven, L. (2003). Learning negotiation skills: Four models of knowledge creation and transfer. *Management Science,* 49(4), 529–540.

Naquin, C. (1999). Trust and distrust in group negotiations. Unpublished dissertation, Kellogg Graduate School of Management, Northwestern University, Evanston, IL.

Naquin, C. (2003). The agony of opportunity in negotiation: Number of negotiable issues, counterfactual thinking, and feelings of satisfaction. *Organizational Behavior and Human Decision Processes,* 91, 97–107.

Nash, J. (1950). The bargaining problem. *Econometrica,* 18, 155–162.

Nash, J. (1951). Non-cooperative games. *Annals of Mathematics,* 54(2), 286–295.

Nash, J. (1953). Two-person cooperative games. *Econometrica,* 21, 129–140.

Neale, M. A., & Bazerman, M. H. (1983). The role of perspective taking ability in negotiating under different forms of arbitration. *Industrial and Labor Relations Review,* 36, 378–388.

Neale, M. A., & Bazerman, M. H. (1985). The effects of framing and negotiator overconfidence on bargainer behavior. *Academy of Management Journal,* 28, 34–49.

Neale, M. A., & Bazerman, M. H. (1991). *Cognition and Rationality in Negotiation.* New York: Free Press.

Neale, M. A., Huber, V. L., & Northcraft, G. (1987). The framing of negotiations: Contextual versus task frames. *Organizational Behavior and Human Decision Processes,* 39(2), 228–241.

Neale, M. A., & Northcraft, G. (1986). Experts, amateurs, and refrigerators: Comparing expert and amateur negotiators in a novel task. *Organizational Behavior and Human Decision Processes,* 38, 305–317.

Neale, M. A., Northcraft, G. B., & Earley, P. C. (1990). The joint effects of goal setting and expertise on negotiator performance. Working paper, Northwestern University, Evanston, IL.

Newman, M. L., Pennebaker, J. W., Berry, D. S., & Richards, J. M. (2003). Lying words: Predicting deception from linguistic styles. *Personality and Social Psychology Bulletin,* 29(5), 665–675.

Nierenberg, G. I. (1968). *The Art of Negotiation: Psychological Strategies for Gaining Advantageous Bargains.* New York: Hawthorn Books.

Nisbett, R. E., Krantz, D. H., Jepson, C., & Kunda, Z. (1995). The use of statistical heuristics in everyday inductive reasoning. In R. E. Nisbett (Ed.), *Rules for Reasoning* (pp. 15–54). Hillsdale, NJ, Lawrence Erlbaum.

Northcraft, G., & Neale, M. A. (1993). Negotiating successful research collaboration. In J. K. Murnighan (Ed.), *Social Psychology in Organizations: Advances in Theory and Research.* Upper Saddle River, NJ: Prentice Hall.

Notarius, C. I., & Levenson, R. W. (1979). Expressive tendencies and physiological response to stress. *Journal of Personality and Social Psychology,* 37(7), 1204–1210.

Notz, W. W., & Starke, F. A. (1987). Arbitration and distributive justice: Equity or equality? *Journal of Applied Psychology,* 72, 359–365.

O'Connor, K. M. (1994). *Negotiation Teams: The Impact of Accountability and Representation Structure on Negotiator Cognition and Performance.* Eugene, OR: International Association of Conflict Management.

O'Connor, K. M. (1997). Groups and solos in context: The effects of accountability on team negotiation. *Organizational Behavior and Human Decision Processes,* 72(3), 384–407.

O'Connor, K. M., & Adams, A. A. (1996). Thinking about negotiation: An investigation of negotiators' scripts. Unpublished manuscript, Northwestern University, Evanston, IL.

O'Connor, K. M., & Arnold, J. A. (2001). Distributive spirals: Negotiation impasses and the moderating role of disputant self-efficacy. *Organizational Behavior and Human Decision Processes,* 84(1), 148–176.

O'Connor, K. M., & Arnold, J. A., & Burris, E. R. (2003). Negotiators' bargaining histories and their effects on future negotiation performance. Working paper, Cornell University, Ithaca, NY.

O'Connor, K. M., and Carnevale, P. J. (1997). A nasty but effective negotiation strategy: Misrepresentation of a common-value issue. *Personality and Social Psychology Bulletin,* 23(5), 504–515.

O'Quin, K., & Aronoff, J. (1981). Humor as a technique of social influence. *Social Psychology Quarterly,* 44(4), 349–357.

Ohtsubo, Y., & Kameda, T. (1998). The function of equality heuristic in distributive bargaining: Negotiated allocation of costs and benefits in a demand revelation context. *Journal of Experimental Social Psychology, 34*, 90–108.

Okhuysen, G., Galinsky, A., & Uptigrove, T. (2003). Saving the worst for last: The effect of time horizon on the efficiency of negotiating benefits and burdens. *Organizational Behavior and Human Decision Processes, 91*, 269–279.

Olekalns, M., Brett, J. M., & Weingart, L. R. (2003). Phases, transitions and interruptions: The processes that shape agreement in multiparty negotiations. Working paper, Dispute Resolution Research Center, Northwestern University, Evanston, IL.

Olekalns, M., & Smith, P. L. (1998). Simple frequency effects? Motivational orientation, strategic choice and outcome optimality in negotiations. Paper presented at IACM, Washington, DC.

Olekalns, M., & Smith, P. L. (1999). Social value orientations and strategy choices in competitive negotiations. *Personality and Social Psychology Bulletin, 25*(6), 657–668.

Olekalns, M., & Smith, P. L. (2003). Testing the relationships among negotiators' motivational orientations, strategy choices, and outcomes. *Journal of Experimental Social Psychology, 39*, 101–117.

Ordeshook, P. (1986). *Game Theory and Political Theory: An Introduction.* Cambridge: Cambridge University Press.

Osborn, A. F. (1957). *Applied Imagination.* New York: Scribner.

Osborn, A. F. (1963). *Applied Imagination,* 3rd ed. New York: Scribner.

Osgood, C. E. (1962). *An Alternative to War or Surrender.* Urbana: University of Illinois Press.

Osgood, C. E. (1979). GRIT 1 (vol. 8, no. 1, 0553–4283). Dundas, Ontario: Peace Research Reviews.

Osgood, C. E., Suci, G. J., & Tannenbaum, P. H. (1957). *The Measurement of Meaning.* Urbana: University of Illinois Press.

Oskamp, S. (1965). Attitudes toward U.S. and Russian actions: A double standard. *Psychological Reports, 16*, 43–46.

Paese, P. W., & Gilin, D. A. (2000). When an adversary is caught telling the truth: Reciprocal cooperation versus self-interest in distributive bargaining. *Personality and Social Psychology Bulletin, 26*(1), 79–90.

Palmer, L. G., & Thompson, L. (1995). Negotiation in triads: Communication constraints and tradeoff structure. *Journal of Experimental Psychology: Applied, 2*, 83–94.

Parks, C. D., Sanna, L. J., & Posey, D. C. (2003). Retrospection in social dilemmas: How thinking about the past affects future cooperation. *Journal of Personality and Social Psychology, 84*(5), 988–996.

Paulus, P. B. (1998). Developing consensus about groupthink after all these years. *Organization Behavior and Human Decision Processes, 73*(2–3), 362–374.

Pennebaker, J. W., Hughes, C. F., & O'Heeron, R. C. (1987). The psychophysiology of confession: Linking inhibitory and psychosomatic processes. *Journal of Personality and Social Psychology, 52*, 781–793.

Pennebaker, J. W., & Sanders, D. Y. (1976). American graffiti: Effects of authority and reactance arousal. *Personality and Social Psychology Bulletin, 2*, 264–267.

Peterson, E., & Thompson, L. (1997). Negotiation teamwork: The impact of information distribution and accountability on performance depends on the relationship among team members. *Organizational Behavior and Human Decision Processes, 72*(3), 364–383.

Philip, G., & Young, E. S. (1987). Man-machine interaction by voice: Developments in speech technology. Part I: The state-of-the-art. *Journal of Information Science, 13*, 3–14.

Pierce, R. S., Pruitt, D. G., & Czaja, S. J. (1993). Complainant-respondent differences in procedural choise. *International Journal of Conflict Management, 4*, 199–122.

Pillutla, M. M., & Chen, X. (1999). Social norms and cooperation in social dilemmas: The effects of context and feedback. *Organizational Behavior and Human Decision Processes, 78*(2), 81–103.

Pillutla, M. M., & Murnighan, J. K. (1995). Being fair or appearing fair: Strategic behavior in ultimatum bargaining. *Academy of Management Journal, 38*(5), 1408–1426.

Plott, C. (1976). Axiomatic social choice theory: An overview and interpretation. *American Journal of Political Science, 20,* 511–596.

Plott, C., & Levine, M. (1978). A model of agenda influence on committee decisions. *American Economic Review, 68,* 146–160.

Poincaré, H. (1929). *The Foundations of Sciences.* New York: Science House.

Pólya, G. (1957). *How to Solve It: A New Aspect of Mathematical Method,* 2nd ed. New York: Doubleday.

Pólya, G. (1968). *Mathematical Discovery, Volume II: On Understanding, Learning, and Teaching Problem Solving.* New York: Wiley.

Popkin, S. (1981). Public choice and rural development—free riders, lemons, and institutional design. In C. Russel & N. Nicholson (Eds.), *Public Choice and Rural Development* (pp. 43–80). Washington, DC: Resources for the Future.

Prentice, D. A., Miller, D. T., & Lightdale, J. R. (1994). Asymmetries in attachments to groups and to their members: Distinguishing between common-identity and common-bond groups. *Personality and Social Psychology Bulletin, 20,* 484–493.

Pruitt, D. G., (1981). Negotiation Behavior. New York: Academic Press.

Pruitt, D. G., & Carnevale, P. J. (1993). *Negotiation in Social Conflict.* Pacific Grove, CA: Brooks-Cole.

Pruitt, D. G., & Lewis, S. A. (1975). Development of integrative solutions in bilateral negotiation. *Journal of Personality and Social Psychology, 31,* 621–630.

Putnam, L. L. (1983). Small group work climates: A lag-sequential analysis of group interaction. *Small Group Behavior, 14*(4), 465–494.

Quinn, S. R., Bell, D., & Wells, J. (1997). Interest-based negotiation: A case study. *Public Personnel Management, 26*(4), 529–533.

Raiffa, H. (1982). *The Art and Science of Negotiation.* Cambridge, MA: Belknap.

Rand, K. A., & Carnevale, P. J. (1994). The benefits of team support in bilateral negotiations. Unpublished manuscript, University of Illinois, Champaign, IL.

Raven, B. H. (1990). Political applications of the psychology of interpersonal influence and social power. *Political Psychology, 11*(3), 493–520.

Redelmeier, D. A., & Kahneman, D. (1996). Patients' memories of painful medical treatments: Real-time and retrospective evaluations of two minimally invasive procedures. *Pain, 66*(1), 3–8.

Reingen, P. H. (1982). Test of a list procedure for inducing compliance with a request to donate money. *Journal of Applied Psychology, 67*(1), 110–118.

Reingen, P. H., & Kernan, J. B. (1993). Social perception and interpersonal influence: Some consequences of the physical attractiveness stereotype in a personal selling setting. *Journal of Consumer Psychology, 2*(1), 25–38.

Robinson, R. J., & Keltner, D. (1996). Much ado about nothing? Revisionists and traditionalists choose an introductory English syllabus. *Psychological Science, 7*(1), 18–24.

Robinson, R. J., Keltner, D., Ward, A., & Ross, L. (1994). Actual versus assumed differences in construal: "Naïve realism" in intergroup perception and conflict. *Journal of Personality and Social Psychology, 68,* 404–417.

Robinson, R. J., Lewicki, R. J., & Donahue, E. M. (2000). Extending and testing a five factor model of ethical and unethical bargaining tactics: Introducing the SINS scale. *Journal of Organizational Behavior, 21,* 649–664.

Rose, C. M. (1994). *Property and Persuasion: Essays on the History, Theory, and Rhetoric of Ownership.* Boulder, CO: Westview Press.

Rose, J. B., & Manuel, C. (1996). Attitudes toward collective bargaining and compulsory arbitration. *Journal of Collective Negotiations in the Public Sector, 25,* 287–310.

Rosenthal, R., & DePaulo, B. M. (1979a). Sex differences in accommodation in nonverbal communication. In R. Rosenthal (Ed.), *Skill in Nonverbal Communication: Individual Differences* (pp. 68–103). Cambridge, MA: Oelgeschlager, Gunn, and Hain.

Rosenthal, R., & DePaulo, B. M. (1979b). Sex differences in eavesdropping on nonverbal cues. *Journal of Personality and Social Psychology, 37*(2), 273–285.

Rosette, A., Brett, J. M., Barsness, Z., & Lytle, A. (2000). Social presence across cultures: E-mail negotiations in the U.S. and Hong Kong. Working paper, Northwestern University, Evanston, IL.

Ross, B. H. (1987). This is like that: The use of earlier problems and the separation of similarity effects. *Journal of Experimental Psychology: Learning, Memory and Cognition,* 13(4), 629–639.

Ross, J., & Staw, B. M. (1993). Organizational escalation and exit: Lessons from the Shoreham Nuclear Power Plant. *Academy of Management Journal,* 36(4), 701–732.

Ross, L. (1977). The intuitive psychologist and his shortcomings: Distortions in the attribution process. In L. Berkowitz (Ed.), *Advances in Experimental Social Psychology,* vol. 10 (pp. 173–220). Orlando, FL: Academic Press.

Ross, L., & Lepper, M. R. (1980). The perseverance of beliefs: Empirical and normative considerations. In R. A. Shweder (Ed.), *New Directions for Methodology of Behavioral Science: Fallible Judgment in Behavioral Research.* San Francisco: Jossey-Bass.

Ross, L., & Samuels, S. M. (1993). The predictive power of personal reputation vs. labels and construal in the prisoner's dilemma game. Working paper, Stanford University, Palo Alto, CA.

Ross, L., & Stillinger, C. (1991). Barriers to conflict resolution. *Negotiation Journal,* 7(4), 389–404.

Ross, L., & Ward, A. (1996). Naïve realism in everyday life: Implications for social conflict and misunderstanding. In T. Brown, E. S. Reed, & E. Turiel, (Eds), *Values and Knowledge. The Jean Piaget Symposium Series* (pp. 103–135). Mahwah, NJ: Lawrence Erlbaum.

Ross, M., & Sicoly, F. (1979). Egocentric biases in availability attribution. *Journal of Personality and Social Psychology,* 8, 322–336.

Ross, W. H., & Conlon, D. E. (2000). Hybrid forms of third-party dispute resolution: Theoretical implications of combining mediation and arbitration. *Academy of Management Review,* 25(2), 416–427.

Ross, W. H., Conlon, D. E., & Lind, E. A. (1990). The mediator as leader: Effects of behavioral style and deadline certainty on negotiator behavior. *Group and Organization Studies,* 15, 105–124.

Roth, A. E. (1993). Bargaining experiments. In J. Kagel & A. E. Roth (Eds.), *Handbook of Experimental Economics.* Princeton, NJ: Princeton University Press.

Roth A. E., Murnighan, J. K., & Schoumaker, F. (1988). The deadline effect in bargaining: Some experimental evidence. *American Economic Review,* 78(4), 806–823.

Rothbart, M., & Hallmark, W. (1988). In-group and out-group differences in the perceived efficacy of coercion and concilliation in resolving social conflict. *Journal of Personality and Social Psychology,* 55, 248–257.

Ruback, R. B., & Juieng, D. (1997). Territorial defense in parking lots: Retaliation against waiting drivers. *Journal of Abnormal Social Psychology,* 27, 821–834.

Rubin, J. Z., Pruitt, D. G., & Kim, S. H. (1994). *Social Conflict: Escalation, Stalemate and Settlement.* New York: McGraw-Hill.

Rubin, J. Z., & Sander, F. E. A. (1988). When should we use agents? Direct vs. representative negotiation. *Negotiation Journal,* 4(4), 395–401.

Rutte, C. G., & Wilke, H. A. M. (1984). Social dilemmas and leadership. *European Journal of Social Psychology,* 14, 105–121.

Sally, D. F. (1995). Conversation and cooperation in social dilemmas: Experimental evidence from 1958 to 1992. *Rationality and Society,* 7(1), 58–92.

Sander, F. E. A. (1993). The courthouse and alternative dispute resolution. In L. Hall (Ed.), *Negotiation: Strategies for Mutual Gain* (pp. 43–60). Newbury Park, CA: Sage.

Saunders, D. G., & Size, P. B. (1986). Attitudes about woman abuse among police officers, victims, and victim advocates. *Journal of Interpersonal Violence,* 1.

Savage, L. J. (1954). *The Foundations of Statistics.* New York: Wiley.

Schatzki, M. (1981). *Negotiation: The Art of Getting What You Want.* New York: New American Library.

Schelling, T. (1960). *The Strategy of Conflict.* Cambridge, MA: Harvard University Press.

Schkade, D. A., & Kahneman, D. (1998). Does living in California make people happy? A focusing illusion in judgments of life satisfaction. *Psychological Science, 9*(5), 340–346.

Schlenker, B. R. (1980). *Impression Management: The Self-Concept, Social Identity, and Interpersonal Relations.* Belmont, CA: Brooks-Cole.

Schmitt, D., & Marwell, G. (1972). Withdrawal and reward reallocation in response to inequity. *Journal of Experimental Social Psychology, 8*, 207–221.

Schneider, A. K. (2002). Shattering negotiation myths: Empirical evidence on the effectiveness of negotiation style. *Harvard Negotiation Law Review, 7*, 143–233.

Schneider, S. C. (1997). *Managing Across Cultures.* Upper Saddle River, NJ: Prentice Hall.

Schofield, J. W. (1986). Black and white contact in desegregated schools. In M. Hewstone & R. J. Brown (Eds.), *Contact and Conflict in Intergroup Encounters* (pp. 79–92). Oxford, England: Blackwell.

Schrage, M. (1995). *No More Teams!: Mastering the Dynamics of Creative Collaboration.* New York: Currency Doubleday.

Schwartz, S. (1994). Beyond individualism/collectivism: New cultural dimensions of values. In H. C. Triandis, U. Kim, & G. Yoon (Eds.), *Individualism and Collectivism* (pp. 85–117). London: Sage.

Schweitzer, M. (2001). Deception in negotiations. In S. Hoch & H. Kunreuther (Eds.), *Wharton on Making Decisions* (pp. 187–200). New York: Wiley.

Schweitzer, M., Brodt, S., & Croson, R. (2002). Seeing and believing: Visual access and the strategic use of deception. *International Journal of Conflict Management, 13*(3), 258–275.

Schweitzer, M., & Croson, R. (1999). Curtailing deception: The impact of direct questions on lies and omissions. *International Journal of Conflict Management, 10*, 225–248.

Schweitzer, M., Hershey, J., & Bradlow, E. (2003). Promises and lies: Restoring violated trust. Working paper, University of Pennsylvania, Philadelphia.

Schweitzer, M., & Hsee, C. (2002). Stretching the truth: Elastic justification and motivated communication of uncertain information. *Journal of Risk and Uncertainty, 25*(2), 185–201.

Schweitzer, M., Ordóñez, L., & Douma, B. (2004). The dark side of goal setting: The role of goals in motivating unethical behavior. *Academy of Management Journal, 47*(3).

Schwinger, T. (1980). Just allocations of goods: Decisions among three principles. In G. Mikula (Ed.), *Justice and Social Interaction: Experimental and Theoretical Contributions from Psychological Research.* New York: Springer-Verlag.

Sears, D. O., & Allen, H. M., Jr. (1984). The trajectory of local desegregation controversies and Whites' opposition to busing. In N. Miller & M. Brewer (Eds.), *Groups in Contact: The Psychology of Desegregation* (pp. 123–151). New York: Academic Press.

Sebenius, J. (2001). Six habits of merely effective negotiators. *Harvard Business Review, 79*(4), 87–95.

Seeley, E., Thompson, L. & Gardner, W. (2003). Power and exploitation in groups: Effects of construal and group size. Paper presented at the Academy of Management Annual Meeting, Seattle, WA.

Segal, M. W. (1974). Alphabet and attraction: An unobtrusive measure of the effect of propinquity in a field setting. *Journal of Personality and Social Psychology, 30*(5), 654–657.

Segil, L. (1999). Alliances for the 21st century. *Executive Excellence, 16*(10), 19.

Selten, R. (1975). Re-examination of the perfectness concept for equilibrium points in extensive games. *International Journal of Game Theory, 4*, 25–55.

Shafir, E. (1994). Uncertainty and the difficulty of thinking through disjunctions. *Cognition, 50*, 403–430.

Shapiro, D. L., Buttner, E. H., & Barry, B. (1994). Explanations: What factors enhance their perceived adequacy? *Organizational Behavior and Human Decision Processes, 58*(3), 346–368.

Shapiro, D. L., Sheppard, B. H., & Cheraskin, L. (1992). Business on a handshake. *Negotiation Journal*, 8(4), 365–377.

Shapley, L. S. (1977). The St. Petersburg Paradox: A con game? *Journal of Economic Theory*, 14, 353–409.

Shaw, M. E. (1981). *Group Dynamics: The Psychology of Small Group Behavior*, 3rd ed. New York: McGraw-Hill.

Shell, G. R. (1999). *Bargaining for Advantage: Negotiation Strategies for Reasonable People.* New York: Viking.

Shell, G. R. (1999, May). Negotiator, know thyself. *Inc.*, p. 106.

Sheppard, B. H. (1984). Third-party intervention: A procedural framework. In B. M. Staw & L. L. Cummings (Eds.), *Research in Organizational Behavior*, Vol. 6. Greenwich, CT: JAI Press.

Sherif, M. (1936). *The Psychology of Social Norms.* New York: Harper and Row.

Sherif, M., Harvey, O. J., White, B. J., Hood, W. R., & Sherif, C. W. (1961). *Intergroup Conflict and Cooperation: The Robber's Cave Experiment.* Norman: University of Oklahoma Press.

Sherman, D. K., Nelson, L. D., & Ross, L. D. (2003). Naïve realism and affirmative action: Adversaries are more similar than they think. *Basic and Applied Social Psychology*, 25(4), 275–289.

Sherman, S. J., Presson, C. C., & Chassin, L. (1984). Mechanisms underlying the false consensus effect: The special role of threats to the self. *Personality and Social Psychology Bulletin*, 10, 127–138.

Shirakashi, S. (1985). Social loafing of Japanese students. *Hiroshima Forum for Psychology*, 10, 35–40.

Siamwalla, A. (1978, June). Farmers and middlemen: Aspects of agricultural marketing in Thailand. *Economic Bulletin for Asia and the Pacific*, pp. 38–50.

Siegel, S., & Fouraker, L. E. (1960). *Bargaining and Group Decision Making.* New York: McGraw-Hill.

Silveira, J. M. (1972). Incubation: The effect of interruption timing and length on problem solution and quality of problem processing. *Dissertation Abstracts International*, 32(9-B), 5500.

Simon, H. (1955). A behavioral model of rational choice. *Quarterly Journal of Economics*, 69, 99–118.

Singelis, T. M. (1998). *Teaching About Culture, Ethnicity, and Diversity: Exercises and Planned Activities.* Thousand Oaks, CA: Sage.

Skinner, B. F. (1938). *The Behavior of Organisms: An Experimental Analysis.* New York, London: D. Appleton Century.

Slovic, P. (1962). Convergent validation of risk taking measures. *Journal of Abnormal and Social Psychology*, 65(1), 68–71.

Slovic, P. (1964). Assessment of risk taking behavior. *Psychological Bulletin*, 61(3), 220–233.

Snodgrass, S. E. (1985). Women's intuition: The effect of subordinate role on interpersonal sensitivity. *Journal of Personality and Social Psychology*, 49(1), 146–155.

Snodgrass, S. E. (1992). Further effects of role versus gender on interpersonal sensitivity. *Journal of Personality and Social Psychology*, 62(1), 154–158.

Snyder, M. (1974). Self-monitoring of expressive behavior. *Journal of Personality and Social Psychology*, 30, 526–537.

Solnick, S. J., & Schweitzer, M. (1999). The influence of physical attractiveness and gender on ultimatum game decisions. *Organizational Behavior and Human Decision Processes*, 79(3), 199–215.

Sondak, H., & Moore, M. (1994). Relationship frames and cooperation. *Group Decision and Negotiation*, 2, 103–118.

Sondak, H., Neale, M. A., & Pinkley, R. (1995). The negotiated allocation of benefits and burdens: The impact of outcome valence, contribution and relationship. *Organizational Behavior and Human Decision Processes*, 64(3), 249–260.

Spencer, S. J., Steele, C. M., & Quinn, D. M. (1999). Stereotype threat and women's math performance. *Journal of Experimental Social Psychology*, 35(1), 4–28.

Sproull, L., & Keisler, S. (1991). *Connections: New Ways of Working in the Networked Organization.* Cambridge, MA: MIT Press.

Stasser, G. (1992). Pooling of unshared information during group discussion. In S. Worchel, W. Wood, & J. A. Simpson (Eds.), *Group Processes and Productivity* (pp. 48–67). Newbury Park, CA: Sage.

Staudohar, P. D. (1999). Labor relations in basketball: The lockout of 1998–99. *Monthly Labor Review,* 122(4), 3–9.

Steele, C. M. (1997). A threat in the air: How stereotypes shape intellectual identity and performance. *American Psychologist,* 52(6), 613–629.

Steele, C. M., & Aronson, J. (1995). Stereotype threat and the intellectual test performance of African Americans. *Journal of Personality and Social Psychology,* 69(5), 797–811.

Steil, J. M., & Makowski, D. G. (1989). Equity, equality, and need: A study of the patterns and outcomes associated with their use in intimate relationships. *Social Justice Research,* 3, 121–137.

Stoppard, J. M., & Gun-Gruchy, C. (1993). Gender, context, and expression of positive emotion. *Personality and Social Psychology Bulletin,* 19(2), 143–150.

Stratton, R. P. (1983). Atmosphere and conversion errors in syllogistic reasoning with contextual material and the effect of differential training. Unpublished masters thesis, Michigan State University, East Lansing. In Mayer, R. E. (ed.), *Thinking, problem-solving, and cognition.* New York: W. H. Freeman and Company.

Strodtbeck, F. L., & Hook, L. H. (1961). The social dimensions of a 12-man jury table. *Sociometry,* 24(4), 397–415.

Stroebe, W., Kruglanski, A. W., Bar-Tal, D., & Hewstone, M., (Eds). (1988). *The Social Psychology of Intergroup Conflict.* Berlin: Springer-Verlag.

Stroebe, W., Lenkert, A., & Jonas, K. (1988). Familiarity may breed contempt: The impact of student exchange on national stereotypes and attitudes. In W. Stroebe, A. W. Kruglanski, D. Bar-Tal, & M. Hewstone (Eds.), *The Social Psychology of Intergroup Conflict* (pp. 167–187). New York: Springer-Verlag.

Stuhlmacher, A. F., Gillespie, T. L., & Champagne, M. V. (1998). The impact of time pressure in negotiation: A meta-analysis. *International Journal of Conflict Management,* 9(2), 97–116.

Suedfeld, P., Bochner, S., & Matas, C. (1971). Petitioners attire and petition signing by peace demonstrators: A field experiment. *Journal of Applied Social Psychology,* 1(3), 278–283.

Sullins, E. S. (1989). Perceptual salience as a function of nonverbal expressiveness. *Personality and Social Psychology Bulletin,* 15(4), 584–595.

Sullivan, B. A., O'Connor, K. M., & Burris, E. (2003). How negotiation-related self-efficacy affects tactics and outcomes. Paper presented at the Academy of Management Annual Meeting, Seattle, WA.

Swann, W. B., Pelham, B. W., & Roberts, D. C. (1987). Causal chunking: Memory and inference in ongoing interaction. *Journal of Personality and Social Psychology,* 53(5), 858–865.

Tajfel, H. (1970). Experiments in intergroup discrimination. *Scientific American,* 223, 96–102.

Tajfel, H. (1979). The exit of social mobility and the voice of social change: Notes on the social psychology of intergroup relations. *Przeglad Psychologiczny,* 22(1), 17–38.

Tajfel, H. (1982). Social psychology of intergroup relations. *Annual Review of Psychology,* 33, 1–39.

Tajfel, H., & Turner, J. (1986). The social identity theory of intergroup behavior. In S. Worchel and W. Austin (Eds.), *Psychology of Intergroup Relations* (pp. 7–24). Chicago: Nelson-Hall.

Taylor, S. E., & Brown, J. (1988). Illusion and well-being: A social-psychological perspective. *Psychological Bulletin,* 103, 193–210.

Taylor, S. E., & Lobel, M. (1989). Social comparison activity under threat: Downward evaluation and upward contacts. *Psychological Bulletin,* 96, 569–575.

Teal, T. (1996). The human side of management. *Harvard Business Review,* 74(6), 35–44.

Tetlock, P. E. (1985). Accountability: A social check on the fundamental attribution error. *Social Psychology Quarterly,* 48, 227–236.

Tetlock, P. E. (1992). The impact of accountability on judgment and choice: Toward a social contingency model. *Advances in Experimental Social Psychology,* 25, 331–376.

Tetlock, P. E., Peterson, R., & Lerner, J. (1996). Revising the value pluralism model: Incorporating social content and context postulates. In C. Seligman, J. Olson, & M. Zanna (Eds.), *The Psychology of Values: The Ontario Symposium,* vol. 8. Mahwah, NJ: Lawrence Erlbaum.

Thibaut, J., & Kelley, H. H. (1959). *The Social Psychology of Groups.* New York: Wiley.

Thibaut, J., and Walker, L. (1975). *Procedural Justice: A Psychological Analysis.* Hillsdale, NJ: Erlbaum.

Thibaut, J., and Walker, L. (1978). A theory of procedure. *California Law Review,* 60, 541–566.

Thompson, L. (1990a). An examination of naïve and experienced negotiators. *Journal of Personality and Social Psychology,* 59(1), 82–90.

Thompson, L. (1990b). The influence of experience on negotiation performance. *Journal of Experimental Social Psychology,* 26(6), 528–544.

Thompson, L. (1991). Information exchange in negotiation. *Journal of Experimental Social Psychology,* 27(2), 161–179.

Thompson, L. (1993). The impact of negotiation on intergroup relations. *Journal of Experimental Social Psychology,* 29(4), 304–325.

Thompson, L. (1995a). The impact of minimum goals and aspirations on judgments of success in negotiations. *Group Decision Making and Negotiation,* 4, 513–524.

Thompson, L. (1995b). "They saw a negotiation": Partisanship and involvement. *Journal of Personality and Social Psychology,* 68(5), 839–853.

Thompson, L. (2004). *Making the Team: A Guide for Managers,* 2nd ed. Upper Saddle River, NJ: Pearson Education.

Thompson, L., & DeHarpport, T. (1994). Social judgment, feedback, and interpersonal learning in negotiation. *Organizational Behavior and Human Decision Processes,* 58(3), 327–345.

Thompson, L., & DeHarpport, T. (1998). Relationships, good incompatibility, and communal orientation in negotiations. *Basic and Applied Social Psychology,* 20(1), 33–44.

Thompson, L., & Fox, C. (2000). Negotiation within and between groups in organizations: Levels of analysis. In M. Turner (Ed.), *Groups at Work: Advances in Theory and Research.* Hillsdale, NJ: Erlbaum.

Thompson, L., & Gonzalez, R. (1997). Environmental disputes: Competition for scarce resources and clashing of values. In M. Bazerman, D. Messick, A. Tenbrunsel, & K. Wade-Benzoni (Eds.), *Environment, Ethics, and Behavior* (pp. 75–104). San Francisco: New Lexington Press.

Thompson, L., & Hastie, R. (1990). Social perception in negotiation. *Organizational Behavior and Human Decision Processes,* 47(1), 98–123.

Thompson, L., & Hrebec, D. (1996). Lose-lose agreements in interdependent decision making. *Psychological Bulletin,* 120(3), 396–409.

Thompson, L., & Kim, P. H. (2000). How the quality of third parties" settlement solutions are affected by the relationship between negotiators. *Journal of Experimental Psychology: Applied,* 6(1), 1–16.

Thompson, L., & Loewenstein, G. F. (1992). Egocentric interpretations of fairness and negotiation. *Organizational Behavior and Human Decision Processes,* 51, 176–197.

Thompson, L., & Loewenstein, J. (2003). Mental models of negotiation: Descriptive, prescriptive, and paradigmatic implications. In M. A. Hogg & J. Cooper (Eds.), *Sage Handbook of Social Psychology.* London: Sage.

Thompson, L., Loewenstein, J., & Gentner, D. (2000). Avoiding missed opportunities in managerial life: Analogical training more powerful than case-based training. *Organizational Behavior and Human Decision Processes,* 82(1), 60–75.

Thompson, L., Mannix, E., & Bazerman, M. H. (1988). Group negotiation: Effects of decision rule, agenda, and aspiration. *Journal of Personality and Social Psychology,* 54, 86–95.

Thompson, L., Medvec, V. H., Seiden, V., & Kopelman, S. (2000). Poker face, smiley face, and rant" 'n" rave: Myths and realities about emotion in negotiation. In M. Hogg & S. Tindale (Eds.), *Blackwell Handbook in Social Psychology,* vol. 3: Group processes. Cambridge, MA: Blackwell Publishers, Inc.

Thompson, L., & Nadler, J. (2002). Negotiating via information technology: Theory and application. *Journal of Social Issues,* 58(1), 109–124.

Thompson, L., Nadler, J., & Kim, P. (1999). Some like it hot: The case for the emotional negotiator. In L. Thompson, J. Levine, & D. Messick (Eds.), *Shared Cognition in Organizations: The Management of Knowledge* (pp. 139–162). Mahwah, NJ: Erlbaum.

Thompson, L., Peterson, E., & Brodt, S. (1996). Team negotiation: An examination of integrative and distributive bargaining. *Journal of Personality and Social Psychology,* 70(1), 66–78.

Thompson, L., Valley, K. L., & Kramer, R. M. (1995). The bittersweet feeling of success: An examination of social perception in negotiation. *Journal of Experimental Social Psychology,* 31(6), 467–492.

Thornton, B. (1992). Repression and its mediating influence on the defensive attribution of responsibility. *Journal of Research in Personality,* 26, 44–57.

Tiedens, L. Z., & Fragale, A. R. (2003). Power moves: Complementary in dominant and submissive nonverbal behavior. *Journal of Personality and Social Psychology,* 84(3), 558–568.

Tietenberg, T. (2002). The tradable permits approach to protecting the commons: What have we learned. In E. Ostrom, T. Dietz, N. Dolsak, P. C. Stern, S. Sonich, & E. U. Weber (Eds.), *The Drama of the Commons* (pp. 197–232). Washington, DC: National Academy Press.

Ting-Toomey, S. (1985). Toward a theory of conflict and culture. *International and Intercultural Communication Annual,* 9, 71–86.

Tinsley, C. H. (1998). Models of conflict resolution in Japanese, German, and American cultures. *Journal of Applied Psychology,* 83(2), 316–323.

Tinsley, C. H. (2001). How we get to yes: Predicting the constellation of strategies used across cultures to negotiate conflict. *Journal of Applied Psychology,* 86(4), 583–593.

Tinsley, C. H., & Brett, J. M. (2001). Managing workplace conflict in the United States and Hong Kong. *Organizational Behavior and Human Decision Processes,* 85(2), 360–381.

Tinsley, C. H., Curhan, J. R., & Kwak, R. S. (1999). Adopting a dual lens approach for examining the dilemma of differences in international business negotiations. *International Negotiation,* 4, 5–22.

Tinsley, C. H., O'Connor, K. M., & Sullivan, B. A. (2002). Tough guys finish last: The perils of a distributive reputation. *Organizational Behavior and Human Decision Processes,* 88, 621–642.

Tinsley, C. H., & Pillutla, M. M. (1998). Negotiating in the United States and Hong Kong. *Journal of International Business Studies,* 29(4), 711–728.

Tinsley, C. H., & Weldon, E. (2003). Responses to a normative conflict among American and Chinese managers. *International Journal of Cross-Cultural Management,* 3(2), 183–234.

Tipton, C. A. (1995). Protecting tomorrow's harvest: Developing a national system of individual transferable quotas to conserve ocean resources. *Virginia Environmental Law Journal,* 14, 381–421.

Tornow, W. W., & Pinto, P. R. (1976). The development of a managerial job taxonomy: A system for describing, classifying, and evaluating executive positions. *Journal of Applied Psychology,* 61, 410–418.

Triandis, H. C. (1994). *Culture and Social Behavior* (pp. 29–54). New York: McGraw-Hill.

Tversky, A., & Fox, C. (1995). Weighing risk and uncertainty. *Psychological Review,* 102(2), 269–283.

Tversky, A., & Kahneman, D. (1973). Availability: A heuristic for judging frequency and probability. *Cognitive Psychology,* 5, 207–232.

Tversky, A., & Kahneman, D. (1974). Judgment under uncertainty: Heuristics and biases. *Science,* 185, 1124–1131.

Tversky, A., & Kahneman, D. (1992). Advances in prospect theory: Cumulative representation of uncertainty. *Journal of Risk and Uncertainty,* 5, 297–323.

Tversky, A., & Shafir, E. (1992). The disjunction effect in choice under uncertainty. *Psychological Science,* 3(5), 305–309.

Tyler, T. R., & Degoey, P. (1995). Collective restraint in social dilemmas: Procedural justice and social identification effects on support for authorities. *Journal of Personality and Social Psychology,* 69(3), 482–497.

Tynan, R. O. (1999, August). The impact of threat sensitivity and face giving on information transfer in organizational hierarchies. Paper presented at the Academy of Management Annual Meeting, Chicago.

Ury, W. L., Brett, J. M., & Goldberg, S. B. (1988). *Getting Disputes Resolved: Designing Systems to Cut the Costs of Conflict.* San Francisco: Jossey-Bass.

Uzzi, B. (1997). Social structure and competition in interfirm networks: The paradox of embeddedness. *Administrative Science Quarterly,* 42, 35–67.

Uzzi, B. (1999a). Access and control benefits through embedded ties and network complementarity: The case of midmarket firms and banks. Manuscript under review.

Uzzi, B. (1999b). What is a relationship worth? The benefit of embeddedness in corporate financing. Manuscript under review.

Valley, K. L., Moag, J., & Bazerman, M. H. (1998). A matter of trust: Effects of communication on the efficiency and distribution of outcomes. *Journal of Economic Behavior and Organizations,* 34, 211–238.

Valley, K., Neale, M. A., & Mannix, E. (1995). Friends, lovers, colleagues, strangers: The effects of relationship on the process and outcome of dyadic negotiations. In R. J. Bies, R. J. Lewicki, & B. H. Sheppard (Eds.), *Research on Negotiation in Organizations: Handbook of Negotiation Research*, vol. 5 (pp. 65–93). Greenwich, CT: JAI Press.

Valley, K. L., & Thompson, T. A. (1998). Sticky ties and bad attitudes: Relational and individual bases of resistance to change in organizational structure. In Kramer, R. M., & Neale, M. A. (Eds.), *Power and Influence in Organizations* (pp. 39–66). Thousand Oaks, CA: Sage.

Valley, K., Thompson, L., Gibbons, R., & Bazerman, M. H. (2002). How communication improves efficiency in bargaining games. *Games and Economic Behavior,* 38, 127–155.

Valley, K. L., White, S. B., & Iacobucci, D. (1992). The process of assisted negotiations:

A network analysis. *Group Decision and Negotiation,* 2, 117–135.

Valley, K. L., White, S. B., Neale, M. A., & Bazerman, M. H. (1992). Agents as information brokers: The effects of information disclosure on negotiated outcomes. Special Issue: Decision processes in negotiation. *Organizational Behavior and Human Decision Processes,* 51(2), 220–236.

Vallone, R. P., Ross, L., & Lepper, M. (1985). The hostile media phenomenon: Biased perception and perceptions of media bias in coverage of the "Beirut Massacre." *Journal of Personality and Social Psychology,* 49, 577–585.

van Avermaet, E. (1974). Equity: A theoretical and experimental analysis. Unpublished manuscript, University of California.

van Boven, L. & Thompson, L. (2003). A look into the mind of the negotiator: Mental models in negotiation. *Group Processes & Intergroup Relations,* 6(4), 387–404.

van Kleef, G. A., De Dreu, C. K. W., & Manstead, A. S. R. (2004). The interpersonal effects of anger and happiness in negotiations. *Journal of Personality and Social Psychology,* 86(1), 57–76.

van Dijk, E., Wilke, H., & Wit, A. (2003). Preferences for leadership in social dilemmas: Public good dilemmas versus common resource dilemmas. *Journal of Experimental Social Psychology,* 39, 170–176.

Van Lange, P. A. M. (1999). The pursuit of joint outcomes and equality in outcomes: An integrative model of social value orientation. *Journal of Personality and Social Psychology,* 77(2), 337–349.

Van Lange, P. A. M., & Visser, K. (1999). Locomotion in social dilemmas: How people adapt to cooperative, tit-for-tat and noncooperative partners. *Journal of Personality and Social Psychology,* 77(4), 762–773.

Van Vugt, M., & De Cremer, D. (1999). Leadership in social dilemmas: The effects of group identification on collective actions to provide public goods. *Journal of Personality and Social Psychology,* 76(4), 587–599.

Van Vugt, M., & Samuelson, C. D. (1999). The impact of personal metering in the management of a natural resource crisis: A social dilemma analysis. *Personality and Social Psychology Bulletin,* 25(6), 731–745.

von Neumann, J., & Morgenstern, O. (1947). *Theory of Games and Economic Behavior.* Princeton, NJ: Princeton University Press.

Vorauer, J. D., & Claude, S. (1998). Perceived versus actual transparency of goals in negotiation. *Personality and Social Psychology Bulletin,* 24(4), 371–385.

Wade-Benzoni, K. A., Hoffman, A. J., Thompson, L. L., Moore, D. A., Gillespie, J. J., & Bazerman, M. H. (2002). Contextualizing environmental negotiations: Uncovering barriers to efficient agreements. *Academy of Management Review,* 27(1), 41–57.

Wade-Benzoni, K. A., Okumura, T., Brett, J. M., Moore, D. Tenbrunsel, A. E., & Bazerman, M. H. (2002). Cognitions and behavior in asymmetric social dilemmas: A comparison of two cultures. *Journal of Applied Psychology,* 87, 87–95.

Walster, E., Berscheid, E., & Walster, G. W. (1973). New directions in equity research. *Journal of Personality and Social Psychology,* 25, 151–176.

Walton, R. E., & McKersie, R. B. (1965). *A Behavioral Theory of Labor Relations.* New York: McGraw-Hill.

Weber, M., Loewenstein, J., & Thompson, L. (2003). Of wolves and sheep: Reputation and negotiation performance. Working paper, Northwestern University, Evanston, IL.

Weber, R. J. (1997). Making more from less: Strategic demand reduction in the FCC spectrum auctions. *Journal of Economics & Management Strategy,* 6(3), 529–548.

Wegner, D. M. (1994). Ironic processes of mental control. *Psychological Review,* 101, 34–52.

Wegner, D. M., Lane, J. D., & Dimitri, S. (1994). The allure of secret relationships. *Journal of Personality and Social Psychology,* 66(2), 287–300.

Wegner, D. M., Shortt, J. W., Blake, A. W., & Page, M. S. (1990). The suppression of exciting thoughts. *Journal of Personality and Social Psychology,* 58, 409–418.

Wegner, D. M., & Wenzlaff, R. M. (1996). Mental control. In E. T. Higgins & A. W. Kruglanski (Eds.), *Social Psychology: Handbook of Basic Principles* (pp. 466–492). New York: Guilford Press.

Weingart, L. R., Bennett, R., & Brett, J. M. (1993). The impact of consideration of issues and motivational orientation on group negotiation process and outcome. *Journal of Applied Psychology,* 78, 504–517.

Weingart, L. R., & Brett, J. M. (1998, April). Mixed motivational orientation in negotiating groups: Convergence and reaching agreement. Paper presented at Society for Industrial Organizational Psychology 13th Annual Conference, Dallas, TX.

Weingart, L. R., Brett, J. M., & Olekalns, M. (2003). Conflicting social motives in negotiating groups. Working paper, Carnegie Mellon University, Pittsburgh, PA.

Weingart, L. R., Hyder, E. B., & Prietula, M. J. (1996). Knowledge matters: The effect of tactical descriptions on negotiation behavior and outcome. *Journal of Personality and Social Psychology,* 70, 1205–1217.

Wellens, A. R. (1989). Effects of telecommunication media upon information sharing and team performance: Some theoretical and empirical findings. *IEEE AES Magazine,* September, p. 14.

White, J. B., Tynan, R. O., Galinsky, A., & Thompson, L. (in press). Face threat sensitivity in negotiation: Roadblock to agreement and joint gain. *Organizational Behavior and Human Decision Processes.*

Whitehead, A. N. (1929). *The Aims of Education.* New York: Macmillan.

Whorf, B. L. (1956). Science and linguistics. In J. B. Carroll (Ed.), *Language, Thought, and Reality. Selected Writings of Benjamin Whorf.* New York: Wiley.

Wicklund, R. A., & Gollwitzer, P. M. (1982). *Symbolic Self-Completion.* Hillsdale, NJ: Lawrence Erlbaum.

Wildschut, T., Insko, C. A., & Gaertner, L. (2002). Intragroup social influence and intergroup competition. *Journal of Personality and Social Psychology,* 82(6), 975–992.

Williams, G. (1983). *Legal Negotiation and Settlement.* St. Paul, MN: West Publishing.

Wills, T. A. (1981). Downward comparison principles in social psychology. *Psychological Bulletin,* 90, 245–271.

Wilson, T. D., Wheatley, T., Meyers, J., Gilbert, D. T., & Axsom, D. (1998). Focalism: A source of durability bias in affective forecasting. Unpublished manuscript, University of Virginia, Charlottesville, VA.

Windschitl, P. D., Kruger, J., & Simms, E. N. (2003). The influence of egocentrism and focalism on people's optimism in competitions: When what affects us equally affects me more. *Journal of Personality and Social Psychology,* 85(3), 389–408.

Woodroofe, M. (1975). *Probability with Applications.* New York, McGraw-Hill.

Woodside, A. G., & Davenport, J. W., Jr. (1974). Effects of salesman similarity and expertise on customer purchasing behavior. *Journal of Marketing Research,* 11(2), 198–202.

Worchel, S., & Austin, W. G., (Eds). (1986). *Psychology of Intergroup Relations.* Chicago: Nelson-Hall.

Wright, S. C., Aron, A., McLaughlin-Volpe, T., & Ropp, S. A. (1997). The extended contact effect: Knowledge of cross-group friendships and prejudice. *Journal of Personality and Social Psychology,* 73(1), 73–90.

Yamaguchi, S., Okamoto, K., & Oka, T. (1985). Effects of coactors' presence: Social loafing and social facilitation. *Japanese Psychological Research,* 27, 215–222.

Yates, J. F. (1990). *Judgment and Decision Making.* Upper Saddle River, NJ: Prentice Hall.

Yukl, G. A. (1974). Effects of the opponent's initial offer, concession magnitude and concession frequency on bargaining behavior. *Journal of Personality and Social Psychology,* 30(3), 323–335.

Zajonc, R. (1968). Attitudinal effects of mere exposure. *Journal of Personality and Social Psychology,* 9 (monograph supplement No. 2, Part 2).

Zuckerman, M., Blanck, P. D., DePaulo, B. M., & Rosenthal, R. (1980). Developmental changes in decoding discrepant and nondiscrepant nonverbal cues. *Developmental Psychology,* 16(3), 220–228.

Zuckerman, M., DePaulo, B. M., & Rosenthal, R. (1981). Verbal and nonverbal communication of deception. In L. Berkowitz (Ed.), *Advances in Experimental Social Psychology,* vol. 14 (pp. 1–59). New York: Academic Press.

Zuckerman, M., Koestner, R., & Driver, R. (1981). Beliefs about cues associated with deception. *Journal of Nonverbal Behavior,* 6(2), 105–114.

Popular Press References

Advertising Age. (Oct. 1, 2001). L. Sanders. Betty Pat McCoy: Senior VP-director of national broadcast, GSD&M, p. S16.

Adweek. (May 1, 2000). M. Larson. Time Warner yanks ABC from 3.5 million cable sets.

Adweek. (June 9, 2003). M. Larson. Atlanta falcon: With his keen business instinct and sharp negotiating skills, Mark Lazarus has soared through the ranks of Turner, p. SR14.

American Bar Association. (2004). Model Rules of Professional Conduct. Accessed May 24, 2004, at http://www.abanet.org/cpr/mrpc/mrpc_toc.html.

Arizona Republic, The. (Jan. 9, 1994). J. Kaplan. Single-offer tactic can be costly, p. E6.

Arizona Republic, The. (Dec. 7, 1999). P. Kossan. Hotel negotiations go nowhere: Marriott won't wait forever, and all parties know it, p. B1.

Ascribe News. (June 5, 2003). Transnational executive education exercise shows Brazilians, Americans must negotiate past cultural difference.

Associated Press. (Sept. 20, 2001). Excerpts from George W. Bush's speech.

Associated Press. (May 16. 2002). M. Gordon. Bankruptcies rise to record level, indication that consumers kept spending in recession.

Associated Press. (Dec. 3, 2002). Doyle, tribes prefer to negotiate tribal compacts as a group.

Associated Press. (Jan. 15, 2003). Bankruptcies rise to record highs.

Associated Press. (Apr. 23, 2003). Challenge: Getting real results from virtual teams.

Augusta Chronicle. (July 12, 2003). M. Mogul. The art of the deal: Professional haggler shares bargaining skills, p. C7.

Australian Financial Review. (Sept. 30, 1998). Managing innovation in the 24-hour laboratory, p. 2.

Baltimore Sun. (May 7, 1991). G. Lewthwaite. Northern Ireland talks deadlock over location, p. 5A.

Baltimore Sun. (Aug. 17, 2003). A. MacGillis. California deal may turn tide in battle for Colorado river water.

Best's Review. (Oct. 1, 2002). L. Goch. Battle of the blues, p. 90.

Bestwire. (July 3, 2002). M. Suszynski. Independence Blue Cross, Pennsylvania hospital agree on contract.

Business 2.0. (Sept. 1, 2002). E. Schonfeld. Second act for a manic CEO, pp. 51–54.

Business 2.0. (Aug. 1, 2003a). O. Malik. And the coolest new PC is made by . . . Best Buy? pp. 47–49.

Business 2.0. (Aug. 1, 2003b). At Starbucks, the future is in plastic, p. 56.

Business 2.0. (Aug. 1, 2003c). How to survive when you've been given up for dead, p. 64.

Business 2.0. (Aug. 1, 2003d). E. Schonfeld & O. Malik. Gulp! pp. 88–95.

Business Wire. (May 22, 2001). CareerJournal.com offers pay and severance package negotiation tips.

Business Wire. (July 30, 2001). Job coaching industry grows in Washington metro area: MyJobCoach offers increasingly popular resource for career changers.

Business Wire. (Dec. 6, 2001). Davel selects INFONXX for directory assistance.

Business Wire. (Dec. 27, 2001). IBEW, CVPS reach deal on three-year contract.

Business Wire. (June 10, 2002). AuntMinnie.com launches SalaryScan compensation research tool for radiology professionals.

BusinessWeek. (Aug. 12, 2002). T. Gutner & M. Hyman. More heat on the masters, p. 75.

BusinessWeek. (Aug. 4, 2003a). S. Reed. Suddenly, the Saudis want to close some deals, p. 51.

BusinessWeek. (Aug. 4, 2003b). S. Rosenbush. Gutsy bet, pp. 53–62.

BusinessWeek. (Aug. 11, 2003a). E. Thornton & M. France. For Enron's bankers, a "get out of jail free" card, p. 29.

BusinessWeek. (Aug. 11, 2003b). R. Berner. Sears: The silent partner who's making himself heard, p. 38.

BusinessWeek. (Aug. 11, 2003c). S. Rosenbush & C. Haddad. MCI is under a new cloud, but it can weather the storm, p. 31.

BusinessWeek. (Aug. 11, 2003d). S. Ante. Blood feud, pp. 50–52.

BusinessWeek. (Aug. 11, 2003e). A. Barrett. Is this banker too brazen? pp. 48–49.

BusinessWeek. (Sept. 1, 2003). B. Elgin. A nasty surprise from HP, p. 80.

BusinessWeek. (Nov. 24, 2003a). D. Henry. A fair deal—but for whom? pp. 108–109.

BusinessWeek. (Nov. 24, 2003b). R. Grover, G. Edmondson, & K. Kerwin. What a difference a phrase makes.

BusinessWeek. (Dec. 1, 2003). Steve Ballmer on Microsoft's future, pp. 72–74.

BusinessWeek. (Mar. 22, 2004). J. Kerstetter. Microsoft versus Linux, p. 14.

Capital Times. (Jan. 1, 2000). S. Kalk. Fine art of negotiating a fact of life, p. 1E.

Century 21 Inc. v. F. W. Woolworth Co., 181 A. D. 2D 620 (NY 1992).

Chicago Sun-Times. (Feb. 10, 1986). Cultural differences can make or break a deal, p. 60.

Chicago Sun-Times. (Oct. 22, 1990). P. Bednarski. When stars need pacts, she's hired, p. 35.

Chicago Tribune. (Nov. 10, 1995). S. Ziemba. American to United: Avoid bidding war, carrier won't draw first in USAir fight, p. 1.

Chicago Tribune. (Aug. 13, 2003). R. Manor. Jewel supermarkets–Union hammer out tentative contract deal.

Christian Science Monitor. (July 29, 2002). F. Hansen. Getting what you're worth: Online salary data helps level the playing field in salary negotiations, p. 14.

Chronicle of Higher Education. (Feb. 9, 2000). S. Carlson. Penn officials use e-mail to negotiate a $10-million gift, pp. 1–2.

CFO Magazine. (Sept. 1, 2001). R. Fisher. Doctor YES, p. 66.

CNN. (Sept. 6, 2001). J. Greenfield. Electronic surveillance: Is it '1984' in the workplace?

CNN. (Mar. 19, 2003). U.S. President George W. Bush has announced that war against Iraq has begun.

Colorado Business. (Apr. 1, 2001). M. E. Stevens. Companies' perks get creative, pp. 31–34.

Commercial Appeal, The. (July 16, 2003). J. Roberts. Northwestern Airlines, pilots open contract discussions.

Crain's Detroit Business. (May 7, 2001). A. Lane. Perking up perks: Options range from fitness centers to same-sex partner coverage, p. 11.

Dallas Morning News. (Apr. 3, 2003). E. Torbenson. American pilots agree to plan to avoid bankruptcy.

Denver Post. (June 9, 2003). G. Griffin & J. Leib. Flying on fumes: A costly pilots contract, the dot-com meltdown and a failed merger put United in a tailspin and sent executives scrambling to recover, p. A01.

Digital v. Desktop Direct, 114 S. Ct. 1992, 1995 (1994)

Dow Jones Business News. (Dec. 27, 1999). T. Hofmann. The year in review: Media players set torrid pace.

Dow Jones Newswires. (Apr. 22, 2003). J. Kim. Negotiating a sweeter college aid deal.

Economic Times. (Nov. 8, 1999). B. Mishra & N. Sinha. Cross-cultural booby traps.

Feldman v. Allegheny International, Inc., 850 F.2d 1217 (IL 7th Cir. 1988).

Final Offer. (1985). S. Gunnarsson & R. Collison (Directors/Producers). National Film Board of Canada.

Forbes. (Sept. 2, 2002a). B. Condon. Home wrecker, pp. 63–66.

Forbes. (Sept. 2, 2003b) E. MacDonald. Hit man, pp. 46–48.

Fortune. (July 21, 2003). A. Lashinsky. Penguin slayer, pp. 85–90.

Fortune. (Aug. 11, 2003a). J. Useem. Power: The 25 most powerful people in business, pp. 57–84.

Fortune. (Aug. 11, 2003b). J. Birnbaum. The persuaders, pp. 121–124.

Fortune. (Aug. 11, 2003c). D. Rynecki. Field guide to power: Power golf guru, p. 126.

Fortune. (Sept. 1, 2003). P. Sellers. The trials of John Mack, pp. 98–104.

Fortune. (Dec. 22, 2003). C. Loomis. The larger-than-life life of Robert Rubin, pp. 114–124.

Globe and Mail, The. (June 17, 2002). V. Galt. Deal makers share their secrets, p. C1.

Guardian, The. (Jan. 15, 2000). A. Perkins. John Wakeham, Lord Fixit, p. 6.

Guardian, The. (July 17, 2003). O. Burkeman. How I failed to make my millions: Mathematician John Allen Paulos on his disastrous foray into the stock market, p. 8.

Inc. (Aug. 1, 2003a). R. Walker. Take it or leave it: The only guide to negotiating you will ever need, pp. 75–82.

Inc. (Aug. 1, 2003b). D. Fenn. I want my company back, pp. 103–108.

Inc. (Aug. 1, 2003c). C. Cannella. Why online exchanges died.

Independent, The. (Mar. 10, 1999). D. McKittrick. Astonishingly, Mr. Adams and Mr. Trimble share a common aim, p. 3.

International Business. (July 1, 1998). A. Pachtman. Getting to "hao!" pp. 24–26.

Investors' Business Daily. (Sept. 22, 1998). T. Dworetzky. Sports superagent Leigh Steinberg, p. A6.

Investors' Business Daily. (Dec. 11, 1998). T. Dworetzky. Explorer Christopher Columbus: How the West's greatest discoverer negotiated his trips' financing, p. 1BD.

Investors' Business Daily. (Nov. 12, 2003). R. Shaw. Workplace messaging offers rewards, risks.

Kitchener-Waterloo Record. (July 29, 2003). R. Simone. Food workers help WLU trim deficit, p. D8.

Los Angeles Times. (Apr. 23, 1996). S. Howard-Cooper. The odd couple: From beginning, friendship between Buss, Johnson has transcended usual relationship between owner, player, p. 1.

Los Angeles Times. (May, 1998). J. Oldham. Conflict and cookies: Companies coax problems out into the open and use them to make working groups more effective, p. 22.

Machine Design. (Feb. 11, 1999). Tips from a negotiation coach, 71(3), p. 96.

Management Today. (Nov. 1, 1998). J. Davies. The art of negotiation, pp. 126–128.

National Journal. (June 3, 2000). T. W. Lippman. Madame Secretary, p. 1736.

National Public Radio. (Nov. 3, 1995).

National Public Radio. (Aug. 28, 2002). Analysis: Business deal between Great Northern Paper and The Nature Conservancy to protect a quarter-million acres of Maine woods from development.

National Public Radio. (Sept. 23, 2002). In New Mexico, a land management 'experiment.'

National Public Radio. (Aug. 12, 2003). Analysis: Environmentalists critical of President Bush's Healthy Forests Initiative.

New Sunday Times. (June 1, 2003). C. Hong. Tough negotiator, dynamic diplomat with a mission in France, p. 3.

New York Daily News. (June 20, 2003). O. Moritz. First Lady Effa Manley chapter 101, p. 33.

New York Times. (Feb. 6, 1998). S. Elliott. Milk promoters agree to cooperate, p. D17.

New York Times. (Sept. 20, 1998). D. Barboza. Loving a stock, not wisely, but too well, p. 1.

New York Times. (Sept. 3, 1999). A. Harmon. Auction for a kidney pops up on Bay's site, p. A13.

New York Times. (Nov. 6, 1999). R. D. McFadden. Daily News error: $100,000 dreams turn to nightmare, p. A1.

New York Times. (July 16, 2003a). E. Wyatt. Officials reach an agreement on rebuilding downtown site, p. 1.

New York Times. (July 16, 2003b). J. Kahn. As U.S. and North Korea glower, China pushes for talks, p. 3.

New York Times. (Aug. 1, 2003). E. Schmitt. Poindexter will be quitting over terrorism betting plan.

Newsday. (Feb. 2, 1987). F. Fessenden. A man who gets them talking, p. 6.

Newsweek. (Nov. 1, 1999). L. Baguioro. Kidneys for sale, p. 50.

Newsweek International. (Nov. 8, 1999). Back to the (dinner) table.

Orange County Business Journal. (Apr. 21, 2003). M. Padilla. Let's make a deal, p. 22.

Orange County Register. (Jan. 6, 2002). H. Quach. "Caveman" and conciliator: Sen. Ross Johnson adroitly plays to both sides of the aisle, and sings, too, p. 1.

Orange County Register. (July 5, 2003). M. Fisher. Why do women settle for less: A researcher says female job seekers hate to haggle over pay, p. 1.

Oregonian, The. (Mar. 7, 1991). P. Koberstein. Deal aims to reduce Los Angeles smog, aid NW salmon, p. D1.

Oregonian, The. (Apr. 30, 1996). M. Trappen. Shopping on a shoestring: How to haggle, p. D01.

Oregonian, The. (May 25, 2003). J. Manning & K. Turnquist. Squabble in 'Toon Town, p. A1.

Pantagraph, The. (June 22, 2003). S. Silverman. Divorce mediation gains popularity, p. A1.

Patriot-News Harrisburg. (Jan. 12, 2003). M. Zielenziger. Crazy like a fox and steel-tough, p. A20.

Pentagon Papers. (1971). As published by *The New York Times*, based on the investigative reporting by Neil Sheehan, written by Neil Sheehan [and others]. Articles and documents edited by G. Gold, A. M. Siegal, and S. Abt. New York, Toronto: Bantam.

Pittsburgh Post-Gazette. (Aug. 29, 2002). T. Lindeman. Del Monte weighed being bought as it worked on buying Heinz units.

Private Equity Week. (June 9, 2003). L. Aragon. Must see TV: Anchor Bay gets $5M for crystal clear picture.

Record, The. (Mar. 12, 2003). R. Feldberg. Curtains come down on Broadway strike.

Reuters. (Aug. 11, 2003). J. Goldfarb. Tough deadline helps Saban's right-hand man ink deal.

Richmond Times-Dispatch. (Feb. 18, 1998). G. Robertson. Creative negotiations pay off, p. J3.

San Antonio Express-News. (Sept. 1, 2003). S. Nowlin. SBC, Time Warner poised to fight over each other's traditional markets.

San Francisco Chronicle. (Jan. 13, 2002). D. Fost. How NBC, KRON deal fell apart: Animosity, mistrust colored negotiations, p. G1.

San Francisco Chronicle. (Aug. 20, 2003). C. Said. Chris Larsen puts the clout behind state's new privacy bill, p. B1.

Seattle Post-Intelligencer. (May 24, 2003). C. Pope. Boeing lands major deal, p. A1.

Seattle Post-Intelligencer. (July 16, 2003). S. Powell. U.S. scrambles to investigate North Korea's nuclear claim, p. A1.

Seattle Times. (Apr. 4, 2002). D. Postman. E-mail reveals labor's plot to foil I-776, p. A1.

Seattle Times. (Apr. 21, 2002). S. Dunphy. MBAs face a tough market: A master's degree doesn't open corporate doors so quickly, p. D1.

Sequim Gazette. (July 9, 2003). D. Ross. City, Wal-Mart united against county during hearing, pp. A1, A5.

Sequim Gazette. (July 30, 2003a). D. Ross. City council says "yes" to developers, pp. A1, A5.

Sequim Gazette. (July 30, 2003b). D. Ross. County proposes mall traffic solution, p. A7.

Slate. (Jan. 23, 2003). W. Saletan. Enron evasions: Lessons from Ari Fleischer in the art of spin. Accessed December 15, 2003, at http://slate.msn.com/?id = 2061084/.

SOEST. (2004). Raising food fish in sea cages: a Hawai'i first! T. Reid. Accessed January 1, 2004, at http://www.soest.hawaii.edu/SEAGRANT/special_projects.html/.

South Florida Sun-Sentinel. (July 3, 2003). J. Holland. Hollywood, Fla., backs off pension fund deal for firefighters.

St. Louis Post-Dispatch. (June 10, 1996). M. Shirk. Women go beyond rhetoric, p. 11B.

Star-Ledger, The. (Apr. 27, 1995). E. Iwata. Negotiating skills. © 1995 Newark Morning Ledger Co.

Star-Tribune. (Apr. 1, 2002). P. Schmid. Director: Oldfield planning to leave, AAU official says 'U' coach to move on, p. 1C.

Star-Tribune. (June 14, 2003). N. Gendler. Hispanic home buyers, p. 4H.

Straits Times. (Nov. 21, 1999). L. S. Hua. She's a master of details, p. 42.

Textron v. United Automobile, 118 S. Ct. 1626 (1998).

Time. (Dec. 2, 1985). E. Thomas. Fencing at the fireside summit: With candor and civility, Reagan and Gorbachev grapple for answers to the arms-race riddle, p. 22.

Time. (Dec. 22, 1997). M. Lemonick. Turning down the heat, p. 23.

Times-Picayune. (June 1, 2003). J. Duncan. The name remains the same: Naming rights for Superdome continue to be a hard sell.

Times Union-Albany. (Mar. 2, 2003). P. Grondahl. Different worlds, same side of bargaining table, p. B1.

Times Union-Albany. (Mar. 9, 2003). P. Grondahl. Offering a lifeline at marriage's end, p. CC17.

Toronto Star. (July 14, 1990). A. Cassel. U.S. Indians flex muscles in making treaty claims, p. D5.

Toronto Star. (June 2, 2003). S. Pigg. How a judge's plain speaking saved Air Canada, p. A1.

Training. (Oct. 1, 1999). K. Kiser. The new deal, pp. 116–126.

Tulsa World. (Apr. 25, 2003). K. Kerr. Carty known as tough CEO who smiled, p. E1.

USA Today. (Jan. 5, 2000). B. Slavin. Negotiators clear first bump in Middle East talks, p. 6A.

US Banker. (Feb. 1, 1997). S. Zuckerman. The best damn dealmaker in banking, p. 28.

U.S. Department of Labor. (2002). Number of jobs held, labor market activity, and earnings growth among younger baby boomers: Results from more than two decades of a longitudinal survey (Release No. 02–497). Accessed December 10, 2003, at http://www.bls.gov/nls/nlsy79r19.pdf/.

U.S. News & World Report. (Nov. 1, 1999). K. Clark. Gimme, gimme, gimme: Job seekers don't realize they can ask for more—lots more, pp. 88–92.

Vancouver Sun. (Nov. 1, 2003). Gaborik wild about re-signing with Minnesota, p. S3.

Wall Street Journal, The. (May 12, 1995). M. Pacelle & S. Lipin. Japanese owner seeks court protection for Manhattan's Rockefeller Center, p. A3.

Wall Street Journal, The. (June 9, 1995). M. Pacelle. Japan's U.S. property deals: A poor report card, p. B1.

Wall Street Journal, The. (Jan. 27, 1998). H. Lancaster. You have to negotiate for everything in life, so get good at it, p. B1.

Wall Street Journal, The. (Sept. 22, 1998). J. Lublin. Web transforms art of negotiating raises, pp. B1, B16.

Wall Street Journal, The. (Mar. 19, 1999). K. Bensinger & D. Costello. Art and money, p. W16.

Wall Street Journal, The. (Dec. 2, 1999). J. Pereira & J. Lublin. 'Toys' story: They ran the retailer as a team for years; then, a nasty split, p. A1.

Wall Street Journal, The. (Aug. 12, 2002). J. Bailey. A CEO's legacy: Sons battle in fight for control of Maritz.

Wall Street Journal, The. (Mar. 12, 2003). N. Boudette. Marriage counseling: At DaimlerChrysler, a new push to make its units work together, p. A1.

Wall Street Journal, The. (June 25, 2003). G. Anders. Upping the ante: As some decry lavish CEO pay, Joe Bachelder makes it happen, p. A1.

Wall Street Journal Europe. (Dec. 11, 2003). K. Johnson. Air alliances get stronger: Combination of Air France, KLM will bolster partnerships, p. A4.

Warehousing Management. (Sept. 1, 1998). S. Turpin. Negotiation: A necessary skill, p. 60.

Washington Post. (Nov. 23, 1985). D. Hoffman. Tense turning point at summit; key Reagan-Gorbachev handshake calmed atmosphere, p. A1.

Washington Post. (June 15, 2003). A. Klein. Lord of the flies, p. W06.

Wisconsin State Journal. (June 4, 2002). J. Wilde. Packers turn Freeman loose, p. C1.

Workforce. (Feb. 1, 2003). S. Gale. Memo to AOL Time Warner: Why mergers fail, 82(2), 60.

Subject Index

Author Index